CW01022023

THE COGNITIVE REPRESENTATION OF SPEECH

ADVANCES
IN
PSYCHOLOGY
7

Editors

G. E. STELMACH

P. A. VROON

NORTH-HOLLAND PUBLISHING COMPANY
AMSTERDAM · NEW YORK · OXFORD

THE COGNITIVE REPRESENTATION OF SPEECH

Edited by

Terry MYERS
Department of Psychology
School of Epistemics
University of Edinburgh

John LAVER
Department of Linguistics
University of Edinburgh

John ANDERSON
Department of English Language
University of Edinburgh

NORTH-HOLLAND PUBLISHING COMPANY
AMSTERDAM · NEW YORK · OXFORD

ISBN: 0 444 86162 9

Publishers:
NORTH-HOLLAND PUBLISHING COMPANY
AMSTERDAM · NEW YORK · OXFORD

Sole distributors for the U.S.A. and Canada:
ELSEVIER NORTH-HOLLAND, INC.
52 VANDERBILT AVENUE
NEW YORK, N.Y. 10017

Library of Congress Cataloging in Publication Data
Main entry under title:

The Cognitive representation of speech.

    (Advances in psychology ; 7)
    Bibliography: p.
    1. Psycholinguistics--Congresses. 2. Speech--
Congresses. 3. Cognition--Congresses. 4. Language
acquisition--Congresses. 5. Grammar, Comparative
and general--Phonology--Congresses. I. Myers,
Terry. II. Laver, John. III. Anderson, John M.
IV. Series: Advances in psychology (Amsterdam,
Netherlands) ; 7.
P37.C58   401'.9   81-18736
ISBN O-444-86162-9 (U.S.) AACR2

PRINTED IN THE NETHERLANDS

INTRODUCTION

A basic proposition in all the behavioural sciences is that, underlying the apparently infinite variability of man's behaviour, there is a systematic orderliness of cognitive structure. The study of this structure is now often called cognitive science. It is tempting to assume that this singular label reflects the unity of the subject: but in fact cognitive science is an outstanding example of a multidisciplinary field unified more by the object of study than by its methodology. This is particularly evident in the case of one of the central topics in cognitive science, that of speech. The editors of this book are committed to the view that the comprehensive study of speech can only be properly achieved by the collaboration of linguists, phoneticians, psychologists, neurophysiologists and communications engineers, and many others. There are of course many aspects of speech which lie outside cognitive science, but our point is that an adequate study of the facets of speech relevant to cognitive science, that is to say the study of the systematic structures and processes whereby speech is produced and perceived, must be based on a multidisciplinary approach.

With this orientation in mind, an international symposium was organized in Edinburgh, in July 1979, of which this book is the product. The aims of the symposium were to gather the leading researchers in the rapidly developing area that we are calling the cognitive representation of speech, in order to promote a synthesis of ideas from the different disciplines involved and to encourage the perception of new research directions. Within the framework of these objectives, this book was intended to provide a coherent and comprehensive account of the state of the art in this area.

The organization of the book follows that of the symposium, and is intended to explore the range and the major dimensions of the subject. The first half examines phonetic and psycholinguistic studies of speech processing. It begins with a consideration of perhaps the most central topic in the subject - namely, the relation between production and perception. This is followed by a discussion of the constraints on the form of representation imposed by properties of the peripheral systems. The third session explores the relation between segmental and suprasegmental levels of representation and the fourth focusses on the influence of information processing limitations on representation.

The second half of the book explores biological, developmental, phonological and machine approaches to the subject. Session V presents a biological perspective, raising the questions: What are the neurolinguistic mechanisms underlying speech processing, and how did they evolve? Session VI considers the development of phonological representations in the child. Session VII discusses the psychological reality of phonological descriptions. Finally, Session VIII poses the question of the extent to which machine representations of speech, in speech synthesis and speech recognition, may plausibly be considered as models of equivalent human processes.

We hope that the book will serve as a basic source for both researchers and students, presenting as it does such a wide variety of conceptual and experimental methodologies, with a commitment to the relevance of an interdisciplinary approach. As a commentary on the state of the art, it reveals that the study of the cognitive representation of speech is perhaps still in a ground-clearing stage. But the scale of the subject, and many of its salient issues, are made thoroughly visible, and many avenues of future research are signposted.

ACKNOWLEDGEMENTS

We owe a considerable debt to many people for advice and assistance towards the organization of the symposium and the preparation of the book. Advisory help with the symposium was given by R.E. Asher, J.K. Anthony, and E.K. Brown of the Department of Linguistics, B. Richards of the School of Epistemics, and D.M. Vowles of the Department of Psychology.

Assistance with the symposium was enthusiastically given by research assistants, and postgraduate and undergraduate students of the Departments of Linguistics and Psychology, particularly including Anne Anderson, Marie Azzopardi, Roger Brown, Robert Byrnes, Nantana Danvivathana, Rebecca Dauer, Helen Daw, John Fisher, Hossein Gorji, Amal Kari, Pamela Rodrigues, Alicia Salazar and Cynthia Shuken. Technical help was given by the technical staff of the Phonetics Laboratory, Department of Linguistics.

The symposium was financially supported by the University of Edinburgh, particularly by grants from the Institute of Advanced Studies in the Humanities, Faculty of Arts, the Social Sciences Faculty and the School of Epistemics.

Preparation of the book was helped by assistance from Norman Aikman, John Fisher, Janet Mackenzie Beck, Frances Macnamara, John McNeill, Morag Mullay and Frances Taylor, and Norman Dryden and Irene MacLeod were responsible for the computer-collated references.

We express our gratitude to all these friends and colleagues.

We also gratefully acknowledge permission from the publishers of Cognition, Elsevier Sequoia S.A., to reprint portions of Eric Wanner's contribution which appeared earlier in that journal.

T.M.
J.L.
J.A.

Edinburgh
October 1981

TABLE OF CONTENTS

LIST OF PARTICIPANTS

Dr. Evelyn Abberton,
Department of Phonetics and
  Linguistics, Annexe,
Wolfson House,
4 Stephenson Way,
LONDON NW1 2HE,
United Kingdom.

Dr. W. Ainsworth,
Department of Communication
  and Neuroscience,
University of Keele,
KEELE,
Staffordshire ST5 5BG,
United Kingdom.

Professor G.D. Allen,
Dental Research Center,
University of North Carolina,
CHAPEL HILL,
North Carolina 27514,
U.S.A.

Dr. P. Bailey,
Department of Psychology,
University of York,
Heslington,
YORK YO1 5DD,
United Kingdom.

Professor A.P. Bengueral,
Faculty of Medicine,
Division of Audiology and Speech
  Sciences,
University of British Columbia,
VANCOUVER B.C.,
Canada V6T 1WS.

Professor T.G. Bever,
Department of Psychology,
Schenehorn Hall,
University of Columbia,
NEW YORK, N.Y. 10027,
U.S.A.

Professor J. Berko-Gleason,
Department of Psychology,
Boston University,
64 Cummington Street,
BOSTON,
Mass. 02215,
U.S.A.

Mr. A. Bladon,
Department of Linguistics,
University College of North Wales,
BANGOR, Gwynedd LL57 2DG,
North Wales,
United Kingdom.

Professor S. Blumstein,
Department of Linguistics,
Brown University,
PROVIDENCE,
Rhode Island 02912,
U.S.A.

Dr. B. de Boysson-Bardies,
École des Hautes Études en
  Sciences Sociales,
Laboratoire de Psychologie,
Centre d'Étude des Processus
  Cognitifs et du Langage,
54 Boulevard Raspail,
75270 Cedex 06, PARIS,
France.

Professor A. Bregman,
Department of Psychology,
Stewart Biological Sciences Bldg.,
McGill University,
1205 McGregor Ave.,
MONTREAL,
Quebec,
Canada H3A 1B1.

Dr. J. Bridle,
Joint Speech Research Unit,
Princess Elizabeth Way,
CHELTENHAM,
Gloucestershire GL52 5AJ,
United Kingdom.

Dr. Cathe Browman,
c/o Professor Fujimura,
Linguistics and Speech Analysis
  Department,
Bell Laboratories,
600 Mountain Avenue,
MURRAY HILL, N.J. 07974,
U.S.A.

Professor Joan Bybee Hooper,
Department of Linguistics,
State University of New York,
C106 Spaulding Quadrangle,
Buffalo,
NEW YORK 14261,
U.S.A.

Dr. R. Carré,
Institut National Polytechnique
  de Grenoble,
E.N.S.E.R.G.,
23 rue des Martyrs,
38031 GRENOBLE, Cedex,
France.

Professor Dr. A. Cohen,
Rijksuniversiteit Utrecht,
Fonetisch Instituut,
Oudenoord 6,
UTRECHT 2506,
The Netherlands.

Professor R.A. Cole,
Carnegie-Mellon University,
PITTSBURGH,
Pennsylvania 15213,
U.S.A.

Professor R. Crowder,
Department of Psychology,
Yale University,
New Haven,
CONNECTICUT,
U.S.A.

Dr. Anne Cutler,
Laboratory of Experimental
  Psychology,
University of Sussex,
BRIGHTON BN1 9QG,
United Kingdom.

Professor B. Derwing,
Department of Linguistics,
Faculty of Science,
The University of Alberta,
EDMONTON,
Alberta,
Canada T6G 2H1.

Dr. B. Dodd,
Speech Unit,
School of Education,
The University of Newcastle
  upon Tyne,
St. Thomas' Street,
NEWCASTLE UPON TYNE
  NE1 7RU,
United Kingdom.

Dr. A. Elliot,
Department of Psychology,
University of Edinburgh,
1 Roxburgh Street,
EDINBURGH,
United Kingdom.

Dr. A. Ellis,
Department of Psychology,
University of Lancaster,
Fylde College,
Bailrigg,
LANCASTER LA1 4YF,
United Kingdom.

Professor E. Evans,
Department of Communication and
 Neuroscience,
University of Keele,
KEELE,
Staffordshire ST5 5BG,
United Kingdom.

Professor Don Foss,
Department of Psychology,
University of Texas,
AUSTIN,
Texas 78712,
U.S.A.

Professor A. Fourcin,
Department of Phonetics and
 Linguistics, Annexe,
University College London,
Wolfson House,
4 Stephenson Way,
LONDON NW1 2HE,
United Kingdom.

Professor H. Francis,
Department of Child Development
 and Educational Psychology,
University of London Institute
 of Education,
24-27 Woburn Place,
LONDON WC1H 0AA,
United Kingdom.

Professor V. Fromkin,
Department of Linguistics,
University of California at
 Los Angeles,
California 90024,
U.S.A.

Dr. O. Fujimura,
Head, Linguistics and Speech
 Analysis Department,
Bell Laboratories,
600 Mountain Avenue,
MURRAY HILL,
N.J. 07974,
U.S.A.

Professor Hiroya Fujisaki,
Department of Electrical
 Engineering,
The Faculty of Engineering,
University of Tokyo,
Bunkyo-Ku, TOKYO,
113 Japan.

Dr. M. Garman,
Department of Linguistics,
University of Reading,
Whiteknights Park,
READING, Berks,
United Kingdom.

Professor T. Gay,
Department of Oral Biology,
Health Center,
University of Connecticut,
Farmington,
CONNECTICUT 06032,
U.S.A.

Professor J.H.V. Gilbert,
Faculty of Medicine,
Division of Audiology and
 Speech Sciences,
University of British Columbia,
VANCOUVER B.C.,
Canada V6T 1W5.

Dr. Louis Goldstein,
Massachusetts Institute of
 Technology,
Room 36-549,
CAMBRIDGE,
Mass. 02139,
U.S.A.

Professor P.B. Gough,
Co-director, Center for Cognitive
  Science,
The University of Texas at Austin,
AUSTIN, Texas 78712,
U.S.A.

Professor M. Haggard,
MRC Institute for Hearing
  Research,
The Medical School,
University of Nottingham,
NOTTINGHAM NG7 2UH,
United Kingdom.

Dr. A. Hendrikson,
15 Lakeside Drive,
ESHER KT10 9EZ,
Surrey,
United Kingdom.

Professor G. Hewes,
Department of Anthropology,
University of Colorado,
BOULDER,
Colorado, 80309,
U.S.A.

Mr. John Holmes,
Head of Joint Speech
  Research Unit,
Princess Elizabeth Way,
CHELTENHAM,
Gloucestershire GL52 5AJ,
United Kingdom.

Dr. P. Howell,
Department of Psychology,
University College London,
Gower Street,
LONDON WC1E 6BT,
United Kingdom.

Dr. S. Isard,
Laboratory of Experimental
  Psychology,
University of Sussex,
BRIGHTON BN1 9QG,
United Kingdom.

Professor Eric Keller,
Département de Linguistique,
Université de Québec à Montréal,
C.P. 8888,
MONTREAL,
Québec H3C 3P8,
Canada.

Dr. Jurek Kirakowski,
Department of Applied Psychology,
University of Cork,
CORK,
Eire.

Dr. D.H. Klatt,
Research Laboratory of Electronics
  and Department of Electrical
  Engineering,
Massachusetts Institute of
  Technology,
CAMBRIDGE, Mass. 02139,
U.S.A.

Dr. R. Ladd, Jr.,
Psychologisches Institut,
Justus-Liebig Universität,
GIESSEN,
West Germany.

Professor P. Ladefoged,
Phonetics Laboratory,
Department of Linguistics,
University of California at
  Los Angeles,
Los Angeles, CA. 90024,
U.S.A.

Professor I. Lehiste,
Department of Linguistics,
The State University of Ohio,
204 Cunz Hall of Languages,
1841 Millikin Road,
COLUMBUS, Ohio 43210,
U.S.A.

Dr. R. Lesser,
Speech Unit,
School of Education,
The University of Newcastle upon
 Tyne,
St. Thomas' Street,
NEWCASTLE UPON TYNE
 NE1 7RU,
United Kingdom.

Professor P. Lieberman,
Department of Linguistics,
Brown University,
PROVIDENCE, Box E,
R.I. 02912,
U.S.A.

Professor C. Longuet-Higgins,
Laboratory of Experimental
 Psychology,
University of Sussex,
BRIGHTON BN1 9QG,
United Kingdom.

Dr. James Lubker,
Institutionen for Lingvistik,
Avdelningen for Fonetik,
Stockholm Universitet,
104 05 STOCKHOLM 50,
Sweden.

Dr. Harry McGurk,
Department of Psychology,
Surrey University,
GUILDFORD,
Surrey,
United Kingdom.

Professor D. MacKay,
Department of Communication
 and Neuroscience,
University of Keele,
KEELE,
Staffordshire ST5 6BG,
United Kingdom.

Professor P.F. MacNeilage,
Department of Linguistics,
The University of Texas,
AUSTIN,
Texas 78712,
U.S.A.

Dr. S. Maeda,
Département des Études et
 Techniques d'Acoustique,
Centre National d'Étude
 des Télécommunications,
B.P. 40, route de Tregastel,
22301 LANNION Cedex,
France.

Professor P. Marler,
Field Research Center for
 Ecology and Ethology,
Rockefeller University,
Tyrrel Road,
MILLBROOK,
N.Y. 12545,
U.S.A.

Dr. John C. Marshall,
Neuropsychology Unit,
Neuroscience Group,
The Radcliffe Infirmary,
Woodstock Road,
OXFORD OX2 6HE,
United Kingdom.

Professor D. Massaro,
University of Wisconsin,
Department of Psychology,
W.J. Brogden Psychology Bldg.,
1202 West John St.,
MADISON, Wisconsin 53706,
U.S.A.

Professor I. Mattingly,
Department of Linguistics,
University of Connecticut,
STORRS,
Connecticut 06268,
U.S.A.

Professor Jacques Mehler,
Ecole des Hautes Etudes en
  Sciences Sociales,
Laboratoire de Psychologie,
Centre d'Etude des Processus
  Cognitifs et du Langage,
54 Boulevard Raspail,
75270 Cedex 06, PARIS,
France.

Dr. R. Moore,
Department of Phonetics and
  Linguistics,
University College London,
Wolfson House,
Stephenson Way,
LONDON NW1 2HE,
United Kingdom.

Dr. T.M. Nearey,
Department of Linguistics,
Faculty of Science,
The University of Alberta,
EDMONTON,
Alberta T6G 2H1,
Canada.

Dr. S.G. Nooteboom,
Instituut voor Perceptie Onderzoek,
P. Box 513, Den Dolech 2,
EINDHOVEN 5612 AZ,
The Netherlands.

Professor John Ohala,
Phonology Laboratory,
Department of Linguistics,
University of California,
BERKELEY, CA 94720,
U.S.A.

Professor Manjari Ohala,
Phonology Laboratory,
Department of Linguistics,
University of California,
BERKELEY, CA 94720,
U.S.A.

Professor S. Öhman,
Department of Linguistics,
Uppsala University,
Kingsgatan 36,
Box 513, S-751 20,
UPPSALA,
Sweden.

Professor J. Perkell,
Research Laboratory of Electronics,
Massachusetts Institute of
  Technology,
CAMBRIDGE,
Mass. 02139,
U.S.A.

Professor K. Pribram,
Department of Psychology,
Stanford University,
STANFORD, CA 94305,
U.S.A.

Professor Dr. von Raffler Engel,
Program in Linguistics,
Vanderbilt University,
NASHVILLE,
Tennessee 37235,
U.S.A.

Dr. Shulamit Reich,
Middlesex Hospital Medical School,
Department of Psychiatry,
LONDON W1P 8AA,
United Kingdom.

Mr. S. Rosen,
Department of Phonetics and
  Linguistics,
University College London,
Wolfson House,
Stephenson Way,
LONDON NW1 2HE,
United Kingdom.

Professor J.Sachs,
Department of Psychology,
U-85 University of Connecticut,
STORRS, CT. 06268,
U.S.A.

Dr. M. Schouten,
Instituut voor Engelse taal-en
  Letterkunde,
Rijksuniversiteit Utrecht,
Oudenoord 6,
3513 UTRECHT,
The Netherlands.

Dr. C. Scully,
Department of Linguistics and
  Phonetics,
University of Leeds,
LEEDS LS2 9JT,
United KIngdom.

Professor E. Selkirk,
Department of Linguistics,
University of Massachusetts,
AMHERST 01003,
U.S.A.

Dr. Linda Shockey,
Language Centre,
University of Essex,
COLCHESTER,
Essex,
United Kingdom.

Dr. P. Simpson,
Department of Psychology,
University of Surrey,
GUILDFORD,
Surrey GN2 5XH,
United Kingdom.

Dr. N. Smith,
Linguistics Section,
Department of Linguistics and
  Phonetics,
University College London,
Gower Street,
LONDON WC1E 7HU,
United Kingdom.

Dr. P. Smith,
Department of Psychology,
University of Reading,
Whiteknights Park,
READING, Berks,
United Kingdom.

Dr. K.N. Stevens,
Director, Speech Group,
Research Laboratory of
 Electronics,
Massachusetts Institute of
 Technology,
CAMBRIDGE, Mass. 02139,
U.S.A.

Professor M. Studdert-Kennedy,
Queens College Graduate Center,
City University of New York,
NEW YORK,
U.S.A.

Dr. Q. Summerfield,
MRC Institute of Hearing
 Research,
The Medical School,
University of Nottingham,
NOTTINGHAM NG7 2UH,
United Kingdom.

Professor David Swinney,
Department of Psychology,
Tufts University,
MEDFORD, Mass. 02155,
U.S.A.

Professor M.A.A. Tatham,
Department of Language and
 Linguistics,
University of Essex,
COLCHESTER,
Essex,
United Kingdom.

Dr. C. Trevarthen,
Department of Psychology,
University of Edinburgh,
1 Roxburgh Street,
EDINBURGH,
United Kingdom.

Professor A. Treisman,
Department of Psychology,
The University of British
 Columbia,
2075 Westbrook Hall,
VANCOUVER, B.C.
Canada V6T 1W5.

Dr. P. Tuaycharoen,
c/o Dr. N. Waterson,
School of Oriental and African
 Studies,
University of London,
Malet Street,
LONDON WC1E 7HP,
United Kingdom.

Dr. J. Vaissière,
Département des Etudes et
 Techniques d'Acoustique,
Centre National d'Etude
 des Telecommunications,
B.P. 40,
22301 LANNION Cedex,
France.

Professor E. Wanner,
Harvard University Press,
79 Garden Street,
CAMBRIDGE,
Mass. 02138,
U.S.A.

Professor R.M. Warren,
Department of Psychology,
College of Letters and
 Science,
The University of Wisconsin-
 Milwaukee,
P.O. Box 413,
MILWAUKEE,
Wisconsin 53201,
U.S.A.

Dr. N. Waterson,
Department of Phonetics and
  Linguistics,
School of Oriental and African
  Studies,
University of London,
Malet Street,
LONDON WC1E 7HP,
United Kingdom.

Professor W. Wickelgren,
Department of Psychology,
College of Arts and Sciences,
University of Oregon,
EUGENE,
Oregon 97403,
U.S.A.

Professor R. Wilbur,
Department of Special Education,
765 Commonwealth Avenue,
Boston University,
BOSTON,
Mass. 02215,
U.S.A.

Dr. Eric Young,
Neural Encoding Laboratory,
Department of Biomedical
  Engineering,
Traylor Research Building,
Johns Hopkins University,
720 Rutland Avenue,
BALTIMORE,
Maryland 21205,
U.S.A.

SESSION I
RELATION BETWEEN PRODUCTION AND PERCEPTION

Seminar 1: Mode of representation in production and perception

Chair	RICHARD WARREN
Speakers	MICHAEL STUDDERT-KENNEDY,
	DENNIS KLATT
Discussants	PETER BAILEY, R. A. COLE,
	LOUIS GOLDSTEIN

Seminar 2: Mode of representation in the feedback control of speech
production

Chair	SVEN ÖHMAN
Speakers	PETER MACNEILAGE, JOSEPH PERKELL
Discussants	PETER HOWELL, MARCEL TATHAM,
	KENNETH STEVENS

THE COGNITIVE REPRESENTATION OF SPEECH
T. Myers, J. Laver, J. Anderson (editors)
© *North-Holland Publishing Company, 1981*

Perceiving Phonetic Segments

MICHAEL STUDDERT-KENNEDY

City University of New York and Haskins Laboratories

Why do we study speech perception? Is the speech signal merely a complex acoustic structure in which we are interested because we happen to use it for communication? Certainly, speech belongs to a natural class of acoustic patterns about which we know very little, namely, patterns structured over time by mechanical events—such as a footstep on gravel, a hand crumpling paper, a glass bottle bouncing or breaking (Warren, in preparation). If we knew more about the temporally and spectrally distributed acoustic properties of such dynamic events, and how we recognize them, would we then understand how we perceive speech? In other words, is speech merely a distinctive set of sounds, shaped, as no other sounds are, by movements of human articulators modulating a characteristic vocal source? Perhaps.

But there are reasons to believe that speech may also be distinctive in some deeper sense than this, and that it may engage distinctive perceptual mechanisms. First, the speech signal is the primary carrier of a language: it is rich in information not only about the abstract phonological structure of an utterance, but also about its syntactic and semantic structure. To perceive speech is to apprehend this structure, an act that can only be accomplished by a listener who knows a language. Just what the listener knows is, of course, very much the question. But, he must, at least, know the abstract linguistic units that compose the message—whether words, morphemes or phonemes—and he must know how such units are realized in the signal. No other natural sound, so far as we know, conveys so complex an abstract message.

A second and simpler reason for suspecting that the speech signal may be uniquely related to the human perceptual apparatus is that each speaker of a particular language can readily reproduce sounds uttered by another. Moreover, he can repeat the sounds so rapidly that we may reasonably hypothesize a privileged relation between elements of perception and elements of production. That the repetition may be far from an acoustically exact imitation, and yet be perceived as a repetition, only strengthens the hypothesis by emphasizing that more than mere acoustic identity is involved.

We should not lightly dismiss the ability to repeat or imitate. Imitation is, in fact, a remarkable skill that requires an animal to parse the behavior of another into components, and then activate its own corresponding motor controls to reproduce the behavior. A general capacity to imitate has evolved only in social animals—for the most part, in certain primates: its adaptive advantages are obvious in, for example, the well-known sweet potato washing of Japanese macaques (Wilson, 1975, pp. 170-171) or the nest-building of young chimpanzees (van Lawick-Goodall, 1971). Vocal imitation has evolved only in certain species of birds and in man: its adaptive advantages can only lie in communication. Moreover, transformation from sensory input to corresponding motor control is less direct for an acoustic signal, shaped by movements within the internal space of a vocal tract, than for an optical signal, shaped by movements in the external space common to observer and observed. Perhaps we should not be surprised that the human infant begins its imitative attempts by tracking the visually available movements of its caretaker's mouth in ''prespeech'' oral play (Trevarthen, Hubley and Sheeran, 1975). In any event, the human capacity to imitate the speech of another implies a specialized sensorimotor device (perhaps analogous to that being discovered in the canary (Nottebohm, 1977) and suggests that phonetic structure may be represented in the brain in a form sufficiently abstract for there to be ready interchange between listening and speaking. Whether this representation is necessarily elicited during normal speech perception is, of course, an open question.

From this introduction, I wish to turn to the question of how listeners parse an utterance into its component linguistic segments. Whether the segments are words, morphs, syllables or phones need not concern us, for the moment, since once we have accepted the onus of describing the relation between linguistic segments and the acoustic signal, the problem is essentially the same. However, I shall concentrate on the phone, and its constituent cues or features, for several reasons, more fully discussed elsewhere (Liberman and Studdert-Kennedy, 1978). First, I assume the abstract elements of phoneme or feature that underlie the phonetic string to be psychologically real, structural units of lexical and grammatical morphemes, essential to the dual structure that makes linguistic communication possible. Second, a solution to the segmentation problem at the phonetic level should lead toward a solution at higher levels. In fact, we already have some evidence that English word juncture is signalled by allophonic variations in the immediate vicinity of the juncture, that these variations occur at onset rather than offset of words (Nakatani and Dukes, 1977) and that acoustic-phonetic structure at word onset is particularly important for lexical access in fluent speech (Marslen-Wilson and Welsh, 1978). Finally, the speed and efficiency of speech as a medium of communication rests, in large part, on coarticulation among phonetic segments, and this coarticulation is the primary source of the segmentation problem (Liberman, Cooper, Shankweiler and Studdert-Kennedy, 1967).

The trouble began with the spectrogram and with the recognition that, as the cliché has it, phones are not strung together like beads on a string, but rather, as Hockett (1958) wrote, like a line of eggs passed between rollers. Historically, there have been two broad responses to the paradox. The first has been to accept the segments of linguistic analysis—whether the features of distinctive feature theory or the static targets of traditional articulatory phonetics—as psychologically real, and then either to attempt an acoustic formulation of the signal isomorphic with those segments or to posit some specialized mechanism for linking signal and message. The second response has been frankly pragmatic, proposing to finesse the linguist's units as little more than analytically useful fictions (perhaps encouraged by the historical ''accident'' of the alphabet) and to go for supposedly simpler groupings such as phoneme dyads, syllables, or even words.

The first line of response has been the more varied and complex of the two, and will be the focus of most of what I have to say. An important contributor here was Fant who early recognized the disparity between signal and message, remarking that a single segment of sound may convey information concerning several segments of the message, and a single segment of the message may draw information from several segments of the sound (Fant, 1962). Moreover, despite the claim of distinctive feature theory that correlates of the features are to be found at every level of the speech process (articulatory, acoustic, auditory), Fant observed that ''. . .statements of the acoustic correlates to distinctive features have been condensed to an extent where they retain merely a generalized abstraction insufficient as a basis for the quantitative operations needed for practical applications'' (Fant 1962, p. 94). He and his colleagues therefore set about describing the actual segments of sound observable in a spectrogram, the presumed elements with which the perceptual system has to work. They developed a terminology for describing these segments as manner or segment type features (e.g., voicing, plosive release, frication, nasal resonance and so on) and place features specified in terms of formant pattern and energy distribution over frequency and time (Fant, 1968). On two general points, central to Fant's position, there now seems to be a growing consensus: first, one-to-one correspondence does not obtain between features of the signal and features of the message (cf. Parker, 1977, Ganong, in press); second, the signal takes effect through its entire spectral array rather than through the pattern of individual formants. However, Fant's approach has not yielded a solution to the segmentation puzzle.

An emphasis on the entire spectral array has also characterized the recent work of Stevens (e.g. 1972, 1975). Stevens has confronted the problem head-on by undertaking to reformulate the acoustic description of the signal to make it isomorphic with the message (that is, the distinctive feature). He has adopted an explicitly evolutionary approach to the presumed link between production and perception. According to Stevens' (1972) quantal theory, phonetic categories have come to occupy those acoustic spaces where (by calculations from a vocal tract model) large articulatory variations have little acoustic effect, and to be bounded by those regions where small articulatory changes have a large acoustic effect. As a simple example, consider the articulatory-acoustic series that carries the speaker-listener from a high front vowel [i], through an alveolar fricative [s], to an alveolar stop [d]. However, most of Stevens' recent empirical work has concentrated on stop consonants. For example, Blumstein and Stevens (1979) derive three invariant spectral templates, determined by integration over a 26 msec. window at the onset of the three voiced stops, /b,d,g/, spoken by two male speakers before five representative vowels. Their terminology explicitly recalls distinctive feature theory: ''diffuse-rising'' for alveolar, ''diffuse-falling'' for labial and ''compact'' for velar. To match these acoustic properties, and as a step toward solving both the invariance and the segmentation problem, Stevens (1975) posits innate property detecting devices by means of which the infant is presumed to latch onto the speech system. We should note that these devices are conceived by Stevens as general to the mammalian auditory system rather than as tuned specifically to speech; in this they differ from the feature detectors to be discussed below.

Nonetheless, there are difficulties with Stevens' approach. First, the proposed stop-consonant templates invoke a fixed ''locus,'' incompatible with the findings of Delattre, Liberman and Cooper (1955). Thus, the supposedly invariant properties are static rather than dynamic and the role of their matching detectors is essentially to filter out ''irrelevant'' variation. Yet there is a mass of empirical data to demonstrate that the perceptual system is not only sensitive to the very information that these detectors are designed to exclude, but also uses it to reach phonetic decisions (see Studdert-Kennedy, 1976 for a review). Second, the proposed property detectors are currently confined to consonant place of articulation, and there is reason to believe that an attempt to specify analogous detectors for, say, consonant voicing or vowel features would run foul of the many acoustic variations induced by phonetic context, rate and speaker. Finally, no integrative mechanism is proposed for aligning the features in the rows of the phonetic matrix within their appropriate segmental columns.

A third approach within this line of response has been that of researchers at Haskins Laboratories. They too have taken the goal of research in speech perception to be specification of relations between signal structure and linguistic units—but the units of traditional articulatory phonetics rather than of distinctive feature theory.

They too early recognized the problem of acoustic segmentation, remarking at the conclusion of a study demonstrating contextual dependencies among plosive release bursts and following vowel: ". . .the irreducible acoustic stimulus is the sound pattern corresponding to the consonant-vowel syllable" (Liberman, Delattre and Cooper, 1952, 516). However, they have been more atomistic in their approach, searching the signal for "minimal cues" (Liberman, Ingemann, Lisker, Delattre and Cooper, 1959) to phonetic contrasts rather than characterizing the entire spectrum.

Two broad lines of research bearing on the segmentation issue have stemmed from this approach: one, deriving from a seemingly plausible account of categorical perception, has issued in recent work on feature detectors; the other, pursuing multiple acoustic cues, has sought to explain how they are integrated within the phonetic segment. Let us consider each in turn.

Early work with speech synthesizers showed that a useful procedure for defining the acoustic properties of a phoneme was to construct tokens of opponent categories, distinguished on a single phonetic feature, by varying a single acoustic parameter along a continuum (e.g., /ba/ to /da/, /da/ to /ta/, etc.). If listeners were asked to identify these tokens, they tended to identify any particular stimulus in the same way every time they heard it: there were few ambiguous tokens. Moreover, when asked to discriminate between neighboring tokens, listeners tended to do badly, if they assigned them to the same phonetic category, well if they assigned them to different categories, even though the acoustic distance between tokens was identical in the two cases. This phenomenon was dubbed "categorical perception" (Liberman, Harris, Hoffman and Griffith, 1957). Recent work has demonstrated that the phenomenon is not purely psychoacoustic, but, in some degree, a function of the listener's language (for a review, see Strange and Jenkins, 1977). Here, however, I want to pursue its possible psychoacoustic implications for segmentation—implications exploited, incidentally, by Stevens in his quantal theory (Stevens, 1972).

These implications have been elaborated (although with an eye to the problem of invariance rather than of segmentation) by recent work in selective adaptation. Following the lead of Eimas and Corbit (1973), several dozen studies over the past five years have demonstrated that listeners, asked to identify tokens along a synthetic speech continuum before and after repeated exposure to (that is, adaptation with) a good category exemplar from one end of the continuum, report fewer instances from the adapting category after than before adaptation. Since this effect is observed on a labial voice onset time (VOT) continuum after adaptation with a syllable drawn from an alveolar continuum, and vice versa, adaptation is clearly neither of the syllable as a whole nor of the unanalyzed phoneme, but of a feature within the syllable. Eimas and Corbit therefore termed the adaptation "selective" and attributed their results to the "fatigue" of specialized detectors and to the relative "sensitization" of opponent detectors. Later studies have replicated the results for VOT and extended them to other featural continua, such as those for place and manner of articulation.

Unfortunately, several lines of evidence and argument undermine the hypothesis that selective adaptation reflects the operation of feature detecting mechanisms, specialized for speech. First, is the fact that adaptation has been shown to depend on spectral overlap between adaptor and test continuum: adaptation of consonantal features is specific to following vowel, syllable position and even fundamental frequency (see Ades, 1976, for a review) demonstrating that the supposed detectors are certainly not context-free (as would be required, if we wished to identify these mechanisms with Stevens' (1975) property detectors). Second, the grounds for arguing that, say, variations in voice onset time or place of articulation are mediated by opponent detectors, analogous to those posited for color perception, are not neurophysiological. On the contrary, the notion of binary opposition is drawn from distinctive feature theory, despite the fact that this theory holds such oppositions to be abstract relations within a phonological system, often realized phonetically by multiple, context-dependent values (cf. Parker, 1977). Finally, the proposed feature detectors lack biological warrant. The communication system of an animal reflects the pressures of its environment and life-history. Animals such as bullfrogs (Capranica,, 1965) or certain songbirds (Marler, 1963) require innate feature detectors or templates, because they must identify their species accurately, and must learn to do so (when learning is involved) within a relatively brief (or non-existent) period of parental care. The message conveyed by their species-specific signals is simple and largely confined to matters associated with reproduction. This is not the case for human infants. The patterns of mother-infant interaction (e.g., Stern, Jaffe, Beebe and Bennett, 1975; Freedle and Lewis, 1977) and of early infant vocalization (e.g., Huxley and Ingram, 1971, 162 ff.; Menn, 1979) suggest a lengthy, epigenetically guided search for sound structure rather than an innate response to species-specific calls.

I take the preceding arguments and evidence to rule out feature or property detecting mechanisms specialized for speech, but to say nothing about property detecting mechanisms in the general auditory system. In fact, selective adaptation studies bear on the segmentation issue precisely by reaffirming the familiar fact that listeners can engage distinct channels of analysis to perceive contrasts between properties of acoustic signals and that, in speech, these properties may be the many-to-one or one-to-many correlates of phonetic features.

Whether or how listeners normally use these channels in listening to speech is both unknown and a separate issue, one that returns us to the second line of research that has developed out of the Haskins work—the search for cues. This work can be seen as, in a sense, coordinate with Stevens' research on spectral properties. Just as Stevens' work raises the question of how diverse spectral properties, said to correspond to distinctive features, are organized and aligned into phonemes and syllables, so the Haskins work raises the issue of how diverse acoustic cues are integrated perceptually into spectral and temporal properties corresponding to features or phonemes.

The puzzle arises because each phonetic distinction is susceptible to manipulation by many acoustic cues. For example, Lisker (1978) has listed sixteen different cues (not all of them tested, it is true) that may serve to distinguish the medial stops of *rapid* and *rabid*. Similarly, Bailey and Summerfield (1978) have shown that perceived place of articulation of a stop consonant (/p/, /t/ or /k/), consequent upon the introduction of a brief silence between /s/ and a following vowel, depends in English on the duration of the silent closure, on spectral properties at the offset of /s/ and on the relation between these properties and the following vowel.

Typically, cues seem to form a hierarchy with one or more cues dominating the others. Thus, presence of voicing during medial closure forces perception of *rabid* rather than *rapid*, but its absence permits other cues to come into play. These cues may then engage in trading relations, so that equivalent percepts result from reciprocal increases and decreases in their values. A well-worked example is provided by the distinction between *slit* and *split*. Here, equivalent percepts of *split* are yielded either by a relatively brief silence (stop closure) after /s/, followed by second and third formant transitions appropriate to /p/, or by a longer silence followed by steady-state vowel formants without transitions (Fitch, Halwes, Erickson and Liberman, in press). (For a review of such work, see Liberman and Studdert-Kennedy, 1978).

At first glance, multiple cue equivalences, or trading relations, seem common-place in light of the familiar intensity-time relations of audition and vision.

However, while constant energy functions are readily rationalized in terms of basilar mechanics or retinal photochemistry, there is no obvious account of why cues as diverse as, say, silence and formant transitions should be perceptually equivalent. No less puzzling is the function of such spectrally diverse and temporally distributed cues in normal perception. Given the multiplicity of cues to any given phonetic distinction, it hardly seems plausible that each cue be extracted by a separate channel and then combined with other cues to yield a phonetic feature—which must then be combined with other phonetic features to form a phone or syllable (Pisoni and Sawusch, 1975). What principle would rationalize these successive integrations?

The quandary was recognized and a rationale for its solution proposed a number of years ago by Lisker and Abramson (1964, 1971). They pointed out that the diverse array of cues which separate so-called voiced and voiceless initial stop consonants in many languages—plosive release energy, aspiration energy, first formant onset frequency—were all consequences of variations in timing of the onset of laryngeal vibration with respect to plosive release—in other words, of voice onset time (VOT). Moreover, they proposed VOT as no more than an instance of a general articulatory variable, timing of laryngeal action, from which the multiple acoustic cues to consonant voicing in all contexts (initial, medial, final/stressed, unstressed) might be derived (Abramson, 1977; cf. Fant, 1960, p. 225). Unfortunately, VOT has often been narrowly interpreted as an acoustic variable, comparable with supposed non-speech analogs, such as the relative onset time of noise-buzz sequences (Stevens and Klatt, 1974; Miller, Wier, Pastore, Kelly and Dooling, 1976) or of two tones (Pisoni, 1977). Such studies have diverted attention from the deeper issue which Lisker and Abramson were addressing, namely, the origins of acoustic cue diversity.

If we extend their account to perception, we have to say that the perceptual counterpart of the unitary articulatory gesture is not an arbitrary collection of cues, but an integral auditory array. In apprehending this array, we perceive the event that shaped it. In other words, we perceive the gesture by means of its radiated sound pattern, just as we perceive the movement of a hand by reflected light—or the articulated gestures of speech by cineradiography. This is not a new notion. Both Paget in his book on human speech (1930) and Dudley (1940) some years later pointed out that the sounds of speech could be regarded as the carriers of articulated gesture.

Yet, attractive as this view may be and important as an account of the origins of speech cue diversity, it still does not explain how we divide the gesture into its underlying linguistic segments. On the contrary, if we regard the consonant-vowel syllable as the product of an integrated, ballistic gesture (Stetson, (1952) and if, further, we regard this gesture as the essential perceptual object which underlies the diverse acoustic cues, we are led to the paradoxical conclusion that the atomistic approach of the Haskins researchers returns us to a view that anchors perception in the entire spectral array rather than in individual cues—a view, moreover, that comes close to that of the more pragmatically directed line of response to the segmentation problem, mentioned at the beginning. This approach makes no attempt to align segments of the signal with the abstract phonetic segments that shape it.

Let us turn briefly to this second line of response. In the first instance, the approach was adopted in order to synthesize or compile speech with "building blocks" (Harris, 1953), formed from half syllables or "phoneme dyads" (Peterson, Wang and Sivertsen, 1958). Given our ignorance of precisley how the consonant gesture merges with the vowel gesture to yield the *motoric* consonant-vowel syllable, this was an eminently practical approach to *acoustic* synthesis, and one that is still viable (e.g., Fujimura, 1975; Mattingly, 1976). Recently, Klatt (1979) has developed a detailed model in which elements larger than the phone are also the elements of perception (cf. Fujimura, 1975). Klatt proposes a store of a few hundred spectral templates corresponding to phone-pairs, as sufficient to bypass application of phonological rules during perception and to enable recognition of a sizeable lexicon. The point of interest to the present discussion is that Klatt's phone-pairs are, in principle, no different than the acoustic counterparts of syllable gestures. He has taken seriously the familiar claim that ''. . . phones are not directly perceived, but must rather be derived from a running analysis of the signal over stretches of at least syllable length'' (Liberman and Studdert-Kennedy, 1978, p. 153), but has elected to sidestep their analytic derivation. What we must ask is whether this brute force solution is our only recourse.

I believe that it is not and that the solution to the problem lies in recognizing that the speech signal can indeed be segmented into acoustic groups corresponding to phonetic segments, but only by an organism that already knows that phonetic segments are there to be found. The point is clearly made by the results of recent work on reading spectrograms (Cole, Rudnicky, Reddy and Zue, 1979). The subject, VZ, is a skilled acoustic phonetician who has devoted some 2500-3000 hours to learning to read spectrograms. What is of interest here is that while VZ's performance on correctly labeling segments seems to hover around 85% (a vast improvement, incidentally, on previous reported work), he identifies the existence of segments with an accuracy close to 97%. What is the basis of this remarkable performance?

A moment's reflection tells us that the performance must rest on two crucial facts: first, VZ knows that the segments are there to be found; second, the spectrographic display must represent sufficient acoustic information for the task to be accomplished. Consider each in turn.

That VZ's skill rests on his knowledge that phonetic segments exist becomes obvious as soon as we imagine a reader who lacks this knowledge and confronts a spectrogram as a cryptoanalyst, knowing nothing more than that it conveys a message. How would he proceed? Let us grant that, being human, the cryptographer would start by looking for units (very much like the epigraphist, confronted with Minoan Linear B (Chadwick, 1958). What he would find would be, of course, what Fant (1968) found, namely, a large number of clearly defined acoustic segments bearing (as we know, but the cryptographer does not) a one-to-many and many-to-one relation to the phonetic message. Since this appears to be precisely the condition of the human infant, we must ask how the infant acquires the knowledge that segments exist.

Before attempting to answer this, consider the second condition of VZ's performance—that the spectrographic display does represent enough information for the task to be done. What information does VZ, in fact, use? Apparently, the primary sources of information are spectral discontinuities (including, we may assume, the brief silences of stop closure, contrasts between friction noise and vowel periodicity, formant transitions, nasal resonances, plosive release bursts, and so on) and duration. These are the properties recommended by Fant (1968) in his prescription for spectrogram reading. They are also the properties described by Bondarko (1969) in her account of within-syllable segmentation as based on auditory contrast, a relational process, rather than on the extraction of absolute, context-free features.

Yet, as we have already argued, use of this contrast for segment recognition rests on the prior knowledge that phonetic segments exist. Only when the cryptographer possesses this key to the code, is he in a position to discover, by prolonged practice, the groupings and divisions of the acoustic stream that relate the signal to its phonetic message. How then does the human infant learn the code?

Perhaps the answer will emerge from a deeper understanding of the development of imitation. The process is epigenetic: it seems to rest on an innate, imitative response to the sounds of speech, gradually shaped by the language to which the infant is exposed. The newborn quickly learns to discriminate sound from silence (Friedlander, 1970), voices from other sounds (Alegria and Noirot, 1977), its mother's voice from a stranger's, intonation from monotone (Mehler, Bertoncini, Barriere and Jassik-Gershenfeld, 1978), and, in due course, syllable from intonation contour. Motorically, within weeks of birth, the infant is able to imitate the facial movements of its caretakers (Meltzoff and Moore, 1977), and soon engages in "prespeech" oral play, watching its mother's eyes and mimicking the movements of her mouth (Trevarthen, et al. 1977). Gradually, it shifts from cooing and crowing to intonated babble, until, before the end of its first year, syllables emerge.

Here, the process of differentiation ends—saving us from the paradoxical claim that the infant can imitate what it cannot perceive: the babbling infant imitates syllables, not phonetic segments. For, as we have seen, phonetic segments exist neither in the articulatory gesture nor (a fortiori) in the acoustic signal. Rather, phonetic segments are abstract control processes that emerge as the links between acoustic syllables and their corresponding gestures.

We do not have to suppose that development requires actual activation of the motor system, although this must surely facilitate the process. That activation is not necessary is shown by several well-attested cases of children who have learned to understand without being able to speak. An impressive case is that of Richard Boydell, a victim of congenital cerebral palsy, who, unable to speak and lacking all use of hands and arms, nonetheless learned by prolonged maternal tutelage to understand speech, to read, and even, when provided at the age of 30 with a foot-typewriter, to express his thoughts in highly literate English (Fourcin, 1975). If the difficulties of purely auditory segmentation are indeed as real as the evidence suggests, we must conclude that what remained unimpaired in Boydell was the sensori-motor center that links sound and gesture, and that permits the imitating infant to discover the abstract components of its language.

If this view has any merit and any import for future research, it lies in the implication that we cannot understand speech perception by simply charting relations between signal and percept. We have to go behind the signal to the gestures that shape the resonant volumes of the vocal tract. We have to understand how consonant movement and vowel movement merge to form the motor syllable. Perhaps we shall then conclude that the sounds of speech do indeed form a natural class of dynamic events—distinctive in that those who perceive them have learned how to speak.

Note

Acknowledgement I thank Alvin Liberman for shrewd comments. Preparations of this chapter was supported in part by NICHD grant HD-01994 to Haskins Laboratories, New Haven, Connecticut.

THE COGNITIVE REPRESENTATION OF SPEECH
T. Myers, J. Laver, J. Anderson (editors)
© *North-Holland Publishing Company, 1981*

**Lexical Representations
For Speech Production and Perception**

DENNIS H. KLATT

Massachusetts Institute of Technology

INTRODUCTION

Each of us possesses a mental lexicon that characterizes thousands of morphemes and tens of thousands of words. The lexicon contains facts concerning the pronunciation of each item, the syntactic form class(es) of the item, semantic relations among items, and special rules to which the item is subject. The mental lexicon must be accessed for speaking, for listening, for reading, for writing, and for making linguistic judgements.

Each of these activities requires, at least in part, a different method for the retrieval of information. One might assume that these differing requirements have resulted in the creation of distinct accessing mechanisms for what is still a single mental lexicon (Morton, 1970; Ellis, 1979; Fay and Cutler, 1977). Besides being intuitively attractive, this assumption avoids the need for storing the same information in several different modules.

Alternatively, one might hypothesize the existence of several distinct lexicons, each specifically designed to serve the special needs of a given activity. For example, in one form of this conjecture, there might be a single syntactic/semantic lexical network with ties to several special-purpose lexicons containing various types of phonemic, phonetic, and orthographic information. Under this hypothesis, it would be difficult (but not impossible) to explain the importance of phonetic skills for the development of reading skills (Kavanagh and Mattingly, 1972), as well as the phonetic basis for many spelling errors in adults and spelling intuitions in preliterate children (Read, 1971), and the acoustic basis of confusions among letters in short-term memory (Conrad, 1965).

Most researchers currently seem to favor the one-lexicon hypothesis. However, in this paper, I will present new theoretical arguments in support of a dual-lexicon hypothesis—in which one lexicon is used for speaking and a second lexicon (or at least a very different *acoustic* representation of words) is used for listening. Arguments to be presented in the body of this paper motivate two conjectures concerning the most likely representation of lexical information (and method of lexical access) for speaking and listening. The first is that:

> The mental lexicon used for speaking represents
> words in terms of sequences of phonemes (rather than
> in terms of syllables or distinctive features).

This same lexicon could be used in the analysis-by-synthesis mode during speech perception, and is probably used for the overlaid functions of reading and writing (assuming suitable accessing mechanisms are developed). The second conjecture is that:

> The normal method of perceiving familiar words does not exclusively make use of this phonemic lexicon, but rather involves, in addition, the frequent use of a special acoustically-based lexical hypothesis module.

In this paper, I will examine psychological data as well as theoretical arguments concerning the requirements for storage and use of lexical information during speaking and listening in order to make the case for our two primary conjectures. Nothing more will be said about reading or writing or how these activities relate to speaking and listening.

LEXICAL REPRESENTATIONS FOR SPEECH PRODUCTION

Grammars as Psychological Models   Linguists are usually careful to point out that a generative grammar is a descriptive device rather than a model, and to make no claims concerning the status of a generative grammar as a model of speech production (Chomsky and Halle, 1968). And well they should, because attempts to measure the psychological reality of abstract form expansion (Ohala, 1974; Hooper, 1976) and deep-structure rules (Cooper and Walker, 1979) as computations performed during speech production have not been very successful (but see Fay, 1979 for arguments concerning the psychological reality of certain kinds of syntactic transformations).

FEATURE NAMES	/ S	P	R	I	NG /
CONSONANTAL	+	+			+
CONTINUANT	+		+	+	
SONORANT			+	+	
STRIDENT	+				
NASAL					+
LABIAL		+			
CORONAL	+				
ANTERIOR	+	+			
DISTRIBUTED					
LATERAL					
HIGH				+	
LOW					
BACK					
SPREAD GLOTTIS	+	+			
STIFF VOCAL FOLDS	+	+			

FIGURE 1   *Abstract linguistic representation for the word "spring" in terms of component binary distinctive features.*

Nonetheless, the forms and rules developed for linguistic descriptions constitute a good starting point for the study of lexical representation and lexical access. A hypothetical lexical entry incorporating many of the abstract concepts useful in linguistic descriptions is shown in Figure 1, where the word "spring" is represented by a matrix in which the columns are phonetic segments, the rows are names for phonological distinctive features, and the entries indicate whether each segment possesses the particular feature or not. (A linguist might wish to leave some feature values unspecified in a lexical form in order to capture redundancies by rule, but there appears to be little psychological motivation for such a move, and it has the effect of making all features into ternary variables so that there is little or no saving of bits in storage.)

A production model which incorporates the principles of generative grammar à la Chomsky and Halle (1968) might be formulated in the following way: (1) words are represented in terms of their meaningful subcomponent morphemes, (2) morphemes are represented in terms of sequences of phonological segments, (3) segments are represented in terms of component phonological distinctive features, (4) lexical stress patterns for words are assigned by rule, (5) morpheme boundary symbols are used to describe word-internal structure, (6) a set of phonological recoding rules is applied to a morpheme sequence to fill in redundant entries in the feature matrix, elaborate or modify the stress pattern, replace abstract phonological segments by surface phonetic forms, and change feature values as a function of phonetic context and stress (e.g. vowel reduction, cluster simplification, etc.), (7) the rules change the binary phonological features into phonetic scales appropriate for interfacing with the speech production apparatus, and (8) the rules erase boundary information. In the following paragraphs, I will attempt to evaluate the psychological status of some of these units / computations.

Speech Error Evidence   Speech errors are a rich source of information concerning sentence planning and execution. The corpus of over 6000 speech errors collected at MIT over the last few years (Garrett, 1975; Shattuck, 1975), and the extensive UCLA corpus (Fromkin, 1971), have been used to study syntactic questions (Garrett, 1975; 1976) and issues of phonological / phonetic representation of words during speech production (Hockett, 1967; Fromkin, 1971; MacKay, 1972; Fay and Cutler, 1977; Shattuck, 1975; Shattuck-Hufnagel, 1979; Shattuck-Hufnagel and Klatt, 1979a). In the first half of this paper, I will examine what the observed error patterns have to say about the representation of words stored in the mental lexicon and how words are modified at various stages of the speech production process.

Shattuck-Hufnagel (1979) has argued that phonetic speech errors take place well after lexical selection and expansion, so that sound error data may say very little about the nature of lexical representations. However, even if sound errors occur after a lexical entry has been changed by phonological rules, it would be quite remarkable if the units being manipulated when errors are introduced were very different from those units out of which lexical items are constructed. For example, if the lexical representation for ''spring'' is a feature matrix similar to (or more abstract than) the one shown in Figure 1, and phonological rules are applied to change feature values, it would be surprising if errors involving the movement of a single feature (a plus or minus entry in the column representing a particular segment) were almost nonexistent (which, I will argue, is true). Of course, it is conceivable that features move about during phonological expansion, and only entire columns (segments) are being moved about when speech errors occur, but such a state of affairs seems less plausible.

Stress Rules   Chomsky and Halle (1968) formulated the stress assignment rules for English without making explicit reference to syllable boundary locations. In order to accomplish this feat, they had to postulate rather abstract underlying forms for vowels (so as to be able to determine syllable types and syllable boundary positions in relation to weak and strong consonant clusters). Thus, if lexical stress rules are normally applied to the stored representation for a morpheme, either abstract forms for vowels are psychologically real, or syllable structure assignments must be stored in the lexicon.

On the other hand, if stress patterns are stored in the lexicon for all morphemes, and there are therefore separate entries for morphemes that change stress pattern during morphological expansion, there is no compelling motivation either for the representation of vowels by abstract underlying forms, or for the representation of syllable structure in the lexicon. Nor is there need for an exceptions dictionary for unpredictable stress patterns.

Speech error data relevant to the psychological status of English stress rules have been discussed by Fromkin (1971) and by Cutler (1979). They observe that there are relatively few stress placement errors, but of those that are observed, the remarkable thing is that almost all are of the type exemplified by ''I put things in that *abstr'act* that I can't justify'', i.e. the error shares the stress pattern and phonetic pattern of another word (in this case, the word ''abstr'act'' or ''abstraction''). If separate entries are in the lexicon for ''abstract'' and ''abstr'act'', the stress error data is due to lexical selection errors, not incorrect execution of stress rules (Cutler, 1979). Since there are virtually no errors of the kinds that would occur if the stress rules were incorrectly applied to polysyllabic mono-morphemic words such as ''problem'' or ''appetite'', it seems doubtful that stress is computed in these cases. The only open issue is the representational status (stored as a unit or morphemic composition by rule?) of words that include a stress-shifting suffix, e.g. ''excitation'' = ''excite + ation''?

TABLE 1 *Possible units involved in lexical representations, lexical expansion, serial ordering, and phonetic recoding stages of the speech production process. The second column indicates our conclusions concerning the status of each unit as an independently movable entity, as revealed in the pattern of speech errors discussed below.*

Unit	Status
1. words	yes
2. morphemes	yes
3. abstract morphophonemic rules	no
4. syllables	no
5. syllable onset and rime	?
6. phoneme	yes
7. context-sensitive allophone	no
8. phonetic features	no

Alternative Phonetic Representations   A list of possible representational units for specifying the segmental form of lexical items is presented in Table 1. In order to use speech error data to establish the psychological reality of one or more of these candidate units, four criteria must be met:

(1)   There must exist errors involving the hypothesized unit,
(2)   which are clearly not changes or movements of a larger unit,
(3)   which are unlikely to be changes in (several) smaller units,
(4)   and the proportion of such errors should be greater than expected, i.e. much larger than would be expected if the speech error data were totally random.

In a pioneering analysis of a large speech error corpus, Fromkin (1971) showed that words, morphemes, certain morphophonemic rules, syllables, segments, and features all met the first three of these criteria, and thus were probably psychologically real units. However, closer examination of the error data suggest that some of the proposed units fail to meet the fourth criterion. The most common units to move about in speech errors are phrases and words (2500/6000 in the 1978 MIT corpus), morphemes (500/6000), and single phonetic segments (2500/6000).[1] But, as detailed below, syllables and phonetic features do not appear to move above independently very often in the "mixed bag" of about 500 remaining errors (such as multiple-segment movement errors, stress errors, and syntactic errors) that cannot be fit into the above categories.

Syllables The status of the syllable as an independently movable unit was called into question by Shattuck (1975). The corpus she discussed contained about two hundred errors in which the moved or changed unit was larger than a single segment or consonant cluster, but smaller than a word. Of this set, by far the largest proportion corresponded to sequences of phonemes which clearly did not correspond to a single syllable. Less than 20 could be called syllabic. This is about the number one might expect if the phonemic sequence errors were distributed randomly with respect to syllable structure. Thus while Fromkin (1971) correctly pointed out that error units do occasionally correspond to syllabic units, the set of submorphemic errors is by no means dominated by syllabic errors. However, syllable structure has some relevance, as will be discussed below in the section on Slots and Fillers; it is only that syllabic sized units do not move about regularly during sentence planning.

Onset and Rime Another way to look at morpheme structure is to divide each component syllable of a morpheme into two phonologically motivated parts—the syllable onset and the rime (Hockett, 1965; Vergnaud and Halle, 1979). In English, there are severe constraints on permitted morpheme-initial consonant clusters (the onset) and on morpheme-final VC (CC) sequences (the rime), but few constraints on putting onsets and rimes together to form syllables, morphemes, and words. Onset and rime constraints are phonotactic generalities that constrain the formation of all morphemes. Is it possible that individual English morphemes are actually represented in terms of such units in the heads of speakers?

The answer turns out to be very difficult to determine from a speech error corpus, since a word-initial single phoneme error usually can be interpreted equally well as a syllable onset error (and such word-initial consonant errors are quite frequent). However, an absolute division of syllables into onsets and rimes cannot be correct because there are several hundred errors in which a single vowel moves or is changed without affecting the remainder of the rime, and there are over fifty errors that clearly involve a single postvocalic consonant without affecting the vocalic portion of the rime.

The onset-rime hypothesis might be reformulated to ask whether errors tend to break the CV connection more often than the VC connection, because the onset-rime hypothesis predicts a looser connection between the initial C and V of a CVC, where the boundary between onset and rime is located. Word-blend errors (e.g. emitting [kənɑkiz] as a blend of two alternative words, "cannollis" and "cookies") are ideal for examining this hypothesis. Note that, in this example, as predicted, the speaker switched to the second word between the C and V of "no", rather than saying [kənokiz]. In a sample of 100 word-blend errors that have been examined, 22 involved clear C/V breaks, 14 contained clear V/C breaks, 56 were ambiguous because of shared segments between the two blended words or because a break at the other position would not have resulted in a detectable word error (e.g. producing "bait" when "beat" and "rate" were intended), and 8 were breaks in consonant sequences (any breaks that occurred at morpheme boundaries were not included in the sample). Apparently, shared segments at comparable positions in competing words (56/100) cases) facilitate the formation of word-blend errors. Secondly, the number of breaks between C/V (22) versus breaks between V/C (14) are not significantly different. Thus, while there is a weak tendency for breaks to occur between onset and rime, there is really little support in speech error data for theories that claim either CV or VC as more basic. Similar conclusions were reached through examination of tip-of-the-tongue data by Browman (1978).

Phonemes   Given the high frequency of single segment speech errors, it seems reasonable to postulate that morphemes are represented in terms of phonetic segments or *phonemes*[2](at least in the stages of sentence planning where speech errors involving sound changes occur). The phoneme is an abstraction in that acoustically rather different phonetic segment types are sometimes grouped together. For example, the /ι/ in "sing" is acoustically quite different from the /ι/ in "will", but they are considered instances of the same phoneme because one believes that they share a common articulatory/acoustic target configuration. The target may not be realized because of coarticulatory constraints with neighboring segments, as in "will".

The number of single-segment speech errors in the MIT corpus, 2500 out of 6000, strongly support claims for the psychological reality of phoneme-sized units during the sentence planning process. These units might be phonemes, less abstract phonetic segments, or even context-sensitive allophones. Consider the phoneme /t/. The /t/ in "cat" may be realized in utterance-final position as a released fully aspirated plosive, while in other sentence contexts, it may be realized as an unreleased stop, as a flap, or as a glottal stop. These allophonic variants do not all share a common articulatory goal structure. Words like "cat" either have several distinct phonetic representations (one of which is selected at any given time according to the nature of the following word), or a single lexical representation that is operated on by a set of rules to introduce an appropriate allophone. The single phonemic /t/ solution seems more attractive from a theoretical standpoint, and is supported by speech error data to the extent that errors seem to occur prior to allophonic selection (Fromkin, 1971).

Context-Sensitive Allophones   Wickelgren (1969) proposed that speech production and perception strategies would be much simpler if the units being manipulated were a large set of context sensitive allophones xAy for each phonetic segment type A, i.e. one allophone for every possible combination of preceding phone x and following phone y. Coarticulatory constraints are built into the allophones, and the serial ordering of segments is specified by default. Speech error data rule out as extremely implausible any claim that lexical entries are stated in terms of context-sensitive allophones in the mental lexicon. An error involving the movement of a single vowel or consonant would result in an inconsistent string of context-sensitive allophones that either could not be pronounced or should lead to deviant productions of the segments involved, whereas segmental errors are typically fluently rendered in a manner appropriate to their new context (Fromkin, 1973).

Abstract Morphophonemic Rules   Fromkin (1971; 1973) cites a number of errors in which the past and plural morphemes are realized in a manner appropriate to the incorrect root morpheme that has exchanged with an intended root. These examples suggest that the phonetic form of the bound morpheme is computed, at least for regular past and plural.

On the other hand, Ohala (1974) tried to determine whether velar softening and morphophonemic rules relating e.g. "divine" and "divinity" are psychologically real in the sense that subjects would generalize these sound patterns to unfamiliar words. The majority of the subjects did not generalize, raising questions concerning any claim that surface forms for "divine" and "divinity" are derived from a single abstract underlying form. It is perhaps more reasonable to suppose that morphophonemic rules that are very productive, have few exceptions, and do not require the postulation of highly abstract base forms will turn out to be psychologically real. But the elegant theoretical framework of Chomsky and Halle (1968) shows little hope of being in the average speaker's head (Mohanan, in preparation; Hooper, 1976).

Phonetic Features   Fromkin (1971) cited a few examples of exchange errors that clearly involved the movement of a single distinctive feature. An example in the MIT corpus is the rendering of "tomato" as [paneto]. The place features of /t/ and /m/ have exchanged, while manner and voicing features have remained in the same position. Fewer than a dozen errors of this type have been observed in a combined MIT/UCLA data base of over 10,000 speech errors. (The exact number of feature blends to be expected in 10,000 speech errors is unclear since there may be a tendency for transcribers to write down only "linguistically interesting" errors after a while.)

How many unambiguous feature exchange errors should be seen if features (rather than whole segments) function as independent movable entities during sentence planning? The only opportunity to observe an unambiguous feature movement error is in an exchange error. We examined the structure of 200 consonantal exchange errors (Spoonerisms) in the MIT corpus to see how often the exchanged elements differed by more than one feature (Shattuck-Hufnagel and Klatt, 1979a). There were (conservatively) at least 70 cases of consonant exchanges where the two consonants differed by more than one feature *and* if a single feature had moved, an unambiguous feature-exchange error would have been produced. For example, "*p*ay Gary" could have come out as a feature exchange ("bay Cary" or "Kay Barry"), or as a segment exchange ("gay Perry").

Thus there were over 70 test cases in which either a feature or phoneme exchange could have occurred. Since the MIT corpus contains only 3 unambiguous feature exchange errors, a single feature exchange seems to occur with a frequency of about 3 times out of 73 opportunities. These results argue strongly for the unity of the segment during those parts of the sentence planning process where segmental exchange errors are generated. Furthermore, Shattuck-Hufnagel and Klatt (1979b) have shown that exchange errors are not idiosyncratic among error types, and that most segmental speech errors appear to occur by a common mechanism. By implication, other types of segmental errors such as additions, omissions, substitutions, and shifts normally involve the movement of an entire segment, even when the error and intended segment differ by only a single phonetic feature. While single features may occasionally be manipulated independently during the production process, the phoneme appears to be the primary unit being manipulated at this level.

Markedness   Linguists such as Jakobson (1968) argue that certain segments or feature values are unmarked in the sense that (1) they are the more natural pole of an opposition, (2) they are acquired earlier, (3) or they are easier to produce. A matrix of 1620 consonantal confusions involving 23 different consonantal phonemes (where both the single intruding consonant and the single intended consonant were known) has been examined for evidence of markedness (Shattuck-Hufnagel and Klatt, 1979a). Results of the analysis indicate that a consonant is rendered incorrectly with a frequency that is very highly correlated with frequency of occurrence of that consonant in English. In addition, a consonant serves as an intrusion with a frequency that is highly correlated with its frequency of occurrence in the language, and this relative frequency is statistically indistinguishable from its frequency of occurrence as an intended consonant.[3] These results would not be expected if the likelihood of an error depended on the phonetic quality of the intended consonant, or if there were a set of "unmarked" consonants which tended to replace marked consonants in errors. The absence of evidence in favor of such strength or markedness concepts (no matter what global linguistic definition of markedness one might favor) is one additional detail in the characterization of the sentence planning process.

"Slots and Fillers" Single consonant errors outnumber vowel errors by a ratio of over 5 to 1 in the MIT corpus. There are virtually no errors where a vowel replaces a consonant, or vice versa. Such errors conceivably might occur during sentence planning, but are aborted as unpronounceable. However, it is more likely that their absence reflects the presence of structure beyond a linear string of segments in the representation of a lexical item. While the precise nature of this structure is a subject of debate, at the very least, it appears to include a distinction between syllabic and nonsyllabic segments.

Single-segment errors are most frequent in word-initial position, in prestressed position, and when competing morphemes have the same syllable-structure and stress pattern (Boomer and Laver, 1968; Nooteboom, 1969; Fromkin, 1971). These tendencies make sense if the segmental insertion component of the speech production process searches the lexicon (or points to entries in a temporary lexical buffer) organized in part according to the supra-phonemic structure of a word, but moves phoneme-sized units about. It is as if concepts such as syllable structure, stress, and the distinction between vowels and consonants form a structural description of a word, or a set of "slots", while individual phonemes are the "fillers" to be located in proper order in these slots. In this sense, the lexical representation for a word is more than just a linear string of segments (see also Liberman and Prince 1977).

Toward a Measure of Consonantal Confusability The detailed pattern of substitutions in the MIT consonantal confusion matrix is far from random. In the matrix representing 1620 errors, 4% of the cells account for over 60% of the errors. These highly confusable pairs tend to share conventionally defined distinctive features (Nooteboom, 1969; MacKay, 1970; Shattuck-Hufnagel and Klatt, 1979b; Goldstein, 1979). Most often, voicing and manner features are preserved in an error, while place-of-articulation features are changed (Shattuck-Hufnagel and Klatt, 1979b). However, this kind of result does not necessarily imply that characterization of the confusion patterns among segments is best described by features. Detailed examination of the error patterns suggest to me that rules stated in terms of features are less descriptive of the data than statements that simply enumerate individual confusable pairs of consonants (or represent confusability by placing consonants in some sort of n-dimensional space). Only a few pairs of consonants account for a majority of the errors; for example, there are many instances of /p/-/f/ confusions, but not nearly as many /b/-/v/ or /t/-/s/ confusions. Unfortunately, an objective test of this conjecture has yet to be formulated.

Consonant Clusters The /r/ or /l/ of morpheme-initial consonant clusters seems to be free to move about independently in speech errors, creating a few errors of the type "pay blasketball". The number of such errors is not large. Do these few errors reflect a random component to the data, or are individual elements of clusters free to move about independently? It is important to know the status of individual segments in prevocalic clusters because it is not inconceivable that clusters function as single units at some stages of speech production.

In particular, postvocalic clusters such as /mp/, /nt/, /nd/, etc. must share the same place of articulation feature in English if they occur in the same morpheme. Such sequences may have a psychological status similar to affricates, i.e. they may involve a complex sequence of articulatory gestures that constitute a single phonological unit. If this were the case, then the articulatory rules that require an earlier time of velar lowering for "sent" versus "send" would be considerably simpler to state, i.e. there would be no need for any "look-ahead" mechanism beyond the next segmental planning unit. (A similar simplicity of control might obtain if the onset and rime were the basic units of articulatory control.)

Models of Speech Articulation This is not the place to review the various theoretical models of articulatory control during speech production (see Kent, 1976 and Perkell, 1977 for reviews). It is probably unwise to even speculate beyond the narrow context of speech errors to the articulatory organization of the speech generation process. Nonetheless, it is tempting to hypothesize that a simple-minded view of phoneme-based articulatory targets might form the basis for a psychologically appropriate model. In this regard, one can question claims that a distinctive-feature based account of articulatory control is desirable; there are too many features that either don't have simple correspondences to muscular commands (e.g. +STOP) or are substantially different in realization depending on the values of other features.

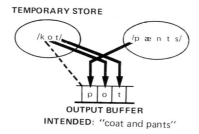

TEMPORARY STORE

OUTPUT BUFFER
INTENDED: "coat and pants"

FIGURE 2   *Many segmental speech errors appear to be the result of two lexical items, represented in terms of phonemes, competing to get into the output buffer.*

How do Speech Errors Occur?   Many segmental speech errors appear to be the result of a malfunction of the segmental insertion process during a serial ordering of the words and segments of an intended utterance. The process is illustrated in Figure 2. When two content words compete for insertion at a particular slot in the planned utterance, one or more segments from roughly the same location in the wrong lexical item can get inserted into the output buffer (Shattuck-Hufnagel, 1979). Frequently, the unused segment is then inserted into a comparable slot in the corresponding lexical item later in the utterance, resulting in an exchange error such as "side and heek" for "hide and seek". Other phonetic errors, such as sub-stitutions and additions, can be explained as the misselection of a segment from elsewhere in the utterance (or from an alternative utterance), while still other "perseveratory" errors are created by the failure of a check off mechanism to keep proper track of which words and segments have been used (Shattuck-Hufnagel, 1979).

Shattuck-Hufnagel envisions the serial ordering process to consist of two stages, the first involving the retrieval of phonemic and stress information from the lexicon for the set of content words to be used in a planning unit, and the placement of items in a temporary store. The second stage involves the specification of a syntactic framework and the insertion of lexical items in the slots by retrieving phonemes one by one from the temporary lexical store. Segmental errors are explained as errors of selection and/or check off during this final phonemic insertion process. The temporary lexical buffer and syntactic framework of the model can be motivated on independent grounds. I.e. a syntactic framework (or response buffer as in Ellis, 1979) is needed to account for syntactic constraints on errors, such as the observation that content and function words do not interact in errors (Garrett, 1975; 1976). The temporary lexical store is needed to account for the availability of source words for anticipatory phonemic errors and exchanges (Lashley, 1951).

The temporary lexical store must have a fairly rich structure in order to ensure that phonemic intrusions come from the same stress and/or syllabic position in another word in the store. One of the most interesting challenges remaining in the modeling of speech production and speech error generation is to provide an explanatory account of the positional constraints on segmental speech errors. An intriguing ''spreading activation'' theory has been offered by Dell and Reich (1979), but there are many details to be worked out before such models can account for the details of error patterns.

Who is Next to Whom in the Mental Lexicon?   During speech production, words are presumably accessed according to syntactic and semantic pointers. Thus it would not be surprising if words in the speaking lexicon were subdivided according to syntactic categories. Misselections involving near neighbors of a desired word would then share syntactic features with the intended word (Fay and Cutler, 1977). But what about phonetic similarity between neighbors in the mental lexicon?

TABLE 2   *Malapropisms with non-initial primary lexical stress.*

	Intended	Error
1	suggest	suspect
2	discussing	disgusting
3	resurrected	rearrested
4	similarity	significance
5	permit	promote
6	expeditious	exhibits
7	described	discovered
8	collecting	correcting
9	constriction	construction
10	detective	defective
11	Viennese	Vietnamese
12	experiments	experience
13	commute	compete
14	reversed	reserved
15	Alaska	elastic
16	affection	infection
17	apply	supply
18	complied	compiled
19	photographic	photogenic
20	underlying	underlining

— 18/20 share the same initial segment
— 15/20 share the same second segment
— 14/20 share the same stressed vowel
— 6/20 share the same prestressed segment
— 6/20 share the same post-stressed segment
— 17/20 share the same final segment

If bound morphemic suffixes and prefixes are ignored:
— 14/20 roots share the same initial segment
— 10/20 roots share the same final segment

Fay and Cutler (1977) and Hockett (1967) argue for the existence of a set of speech errors called malapropisms (sound errors resulting in a word that is *not* semantically related to the intended word) and that these errors are phonemically very similar to the intended word in terms of number of syllables, stress pattern, and phonetic segments. In fact, they are so similar (relative to the control condition of phonetic similarity among word errors that *are* semantically related to the intended word) that, they argue, the mental lexicon accessed during speech production must be ordered according to both syntactic category and phonetic similarity within syntactic categories.

I have examined 100 potential malapropisms in the MIT corpus to determine in greater detail the properties shared by a malapropism and the intended word. The hypotheses to be examined include the possibility that near neighbors in the lexicon (1) share word-initial segments, (2) share segments in their stressed syllable, or (3) share segments in their final syllable. Twenty polysyllabic malapropisms having primary lexical stress not on the first syllable were examined, see Table 2.

There are many problems with the analysis, the most serious of which is the determination of a true malapropism. There are uncertainties concerning (1) possibly remote semantic ties, (2) other things that the subject may have been thinking about while speaking which, if phonetically similar, may have intruded upon an intended word, and (3) the fact that a simple sound error will often result in an English word. It is in fact not inconceivable that there is no such thing as a malapropism (defined as the accidental retrieval of a word close to the intended word in the mental lexicon), but that malapropisms are artifacts of deficiencies in the error transcription/classification process. This is an issue of major significance (see below), but one for which no easy answer is apparent.

If malapropisms do exist, and the ones listed in Table 2 are a representative sample, the following general statement can be made. Phonetic similarity at the beginning of words is stronger than that associated with stressed syllables or word endings (especially true if suffix effects and the high probability of certain word-ending consonants are taken into account). It is almost as if the lexicon is arranged in the form of a tree in which all words that share initial segments are grouped together until they diverge in terms of stress or segmental composition. However, the similarity is more complex than can be explained by a simple tree, and details remain to be worked out.

Why should phonetic similarity be an organizational principle for a lexicon used for speech production? Fay and Cutler suggest that the reason is to facilitate search of the same lexicon during speech *perception*. This is a not unreasonable hypothesis, but there remains a puzzle — if the lexicon is subdivided by syntactic categories for purposes of speech production, wouldn't this interfere with efficient search based on phonetic analysis during speech perception? Perhaps the phonemic similarity among near neighbors is for an entirely different reason, such as to facilitate phonological rule application for morphological expansion or the application of phonetic recoding rules across word boundaries during speech production.

Discussion (Speech Production) In summary, I have argued that words in the mental lexicon used for talking are represented phonemically, and that stress patterns for morphemes are stored rather than being computed. Syllables, distinctive features, and markedness concepts play at most a limited role in representing morphemes. The lexicon is probably partitioned according to syntactic categories, and individual words within a syntactic category may be grouped according to phonetic similarity.

The strong evidence in support of phonetic segments (and absence of evidence in support of distinctive features) in speech error data is somewhat surprising and contrary to intuitions. Linguists can make a very strong case for the advantage of stating phonological rules in terms of features, and a strong case for the common articulatory gestures to be found in many classes of phonetic segments. We must now examine these claims more carefully to determine the disadvantages of a strictly segmental account of the speech production process.

In this reexamination, one must be careful to distinguish between two roles that distinctive features might play. The role that has been argued against in this paper is that of the distinctive feature as an independently movable component of a segment. The second role concerns the use of distinctive features as names for sets of segments that participate in rules. For example, the plural rule of English is most efficiently stated by postulating the existence of two natural classes of segments, sibilants, and voiceless consonants. To the extent that speakers apply the plural rule productively when encountering new words, they are aware of these natural classes, but such behavior has no bearing on the status of distinctive features as independent building blocks or components of segments.

For those features that involve a more-or-less identical articulatory gesture across several phonetic segment types, such as the voicing onset delay for English /p, t, k/, it is more efficient, but not logically necessary, to call a common articulatory subroutine for delaying voicing onset. Given the minimal number of cases where such subroutines are completely independent of values of other features, it seems questionable that the organism should evolve to capture such regularities by subroutines associated with distinctive features.

On the other hand, if segmentally based rules are indeed the way in which the nervous sytem is organized to produce speech, how is one to account for the evolution of natural classes of consonants (Stevens, 1972), or for why dialects e.g. devoice *all* utterance-final voiced fricatives rather than just e.g. /z/?[4] In addition, why are some pairs of consonants more easily confused in the speech error data? These and many other questions must be answered before we can be sure that we have the whole story concerning the psychological form of lexical representations for speech production.

LEXICAL REPRESENTATIONS FOR SPEECH PERCEPTION

I have concluded that a phonemically represented lexicon is accessed during speech production. Is the same mental lexicon examined during speech perception, or does there exist a separate lexicon especially organized for perceptual purposes? The point of the second half of this paper is to show that, although analysis-by-synthesis at the lexical level (Klatt, 1979) and the attitude represented by the motor theory of speech perception (Liberman *et al.*, 1967) are philosophically well motivated, theoretically attractive alternatives exist, and there is presently little psychological data that distinguishes among these alternatives.

The perceptual model, whose description will take up the body of this section, is offered as a direct challenge to a number of assumptions that have traditionally been made concerning mechanisms of speech perception (Liberman and Studdert-Kennedy, 1978). Specific challenges concern the likelihood and desirability of feature detectors, formant frequency estimation, phonetic segmentation, and phonetic labeling as steps in the bottom-up hypothesization of familiar words.

Top-down and Bottom-up Mechanisms in Speech Perception The phonemic talking lexicon might be employed in two different ways during speech perception: (1) by strictly bottom-up analysis of the input acoustic waveform in order to derive a phonetic or phonemic transcription to be compared with the lexical entries, and (2) by top-down analysis-by-synthesis at the lexical level.

Reasonably accurate bottom-up phonetic analysis of an utterance appears to be possible. For example, Cole *et al.*, (1979) have shown that an expert spectrogram reader can perform phonetic transcription with an accuracy approaching 90 percent correct. Nevertheless, it is hard to imagine how the phonetic ambiguity resulting from common phonological recoding rules of the sentence production process (rules of the type that flap /t/ and /d/, collapse identical or similar consonants across word boundaries, palatalize adjacent alveolar consonants, etc.) can be "undone" to find the correct (phonemic) lexical entry, or how inevitable transcription errors are overcome.[5]I describe now a new model of bottom-up acoustic analysis of speech that provides solutions to the phonological recoding problem, as well as to the other problems listed in Table 3.

TABLE 3   *Eight problem areas that must be dealt with by any model of bottom-up lexical access.*

1. Acoustic-phonetic non-invariance
2. Segmentation of the signal into phonetic units
3. Time normalization
4. Talker normalization
5. Lexical representations for optimal search
6. Phonological recoding of words in sentences
7. Dealing with errors in the initial phonetic representation during lexical matching
8. Interpretation of prosodic cues to lexical items and sentence structure

The LAFS (Lexical Access From Spectra) Model   LAFS is a model of lexical hypothesis formation that specifies in detail algorithms for recognizing words of conversational speech directly from a spectral representation of the speech waveform, without making intermediate decisions concerning phonetic segments or phonetic features. The model is described and motivated in greater detail elsewhere (Klatt, 1979).

Preliminary Perceptual Representation of Speech Waveforms   There have been several recent attempts to define a spectral representation of speech that better reflects visually the simple kinds of psychophysical constraints that limit the performance of the perceptual apparatus (Zwicker, 1974; Klatt, 1976; Dolmazon *et al.*, 1977; Zwicker *et al.*, 1979; Searle *et al.*, 1979). One such representation is shown in Figure 3. A *Mel-like* frequency scale [f' = 2000*log(l + f/1600)] is used to reduce the relative importance of high frequencies. A *Sone* amplitude scale is used to account for the nonlinear growth of loudness. Since the equal loudness contour at typical speech levels is nearly flat, use of the sone scale implies that no preemphasis filter need be employed to boost the energy at higher frequencies (filter bandwidths increase with filter center frequency, and this has the effect of introducing some high-frequency preemphasis for speech sounds).

Detailed shapes and bandwidths of the critical-band filters have been designed to match the 40-Sone masking data of Patterson (1976). If Fc is the filter center frequency, then the 3-db down bandwidth is 0.87 Fc to 1.13 Fc. For filters below 1000 Hz, the critical bandwidths are somewhat larger, i.e. BW' =(BW + 130)/2. The bandwidth values asymptotically approach 65 Hz, which minimizes the likelihood that individual harmonics will be resolved at low frequencies. Filter skirts are symmetrical if plotted on a linear frequency scale. Filter skirt attenuation is -35 dB at 0.6 Fc and 1.4 Fc, and skirt attenuation is somewhat more gradual thereafter.

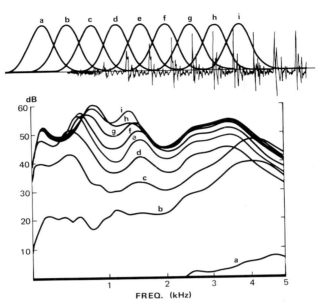

FIGURE 3   *The waveform at the release of the syllable* [da], *shown at the top, has been processed by computing spectra every 10 msec.*

The time weighting window currently used to compute the critical-band spectrum is a 25.6 ms Kaiser window (i.e. the window has about a 10 ms effective averaging duration). It may be necessary to use a shorter window at higher frequencies in order to account for some psychophysical data (see Searle et al., 1979), but for our purposes, the 10-ms averaging window is fast enough to see the spectral changes associated with the most rapid formant transitions in stops, and, at the same time, it encompasses enough of the waveform to get an accurate spectral estimate that does not fluctuate with changes in alignment of glottal pulses with respect to the center of the window.

If this is the nature of the "neural spectrogram" internal representation of a chunk of speech waveform, then we can get some idea of the representation of speech spectra over time by computing static spectra every 1 to 2 msec. Of course, with a time weighting window of 10 msec effective duration, the spectrum cannot change very much in 1 to 2 msec. Thus, if spectra are sampled at discrete 10 msec intervals, as in Figure 3, essentially no information is lost.

Spectral sequences like the one shown in Figure 3 can be thought of as the input representation to the decision processes of the speech decoder. Why not postulate that the strategy of the auditory system is to memorize spectral sequences of this sort for every possible phonetic transition observed in a language? I am proposing a model of phonetic perception that is functionally equivalent to this view. For example, one way to represent the important features of the acoustic transition from /t/ to /a/ is illustrated in Figure 4. A sequence of five representative spectral

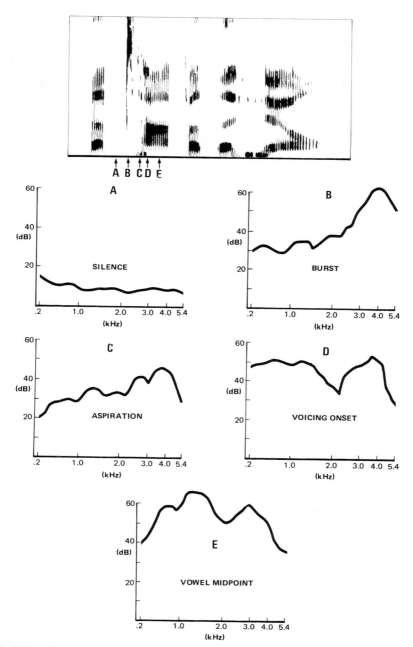

FIGURE 4   *Spectra selected to characterize the transition from /t/ to /a/ of "top" in the phrase "On top of the hill".*

"templates" have been selected to characterize the most important acoustic aspects of all /ta/ transitions. In order to recognize a /ta/, one must match input spectra to one or the other of these ordered spectra; any mismatches would be penalized by computing a cumulative measure of spectral distance between input and templates.

Lexical Representations   The first step in the design of LAFS is to construct a tree of expected *phonemic* sequences for all words of the lexicon, as shown in Figure 5a[6] An abstract phonemic lexicon is assumed as a starting point because of the many theoretical advantages of postulating abstract underlying forms for words and morphemes (Chomsky and Halle, 1968), even though the psychological lexicon may not include some of the more abstract, less productive rules (Ohala, 1974). The phonemic lexicon is organized into the form of a tree (Figure 5a), such that words having the same initial phoneme sequence share nodes (phonemes) and branches until the words diverge in phonemic representation. Initial portions of words are shared so as to save storage, increase search speed, and facilitate application of phonological rules. Of course, a pair of words cannot share tree nodes if the words react differently to phonological rules due to stress differences or other factors.

Precompiled Phonological Rules   Phonological rules are used to derive phonetic forms for each word. Rule application often depends on characteristics of adjacent words, so the lexical tree is first modified in the following way. The end of each word in the tree is attached to all word-beginning states. Then a set of phonological rules are applied to replace each phoneme by an appropriate phonetic allophone, delete or replace some segments, and modify the connectivity pattern (Klovstad, 1978). The result is a phonetic-sequence lexical decoding network of the type shown in Figure 5b, representing expected phonetic properties of all possible (grammatical and ungrammatical) word sequences of the lexicon. Cross-word-boundary phonological phenomena that must be described include the possible insertion of a silence or juncture phone such as the glottal stop, normal phonetic coarticulation, and various simplifications such as palatalization, flapping, [t]-deletion, etc. (Oshika *et al.*, 1975).

For example, the effect of the [s t # s] —> [s] phonological rule in Figure 5b is to create an extra path from near the end of words ending in [st] to the second phonetic segment of words beginning with [s], so that a word pair such as "list some" can be recognized when spoken in the normal way, i.e. without the [t]. Since the rule is optional, the network must represent both alternatives, and the path from the final [t] of "list" to words beginning with [s] is therefore not broken. In the past few years, phonologists have developed formal rules of considerable predictive power (Chomsky and Halle, 1968; Cohen and Mercer, 1975; Oshika, *et al.* 1975; Woods and Zue, 1976) that should prove useful in the context of lexical access.

Precompiled Acoustic-Phonetic Relations   If lexical access is attempted from a phonetic transcription, even given this decoding network in which words are represented in terms of phonetic segments, and phonological rule phenomena are represented by the connectivity pattern in the network, one still requires a fairly sophisticated matching strategy to select precisely those words corresponding to the derived phonetic string. A metric is needed to determine penalties for mismatches and for segmental intrusions or deletions because the automatic phonetic analyzer will make many errors of these types. Experience with the BBN lexical decoding network has shown that metrics to handle errors are very important in that unexpected transcription errors frequently result in a fatal rejection of the correct word (Wolf and Woods, 1978).

The ideal way to deal with transcription errors would be to go back to the original acoustic data to see if the expected phonetic sequence for a word agrees reasonably well. A phonetic transcription intentionally throws away this information, reducing

Step 1: LEXICAL TREE (Phonemic)

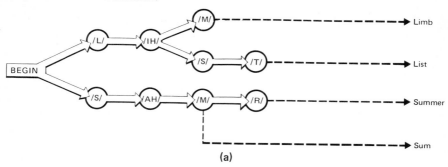

(a)

Step 2: LEXICAL NETWORK (Phonetic)

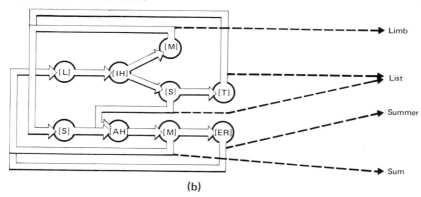

(b)

Step 3: LEXICAL ACCESS FROM SPECTRA (Spectral Templates)

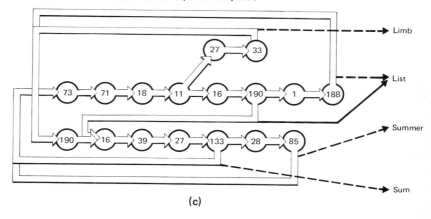

(c)

FIGURE 5 *The LAFS decoding network (c) is derived from a tree of phonemic representations (a) via a phonetic sequence lexical decoding network (b).*

large amounts of acoustic data to a sequence of discrete phonetic elements, and thus, it has been argued, makes the lexical search problem computationally tractable. Why not avoid the problem of recovering from errorful intermediate phonetic decisions by not making phonetic decisions at all? To accomplish this goal within LAFS, each state transition in Figure 5b is replaced by a mini-network of spectral templates of the type shown in Figure 4.

The result is shown in Figure 5c, a lexical-access-from-spectra decoding network that has no intermediate phonetic level of representation. The network is quite large, but only on the order of three times as large as the lexical decoding network made up of phonetic segments that is shown in Figure 5b (i.e. there are, on the average, about three new states (spectral templates) required to represent a phonetic transition).

Recognition Strategy   The input waveform is analyzed by computing a critical-band spectrum every 10 ms (using overlapping 25.6 ms chunks of windowed waveform). The recognition strategy consists of comparing this input spectral sequence with spectral templates of the network. The idea is to find the path through the network that best represents the observed sequence of input spectra. This path defines the word sequence that best matches the input.

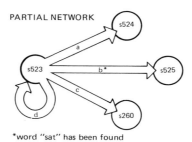

CURRENT HYPOTHESIS BUFFER

HYPOTHESIS	NETWORK STATE	DISTANCE SCORE	PREVIOUS WORDS IMPLIED BY PATH TAKEN THRU NETWORK
1.	s523	80	"THE OLD MAN"
2.	s347	86	"THE OLD MAN"
3.	s520	97	"THE OLD MEN"
4.	s472	114	"THE ALL MEN"
5.	....		

PARTIAL NETWORK

*word "sat" has been found

FIGURE 6   *The LAFS recognition strategy is illustrated by showing a portion of the current hypothesis buffer and a portion of the decoding network relevant to an attempt to extend Hypothesis One by processing the next unknown input spectrum.*

Some details of the recognition strategy can be explained with the aid of an example shown in Figure 6. Let the sequence of input spectra be labeled by the integers 1,2,...,n,...,N. After processing input spectrum n, the "current-hypothesis" buffer might contain the information shown at the top in Figure 6. In order to process input spectrum n + 1, each hypothesis in the hypothesis buffer would be extended by trying all paths leading from that network state. For example, to extend the current best-scoring hypothesis involving network state s523 shown in the lower half of Figure 6, paths a,b,c, and d are tried by matching spectrum n + 1 to spectral templates s524, s525, s260, and s523, and adding the observed spectral distance to the cumulative distance score in each case. Hypothesis One is erased from the hypothesis buffer, and four new hypotheses are inserted in the buffer in the order dictated by the resulting cumulative distance scores. Poorly-scoring hypotheses are pruned from the buffer when it becomes clear that they are unlikely to ever score better than the current best hypothesis. LAFS also makes lexical decisions as it goes along (with a delay of about two words to guard against missing long words), and prunes theories from the theory buffer that are inconsistent with the optimal word string.

As described above, LAFS pays no attention to durations of acoustic events or to rate of spectral change. Methods for incorporating temporal constraints within LAFS are discussed in Klatt (1979).

The search strategy of Figure 6 is almost identical to one employed in the HARPY sentence recognition system (Lowerre and Reddy, 1979). Of course there are major differences between HARPY and LAFS. Harpy represents each phone by only a single spectral template from a rather small inventory of template types, and Harpy can only recognize a finite set of acoustically rather dissimilar sentences with its limited phonetic discrimination abilities. However, the strategies implicit in HARPY, including adaptive talker normalization, seem to me to have much more general application to models such as LAFS.

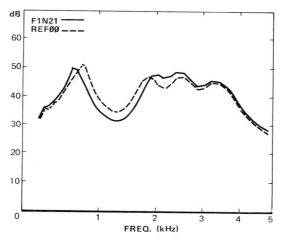

FIGURE 7   *Two spectra differing in terms of the frequencies of first and second formant frequencies and normalized to have the same overall energy.*

Spectral Distance Metrics   A spectral comparison metric is needed to compute matching scores for each input spectrum with the spectral templates. We have begun to collect psychophysical data that may aid in revealing properties of a good spectral comparison metric (Carlson, Granstrom, and Klatt, 1979). It is hoped that a metric can be devised that (1) is independent of the details of the spectra to be compared, and (2) does not require making decisions such as formant frequency estimation, extraction of relational properties such as the direction of a rapid spectral change, or calculation of phonetic feature values. An example of the kind of metric that we have in mind is shown in Figure 7. Two spectra to be compared would first be normalized to have the same overall energy. In this way, differences in overall energy between an expected spectral template and an input spectrum could be entered into the overall distance metric as a separate factor.

The area between the two curves in Figure 7 is one possible measure of psychological distance between the two sounds. We have begun to examine the extent to which the area between the two curves, or area squared, correlates well with perceptual distance (Carlson, Granstrom, and Klatt, 1979). The results are encouraging in that simple metrics can account for over 80% of the variance in distance judgements of subjects who compared vowel pairs within a set of 66 synthetic vowel stimuli, although a few departures from this simple-minded approach are already indicated. Differences in the valleys between energy concentrations are not as important as differences between the two curves in the region of an energy peak, and general spectral tilt does not influence listener's perceptual judgements very much.

Any static metric that is devised will then have to be modified to take into account changes in average speech spectrum and noise background associated with a new speaker or a new recording environment (Klatt, 1976). Modifications may also be needed for comparison of template sequences so as to emphasize dynamic over static properties of the speech signal. For example, a long vowel probably should not contribute much more to cumulative distance than a brief plosive burst.

Template theories of this sort have been criticized in the past as requiring too much storage (but not so much compared with modern computers), of not explicating how the infant learns to group together acoustic sequences into the appropriate phonemes (but motor theory arguments and a good deal of acoustic similarity among most phonetically related sets of acoustic transitions probably can answer this criticism), and that the decoder must make decisions in the face of considerable acoustic variability (true of any model, but more obvious in this case where the input is to be compared with fixed templates). There is variability of at least four kinds: that induced by (1) phonetic context, (2) speaking rate and stress, (3) speaker-dependent differences, and (4) background noise and transmission system distortions. I suggest that there exist in the Harpy speech understanding system (Lowerre and Reddy, 1979) normalization and learning procedures that seem to be capable, in theory, of dealing with variability of these kinds.

Discussion (*Speech Perception*)   LAFS has been designed to provide computational solutions to the eight problems identified in Table 3. In theory, a LAFS processor has the capability of representing all of the acoustic-phonetic and phonological knowledge needed to recognize words in spoken sentences. Lexical hypotheses can be generated rapidly and more accurately in a LAFS structure than in any two-step model (phonetic recognition followed by lexical access) containing the same acoustic-phonetic and phonological knowledge. Two-stage models violate the principle of delaying absolute decisions until all of the relevant information is available, and errors thereby introduced cannot always be overcome. LAFS will make fewer errors than a system that employs a phonetic recognizer for another reason: LAFS does not evaluate all phonologically possible phonetic sequence alternatives—only phonetic sequences that make up English words—and the consideration of fewer alternatives means fewer chances to make an error. The cost of recasting LAFS as a two-stage model would be both a decrement in performance and a need to add strategies for comparing errorful phonetic strings with expected phonetic strings; these strategies are totally unnecessary in a model that does not make phonetic decisions.

LAFS has been presented as if it were a computer system for automatic word recognition in sentence contexts. The advantage of this expository choice is that very explicit solutions to implementation issues must be provided. The disadvantage is that it is hard to visualize how the human auditory system might learn and use such algorithms. How the computational equivalent of LAFS might be acquired by infants learning to listen and speak is an interesting question. The initial perceptual representation of words by an infant is probably close to a simplified neural spectrogram representation, just as in LAFS. The trick will be to explain how a speaking lexicon evolves and how the effects of phonological recoding rules are entered into LAFS.

I have argued elsewhere (Klatt, 1979) that LAFS is a mechanism for implementing three popular (but ill-specified) earlier models of speech perception, the motor theory (Liberman *et al.*, 1967), analysis by synthesis (Stevens and Halle, 1967), and the Logogen (Morton, 1970). All three models are *functionally* equivalent to LAFS, but LAFS uses precompiled information to avoid active on-line synthesis that is characteristic of analysis by synthesis and the motor theory.

LAFS is not the only method of bottom-up speech analysis that is needed to account for the speech perception abilities of man. There must exist a phonetic analysis system for dealing with unfamiliar words (in order to determine a phonemic representation to be placed in the segmentally based talking lexicon, among other reasons). Thus, while it has been argued here that the phoneme is the basic unit for speech production, and the "acoustic morpheme" is the basic unit for speech perception, it would be foolish to suppose that these oversimplified generalizations constitute the whole story.

Notes

1.   It might be argued that segment errors involve the movement of one or two distinctive features because error and intended segment are so often phonetically similar. I will deal with this question below and show that the feature movement explanation is unlikely.

2.   It is notoriously hard to come up with an objective definition of a phoneme (Halle, 1964). One possible view is that phonemes are the psychologically real inventory of segment types that is used by talkers to represent lexical items for speech production. I will use the term in this way in the remainder of the paper.

3.   There is an exception to this generalization involving the four consonants /s,š,č,t/ for which there is a strong localized asymmetry: across this set of consonants, palatalizing errors are much more likely to occur than alveolarizing errors. One possible explanation for these extra palatalizing errors is the misapplication of a common pronunciation rule of English that e.g. causes "gas shortage" to come out as [g æ š: o . . .] (such an utterance would not be considered an error, of course).

4.   These factors argue strongly for the second role of distinctive features, as names for sets of related segments.

5.   See Klatt (1979) for detailed arguments concerning the non-unique inverse of many rules of speech production and the search problems faced by the decoder.

6.   A phonemic tree is the first step in the *computer* design of LAFS, but obviously would not be the first step in the acquisition of LAFS perceptual skills by the infant.

Acknowledgement   Research supported in part by an NIH grant. I am grateful for the critical comments concerning an earlier version of this paper that were provided by Vicki Fromkin, Louis Goldstein, Jola Jakimik, David Pisoni, Ken Stevens, and especially Stefanie Shattuck-Hufnagel. I alone take responsibility for the views expressed here.

Discussion

Peter J. Bailey Studdert-Kennedy and Klatt are in broad agreement with each other about the issues which an adequate model of speech perception must address, for example the traditional problems of segmentation, acoustic-phonetic non-invariance, and talker and rate normalisation, but their contrasting approaches to these problems merit comment.

Klatt's model, incorporating elements of the HARPY speech understanding system (Lowerre and Reddy, 1979), is an illuminating source of ideas for experimentation to test the hypothesis that, in normal adult speech perception, significant gains in accuracy will be achieved by abandoning the traditional requirement that phonetic recognition necessarily precedes lexical access. Certainly, the storage economy implied by phonetic recognition strategies is not specifically motivated on physiological grounds, but, as Klatt acknowledges, there is more than one way to skin a rabbit, and the *growth* of a decoding network for lexical access from spectra is likely to require a capability for phonetic analysis, as will the process by which the representations of new words are entered into the lexicon. Clearly the plausibility of Klatt's scheme as a psychological model will depend on a more detailed specification of, for example, the consequences of *failure* to achieve successful lexical access from spectra, and, in general, of the factors which influence the choice of a particular lexical access strategy. Similarly, since the model depends heavily on the success of HARPY's approach to normalisation of spectra from different talkers and rates of speech, it will be of interest to establish the limits of these techniques. A considerable virtue of Klatt's proposals is that they can be wrought in the precise, specific terms of a computer program, whose predictions can guide empirical investigation or be compared with existing psychological data. For example, we may ask whether the model exhibits the trading relationships between very diverse cues which pervade the results of multi-dimensional speech perception experiments.

Studdert-Kennedy's comments raise important questions for any attempt to characterise, in a model such as Klatt's, what is involved in the development of strategies for lexical access. Introducing a discussion of segmentation of the acoustic array into phonetic segments, Studdert-Kennedy emphasises the importance for acquisition of this skill of a pre-disposition on the part of the infant to imitate (initially the visual) concomitants of articulation. It is probably fair to say, however, that perceptual sensitivity for speech sounds is surprisingly well developed before these imitative behaviours are enlarged into a capacity for speech production. Nevertheless, the implication that there exists in infants an abstract cerebral representation of phonetic structure is congruent with a later argument that the recovery of information for phonetic segments from the acoustic array is predicated upon a sensitivity to the existence of such segments. It is encouraging to find some suggestions about potential specialisations for speech perception (a surprisingly unfashionable position in view of the manifest specialisation for speech production found in the vocal tract morphology of humans) in company with a cogent criticism of claims that speech perception is built upon speech-specialised feature or property detecting mechanisms.

It seems that considerable benefit in the form of testable hypotheses about the form of the cognitive representation of speech would be derived from a formalisation of the knowledge which must be assumed to be available to a model such as Klatt's for it to be able to develop psychologically plausible strategies for lexical access.

Chairman's Comments

Richard M. Warren Humans can function both as producers and receivers (perceivers) of speech. This session is concerned with the relations and differences between these two functions. Certainly, members of a producer-perceiver dyad must share a common lexicon and linguistic conventions. But there are basic differences in the tasks of production and perception: in one case a concept of the material to be communicated precedes (or should precede) verbal organization and production by the speaker; in the other case the concept must be extracted during and following reception by the listener. Are strategies used for one task employed for the other? Michael Studdert-Kennedy sees a close relation between the mechanisms for production and perception, while Dennis Klatt sees a fundamental difference between the units of linguistic organization and lexical access for the two tasks.

Perception of speech is in some respects a more fundamental problem than speech production. There has been an attempt to gather evidence indicating that mechanisms used for speech perception are based upon prelinguistic abilities for perception of auditory sequences which are shared with other animals (Warren, 1976a). Stevens (1975) has looked more closely at the speech signal and has attempted to show how phonetic categories reflect general perceptual mechanisms used by other mammals. It seems quite reasonable to consider that production of speech, if it is to be effective as a means of communication, must conform to the auditory capacities of the target listener and must build upon these abilities. Hence, studies of human nonlinguistic auditory abilities can provide useful information relevant to the perception of speech, and the restrictions and rules which must be followed for any sequence of sounds to be used effectively for linguistic communication.

Knowledge of nonlinguistic auditory abilities may be necessary for a more complete understanding of speech perception and speech production. But the topic of this session, the relation between production and perception of speech, needs to be addressed on a linguistic level.

Michael Studdert-Kennedy's paper is concerned chiefly with the ability of listeners to break down a speaker's utterance into phonetic segments at an early stage in speech perception. Starting with K. N. Stevens' quantal theory, and moving on to lines of research which have emerged from studies of the Haskins group and members of other laboratories, Studdert-Kennedy attempts to integrate and evaluate a large amount of recent data. His conclusions represent a modified motor theory of speech perception — we cannot consider simply the relation between the acoustic signal and what is perceived, but must consider how articulatory gestures enter into the system. While perceptual mechanisms for speech may be shared with other nonlinguistic sounds, a more complete understanding, Studdert-Kennedy concludes, should include the fact that a perceiver of speech (in general) also can function as a producer of speech, and these motor skills are of considerable importance to perceptual skills.

Dennis Klatt's paper represents a rather different approach. He examined speech errors in some detail to argue that phonemes and morphemes correspond to the units of representation in the production of speech. Despite the importance he sees for phonemic units in production, they do not appear attractive to Klatt as units for speech perception. He proposes his LAFS (Lexical Access From Spectra) as a model for going directly from the acoustic spectrum to word recognition without the need to bother with intermediate decisions concerning lower levels of perceptual organization such as phonemic features, phonemes, or syllables. While Klatt is careful to specify that the experimental evidence is not yet available to favor the LAFS perceptual model over other alternatives, nevertheless it shows promise as a computer algorithm for automatic speech recognition. While LAFS as a computer algorithm may prove useful, it seems to me that great care must be exercised in separating such potential usefulness from its validity as a model of perceptual processing. A lesson we should have learned from earlier attempts to go from formal models representing information processing by artificial devices to actual perceptual mechanisms is that what constitutes a simple task for a computer can be extremely difficult for a human, and more importantly for the problem of speech production and perception, what a human can master with seeming ease can be extremely difficult for today's computers. Of course, since the same problems may confront an artificial device and a brain, analyses of the logical requirements of the task may be useful in working with both. But the strategies available for solving problems are quite different. Hence, such strategies as top-down versus bottom-up analysis, and lexical access from spectra, which are treated as related factors for perception and for artificial intelligence by Klatt, should be carefully isolated from each other unless justified quite specifically by direct evidence. Klatt is aware of these risks, but temptation has overwhelmed caution: elsewhere he states, "Perhaps it is not wise to draw conclusions about the functioning of the human brain from analogies to computer algorithms, but the theoretical advantages of combining some of these strategies into a perceptual model are overwhelming'' (Klatt, 1979).

The phoneme appears in several contexts in both Studdert-Kennedy and Klatt's papers as an important, but controversial, entity. I find myself in agreement with Klatt's position that phonemes are not basic units for speech perception, and most of his statement that ". . . it is tempting to hypothesize that a simple-minded view of phoneme-based articulatory targets might still form the basis for a psychologically appropriate model.'' My main disagreement is with Klatt's designation of his hypothesis as "simple-minded.'' I would like to spell out some reasons why I believe the phoneme is basically an articulatory unit, not a perceptual unit. The phoneme appears to be linked conceptually to the alphabet as a set of instructions for speech production. An unfamiliar word can be articulated simply by proceeding through the series of instructions given by the letters within a word (at least for languages in which spelling has not diverged as far from pronunciation as in English). The brilliant unknown inventor of the alphabet must have carefully observed the limited number of articulatory gestures associated with a particular language, and produced a separate symbol for each. Of course, the permuted arrangements of this set of symbols not only provides instructions for production, but also serves the same function as pictographs or hieroglyphics. . . a permanent visual record corresponding to speech. However, while the symbolic systems used for nonalphabetic writing could not be confused with attempts to represent acoustic components of speech, such confusion has occurred with the alphabet and with phonemes, these symbols often taken as representing *sounds* rather than *gestures* leading to production of speech. Even after sound spectrographs demonstrated that phonemes were not generally recognizable in the acoustic signal, they were not abandoned as units of auditory perception. The "acoustic-phonetic non-invariance problem'' (Klatt, 1979) is a legacy of this confusion.

Much of Klatt's paper deals with evidence concerning the nature of speech production provided by errors made by speakers which provide ". . . a rich source of information concerning sentence planning and execution.'' Over a period of years a rich corpus has been collected at MIT and at UCLA. This information is difficult to collect since the occurrence of errors is relatively rare, and much correct speech must be monitored before the errors can be gleaned. I wish to suggest that there is a source of comparable information concerning speech *perception* which can be gathered with much greater ease using a phenomenon which I have called "verbal transformation''.

When a listener hears a word, phrase, or sentence repeated clearly over and over on a loop of tape (or better, a recirculating digital delay line), listeners believe that they hear clear changes in what the voice is saying. These changes occur several times a minute. The nature of changes is lawful, and follows rules which appear to differ from those governing errors in speech production. When sentences are used as stimuli, semantic restraints are strong. Listeners will generally experience changes to acoustically similar forms only if the meaning is closely related. For example, with the sentence "Our side is right" repeated clearly over and over (Warren, 1961), forms such as "I'll side his right" are reported, but forms such as "Our cider's right" were reported very infrequently despite the great acoustic similarity (the experiment was done in England with a speaker who would not pronounce "cider" with a final /r/). The initial meaning inhibits organization into phonetically similar but semantically different responses, and the listener becomes locked into a particular meaning. The listener's cortex does not contain an unabridged lexicon; rather it seems to contain a library wherein are stored many volumes consisting of specialized lexicons devoted to particular topics: once one is opened, we are reluctant to close it and open another. This phonetic/semantic restriction is also found for verbal transformations involving single repeated words. Despite the fact that the only stimulus heard is a single word iterated again and again (corresponding to a particular sequence of articulatory gestures by a speaker), the listener tends to respond in terms of the topic indicated by the meaning of the particular word heard initially.

Verbal transformations correspond to a highly selective aphasia brought on by repetition, followed by reorganization to related alternate forms. The term "related" is crucial — for here we can examine the nature of perceptual relatedness. Verbal transformations appear to reflect linguistic rather than acoustic adaptation or fatigue, for after hearing an alternate word, the original form can (and usually does) reappear: a strictly acoustic adaptation would not be reversed while the stimulus continues. A sizable corpus of errors is easily obtained with verbal transformations for any linguistic stimulus, and I have examined many based on stimuli of graded phonetic and semantic complexity (for a review of the pertinent literature on verbal transformations, see Warren, 1976b). I have not seen any evidence appear suggesting a motor theory of speech perception — that is, there does not seem any favoring of transforms which correspond to neighboring articulatory positions, or motor transitions which are more readily achieved than others.

An examination of the nature of speech perception errors with verbal trans-formations indicates that explanations for these errors won't work which consider either that speech perception is initiated at higher level and then works down, or that initiation is at lower level and then proceeds upwards. Both top-level (semantic) and bottom-level (acoustic-phonetic) factors are evident in the verbal transformation errors observed.

Speech perception cannot be simply a synthetic process (combining lower level units to produce higher order structures) or an analytic process (starting at a higher level organization and then breaking this down into simpler components). Either process alone would be of little value. I suggest that speech perception proceeds neither through analysis-by-synthesis nor through synthesis-by-analysis, but by both at the same time. A bottom-up synthesis couldn't work unless there was guidance toward the correct higher level organization together with a rejection of possibilities leading to incorrect syntheses. A pure top-down analysis would be useless — if there was a way meaning could be found by some sort of template matching without involvement of lower-level aspects of the speech signal, then there would be no need for a listener to proceed with an analysis into components.

What appears appropriate for speech perception is neither a top-down nor a bottom-up model, but a side-by-side model, whereby chunks of different sizes from the incoming message corresponding to higher and lower levels of organization are aligned with corresponding stored engrams, so that simultaneous comparisons can occur at higher levels, at lower levels, and across levels. This Lateral Access to Multilevel Engrams (LAME) model would be more difficult to implement at the level of a computer algorithm than Klatt's bottom-up LAFS model, but LAME may correspond more closely to the nature of perceptual processing.

There is one more suggestion concerning the nature of speech perception which has emerged from study of verbal transformations. Profound age differences exist in the nature of error data obtained at different ages. Perceptual reorganization by children 6 to 10 years of age follows different rules than those for young adults, and both differ considerably from the aged (Warren, 1976b). This suggests that speech perception is not a static skill acquired during childhood, and maintained in this form throughout life. It appears rather that perceptual strategies change with both linguistic experience and functional capacities during the normal life span. While performance may remain similar (that is, the different age groups each have mastery of speech perception) this mastery may be achieved through different mechanisms, perhaps through use of different size linguistic chunks for the processing suggested by the LAME model. I suggest that care should be taken not to assume that equivalent accuracy in speech comprehension implies use of the same perceptual strategies.

THE COGNITIVE REPRESENTATION OF SPEECH
T. Myers, J. Laver, J. Anderson (editors)
© North-Holland Publishing Company, 1981

Feedback in Speech Production:
an Ecological Perspective

PETER F. MACNEILAGE

University of Texas, Austin

One of the most spectacular findings in recent experimental phonetics is the great ability of experimental subjects to compensate for interference with the operation of the speech apparatus. There has been a number of studies of the effects of placing bite blocks of various sizes between the teeth and asking the subject to produce steady state vowels immediately afterwards (Lindblom and Sundberg, 1971b; Lindblom, et al. 1977; 1979; Gay and Turvey, 1979; Kelso and Tuller, cited in Kelso, et al. 1979). These studies have been unanimous in showing that even with bite blocks 22-25 mm in height, subjects were able to produce vowels with appropriate formant frequencies, as early as the first pitch period of phonation.

The results of the bite block studies appear to demand the use of peripheral somatic sensory feedback to inform the control mechanism about the state of the articulators prior to the generation of control signals compensating for that state. (Under the term "somatic sensory" are lumped tactile, joint, tendon, and muscle receptors. Differentiation of the function of these receptors in speech production has not yet been made).

In an attempt to define the role of peripheral feedback more precisely, some of these studies have included the use of various forms of anesthesia. The evidence provided by these attempts has been inconclusive. In one study, topical anesthesia of the anterior portion of the oral cavity produced some production deficit (Lindblom, et al. 1977). In another only the combined effect of topical anesthesia and temporomandibular joint blockade produced a transient deficit (Gay and Turvey, 1979). But in the third study (Kelso, et al. 1979) even the combination of topical anesthesia and temporomandibular joint blockade was not sufficient to produce a production deficit. Kelso et al. believe that this result shows that compensation is possible without feedback. (For their alternative theoretical viewpoint see also Kugler, et al. 1979). I prefer to believe that even in this case considerable sensory information remained available to guide the computation of control signals. This information could come from muscle receptors, peridontal receptors and tactile receptors remote from the topical anesthetic. Nevertheless it is quite remarkable that in the presence of a constraint which, in magnitude at least, must have been unique for the subjects, and in the absence of complete sensory information, correct production was possible. These facts tell us that we are dealing with an adaptive mechanism of great versatility, which, though it may require peripheral feedback does not require the *integrity* of the peripheral somatic sensory apparatus.

There appear to be two possible explanations for these elegant compensatory behaviors. The first is that a central control mechanism is capable of spontaneously generating an entirely new pattern of correct adaptive behavior. The second is that the mechanism makes use of adaptive procedures that are already available because they have been developed for related purposes. Lindblom, et al. (1979) favor the second explanation on the ground that normal speech motor programming is compensatory in nature. As evidence for this they point to the versatile context sensitivity of the speech motor control mechanism and the apparent necessity for a creative generative mode of operation to achieve this context sensitivity. They agree with the present author (MacNeilage, 1970) that a huge set of stored motor commands serving the purpose is implausible. They consider that both peripheral closed loop control and a predictive simulation mode are required in this compensatory behavior.

It is the main thesis of this paper that there is another set of speech-related compensatory maneuvers commonly associated with speech that also give us the ability to compensate in the bite block situation. If one considers the ecology of speech movements, that is, the circumstances in which speech occurs in everyday life it becomes apparent that speech is produced over a wide range of bodily postural contexts. It is the present contention that extensive compensatory maneuvers are required to produce speech intelligibly in all these postural contexts, and it is the ability to make *these* maneuvers that primarily underlies compensation in the bite block situation. The importance of this contention for the present paper is that such maneuvers presumably require peripheral somatic sensory feedback and therefore feedback presumably plays an important role in the control of speech production under normal circumstances.

First consider the postural contexts underlying initiation of speech under everyday conditions. It is a truism that speech is an overlaid function, imposed on structures initially developed for respiration, swallowing, mastication and olfaction. A consequence of this overlaid status is that whenever we initiate speech, we do so in a biomechanical context provided by the respiratory cycle and positions or postures of the moveable structures of the speech apparatus adopted for other purposes.

When initiating speech following a period of silence, the necessary prespeech inspiratory maneuver, usually involving deeper inspiration than that of quiet breathing, (Hixon, 1973) is presumably synchronized with what would have been the inspiratory phase of the respiratory cycle. It is not clear at present whether this adaptation of the respiratory system requires peripheral feedback. It may be achieved by direct modification of the activity of centers controlling the respiratory cycle.

Particular prespeech positions of the phonatory and articulatory structures have often been noted (see the summary in Fowler, 1977). Such positions have not been systematically studied. If these positions were invariant, the initial movement for speech could in principle be produced entirely in an open loop mode, as the control system could, in some sense, know the prespeech position and thus know what was required to get to the initial speech position. Peripheral feedback would presumably be necessary to attain the invariant prespeech position, as the particular movements required would depend on the positions of the moveable structures prior to the movements. On the other hand, if there was no fixed prespeech position, feedback would presumably be necessary to note the particular prespeech position preceding each utterance, as this position would determine precisely what initial speech movement needs to be made. In a preliminary study of this issue in the mandible (MacNeilage, et al. 1969), we found no invariant prespeech position, but found that both velocity and displacement of the initial mandibular movement were directly related to the distance between mandible position at movement onset and "target" position for the first speech segment. Thus, in this case at least, "correction" for prespeech posture was made during speech itself rather than in a preliminary maneuver, and the correction was presumably based on feedback information.

The situation discussed so far is one in which the compensation for particular prespeech positions or postures of the speech apparatus is made during the process of initiating speech. In addition to these prespeech contextual influences which could be labelled adventitious, there is an additional large class of contextual influences that we voluntarily impose on ourselves and do not choose to eliminate when initiating speech. These effects will be discussed first for the respiratory system and then for the phonatory and articulatory systems.

Hixon (1973) has pointed out that there are considerable effects of voluntarily imposed postures on the control of respiration during speech, largely due to the variable role of gravity. For example, whereas in the upright position the effect of gravity on the abdominal contents is inspiratory in direction, (tending to increase lung volume) in the supine position the effect is expiratory. The abdominal contents flow headwards to the extent permitted by the diaphragm, and resting lung volume thus becomes a good deal smaller than in the upright position. Consequently a different pattern of active muscular forces is necessary to control the expiratory phase of respiration for speech in the supine position from that required in the upright position. This difference lies not simply in the greater magnitude of negative muscular forces required to modulate passive forces towards expiration at a given lung volume, but in the pattern of forces. The diaphragm, which is not active during expiration in upright speech, is required to be active in supine speech to combat the gravity-induced headward forces exerted by the abdominal contents (Hixon, 1973).

So far only 2 postures of the respiratory system have been considered. But, as Hixon (1973) points out; "the complexity of respiratory function in speech becomes staggering when consideration is given to the innumerable postures in which the body is oriented and reoriented with respect to gravity" (p. 114). To support this voluntarily induced versatility of function it would appear necessary to make extensive use of peripheral feedback in order for the control system to adequately note the condition to which an adaptive response must be made. Furthermore, it seems plausible that, rather than computing in advance an adaptive response adequate to an entire following utterance, the control system makes use of on-line peripheral feedback during the utterance to monitor its attempts at adaptive response.

Consider next the effects of voluntarily imposed postures on the phonatory and articulatory systems. The fact that these two systems are mechanically linked via the hyoid bone presumably means that the precise position of the head with respect to the thorax must be taken into account for both systems by means of peripheral feedback. Only thus would it appear possible to account for our ability to speak fluently while looking upwards, downwards, or to the side. Voluntary constraints centering on the articulatory system are quite frequently observed. Pipe smoking has often been cited. Holding the chin and holding the hand over/on the mouth are others. Speaking with food in the mouth is another. As in the case of respiration it is plausible that peripheral feedback is necessary not only to note postural constraints prior to speech but also to monitor the system's attempts at adaptive motor response during the course of utterances.

I am aware of 2 studies in which an involuntary postural constraint (bite block) was imposed across an entire utterance (Kelso and Tuller, cited in Kelso, et al. 1979; and Netsell, et al. 1978). (This excludes experiments using artificial prostheses — e.g. Hamlet and Stone (1976) — where the shape of a nonmoving part of the vocal tract is changed). In these studies, remarkable compensation for the presence of bite blocks was observed. It is difficult for me to imagine this being achieved entirely on an open loop basis (again see Kelso, et al. for an alternative viewpoint).

So far we have considered primarily two types of postural constraints that are frequently imposed on the speech production system; 1. adventitious constraints related to other functions of parts of the speech apparatus, which are apparently removed at or prior to speech initiation; and 2. voluntarily imposed prespeech constraints which are maintained throughout utterances. A third and perhaps most interesting type of constraint is that which we voluntarily impose *during* an ongoing utterance. Just as one can speak while lying down, one can lie down while speaking. Within limits, there seems to be no obvious postural constraint imposed on us once we begin an utterance. We nod and shake our heads and smile while talking. When lecturers use the blackboard, head rotations of close to ninety degrees in an alternation between viewing the blackboard and viewing the audience are not uncommon during an utterance. More spectacular examples from calisthenics instructors, and cheerleaders, have been noted by Abbs (1979). The reader can readily provide further examples.

In these cases, the speaker must know within certain limits what postural modification he will impose on the mechanism and, in principle, would be capable of preprogramming an adaptive response. But as in the case of prespeech constraints that are maintained throughout utterances, it seems likely that peripheral feedback is necessary to monitor the success of this preprogramming across the remainder of the utterance. Furthermore, postural modification during an utterance involves a demand in addition to the demands of prespeech postural constraints. Ongoing speech production must be successfully continued *during* the time that the postural change is being made. Intuitively, this seems the most difficult of all the maneuvers discussed so far. Could it be achieved in an entirely open loop mode without requiring correction on the basis of its peripheral consequences? Only if it could be done without significant error. But, as Miles and Evarts (1979) recently pointed out in a discussion of principles of motor control, the main problem with an open loop control system is the problem of error. And given the wide range of possibilites for voluntary postural adjustments and the wide range of segmental and supra-segmental states that could accompany these adjustments and follow them, a totally open loop mode of control in all of these circumstances would seem a remote possibility.

So far we have discussed two types of feedback-based control of the speech apparatus; an off-line mode where feedback can serve to assist corrective adjustments programmed *prior* to speech onset, and an online mode in which feedback serves to assess the need for further corrective adjustments during speech. The question can be raised as to whether these two roles of feedback are qualitatively different. For example in reference to the off-line mode, Perkell (1979) warns that "a steady state paradigm which allows the subject time to "organize" his response before presenting it may reflect functions which are not part of normal dynamic speech motor processes." We presently know too little about how feedback operates to prejudge the answer to this question. But even if the two situations are qualitatively different, this does not mean that the off-line mode is any less important in the successful production of speech. The contention being made in this paper is that *both* the off-line and on-line mode of feedback based control are typically in use in normal circumstances and are therefore important modes of control of speech.

It is only fair to note that so far in this paper no *direct* evidence has been presented for participation of peripheral feedback in either off-line or on-line control processes. In the absence of such evidence, the logical basis of the argument that peripheral feedback is involved in off-line control seems stronger than for the on-line case. It seems that in the off-line mode the system must take into account postural state prior to speech initiation to initiate speech successfully, and that typically no central indicant of that state would be available that did not include a contribution from peripheral feedback. Fortunately, in the on-line case one piece of *direct* evidence *is* available. This comes from an experiment by Folkins and Abbs (1975) in which they unexpectedly impeded jaw closing movements during the production of bilabial stop consonants in three speakers. They found that speakers were capable, even on the occasion of the first disturbances, of making on-line compensatory adjustments involving increased displacement of upper and lower lips in order to achieve bilabial closure. Although more evidence of this kind is obviously desirable, this experiment does suggest that an on-line control mechanism using peripheral feedback was in operation in this experiment. The time constant of this system is of considerable interest. The most direct information on this question from the Folkins and Abbs study comes from an EMG recording from one subject (Fig. 6 in their paper) in which the jaw closing muscle, medial pterygoid, showed an additional burst of activity about 50 milliseconds after the application of the load.

The contention of the present paper that both the off-line and the on-line mode of feedback based control are typical during speech is in opposition to the often expressed opinion that there is "open loop control of well learned speech patterns under normal circumstances" (Borden, 1979, p. 307). Much of the disagreement here might center on the definition of the term "normal circumstances." The author cited above appears to have either not taken into consideration the ecological factors outlined earlier in this paper, or believes them to be relatively unimportant. The present view is that these factors make the definition of a single *normal* speech posture very difficult. And even if such a definition could be agreed upon it may only apply to a small proportion of the occasions on which speech is uttered. The present view is that because of the wide range of postural circumstances under which we speak and the frequent changes in these circumstances, closed loop control is typically in operation. This is not to deny that there might be some periods of time during which no feedback based *corrections* are being made. But these periods may be infrequent.

A question which remains unanswered is of the extent to which postural constraints result in distortions in speech output which are *not* corrected by the control mechanism but are "tolerated" by the listener because of the listener's extensive use of top-down information in interpretation of the speech wave. So little attention has been paid to the postural constraints discussed here that even a relatively gross biomechanical model of the speech production apparatus, from which one could derive effects of postural perturbations on the speech wave, would be extremely useful.

Unfortunately when one comes to relate the present contentions regarding the role of peripheral feedback to the theme of this monograph — the Cognitive Representation of Speech — very little can be said. It is obvious from the preceding discussion that there is a level of representation for speech production which is independent of postural constraints and therefore independent of the detailed movements of the speech apparatus. However, the movements which actually occur are *guided* by the specification of relatively invariant goals at this underlying level. The independence of an underlying representation in terms of goals, and the actual speech movements can also be observed in an analysis of spoonerisms. Here we observe that after the permutation of segments or other units, the movements associated with inserting the units into their new contexts are appropriate to the *new* contexts (MacNeilage, 1979a). I have discussed the question of the means of representation of these goals in some detail elsewhere (MacNeilage, 1979b). The primary candidates for representation at this underlying level are Spatial Targets, Auditory Targets and configurations achieved by Coordinative Structures (Fowler, 1977; Kelso, et al. 1979; Kugler, et al. 1979). Suffice it to say that at present very little evidence is available to allow a choice between these hypotheses, or between these hypotheses and any other.

SUMMARY

It is argued that successful speech observed under bite block conditions, and also under a wide range of self imposed postural constraints which typically precede and accompany ordinary speech, requires a speech control mechanism which uses (both off-line and on-line) peripheral somatic sensory feedback. Three types of postural constraints are discussed: 1. Adventitious constraints resulting from positions adopted by parts of the speech apparatus associated with other uses of the apparatus such as respiration, swallowing, mastication, and olfaction. 2. Voluntary constraints on body and head position adopted prior to speech. 3. Voluntary changes in body and head position during the course of an utterance. It is argued that the first two types of postural constraint require off-line peripheral somatic sensory feedback to note the particular prespeech posture as a necessary prelude to programming of an adaptive response. In addition all three types of constraint probably require on-line peripheral feedback in order to monitor the outcome of the adaptive response. The nature of the underlying cognitive representation which guides the adaptive maneuvers required to overcome postural constraints remains elusive.

Acknowledgements   I would like to thank Randy Diehl, Jerry Lame, Sarah Lasater and Harvey Sussman for their comments on an earlier draft of this paper.

THE COGNITIVE REPRESENTATION OF SPEECH
T. Myers, J. Laver, J. Anderson (editors)
© *North-Holland Publishing Company, 1981*

On the Use of Feedback in
Speech Production

JOSEPH S. PERKELL

Massachusetts Institute of Technology

INTRODUCTION

Very little is actually known about how feedback is used in the control of movement, particularly skilled movement. However, progress in work on the control of movement in recent years has been accelerating, and movement control physiologists now offer a number of examples, hypotheses and paradigms which are extremely interesting to speech physiologists. Considering this state of affairs, any remarks on the use of feedback in the control of speech production have to be speculative, but we can begin to relate our speculations to movement control principles at least in a tentative fashion.[1]

In this chapter, the discussion is focused primarily on the use of *peripheral* feedback in the control of speech production. The term "orosensory" is used to mean the vocal-tract equivalent of somatosensory, that is, tactile and proprioceptive feedback from the vocal tract. The use of orosensory feedback is considered in two categories which are defined by whether the feedback operates in an "on-line" or "off-line" fashion. The expression "on-line" refers to feedback which is used in the direct, moment-to-moment control of movements which are in progress, whereas "off-line" refers to feedback which is used to help control programming of future movements.

OFF-LINE USE OF OROSENSORY FEEDBACK

The off-line use of feedback may be considered in two sub-categories: 1) the role which feedback patterns might play in defining goals toward which articulatory movements are programmed, and 2) the role of feedback in a monitoring function to help refine and adjust motor control strategies.

Orosensory feedback goals as underlying articulatory movements [2] Stevens (1972) has pointed out that there are a number of discontinuous relationships between articulation and sound; that is, for some continuous change in articulation there is a discontinuous change in an acoustic characteristic of the sound output. One way of producing the distinction between the sounds [s] and [š] provides a good example of such a relationship. Figure 1 is a spectrogram of the sound produced by a subject who is asked to pronounce an [s] and then gradually and continuously move his tongue blade back along the surface of the hard palate while continuing to make the fricative sound. At the point during this maneuver marked by the vertical arrow in Fig. 1 there is an abrupt intensification of acoustic energy at about 3 kHz.

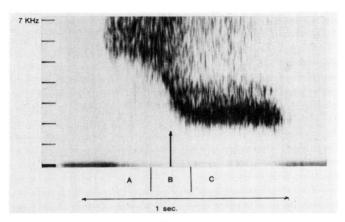

FIGURE 1   *A spectrogram of a* [s - š̌] *transition made by forming an* [s] *and gradually and continuously moving the tongue blade back along the hard palate.*

Figure 2 is a diagram illustrating a hypothesis about a mechanism to account for the acoustic pattern seen in Fig. 1. The diagram shows a hypothetical midsagittal section through the upper and lower incisors, hard palate and tip of the tongue. The [s] is produced by forming a constriction with the tongue tip against the maxillary alveolar ridge and with the inferior aspect of the tongue blade in contact with the lower incisors, as illustrated in Fig. 2a. The [š̌] is produced by forming a constriction a few millimeters posterior to the location for [s], but with the lower part of the tongue blade out of contact with the lower incisors, thus forming a space between the underside of the tongue blade and the incisors and mandibular alveolar ridge, as shown in Fig. 2b. The turbulence noise source that is created by directing the airstream toward the lower incisors acts as an excitation for the acoustic cavities anterior to the constriction. The front cavity is considerably smaller for [s] than it is for [š̌] For an adult male speaker, the volume of the airspace between the tongue constriction and the incisors is estimated to be 4 cc for [š̌] and 1cc for [s]. Spectra (Hughes and Halle, 1956) show a lowest major peak at about 2500 Hz for[š̌]and 4500 Hz or higher for [s]. These values are consistent with calculated natural frequencies for the acoustic cavity anterior to the constriction formed by the tongue blade (Fant, 1960).

FIGURE 2   *Schematic midsaggital views of the positions of the lips, upper and lower incisors, alveolar ridges and blade of the tongue for* [s] *(A) and* [š̌] *(B).*

Thus, a discontinuous acoustic change is produced by a quantal change in the pattern of articulatory contact which results from continuous forward and backward movement of the tongue blade. It is hypothesized that the difference in tactile sensation (corresponding to contact of the tongue tip with the lower teeth versus the lack of contact) is the primary articulatory correlate of the distinction between the two sounds. The implication of this and other examples (Stevens and Perkell, 1977) is that there are states which are defined by certain critical aspects of articulation (such as relatively limited or discrete pattern of contact) that produce sounds with stable acoustic characteristics, regardless of changes or differences in other aspects of articulation. In the above example, two such states would be the articulations illustrated in Fig. 2, which produce the sounds in regions A and C in Fig. 1. These states are opposed to intermediate ones in which a change in the critical aspect of articulation produces a large acoustic change (as represented in our example by articulation around the transition marked as region B in Fig. 1).

States that produce sounds with relatively stable acoustic properties can be called *quantally preferred* states, meaning that they are preferred by virtue of the corresponding stable acoustic output. It is also hypothesized that the same stable acoustic properties can be detected and perhaps even enhanced or selected out by the perceptual mechanism (Stevens, 1972). Presumably languages take advantage of this property of speech production and perception. Quantally-preferred articulatory states define *goals* which are the articulatory correlates of the phonetic features that delineate sound categories. The speech motor control mechanism tends to program movements toward quantally-preferred goals to produce sounds that have stable, perceptually-salient acoustic characteristics.

As has been implied, the articulatory goals are most likely defined in terms of orosensory patterns, and these patterns would come as close as possible to defining the nature of the sound output. The kind of goal illustrated above is a pattern of contact of articulators with one another as this pattern influences the vocal-tract area function (although not all contact patterns may be all-or-none in nature). Compensatory articulation experiments (discussed in the next section) suggest that contact of the tongue with the palate or vocal-tract walls, especially at the point of maximal constriction, constitute articulatory goals for vowels. Other types of goals may be articulator shapes (of the lips or tongue dorsum), levels of vocal-tract wall stiffness, and intraoral air pressure and flow. These parameters influence the characteristics of noise sources or vocal tract resonances and they also can lead to distinctive sensory responses in receptors in vocal-tract muscles and mucosa. Sensory patterns such as these should be less subject to variation from context effects than parameters such as muscle activity or the positions of structures like the mandible which have a less direct influence on sound properties.

This view of the quantal nature of speech production and perception has considerable theoretical appeal; however, our initial experiences in testing it have produced mixed results. Experimentation has shown that subjects demonstrated the hypothesized [s] - [š] distinction under some circumstances, but when the sounds were embedded in words and sentences, the results varied with different subjects and phonetic environments (Perkell, et al. 1979). The work of other investigators also suggests that additional factors such as the location of the constriction between the tongue tip and alveolar ridge may play a role in differentiating sibilants from one another (cf. Catford and Krieg, 1979). In a test of the articulatory correlates of vowel height categories, it was found that hypothesized quantal differences in contact between the sides of the tongue and the maxilla appeared to be much less important than acoustic and individual anatomical factors in differentiating groups of high, mid and low vowels from one another (Stevens, 1975, Perkell, 1979a).

Results like these suggest that any future investigation of orosensory patterns as articulatory goals will have to consider several modifications to or reservations about a strong theory of the quantal nature of speech production and perception. It is possible that there is variation in the relative importance of articulatory and acoustic bases for different features as well as variation of the degree of sharpness of quantal effects (Lieberman, 1971, 1976c). In fact, some features may be defined in part along continuous dimensions, as has been suggested for vowels (Lindblom, 1975; Lindau, 1978). In addition, *expressions* of feature correlates may depend on language-specific phonotactic rules and phonetic inventories as well as on individual variations in anatomy and motor strategies. Thus any single influence on a sound category such as an orosensory pattern may be obscured by a number of other factors. Because of the many possible influences on sound categories and sources of variability, any quantally-preferred orosensory goal such as a pattern of articulatory contact may only be manifested on a statistical basis in some percentage of speakers (Perkell, 1979a). Its influence would be expressed more generally by its effect on sound patterns, as reflected in acoustic targets and possibly by its use during language acquisition.

There is an approach to studying articulatory goals which might be more revealing than the methods used to produce the above-described results. Hughes and Abbs (1976) made measurements of lip and mandible displacement corresponding to vowel production for numbers of repetitions of the same utterance. The results showed variable, but reciprocal amounts of movement of the lower lip (relative to the mandible) and of the mandible in achieving the relatively stable acoustically-important lip opening "goal". Variability of lip and mandible movements across repetitions was found to be significantly greater than variability of the measurement of distance between the lips. These results were interpreted as evidence for operation of the principle of "motor equivalence", or motor programming on a goal-oriented rather than movement-oriented basis. Although there may be methodological problems with the experiment of Hughes and Abbs (Sussman, 1979), their findings do suggest less repetition-to-repetition variability for a parameter with acoustic significance (lip opening) than one with less direct significance (mandible height). If other analogous results can be found, these results could help identify minimally-varying articulatory parameters that serve as important underlying control elements. These parameters could then be compared to those proposed on the basis of quantal effects.

Use of feedback in a "monitoring" function [3] A "monitoring" function of orosensory feedback is suggested by the results of experiments on what is called "compensatory articulation". Several of these experiments have used bite blocks to constrain the mandible in abnormally open (or closed) positions while the subjects produced *steady state* vowels ([i], [a], and [u]) (cf. Lindblom et al. 1971b; Lindblom et al. 1977; Lindblom et al. 1978; Gay and Turvey, 1979). The resulting formant patterns were measured at the first glottal pulse to avoid any possible effects of auditory feedback (which was not masked out). It was found that vowels produced with significantly abnormal jaw openings (i.e. 22-25 mm open for [i]) were essentially the same in quality as those produced normally by the same subjects. However when bite blocks were used in conjunction with oral topical anesthesia (Lindblom, et al. 1977) or with a combination of oral topical anesthesia and anesthesia of the temporo-mandibular joint (Gay and Turvey, 1979), subjects needed several attempts to produce appropriate vocal tract configurations and sound outputs. In the latter experiment, the application of oral topical anesthesia alone was not enough to impair subjects' ability to produce vowels appropriately.

Lindblom and his co-workers interpret their findings as support for the following claim about the role of orosensory feedback. Tactile information from the labial and oral mucosa can be utilized in the motor programming of speech. Vowel "targets" may be encoded as (oro)sensory goals which reflect a neuro-physiological encoding of area functions. These goals serve as a basis for the elaboration of motor commands by structures which "can generate appropriately revised motor commands on the basis of the feedback positional information available before onset of phonation" (Lindblom, et al. 1978).

These results and their interpretations must be viewed with caution for a number of reasons. For example, a generous application of topical anesthesia to the oral and pharyngeal cavities can have a distracting effect on the subject (Lindblom, personal communication). Perhaps more importantly, a steady-state paradigm which allows the subject time to "organize" his response before representing it may reflect functions which are not part of normal dynamic speech motor processes (cf. Leanderson and Persson, 1972; Abbs and Eilenberg, 1976). Nevertheless, the results are provocative enough to warrant further examination, particularly in light of a recent experiment on arm movements.

Polit and Bizzi (1978) have performed an experiment in which 3 adult monkeys were trained to point to a target light with the forearm and hold the position for about 1 second in order to obtain a reward. The monkey could not see its forearm which was fixed to an apparatus that permitted only flexion and extension about the elbow in the horizontal plane. Performance was tested before and after a dorsal root section which eliminated somato-sensory feedback from both upper limbs. In both intact and deafferented animals, the arm was unexpectedly displaced within the reaction time of the monkey, and in both cases the displacement of the initial arm position did not affect the attainment of the intended final steady-state position. These results suggested to the authors that a central program specified an equilibrium point corresponding to the interaction of agonist and antagonist muscles. A change in the equilibrium point leads to movement and attainment of a new posture.[4] However, it was also found that when the spatial relationship between the animal's arm and body was changed, the pointing response of the deafferented monkeys was inaccurate, and remained so even when visual feedback was allowed. In contrast, the intact monkeys were able to compensate within a few tries to the new position without visual feedback. This finding suggested that one major function of afferent feedback is in the adaptive modification of learned motor programs (Polit and Bizzi, 1978).

Following these authors' interpretation of their results, we might consider that in establishing the central program for the performance of the motor task (i.e., in learning the task), the monkeys were incorporating a subconscious "knowledge" of the relationships between the target points with respect to the apparatus and the muscular settings which would result in correct pointing. In doing so, the monkeys were calibrating the biomechanical properties of the system with respect to a particular *frame of reference* (i.e. orientation in space in relation to the body) with the use of somatosensory feedback from the system. When the frame of reference changed, only the monkeys with intact somatosensory pathways were able to "recalibrate" the central program to the new frame of reference.

This line of reasoning and the interpretations of Lindblom and his colleagues lead to a plausible, slightly more specific explanation of the compensatory articulation results. In the case of steady-state vowel productions, the *frame of reference* is defined as the configuration of the dorsal walls of the vocal tract and the position of the mandible. The target (or goal) consists of a vocal-tract area function as sensed by a complex pattern of sensory feedback from the vocal tract. Normally, to produce a steady-state configuration, the control mechanism has a choice of: 1) using a pattern of peripheral feedback to compare with one that has been learned in association with a particular area function and vowel quality, of 2) using a set of equilibrium levels of muscle excitations. These muscle excitation levels can be stored or computed on the basis of an overlearned knowledge of the vocal-tract geometry and biomechanical properties.

In light of these comments, we can consider the three possible combinations of the anesthesia and/or bite blocks. With only (complete) anesthesia, the controller uses option 2. In other words, with a frame of reference which is assumed to be normal, the controller is still capable of specifying equilibrium muscle excitations which it "knows" will produce the correct area function. On the other hand with only the bite block, the controller uses option 1. The appropriate area function is produced by comparing peripheral feedback with the "known" pattern. With anesthesia and the bite block, neither option is available. The frame of reference has been changed. The absence of feedback about the new frame of reference precludes an *a priori* recomputation of appropriate equilibrium muscle excitations, and the absence of tactile feedback precludes a direct comparison with the known pattern. This latest statement is reinforced by the results of Gay and Turvey: only combined anesthetization of the oral mucosa and the temporomandibular joint (along with the bite block) rendered the subject incapable of producing the vowel correctly on the first try. The loss of joint sensation would eliminate the feedback about the frame of reference, needed for a recalibration of the central program, and the loss of sensation from the oral mucosa would preclude using such feedback directly in an error-minimizing feedback loop.[5]

The hypothetical use of afferent information to keep the controller informed about the frame of reference would be equivalent to the function proposed by Polit and Bizzi (1978) in the adaptive modification of learned motor programs. Presumably, the predictive simulation mechanism proposed by Lindblom, et al. (1978) also needs to use feedback in a similar way. It has been suggested that learning a motor activity consists in part of substituting central programming for the use of peripheral feedback (cf. Allen and Tsukahara, 1974). This use of central patterning presumably incorporates an ability to adjust the parameters of the central program to account for changes in the frame of reference. In the case of speech, such changes correspond to speaking with a pipe clenched between the teeth, with the head tilted to one side, or resting one's chin in his or her hand.

Thus, feedback could be used over a time span corresponding to hundreds of milliseconds to inform the control mechanism about changes in the frame of reference (Larson, personal communication; Polit and Bizzi, 1978; Borden, 1979) and about discrepancies between the expected and actual results of motor programs (Luschei, personal communication). Both auditory and orosensory feedback could be used to make adjustments for programming of movements which will occur in the immediate future, but not necessarily on a moment-to-moment basis (Hamlet and Stone, 1978).

THE ON-LINE USE OF PERIPHERAL FEEDBACK

Feedback can conceivably be used on a moment-to-moment basis in "autogenetic" and "coordinating" functions. The term "autogenetic" refers to feedback from receptors within or associated with a muscle which can help to control the contraction of that same muscle with time delays which are limited only by neural conduction and muscle contraction, with little or no neural "integration" times (cf. Houk, 1979). The same feedback might be used to help control the more or less simultaneous contractions of groups of muscles (cf. Henneman, 1974). This "coordinating" use of feedback is presumably accomplished by more neural integrative activity which involves somewhat longer delay times.

Experiments on the moment-to-moment use of feedback are most often performed by exciting afferent neurons (with electrical stimulation of the afferent nerve or mechanical stimulation of the tissue containing sensory receptors) and looking for short-latency EMG responses. Netsell and Abbs (1977) have found that orbicularis oris reflex (EMG) responses to electrical stimulation of the infra-orbital nerve (which carries facial reflex afferents) were greatest in amplitude during closure for a [p], at an intermediate level when the lips were passive, and lowest when the lips were being opened. They suggested that one interpretation of this result is that ''the CNS actively and dynamically facilitates and inhibits the perioral afferent-to-efferent pathway during the ongoing pattern of voluntary labial muscle contraction.'' In other words, this result might be interpreted as evidence that a motor goal (lip closure) is being elaborated in part by a facial reflex pathway. Similar results in response to mechanical stimulation were found by McClean (1978), but he concluded that the increase in reflex excitability before a speech gesture was mainly due to alpha motorneurons' depolarization from descending signals. On the other hand, Kennedy (1977) has obtained results on the autogenetic use of feedback which seem to contradict those described above. Kennedy mechanically interrupted lip movements and looked for short-latency compensatory responses in the EMG of the orbicularis oris muscle. Three different tasks were used, a postural maintenance task, a visual tracking task and a speech task (closure for [p]). In general, responses varied depending on the type of task, with the utilization of feedback appearing to be a ''function of the dynamic requirements of the motor task.'' Responses were minimal for the speech task indicating the absence of a ''servo-like mechanism. . .'' suggesting ''open loop'' operation of the motor control mechanism during [p] closure.

From these preliminary results we can suggest that while the mechanisms are available for the autogenetic moment-to-moment use of peripheral feedback (see also McClean, et al., in press), these mechanisms may not be used in speech. This notion is consistent with the observation that autogenetic reflex loops may be useful in adjusting muscle stiffness to aid in absorbing abrupt load changes (Houk, 1979) which are not usually encountered in speech.

There is one set of experiments in speech production which suggests that feedback information from one structure is used to control or coordinate concurrent movements of another structure. Folkins and Abbs (1975) applied sudden resistive loading to the mandible during bilabial stop closure for randomly selected tokens. They found that the vertical movement of the lips increased in order to complete the closure, even on the first trial. In a later analysis (Folkins and Abbs, 1976), increases in integrated EMG activity were found to accompany the increased lip movements. These results seem to show that the overall gesture is programmed to achieve the goal of lip closure and that ''motor control signals to the lips are adjusted on the basis of on-line information concerning the relative positions of the lips and jaws. . .'' (Folkins and Abbs, 1975).

To date there is only one other demonstration of such coordination, from experiments on head and rapid (saccadic) eye movements in monkeys. With presentation of a visual stimulus, approximately simultaneous initial bursts of EMG occur in neck and eye antagonist muscles, initiating head and eye rotation (in the horizontal plane) toward the target. The eyes reach the target first, and as the head completes its rotation, a compensatory reverse eye movement occurs to keep the eyes on target. This coordination has been found to be initiated by a central program, but the compensatory movement is under peripheral reflex control, using pathways which include the vestibular apparatus (Bizzi, 1975).

Although a mechanism comparable to the vestibular apparatus may not be required for analogous coordination of vocal-tract movements, it seems reasonable to examine ways in which the neural organization for speech might be specialized for such an apparently unusual function. There are a few possibilities. The proximity of the vocal-tract to bulbar and suprabulbar neural centers means that neural conduction delays are very short. For example, monosynaptic loop times can be as short as 12 msec. (Dubner, et al. 1978). Many more complex, even transcortical reflex responses can be elicited with delays as short as 25-40 msec. With muscle contraction times in the range of 30-50 msec, a conservatively-estimated total loop time of 80-100 msec could conceivably allow enough time for some coordinating use of peripheral reflex mechanisms. It has also been observed that there are complex reflex interconnections among vocal-tract sensory and motor-control mechanisms (cf. Dubner, et al. 1978; McClean, et al. in press). It is not inconceivable that speakers learn how to exert ''adaptive control'' over such circuitry as part of learning how to control speech movements.

On the other hand there are reasons for being cautious in suggesting that peripheral feedback is used in this way. Speech experiments which show short-latency reflex responses require an elaborate apparatus which must be attached to the subject. It could be that under these experimental conditions subjects are using mechanisms which they have available but do not usually use in speaking. In fact, experiments on patterns of respiration (Conrad and Schonle, 1979) suggest that we may use somewhat different control strategies under different speaking circumstances (i.e. formal, ''automatic'' and ''spontaneous'' speech or first and second language learning). These different strategies might utilize somewhat different neurological mechanisms. However, as we have noted, the usual absence of unanticipated physical disturbances to speaking suggests that we ordinarily do not use peripheral reflex mechanisms which might be used primarily to compensate for such disturbances.

As mentioned above, variations which are usually encountered in speaking consist of *self-imposed* postural changes, insertions of cigarettes, pencils and chewing gum into the mouth and small fluctuations that result from a less than perfectly precise control over every movement subcomponent (as demonstrated by Hughes and Abbs, 1976). While we could use peripheral feedback mechanisms to deal with such variation, we probably learn how to replace most of the moment-to-moment use of peripheral feedback with internal feedback and efferent copy (cf. Evarts, et al. 1971). These mechanisms are entirely internal to the central nervous system (in the form of interconnections among the cerebral cortex, basal ganglia, cerebellum and brainstem). Their function does not directly include peripheral biomechanics, so they offer a more efficient means of coordinating speech movements which are rapidly sequenced and very complicated.

SUMMARY: A SPECULATIVE OVERVIEW

A great deal of movement control for ongoing adult speech production is probably accomplished through preprogramming. We use basic motor patterns which might be stored in word or morph-size ''skeletal'' form. The basic patterns are constructed of segment-sized units and they are established and maintained with reference to auditory sensory and orosensory goals which help to differentiate sound categories from one another. When we speak, the basic patterns are concatenated and elaborated, partly during pauses and partly on the fly to produce motor programs which incorporate context-dependent phonetic variation. The parameters of programming strategies are adjusted for slowly-varying conditions such as postural changes using efferent copy as well as ''off-line'' feedback about: a) the frame of reference and b) differences between actual and predicted results of the motor programs.

Discussion

Peter Howell: Feedback and the central representation of speech   In the present contribution I want to indicate why the acoustic product of phonemes spoken with differences in speaking rate and stress (Lindblom, 1963), with differences in phonation type (Howell, in press) as well as a result of phonological constraints need to be considered with respect to the feedback they require. In contrast with interferences which give the same acoustic output for a known phonetic input these have received much less attention. The latter require a versatility in the articulatory system while the former might just reflect the auditory tolerance for that segment by the perceiver. In this respect the findings would not be very interesting from the point of view of the production theorist.

If these findings feature in theories of speech production at all they do so in terms of the target representation which is sent to the peripheral articulatory system. They are supposed to be achieved by open-loop control (the target specification is sent to the articulators where, because of mechanical and/or neuromuscular constraints, they have insufficient time to reach the required position before another target configuration opposes the articulatory movement) or by an acoustic target which must (at least in the long-term) be controlled by exteroceptive (in this case, auditory) feedback.

It is clear that an open-loop explanation of these findings is wrong. This will be illustrated by considering the systematic differences which occur with a change in speaking rate. With a change in speaking rate more phonemes have to be produced per unit time. The important acoustic properties of stop consonants are largely insensitive to changes with rate (Klatt, in press) while those of vowels change markedly (Lindblom, 1963). These changes were originally attributed to inertial properties of the articulators, i.e., they were not thought to be under the control of feedback. There are two consequences of an open-loop explanation for vowel production at different speaking rates. First, vowel duration should be determined by inertia (if there were any slack time in the vowel this could be lopped off at high speaking rates without changing the acoustic properties of the vowel). Second, the same muscle groups should be used to move the articulators involved in produced a segment irrespective of speaking rate.

Data on vowel duration for different speaking rates has recently been reported by Gay (1978). It is a well known fact that vowel duration varies with the degree of openness of a vowel and this has been attributed to inertia because of the larger jaw movement required for open vowels (MacNeilage, 1972). If vowel duration arises from inertia in the movement of the jaw then changes in speaking rate should have a bigger effect for the more open vowels (i.e., an interaction between speaking rate and degree of openness is expected). In Figure 1 Gay's (1978) data is presented with vowel duration as a function of first formant frequency for two different speaking rates. (The first formant frequency is an acoustic indicator of degree of openness of a vowel). The estimates of first formant frequency are taken from Lehiste and Peterson (1961) because the figures for the first formant frequencies are not tabulated in Gay (1978). Note that there is a tendency for there to be a positive relation between first formant frequency and duration indicating that segment duration increases with openness. Note that there is clearly no interaction with speaking rate so vowel duration does not appear to be a consequence of inertial

53

properties of the articulators. The second implication of the open-loop explanation is that the same muscle groups are involved in the production of a segment at any speaking rate. EMG studies by Gay and Ushijima (1975) show that this is not true. Speakers reorganize their articulators in complex ways when speaking at different rates recruiting different muscle groups.

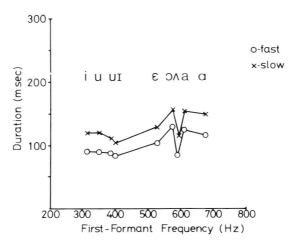

FIGURE 1   *Vowel duration plotted against first formant frequency (an approximate acoustic indicator of degree of openness of a vowel) for the fast and slow speaking rate data of Gay (1978).*

Marcel A. A. Tatham   The linguistic control of speech production: The mechanisms described so adequately by MacNeilage and by Perkell in their papers form part of a device operating somewhere near the end of the encoding system we call language. That system is designed to encode our thoughts into a soundwave able to be decoded by a complementary system back to some copy of the original thoughts. Linguistics is properly concerned with this encoding system, and finds it convenient to subdivide the system into various stages or components. Thus in initial stages thoughts are encoded symbolically and according to their internal logical structure (semantics), and subsequently into symbols which are recognisable as words together with an ordering of those symbols which encodes much of the logical structure (syntax). Even a cursory examination of the output of these initial stages reveals that encoding is not a matter of correct selection of sentences to match the underlying thoughts from a store of some set of such sentences, but rather, for the most part, a process of creation of novel sentences encoding thoughts on a one-off basis. Such a system could only operate if for the encoding of any one particular thought a set of rules were employed (or consulted) which together form the means of creating all possible sentences of the language. That set of rules embodies of course the potential of the entire language, and is by definition unimpeded by locally operating constraints on its actual use for any one encoding operation. This system is mental, and any theory describing it is called psychological

Also mental is that part of the encoding device which accepts such sentential encodings and conditions them such that they can be used to drive the mechanisms described by MacNeilage and Perkell. This stage of encoding must clearly look back to consider aspects of just how the semantic and syntactic encoding was done, and of course look forward to see what are the capabiliites of the final stages (the phonetics). This all is the business of phonology — itself a mental component of the encoding system. Access to the nature of constraints deriving from the mechanisms of articulation, the nature of acoustics and the control of the neuro-muscular/ mechanical system we include under the heading phonetics enables a phonology to produce an output for all possible sentences (as a potential encoding), and for one single sentence (as an actual encoding), which is both a satisfactory rendering of the input sentence and a satisfactory trigger for control of the vocal apparatus.

The output of the phonology (as a potential, or on any actual occasion) has some interesting properties which are by no means apparent from inspection, however close, of the *final* output of the entire system (the potential or actual soundwaves). The discovery of these properties has to do with their psychological reality, and anything beyond this level has no psychological reality. The most striking (for the purposes of this paper) property here is the reality of identifiable objects which make up the sound patterns of words or sentences, and the *smallness* of that set. Mere tens of objects only are discoverable, and therefore, since they participate in the encoding of an infinite number of sentences, invariance is the order of the day. Invariance has two aspects: a same phonological object may occur in different contexts to contribute to the encoding of different words, and the same phonological object may occur in the same context to form encodings of the same word on different occasions.

No-one at our present state of understanding of neurology would claim that there was neural sameness for these objects, but it must surely be unarguable that there *is* psychological sameness. But even if there is neural variability for some representation of these objects at the output level of the phonology, that variability is *minute* compared with the variability readily observed during and at the output of the phonetics.

The variability generated in MacNeilage's and Perkell's mechanisms and in the mechanical and any other mechanisms involved in the conversion of the psychologically-real phonological output into soundwaves can in principle be attributed to the input of that control. Indeed if it *is*, then the variability we *know* to be attributable to such mechanisms would be denied — and that is impossible.

We can examine these systems in the manner of MacNeilage and Perkell; but we can also determine how they must operate in language by hypothesising their role in their immediate task — the encoding of what is mental into something physical.

Psychologically real objects relate to each other in a space. It is worthwhile to associate this space (which is abstract) with the space (which is not) in which articulations find themselves. One thing is apparent: discrimination within the psychological space is finer than that within the articulatory space. This is because constraints on location and precision of location within the spaces are severer physically than mentally. Because the psychological space is destined (as part of the encoding which is language) to be realised as physical space it must be constrained beyond *its* intrinsic limitations. And that is why phonology must look forward to phonetics to determine what is possible.

But under certain conditions the physical constraints can be tamed. Whether they *need* to be to provide an adequate set of locations in the underlying psychological space is arguable: but the fact remains that they can be and are both inhibited and enhanced. In other words MacNeilage and Perkell have described systems which have intrinsic limiting properties: the phonology can and does inhibit and enhance those properties to its own ends. Specific examples of this inhibition and enhancement have been given elsewhere (Morton and Tatham, 1980a), but suffice it

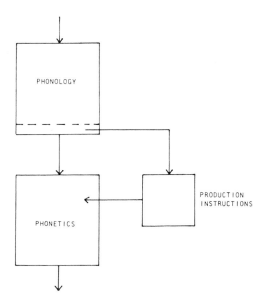

FIGURE 1   *Production Instructions stabilise phonetic processes*

to say here that for *linguistic purposes* intrinsic variability (which might perhaps under other circumstances be considered a defect) is manipulated.

It has been proposed that such manipulation be characterised in the linguistics as a set of Production Instructions (Morton and Tatham, 1980b). This set is, of course, static in the spirit of the overall model of language favoured (Trans-formational Generative Grammar), and exists aside from the phonological and phonetic rules, at a phonetic level (and therefore not deriving psychologically real objects), with an input derived from the phonology's output level and with an output intervening in phonetic processes (Figure 1). A phonetic output is thus the result of an invariant input, whose invariant realisation is rendered impossible by phonetic constraints, but whose potential variance has been somewhat inhibited or somewhat enhanced by the application of phonologically-driven Production Instructions. These Production Instructions, for *linguistic purposes*, stabilise or govern phonetic realisations and are candidate users of the feedback stabilising mechanisms described by MacNeilage and by Perkell.

In order to compensate for natural fluctuations in otherwise undisturbed articulatory movements some moment-to-moment feedback function seems necessary. This function could include peripheral feedback mechanisms and it probably includes internal feedback. The substitution of internal feedback for peripheral feedback might be part of learning how to speak; and there is most likely a fluctuating use of all forms of feedback depending on the demands of the particular speaking situation.

Notes

1.   See Abbs and Eilenberg (1976), Borden (1979), McClean, et al. (in press) and Kent (1976), for reviews of experimental and theoretical work on the use of feedback in speech production.

2.   Much of the discussion in this section has appeared in Stevens and Perkell (1977) and Perkell (1979a, 1980).

3.   This discussion has also appeared in Perkell (1979b).

4.   The existence of additional processes related to the dynamic aspects of the movements is acknowledged, but not treated by Polit and Bizzi (1978).

5.   The fact that only topical anesthesia in combination with bite block was sufficient to impair vowel production in the subject of Lindblom, et al. (1977) might be due to individual differences or differences in the extent and depth of topical anesthesia.

Acknowledgements   I am grateful to Professors Kenneth Stevens, Emilio Bizzi, and Stefanie Shattuck-Hufnagel for their helpful comments. This work was supported by National Institutes of Health Grant No. NS04332.

SESSION II
PERIPHERAL CONSTRAINTS ON THE FORM OF REPRESENTATION

Seminar 3: Auditory constraints

Chair	MARK HAGGARD
Speakers	KENNETH STEVENS, ERIC YOUNG
Discussants	STUART ROSEN, HIROYA FUJISAKI, M. E. H. SCHOUTEN

Seminar 4: Articulatory constraints

Chair	JOHN LAVER
Speakers	OSAMU FUJIMURA, JOHN OHALA
Discussants	ANDRE-PIERRE BENGUEREL, R. A. W. BLADON, JAMES LUBKER, JOSEPH PERKELL

THE COGNITIVE REPRESENTATION OF SPEECH
T. Myers, J. Laver, J. Anderson (editors)
© North-Holland Publishing Company, 1981

Constraints Imposed by the Auditory System on the Properties Used to Classify Speech Sounds: Data from Phonology, Acoustics, and Psychoacoustics

KENNETH N. STEVENS

Massachusetts Institute of Technology

The purpose of this paper is to review some of the psychophysical data and acoustic data that shed light on how the peripheral auditory system creates some form of representation of the speech signal. There are two motivations for engaging in this kind of activity. The first is simply to gain an understanding of how speech signals are processed in the peripheral auditory system, so that one can know what aspects of the signal become distinctive or highlighted in an auditory representation, and what aspects become suppressed. A second, and perhaps more fundamental, motivation is to gain some insight into how the constraints imposed by the auditory system shape the inventory of sounds that are used in language, and how the auditory processing imposes a classificatory structure on the sounds — a structure that plays an important role in determining the organization of the phonological component of language.

Before proceeding to discuss specific evidence for peripheral constraints on the auditory representation, we first consider the kinds of data we plan to use as evidence, and how we propose to interpret these data. One of these kinds of data comes from acoustic measurements on speech sounds, and the other comes from studies of the perception of speech and speechlike sounds. We omit discussion of data from electrophysiological and mechanical studies of the processing of auditory signals — that is the domain of Dr. Young in this symposium (refer to Young-Sachs chapter in this volume).

PHONOLOGICAL EVIDENCE AND ACOUSTIC MEASUREMENTS

In their studies of phonological regularities in different languages, linguists have observed that phonological rules commonly involve groups of sounds. These groups of sounds figuring in different rules in different languages exhibit striking overlaps, and frequently the different sounds within a group undergo the same kinds of modifications as a consequence of application of the rules (Jakobson, Fant, and Halle, 1951; Chomsky and Halle, 1968). Thus, for example, in English, the consonants [s z š ž č ǰ] form a natural class because of the role they play in formation of the plural — when one of these sounds appears at the end of a noun, the plural is formed by adding [ɪz]. Or, in English again, the consonants [p t k f θ] form another natural class — the plural for nouns ending in one of these consonants is formed by adding [s]. These and other natural classes of speech sounds or phonetic segments appear again and again in the phonological rules of a variety of languages. It is not unreasonable, therefore, to suppose that there is some biological predisposition for this organization of phonetic segments into classes. (For further discussion, see Halle and Stevens, 1979.)

One form of this biological predisposition is assumed to arise from the nature of the auditory processing system. The hypothesis is that some component of that system gives a distinctive response to all segments that are placed in a class on the basis of the phonological evidence. According to this hypothesis, all the segments in a given class have some acoustic property in common, independent of the phonetic context in which the segments appear, and that the auditory system responds in some distinctive way when this property is present in the signal. Thus, for example, we would expect there to be some acoustic property or properties in common with the segments [s z š ž č ǰ] or with the group of segments [p t k f θ].

Linguists have described each of these natural classes of phonetic segments as having a particular *feature* in common (Jakobson, Fant, and Halle, 1951). A given phonetic segment, then, is specified in terms of a bundle of features, reflecting the fact that the segment is a member of several intersecting natural classes. About 10 or 15 different features are needed to classify the phonetic segments in all languages. A particular word in a language is represented in the lexicon as a matrix of features: each segment of the word is characterized by a bundle of binary features.

The hypothesis, then, is that phonetic segments within a particular natural class have some acoustic property in common, and that the auditory system responds in a distinctive manner when this acoustic property is present in the sound. A stronger hypothesis would be that this common acoustic property is used in the ongoing process of speech perception. That is, speech perception proceeds by identifying features and then using the feature specification to identify the words. This stronger hypothesis that the features play a central role in ongoing speech perception is often made by linguists and psychologists, but it is not an essential   requirement of a theory that postulates a biological basis for the features. The distinctive response of the auditory system to a particular class of segments could constitute a mechanism for organizing segments into classes for describing phonological regularities or constraints, without necessarily being a vehicle (or, at least, the exclusive vehicle) for instant-by-instant perception of speech.

In this paper, we take the position that the stronger hypothesis is valid, at least under certain speech perception tasks. As we shall observe, there is evidence from experiments on speech perception that the auditory processing of speech proceeds through the identification of particular acoustic properties in the signal — properties that are related directly to the natural classes of segments, or to the features.

PSYCHOACOUSTIC EVIDENCE

For the past 25-30 years, spurred by the work at the Haskins Laboratories, techniques have evolved for using synthetic speech and speechlike sounds for the study of speech perception and, in particular, for investigation of the cues used by listeners in the decoding of speech. One of the techniques that has been used involves generating an ordered sequence of sounds such that one sound differs from its neighbor by a fixed, specified distance along some acoustic dimension. Typically, the sounds that are used have the structure of monosyllabic or bisyllabic utterances, and the sequence spans a range that includes the characteristics of one phonetic category at one end of the range and another, adjacent, phonetic category at the other end of the range. In some experiments the sounds are heard as speech, whereas in others they are nonspeech.

The psychophysical procedures usually involve obtaining measures of the ability of listeners to discriminate adjacent stimuli in the continuum. With particular kinds of acoustic continua, the data show that the ability of listeners to discriminate adjacent pairs of stimuli is not constant. There are some regions along the continuum where discrimination is poor, and other regions where discrimination of adjacent stimuli is very good (Liberman, et al., 1957; Pastore, et al., 1977). That is, even though the physical differences between adjacent stimuli remain the same over the entire series, the listener's ability to discriminate stimuli with these differences shows large variations over the continuum. The auditory system apparently looks at the stimuli in a way that is quite different from the measuring instruments that we use to specify the attributes of the stimuli. In some sense, the auditory representation of the stimuli is a warped or distorted version of the physical representation that we would obtain, for example, by making a spectrogram of the stimuli. Over some portion of the series of sounds, it is difficult to discriminate differences in the auditory representation; over another portion of the series, differences in the auditory representation are very obvious.

The situation is schematized in Fig. 1, in which a sequence of eight sounds is shown as being equally spaced along some physical continuum, but not equally spaced in an auditory representation. Stimuli 1 and 2 would be difficult for a listener to discriminate, whereas stimuli 4 and 5 would be easy to discriminate, even though the physical difference between the two pairs is the same.

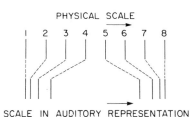

FIGURE 1   *The upper scale depicts a series of acoustic stimuli that are spaced a fixed distance apart according to some acoustic measure. In an auditory representation of these stimuli the distances between adjacent stimuli may be modified in a way that groups the stimuli into categories, as shown in the lower scale.*

If we wish to specify a representation of the stimuli that is more like the auditory representation, we need to define a different way of measuring or describing the sound. For all stimuli in the region where discrimination is poor such as in the region of stimuli 1 - 3 in Fig. 1, we would like to be able to specify some common property, or perhaps to specify some plausible peripheral analysis procedure or transformation that makes these stimuli appear to be very similar. The output of this transformation or property should change abruptly for adjacent stimuli in the region where discrimination is good, as in the region of stimuli 4-5 in Fig. 1.

It is reasonable to suppose that, as inventories of speech sounds have evolved for use in language, preference is given to sounds with physical characteristics spanning the range where differences in these characteristics are difficult to discriminate. Within this range of characteristics, all stimuli presumably sound alike, or at least are very similar, so that deviations in production are not detected as long as they lead to an acoustic output with characteristics that remain within this region. Furthermore, the response of the auditory system when the sound has this acoustic property is distinctively different from the response when the acoustic parameters of the sound lie in an adjacent region (Stevens, 1971a, 1972). If this point of view is correct, we would expect to find these same properties when we measure the sounds that occur in natural speech. That is, the acoustic data that emerge from the study of classes of segments based on phonological rules should yield the same properties as those obtained from the psychoacoustic studies.

SOME EXAMPLES

Rapid-Spectrum Change Versus Slow-Spectrum Change   In general, the speech
stream consists of regions in which the spectrum changes relatively slowly bounded
by narrow time intervals where the spectrum changes rapidly, possibly within a time
span of 20-30 msec or less (Stevens, 1971b; Stevens and Blumstein, 1980). The
regions of rapid spectrum change occur whenever there is an articulatory movement
between a relatively constricted vocal tract and an unconstricted tract. One possible
source of the rapid spectrum change is the rapid increase in frequency of the first
formant that always accompanies an increase in the size of the constriction when the
constriction is in the oral cavity (Fant, 1960). Rapid spectral changes can also occur
at higher frequencies as a consequence of changes in the source of noise in the
vicinity of the constriction or changes in the frequencies of the higher formants.
Vowels are produced with a relatively open vocal tract, and the acoustic consequence
of this configuration is a well-defined formant structure with relatively slow changes
over time.

Segments that exhibit rapid spectrum change and are produced with a narrow
constriction along the midline of the vocal tract are identified by linguists by the
feature *consonantal*. Vowels and glides, which are produced with a less constricted
vocal tract and do not give rise to a rapid spectrum change, are *nonconsonantal*.
As we shall observe later, the points in time where rapid spectrum changes occur
can be regarded as special events or landmarks in the signal, and it is suggested that

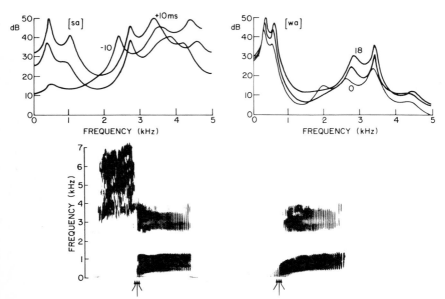

FIGURE 2   *Spectrograms of the two consonant-vowel syllables* [sɑ] *and* [wɑ] *are
shown at the bottom. The spectra at the top are sampled at three points in time from
each utterance, spaced at approximately 10-msec intervals, in the vicinity of the
point where the spectrum is changing most rapidly. Each spectrum is sampled over
a time interval of about 15 msec with some high-frequency preemphasis, and is
smoothed using a linear prediction procedure. The spectra for* (sɑ) *are changing
more rapidly than those for* [wɑ].

the listeners use a speech perception strategy that directs attention to attributes of the signal in the vicinity of these events. In the spectrogram at the left of Fig. 2, for example, we can observe a narrow time region or event where there is a rapid spectrum change. The regions where there is rapid spectrum change are joined to other regions where the spectrum changes are relatively slow. The regions between the slow and rapid spectrum changes constitute the so-called transitions, and these may vary in duration from a few tens of milliseconds to over 100 msec. In the case of the syllable [sɔ] in Fig. 2 there are rather abrupt changes in the spectrum in the vicinity of the consonantal release, whereas for [wɑ],which is nonconsonantal, there are changes in spectral amplitude at low and at high frequency but the changes in spectrum *shape* are relatively slow.

The acoustic attributes that correlate with the identification of the feature *consonantal* have been examined in a series of speech perception experiments (Liberman, Delattre, Gerstman, and Cooper, 1956; Miller and Liberman, 1979). In these experiments, the rate of movement of the formants at the onset of a synthetic consonant-vowel syllable was manipulated to produce a series of stimuli ranging from those with rapidly moving formants to those with slowly moving formants. One of the stimulus continua, schematized in Fig. 3, was characterized by rising

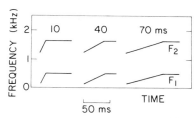

FIGURE 3 *Schematic representation of three two-formant stimuli selected from a series of stimuli in which the durations of the initial transitions varied from short (10 msec, at left) to long (70 msec or more, at right). The formant trajectories for only the initial parts of the stimuli are shown. (After experiments reported by Liberman, et al., 1956.)*

transitions of the formants, and encompassed a range corresponding to the consonants [b] and [w]. Listener responses to the stimuli showed that fast transitions were identified as [b], which is consonantal, whereas slow transitions gave the nonconsonantal response [w]. The boundary between these two classes occurred when the duration of the transitions was about 40 msec. Other experiments with similar kinds of stimuli have shown that the identification of stimuli close to the boundary is equivocal, and can be influenced by the duration of the following vowel (Miller and Liberman, 1979).

Rapid Amplitude Change Versus Slow Amplitude Change Another acoustic property that is common to a particular class of speech sounds is an abrupt rise or fall in the amplitude of the sound, whether or not there is a rapid change in spectral shape. This class of *interrupted* (or stop) segments, includes the set [p t k b d g č ǰ m n ŋ ʔ]. All of these consonants except [ʔ] are consonantal segments as well as being interrupted, i.e., they show a rapid spectrum change as well as an abrupt change in amplitude. For the affricates [č] and [ǰ], however, the abrupt onset (at the initial release following the consonantal closure interval) and the rapid spectrum change (as the following vowel is initiated) occur at different times. Interrupted consonants are produced by completely blocking the airstream at some point along the midline of the vocal tract, including the glottis. Consonantal segments, on the other hand, are produced by creating a complete or partial blockage of the airstream at a point in the vocal tract above the larynx, and the release of this constriction into a following more open vocal-tract configuration gives rise to a rapid change in the spectrum.

The primary acoustic attribute that characterizes interrupted segments is an abrupt rise in amplitude at the release (or an abrupt fall in amplitude at the implosion). The difference in rise time for one example of an interrupted-continuant contrast is illustrated in Fig. 4 for the syllables [čɑ] (interrupted) and [šɑ] (continuant). The amplitude envelope versus time for each consonant is schematized by the piecewise-linear function at the bottom of the figure. The rise in amplitude for an interrupted segment occurs at all frequencies; that is, there is no frequency band for which the amplitude is greater before the release than after the release. This property seems to exist for the nasal consonants as well as for the stop consonants, since the spectrum for the nasal murmur is lower in amplitude than the spectrum immediately following the release at essentially all frequencies, and consequently nasal consonants are classified as interrupted.

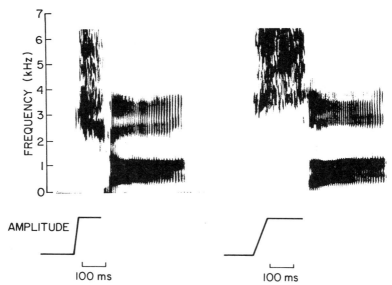

FIGURE 4   *Spectrograms of the syllables [čɑ] (left) and [šɑ] (right). The amplitude envelope at the onset of each syllable is approximated by the piecewise-linear functions shown below the spectrograms.*

Several experiments have investigated listener responses to stimuli in which the abruptness of an onset or the duration of the silent interval preceding the onset is manipulated. The experiments indicate the rate of increase of amplitude at the onset and the duration of the interval of low intensity prior to the onset that are necessary to elicit a distinctive response corresponding to an interrupted or stop consonant.

One such experiment utilized nonspeech stimuli with onsets for which the rise time varied from a few msec to several tens of msec (Cutting and Rosner, 1974). The onsets of the stimuli are schematized at the bottom of Fig. 5, and the discrimination performance is shown by the solid line in the graph at the top of the figure. These stimuli were categorized systematically by listeners: those with rise

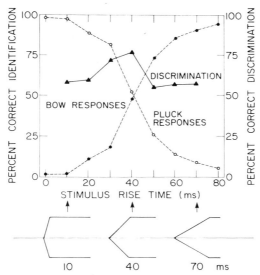

FIGURE 5 *Shown at the bottom are schematized amplitude envelopes at the onsets of three different acoustic stimuli in a series of stimuli with rise times varying from short (10 msec, at left) to long (70 msec, at right). The curves at the top give the responses of listeners to these stimuli in terms of their identification of the sounds as being "plucked" or "bowed" (dashed lines) and in terms of their ability to discriminate pairs of sounds (in an ABX paradigm) with rise times differing by 20 msec (solid line). (The identification and discrimination functions are taken from Cutting and Rosner, 1974.)*

times less than 40 msec sounded like "plucked" musical sounds, whereas those with longer rise times were identified as "bowed" sounds. Pairs of stimuli that occurred within each class were essentially nondiscriminable by listeners, whereas two stimuli with rise times of 30 and 50 msec (i.e., stimuli that were classified differently by the listeners) were more easily discriminated. These results suggest that the auditory system is predisposed to categorize sounds with different rise times into two different classes — those with rapid rise times and those with slow rise times. It is not unreasonable to suppose that the phonetic distinction between *interrupted* and *continuant* consonants (Jakobson, Fant, and Halle, 1963) is based in part on this property of the auditory system.

Experiments in which natural speech stimuli are manipulated in various ways have also provided evidence that helps to define the acoustic property associated with the feature *interrupted*. For example, Cutting and Rosner (1974) have shown that a syllable [šɑ], for which the onset of the amplitude of the [š] is rather gradual, can be changed to [čɑ] by removing the initial part of the frication and by leaving an abrupt amplitude rise in the noise. In another experiment (Bastian, Delattre, and Liberman, 1959), the word *slit* was generated, and the acoustic waveform was then modified by creating a gap of successively increasing duration between the end of the frication noise in [s] and the onset of voicing in [I]. When this duration of silence extended about 50-odd msec, the word was heard as *split*. Apparently the onset of voicing in the [I] was sufficiently abrupt that a stop consonant was heard if the preceding silent interval was long enough. It would appear that about 50 msec of silence or of low amplitude is needed preceding an abrupt onset if the onset is to be heard as an interrupted consonant. This effect of introducing a silent interval preceding an onset was examined further by Bailey and Summerfield (1978) and by Repp et al. (1978). The duration of a gap between [s] and a following vowel was manipulated, to determine the point at which a stop consonant was heard. It was found that the duration required to elicit a stop consonant response depended to some extent on the physical characteristics of the onset following the silent interval. If the onset exhibits a rapid spectrum change, it appears that it is a "stronger" onset than one that shows an abrupt amplitude increase without a spectrum change, and thus requires less of a preceding silent interval.

Nasal-Nonnasal   Within the class of interrupted consonants, we can distinguish two categories — nasal and nonnasal. The nonnasal (interrupted) consonants in English are the stops [p t k b d g č ǰ], and the nasals are [m n ŋ]. The principal acoustic characteristics that distinguish nasals from nonnasals is the presence or absence of an appreciable amount of energy within the closure interval, as illustrated in Fig. 6.

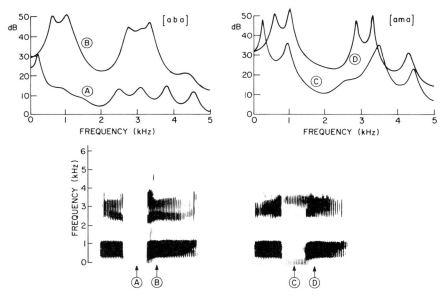

FIGURE 6   *Spectrograms of the two utterances* [ɑbɑ] *and* [ɑmɑ] *are shown at the bottom. Spectra sampled at the points indicated on the spectrograms during the closure interval and in the adjacent vowel are shown at the top. These are linear prediction spectra, as in Fig. 2.*

In nasal consonants, although the amplitude within this interval is lower than that in the adjacent vowel, the lowest spectral peak may only be a few dB lower than the first-formant amplitude of the vowel. There is also an appreciable amplitude in the spectrum of the nasal murmur in higher frequency regions. Some low-frequency energy may also be present in the spectrum sampled during the closure interval for an intervocalic voiced stop consonant. The amplitude in this low-frequency region is, however, considerably lower for voiced stops than for nasal consonants.

The distinction between nasal and voiced stop consonants has been studied perceptually by Mandler (1976). He generated oral-nasal continua by manipulating the amplitude of the nasal murmur relative to the vowel, and found that listener responses shift from nasal to stop when this relative amplitude was in the range -8 to -15 dB. Further studies are needed to determine whether there is some natural perceptual boundary when this relative amplitude reaches a particular value, or whether some other acoustic attribute forms the primary cue for distinguishing nasals from stops.

Voiced-Voiceless   There are a large number of languages that distinguish voiced from voiceless segments. Thus, for example, in English the consonants [p t k č f ɵ s š] are voiceless, and are in opposition to the voiced consonants [b d g ǰ v ð z ž]. For voiced segments there is low-frequency spectral energy or periodicity in the speech signal due to vibration of the vocal folds, whereas for voiceless sounds there is no such periodicity. In the case of voiced consonantal segments, the low-frequency spectral energy or periodicity occurs during the closure or constricted interval for the consonant, i.e., between the time the consonant constriction is achieved (usually from a preceding vowel) and the time of release of the consonant. The presence of this low-frequency periodicity is illustrated by the spectrogram and spectrum for a voiced stop consonant in Fig. 6. Whereas the low-frequency periodicity usually persists throughout the constricted interval for the consonant, it may often occur during only a portion of this interval, usually in the initial part of the interval. For a voiceless consonant, there is no low-frequency periodicity within the closure interval.

In some languages, such as English, there is a class of stop consonants for which there is a lack of low-frequency periodicity in a time interval immediately following the release. That is, there is a time delay from the rapid onset at the consonant release and the onset of low-frequency energy corresponding to the initiation of vocal-fold vibration (Lisker and Abramson, 1964). This class of sounds is called *aspirated* because "aspiration" noise is generated at the open glottis during this time interval from consonantal release to voicing onset. The contrast between an aspirated and an unaspirated stop consonant (both voiceless) is illustrated in Fig. 7.

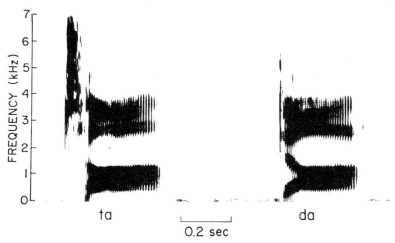

FIGURE 7   *Spectrograms of the syllables* [tɑ] (*left*) *and* [dɑ] (*right*) *in English, showing the longer delay in onset of low-frequency periodicity for the aspirated consonant.*

In English, the unaspirated stop consonant is optionally voiced in utterance-initial position, and, indeed, is generally thought of as a voiced consonant.

Speech perception experiments in which the time from release to voicing onset (voice-onset time) is manipulated to produce a series of synthetic consonant-vowel syllables show that the consonants are identified as unaspirated or aspirated (e.g., [b] or [p] in English) depending on whether the voice-onset time is less than or greater than about 20 msec (Abramson and Lisker, 1970). These and other experiments have suggested that if the timing of a sequence of two onsets of different components of a stimulus (such as noise burst and voicing initiation) is within 20-odd msec, listeners judge the onsets to be simultaneous (Hirsh, 1959), and have difficulty discriminating between stimuli that have onsets within this time interval. On the other hand, if the time delay between onsets is greater than 20 msec, they are judged to be successive. The discriminability of stimuli characterized by two

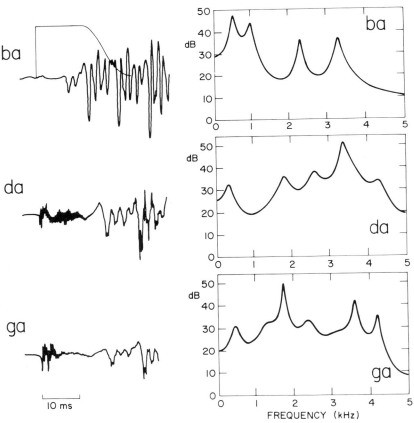

FIGURE 8 *Examples of waveforms and spectra sampled at the release of three voiced stop consonants as indicated. Superimposed on each waveform is the time window (with an effective width of about 15 msec) that is used for sampling the spectrum. Short-time spectra are preemphasized at high frequencies and are smoothed using a linear prediction algorithm. (From Stevens and Blumstein, 1978.)*

onsets with different times between the onsets has been examined by Miller et al. (1976) and by Pisoni (1977), with results that show regions of poor discrimination separated by regions in which differences in onset times can be discriminated well.

Place of Articulation for Stop Consonants   Place of articulation for stop consonants in syllable-initial position seems to be determined by acoustic events in the vicinity of the consonant release — probably within 10-20 msec of the release. It has been hypothesized by Fant (1960), by Stevens and Blumstein (1978), and by others (Halle, Hughes and Radley, 1957; Zue, 1976) that the gross shape of the spectrum sampled at the consonant release signals the stop consonant place of articulation. This gross shape reflects the acoustic attributes of the initial noise burst and the frequencies of the vocal-tract resonances immediately following the release.

In Fig. 8 we show the waveforms at the release of several different stop consonants in English. The smoothed spectra sampled at onset, using a time window like that illustrated in the figure, show quite different shapes depending on the place of articulation of the stop. Thus the spectrum for [b] is diffuse or spread out in frequency, and is flat or falling, while that for [d] is diffuse but is rising. On the other hand, the [g] spectrum shows a distinctive rather narrow or compact spectral peak in the midfrequency range, with other subsidiary peaks being smaller and well separated from the midfrequency spectral prominence.

The onset spectra for [b], [d], and [g] generally have the gross shapes shown in Fig. 8 independent of the vowel that follows the consonant, although certain details like the frequencies of the spectral peaks (corresponding to onset frequencies for the formants in the vowel) may vary from vowel to vowel (Blumstein and Stevens, 1979). The gross shapes for a particular place of consonant articulation are usually also similar to those in the figure when the consonant is voiceless aspirated or nasal. Examples of smoothed spectra sampled at the consonant release for the labials [p b m], the alveolars [t d n], and the velars [k g] are given in Fig. 9. Certainly for each of the pairs [p t], [b d], and [m n] the spectrum for the labial shows a more downward sloping shape than that for the alveolar. The nasal spectra, however, have less high-frequency energy than do the corresponding spectra for the stop consonants, presumably because the nasals lack a burst, which usually has high-frequency energy. It might be argued, however, that the presence of the low-frequency nasal murmur in the time interval immediately preceding the release of the nasal consonant causes a partial masking of the lower frequencies in the onset spectrum, giving rise to an auditory representation for nasals that slopes downward less than the spectra shown in Fig. 9 (Blumstein and Stevens, 1979; Delgutte, 1980). Such a modification in the nasal onset spectra would bring those spectral shapes more in line with the shapes for the stop-consonant onset spectra.

If perceptual experiments are carried out in which listeners are exposed to sounds with onset spectra like those illustrated in Figs. 8 and 9, they will categorize them appropriately. In fact, experiments have shown that place of articulation for a voiced stop consonant can usually be heard by a listener based only on the initial part of the stimulus up to 10-20 msec of voicing (Blumstein and Stevens, 1980). Perceptaul experiments with stimuli organized along a place-of-articulation continuum from [b] to [d] to [g] (by modifying systematically the characteristics of the spectrum at stimulus onset) show that there is a shift in identification from one category to another when the gross shape of the onset spectrum shifts from one type to another (e.g., from diffuse-falling to diffuse-rising, or from diffuse-rising to compact). Other experiments with similar kinds of stimulus continua show peaks and valleys in discrimination similar to those for other acoustic continua described earlier in this paper (Liberman, et al., 1957; Stevens, et al., 1969).

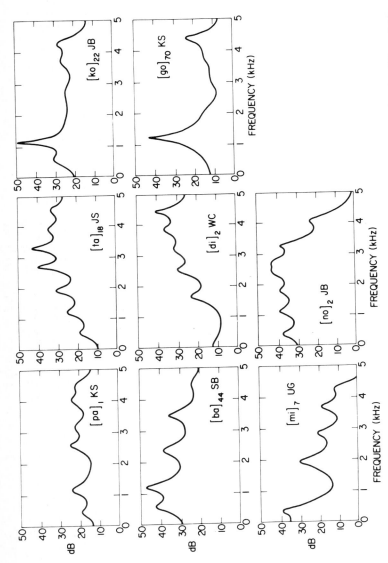

FIGURE 9   Spectra sampled at the release of several different stop and nasal consonants spoken by different American English talkers. The rows depict (from top to bottom) voiceless consonants, voiced consonants, and nasal consonants, arranged with labials at the left, alveolars in the middle, and velars at the right. The spectra are pre-emphasized and smoothed by a linear prediction algorithm, and are sampled over an effective time window of about 15 msec for the stops and 5 msec for the nasals.

Vowel Features　To deal adequately with the properties of vowels would require a much more extensive discussion than is possible here. However, we can discuss the acoustic nature of just two of the basic vowel features: high-low and front-back (Jakobson, Fant, and Halle, 1963; Chomsky and Halle, 1968). We have already seen in Fig. 8 the nature of the vowel waveform — with its periodicities corresponding to the fundamental frequency and the formant frequencies. One way of looking at vowel contrasts is to examine the spectral characteristics above and below some midfrequency dividing line — say around 1000 Hz, as shown in Fig. 10. These are smoothed spectra or spectrum envelopes for the three vowels [i ɑ u]. If we look to the left of the dividing line, we observe two possibilities: the lower half of this region is filled with spectral energy (as in [i] or [u]) or it has a hole or valley (as in the [ɑ] spectrum). A more conventional way of saying this is that the first formant frequency is low or high. This acoustic attribute at low frequencies provides the basic contrast between vowels that are produced with the tongue body high in the mouth — the *high* vowels — and those produced with the tongue body low in the mouth — the *low* vowels.

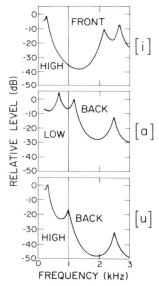

FIGURE 10　*Idealized spectrum envelopes for the vowels* [i], [ɑ], *and* [u] *as indicated. The line at 1 kHz divides the spectrum into a low-frequency region which signals the high-low contrast, and a high-frequency region which signals the front-back contrast. (From Stevens, in press.)*

A different contrast between vowel categories is signalled by events to the right of the midfrequency line. If there is a hole or a valley immediately to the right of this line, with appreciable energy well above this valley (as in the vowel [i]), then the vowel is in one class — we call it a *front* vowel because the tongue body is pushed to the front of the mouth. On the other hand, if there is appreciable spectral energy immediately to the right of the line with relatively weak spectral amplitude at higher frequencies (as in [ɑ] and [u]), then the vowel is in the opposite class — a *back* vowel. More conventionally, the distinction between front and back vowels is regarded as a distinction between vowels with a high second formant frequency and vowels with a relatively low second formant frequency.

In summary, then, we have reviewed two independent ways of classifying vowels depending on the locations and relative amplitudes of spectral valleys and prominences. One of these classification procedures involves a determination of the presence or absence of low-frequency spectral energy in relation to midfrequency energy (in the range 500 - 1000 Hz). The other tests whether the midfrequency range contains a spectral peak or a broad valley. (The definition of the midfrequency range may be influenced somewhat by the fundamental frequency and possibly by the average spacing of the formants, particularly the higher formants.)

CONCLUDING REMARKS

We have discussed a frew rather simple but basic properties that help to distinguish one class of speech sounds from another, and we have touched on a few experiments to indicate how the auditory perception system discriminates physical differences in speechlike sounds organized along various continua. Our point of view is that the auditory system is predisposed to provide some kind of distinctive pattern of response when the sounds have these attributes. This predisposition in fact may impose constraints on the kinds of acoustic distinctions that are used in language to form phonetic contrasts.

Note

Acknowledgements   Many of the ideas in this paper have grown out of collaborative research and discussion with Sheila Blumstein and with Morris Halle, and their positive influence is gratefully acknowledged. The preparation of this chapter was supported in part by Grant NS-04332 from the National Institutes of Health of the United States Public Health Service.

THE COGNITIVE REPRESENTATION OF SPEECH
T. Myers, J. Laver, J. Anderson (editors)
© *North-Holland Publishing Company, 1981*

Processing of Speech in the Peripheral Auditory System

ERIC D. YOUNG AND MURRAY B. SACHS

Johns Hopkins University School of Medicine

The first step in the auditory processing of speech is conversion of the acoustic speech signal into patterns of activity in the neurons of the auditory nerve. Ideally, this transduction process would provide the central nervous system with complete information about the acoustic speech signal. In this paper, we will consider some aspects of the internal representation of speech at the level of the auditory nerve; in particular, we will show how information about the spectrum of a complex acoustic signal like a vowel is encoded and how the physiological properties of the cochlea affect the representation.

The results to be described were obtained in experiments in which responses to steady-state synthetic vowels were recorded from large populations of single auditory-nerve fibers in anesthetized cats (Sachs and Young, 1979; Young and Sachs, 1979). This technique, introduced by Pfeiffer and Kim (1975), allows a direct estimate of the population response of the entire ensemble of auditory-nerve fibers to be obtained. The synthetic vowel stimuli used were perfectly periodic with steady formant frequencies. They are a considerable simplification of natural speech, but by simplifying our stimuli in this way, we have been able to focus our attention on fundamental questions which otherwise would have been obscured by complexities in the stimulus.

The basic principles of the physiology of the auditory nerve have been extensively worked out using simple stimuli like pure tones, clicks and broadband noise (see reviews by Evans, 1978; Kim and Molnar, 1975; Kiang, 1975, 1979). One fundamental feature of the response properties of auditory neurons which is of importance to the problem of the representation of complex stimuli is tuning (Kiang and Moxon, 1974; Evans, 1974b). The graph in Fig. 1B shows the tuning curves of three auditory-nerve fibers. These curves show the threshold (for an increase in discharge rate of about 20 spikes/second) as a function of the frequency of a tone burst stimulus. They have a minimum at the "characteristic frequency" (CF) of the fiber. The tuning properties of auditory-nerve fibers result from the fact that each fiber innervates one point (or a short distanc) on the basilar membrane (reviewed by Spoendlin, 1973, 1974) and that the motion of each point on the basilar membrane is tuned to a different frequency (Bekesy, 1960; Rhode, 1971; Johnstone et al., 1970; Wilson and Johnstone, 1975); other non-mechanical factors may also be involved (Evans, 1974b; Kiang et al., 1970; Evans and Wilson, 1973; Zwislocki and Sokolich, 1974). The tuning of the basilar membrane provides the basis for a *place* representation of acoustic stimuli (Holmholtz, 1863) whereby a crude frequency decomposition of the signal is performed and stimulus frequency is mapped into position, or place, along the basilar membrane. This mapping of frequency into place is preserved throughout the entire auditory system by the tonotopic organization of central auditory nuclei (Clopton et al., 1974; Merzenich et al., 1977). In the simplest statement of the place representation, the amount of energy in an acoustic stimulus in a particular frequency region is represented by the activity of the auditory-nerve fibers innervating the corresponding place along the basilar membrane. Thus, a profile of response as a function of CF for auditory-nerve fibers should, qualitatively at least, resemble the spectrum of the acoustic stimulus.

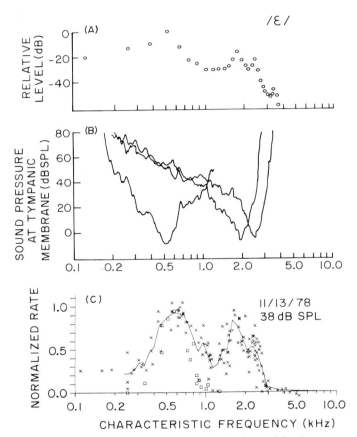

FIGURE 1   A: Amplitude spectrum of synthetic / ɛ / used in these experiments. B: Tuning curves from three auditory-nerve fibers whose CFs are near the formants of the / ɛ /, provided by Eaton-Peabody Lab. C: Plot of normalized rate versus CF for units studied on 11/13/78 using / ɛ / at 38 dB SPL as stimulus. [1]

Figure 1 illustrates the workings of the place scheme for the case in which the response of auditory neurons is measured in terms of their average discharge rate. The top plot shows the spectrum of a synthesized / ɛ / with formant frequencies of 0.512, 1.792 and 2.432 kHz. The three units whose tuning curves are shown in Fig. 1B have CFs near the formant frequencies. Because the vowel has more energy in the vicinity of their CFs, these units should begin to respond to the vowel at lower stimulus levels than units with CFs between the formants and should respond at higher discharge rates at all stimulus levels. The plot in Fig. 1C shows an example of the profile of discharge rate in a population of auditory-nerve fibers recorded in one cat when the stimulus was the synthetic / ε / whose spectrum is shown in Fig. 1A; the vowel stimulus was presented at a relatively low level of 38 dB SPL. There is one point in this plot for each unit studied in the experiment; it shows the discharge rate of that unit in response to the 38 dB / ε / (ordinate) plotted against the unit's CF (abscissa). The line is an average of the points computed with a sliding triangular window 0.25 octaves wide. Discharge rate is normalized in this figure by subtracting spontaneous rate (R_S in Fig. 2A,B) and dividing by maximal (saturation) discharge rate (R_M in Fig. 2A,B) minus spontaneous rate; thus each fiber's rate increase to the vowel is plotted as a fraction of its maximal rate increase. There is some evidence that auditory-nerve fibers with very low spontaneous rates form a separate population (Liberman, 1978; Kim and Molnar, 1979); for this reason, data from fibers with spontaneous rates less than 1/sec are plotted with open square symbols and data from higher spontaneous rate units with Xs. The average curve was computed from the high spontaneous population only. In this situation there is a good representation of the spectrum of the vowel; clear peaks can be seen in the rate profile at places corresponding to the first two formants of the vowel and a smaller peak is evident near the third formant place.

As sound level is increased, the representation of the stimulus spectrum in terms of rate profiles degenerates. The principal cause of this degeneration is the limited dynamic range of auditory-nerve fibers (Kiang et al., 1965; Sachs and Abbas, 1974; Evans, 1978b) which is illustrated by the rate versus level functions in Figs. 2A and 2B. These figures show the discharge rates of two single fibers to tone bursts at their CFs as functions of sound level. As sound level is increased, the response rate increases monotonically from spontaneous (R_S) to a maximal, saturation value (R_M). Further increases in sound level evoke no change of discharge rate. The effect of saturation on rate profiles can be seen in Fig. 2C for the vowel / ε / and in Fig. 2D for the vowel / α /. These plots show the average curves computed from response profiles like the one in Fig. 1C; in each case average profiles are shown for responses to the vowel presented over a wide range of sound levels. The first three formant frequencies of the vowels are indicated by the arrows. In the case of the / ε /, clear peaks corresponding to the formants can be seen at 28 and 38 dB SPL. As sound level is increased, fibers with CFs between the first and second formants increase their discharge rate as the energy within their tuning curves increases; this potentially includes not only energy in the vowel at frequencies near their CFs, but also energy remote from CF which is included as the tuning curves broaden at higher sound levels (Fig. 1B). At about 58 dB SPL the response rate of fibers with CFs near the formants saturates and the continued increase in the discharge rate of fibers with CFs between the formants causes the rate profiles to flatten out. The behavior of the rate profiles of responses to / α / shown in Fig. 2D is similar. In this case the first and second formants are close together and the separation between the corresponding peaks in the rate profiles is small even at low sound levels.

Notice that for both vowels shown in Fig. 2 the rate profiles saturate at values of normalized rate less than 1.0 in the frequency range above the first formant; i.e., fibers with CFs in the vicinity of the second and third formants do not reach rates as high as their maximal rate even at high stimulus levels. In fact, for the / ε / (Fig. 2C), the height of the rate profile in the vicinity of the second and third formants is actually a slightly nonmonotonic function of stimulus level: rate is higher at 59 dB SPL than at 78 dB SPL. In the vicinity of the first formant, however, the profiles saturate at normalized rates near 1.0. The behavior of units with CFs above the first formant can be explained as resulting from the phenomenon of two-tone suppression (Sachs and Young, 1979). This term refers to the fact that an increase in discharge rate evoked by a tone at CF can be suppressed by a second, more intense, tone at a

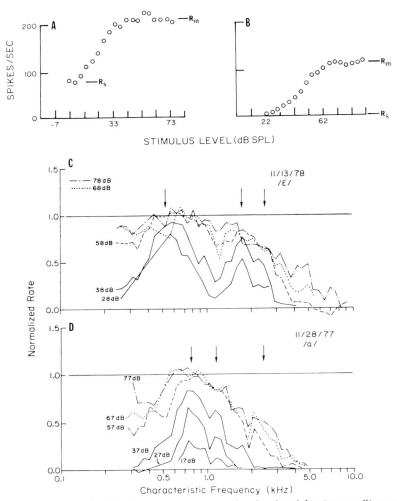

FIGURE 2   *A and B: Discharge rate versus stimulus level for two auditory-nerve fibers. C and D: Average rate profiles for* / ε / *and* / ɑ / *respectively, for several levels of the vowel.*[2]

frequency above or below CF (Sachs and Kiang, 1968). Figure 3B shows an example of the tuning curve of a fiber (plotted with filled circles) and its two suppression areas (shaded). Presentation of a tone with frequency and sound level anywhere within the shaded areas caused a reduction (suppression) of the response evoked by the CF tone indicated by the square.

The two-tone case most relevant to the discussion of vowels is that of a suppressor tone below CF which is 10 to 20 dB more intense than the excitor tone at CF (Abbas and Sachs, 1976). This serves as a crude approximation to the case of a unit with CF near the second or third formant of a vowel whose responses are being suppressed by the energy in the stimulus near the first formant. Comparison of the low frequency suppression area of the unit shown in Fig. 3B with the spectrum of the vowel / ε / shown in Fig. 3A demonstrates that energy at the first formant can be expected to suppress the responses of fibers with CFs near the second and third formant peaks. A typical rate versus level function for a two-tone stimulus consisting of an excitor tone at CF and a lower frequency suppressor tone, which is always 20 dB more intense than the CF tone, is shown in Fig. 3C. The circles show the rate response to the CF tone alone and the triangles show the rate response to the two-tone combination. In both cases, the abscissa is the level of the CF tone. The

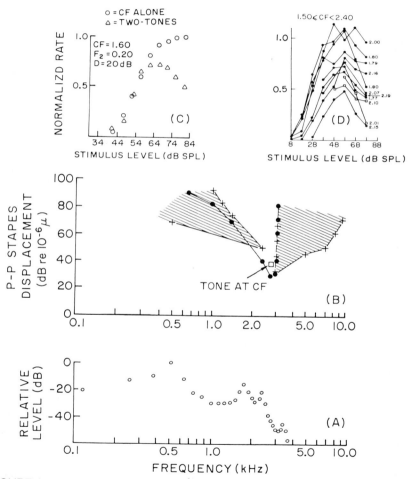

FIGURE 3 A: Amplitude spectrum for / ε /. B: Tuning curve and "suppression areas" for one auditory-nerve fiber (redrawn from Sachs and King, 1968). C. Rate-level functions for CF tones presented alone (circles) and for two-tone stimuli (triangles). D: Normalized discharge rate versus sound level for individual units taken from the experiment of 11/13/78 with / ε / as stimulus. [3]

effect of the low-frequency suppressor is to reduce the maximal response rate of the fiber and actually make the rate versus level function nonmonotonic at higher stimulus levels. This is suggestive of the behavior of the rate profiles of Figs. 2C and 2D. Figure 3D shows rate versus level functions for single units taken from the population of Fig. 2C; all of these units had CFs near the second or third formants. Notice that most of them reach maximum rates significantly less than their saturation rates (corresponding to a normalized rate of 1.0) and most of them are nonmonotonic. By contrast the units with CFs near the first formant in the same population have monotonic normalized rate versus level functions which saturate near 1.0 (Sachs and Young, 1979). The evident similarity of two-tone rate versus level functions like Fig. 3C and the vowel rate-level functions in Fig. 3D strongly suggests that the mechanism underlying the suppressed saturation and nonmonotonicity of vowel responses at CFs above the first formant is the same as the mechanism of two-tone suppression.

Suppression has frequently been considered to be a mechanism for maintaining or even sharpening peaks in the response profiles to stimuli like vowels (Karnickaya et al., 1975; Houtgast, 1974). By retarding the growth of discharge rate for units with CFs between the formants, suppression might maintain the formant-related peaks in rate profiles at high stimulus levels. Examination of Figs. 2C and 2D shows that units with CFs between the first and second formants are suppressed in that they do not reach their maximal discharge rate. However, this mechanism is not sufficient to maintain the formant peaks in the rate profiles because units with CFs near the second and third formants are suppressed as much or more. Thus two-tone suppression actually contributes to the loss of formant peaks in rate profiles, rather than acting to preserve them.

The loss of formant peaks in rate profiles such as those in Fig. 2 occurs at sound levels within the conversational range. This is a serious problem for a theory of vowel perception based on rate and place, since speech intelligibility is stable at levels up to 100 to 120 dB SPL, depending upon the integrity of the middle ear muscle reflex (Pollack and Pickett, 1958; Borg and Zakrisson, 1973). Representation of vowels based on rate must still be considered a possibility, however, because of the following uncertainties:

1.   The gross shape of the rate profiles for different vowels differ at high levels. In Fig. 2, for example, the 77 dB profile for responses to / ɑ / falls off more rapidly at high frequencies than the 78 dB profile for / ɛ /. The difference in gross shapes for vowels like / ɛ / and /ɪ/ is relatively small, however, and it is not clear that all the possible vowel distinctions could be supported by this mechanism (Sachs and Young, 1979).

2.   The fibers in the population of low-spontaneous rate units mentioned earlier have higher thresholds (Liberman, 1978) and wider dynamic ranges (Schalk and Sachs, in preparation) than the higher spontaneous rate fibers from which the rate profiles in Fig. 2 were computed. Thus formant-related peaks might be observed in rate profiles for this population at levels above those at which the high spontaneous population has saturated. Because the low spontaneous rate fibers constitute only a small fraction of the population, we have not yet studied a large enough sample of them in one animal to allow firm conclusions about their responses to be reached. Rate profiles for the low spontaneous rate fibers from the same population as the data in Fig. 2C are shown in Fig. 4. Although the data are sparse, there are clearly formant-related peaks in these profiles at 78 dB, at which level they do not exist in the high spontaneous rate population. The low spontaneous rate units show the effects of suppression more strongly than high spontaneous rate units (Sachs and Young, 1979;

the two units plotted with unfilled squares in Fig. 3D are typical); because of this the peak in the 78 dB rate profile in Fig. 4 is quite small and it is doubtful that it would remain at a 20 dB higher level.

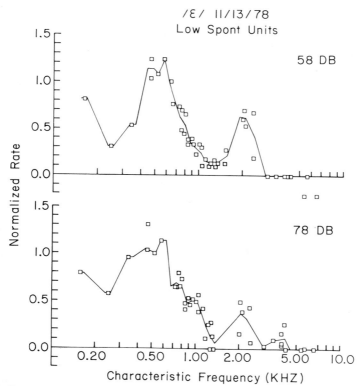

FIGURE 4 *Normalized rate versus CF for low spontaneous rate units (less than 1 / Sec) studied on 11 / 13 / 78 with | ε | as stimulus.*

3. The effect of the human external ear is to increase the level of the acoustic signal for frequencies above about 2 kHz (Wiener and Ross, 1946). This should increase the level of the second and third formants of many vowels with respect to the first formant and would result in a weakening of the two-tone suppression effect of the first formant on units with CFs near the second formant. This might act to preserve formant peaks in rate profiles. The effects of the external ear resonance on rate profiles will be discussed later.

4. Contraction of the middle ear muscles reduces the transmission of low frequencies through the middle ear (Wever and Vernon, 1955; Borg, 1978), and thus might have the same effect as the external ear resonance by reducing the first formant energy. The middle ear muscles have been shown to be important in speech intelligibility at very high levels (greater than 100 dB SPL, Borg and Zakrisson, 1973).

Despite the uncertainties mentioned above, it is clear that the representation of a vowel's spectrum in terms of profiles of discharge rate is highly unstable as sound level changes. It is natural to question whether other information is present in the discharge patterns of auditory neurons which could be utilized to provide a more stable representation of the spectrum of a vowel stimulus. The classical alternative to representation of stimuli in terms of rate and place in the auditory system is representation in terms of the temporal patterns of response of single neurons (Wever, 1949). The instantaneous rate (or probability of discharge) of auditory-nerve fibers responding to stimuli with frequencies below about 6 kHz is modulated by a rectified version of the stimulus waveform, as modified by cochlear filtering and nonlinearities (Rose et al., 1967, 1974; Hind et al., 1967; Brugge et al., 1969). Thus if an auditory-nerve fiber is responding to a 1 kHz tone, there will be alternate 0.5 msec periods of increased and decreased probability of discharge which will be phase-locked to the stimulus; as a consequence of this alternating drive, the unit will tend to discharge at intervals of about 1 msec and multiples of 1 msec (since the unit will not fire on every cycle of the stimulus, (Rose et al., 1967). It is clear that considerable information about the stimulus spectrum can be extracted from temporal patterns of response. A convenient way to analyze the temporal responses of auditory neurons is the *period histogram* which estimates the instantaneous rate (or probability) of discharge of a fiber as a function of time through one cycle of a (periodic) stimulus. It is constructed from the data record by dividing one cycle of the stimulus up into a number of bins and then tallying in each bin the number of spikes which occurred in the data record with the same phase relationship to the stimulus as the bin.

Examples of period histograms of responses of four single units to the vowel / ɛ / are shown in the left column of Fig. 5. The waveform of one cycle of the vowel is shown at the top of the column. The CFs of the units are shown in the center column and the magnitudes of the Fourier transforms of the period histograms are shown in the right column. The spectrum of this vowel is shown in Fig. 1A; since it is periodic, it contains energy only at the harmonics of its fundamental frequency (128 Hz). In discussing responses to the vowel, we will refer to aspects of its spectrum in terms of their harmonic numbers. Notice that the first formant frequency is harmonic 4, the second is harmonic 14, and the third is harmonic 19.

The top unit in Fig. 5 responded to the vowel with four phases of increased discharge rate; this unit seems to be responding principally to the fourth harmonic of the vowel. The frequency of the fourth harmonic, 0.512 kHz, is near the unit's CF. The second unit in Fig. 5 has a CF near the 14th harmonic of the vowel and its response contains 14 peaks, indicating that it is principally responding to the 14th harmonic. Responses such as these, in which one frequency component dominates, are seen most often in units whose CFs are near a formant frequency. They are quite similar to period histograms of responses to pure tones at the same frequencies. The Fourier transforms of these two period histograms (right column) have a large component at the frequency of the dominant harmonic (4 in the top histogram and 14 in the second histogram). They also have significant energy at integer multiples (harmonics) of the dominant harmonic (8, 12, 16, 20 in the top histogram and 28 in the second histogram). The components at integer multiples of the dominant harmonic arise, at least in part, from the rectification inherent in the fact that auditory neurons cannot discharge at negative rates; the inhibitory half cycles of period histograms such as these are therefore clipped at zero rate, resulting in the production of frequency components in the response histogram at the harmonics of the actual stimulus frequency (Goldstein, 1972; Littlefield, 1973; Molnar, 1974; Johnson, 1974; Young and Sachs, 1979). This distortion must be kept in mind when considering our results below; it will be referred to as *rectifier distortion*. Responses to frequency components not present in the stimulus can also be produced by *combination tones*, which are generated by cochlear nonlinearities and seem to produce stimulus-like propagating excitation patterns in the population of auditory neurons (Kim et al., 1979; Siegel et al., 1977).

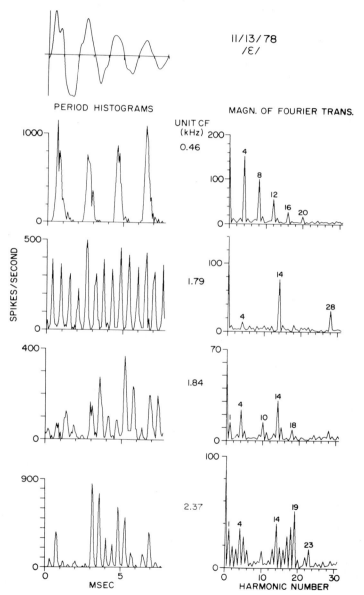

FIGURE 5 *Period histograms (left column) and amplitude spectra of Fourier transforms for the period histograms (right column) for four single fibers studied on 11/13/78 using / ε / as stimulus.* [4]

The third and fourth histograms shown in Fig. 5 are examples of units which responded significantly to more than one stimulus component. The third histogram has 14 peaks which are strongly modulated in amplitude; its Fourier transform contains a large component at the 14th harmonic, as expected, and another large component at the 4th harmonic. Two of the remaining significant components, the 10th and the 18th harmonics, most likely are rectifier distortion products produced by the responses at harmonics 4 and 14. Such responses are expected because a unit simultaneously responding to two tones f_1 and f_2 should have a series of rectifier distortion products in its response at frequencies like $f_2 \pm f_1$, $2f_1 \pm f_2$, etc.,; the components at $f_2 \pm f_1$ should be the largest (Johnson, 1974). The fourth histogram in Fig. 5 is an example of a pattern of response which occurs frequently in units with CFs above 1.5 to 2.0 kHz. The period histograms have a large peak which may be followed by damped oscillations; the Fourier transforms contain significant components over a broad range of frequencies, among which the formants are usualy prominent.

The magnitudes of the components in the Fourier transforms of period histograms provide a good measure of the temporal response strength of auditory-nerve fibers to the corresponding frequency components of the stimulus, if adequate account is taken of rectifier distortion and combination tones. Figure 6 shows how the responses at three harmonics of the stimulus were distributed in a population of auditory-nerve fibers when the stimulus was / ε /. These temporal response distributions were computed from the same data as the rate profiles in Fig. 2C. Each column shows the distribution of temporal response to one of three harmonics, the 4th (first formant) in the left column, the 10th in the center column and the 14th (second formant) in the right column. Each row shows the responses to the three harmonics at one of three different sound levels (38, 58 or 78 dB SPL, indicated at right). The plots in Fig. 6 were constructed in the same fashion as the rate profile in Fig. 1C; there is one point for each unit which shows the amplitude of the 4th, 10th or 14th harmonic in the Fourier transform of the unit's period histogram (ordinate; normalized by dividing by the average discharge rate, Young and Sachs, 1979) plotted against the unit's CF (abscissa). The lines are averages of the points computed with a triangular weighting function whose base was 0.25 octaves wide (both high and low spontaneous rate units were included in the averaging computation). The arrow in each graph points to the CF which is equal to the frequency of the harmonic plotted in that graph; this will be referred to below as the "place" of that harmonic.

The temporal response distributions in Fig. 6 have been chosen to illustrate the behavior of responses to all harmonics. At the lowest stimulus level (38 dB, top row) the response to each harmonic is maximum in the vicinity of its place; i.e., the largest amount of response to each harmonic is found among fibers whose CFs are approximately equal to the frequency of the harmonic. The strongest responses are seen at the formant frequencies, in this case the 4th and 14th harmonics; the first formant response is particularly strong and widespread. As stimulus level is increased, the response to the first formant spreads over a wide range of CFs; at 78 dB, almost the entire population of fibers is responding to the first formant. Response to the second formant near its place stays roughly constant from 38 to 58 dB although some changes in its distribution occur. At 78 dB, the response to the second formant is reduced slightly near its place, but significant response to this harmonic remains.

In contrast to the behavior of the formant harmonics, the response of the 10th harmonic near its place decreases monotonically as sound level is increased until at 78 dB there is no sign of the peak which was observed at 38 dB. Instead, units with CFs near the 10th harmonic's place are responding to the 4th harmonic, the first

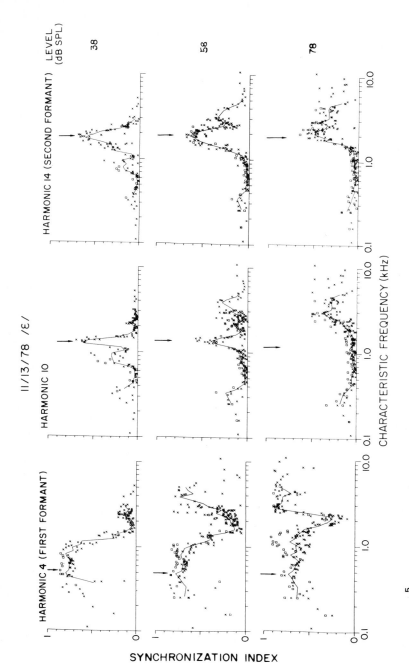

FIGURE 6 ⁵ *Distribution of temporal response as a function of CF for units studied on 11/13/78 with / ε / as the stimulus.*

formant. This behavior is similar to the behavior of two-tone synchrony suppression which has been previously described in detail (Brugge et al., 1969; Rose et al., 1974; Arthur, 1976; Johnson, 1974; Kim et al., 1979). When a two-tone stimulus consisting of one tone at CF and a second tone at a lower frequency and 10 or 20 dB more intense is presented to an auditory-nerve fiber, the fiber's temporal responses are dominated by the CF tone at low sound levels; as the overall level of the complex is increased, keeping the relative level of the two tones constant, the response to the CF tone is suppressed and the unit's responses become dominated by the lower frequency tone (Brugge et al., 1969; Rose et al., 1974; Reale and Geisler, 1979). This is the behavior observed for the 10th harmonic in Fig. 6; it is typical of non-formant harmonics in our data (except for harmonics of the first formant discussed below). Although there is no response to the 10th harmonic near its place at 78 dB, there is significant response to this harmonic at CFs between about 2.5 and 5.0 kHz. Notice that this is the frequency region in which units are responding strongly to both the 4th and 14th harmonics and the distribution of the 10th harmonic has roughly the same shape as the distribution of the 14th harmonic. As we have discussed in detail previously, this is the behavior expected of a rectifier distortion product (Young and Sachs, 1979).

At levels of 70 to 80 dB, responses to all the vowels we have studied are dominated by the first and, to a lesser extent, the second formants of the vowel (Young and Sachs, 1979). Responses to non-formant harmonics are suppressed, so that peaks of response occurring near their places at lower levels are gone, replaced principally by responses to the first formant. The only non-formant harmonics at which significant responses are observed at high levels are various distortion products of the first and second formants (such as $2F_1$, $3F_1$, $F_2 \pm F_1$, etc.).

The fact that the formant harmonics dominate the patterns of temporal response of auditory-nerve fibers suggests that a good idea of the spectrum of a vowel stimulus could be gained by comparing the amount of temporal response at various harmonics of the stimulus. Examination of the top line in Fig. 6 suggests that it is appropriate to look for response to each harmonic in a restricted region centered around that harmonic's place in the population, because when a response occurs to a particular harmonic, it will be maximal at this place. Using a restricted region centered on a harmonic's place has the added advantage that it discriminates against responses which are rectifier distortion products, such as the 10th harmonic in the bottom row of Fig. 6; a response which is a rectifier distortion product is distributed in the population according to the frequency of the primaries from which it is produced, not according to the frequency of the distortion product itself (Young and Sachs, 1979). The average temporal response contours shown in Fig. 7 were motivated by these considerations. The *points* show the average value of temporal response in distributions like those of Fig. 6 (except not normalized but expressed as discharge rate) for each harmonic (ignore the lines for now); the average was computed only over fibers whose CFs were within 0.5 octave of the frequency of the harmonic. Thus these curves show the average temporal response to each harmonic among fibers with CFs within 0.5 octave of the harmonic's place; they reflect a combination of rate, place and periodicity information. One curve is shown for each stimulus level used in this experiment; the curves are plotted on a logarithmic ordinate and displaced by one order of magnitude from each other for clarity. The ordinate scale is appropriate to the 78 dB curve; in each curve the maximum response is about 100 spikes/sec. For convenience we will refer to these temporal response contours as ALSR (for average localized synchronized rate) curves. The points at the first three formant frequencies harmonics (4, 14 and 19) have been plotted with filled circles. Notice that the ALSR is always largest at the first formant. At lower sound levels the profile of the ALSR is a good reflection of the spectrum of the / ε / (Fig. 1C), with local maxima at the first three formant frequencies. The only serious deviation is the slightly elevated response at the second harmonic of the first formant (harmonic 8). At higher levels the first and second formants continue to stand out; the salience of the third formant is reduced, as response to it is suppressed. Responses to the second and third harmonics of the first formant (8th and 12th harmonics) grow considerably at higher levels until they are larger than the second formant response at the highest level. Except for these two distortion products related to the first formant, however, all response components between the first and second formants are suppressed at higher levels. For example, at 38 dB, the response to harmonics 6 through 13 (excluding 8 and 12) averaged about 22 spikes/sec; at 78 dB, the responses to these same harmonics ranged between 6 and 11 spikes/sec, a reduction of more than 50%. This is the suppression which was illustrated by the responses to harmonic 10 in Fig. 6.

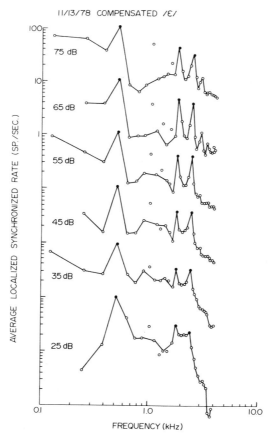

FIGURE 7   *Average synchronized rate for responses to / ɛ / at all sound levels used in experiment on 11/13/78.* [6]

The lines drawn through some of the points in Fig. 7 are meant to show the extent to which the ALSR resembles the stimulus spectrum if presumed distortion components are ignored. The lines are drawn through all the points except those at the second and third harmonics of the first two formants and the first sum and difference tone of the first two formants (i.e., excluding $2F_1$, $3F_1$, $2F_2$, $3F_2$, and $F_1 \pm F_2$). The first formant was taken to be the harmonic at which the largest response was observed; the second formant was taken to be the harmonic above the first formant at which the largest response (relative to adjacent harmonics) was observed after elimination of the harmonics of the first formant. The similarity of these plots to the spectrum of the stimulus (Fig. 1C) is clear. Notice particularly that changes in stimulus level over a 50-60 dB range do not greatly alter the qualitative aspects of these plots; they continue to reflect the first two formants of the stimulus. This stability is in marked contrast to the behavior of response profiles based on discharge rate alone (Figs. 2C, 2D, 4) where saturation and suppression limit the representation of the formants at higher levels.

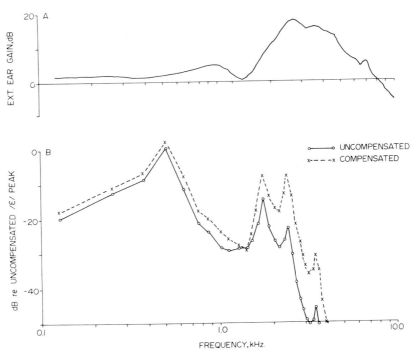

FIGURE 8   A: Transfer function of human external ear (from Wiener and Ross, 1946). B: Spectrum of / ε / with (dashed line) and without (solid line) compensation for human external ear transfer function. [7]

The human external ear has a broad resonance in its transfer function at frequencies above 2 kHz (Fig. 8A; Weiner and Ross, 1946); as a consequence, the acoustic signal at the tympanic membrane is boosted in the frequency range occupied by the third, and frequently also the second, formant by as much as 20 dB over free-field values. As was discussed above, boosting the amplitude of the second and third formants with respect to the first would weaken the suppressive effects of the first formant energy on both rate and temporal responses to the second and third formants; it would also increase the suppressive effects of the second and third formant energy on responses at frequencies between the formants. Both effects would serve to sharpen the representation of vowels' spectra in either rate or temporal response profiles. Thus far we have presented results for synthetic vowels whose spectra at the cat's tympanic membrane were approximately that of average free-field vowels (Peterson and Barney, 1952); no corrections for the effects of the human external ear were applied. The external ear transfer function (Fig. 8A) was applied to the / ε / whose spectrum is shown in Fig. 1A; the resulting compensated vowel, in which the balance of energy in the first and higher formant regions is about what it would be at the input to the human middle ear, was used in the same experiment as the normal / ε / for which results have been presented. The spectra of the original / ε / and the compensated / ε / are compared in Fig. 8B.

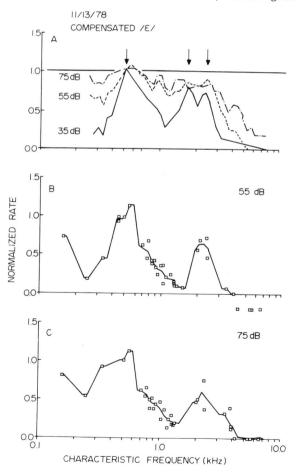

FIGURE 9 *A: Averaged normalized rate profiles for units studied on 11/13/78 with compensated / ε / as the stimulus. B and C: Rate profiles for the low spontaneous units from the same data as in A at 55 and 75 dB SPL.*

Rate profiles for the responses of the high spontaneous fiber population to the compensated / ε / are shown in Fig. 9A. The principal difference between these and the profiles for the uncompensated / ε / in Fig. 2C is the rather prominent third formant peak at 35 dB which is observed in the responses to the compensated vowel. At higher levels, the effects of rate saturation and suppression are quite evident in the data of Fig. 9A; the separate peaks in the rate profiles corresponding to the formants are lost, just as they were for the uncompensated vowel. Rate profiles for the responses of the low spontaneous population to the compensated / ε / are shown in Figs. 9B and 9C. Once again there are clear formant-related peaks in this population at levels where they have disappeared in the higher spontaneous rate group. The effect of strengthening the second and third formants appears to be principally an increased resistance of the second and third formant peak to the effects of suppression, since the amplitude of this peak does not decrease from 55 to 75 dB as much as it did for the uncompensated vowel (Fig. 4). Figure 10 shows the ALSR functions for responses to the compensated / ε /. The responses at the second and third formants are now much stronger than in the case of the uncompensated

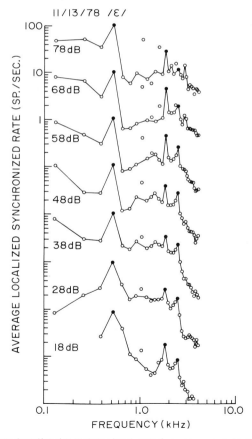

FIGURE 10   *Average localized synchronised rate for responses to the compensated / ε / at all sound levels used in experiment 11/13/78.* [8]

/ ɛ / (Fig. 7). The third formant, in particular, stands out clearly even at the highest level, whereas in the uncompensated vowel, it was strongly enough suppressed that response to it was not significantly larger than the response to adjacent, non-formant harmonics at this level. It is quite clear from Figs. 9 and 10 that the effects of the external ear resonance on the representation of the second and third formants of speech sounds in the auditory nerve are likely to be quite important.

In this paper we have discussed two ways in which the spectra of complex stimuli such as vowels might be obtained from the response patterns of auditory-nerve fibers. Although sufficient information to determine at least the first two formants is present in profiles of discharge rate, this representation is highly sensitive to stimulus level; there is no single set of features of rate responses which corresponds directly with the vowel spectrum at all stimulus levels. Instead, one population of fibers serves best at low levels and a second at higher levels. Yet vowel quality is a stable and strong percept over a wide range of levels, extending at least 40 dB above the highest levels used in our studies (Pollack and Pickett, 1958). There is no evidence which we know of to indicate a change of vowel quality or a shifting of encoding mechanisms, as the rate data would seem to require. On the other hand, if temporal aspects of the responses are considered, a stable representation of vowel spectrum which provides a clear indication of the first two and sometimes the third formant can easily be derived. This representation is good to at least 80 dB SPL in our data. The robust nature of the temporal representation of vowel spectra makes it worthy of serious consideration in future studies of vowel perception.

Finally, we mention that the temporal representation which we have advanced is similar to at least one previous model of vowel perception, that of Carlson et al. (1975) which is based on counting zero-crossings in the output of a bank of filters. Furthermore, it is essentially the same as a recent model for periodicity pitch (Goldstein, 1973; Goldstein and Srulovicz, 1977; Srulovicz, 1978) which has succeeded in predicting a number of aspects of a psychophysical phenomenon which bears some general similarity to the problem of vowel perception.

Notes

1. A: / ɛ / was synthesized digitally using a terminal analog synthesizer provided by J. Heinz. The vowel was perfectly periodic with fundamental frequency of 128 Hz and first three formants at 512, 1792, and 2432 Hz. C: Each point is normalized rate (see text for normalization procedure) of one unit plotted at the unit's CF. Units with spontaneous rate less than 1/sec. plotted with open squares; other units with Xs. Line is average rate of units with spontaneous rate greater than 1/sec.

2. A and B: Stimulus was pure tone at CF, rate was averaged over 400 msec. tone burst. In each plot R_m is the saturation rate of the unit; R_s is the spontaneous rate. C: The profiles are for high spontaneous rate units from data of 11/13/78. Sound levels are given by the numbers next to the curves. Positions of the formant frequencies of the vowel are shown by the arrows. D: Same as C except for data of 11/28/77.

3. B: Suppression areas are regions in the stimulus-level frequency plane in which a tone, when added to a tone at CF, produces a rate at least 20% below the rate to the CF tone alone. C: The two-tone stimuli had the form $p(t) = P(\sin 2\pi f_{cf}t + 10 \sin 2\pi f_2 t)$. Abscissa shows P. Note f_2 is below f_{cf}. (Replotted from Sachs and Abbas, 1976): D. Units all have CFs in the vicinity of the second and third formant frequencies.

4. CFs of the units are shown in the center column. Period histograms are estimates of instantaneous discharge rate as a function of time through one cycle of the vowel; computed with 128 bins per cycle. One pitch period of the vowel (electrical signal at earphone input) is shown at the top of the left column; time scale is the same as the period histogram. Fourier transforms computed from two cycle period histograms which introduces a "noise" point between each adjacent pair of stimulus harmonics. Frequency scale on the abscissa of the Fourier transforms is given in terms of multiples (harmonics) of the vowel's 128 Hz. fundamental.

5. Each plot shows distribution of synchronization to one harmonic of the / ε /. Synchronization is defined as the value of the Fourier transform of a particular harmonic divided by the average rate; it ranges from 0 to 1 (Johnson, 1974). Distributions are shown for the fourth, tenth and fourteenth harmonics at 38, 58 and 78 dB SPL. Arrows point to the CF which is equal to the frequency of the harmonic (i.e., place of the harmonic). Each point derived from response of one unit. Points plotted with open square symbols are from units with spontaneous activity less than 1/sec; points plotted with Xs are from higher spontaneous units. Lines are averages of all points computed with a triangular weighting function whose base was 0.25 octaves wide.

6. There is one point for each harmonic up to the 32nd. Points corresponding to formant frequencies are plotted with filled circles. Ordinate is scaled logarithmically. Plots are shifted vertically from one another by one order of magnitude for clarity. Maximum response in each plot is about 100 spikes/sec. The lines are drawn through all points except those corresponding to the formants' 2nd and 3rd harmonics and the sum and difference tones of the first two formants. See rules given in text.

7. The "compensated / ε /" was obtained from the normal / ε / by multiplying its spectrum by the transfer function given in A.

8. Lines are drawn through points in accordance with rules given in text.

Acknowledgement   This work was supported by a grant from the National Institute of Neurological and Communicative Disorders and Stroke. E.D. Young and M.B. Sachs held N.I.H. Research Career Development Awards.

Discussion

Stuart Michael Rosen   With reference to Ken Stevens' stimulating paper, I would like to make one point which casts considerable doubt on the use of certain types of perceptual experiments in the search for natural sensitivities of the auditory system.

The data of Cutting and Rosner (1974) using "pluck"-"bow" stimuli would seem to suggest the existence of a natural boundary near 40 msec due to properties of the auditory system. Not only do subjects change their labelling of stimuli at that point, they also seem to have the best discriminability there. This suggestion is even more strongly put by comparing this data to that obtained with a /tʃ / - / ʃ / continuum signalled by rise time in the same way, also reported in the Cutting and Rosner paper. The same steep labelling and peaked discrimination functions occur, although the boundary is slightly, but not markedly, different at about 45 to 50 msec. The resemblance is striking, the conclusion seemingly inescapable: this particular distinction has evolved to make use of a natural sensitivity of the auditory system. Correspondances of this kind are at the heart of Stevens' paper.

Alas, the story is not so simple. Figure 1 shows the results of a pilot (one subject) experiment using "pluck"-"bow" stimuli similar to those used by Cutting and Rosner. The dashed line shows the typical steep function when the subject is asked to label all the stimuli in the range (8 trials per point). The solid lines show categorization functions (20 trials per point) obtained when only a subset of five of the stimuli (rise times of 0 to 40 msec, 20 to 60 msec or 40 to 80 msec) are presented to the subject. If there were something "natural" about the boundary between "plucks" and "bows", we should expect all these functions to lie on top of one another. In fact, the boundaries seem to be primarily determined by the range of stimuli presented. Similar (though smaller) effects have been shown for consonant categorization by Rosen (1978) and Brady and Darwin (1978).

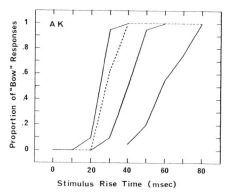

FIGURE 1   *"Pluck-bow" labelling functions*

Such considerations are also important in the recent work exploring the perception of speech sounds by animals. Kuhl and Miller's (1975) study using chinchillas was greeted with much interest since it seemed to reveal the natural sensitivities of the auditory system without the interference of higher level speech processes. Although speech processes could not intervene, this does not mean that other higher level processes could not. Waters and Wilson (1976) in fact showed range effects for consonant categorization in monkeys. Thus, the category boundaries obtained in these experiments are not evidence for natural sensitivities in the auditory system, but are highly dependent on the range of stimuli presented.

Hiroya Fujisaki   Before discussing specific topics concerned with peripheral (especially auditory) constraints on the form of representation, it may be useful to analyze the types of constraint that are involved in the whole process of speech perception whereby the speech signal is converted into a linguistic code. The analysis may be based on a functional representation of the process of auditory information processing consisting of three stages: reception and processing, memory, and decision.

Constraints on signal reception and processing are such factors as auditory threshold, spectral and temporal resolution, masking, etc.

Memory constraints may be divided into those related to short-term and long-term memory systems which hold both auditory and phonetic information. Limited span, temporal decay, noise or inaccuracy in retrieval, and mutual interference among items, etc. are the major constraints at this stage.

Decision constraints may be divided into those related to identification (i.e. categorical, absolute judgment) and those related to discrimination (i.e. comparative, relative judgment). Both statistical and deterministic disturbances in these judgments constitute the constraints at this stage.

Although the theme of the present session is "peripheral auditory constraints," it may be necessary to define what one means by *peripheral* constraints. Does it include constraints on signal processing such as the ones I mentioned above? In fact, the distinction between "peripheral" and "central" constraints is sometimes not clear-cut and somewhat misleading. I would rather consider *all* the constraints inherent in the perceptual process.

I should also like to point out that there seem to exist two distinct forms of categorical judgment of speech sounds. One form is based on psychophysically *discrete* pheonomena (i.e. on the presence/absence of certain elementary percepts), while the other is based on acquired criteria established on a perceptual continuum. I consider that the former is responsible for a major part of consonantal identification as well as to categorization of certain non-speech stimuli, and is more or less universal, while the latter is responsible for vowel identification, and is mostly language-specific.

The following remarks are made in connection with K.N. Stevens' paper:
a) It may be worthwhile to ask whether the "non-uniformity of discriminability along certain auditory continua" really originates from the auditory periphery, or, as I have pointed out elsewhere (Fujisaki, 1979), reflects certain constraints at higher levels (involving short-term memory and the decision process). Unless one can prove the former alternative, the non-uniformity of discriminability may not serve as evidence for the existence of auditory property detectors.
b) Yet the concept of auditory property detector may be a useful working hypothesis. I should like to ask about the structural relationships among those property detectors. Are they all situated on one level, working more or less in parallel, or are they arranged in some sort of hierarchy? If the property detectors are arranged in a hierarchical structure, I find that the difference between Prof. Stevens' property detectors and the channels of analysis posited by Simon and Studdert-Kennedy (1978) is rather small.

c) I consider it necessary to examine critically whether a certain constraint in the form of signal representation stems from characteristics of the perceptual mechanism or from those of the production mechanism. In fact, some of the constraints mentioned by Prof. Stevens may stem from the production mechanism rather than from the perceptual mechanism.

M.E.H. Schouten: Speech Perception is Timbre Perception There is hardly any empirical evidence to support the view that speech is perceived in a special way. Elsewhere I have attempted to show that virtually every argument produced so far in favour of a speech mode of perception is based on a dubious interpretation of data. Whether or not one believes in a speech mode is just that: a question of belief. Having found all arguments supporting a speech mode wanting, I find it very easy to believe that there is no such thing, and to conclude that speech research should be a branch of psychophysics and physiology. Unfortunately, both of the latter have mainly restricted themselves to pure tones and noise bursts, so that very little is known about the perception of timbre, let alone that of rapidly varying timbre, which is what speech is. As a result, the misunderstanding has arisen that speech sounds and other sounds are perceived in different ways. Another cause of that misunderstanding is the tendency of people to regard their own separate discipline as something corresponding to something separate in reality. This tendency seems to be especially strong among my fellow-linguists: I can think of no other reason why so many descriptive accounts of the syntax of written language have been assigned psychological reality.

I do not want to deny that speech and language are rather specialised functions of the human brain — their assumed innateness is what I reject. Again, it is a matter of faith which side of the chicken-and-egg argument about language and intelligence one is on, but I prefer to think that language presupposes certain forms of intelligence, such as the ability to process information linearly, rather than the reverse.

Phonetics and linguistics have no right to exist outside psychophysics/physiology and psychology respectively. It is for that reason that I welcome every psycho-physicists's and physiologist's interest in the perception of timbre, especially if it happens to be speech timbre. If more of them had been interested in the past, the issue of speech versus non-speech would long ago have been buried; indeed, it might even have failed to arise. As for linguistics, its task remains to explain why it takes children such a long time to learn such a simple code as language.

Chairman's Comments

M.P. Haggard In the past the term 'auditory phonetics' referred to the phonetician's use of the auditory sense to make expert judgements about his material. Concern for the nature of those skills has now largely yielded way to concern with a triad of fundamental issues. These in turn impinge on the procedural question of whether or not someone interested primarily in the reception of the spoken medium has anything to learn from or contribute to the study of hearing. The three issues that have appeared with different wordings and emphases over the years may be expressed as:
1. Are sounds with the spectral and temporal properties of speech coded by the auditory system in a way that is emergent and surprising relative to the coding of simpler signals and if so is this also relevant to the extraction of linguistic infor-mation?
2. Do the phenomena of speech perception, when subject to experimental scrutiny, justify the invocation of "special" principles — ie. special modes of brain function —

in addition to those found necessary to explain the phenomena of perception of non-speech sounds?

3.   Is the selection of the general types of feature contrast used in languages and more particularly the location of phoneme boundaries, determined by auditory constraints?

Although these issues are related it gives most insight to attempt to separate them. Young and Sachs' paper is a fine example of physiological investigation relevant to the first — perhaps more relevant even than they would wish to claim. Schouten's comments are concerned directly with the second, and Stevens' paper is a new version of a position on the third which he has held for some 15 years. I shall take these issues in turn and attempt to set them in context, giving least space to the third only because Stevens' paper is comprehensive and provides a statement of its own context and objectives readily appreciable to psychologists and linguists.

Some writers have paid lip service to the desirability of a psychophysiologically veridical measurement system or scaling procedure more adapted to the information-bearing aspects of speech sounds than the applied mathematicians' spectrograph. Those interested in automatic speech recognition have sought the philosopher's stone of ''revelatory'' transformations in general while speech researchers interested in production and perception have mainly been content to have an agreed specification without pressing for a realistic one. Auditory phonetics survived in the face of improvements in instrumental phonetics partly because instruments apparently furnished too much linguistically irrelevant detail. In the prodigal 1950's the definition of realistic parameters could be seen as a phonetic garbage disposal problem. The early work of Haskins Laboratories and elsewhere on a *limited* set of caricature features for speech sounds underpinned the garbage disposal view. In contrast it now appears that the auditory system and the speech perception system are jointly sensitive to a great quantity of detail previously thought irrelevant — to almost any aspect of the stimulus that distinguishes contrasted feature values and that can be isolated in an analysis and resynthesised in a perceptual experiment (eg. Haggard *et al* 1980). The scientific and pedagogical value of the short inventory of speech cues has been immense but it may have sold short the sensitivity of the auditory system. The problem formerly seemed to be: Is there a mathematical transformation of a physical dimension (eg. frequency) that will *throw away* in a fashion that is well-justified (eg. the pitch scale, or the travelling-wave-frequency to inner-ear-place transformation) a lot of the detail that does not appear to be important (eg. spectral structure above 3 kHz)? Now it seems better to say: Is there a way of *keeping* the maximum amount of information so that it can be used later by a plausible mechanism in any way found to be useful? This leads eventually to the realisation that there is probably no *single* best transformation for all purposes but that the physical primitives may be coded in the auditory nerve in multiple ways, for subsequent weighting and scaling in different ways for different functions.

In this somewhat abstract discussion it is not stated whether I am talking about a linguist/engineer with a job of representing speech sounds or a psychologist/physiologist with the job of describing and explaining the auditory system. In fact, unless one's vision is limited to costs and implementation, the problems should be the same. Young and Sachs started from the latter viewpoint. In a nutshell they are saying the following: (a) there is a whole new way of looking at auditory coding that postulates a temporal mechanism more equal to the task of handling speech sounds than the simple place coding of energy maxima; (b) the apparent virtues of this mechanism are to be measured by mapping the information which it preserves back into a simple form as similar as possible to the generally accepted physical metric (the short-time intensity spectrum); when this is done the temporal mechanism performs *better* than the traditional place mechanisms even though the place distribution of firing rates is a more direct analogue of the generally accepted spectral metric; (c) we must believe that the central auditory pathway contains mechanisms that embody some version of a mathematical retrieval procedure that effectively uses the temporal form of representation: (d) this belief is justified at present by the relatively good job the new mechanism does of preserving spectral definition in vowel sounds at high levels. The traditional place mechanism just does not preserve definition at high sound levels — yet behavioural responses in human perception and the temporal mechanism apparent in animals do preserve it well.

As in the classical debate over periodicity theories for musical pitch, some of our physiological colleagues will be reluctant to accept (c) on faith alone, but (a) - (d) will all be acceptable to me until I learn of something better! Particularly interesting ideas are that distortion products might serve as an extra source of information on the main formant frequencies and that significant formant information is carried by synchronised firing in place-frequency regions quite remote from, and generally higher than, the frequency concerned. The latter would explain difficulties in relating audiometric patterns of hearing loss to speech identification scores and, in particular, both the relatively good performance available in low frequency hearing loss and poor performance in high frequency loss. I predict that Young and Sachs' sets of figures for each information-frequency (*ie.* the harmonic-number in their work) displaying synchronised response as a function of place-frequency will be found increasingly useful in examining auditory coding.

Finally it is worth noting that the Young and Sachs' findings support the idea now ascendant in work on the speech cues that no stimulus parameters should be discarded as waste until we have explored uses for them. The conservationist 1980's are here!

I give equal space to the comments of Schouten because they concern an enduring issue which might well have justified a full paper. In his comments and his fuller article (Schouten, 1980) an opportunity was missed to criticise the process of *interpretation* of previous experiments in the literature which were taken as justifying the view that "speech is special", and the way in which the related assumptions distorted the investigation of phenomena of interest. This view has had primarily didactic value through generating interest and understanding among those who knew little about speech, and was only taken as a serious scientific proposition among speech researchers if they failed to appreciate the proselytising context in which it emerged. Certainly formal similarities in the structure of speech and language processing can also be found in other types of behaviour; ultimately the same brain tissue has to cope with both, so where does the special/not so special argument get us?

It is surprising that Schouten quotes the evidence on the voicing distinction in chinchillas, which is sometimes (over)interpreted as dismissing the characteristic linguistic role of categorical perception; yet he does not quote the evidence (Sinnott *et al.,* 1976) on the place distinction in monkeys and humans which indicates that on top of certain psychoacoustical similarities an extra stage has to be postulated to explain the way humans handle formant transition patterns.

Schouten usefully lists some of the fields such as adaptation, discrimination and processing-time in humans where the speech-mode concept has been incautiously or irrelevantly applied. He is absolutely correct to dismiss the fallacy that the adaptation effect *per se* provided evidence of qualitatively distinct processes for speech perception. However, he does not cite the work of Remez *et al* (1980) showing a failure of the adaptation to generalise in a speech continuum to a non-speech continuum and vice versa. Alas, he falls into the same trap as those he criticises when he assumes that 'special/non-special' is a simple empirical issue to be decided on the basis of the quantity of evidence apparently supporting one or the other position. Unfortunately, everything could be said to be special. The real question is a philosophical one: is the meaning of "special", when someone says that speech patterns are special processes, an important or useful meaning?

The issues faced by Stevens and Schouten come together when we contemplate basic acoustical parameters that play a role in both speech and non-speech distinctions, e.g. rate of intensity growth. In speech this dimension gives us stop/ semivowel and in music it gives us pluck/bow; in both cases there is a degree of categorical perception. Speech is characteristically categorical according to *statistical* criteria. To find categoricality elsewhere in no way undermines this characterisation of speech. To imagine that it does is to think in an inappropriately categorical mode about essentially statistical phenomena. Cutting (1977) emphasised the similarity of the average boundary values in the speech and the musical distinction; but as Rosen's comment here elegantly shows, the particular value at the boundary is not sufficiently fixed to justify strong psychoacoustic determinism — *i.e.* the view that all the parameter values are set by the inherent structure of the auditory system. Haggard *et al* (1980) argue analogously in the context of a different phonetic distinction. Does it matter then that the perceptual subsystems for music, bird song, or other mechanical events use the same distinction? Which is the chicken and which the egg?

We need not believe that in every case the use of a class of information in speech must ontogenetically precede the use in other perceptual subsystems. However in some cases at least, one could be excused for believing that the use in speech is in some way more basic. When listeners are presented with sounds of a borderline speech-like structure they perform *better*, and display more categoricality and other useful properties such as equivalence of cues, in so far as they realise that the sounds can be best coded for memory and decision by representing them as speech sounds (Best *et al* 1980). A trumpet has neither the spectrum nor the source characteristics of speech, but when a big band trumpet-player alternately blocks and frees the orifice while playing, do you not think "wa wa wa"? I do. In so far as any reader replies "no" we differ in our predisposition to activate the set of subroutines named "speech mode". The predisposition to activate the speech mode is determined by the sum of (a) stimulus naturalness (b) immediate acoustical context (c) past learning and (d) individual differences, and it can only be demonstrated with borderline speech-like stimuli precisely because one is otherwise categorically in it or not in it.

Each more virtuoso demonstration that chinchillas can do things previously assumed to be unique to humans (Kuhl and Miller, 1978) will be followed by an elegantly controlled experiment in which human listeners find it natural and informationally profitable to behave in subtle ways that are different from how they behave with the nearest possible stimuli that are not heard as speech (Best *et al* 1980). The experiments are fine, but do the interpretations really need to handle such simplistic issues as special/non-special in order to create the scientific motivation for doing the experiments?

Ideological oppositions have also in the past penetrated, although not to the same extent, the third issue of the auditory constraints upon the evolution of language to which Ken Stevens partly addresses himself here. I detect a very careful wording of his thesis to preclude any reader taking him as literally proposing that all the details of how people perceive particular speech distinctions, follow from a fixed universal auditory code. Because this latest account appears, appropriately, not directed at the details of speech perception in adults in particular languages I have accommodated Rosen's comments on it in a different context. What we have instead is a masterly digest of a great diversity of evidence about speech perception, drawing some descriptive generalisations from experimental findings. These generalisation have many uses for the student, the speech researcher, and the communication engineer and part of their value comes from describing the spectrum in a way more general than the terms denoting formant synthesiser parameters do. There is less emphasis than in his previous formulations on the implications for phonology and for the evolution of language. The generalisations are now sufficiently firm to delimit the rough extent of the considerable influence which inherent auditory factors must have had upon the evolution of languages. Within this extent we can now proceed to a more detailed understanding of the roles that have also indubitably been played by limitations of vocal tract anatomy controlling musculature, central information capacity for both input and output, and purely arbitrary cultural factors in particular languages, as suggested by Fujisaki in his comments.

Ken Stevens' overview of auditory factors recalls that speech perception also incorporates non-auditory cues. At present the details of optical speech perception are only just beginning to be worked out (Summerfield 1980) so it will be some time before we will have generalisations that can be brought into complementary relationships with those which Stevens draws or be compared with them for breadth.

Having made distinctions between the auditory level of analysis and a more abstract integrated level of analysis of speech sounds, it is interesting to determine whether the various phenomena of speech perception give us a set of agreed techniques for probing the distinguishable levels. We need paradigms for probing events at each level of analysis and the adaptation paradigm has withstood the reaction to its early overinterpretation to emerge as a paradigm sensitive to auditory pattern properties. The Remez *et al* result shows contextual effects of speech mode but does not undermine this view of the essential contribution of the adaptation effect. Summerfield and Roberts (Personal communication) confirm this role for it by showing that audiovisual presentation can be used profoundly to alter the perceived nature of an adapting auditory stimulus, but that the form of adaptation then observed still follows simply the expected unimodal form for the auditory part of the stimulus. We may therefore hope that the adaptation phenomena, with appropriate controls for response adaptation, now settles down to a period of exploitation in defining the phenomena of auditory pattern perception. I express the hope that this objective will be followed because otherwise those interested in speech and hearing will be unable to interact with physiologists now making progress in the physiology of the auditory cortex. The garbage disposal view was based largely on the assumption that the interesting transformations are peripheral and the parts of the auditory brain concerned with extracting the properties catalogued by Ken Stevens have remained an unfathomable mystery. There are signs that this is changing with recent progress in the mapping of fields of primary auditory cortex. It appears, for example, (Middlebrooks *et al* 1980) and that there are interdigitated sub fields of neurons both having a tonotopic frequency map but differing in their binaural response properties. One set (excitatory/excitatory) would be valuable for binaural averaging for pattern analysis, while the other (excitatory/inhibitory) would be valuable for localisation. Here then is a physiological basis for resynthesising the dissociated results of the analysis of 'where?' and 'what?' information. These analyses are at some stage dissociated, as shown by a number of dichotic experiments on fusion, including speech experiments with different formants fed to different ears (Cutting, 1976), yet they must also come together to mediate such performances as selective listening to speech. Central auditory physiology and auditory perception including speech perception studies can presumably interact profitably in many other respects.

As Fujisaki correctly points out in his comments there are central auditory factors of interest to those concerned with the roles of analysis, storage and decision in speech communication. Single unit mapping studies can, of course, only be done in animals, which of necessity means that not all of the interesting processes in speech perception can be tackled in this way. But cortical physiology is moving away from a superficial fascination with such uninterpretable findings as single units responding to highly specific patterns (e.g. particular conspecific vocalisations). There seems accordingly to be hope for a systematic exploration of cortical areas mediating the extraction of pattern properties such as those described by Ken Stevens. To ensure that this growing knowledge can be used, the psychologically oriented speech researcher will have both to sharpen his available tools, such as adaptation, and abandon the misconception that *only* those phenomena unique to speech tell us things of interest to the internal representation of speech.

THE COGNITIVE REPRESENTATION OF SPEECH
T. Myers, J. Laver, J. Anderson (editors)
© North-Holland Publishing Company, 1981

Elementary Gestures and Temporal Organization —
What Does an Articulatory Constraint Mean?

OSAMU FUJIMURA

Bell Laboratories

Abstract

A model of temporal organization of speech that manifests a syllable based phonological representation is discussed. Realization of phonological features that compose each syllable core is assumed to constitute elementary articulatory gestures. Based on preliminary observations of articulatory data recently acquired by the use of a computer-controlled x-ray microbeam system, some details of interactions between such elementary gestures are discussed. The notion of articulatory constraint is reexamined from this point of view.

Constraints of articulatory dynamics constitute an important aspect of speech. The notion of coarticulation must be clarified with exact definitions, and the choice of phonetic units for such discussion has to be revisited. We are beginning to have powerful new tools for obtaining sufficient data for systematic studies of articulatory dynamics in normal (and pathological) speech, and also computational means to simulate the complex processes of natural speech by simplified models (Fujimura, 1976a). Linguistic characteristics of phonetic units have to be examined because often both the apparent constraints and free variations are related to the permissible phonological paradigm, and their interpretation has to be based on an appropriate phonological description for the language in question.

In this paper, our tentative analysis of the phonetic structure of English syllables will be used in interpreting the articulatory data we have acquired with the computer-controlled x-ray microbeam technique (Fujimura, et al. 1973). We hypothesize that elementary articulatory gestures, as temporal patterns, of the most pertinent articulatory "organs" are the primary units representing the minimal distinctive functions of syllables. Segmental characteristics as total articulatory or acoustic states are often affected by the looseness of temporal relations of such elementary gestures, reflecting to a large extent physiological conflict between articulatory gestures or disfavoring of certain combinations of gestures. Temporal organization of speech is thus subject to the constraints caused by interactions among different articulatory dimensions, which give rise to a "distortion" of their temporal patterns, as well as to so-called coarticulatory or smoothing effects within each dimension.

Temporal organization of articulatory gestures — an hypothetical model For the sake of clarity about the types of assumptions we will need in order to discuss temporal characteristics of speech, I will outline a speculative model of phonetic realization (see Fujimura and Lovins, 1978). I do not have any intention to claim that the validity of this model is proved by the fragmental data I will discuss here; the purpose of this paper is to clarify what kind of implications a well-defined notion of "articulatory constraints" can have in relation to some other basic notions in speech research, rather than to propose a specific framework for phonetic description.

(1)　Phonetic forms are specified as an organization of phonological units, composed as a tree, in which the nodes represent units at different hierarchical levels, such as (phonological) phrases and words, syllables, cores and affixes, syllable (core) features (see Fig. 1 for an illustrative example; cf. Fujimura; (1976b) Fujimura, (in press)). Such a "segmental" tree is associated with a metric interpretation which determines "prosodic" or "suprasegmental" characteristics of the form (see Liberman and Prince, 1977; Selkirk, 1978a).

(2)　In accordance with such specifications, individual phonetic features, or combinations of different classes of features such as place x manner, are retrieved from an inventory of elementary temporal patterns of articulatory gestures. Each of such stored patterns is in one of the prespecified and physiologically natural articulatory dimensions and contains a set of parameters (such as time constants and "durations" of "stationary" portions) which is in general sensitive to the prosodic specifications as well as extra-linguistic conditions.[1]　A subset of such parameters refer to "phonetic dispositions" of the language, the dialect, or the speaker idiosyncrasy, representing "neutral conditions" of those physiologic/physical dimensions to which specifications of phonetic values always refer in their realizations.

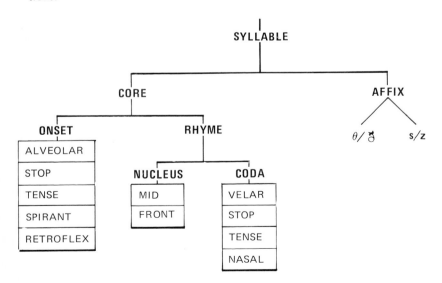

/s t r e N k θ s/: 'strengths'

FIGURE 1　*Part of "segmental tree" according to a core-affix analysis. Syllable feature representations in the boxes are only indicative.*

(3)   Elementary gestures are assembled into a syllabic unit of phonetic events according to a temporal principle of "segmental" organization. The principle controls the sequential ordering of events according to the syllable-initial and final element specifications for each syllable core with its nucleus specifications as its basic quasi-static features. Vowels in the phonemic sense may contain "consonantal" elements such as glides and elongation, which in our framework will be treated much in the same way as core-final sonorant elements are.[2]

(4)   The temporal assembly within a syllable core is loosely (but to a large extent regularly) organized in the sense that exact synchrony is not required between different articulatory dimensions for the same "phonemic segment". The phonetic affixes, in contrast, have relatively stable segmental characteristics and their specified order is respected strictly in the process of concatenation.

(5)   The inherent gestures are contained basically within the syllable core, and the distinction between initial and final elements is respected in assembling the core pattern. Relative temporal positions are assigned to individual gestures by realization rules according to their vowel affinity values (see Fujimura, 1975).

(6)   In the phonetic realization process, a balance is obtained between the inherent influences of elementary gestures via physical and physiologic principles. Conceptually, it is similar to the principle in physics that describes the real physical event as the most stable path in the spatio-temporal domain of all conceivable events, in conformity with the choices of boundary (e.g. durational, in our case) conditions given to the system under consideration (syllabic frames, for example, in our case). Such a balance is evaluated for a larger structure containing an ordered set of syllables (cores and affixes) as well as higher node units, in conformity with the metric interpretation, which gives the input to pitch and duration rules, rather than individually for each syllable core.

Figuratively, the vowel affinity principle as a principle of segmental organization works like the gravity law in a situation when liquids (consonantal features, or partial bundles thereof) with different densities (vowel affinity values) are mixed in a glass cylinder. The exact positions of boundaries are determined according to the quantities of the liquids, in this analogy. In the case of speech, boundaries are well defined partly because the phenomena are multidimensional and individual dimensions have different temporal characteristics, and partly because gestural patterns blend with one another under more complex physiologic/physical transition laws than simple repulsion. The manner of blending as well as quantities of individual liquids, viz. the interrelation between elementary articulatory gestures, are determined as functions of parameters specified for the prosodic and other environmental conditions, as well as some of the parameters representing phonetic dispositions.

Articulatory constraints may thus be pictured as such rules of physiologic/physical interactions between elementary gestures in temporal organization of phonetic forms. Let me give a few examples to explain the types of interactions I have in mind here.

Articulatory data   The articulatory data we will discuss here have been obtained by the use of a computer-controlled x-ray microbeam system which is in operation at the University of Tokyo (see Fujimura, et al. 1973; Kiritani, et al. 1975). The data pertain to utterances of words and sentences containing occurrences of nasal consonantal elements, as spoken by three native speakers of American English (see Fujimura, et al. 1977). Each session contained 6-8 minutes worth net speech. We have a recent addition to this data base in the form of five similar sessions by two more speakers.

Six (five for one of the three speakers) lead pellets were placed on the tongue (posterior, middle and blade portions), the lower lip, a lower tooth (for the mandible) and the velum (on its upper surface), as well as two additional reference points on

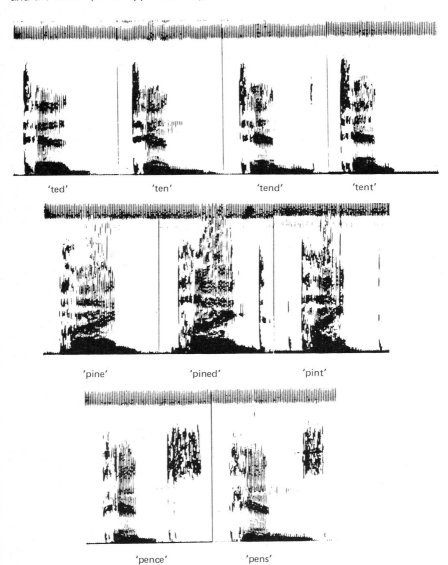

FIGURE 2 *Sound spectrograms of words (from the simultaneous recording of x-ray data). The striation at top shows individual "frames" for the articulatory measurements.*

the bridge of the nose and an upper tooth for correcting for head movements, all in the midsagittal plane. The two-dimensional pellet positions as viewed from the side of the subject's head were automatically tracked and digitally recorded in real time. The time functions representing pellet coordinates were smoothed and displayed on an oscilloscope surface for close examination, and simultaneously recorded sound was available for auditory examinations.

English final cluster — nasalization and tenseness   It is known (Malecot, 1960) that in American English the temporal structure of syllables containing final nasal-obstruents differs drastically depending on the final (consonantal) tenseness. In 'pined', in contrast to 'pint', for example, there can be seen a distinct period of nasal murmur, as we see in the spectrograms shown in Figure 2. The former is very much like an utterance of 'pine' except that it has the final "segment" [d], and that the [n] of 'pine (in isolation) may show additional phrase-final lengthening effects. The pattern of 'pint', in contrast, is inherently different from 'pine' or 'pined'. This point may be even more apparent in the comparison of 'ten, tend, tent'.

From an acoustical point of view, this means that a phonemic concatenation model complicates, for example, speech synthesis by rule.[3] One may introduce an *ad hoc* rule which shortens or eliminates nasal murmur in the context of the following tense consonant (only when it is tautosyllabic, see Lovins, 1978), but this is not the only *ad hoc* difference. If we compare the spectrograms of 'tend' vs. 'tent' and 'pined' vs. pint' again, we find further that, as is well known, the duration of the voiced portion is very different depending on tenseness of the final consonantal element (d/t). We also see in the comparison of 'pined' and 'pint' that the transitional part representing the diphthongization is hardly affected by the tenseness contrast, in spite of the phonemic contiguity of the glide to the stop consonant, whereas the steady vowel portion, located far apart from the pertinent consonant with two intervening "phonemic" segments in between, is affected considerably, and hardly exists for 'pint' in contrast to 'pined'. Such differences in manifestations of the t-d contrast may seem beyond any possible explanation in terms of concatenation of phonemic segments subject only to "articulatory constraints", but, to make sure that we are not misled by superficial acoustic phenomena, let us see if we can gain any insight into these seemingly totally *ad hoc* phenomena by examining the articulatory processes involved.

Figure 3 compares the relevant articulatory events. Here the time functions showing pellet movements are superimposed for comparison of 'pint' (dashed curves) with 'pined' (solid curves). We see that the tongue shape (represented by the three lowest curves) changes relatively similarly in time, if we superimpose the two sets of time functions for the best match in this temporal portion of the words. The tongue body may be moving slightly more vigorously for /t/ than for /d/, whereas the blade seems to move more for /d/, if the differences are significant. The lip, a nonpertinent articulator for this portion of the syllables (i.e. the final demisyllables) seems to move somewhat differently, but we will ignore this difference for the moment.

The most striking difference is seen in the velum movement. The final /t/ seems to be accompanied by a glottalization which stops voicing suddenly near the beginning of the oral closure for what would be an [n] if the voice were there, causing silence while the velic port is still open. One may argue that the "segmental sequence" including the segment [n] is there for 'pint' as well as for 'pined', except that one does not hear it for the former because of the peculiar laryngeal maneuver for /t/. From this point of view, the only difference between the syllables would be in laryngeal control, which shows a notable (and obviously language dependent) "asynchrony" with respect to the movements of other articulators, and "vowel duration" that determines the temporal distance between the initial /p/-gesture

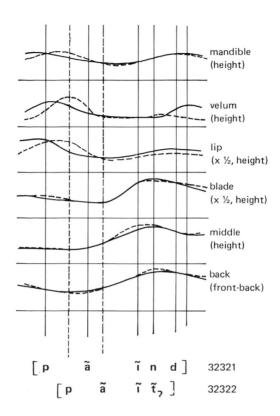

$$[\; p \qquad \tilde{a} \qquad \tilde{\iota} \quad n \quad d \;] \qquad 32321$$
$$[\; p \qquad \tilde{a} \qquad \tilde{\iota} \quad \tilde{t}_{\gamma} \;] \qquad 32322$$

FIGURE 3 *Tracings of the time functions representing pellet positions for 'pined' (solid lines) and 'pint' (broken lines).*

and the final lingual gestures. Based on our descriptive framework, we argue that the feature realization processes for the cores /paJNt/ and paJn/ of /paJnd/, the /d/ being a phonetic affix, adopt the same articulatory gesture with respect to the tongue tip movement because both forms have a place specification of "apical" as well as the "stop" feature. The temporal parameter for specifying the duration of quasi-stationary event for the nucleus /a/ is sensitive to the concomitant syllable-final tenseness feature, and causes a difference in the temporal location of the initial /p/-gesture. From this point of view, /paJNt/ as a core should be compared with /paJt/, the former having an additional "nasal" feature (represented by /N/). The velum lowering as its physical manifestation is "squeezed into" the temporal frame of /paJt/, nasalization being truncated early due to the "repulsion" of the final tenseness of the same core (see the section below on 'Physiologic interactions'). It should be mentioned that in certain dialects, the apical gesture for /t/ may be totally absent, but the variation can be continuous in terms of combinations of such factors as extent of aspiration, degree of glottalization, completeness of apical or velic closure, etc., rather than a choice between a discrete set of allophones. Also, here we should note that it seems unlikely that some allophonic variations (for example, the initial and final /l/'s in English) can be even qualitatively explained by physical or physiological considerations (see Fujimura and Lovins, 1978).

If we look for other differences between the two words in the entire syllabic pattern of articulation, we find that the mandible and the velum show noticeably slower movements for 'pined' than for 'pint' in the initial C-V transition, even though acoustically this difference is hardly discernible. On the other hand, the lip, the pertinent articulator for the initial consonant here, moves more or less the same way with a similar speed of labial separation, and the main difference seems to exist in timing of this movement. In this pair of words, the main features of the initial and final consonants do not overlap in the same articulatory dimensions, and the patterns of elementary gestures for each consonantal feature, such as initial labial stop-plosion, final nasalization, and final alveolar stop, are more or less independent from each other. But in this example, too, an indirectly involved gesture e.g. of the mandible does seem to show some interference effect between the initial and final parts of the core. The direct influence of the final tenseness on mandible movement is relatively small in this subject, but in some speakers it has been found quite strong (Fujimura and Miller, in press). In the case of the velum, the syllable nucleus in its quasi-stationary manifestation (around the vertical lines, solid or broken, corresponding to the symbol [ã] at the bottom in Fig. 3) in general exhibits a lowered position according to the final nasality specification. The temporal change of velum height for the transition from denasalization for the initial consonant to the nasalization of the final consonant seems rather unspecific, and the slope seems sensitive to the amount of time available for the transition as determined by other factors.

Physical interaction between articulatory dimensions Interaction or conflict between different articulatory dimensions can be direct and visibly obvious. For example, we have observed in our data for words like 'among' and 'bungs', that when the final nasal element is accompanied by a velar consonantal element, velum height shows a slight upward movement in conformity with the tongue surface height, due to the obvious mechanical conflict between velum lowering and high tongue body surface.

As a somewhat similar but less obvious case, a comparison is given in Figure 4 between 'pence' and 'pens'. The difference observed in the tongue surface shape (in particular for the back of the tongue) between the two words seems to reflect an interaction between the tongue and the velum. Probably in this case, part of the posterior surface of the tongue is in contact with the velum (and/or the two organs are linked to each other through musculature), and the tongue surface moves upward as the velum is raised (the correct causal relation being unknown). Likewise, lower lip height often reflects mandible height when there is no strong labial gesture. Such direct mechanical interactions between elementary gestures in different articulatory dimensions are commonly observed in apparent articulatory movements, and constitute one type of articulatory constraint. These effects are probably so common that the inherent independence of elementary gestures, if this notion is correct, is not readily visible in most real life situations, particularly when combined with another type of inter-gesture interaction which we will discuss below.

Physiologic interactions The second type of interaction is also an interference observed at the physical level, but is not a direct positional conflict between two articulators as discussed above, nor is it a conflict in the temporal course of movement of the same articulator in the same physical dimension, as we will discuss in the following section. It is characterized by more complex and inherently physiologic factors. Consider, for example, a case where the surface of the tongue shape is stiffened by the contraction of intrinsic lingual muscles, let us say forming noncompliant lateral ridges with midsagittal groove. If this condition is combined

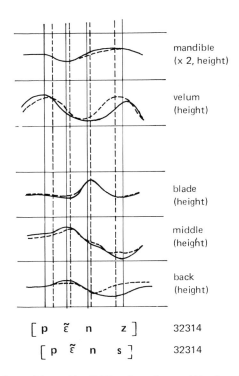

FIGURE 4   *Comparison of 'pens' (solid lines) vs. 'pence' (broken lines).*

with a contraction of the anterior portion of the genioglossus muscle which pulls the tongue surface downward in the region near the midsagittal plane of the blade, even an extreme gesture of tongue fronting by tongue body control does not result in the highest midsagittal coronal surface, because the movement is blocked by the supporting linguapalatal contact on the sides. This is probably one of the characteristics of tense front vowels, even though there are other major factors involved in the characterization of such vowels when we consider the three dimensional structure of the tongue (see Fujimura and Kakita, 1979).

A similar situation seems to exist with respect to the interaction between velum lowering and general tenseness of consonantal gestures in syllable (or word) initial position. Velum height has been observed to be systematically lower for syllable final nasal elements than for syllable initial nasals, in at least English and Japanese (see Fujimura, et al. 1975, 1977; Fujimura, 1977). It is quite possible that the physiologic structure surrounding the velum is generally stiffened in the initial part than in the middle or final part of the syllable (this applies also to word or phrase), and this stiffness counteracts a full lowering of the velum even when the pertinent primary muscle is set for full manifestation of nasality in the form of relaxation of the levator palatini muscle (see Fujimura, 1977). The coexistence of the final tenseness with nasalization as in the example 'pint' we discussed above may be a similar case of interdimensional conflict. If the inherent ''weakness'' of syllable final position favors ''laxness'' of nasalization feature and disfavors ''tenseness'' of the /t/-element, one may not be surprised to see a "nasalized" /t/ with an incomplete articulatory closure.

In addition to the interactions discussed above, some physiologic interactions may have to be described specifically in terms of characteristics of neural control mechanisms, in the form of naturally preferred linkage between potentially independent physiologic dimensions. On the other hand, it must be true that some phonetic facts have to be explained by referring to auditory (and tactile or orosensory, see Perkell (1977); Stevens and Perkell (1976)) effects also. If "tenseness", the yet undefined notion, has to do with some perception of "force", aspiration of tense stop consonants in some languages (e.g. English, in contrast to the case of Korean nonaspirate forced stops, see Kagaya (1974)) may be related to such acoustic effects rather than direct physiologic factors, even though it is also possible that the glottal opening via raising intra-oral pressure is used for a more 'vigorous' movement in articulatory release.

Temporal interaction — hard coarticulation Assimilation is a common type of interaction between sequentially consecutive phonologic units. In phonology, on the other hand, we also see cases of the opposite effect — dissimilation. In the domain of articulatory dynamics, interaction between consecutive articulatory events using the same (or physically interacting) articulators may be described as what we may call hard coarticulation (Fujimura and Lovins, 1978). Much has been discussed about the effective temporal domain of such interaction (see Kent and Minifie (1977) for a review). Hard coarticulation, defined as a direct mechanical smoothing effect, which may contain for example language-dependent and speaker-dependent time constants, would account for only part of the so-called coarticulation phenomena. The Henke type look-ahead mechanism (Henke, 1966), for example, goes beyond this notion, and should be described as a feature-copying (or agreement) process, i.e. soft coarticulation.

CONCLUDING REMARKS

Consideration of all types of interaction discussed above would give us a rather complex picture of temporal organization, as we actually see in articulatory data, but the underlying principle could still be simple and straightforward. It will be a matter of minimizing conflicts and efforts, within the bounds of the phonological framework, specifically using syllabic frames as well as other metric units. Within each frame, the temporal organization is inherently multidimensional and almost liquid, perhaps describable as "smashed raw Easter eggs" (Hockett, 1955). Individual elementary gestures in speech production manifest phonological features, via physiologic processes in the form of proper motor commands. For containing crucial articulatory events within the prescribed frame both spatially and temporally, it seems essential to use various feedback mechanisms (see MacNeilage, 1970).

The complexity of observable phenomena makes it mandatory that we compare a large number of utterance samples that are collected according to a systematic design. Since such comparison can be made only within the same subject, due to anatomical, physiological, and phonetic idiosyncrasy of human speakers, the availability of the new x-ray microbeam system is often an indispensable condition for conducting such studies without giving dangerous radiation doses to the subjects, as far as the use of x-rays for articulatory data collection is concerned. This is why we claim that we are just beginning to be in a position to study speech production.

The basic difference between articulatory events and acoustic events is the continuity of the articulator movements in contrast to apparent discontinuity of acoustic signal characteristics. Because of the nonlinear nature of voice source with respect to voice onset/offset and the sensitivity of the acoustic output to the relatively rapid release of oral closure that is caused by a basically slow movement of the main body of the articulator, the contrast in terms of continuity is quite remarkable (see Miller and Fujimura, 1979; Nelson, 1979).

The notion of articulatory constraint is based on this inherent continuity of the physical events involved in speech production. The apparent segmental nature of speech should not mislead us to the notion that the acoustic segments directly reflect the invariant nature of phonetic units. The observable characteristics of output signals obviously are variable depending on various contextual factors, and articulatory constraints in the sense above are responsible for a large part of such context dependence. They do not, however, account for all variability especially if we take a phonemic segment as the basic phonetic unit. One aim of our work is to clarify the limits of such an explanation based on articulatory continuity.

Notes

1. The "natural" physiological dimensions need not be orthogonal to each other (i.e. different features may refer to a common "organ" or one feature may refer to more than one organ) or universally common among different languages. One could set up a universal articulatory space with common dimensions as a phonetic framework and represent each "articulatory dimension" in the sense above for a given language e.g. as a linear combination of such universal elementary dimensions.

2. Since the phonetic interaction between the initial and final consonants seems very limited, we can further subdivide a core into initial and final demisyllables assuming minimal (hard) coarticulation (Fujimura, 1976b; Lovins, et al. 1979). In conformity with Selkirk's phonological discussion (1978a, also personal communication), Fig. 1 reflects this phonetic characteristic by branching a core into onset and rhyme. Based on this representation, the phonetic realization (see below) can be said to be processed for initial and final demisyllables separately.

3. An effective acoustic appraoch for practical purposes of speech synthesis is to treat the final demisyllable (i.e. the syllable core except the initial consonant-vosel transition, representing the rhyme in Fig. 1) as a holistic pattern (Fujimura 1976; Lovins, et al. 1979).

THE COGNITIVE REPRESENTATION OF SPEECH
T. Myers, J. Laver, J. Anderson (editors)
© *North-Holland Publishing Company, 1981*

Articulatory Constraints on the Cognitive Representation of Speech

JOHN J. OHALA

University of California, Berkeley

INTRODUCTION

This is a story in the Sherlock Holmes tradition.[1] As every reader of the Holmes stories knows, the detective's greatest challenge was discovering the activity of the master criminal Professor Moriarty. Professor Moriarty was what we in America would call a "godfather": a behind-the-scenes director of a vast criminal organization—so much behind-the-scenes that only Holmes could deduce his presence and trace a seemingly isolated crime to his doorstep. Holmes' main tools were his knowledge of the world (cultivated by somewhat exotic research), his deductive powers, and his imagination. In spite of his dabblings in chemistry and such, he relied rather little on sophisticated technology; the simple magnifying glass was his principal technical aid.

This is a fairly good model for the task that faces us in trying to discover the

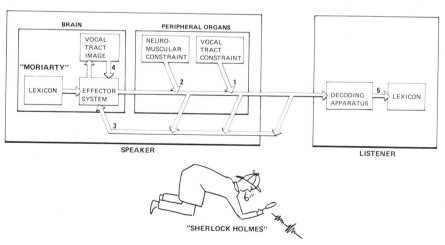

FIGURE 1 *The five routes whereby articulatory constraints can leave their imprint on speech: (1) vocal tract constraints (2) neuromuscular constraints, (3) feedback, (4) feedforward, (5) sound change. In imitation of Sherlock Holmes we must examine the speech signal, the product of these many mechanisms, and isolate the contribution of the lexicon.*

cognitive representation of speech. Somewhere up in the brain there exists the ultimate authority on how to pronounce words; we call this the lexicon. This lexicon —my Moriarty analogue—does its work indirectly through neurological, muscular, and articulatory agents. We are in the position of Holmes in that we can observe the activity of some of these agents and have to deduce the master*mind* behind it all. Like Holmes, I believe that imagination, not engineering, will be our most effective tool in this task.

The particular subquestion I address in this paper is: how is the representation of speech in the brain, i.e., its lexical form, affected by articulatory constraints? We can't really answer this question, however, until we know what the lexical representation of speech is, and we can't know that until we can examine the speech in its acoustical and physiological form and differentiate those features due to lexicon from those added on further downstream. So let's attack that question first.

I think it is possible to identify at least five routes whereby "down-stream" constraints may influence pronunciation. Our task is to examine various features of pronunciation, and assign them to one of these five sources or to the lexicon. I will briefly list and offer examples — in some cases hypothetical — of each of these five. (In the discussion to follow it will be helpful to refer to Figure 1).

VOCAL TRACT MECHANISMS

Some features of the speech signal are probably present due to purely mechanical, i.e., physical, constraints of the vocal tract, e.g., inertial properties of the articulators, the anatomical connections between articulators, the elasticity of articulator tissues, aerodynamic factors, etc. I will discuss two probable examples.

VOT variations   It has been found that the voice onset time (VOT) of voiceless stops in various languages shows systematic variation as a function of vowel quality, i.e., slightly longer (more positive) VOT before high, close vowels and lesser VOT before low, open vowels (Halle and Smith, 1952; Summerfield, 1975; Smith, 1978; Ohala, 1975a). Figure 2 shows more data obtained in our laboratory (by Robert Gaskins and Mary Beckman) which show this vowel-dependent variation in VOT (for individual speakers of English and Japanese). It has been hypothesized that this effect is due primarily to the fact that the high close vowels offer greater resistance to the air escaping from the oral cavity which, in turn, delays the achievement of a transglottal pressure suitable for voicing (Kozhevnikov & Chistovich, 1965:186ff.; Ohala, 1976).

Fundamental frequency perturbations   The small variations in fundamental frequency (F0) of voice on the vowels following voiced and voiceless stops, i.e., higher F0 following voiceless stops and lower F0 following voiced, especially breathy-voiced, stops can probably be traced to some change in vocal cord tension induced by the gestures required for the voiced/voiceless distinction (Ohala, 1978b; Hombert, Ohala & Ewan, 1979).

NEUROMUSCULAR CONSTRAINTS

Another possible influence on the form of speech is limitations of the neuro-muscular system, e.g., the frequency response of the muscles, the transmission time of neural impulses, etc.

The time constant in feedback loops   Kozhevnikov & Chistovich (1965:93), following Lashley (1951), suggested that the time it would take to issue a 'command' to a speech muscle and then receive sensory information on the resulting movement would be something on the order of 100 msec. From this basis they argued that feedback could not be used to regulate the timing of speech since speech gestures follow one another at intervals shorter than 100 msec.

Setting the lower limit of the speed of the efferent-afferent loop to around 100 msec in the case of speech seems to be unjustifiably high, especially when one considers that there are some very fast reflexes served by the cranial nerves: the eye blink reflex (< 10 msec) and the masseter reflex (~ 12-15 msec); see Ohala (1970:124) for a review of this issue.

Inherent phase lag between motor cortex and speech muscles Lenneberg (1967:96) proposed that because of presumed variations in the transit time of nerve impulses over the various nerves serving the speech muscles there could be a 'phase lag' (synchronization error) of some 30 msec between the muscles near the brain (e.g., tensor palatini) and those distant from the brain (e.g., posterior cricoarytenoid) and that this would necessitate a rather complex temporal staggering of the delivery of these motor commands at the center. However, there seems to be little empirical support for this conjecture. Ohala (1970:129ff.) reviewed this issue, made his own estimates of the transit time of neural impulses over the cranial nerves, and arrived at estimated synchronization errors of from 5 to 9 msec — too small to make much of a difference. Subsequent measurement of neural impulse speed over the recurrent nerve by Flisberg and Lindholm (1970) coincided

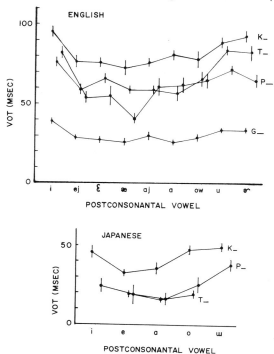

FIGURE 2   *Voice onset time (VOT) for English (top) and Japanese (bottom) stops in the environment of different vowels.*

remarkably well with Ohala's estimates and tended to support the lower value for synchronization error.

Additional examples could be added, e.g., Lenneberg's hypothesis that all speech articulation is superimposed on a 6Hz oscillation in the brain's electrical state, which claim has also been found to be empirically unsupported (Ohala, 1970:156ff, 1975b).

More recent work in this area has progressed beyond pure speculation, e.g., Hirose, Ushijima, Kobayashi, and Sawashima (1969) and MacNeilage and his associates (MacNeilage, Sussman, Westbury, and Powers, 1979) are contributing important data on the response time and other dynamic properties of specific speech muscles and the motoneurones that drive them.

FEEDBACK

Discrepancies between the centrally intended activity and the activity at the periphery can be sensed via feedback and trigger compensatory activity. The following is a hypothetical example.

Voiced stops are difficult to produce because of the small volume of the oral cavity and limited compliance of its surfaces (Passy, 1890: 161; Ohala and Riordan, 1979). These conditions make it inevitable that the glottal air flow necessary for voicing will lead to the build-up of oral pressure which in turn will lead to the cessation of voicing. The extinguishing of voicing can be avoided though, if the speaker makes more room for the glottal air flow, e.g., by lowering the larynx. Presumably the need to implement such compensatory gestures could be signaled to the speaker's brain by sensory feedback e.g., pressure sensation. Thus the presence of purposeful larynx lowering during voiced stops might in some cases stem indirectly from articulatory constraints.

THE VOCAL TRACT IN THE BRAIN OR 'FEEDFORWARD'

It is obvious that the speaker's brain has long experience with the vocal tract and its constraints; it 'knows the ropes', so to speak. We may guess that the brain possesses some kind of image of the vocal tract, i.e., of the various articulators, their connections, the muscles supplying the articulators, etc. Working with this 'model' of the tract, the brain can no doubt figure out how to accomplish its goals, i.e., reproduce the lexical image of a word, given the capabilities and constraints of the tract. We don't know for sure what this lexical image is, whether muscle contractions, vocal tract shapes, aerodynamic states, acoustic-auditory shapes, or some combination of these. We must assume though, that the speaker knows how to control the speech production apparatus in order to produce these images. This type of 'anticipation' of the constraints of the effector structures has been called 'feed forward', and I will henceforth use this simpler term in referring to this concept. To clarify the distinction I'm making: all phonetic activity that is done for the sake of achieving these lexical images can be attributed to 'feedforward': the action which is isomorphic to the stored lexical image is not due to feedforward. If, for example, the image were acoustic-auditory, and the event of interest were a [w], then the labial and velar constrictions (as well as all the neuromuscular activity underlying them) would count as phonetic activity motivated by feedforward. The lowered F1 and F2 would be motived by the stored lexical image.

SOUND CHANGE

An indirect but extremely interesting mechanism whereby the constraints of the vocal tract may influence even the most central representation of speech is sound change. I have reviewed above some ways that the purely mechanical constraints of the speech production apparatus can leave its imprint on speech. We can think of these as distortions of the speech signal since they are unintended by the speaker. In some cases, the listener may not be able to figure out which features of the speech signal are intended and which are unintentional distortions. When repeating what he heard, he may produce intentionally what was previously unintentional (Ohala, 1974, 1975c, 1978a, 1979; Hombert, et al. 1979; Ohala and Lorentz, 1977). This process is represented schematically in Figure 1, where it is indicated that the speech signal reaching the listener consists of the lexical image plus detectable consequences of all the previously discussed four mechanisms: vocal tract and neuromuscular constraints, feedback and feedforward. This 'distortion'-encrusted signal may form the basis of the listener's lexical image of the word.

The philological literature is filled with examples of this process. As mentioned above, the F0 of vowels varies systematically after voiced and voiceless consonants. This mechanically-caused distortion has been reinterpreted centuries ago by the speakers of Chinese, Thai, Vietnamese, and many other languages, as intentional tonal distinctions (Hombert, et al. 1979).

I believe this type of misperception or misjudgment, if you will, on the part of the listener regarding what the intended parts of the speech signal are, goes on all the time — potentially, at least, every time one person speaks and another listens. These I have called 'mini-sound changes'. Most such errors are eventually corrected (because the listener has other sources of information regarding the 'true' pronunciation of words). The few errors that don't get corrected may come to be characteristic of an individual speaker who may then transmit the new pronunciation to other speakers via normal sociolinguistic mechanisms. If the transmission is extensive enough it may become what the linguist recognizes as a sound change proper.

An example of a rather dramatic 'mini-sound change' is provided by a case of a normal Spanish-speaking child who spoke English with characterisitcs of a cleft palate because his only model for English pronunciation was his English-speaking playmate who had a real cleft palate (Klinger, 1962).

DIFFERENTIATING THESE INFLUENCES

To recapitulate: our task is to find out how articulatory constraints may influence the cognitive representation of speech. But we have just seen that articulatory constraints may leave their imprint on the speech signal in a variety of ways and only one, sound change, affects what we would presumably count as the most central, the lexical, representation of speech. We must therefore seek ways to assign any given aspect of pronunciation — suspected of being due to articulatory constraints — to one of the five mechanisms discussed above.

This is a complex problem because in many cases the action of two or more of these mechanisms may be superficially very similar. This has led some writers on the subject to ignore or deny the differences between these mechanisms. For example, Harms (1973) seems to believe that if a certain aspect of pronunciation *can be* attributed to low-level phonetic mechanisms, then it *has to* be so explained; it cannot be counted as a feature of the more central representation of speech. That is, in the jargon of the modern phonologist, phonetically-motivated changes in pronunciation are not to be considered 'rules' in the grammar of the language. Donegan and Stampe (1979) on the other hand, seem to deny that any phonetically-motivated aspects of pronunciation, e.g., stop voicing, vowels nasalizing before nasals, can occur without contribution of the highest levels of the speaker's cognitive system;

for them, presumably, there can be no purely mechanical distortions of the speech signal. I hope to show below that both views oversimplify a complex situation, and, furthermore, that questions about the cognitive/mechanical causes of certain aspects of pronunciation should be decided by empirical evidence, not by decree.

VOCAL TRACT MECHANICS

There are a variety of ways which have been used to reveal whether a certain aspect of pronunciation is present due to vocal tract mechanics.

Control independent variable; observe effect on dependent variable   One set of techniques has in common the following principle: one can remove or alter a given vocal tract constraint (the independent variable) and see if the particular feature of interest (the dependent variable) disappears or changes. If it does then it probably owes its existence to the constraint; if there is no change, then it is probably unrelated to the constraint.

Vowel height and vowel duration   It has been hypothesized that the often-found direct correlation between vowel duration and the openness of the vowel, that is, open vowels longer than close vowels (other things being equal), stems from the fact that the jaw has to travel a greater distance for open vowels and this takes longer (Lindblom, 1967). This hypothesis was tested by Nooteboom and Slis (1970) by having subjects speak test words normally and with their jaw clenched, i.e., by removing the hypothesized cause of the effect. As it turned out, the variation in vowel duration was the same whether the jaw was closed or not. Thus the vowel duration differences could not be attributed to extent of jaw movement (although it leaves open the questions of whether the movement of other articulators, e.g., the tongue, may be the cause and whether the origins of the effect, via sound change, may not have been the physical properties of the jaw).

Vowel height and F0   As is well known, there is a small but systematic correlation between the height of a vowel and its average F0. There have been at least two hypotheses which have attempted to account for it by peripheral factors. One attributes it to the pull of the tongue on the larynx (Ohala, 1972, 1977, 1978b). Ohala and Eukel (1978) found that by having subjects speak with their jaw propped open by bite blocks (and thus presumably making the tongue pull more forcefully on the larynx during the production of high vowels), the difference in F0 between high and low vowels was enhanced. They interpreted this result as favoring the tongue-pull hypothesis. In this case, a change in the dependent variable, tongue pull, was used to support a claimed causal relationship between a peripheral constraint and an aspect of pronunciation.

Many other studies of this type could be cited (Kozhevnikov & Chistovich, 1965: 186ff; Houde, 1968:88ff; Putnam, Doherty & Shipp, 1976; Ohala and Riordan, 1979).

Looking 'upstream' from the vocal tract   Another class of studies uses electromyography (EMG) for the purpose of finding out whether a certain aspect of speech originates in the vocal tract or higher 'upstream'. If the EMG records show that certain muscles actively contribute to a given gesture, then one can conclude that the gesture has a more central origin and is not caused by a purely mechanical factor.

F0 variation in sentence intonation   Lieberman (1967) claimed that the fall in F0 at the end of declarative sentences was purely a mechanical consequence of falling subglottal air pressure, itself a consequence of the approaching inspiratory phase of breathing. The finding, from various EMG studies, that such rapid drops in F0 are invariably accompanied by contraction of one or more of the laryngeal strap muscles (along with other evidence) helped to disprove Lieberman's claim. See Ohala (1970, 1977, 1978b) for a review of this issue.

Velic elevation vs. vowel height It has been hypothesized that the well known correlation between the degree of soft palate elevation and the 'height' of the vowel is due to some sort of mechanical pull of the tongue on the soft palate (or, possibly, vice-versa), presumably via the palatoglossus muscle (Moll, 1962). This hypothesis can be discarded however, since several EMG studies (e.g., Lubker, 1968; Fritzell, 1969) found that the muscles controlling soft palate position are themselves responsible for the vowel-specific variation (cf. Ohala, 1974, 1975c).

Other methods of estimating the mechanical constraints of the articulators Some amount of coarticulation (the values of one or more articulatory parameters of one segment 'spilling over' onto neighboring segments) is probably inevitable due to the inertia of the articulators. How much co-articulation is physically necessary can be estimated either by measuring the frequency response of various articulators or by finding the minimum time required to accomplish specific speech gestures.

In an informal study some years ago, Valerie Mamini and I attempted to estimate the frequency response of my own jaw during speech and non-speech. Jaw

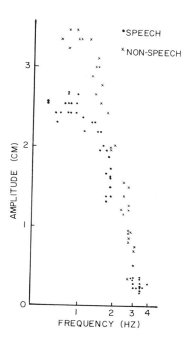

FIGURE 3 *Frequency response of one subject's jaw measured with speech gestures ([sasasa. . .]) and non-speech (opening and closing of the jaw). Amplitude scale, which refers to separation between the incisors, is approximate.*

movement was transduced photo-electrically (Ohala, Hiki, Hubler, and Harshman 1968). Figure 3 shows a plot of jaw movement amplitude vs. frequency ($1/t$, where t = time taken to make one complete opening-closing movement). From this and the results of studies which show that the modal rate of syllable production is about 4/sec (Ohala, 1975b), we can conclude that the jaw must be operating at or near its frequency limit in speech. This would tend to explain the necessity for synergistic action in speech between the jaw and the articulators attached to it, the lower lip and the tongue (Kozhevnikov & Chistovich, 1965: 184; Takahashi and Nigauri, 1962; Lindblom and Sundberg, 1971a; Folkins and Abbs, 1975).

Clumeck (1976), in a cross-language study of velic movement using the nasograph, found that the minimum time required to move from closed to open velopharyngeal port was on the order of 30 to 50 msec. This being the case, we may judge that the extreme anticipatory lowering of the soft palate in American English on vowels before nasal consonants (often 250 msec before the nasal) is *not* caused solely by inertial characteristics of the soft palate.

In a similar vein, the observation that such anticipatory velic opening can be blocked by word or syllable boundary (Ohala, 1971) also argues against such vowel nasalization being due to mechanical characterisitcs. (Cf. similar arguments by Ghazeli (1977:113) regarding coarticulated pharyngealization in Arabic.)

Correlation Analysis   If a hypothesis is stated in the form: 'a variation in x causes, through mechanical factors, a proportional variation in phonetic feature y', then the testing of the hypothesis can be done by seeing whether the stated correlation holds over a wide range of values for x. This was done, qualitatively, in testing various hypotheses which proposed mechanical explanations for the 'declination effect', i.e., the slow drop in F0 from beginning to end of a phrase or breath group. It was proposed, for example, that this F0 slope was caused by the gradual lowering of subglottal air pressure (itself a mechanical consequence of respiratory constraints) or by the gradually increasing pull of the sternum on the larynx, via the sternohyoid muscle (as the chest volume decreases), etc. However, there is widespread evidence that the magnitude of F0 declination is approximately constant over phrases of different durations. That is, the *rate* of declination is greater for short phrases than for long phrases. Such careful regulation of F0 slope argues for its being centrally controlled (cf. Ohala, 1978b).

NEUROMUSCULAR CONSTRAINTS

In principle, many of the same type of techniques used to identify vocal tract constraints could be used to discover neuromuscular constraints, but ethical and technical limitations make it difficult to control most of the relevant independent variables. Nevertheless, a Sherlock Holmes in speech science would still find enough investigative tools at his disposal for this task: using noninvasive techniques (McClean, 1978), electromyography and related techniques (MacNeilage, et al. 1979), pharmacological and surgical techniques which are a regular part of the physician's healing art (Flisbert & Lindholm, 1970), and finally, exploitation of 'controls' introduced by nature as an unfortunate by-product of disease or injury (Critchley & Kubik, 1925).

FEEDBACK

One obvious way to find out if a given speech gesture is influenced by feedback or not is to interrupt the feedback loop (or reduce the amount of sensory information getting back to the brain) and seeing if the given gesture changes in some way (Ringel and Steer, 1963, Ohala, 1975b). This cannot be used conveniently for all possible feedback channels from all parts of the vocal apparatus, however.

A second method involves the detection of a more or less fixed delay between two events, where it is sensory information from the first event that is suspected of triggering or modulating the second event. This technique was used convincingly by Kozhevnikov & Chistovich (1965:133) in suggesting that the second of two closely spaced consonantal movements must have been triggered by sensory information from the release of the first. Another classic instance of this, although not concerned with speech as such, is the study of Sears and Newsom Davis (1968). They had a subject blow into a tube with an initially high resistance while maintaining a constant pressure which the subject could monitor by seeing the output of a pressure transducer. The activity of the expiratory muscles was monitored via EMG. When the resistance of the tube was suddenly and unexpectedly changed, a corresponding compensatory change in the activity of the breathing muscles was detected within 33 to 80 msec, i.e., a delay time so short that pressure sensing mechanisms within the respiratory tract must have provided the initial triggering of the corrective action.

A third, potentially interesting, way to discover whether feedback was used in the control of the timing of speech was introduced by Kozhevnikov & Chistovich (1965:94ff). They used statistical analysis of the temporal variation of the various speech intervals in a sentence repeated many times. As noted by Ohala (1975b) and Ohala and Lyberg (1976) there are many problems with this type of analysis which call into question most of the results obtained with it. Cooper, Sorensen, and Pacia (1977) have made progress in solving some of these problems.

DIFFERENTIATING PERIPHERAL VS. CENTRAL EFFECTS

Those influences on speech which have been discussed so far require an actual physical human vocal tract for their manifestation. The remaining influences do not. If it were somehow possible to disconnect a speaker's brain from his vocal tract it ought to be possible, in principle, to detect the effects which I have put under the headings of 'feedforward' and 'sound change'. Although it is obviously not possible to decerebrate our speakers, it is possible to create circumstances where the speaker doesn't need to use parts of his vocal apparatus in the normal way; if the speaker nevertheless continues muscle contractions, etc. as usual, this can be taken as evidence that those muscle contractions are due to feedforward (Folkins, 1979).

Elimination of alternatives   One way to make this differentiation is the process of elimination of alternatives and, in fact, it is a technique much employed by Holmes. If tests show a given feature of speech cannot be due to vocal tract constraints, neuromuscular constraints, or feedback, then only the central causes remain as viable explanations for it. Many of the cases discussed above have been decided in just this way.

Timing   If we can accept the principle that certain aspects of the timing of speech are centrally programmed, then there are special cases where we can use this as a touchstone to help us determine whether some speech event is centrally programmed or simply the product of peripheral constraints.

Consider the case of the intrusive stops in words such as 'warmth' [wɔɹmpθ], 'length' [lɛŋkθ] etc. These stops may be produced unintentionally due to an anticipatory denasalization (and devoicing) of the latter portion of the nasal consonant. Through sound change, however, these unintended stops may come to be intended features of the pronunciation of these words, as the written 'p' suggests in such words as 'Thompson', 'dempster', 'glimpse', (cf. 'Clemson', 'teamster', 'rinse'; Grandgent, 1896). The durational characteristics of such words may be able to reveal whether in any given word, in the speech of any given speaker, such stops are intended (centrally-programmed because of the action of sound change) or unintended (due to physical phonetic constraints). For a concrete example, consider the word 'teamster'[ˈtʰĩmpstəʲ] We know from numerous studies that in English VN sequences are longer in open syllables than in closed syllables, especially those closed with voiceless obstruents (Lehiste, 1970, Lovins, 1978). Therefore, if the [ĩm] sequence in a given speaker's rendering of this word is characteristically short (in comparison to some reference duration), we could conclude the [p] was a 'true' [p] (an 'underlying' /p/, if one prefers such jargon). If, on the other hand, it was characteristically long, we could probably conclude the [p] was unintentional (a 'surface' [p]).

To demonstrate the viability of this approach, the following study was done: twenty-five American English speakers were asked to form, orally, several novel English words by adding suffixes to existing words. In the early part of the interview the form 'clam + ster' was elicited ("Please add the suffix [stəʲ] to 'clam'."). At the end of the interview the form 'clamp + ster' was elicited. Since these were completely new words, I felt that whatever [p] might show up in 'clamster', it would not yet have a chance to be a fossilized [p]; it must of necessity be unintentional. In 'clampster', on the other hand, the [p] must be intentional. Would the durations of the [ǽm] sequences in the two words be different as predicted? The results, based on the subset of tokens that were measurable, are shown in Figure 4.

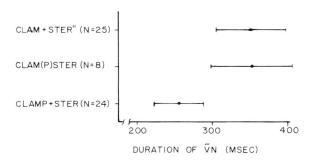

FIGURE 4   *Duration of* [ǽm] *sequence in 25 utterances of* clamster *(top), in 8 tokens of the previous 25 which exhibited an epenthetic* [p], *i.e.,*[kʰlǽmpstəʲ] *(middle), and in 24 tokens of* clampster *(bottom). Horizontal lines indicate the standard deviation associated with each distribution.*

The prediction was borne out. The mean duration of the VN sequence in 'clamster', whether it was said with a clear [p] or not, was about 95 msec longer than the VN sequence in 'clamster', where the [p] was always present because it was intended. In spite of the fact that no normalization of these durations was attempted to correct for inter-subject variations in speaking rate, etc., this difference is highly significant, $p < 0.001$.

Word games and speech errors   Evidence relevant to this issue might be provided by word games and speech errors but there are difficulties in interpreting the results.

Chao (1934) reports that a common word game used by speakers of Mandarin separates word initial consonants from their following vowels by inserting a sequence such as [aik] between them. By this process, [pei] becomes [paikei] but [mi] becomes [meitɕi] This does reveal that the phonetically plausible change of [ki] to [tɕi] is an automatic one but it doesn't unambiguously reveal the level — whether central or peripheral — that this process occurs at. Hombert (1976) provides a review and critique of the use of word games in phonology.

Much the same difficulty surrounds the interpretation of speech error data.

DIFFERENTIATING FEEDFORWARD AND SOUND CHANGE

There remains the task of trying to differentiate speech events motivated by feedforward as opposed to those specified in lexical storage, which can itself be influenced by sound change.

It seems to me that this problem can be approached if we first know the form of lexical representations, i.e., whether they are auditory-acoustic, articulatory, etc.

Nature provides some evidence on this issue. Speakers can often overcome rather severe articulatory handicaps and still achieve intelligible speech. The prognosis is not as good for those born deaf, however. This might suggest that the lexical image is acoustic-auditory, not articulatory. Unfortunately, Nature does not bother to run carefully controlled experiments and so the results of her temperings with human speakers do not unambiguously and unqualifiedly support one view of the other. See Riordan (1978) for a review.

One basic technique of use here is a classic one used by physiologists to study homeostasis in living systems: one creates obstacles for normal behavior and then observes what aspects of behavior remain the same in spite of the obstacle and what aspects change, adapting to the obstacle. Those that remain unchanged are fair candidates for being isomorphic to the ultimate goal of the organism — in our case, the specification of speech in the lexicon (Bernstein, 1967).

A variety of recent experiments, e.g., those by Lindblom and Sundberg (1971a) and Riordan (1977), which show that speakers can quickly overcome artifical articulatory handicaps, seem to rule out conclusively that the lexical image is in the form of an invariant configuration of the articulators.

SOUND CHANGE VS. EVERYTHING ELSE

I think the influence of sound change on speech can, in many cases, be differentiated from other influences by considering the notion of *relatedness* between two or more speech events. In the case of effects due to the purely mechanical or neuromuscular constraints we can say that some speech event, say the F0 perturbation after obstruents, is necessarily related to some other speech event, in the example given, to the voicing distinction on the obstruents. In the case of effects determined by feedback or feedforward, one speech event, say the lowering of the larynx during a voiced obstruent, is necessarily related to another speech event, the continued voicing during the obstruent. Effects due to sound change, however, may lack any necessary relation or connection to other speech events immediately present in the chunk of speech under consideration. For example, the tonal distinctions which developed in Chinese and other languages from the F0 perturbations caused by the voicing distinction of syllable initial obstruents, are now preserved independently of the voicing distinction. In the majority of such cases, in fact, the voicing distinction has been lost from initial obstruents. Likewise, the nasalization of vowels in French, Hindi, Yoruba, and many other languages now exists completely independently of neighboring nasal consonants, which, centuries ago, were the initial cause of the nasalization and which have now been lost.

The investigation of the effects of sound change on speech must start with a knowledge of all the other influences on speech, i.e., vocal tract mechanics, feedback, etc. Before we could make sense of the sound change which led to the development of tones in Chinese, we had to know that the voiced/voiceless distinction on obstruents produces small F0 perturbations even in non-tonal languages such as English and French. In this sense, part of the study of sound change — today, at least — is based in the laboratory. The other part, however, requires the gathering of evidence that the pronunciation of the language has changed. This evidence may come from dialect studies or studies of distinct but genetically related languages, or from language-internal evidence (so-called 'internal reconstruction'), supplemented where possible, by ancient written materials.

CONCLUSION

Although it cannot be said that all aspects of speech can be properly accounted for, i.e., attributed to the lexical representation, to vocal tract or neuromuscular constraints,[2] to feedback or feedforward, we can probably return to the original question 'how can articulatory constraints influence the lexical representation?' and find that it has already been answered. Through *sound change*, any downstream activity — the creakings of the encoding machinery —, that can be detected by the listener may get fixed in his lexicon. Looking at sound patterns cross-linguistically it is difficult to escape the conclusion that this is exactly what has happened to all human languages. To turn our original analogy around, if a Sherlock Holmes were to have presented to him all the structure and details of the lexicon and from this had to discover the properties of the encoding mechanisms, he could probably do fairly well at it. The reason is that our Moriarty figure, the lexicon, keeps getting replaced in generation after generation by a new Moriarty and each new one gets his information only through the agents of the previous one, not directly from the boss himself. Over the centuries then, it is inevitable that the information possessed by these Moriartys should bear the imprint of the agents as much as that of the boss.

Notes

1. This theme was deemed appropriate for a symposium in Edinburgh since Conan Doyle, the author of the Sherlock Holmes stories, was born in Edinburgh and studied there. In fact, the apparent real-life model for Holmes was also a native of Edinburgh, a medical doctor named Joseph Bell who taught medicine at Edinburgh University and amazed his students with his deductive abilities when making diagnoses. May his memory — and the inspiration it provides — live on.

2. Entirely missing from this discussion are auditory constraints. These are covered elsewhere in this volume.

Acknowledgements   This work was supported in part by the National Science Foundation and the Committee on Research, University of California, Berkeley.

Discussion

André-Pierre Benguerel It is difficult to find any major disagreement with John Ohala's insightful presentation, which is so rich in ideas on how to test specific hypothesized constraints in speech production and perception. I will thus limit my comments to a few points along these lines which seem important to me.

In testing hypotheses about the representation of speech, the experimenter must always keep in mind the strong possibility of his contaminating the data through many types of bias, such as in asking the questions to the subject, or in selecting the response mode (and creating uncontrolled interference(s) between phonetic, phonemic orthographic, and/or morphemic representation). At worst, certain hypotheses may be completely untestable unless reasonably intelligent but totally illiterate and linguistically naïve subjects can be found. It is likely that no such subjects can be found for English or for most other European langauges.

The suggested and possible difference between the feedforward image(s) and the lexical image(s), and their being separate and distinct in the speaker's mind appears to be a moot point at this stage. Here, clearly, some ingenious and probably difficult experiments of the sort described by Ohala would be required before we can support such an assumption, but it should not be concluded, of course, that for every hypothesis we may make, there always exists some experiment just waiting to be designed.

Last, but not least, the importance of auditory constraints on articulatory constraints, although not brought up so far in this symposium, must be emphasized, particularly in the area of sound change. For instance, in the case of nasalization in French or Hindi, the auditory constraint of a categorical, thus quasi-discrete, contrast between oral and nasal imposes an articulatory constraint on the gradual time course of velopharyngeal port opening. It would be of interest to discover the nature of the function which maps these articulatory and acoustic patterns onto the two perceptual categories.

Osamu Fujimura's presentation reminds us of a necessity too often forgotten: that of looking at the speech process through as many variables as we practically can. Failure to do so may otherwise make us very similar to the blind monkeys studying the elephant, each in his narrow and particular way. I will present an example of what may happen in such a case in the discussion of the next seminar.

As for the distinction between time effects and spatial effects of coarticulation, I think it may be futile and potentially unproductive to attempt to separate them: for instance, failure for the movement of a particular (point of an) articulator to reach a certain amplitude can be seen both as a spatial effect (due to a lesser muscular activity for example) and/or as a time effect (due to a faster tempo for example). Unless we can look at a higher (than EMG) level of organization, it seems premature to attempt to separate time effect and spatial effect.

R.A.W. Bladon I have two main comments on the papers of Ohala and Fujimura.

First under the heading of *articulatory distance*: would Ohala wish to incorporate into his "ways in which articulatory constraints may influence the form of speech" the notion of articulatory distance? The notion might be illustrated as follows: in Donegal Irish there are three lateral consonants to be kept in contrast, and the

123

extent to which they allow coarticulation of quality with a neighbouring vowel is correspondingly slight. The one single lateral consonant of American English, on the other hand, undergoes very substantial vowel-quality coarticulation. Swedish and Italian, with two laterals each, fall in between with respect to coarticulation. The constraints on coarticulation in these cases could be expressed as a function of the varying articulatory distance available in each language's system.

Secondly, it is important for both speakers to examine the question: *how predictive are explanations based on articulatory constraints?* Consider three examples. The first derives from our observations of Brazilian Portuguese: here the degree of nasality carrying over from a nasal consonant onto the following vowel is greater than that occurring in the opposite direction, that is, on a vowel anticipating a subsequent nasal. An articulatory explanation could be adduced, in that velum raising is typically accomplished faster than the lowering (opening) gesture. Nasality would therefore persist longer into a following vowel. Generalizing from this behaviour onto a VNV sequence in this language, however, produces the wrong predictions, since in such a sequence we observe the opposite effect, with the first of the two vowels displaying the greater nasality.

As a second example we cite the report by Ladefoged that in both French and English /k/ is advanced before /i/ and an explanation in coarticulatory terms, or an 'ease' principle, suggests itself. However, to predict the same effect *after* /i/ would be partly unsuccessful, because while French shows it in such a position, English does not.

Thirdly, it can be hypothesized on the basis of several published studies that the articulatory target for English /s/ is highly constrained, in that disruption of the friction passage is not readily tolerated. For instance, /s/ in CCC clusters blocks the spread of jaw-opening anticipating English /a/; and a blade-articulated /s/ resists any assimilatory shift to tip articulation. On the other hand, however, such articulatory constraints can apparently not be explained as a generalized property of the /s/ manoeuvres, since in the matter of the forward spread of labialization anticipating /u/, English /s/ freely allows the coarticulation.

Data such as these then lead us to conclude that the predictive capacity of explanations based on articulatory constraints is limited; or at least, that other forces sometimes operate with a countervailing effect. And yet, we are reluctant to abandon our search: it seems fair to state as an assumption by all of today's contributors that we seek to reduce as many as possible of our observations about articulatory behaviour in speech to generalizations concerning motor system constraints. There follows a trading relation between the complexity of the rules (generalizations) we set up, and the range of behaviours (what Ohala calls the 'lexical complexity') remaining to be specified as part of a 'cognitive' representation.

Given this position, and the data above, we may have to accept counteracting rules of articulatory constraint, or ones of very considerable complexity. One thing is perhaps inescapable, and that is the postulating of some global 'override' facility in the speech encoding mechanism, which while allowing certain speaker- or language-specific long-term patterns of articulatory representation, would also provide, in individual cases such as the Brazilian Portuguese VNV one, for the relaxation or overriding of articulatory constraints.

SESSION III
RELATION BETWEEN SEGMENTAL AND
SUPRASEGMENTAL REPRESENTATION

Seminar 5: Representation and context sensitivity

Chair	KARL PRIBRAM
Speakers	JAMES LUBKER, THOMAS GAY
Discussants	ANDRE-PIERRE BENGUEREL,
	WAYNE WICKELGREN

Seminar 6: Suprasegmental constraints on segmental representation

Chair	ILSE LEHISTE
Speakers	S. G. NOOTEBOOM, GEORGE ALLEN
Discussants	CATHERINE BROWMAN, ANTHONY COHEN,
	PHILIP SMITH, MANJARI OHALA

THE COGNITIVE REPRESENTATION OF SPEECH
T. Myers, J. Laver, J. Anderson (editors)
© North-Holland Publishing Company, 1981

Representation and Context Sensitivity

JAMES F. LUBKER

University of Stockholm

Abstract

The paper does *not* represent an attempt to summarize the current status of research in the area of co-articulation. Several good summaries are already available in the literature. Rather, after first establishing that the paper will be concerned solely with that aspect of context sensitivity known as co-articulation, the following main points are taken up:

1. Brief definition of terms used in describing the direction of co-articulation effects.
2. A discussion of the perceptual effects of co-articulation.
3. Some comments on synchronous or interarticulator programming.
4. A consideration of some of the current issues in co-articulation research and how they relate to some models of speech production theory.

Since "context sensitivity" is a term that can mean different things to different people, it is perhaps wise to provide an operational definition for the purposes of this discussion.

As Daniloff and Hammarberg (1973) have pointed out, the term can be considered in at least the following ways:

1. Context sensitivity in terms of syntactic entities with no "personal" phonological features. For example, /k/ → /s/ before /ɪti/, as in /taksɪk/ + /ɪti/ → /taksɪsɪti/.
2. Context sensitivity as the spreading of features but without any clear phonological explanations, as in the lengthening of vowels before voiced consonants.
3. Context sensitivity as the spreading of features across or between segments, as in co-articulation.

In the following discussion, I will be concerned with only the third of these viewpoints: co-articulation. That is, the very well established fact that during the generation of running, connected speech, segments or elements are influenced by, or are sensitive to, other segments or elements of the speech signal being produced. Stated somewhat more specifically, we have long known that certain acoustic and physiologic features of speech elements will undergo often times rather dramatic alterations, or will spread to temporally adjacent or nearby elements when the speech elements are produced dynamically as part of connected speech.

Now, if Hockett's (1955) easter-egg analogy of "smeared phonemes" at the acoustic or physiologic level were recounted to a physicist or physiologist, they might well express a "so-what" reaction. That is, they might say: "What else, really, would you *expect* to happen?" When static physical/physiological behaviors are strung together to form a dynamic sequence or serially ordered set of behaviors, some "blurring" of those behaviors must occur. Thus, the hand, arm and finger movements of the deaf speaker "co-articulate", sometimes to a very considerable extent, when her individual signs are formed as a serially ordered sequence of signs, just as the tongue, jaw, lips and velar movements will co-articulate during the generation of some *sequence* of phonemes. The implication is, of course, that such "co-articulations" are a sort of "slop" behavior largely, if not entirely, due to such factors as inertia, mechanical restraint and timing limitations. This, in turn, implies that co-articulation is an entirely peripheral phenomenon and thus, context sensitivity, both physiological and acoustic, would be a rather uninteresting issue.

But, it *is* an interesting issue, and an important one, for at least two reasons:

(i) In the first place, we are by now quite sure that co-articulatory behaviors are not by any means *entirely* the result of mechanico/inertial constraints. On the contrary, at least some aspects of co-articulation appear to be integral to the programming of speech and language. Thus, the careful study of this aspect of context sensitivity can be expected to shed some useful light on such questions as the nature, or size, of the programming units in speech generation and on the value of co-articulated features as perceptual cues. In a larger sense, co-articulation data has proven and will continue to prove useful in the testing of speech production models.

(ii) In the second place, the "blurring" of the production and acoustic units of speech would be acutely interesting even if that "blurring" were entirely peripheral and non-programmed; even if *all* of this sort of context sensitivity were a result of mechanico/inertial factors. This is true since the "blurred" acoustic signal provides all of the perceptual information the listener is going to get. To the extent that context sensitivity has been evidenced by a co-articulatory "blurring" of the acoustic segments, then the listener must be able to remove the "blurring", or decode the signal into a linguistically meaningful form. Clearly, this also leads to some very interesting questions and demands a detailed understanding of the "blurring".

The importance and high interest-level of the many questions revolving around the topic of co-articulation is reflected in the truly vast amount of research devoted to such questions in recent years. I shall not attempt here to provide a comprehensive survey of that literature, in part simply because of its sheer size. In addition, several reviews have recently been provided (Daniloff and Hammarberg, 1973; Kent and Minifie, 1977) and thus not much is to be gained by another review at this time. Instead I will discuss certain issues in a way that is neither exhaustive nor, I hope, exhausting, but that will stimulate some discussion.

First, I will, after all, spend a few moments simply stating a few "ground-rule" operational definitions of things co-articulatory.

Secondly, I will consider with you some aspects of co-articulation as they have been posited to relate to perception.

Thirdly, I will briefly touch on the issue of synchronous programming as that issue relates to co-articulation.

Finally, I will take up some of the issues and models which appear to be most current in this area of research.

Regarding the "ground-rule" definitions, I will be concerned here only with terms for the temporal direction of co-articulatory effects. As I am sure you all know, there is a good deal of evidence, although perhaps not complete agreement concerning that evidence, for the existence of two separate types of co-articulation. In one, features are *carried-over* from a given segment to segments which *follow* it in time. This has been called "Carry-Over", "Retention", "Left-to-Right", or "Backward" co-articulation. Many ascribe the cause of this form of co-articulation to mechanico/inertial effects, and hence the terms "Carry-Over" and "Retention". In this paper I will use the terms "Left-to-Right" and "Carry-Over" as alternatives. The second generic type of co-articulation occurs when features of a segment are *anticipated* by segments which *precede* it in time. "Anticipatory", "Right-to-Left" and "Forward" are the terms most commonly applied to this type. Co-articulatory behaviors of this type are usually considered to be timing effects which are programmed into the speech generation process. Major arguments revolve around the nature of that timing and programming. I will in this paper use the terms "Anticipatory" and "Right-to-Left".

Given that both anticipatory and carry-over co-articulatory effects are well documented in human speech behaviors, then one is compelled to ask two often inseparable and very general questions: *How* do we do that? and, *Why* do we do that?

Let me now spend a few minutes with some of the viewpoints regarding *why* we might "do" co-articulation. Basically, there are two points of view. The first, and probably the most frequently discussed, is that being able to spread features from segment to segment makes the serial ordering of segments in running speech much easier, or perhaps even possible. Parallel processing (Cooper, 1966) rests on this view, but, of course, virtually all models of speech production incorporate co-articulation behaviors. Witness Kozhevnikov and Chistovich's (1965) articulatory syllable and Henke's (1966) "look-ahead" mechanism, as well as the many more recent extensions and ramifications of these views. I will return to this issue, or issues, in the final part of this paper.

A second answer to the "Why?" question involves the view that co-articulatory behaviors may be important to the *perception* of speech. It is intuitively appealing to assume that if a parallel processing-like mechanism is important to the generation of speech, then a similar process would be important to the perception of speech. We know that it is virtually impossible to perceive individual entities of phoneme size at the rate at which phonemes occur during normal connected speech. Obviously, there is something in the acoustic speech signal or in the processing of it that very much aids our perception of that signal. To exactly what extent are co-articulatory cues entering the picture? One can easily imagine anticipatory cues allowing a listener to make preliminary categorizations of segments before they have actually occurred, and one can also easily imagine carry-over cues providing redundancies to aid in the clarification of segments already produced. And, there is a very considerable body of literature relevant to the perceptual effects of co-articulation. For example, the locus-theory research of Delattre and his associates (Delattre, Liberman and Cooper, 1955; Liberman, Delattre and Cooper, 1958), Lindblom and Studdert-Kennedy's (1967) research on the value of formant transitions in vowel perception, and Stevens and Klatt's (1974) report on the importance of transitions to the voicing distinction. In addition, there have been a number of efforts devoted quite specifically to the co-articulation/perception relationship. Fant, et al (1970), Kuehn and Moll (1972), Lehiste and Shockey (1972), Haggard (1974), and Ostreicher and Sharf (1976), to mention only a few.

Taken together, this research seems in general agreement that there *are* perceptually quite important effects of co-articulation, but that there is also some lack of clarity concerning such issues as (1) the temporal extent of such perceptual effects; (2) the relative importance of anticipatory vs. carry-over effects; and (3) the influence of varying context on the perceptual effects of co-articulation.

Regarding, for example, the extent of the perceptual effects of co-articulation, most work seems to favor a very limited range, that is, only to adjacent phonemes (see, for example, Ostreicher and Sharf, 1976). However, Kuehn and Moll (1972) suggest perceptual effects of co-articulation to extend for at least two phonemes, right-to-left. If only for the sake of debate, one might *suggest* a language dependent factor for the extent of such perceptual effects. For example, we have noted that in

Swedish lip rounding is consistently initiated earlier for the front than for the back rounded vowels. Given the rich supply of both rounded and front vowels in Swedish, it is at least possible that speakers of Swedish attempt to provide the listener with as much acoustic information as possible as soon as possible, in order to allow more time for choosing among the several possible vowels. It seems, at least, an interesting idea to test.

However interesting the perceptual effects of co-articulation might be, time dictates that I move on. Hopefully the perceptual issues will be expanded upon during the discussion period to follow. For now I will turn to some issues more related to *How* co-articulation occurs.

I have been discussing co-articulation in terms of the spreading of features across segments. The implication has been that this is for one articulator at a time: for example, the lips in the co-articulation of lip rounding, the velum in the co-articulation of nasality, or the jaw in the co-articulation of open or close vowel characteristics. And, indeed, I will continue to discuss co-articulation in that way throughout most of the remainder of this paper. However, I would like to make a short departure from that approach, in order to simply mention the temporal and spatial co-ordination of *several* articulators. That is, the functioning together of groups or sets or articulators in order to accomplish some specific speech target. Such behaviors have generally been referred to as synchronous programming or inter-articulator programming and represent examples of the principle of motor equivalence (Hebb, 1949) by which sets of articulators are able to reach constant target configurations or target acoustic patterns via quite variable contributions from the several members of the articulator set. Studies by Kent and Moll (1975) and by Gay (1977) have, for example, provided evidence of interarticulator programming on the temporal plane while the bite-block work of Lindblom and Sundberg (1971b) and Lindblom, Lubker and Gay (1979) has demonstrated spatial articulatory alterations in order to accommodate articulatory perturbations. Models purporting to explain such behaviors are currently much debated (e.g. Lindblom, et al. 1979; Turvey, 1977; and Fowler, et al. 1977). These issues and models are sure to be discussed at length next week at the IXth International Congress of Phonetic Sciences in Copenhagen, and I will therefore pass by them now. However, in passing, we might note that both anticipatory co-articulation and interarticulator programming behaviors can occur substantially in advance of the target act or goal, and, further, both may be argued to be important or even vital to successful serial ordering. Perhaps it is wise to at least keep in mind the possibility that they may be explained via similar or even identical mechanisms. This, too, may warrant some further discussion later on.

And so, finally, I will take up a few of the current issues in co-articulation research. Many of these questions and issues are of the "How?" variety: Over how great a temporal distance do co-articulation effects occur? Is there an asymmetry in terms of extent of anticipatory vs. carry-over co-articulation? Are some segments more or less resistant to co-articulation effects? And so on. I think it is fair to say that the relative importance of such questions can be measured in terms of to what degree answers to them contribute to solving questions of a "Why?" nature. Stated somewhat differently, they are a number of models of speech production, but in their most basic form most of them can be placed into one of two very broad categories: those which posit some sort of syllabic input and those which posit some sort of phonemic input (see also the discussion by Gay, 1978). Kozhevnikov and Chistovich (1965) are usually cited as the prototype model of the first type while Henke (1966) is usually the primary example of the second type. Questions in co-articulation that aid in selecting among such models are usually considered more interesting than questions which do not offer much to the selection process.

Thus, there is interest in both the temporal extent of co-articulation and in whether or not it is influenced by syllable and word boundaries. Most such research seems to suggest that when an articulator is "free" to begin producing its part of a segment, it will do so, even if that segment is a very long way in the future and with word and syllable boundaries in between. Just as one specific example, in French (Benguerel and Cowan, 1974), English (Daniloff and Moll, 1968), and Swedish (Lubker, McAllister and Carlson 1975b) it has been shown that lip rounding will begin for a rounded vowel close to the onset of the consonant string preceding the vowel, even when that string is six consonants (Benguerel and Cowan, 1974) or 600 ms (Lubker, et al. 1975) in duration. Actually, and perhaps speaking against the Kozhevnikov and Christovich model, such activity often begins in the non-rounded vowel *preceding* the consonant string. Further, the rounding onset is generally unaffected by traditional syllable and word boundaries. Similarly, Moll and Daniloff (1971) have shown velar lowering for a nasal consonant to begin substantially in advance of the nasal in a *vowel* string preceding the nasal consonant, and, again, across traditional syllable and word boundaries. This latter observation is also usually used to counter the Kozhevnikov and Chistovich model since it uses a /VC/ sort of articulatory grouping as opposed to their /CV/ articulatory syllable. Gay (1978) has recently proposed an alteration that would accept both of these observations: "the forward (anticipatory) extent of co-articulation is limited by the forward boundary of the preceding phonetic category"; a look-ahead mechanism *à la* Henke, but with a definite temporal boundary on the duration of that look-ahead mechanism. This whole issue, however, remains in controversy since, (i) investigators are not in complete agreement concerning the data, and (ii) the data have not allowed a particularly clean separation between syllabic and phonemic input models.

A second issue has been the *direction* of the co-articulatory effects. Specifically, are co-articulatory effects more extensive in the Right-to-Left or in the Left-to-Right direction? Again, the search is for a segmentation of the input units. *In general,* the evidence seems to point to more extensive anticipatory than carry-over co-articulation (see, e.g., McAllister, 1978). For example, Gay (1978) and McAllister (1978) have both shown that when two identical rounded vowels are separated by non-labial consonants, the integrated labial EMG activity for that utterance will resemble a ramp-like trough. Their observations offer some support to the modified phonemic input model of Gay (1977), but certainly they can also be interpreted in the light of a syllabic input. Again, there are some conflicts in the data and a lack of clear choice between models.

At this point I want to mention one other issue that is certain to be discussed in Copenhagen, also. Specifically, the *nature* of the input units. We treat them as if they were abstract linguistic units. And we are simply never able to find any measurable, definable evidence for the existence of such units, outside of our own aching heads. When a theory continually fails to match reality, with any reasonable degree of success, one naturally begins to wonder about the theory. Perhaps it is time for production theorists to begin to model in terms of their own units, which may or may not show equivalence with existing linguistic units? (See Moll, Zimmerman and Smith, 1977, for a further discussion.)

THE COGNITIVE REPRESENTATION OF SPEECH
T. Myers, J. Laver, J. Anderson (editors)
© *North-Holland Publishing Company, 1981*

Temporal and Spatial Properties of Articulatory Movements: Evidence for Minimum Spreading Across and Maximum Effects within Syllable Boundaries

THOMAS GAY

University of Connecticut

The search for articulatory equivalents of linguistic units has been in progress for the past fifteen years or so. Even early on it was recognized that the task of finding a simple linguistic-articulatory correspondence would be a difficult one: the speech string that enters the articulatory mechanism as a set of discrete phonological units emerges at the periphery as a highly encoded stream. The effect of this encoding on the production of a given phone can be observed in the form of a temporal spreading of its features to, or coarticulation with, adjacent phones.

Coarticulatory feature spreading is bidirectional, with effects appearing from right-to-left and left-to-right, and presumably extending across several segments and even syllable and word boundaries. Right-to-left, or anticipatory, effects are observed as the appearance of a phonetic feature (or features) of a given phone during the production of preceding ones. Right-to-left effects are essentially timing effects and because they appear ahead of the fact, so to speak, they are usually considered to reflect an early stage of the speech production process and the *size of the articulatory planning unit*. Left-to-right, or carryover, effects on the other hand, appear as differences in the dynamic properties of articulatory movements as a function of different preceding contexts. Although originally considered mechanical or inertial in origin, left-to-right coarticulation effects also reflect the plasticity of the speech motor control system in linking successive speech gestures, and as such, are related to the *form of the articulatory unit.*

This paper will discuss some of the issues related to the peripheral representation of linguistic units in terms of both the temporal and spatial effects of the surrounding context, in particular, the form of target representation, the physiological adjustments used to ensure target attainment, and the rules that govern the size of the coarticulatory field.

REPRESENTATION OF LINGUISTIC UNITS: ARTICULATORY OR ACOUSTIC TARGETS?

During the past ten years, the basic premise underlying research in speech organization has been that all articulatory movements are directed toward the attainment of a *spatial target*. This view was convincingly established by MacNeilage (1970), who argued that the neuromuscular variability evident in the production of a phone, rather than reflecting motor inefficiency or stochasticity, reflected instead a highly organized response to demands for a constant end: the attainment of an articulatory target, internalized as a set of spatial coordinates. Spatial invariance, for vowels at least, has since been demonstrated in a number of x-ray motion picture studies (Gay, 1974; Gay, 1977), and in studies of speech motor control. For example, both Lindblom and Sundberg (1971b) and Lindblom, Lubker, and Gay (1979) have shown that the F-patterns of isolated vowels produced under even extreme bite block conditions match those for vowels produced naturally. Obviously, either of two alternative compensatory articulatory strategies could be invoked to produce the equivalent bite block F-patterns: One strategy would produce an articulatory ''super-shape'', or exaggerated articulatory movement, directed towards reaching the original vocal tract shape. The second strategy would use an entirely different vocal tract shape that would nonetheless produce an equivalent acoustic output (Stevens and House, 1955). To determine which strategy speakers invoke, the acoustic study of Lindblom, Lubker, and Gay (1979) was repeated using still x-rays to compare vocal tract shapes for the two conditions (Gay, Lindblom, and Lubker, 1979). Analysis of the x-rays showed that for all subjects, maximum compensation (minimum variability) occurred at the point of maximum vocal tract constriction, the cross-dimensions and locations of which were almost always perfectly reproduced during bite block vowel production. This finding is illustrated in Figure 1 which shows the cross-dimension plots for both normal and bite block conditions for four of the subjects. We interpreted these data as relevant to the relationship between context sensitivity and target attainment — the bite block imposes a far greater physiological constraint than any normal context variation — and as supportive of an articulatory target representation, specifiable in terms of the points of maximum vocal tract constriction.

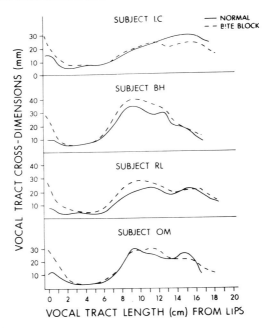

FIGURE 1   *Vocal tract cross-dimensions for the steady state vowel /i/ produced normally and with a 22.5 mm bite block.*

An alternative to an invariant spatial coordinate view is that a speaker instead tries to reach acoustic targets. This point of view has been suggested specifically by Ladefoged, et al. (1972), Nooteboom (1970), and Lieberman (1973). It is also implicit in Steven's (1972) quantal theory of speech production which provides a well developed theoretical basis for such a view. Briefly, quantal theory states that the perturbation of a constriction in the vocal tract will have different effects on the acoustic output depending on where in the vocal tract the constriction is located. At some points along the tract, a small change in the position of a constriction will have a large effect on the acoustic output, whereas at other points it will have relatively little effect. In consequence, the quantal positions have phonetic significance; they correspond to the "point" vowels /i/, /a/, and /u/. Thus, for the point vowels, acoustic output may be stable even if the idealized spatial target is not reached. For the intermediate vowels, a different type of acoustic equivalence might be realized in the absence of target attainment. In an earlier analysis, Stevens and House (1955) showed that for these vowels, equivalent acoustic outputs could be achieved using a variety of vocal tract shapes. Thus, for different reasons the correspondence between vowels and their acoustic representation might be more invariant than a correspondence between vowels and their articulatory representation. Support for an invariant acoustic target appears in the data of Riordan (1977) who showed that when the lips were mechanically restrained during the production of /u/, compensatory vocal tract lengthening was achieved by larynx lowering. However, Woods (1978) suggests that larynx lowering is positively correlated to lip rounding anyway and further, that the lower lip alone can compensate for any disturbances to lip rounding. Also, the x-ray study of Gay, Lindblom, and Lubker (1979) failed to demonstrate compensatory larynx lowering for rounded vowels; compensatory lip rounding (both upper and lower) was the only strategy used to preserve vocal tract length under bite block conditions.

LEFT-TO-RIGHT COARTICULATION: THE EFFECTS OF CONTEXT ON TARGET ATTAINMENT

Regardless of the nature of target representation at the periphery, changes in context affect movements toward these targets. Obviously, the primary preceding context effect is a change in the course and extent of transition movements, the trajectories of which depend on preceding articulatory targets. However, secondary context effects which probably exist to facilitate the primary ones, have also been identified. These appear in the form of differences in the *velocity* and *timing* of articulatory movements from one segment to the next. Kuehn and Moll (1976) for example, have shown that transition velocity is positively correlated to degree of articulatory displacement. Likewise, the co-existence of both positional and timing coarticulation effects was suggested in a paper on stops in CV syllables published by Gunnar Fant (Fant, 1969). In his paper, Fant suggested that differences in the range of F2 onset transition frequencies between voiced and voiceless labial stops, for example, were due to differences in the *relative timing* of tongue body movements from consonant to vowel, with those for /b/ occurring earlier, or coarticulating more than those for /p/. Corresponding timing differences for these and other contrasts have since been observed in other experiments. For example, both tongue and jaw movement from a labial stop to either a close or open vowel have been shown to begin up to 30 msec earlier for the voiced cognate (Gay, 1979). The onset of articulatory movements toward the vowel is also earlier for labials as a class as opposed to alveolars, and for open in contrast to close vowels. While differences in timing between labials and alveolars might be due to tongue tip constraints on the latter, the displacement related differences between open and close vowels are not readily explainable — they might relate to the intrinsic durations of the different segments or to some other temporal or acoustic feature.

If left-to-right coarticulation is the result of a strategy to link two contiguous articulatory targets, then it is reasonable to assume that such effects would be contained within the boundaries of the two targets. This view is supported by some x-ray data that show carryover effects of both a vowel on consonant targets and a consonant on vowel targets and even before the time of consonant release or when the vowel target position is reached, respectively (Gay, 1977). However, other data show carryover effects to extend beyond immediately adjacent segments. For example, Sussman, MacNeilage, and Hanson (1973) showed that for two of their five subjects, jaw displacement for the second vowel in VCV sequence was affected by the openness of the first vowel: apparently, because of its sluggishness, jaw targets were undershot. Perhaps these different findings reflect the existence of two parallel left-to-right effects: one, the adjustment of articulatory movements according to previous positions, and the other, the inefficient response of the mechanism to those adjustments. The former seems to be the more pervasive effect and the one with the greatest acoustic consequences.

RIGHT-TO-LEFT COARTICULATION: THE FORWARD SPREADING OF ANTICIPATORY FEATURES

While left-to-right coarticulation represents a strategy to link successive speech units, right-to-left coarticulation reflects a strategy to spread articulatory features to immediately preceding ones. Anticipatory coarticulation has been studied primarily in terms of three different articulatory features: lip rounding for a rounded vowel, tongue body movements for a postconsonantal vowel in a VCV sequence, and velar lowering for a nasal consonant. Most of the research has been directed to the question on how far in advance of the particular segment these anticipatory movements begin.

As is well known, in one of the earliest studies of anticipation in speech, Kozhevnikov and Chistovich (1965) found that the onset of lip rounding for a rounded vowel in CV, CCV, and CCCV sequences usually began at the beginning of the consonant string even if a syllable boundary appeared within the string. Since the position of the syllable boundary was irrelevant to the timing of the protruding gesture, Kozhevnikov and Chistovich advanced the notion that the basic articulatory programming unit in speech was of a CV form with a C corresponding to any number of consonants (C. . .C) and V corresponding to a vowel. Other data have supported Kozhevnikov and Chistovich's (1965) basic findings. In extending the observations of Kozhevnikov and Chistovich (1965) to American English, Daniloff and Moll (1968) showed that the onset of lip rounding for the vowel /u/ can begin across as many as four consonant segments ahead of the vowel. In their cinefluorographic experiment, the onset of lip protrusion for /u/ was studied for a number of monosyllabic and disyllabic utterances of one and two words embedded in sentence frames. Onset of lip rounding usually began with the first consonant in the string, and was not affected by the position of either syllable or word boundaries that appeared in the string. Similar anticipatory lip rounding effects have been demonstrated by Lubker, McAllister, and Carlson (1975a) at the muscle contraction level and by Benguerel and Cowan (1974) at the movement level. Lubker, McAllister, and Carlson's data showed that the onset of electromyographic (EMG) activity for the orbicularis oris muscle (a primary lip rounding muscle) associated with /u/ began with the first consonant in the string, and as early as 600 msec prior to the onset of the vowel. In the Benguerel and Cowan study, the onset of lip protrusion for /u/ in a number of similar utterances for speakers of French likewise usually appeared at the time of the first consonant. Benguerel and Cowen also observed further that the lip rounding gesture sometimes began as early as the preceding vowel segment.

In contrast to these and other studies, a number of other reports have suggested that the temporal spreading of anticipatory movements in both simple consonant-vowel and more complex consonant cluster-vowel sequences might be contained within a somewhat more limited field (Gay, 1976; Gay, 1978; McAllister, 1978; Bell-Berti and Harris, 1979; Gay, 1979). One of the findings of these studies was that in a symmetrical VCV containing the rounded vowel /u/ and an intervocalic consonant unmarked for rounding (as in /utu/), lip muscle activity associated with the rounding gesture would cease during the production of the intervocalic consonant. An example of this is shown in Figure 2. This figure shows the activity

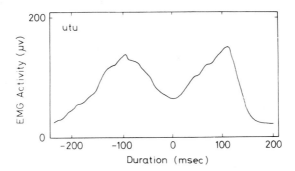

FIGURE 2 *Averaged EMG curve of the orbicularis oris muscle for the utterance* /utu/. 0 *on the abscissa represents the offset of voicing of the first vowel.*

of the orbicularis oris muscle for the utterance /utu/, averaged over sixteen token repetitions. The point '0' on the time scale corresponds to the time of voicing offset of the first vowel. This slide shows a deep trough in the EMG envelope during the time of consonant production. The presence of the trough was interpreted as an interruption of muscle activity corresponding to the time of production of the intervocalic consonant and was used to argue against the interpretation that the onset of rounding is controlled by a look ahead mechanism of the type proposed by Henke (1966). Since the first vowel is marked for rounding while the intervocalic /t/ is unspecified for labiality, Henke's model would predict that the rounding feature would be retained during the production of the consonant. In terms of muscle activity, this would be reflected by a single broad EMG envelope from the beginning of the first /u/, through the consonant, to the end of the second /u/. This does not seem to happen, however. The two vowels are each marked by a separate and distinct muscle pulse, with the onset of the lip rounding gesture for the second vowel constrained by the time of closure of the intervocalic consonant.

Because the onset of lip rounding in a VCV sequence seems to occur considerably closer to the vowel than it does in a CCV sequence, the question arises whether the two types of sequences are governed by the same rules. The results of two recent studies bear directly on this question. In one experiment, Bell-Berti and Harris (1979) showed that the onset of lip rounding for a rounded vowel was synchronized with features of the vowel only, and independent from the type or number of preceding consonants. Essentially the same results appeared in a similar study where EMG recordings were obtained from the genioglossus and orbicularis oris muscles during the production of a number of VCV, VCCV, and VCCCV sequences containing the rounded vowel /u/ in both pre- and post-consonantal positions (Gay, 1979).

The findings of this study are summarized in Table I which shows the onset times of both genioglossus and orbicularis oris muscle activity during the production of a number of these words. The onsets were measured in two ways: first, relative to the

	Consonant Duration	Onset of Muscle Activity (V1 Offset = 0)		Onset of Muscle Activity (V2 onset = 0)	
		OO	GG	OO	GG
A Tutor	80	55	70	-90	-70
Odd Tutor	165	75	85	-90	-80
Old Tutor	245	220	240	-95	-65
A Suit	175	115	95	-80	-60
Loose Suit	285	235	230	-60	-55
Used Suit	400	365	330	-90	-60

TABLE I   *Consonant durations and muscle activity onset times for the vowel /u/.*

offset of voicing of the first vowel, and second, relative to the onset of voicing of the second vowel. Two types of utterances were used: one built around the alveolar stop /t/ and the other around the fricative, /s/. The duration of the consonant component in each set was increased by creating clusters. All measurements represent the mean of ten token repetitions.

As expected, total consonant duration increases with an addition of consonant segments, from 80 ms to 400 ms. However, both the genioglossus and orbicularis oris muscle activity onsets of tongue body movement and lip rounding for the following [u] are delayed relative to the offset of the first vowel, but remain fairly uniform when measured relative to voice onset time for the second vowel. The range in onsets is 310 ms when measured relative to the beginning of the consonant and only 35 ms when measured relative to VOT. It might be argued of course, that the delay in muscle activity onsets is due to the fact that the tongue is involved in the production of the consonant and thus unable to move during its production. This explanation is unlikely, however, for two reasons. First, the delay was observed in other clusters where one or more elements did not require tongue body involvement, [sp] for example. Second, in every utterance containing [u] as the postconsonantal vowel, the delay in genioglossus onset is accompanied by a corresponding delay in orbicularis oris activity; lip activity should not be constrained during these cluster productions. Contrary to some other reports in the literature, these data and those of Bell-Berti and Harris (1979) suggest that a fixed temporal relationship exists between the consonant and vowel segments in both simple and complex syllable constructions, and that the timing of anticipatory movements toward a vowel target seems to be linked, not to the duration or structure of the preceding consonant string, but rather to the time of release of the consonant or to the voice onset time of the vowel itself. These findings also suggest that if the speech string is organized on a phoneme-by-phoneme basis, phonetic features are not scanned as far in advance as present theories suggest; alternatively, these findings could also be used to support the concept of a simple CV syllable as the basic unit of articulatory programming.

In summarizing this paper, the following suggestions are proposed: 1) that while context dependent coarticulation spreads in both directions, the ordering of successive speech gestures is nonetheless programmed for *minimal* rather than maximal coarticulation, and 2) that the greatest effects of both anticipatory and carryover coarticulation on the articulatory and acoustic features of a given segment seem to appear at the boundaries and not at the target of that segment.

Acknowledgement   This work was supported by a grant from the National Institute of Neurological and Communicative Disorders and Stroke, NS-10424.

Discussion

André-Pierre Benguerel Jim Lubker's paper, drawing from his own work as well as from others, has presented to us a useful summary of some important distinctions in coarticulation research. I would like first to emphasize a point which is too often overlooked: the difficulty to separate, in many situations, anticipation from carryover. Let's assume that we are looking at lip protrusion in a polysyllabic utterance, say on the nth syllable, which is presumably rounded. What is happening between this syllable and the following one cannot be assumed, as it has by some, to be simply a carryover from the nth syllable, even if none of the intervening consonants has any intrinsic lip protrusion. It is also an anticipation of the n + 1th vowel, which depends on its parameter value for rounding. This parameter value can have a considerable importance, as has been shown recently by Sussman and Westbury (1978).

My second point is a caveat pertaining to the interpretation of the results of many perceptual studies of coarticulation involving, by necessity, forced choice responses. The listening subjects may be able to use whatever cues are present in the stimulus, together with the information available from the forced choice paradigm. However there is no warranty that the strategy used in such a difficult and unnatural situation is the same as that used in a real life situation. The high inter-subject variability observed (Benguerel and Adelman, 1976) suggests that in fact few subjects can come up with a successful strategy.

Regarding Tom Gay's presentation, I would like to discuss the interpretation of some of his data which are both in agreement with that of Bell-Berti and Harris (1979) and in conflict with that of McAllister (1978) and that of Sussman and Westbury (1979). Gay's proposal, similar to that of Bell-Berti and Harris, suggests that anticipatory coarticulation of lip protrusion is time-locked (to the rounded vowel) rather than dependent on the number of preceding consonants. Even if we leave aside the discrepancy between the two sets of data, Sussman and Westbury's experiment sheds some light on the interpretation of the data by looking at EMG activity of both the agonist (orbicularis oris superior m.) and the antagonist (risorius m.) muscles for lip protrusion. They found that in both /-iC (CC) u-/ and/-aC (CC) u-/ sequences, the EMG patterns of orbicularis oris superior m. were similar, with a small lead in the former case, but that the EMG patterns of risorius m. were markedly different for the two types of sequences: whereas in the first case, the two muscles showed reciprocally innervated on-off bursts of activity, in the second case, risorius was quiet and only orbicularis oris superior activity was present in anticipation for /u/. The conclusions one would draw in the absence of data from the antagonist muscle would obviously not be the same as in their presence. As pointed out in the previous seminar, it is essential to record, or at least to control, as many variables as possible. In particular, prosodic features may have a significant effect on some of the variables observed. For instance, in a study of coarticulation in German, we found that in /-iCCCCCu-/ and /-iCCCCCy-/ sequences, the upper lip protrusion gesture started in many cases on the first consonant of the cluster when /i/ was stressed. However, when /i/ was not stressed, protrusion started even earlier than /i/, hence the importance of controlling stress, even though it may be quite difficult. Similarly, in the sequence /-utu-/ pronounced (by French speakers) with equal stress on both syllables, protrusion of the upper lip showed a trough for /t/, but when stress was greater on the second syllable, no trough was found. In many coarticulation studies, particularly on English, nonsense sequences have been

139

or must be used because of the difficulty, or impossibility, to find appropriate meaningful sequences, thus an even greater care must be taken to monitor prosodic features, since nonsense utterances are less natural for the subject(s) to say than meaningful ones: consequently, a subject is unlikely to be as consistent in his production as in the case of natural utterances.

Wayne A. Wickelgren   How do we recognize the order of the phonemes in a word? It will not suffice to recognize only the unordered set of phonemes, else we could not distinguish "cat" from "tack" from "act". Many considerations weigh against the hypothesis that we somehow time label the set of features occurring at times t, $t + \triangle$, $t + 2\triangle$, . . . with some ordered set of labels, among which is the evidence of Warren (Warren 1974a, 1974b). Accordingly, I have proposed a different theory of the coding of the serial order of phonemes in words, namely, that the segmental units of words are overlapping phoneme triples or context-sensitive allophones (Wickelgren, 1969a, 1969b, 1972, 1976). For example, "cat" would have as its segmental constituents, $\#$ $^k a$, $_k a t$, $_a t$ $\#$. Without any need to time label these segmental nodes, and regardless of the temporal order of activation of such nodes the necessary order information for distinguishing "cat" from "tack" and "act" is contained in the *unordered set* of these overlapping-triple nodes.

Context-sensitive segmental coding explains many important phenomena in both speech recognition and articulation as I have discussed in the papers referred to. Among these are how we perceive segmental order, the difficulty of segmenting the speech stream into phonemic units within a syllable, the context-conditioned variation in acoustic cues for phonemes, how contextual feedback can be used in recognition without disrupting the encoding of order information, intentional (mentally directed) coarticulation, advance priming of long sequences of segments in articulation while retaining the segmental order information, the functions of accent and syllable juncture, a variety of speech error phenomena, and others.

Context-sensitive coding can be extended to the feature level to achieve Gestalt-like grouping of features occurring in temporal proximity. During any slice of time ($\approx$ 10 msec) assume an encoding of the speech signal by strength values from 0 to 1 on each of f atomic (context-free) feature dimensions, such as the spectral frequencies of a Fourier analysis. Now define the context-sensitive features to be the set of all pairs of such atomic features within the same $\triangle$ time window and for $i \triangle$ - windows before and after. If there are f atomic feature dimensions, there will be $\frac{1}{2}f$ (f-1) simultaneous unordered-pair feature dimensions (within the same $\triangle$ -window) if^2 forward-successive ordered-pair features, and if^2 backward-successive ordered-pair features. If $i = 1$, then only adjacent time windows are chunked into coding feature transitions (such as frequency transitions). If $i \geq 2$, then a variety of more extensive feature transitions are directly encoded. If $i = 10$ and $f = 1000$ (e.g., 1000 different frequency dimensions), then the total number of context-sensitive feature dimensions would be about 2.5×10^7. That's a very modest number in relation to 10^{10} neurons in the brain, so I think we could safely assume at least this number of feature dimensions for the analysis of auditory signals including speech.

A suitable mathematical definition of the strength of a pair feature s(x,y) in terms of the strength of its two atomic features s(x) and s(y) might be the fuzzy-logic multiplicative rule, $s(x,y) = s(x) \bullet s(y)$. This gives a pair feature high strength only if both component features have high strength. A strong, but unproven, conjecture is that one only needs to consider feature pairs, not triples or higher-order combinations and permutations, to discriminatively activate the correct context-sensitive segmental units.

Chairman's Comments

Karl H. Pribram The problem of coarticulation as presented by Benguerel and Wickelgren appears similar to that which characterizes other motor functions of the nervous system. An encompassing frame can therefore be provided by current "action theory" (Bernstein, 1967; Gelfand, et al., 1971; Fowler & Turvey, 1977; Pribram, 1971) in which coordinate structures are seen to be fitted hierarchically into larger and larger units. At the cortex the variables that determine the unit are the environmental relationship engendered by the operations of the coordinate structures — i.e. the consequences of the action (Pribram, et al., 1955-56; Pribram, 1971). As in the case of Wickelgren's overlapping allophones, motor equivalences are readily explained since the totality of the consequences of the operations of the coordinate structures (allophones) are encoded in the cortical representation.

A final word. As suggested in Tom Gay's paper and by Benguerel in his discussion segmentation is an aspect of prosodics. Elsewhere, I have made a case for considering prosodics as integral to the regulatory pragmatics of language which is to be sharply distinguished from its referential semantics (Pribram, in press). There is good evidence that this regulatory pragmatics operates by way of segmentation and that the anterior frontal cortex is critically involved in this process (Pribram & Tubbs, 1967; Pribram, 1971). This same part of the brain has been shown to be involved whenever context sensitive behavior is examined (Anderson, et al., 1976; Pribram, et al., 1977; Brody & Pribram, 1978). While these are strong arguments in favor of a top-down interaction, they do not negate the equally important and ordinarily prepotent bottom-up interactivity of the kind proposed by Wickelgren in his overlapping allophone model. What needs to be specified are the triggers that initiate and terminate the top-down process.

Clearly we know a good deal more about how segmentation and coarticulation interact than we did a few decades ago. Not only have we some plausible models of that interaction such as that which relies on overlapping triplet allophones, the coordinate structures of languages but we can even point to the involvement of specific brain loci in the operations of the model. What is lacking is a set of data that test the model at the neural level. Such tests are not beyond current technical capability. Perhaps by the time that the next Edinburgh symposium on speech convenes such tests will be in progress.

THE COGNITIVE REPRESENTATION OF SPEECH
T. Myers, J. Laver, J. Anderson (editors)
© *North-Holland Publishing Company, 1981*

**Speech Rate and Segmental Perception
or the Role of Words in Phoneme Identification**

S.G. NOOTEBOOM

Institute for Perception Research, Eindhoven

INTRODUCTION

Suprasegmental properties of speech, for example those related to intonation, rhythmical grouping and speech rate, form one class of factors causing acoustic variability of linguistically invariant units. Studies of the effects of suprasegmental properties of speech on the perception of discrete linguistic units may therefore in principle be used to gain insight into the general problem of how such discrete units are extracted from the variable speech waveform. By way of example, one particular class of such studies, those concerned with the effect of speech rate on phoneme perception, will be examined in some detail. This class of studies is typical of a much wider range of speech perception studies because of the unquestioned assumption that phonemes are immediate and natural response categories in speech perception tasks, and that studying the perception of phonemes is essential to our understanding of speech perception in general. In fact, it can be said that most perception researchers are eagerly trying to find out how phonemes are extracted from the speech waveform. My present view of this is that they are most probably on the wrong track. I will argue in this paper that linguistic processing of speech, and particularly word recognition, is not mediated by phonemes, but that rather phoneme perception as studied in phoneme identification tasks is mediated by word recognition. If this is correct, it leads to a reinterpretation of current data obtained in phoneme identification experiments. More importantly, it suggests that it may be high time to replace phonemes by words as the main focus of attention in speech perception research.

In what follows I shall first indicate the class of studies of speech rate and segmental perception used by way of example in this paper. I shall then attempt to account for these data within a phoneme-based view of speech perception, concluding that any such attempt is unsatisfactory. Next I will argue that a satisfactory account of these and other data from phoneme identification experiments can be based on the view that phoneme identification is mediated by word recognition or word identification. Finally I make a plea for being careful in interpreting data from identification experiments and for increasing our efforts in the area of word recognition studies.

SPEECH RATE AND SEGMENTAL PERCEPTION

The experiments to be considered here are conceptually very simple. Generally, there are two experimental variables. One is the duration of a particular acoustic segment, for example vowel segment duration, chosen so that at one extreme of the scale of durations a particular categorical response, say a phonemically short vowel, is favoured, whereas at the other extreme the opposing categorical response, a phonemically long vowel, attracts most perceptual judgements. The segment duration at which 50% of responses in either response class are obtained in a forced choice identification task is defined as the perceptual boundary or phoneme boundary. The other experimental variable is speech rate of the utterance or part of the utterance the test segment belongs to. The dependent variable of interest is the shift in perceptual boundary corresponding to a shift in speech rate. Figure 1 presents an example of some data obtained in our Institute. The test vowel segment was embedded in the last syllable of a meaningful carrier phrase. Both the duration of the test segment and the rate of the vocoderized carrier phrase were experimentally varied. The mean phoneme boundary for 10 subjects is plotted as a function of speech rate. It may be seen that the perceptual boundary, defined as the estimated duration giving 50% of either response type, depends on the speech rate. A faster speech rate gives a shorter duration for the perceptual boundary.

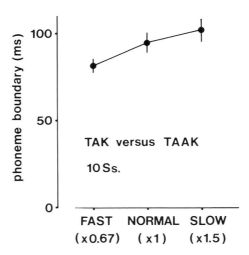

FIGURE 1   *Phoneme boundaries between dutch /a/ and /a:/ on the dimension of acoustic vowel duration. Test segments were embedded in a monosyllable word /tak/ or /taak/ placed at the end of a meaningful carrier phrase. The duration of the carrier phrase up to and including the consonant preceding the test segment was made 0.67, 1, or 1.5 times normal by changing the readout speed of the synthesis part of a computer controlled channel vocoder. Standard deviations over 10 subjects are indicated.*

Similarly, Picket and Decker (1960) showed that the perceptual boundary value between a single and a geminate stop cued by the stop closure duration falls at systematically decreasing durations with increasing speech rate. A qualitatively similar relation was found for the phoneme boundary between voiced and voiceless stops on the dimension of voice onset time (Summerfield and Haggard, 1972), the phoneme boundaries between long and short consonant and vowel phonemes (Ainsworth, 1972, 1974; Fujisaki, Nakamura and Imoto, 1975; Nooteboom, 1977, 1979), the boundary between fricative and affricative as cued by noise duration (Repp, Liberman, Eccardt, and Pesetsky, 1978), the boundary between intervocalic voiced and voiceless stop cues by silent interval duration (Port, 1977, 1978). An exception is reported by Marcus (1978) who found no effect of speech rate within one-word utterances *slit* and *split* on the perception of a /p/ as cued by a silent gap introduced between /s/ and /l/, possibly because the perception of a stop consonant is not cued by the perceived duration of a silent gap but rather by the presence or absence of a silent gap. In all cases where the perceptual distinction depends on the perceived duration of a particular acoustic segment, the perceptual boundary varies with speech rate. How can we account for this rather general phenomenon?

SOME ATTEMPTS TO ACCOUNT FOR RATE EFFECTS ON PHONEME IDENTIFICATION

A simple model predicting the relation between perceptual boundary and speech rate is this: suppose that the transformation of physical time into perceptual time is controlled by a clock, and that the pace of this clock is set by the speech rate of the attended utterance (cf. Summerfield and Haggard, 1972). In its simplest form this model would predict that if we increase speech rate by a factor of two, the perceptual boundary on a durational boundary would be halved. This prediction is at variance with all relevant data, except those obtained by Fujisaki et al. (1975) who assessed phoneme boundaries between Japanese long and short phonemes, both vowels and consonants, at four different rates of speech. Their data show perfect adjustment of the phoneme boundaries to speech rate. However, in all other cases the shifts in perceptual boundary are smaller than predicted by a simple external clock whose pace is completely adjusted to speech rate.

The employment of a rate-controlled clock would, of course, be unrealistic from the standpoint of an efficient use of the cues available in the speech waveform. It is known that not all segment types in speech are equally affected by speech rate in the production of speech (Kozhevnikov and Chistovich, 1965; Lehiste, 1970). At least equally important is the observation that often the size of rate-induced shifts in perceptual boundaries cannot easily be predicted from the size of changes in speech rate in the surrounding speech material. Although there is a good correspondence between the production and perception data of Picket and Decker (1964), Summerfield (1975) found rate-induced shifts in the produced voice-onset time of the order of tens of milliseconds, whereas the corresponding shifts in perceptual boundaries were an order of magnitude smaller. Similar discrepancies were observed for systematic effects of speech rate on spoken vowel duration and the corresponding shifts in perceptual boundaries between short and long vowel phonemes in Dutch (Nooteboom and Doodeman, 1979). Apparently, the relation between speech rate and durational perceptual boundaries is not as straight-forward as suggested by the clock model.

Öhman (1975) proposed a view of speech perception according to which a listener decodes the speech signal by projecting it into his internal model of the vocal apparatus of the speaker. Thus the perceptual model would partly be a production model associated with a set of physical states definable in terms of physical concepts. Speech perception, just as the perception of moving cars, or walking people, would be the perception of physical system-state histories: in perceiving speech we hear another person's vocal organs move. A similar view of speech perception, expressed in somewhat less general terms, seems to be taken by Repp, Liberman, Eccardt, and Pesetsky (1978), and by Summerfield (1979), in relation to, among other things, data on speech rate and segmental perception. Repp et al. provide some data showing that the "listeners integrate a numerous, diverse, and temporally distributed set of acoustic cues into a unitary phonetic percept. These several cues have in common only that they are products of a unitary articulatory act. In effect, then, it is the articulatory act that is perceived". This view of speech perception is basically at variance with the earlier attempts to account for effects of speech rate on segmental perception. This is so, because within this view one cannot distinguish between cues to segmental perception and cues to speech rate. As Summerfield (1979) puts it: "the acoustical substrate for the direct perception of rate and the acoustical elements whose interpretation rate must mediate not only co-occur, they are one and the same". It follows, then, that rate-induced shifts in perceptual boundaries are not caused by differences in perceived speech rate, but rather by rate-induced changes in other acoustic cues which follow from the same articulatory act as the one under investigation. Therefore the time-window over which speech rate may seem to be effective would reflect the time window over which "unitary articulatory acts" have acoustic results.[1]

A test of the hypothesis that speech rate affects segment identification only via its effect on durational cues immediately resulting from the articulation of that segment is provided by Summerfield (1979). Summerfield showed that the perceptual boundary on the dimension of voice-onset time between /b/ and /p/ in the utterance *why are you* /biz/? versus *why are you* /piz/, is affected by the duration of the syllable *you* and the duration of the vowel /i/, but not by the durations of *why* and *are*: the effect of rate appeared to be entirely due to those segment durations which are regularly affected by the production of a voiced versus a voiceless stop. This may be taken to support the perception-of-articulation-model in the strict form that speech is perceived as sequences of articulatory acts each of which is cued by all acoustic attributes regularly associated with its occurrence in the production of speech. Speech rate can only affect segmental perception via its effect on these acoustic attributes, but does not in itself control the processing of these attributes.

So far the perception-of-articulation-model seems to be quite satisfactory. I will now mention two sets of data which, although not immediately concerned with speech rate, refute the model. The first set of data has been described by Nooteboom and Doodeman (1979), and concerns the perceptual boundary between a Dutch short vowel /a/ and a long vowel /a:/ on the dimension of vowel duration. The test segments were part of a monosyllabic real word, being either *tak* (Engl. branch) or *taak* (Engl. task), which was embedded in a meaningful carrier phrase. There were two experimental variables, the duration of the test segment and the duration of a silent gap introduced immediately after the monosyllable containing the test segment. The perceptual boundary value increased with increasing silent gap duration. This poses a problem to the perception-of-articulation-model in its strict form, because the silent gap cannot reasonably be intrepreted as an acoustic result of the articulation of a short or a long vowel. The association between vowel duration and silent gap duration is not that both result from the same unitary articulatory act required by the to-be-identified phoneme, but is of a different order. Vowels in prepausal syllables are regularly lengthened, and therefore the occurrence of a perceived speech pause increases the expected duration in the prepausal syllable, thus causing a shift in the perceptual boundary between short and long vowels.

The second set of data has been reported by Ganong (1978) who showed a clear and consistent bias towards categorization that made words as against categorization that made nonwords in a phoneme identification experiment. Thus in the pair *gift* versus *kift* there was a bias towards *gift* and in the pair *giss* versus *kiss* there was a bias towards *kiss*. Such lexical effects on phoneme identification, even in a binary forced choice task that in many respects resembles a simple discrimination task, cannot easily be explained by assuming that speech perception is the perception of articulatory acts. More likely, speech perception is the perception of words, or in the case of nonsense items, word-like units.

PHONEME IDENTIFICATION VIA WORD RECOGNITION

The tentative explanations given so far of current data on segmental perception and speech rate have one property in common. They are in line with the assumption that phonemes are natural and immediate response categories in a speech perception task. This is a corollary of a basic idea underlying much contemporary work in the domain of speech perception, namely that linguistic processing of speech, and particularly recognition of spoken words, is mediated by phonemes. I propose to reject that view and instead to start from the not altogether original, but perhaps to some speech researchers heretical, assumption that word recognition is not mediated by phonemes but, on the contrary, phoneme identification is mediated by word recognition. This proposal has some nice analogies with the relation between words and phonemes in phonological analysis: phonemes are secondary units of analysis, words are primary units of analysis. Phonemes are found by comparing minimally distinct words, words are not found by combining phonemes. The assumption that in a speech perception task, even in a phoneme identification task, words become available as responses before phonemes do is supported by reaction time experiments showing that listeners react faster to meaningful units than to phonemes or meaningless syllables (McNeill and Lindig, 1973; Foss and Swinney, 1973; Rubin, Turvey and Van Gelder, 1976) and by experiments showing that reaction times to phonemes in spoken sentences are sensitive to transitional probabilities of the words in which these phonemes are contained (Morton and Long, 1976). Further arguments against phonemes as discrete units necessarily mediating between the acoustic signal and word recognition may be derived from the course of language acquisition (Morton and Smith, 1974), from the less complex relation between the acoustic signal and words on the one hand than between the acoustic signal and phonemes on the other, and from the earlier mentioned experiment of Ganong (1978) showing lexical effects in a phoneme identification task. One way of interpreting the dependence of reaction times to phonemes on properties of the words these phonemes belong to is to assume that a phoneme comes available as response only after the word has been recognized. Thus phoneme identification would depend on word recognition.

An immediate consequence of adopting the idea that phoneme identification depends on word recognition is that one must have some ideas about word recognition in order to interpret data of phoneme identification experiments. I assume, then, that word recognition is mediated by a whole array of independent, parallel word recognition elements which actively respond to features from different sources (cf. Morton, 1969; Marslen-Wilson and Welsh, 1978). For the present purpose it is most relevant to consider the nature of that part of the internal specification of these word recognition elements tnat makes them respond to the acoustic input. I suggest that this internal specification is not in terms of phonemes, but rather in terms of areas in a recognition space defined by the set of auditory features which each individual language user has acquired in order to distinguish between the lexical units of his language. As language users in the course of language acquisition are forced to learn that many different acoustic forms have to be recognized as a single lexical unit, each area in auditory recognition space may cover a whole range of auditory feature combinations. Each point in such an area corresponds to a particular combination of auditory feature values and may have a particular strength of its association with the corresponding word response: some auditory feature combinations lead more easily to a word response than others.

How does this relate to phoneme identification experiments? In such experiments phonemes are embedded either in real words or in nonsense items. In the case of real words, a subject has recourse to existing word recognition elements and can respond with one of the alternative phonemes each time he identifies the word containing that phoneme. Note that often no phoneme response is required, but a phoneme perception is inferred by the experimenter from a word response. In the case of nonsense items, the subject has to set up ad-hoc recognition elements for these nonsense items on the basis of the instruction and the initial presentations. These ad-hoc recognition elements can then be used in the same way as the regular ones. The ability to create new recognition elements is essential to language acquisition and therefore must naturally belong to a language user's competence.

WORD RECOGNITION, SPEECH RATE, AND PERCEPTUAL BOUNDARIES

Let me now attempt to relate the present view of phoneme identification to the earlier discussed data on speech rate and segmental perception. I assume that in the internal specification of a word or a word-like unit for each auditory segment that can have a perceptual duration the whole range of potential durations is specified. Each sequence of segment durations (durational pattern) has a particular strength of its association with the word response (response strength). Those durational patterns that are most to be expected in normal speech for the word concerned have the greatest response strength, less likely durational patterns have a smaller response strength. For example, a durational pattern that would be normal within a given speech rate would have a great response strength, just as great as a durational pattern that would be normal in another speech rate. But a durational pattern that belongs partly to one and partly to another speech rate would have a relatively small response strength. In this way detailed tacit knowledge on systematic covariations of segment durations in speech is contained in the distribution of response strength over auditory recognition space for each word recognition element. If two auditory word forms corresponding to two different word responses differ only in the duration of a single auditory segment, there is, when the set of values of all other segment durations is fixed, one duration of that segment for which the association with both word responses is equally strong. This duration corresponds to the perceptual boundary measures in a phoneme identification experiment. Its value on the dimension of auditory segment duration will be the mean of the two values that would correspond to the highest response strengths for the two words in the given durational pattern. Of course, when this durational pattern changes, for example with a change in speech rate, the two optimal values will also change, probably both in the same direction, and therewith the point of equal strength will also shift. In this way shifts in perceptual boundaries can be explained as immediate and passive effects of the distribution of response strengths for different words over the entire set of possible combinations of auditory feature values. No active normalization processes, either operating on subjective durations or operating on internal criteria, are called for. This cheapness in mental calculations is bought at the expense of a very uneconomical storage of word recognition elements. But precisely because of the lack of necessary mental calculations this uneconomical storage has the great advantage that matching between acoustic input and word recognition elements does not take more time than strictly necessary. This means that the effect of memory noise on stimulus presentation is reduced to a bare minimum.

Because the distributions of response strengths must, in the acquisition of language, have arisen from systematic covariations of auditory feature values in the past experience of the individual language user, the present model accounts for all of the data on speech rate and segmental perception that are accounted for by the earlier discussed perception-of-articulation-model, without making the assumption that listeners construct an internalized model of the vocal organs of each speaker they are listening to. In addition the model can naturally handle effects of other sources of information, be they prosodic, lexical, syntactic, or semantic, on phoneme identification, because in speech perception different sources of information come together at the level of word recognition (cf. Cole and Jakimik, 1978; Marslen-Wilson and Welsh, 1978).

If both the model and the data are taken seriously, they together confirm that recognition elements contain detailed information on systematic covariations of auditory feature values in normal speech. Interestingly, this is not only true of regular words but also of nonsense items which have never been heard by the subjects before the experimental session. This suggests that the pattern of response strengths associated with potential configurations of auditory feature values for a particular word recognition element, does not necessarily arise from extensive auditory experience with the word concerned, but may be generated by the subject on the basis of his experience with other words. Thus, whereas the identification or recognition of a particular word or word-like unit may be completely passive, the creation of a new recognition element has to be an active process generalizing from the information patterns of existing recognition elements.

FROM SHIFTING PHONEME BOUNDARIES TO WORD RECOGNITION

There are three major points that emerge from the present reinterpretation of data on speech rate and segmental perception. The first point is this: speech rate as such does not control the processing of acoustic cues to segmental perception, i.e. listeners do not derive from the input speech a measure of the current speech rate which then in turn affects the processing of further acoustic material. The seeming effect of speech rate on the contribution of durational cues to speech perception apparently stems from the effect of speech rate on the production of other durational cues which together with the one under investigation determine what is being perceived. The implication of this finding is that no process of perceptual normalization on speech rate is called for to explain the shifts in perceptual boundaries brought about by changes in speech rate.

The second point is a criticism of the overemployment of forced choice identification as an experimental task in studies of speech perception. I see at least three reasons why one should be hesitant in generalizing from phoneme identification to the normal perception of speech:

1) Due to the lack of useful information in the neighbourhood of the perceptual boundary, the subject may be forced to employ sources of information which in the normal perception of speech never, or hardly ever, play a role.
2) For the same reason responses to stimuli in the neighbourhood of the perceptual boundary are delayed in time, often several hundreds of ms. This makes perceptual boundaries sensitive to information following the test segment in a way which is probably not representative for normal speech perception.
3) Due to the forced-choice character of the task, the limited number of alternatives and the employment of overlearned, highly stable internal criteria, phoneme identification is extremely accurate, often more accurate than one would expect from discrimination measurements. Phoneme identification seems to be an excellent way of measuring just noticeable differences (cf. Schouten, 1978) but these may have little bearing on normal speech perception.

In view of these caveats, it is fair to say that phoneme identification may be a valuable and precise analytical tool for probing a subject's tacit knowledge of, among other things, the sound structure of his language but it is a much less valid tool for studying how this tacit knowledge is applied in the normal perception of speech. This conclusion, of course, reaches much farther than the limited class of speech perception studies used as an example in this paper. Phoneme identification is the most popular experimental task among students of speech perception (not among their subjects).

Thirdly, I would like to make a plea for giving more attention to word recognition in studying suprasegmental effects on segmental representations. If indeed word recognition is as central to speech perception as is argued by Cole and Jakimik

(1978), Marslen-Wilson and Welsh (1978) and Marslen-Wilson (1979b) and as I have assumed in this paper, the effects suprasegmental structures have on recognition may be more interesting than the effects they have on phoneme identification. Although some work has been done relating to this topic (cf. Kozhevnikov and Chistovich, 1965; Blesser, 1969; Cutler, 1976; Brokx, 1979), it is fair to say that only little is known about the features extracted from the speech waveform and contributing to the recognition of words, prosody, syntax, and meaning, and how these features together determine what is perceived. I am convinced that further theorizing and experimental work in this area will benefit if the word instead of the phoneme is made the primary focus of attention.

Note

1. Data from Repp et al. (1978) can be understood in this way. Perceptual boundaries were measured between *shop* and *chop* in *why don't you say shop/chop again*? in a two-dimensional plane, defined by noise duration and silence duration, for both a slow and fast speech rate. Within the same speech rate boundary values for noise and silence duration were positively related, but, for equivalent values durations, more silence was needed in the fast utterance frame than in the slow frame to convert the fricative into an affricative. This may seem paradoxical when one tries to explain it from an effect of perceived speech rate on the cue value of silence duration. Assume, however, that the alleged effect of speech rate is entirely due to the difference in duration of the vowel in *say*, immediately preceding the silence, and that in production there is a regular negative correlation due to compensation between this vowel duration and the following silence duration of the type found by Kozhevnikov and Chistovich (1965) and De Rooij (1979). In that case the shortened vowel in *say* will create an expected longer silence duration for the listener and vice versa. This would explain the data in a natural way, and remove the paradox. Unfortunately, Repp et al. do not provide production data. The point I want to make, however, is that we have to consider the possibility that all so-called rate effects on segment identification can be explained from a subject's tacit knowledge about production regularities immediately related to the segments concerned, without perceived speech rate having any part in it.

Acknowledgement   Some of the ideas expressed in this paper were inspired by discussions I have had with my colleage Steve Marcus on the human recognition of spoken words.

THE COGNITIVE REPRESENTATION OF SPEECH
T. Myers, J. Laver, J. Anderson (editors)
© *North-Holland Publishing Company, 1981*

Suprasegmental Constraints on Segmental Representation: Research Involving Speech Production

GEORGE ALLEN

University of North Carolina, Chapel Hill

INTRODUCTION

This session (Session III) is devoted to the relation between segmental and suprasegmental representation, an interesting and worthwhile question to pursue. However, whereas the earlier of the two seminars devoted to this issue (Representation and context sensitivity) is neutral with respect to directionality between segments and suprasegmentals, the title of the present seminar, ''Suprasegmental constraints on segmental representation'' indicates a decided bias. That the segment is primary and merely ''constrained'' by the prosodies is a view which has (unfortunately) dominated phonetics and phonology from their beginnings and only now is beginning to be replaced widely by more balanced approaches. Thus, although the title of this seminar would have been appropriate ten or perhaps even five years ago, a better title today would be ''Interactions among levels.'' There has recently been a great increase in the activity devoted to discovering information about, and developing descriptive systems for, such suprasegmental phonological constructs as the syllable, the word, accent, tone, intonation, and rhythm. Presumably much of this activity will be described in other sessions of this symposium, such as seminars 8 and 14, and it will therefore not be dealt with directly here. We shall instead devote this paper to a brief review of the variety of ways segmental structure has been seen as dependent on ''higher'' levels of structure and process.

Two Prior Questions   There are two prior issues which must be noted, the first of which is just *whose* cognition we are referring to in this symposium. At least four different minds are present in the overall equation, namely the speaker's, the listener's, the phonetician's, and the phonologist's, and although there must be a great deal of common ground, each has its own peculiar needs as well. For example real speakers and listeners have little use for rewrite rules and the IPA alphabet, yet it is through manipulations of speech data with such mental tools as these that we glimpse the minds of others. This paper will not address directly these differences among the metalanguages required for discussing cognitive representations of these various sorts, yet we must all remain both aware that such differences do exist and alert to the possible futility of bringing inadequate or inappropriate tools to bear on questions of interest.

The second issue worthy of note prior to the review section of this paper is the complex question of what units, features, and processes are to be discussed for each structural level. We do not wish to review the entire field here, and so we must limit the discussion, either explicitly or implicitly, to those subareas which we feel are particularly relevant to this symposium and to this seminar. Such limits are hard to set. Sometimes they are set for us, by the body of work which exists for us to contemplate. Other areas we exclude as the result of a conscious judgement of their value. Most commonly, however, we omit areas from ignorance of subconscious bias. You should therefore regard this chapter as a projection of the writer's knowledge and biases onto the questions at hand and be particularly ready to question the boundaries it defines.

We now turn to more substantive issues concerning constraints on representation at the segmental level by processes at another, "higher" level. Section 1 will deal with "local" constraints, deriving from the syllable or consonant cluster within which a segment is found. Section 2 then discusses more "global" constraints, deriving from processes at the level of the phrase or higher.

1. SYLLABIC CONSTRAINTS ON SEGMENTAL REPRESENTATION

There has recently been a substantial (and gratifying) increase in the attention devoted to syllabic processes in phonology, perhaps as a result of normal development within linguistics, but more likely as a response to new data from phonetics and child language research. Whatever the causes, syllabic phonology is now solidly center-stage, after decades of fidgeting in the wings. Since Session VII, devoted to phonological representations, in part affirms this new status of the syllable, we shall refer here just to some of the ways in which syllable structure constrains segmental representation.

Segmental composition of syllables Bell and Hooper (1978b) have recently reviewed the phonotactic evidence we have concerning segmental distribution within syllables. They point out, among other things, that the CV sequence has a special "preferred" status among syllable types and that different consonant types and processes are "preferred" in syllable-initial vs -final position. "Preference" is to be taken here in both the statistical sense, so that "preferred" structures are found more commonly among languages of the world, and the implicational sense, in that "less preferred" structures are found in a given language only if "more preferred" ones are found in that language, too.

Bell and Hooper's (1978b) paper is the introduction to a book devoted to the topic of the interrelationship between syllables and segments, and there are therefore many other papers therein that could legitimately be reviewed here. Instead, I shall mention just one, as an example, namely Rensch's (1978) paper on "ballistic" vs "controlled" syllables in Otomanguean languages. For the production of ballistic syllables, he lists the following as seven important features, various combinations of which may be used for different contrastive realizations:

1. post-syllabic aspiration
2. breathy articulation of the vowel
3. voicelessness of syllable-final nasal
4. fortis articulation of syllable-initial consonants
5. differences in vowel duration
6. late peak of intensity with sudden decrescendo
7. variant realizations of the tones

The use of such a variety of segmental process to mark a single phonological distinction is reminiscent of the ever-expanding list of acoustic cues comprised by the term "voice onset time" in phonetics. This kind of diversity is probably the rule, rather than the exception.

Effects of Syllable Weight on Segmental Composition Most languages have at least two types of syllables, differing along a "strength" dimension; the adjectives "strong", "heavy", or "stressed" are usually applied to the syllables at the positive end of the scale, "weak", "light", or "unstressed" at the other. The origin and function of such differences have been widely discussed (cf., e.g., Lehiste, 1970; Hyman, 1977b).

For our purposes here, we wish to note the segmental differences that correlate with this dimension of syllable weight. Such differences are highly language dependent, but range from length (acoustic duration), for continuant sounds, to force of articulation (marked, for example, by aspiration), for stops. Many languages use a different (usually more restricted) set of vowel qualities (timbres) for light syllables than for heavy, and the permissable complexity of segmental structures (e.g., consonant clusters) may also differ. Further, although some of these variations are merely allophonic in nature, others are large enough and regular enough to have achieved phonotactic status.

Although many of the characteristics of light syllables quite rightly lead us to think of them as "reduced", for example that their component segments are drawn from a subset of (or a set of lower cardinality than) the segments composing heavy syllables, or that their articulations may be described as "undershooting" the "target" for a heavy syllable (cf. below), we must not be misled by this correlation. In some other ways, such as temporal precision or allophonic selection, these light syllables are just as reliably produced as heavy ones, and some of their characteristics may be just as "strong" as for heavy syllables. From the point of view of segmental composition we are perhaps better off regarding syllable weight as just another conditioning factor, at least for fluent adult speech, since the processes involved are so hidden by perceptual-motor overlearning. We shall return to this point later, when discussing speech rate.

Effects of Syllable Tone on Segmental Composition   The interaction of syllabic tone and segmental features, especially initial or final consonant voicing, has been studied actively for many years, but since this writer has not followed that work closely, we shall refer the reader to a recent annotated bibliography (Maddieson, 1974b). There does seem to be some disagreement as to the extent and direction of influence of tone and segments on each other, and Maddieson (1974a) describes Hyman and Schuh's (1974) dictum, that "consonants affect tone, but tone does not affect consonants," as "hasty". He cites a number of examples showing influences in the opposite direction and exhorts us not to blind ourselves to the many other instances which he believes must exist. He also describes the two requirements for an adequate model of this interaction, the first being a dynamic physical and physiological model relating subglottal air pressure, supraglottal pressure, glottal area, and vocal cord tension, the second a psychological model describing how such physical differences become linguistically distinctive.

Development Data on Syllabic Constraints   Another important source of data on these questions of representation in general, and syllabic constraints on segmental representation in particular, is studies of how children acquire their first language. Since Session VI is devoted directly to the issue of speech and language acquisition, I shall again restrict my remarks here just to the questions of this session.

The most common observation in developmental studies, of any sort, is how differently from one another, and sometimes even from themselves, children acquire knowledge and skills. This variability, combined with the necessity of sampling a relatively wide range of communicative behaviors in each child, has made it difficult to establish any but the most simplistic of norms for language and speech development. Even after many years and hundreds of serious attempts at developing valid scales of language development, for example, the MLU (mean length of utterance) remains the most reliable measure and the most useful for many of our purposes, even though we know it to be a composite of linguistic and non-linguistic factors.

In spite of this inter- and intra-individual variability, a few general syllabic constraints on segmental representation have emerged (cf. Ingram (1976b) and Menn (1978b) for recent reviews). For example, the preference of young children for CV and so-called "reduplicated" $(CV)^2$ syllables results in an overall bias towards consonants being learned first in syllable-initial position. This bias is not uniform, however, in that it is apparently subject to a consonant-type-by-syllable-position interaction. Specifically, using a $C_1VC_2VC_3$ for reference, voiced obstruents and liquids are favored in initial position (C_1), voiceless obstruents in final position (C_3), and glides (including [h] and [?] intervocalically (C). The origin of these tendencies in articulatory constraints, as well as their correspondence with certain phonological universals, have been duly noted in the literature.

Constraints on Consonant Clusters and their Development   Conceptually quite closely related to the issue of syllabic constraints on segments is that of constraints on consonant sequences, or clusters. As Bell and Hooper (1978) note, in most languages any word-medial intervocalic consonant sequence can be divided (often non-uniquely) into an allowable word-final sequence followed by an allowable word-initial sequence. Thus, the word *monstrous* can be divided as *mon.strous* or *mons.trous*, but not *mo.nstrous* or *monstr.ous*. (The other possibility, *monst.rous*, is currently an interesting problem, since the only word final /nst/ sequences in English include a morpheme boundary before the /t/ (e.g., *danced*); Fujimura (this volume) discusses articulatory constraints on such sequences within the context of his model of English syllable structure.) Because medial clusters are constrained in this way, the majority of the work on consonant sequences has therefore quite correctly focused on word initial and word final clusters and their interactions.

Much information of interest has come from studies of how children acquire consonant clusters. Although the earliest work on the acquisition of clusters was oriented toward the "time table" or "milestone" point of view (e.g., Templin, 1957), more recent studies have used children's developmental peculiarities as evidence toward asking and answering more general linguistic and psycholinguistic questions. For example, Ingram (1976b), citing the work of Olmsted (1971), Greenlee (1974) and others, notes that when children "reduce" a cluster, by deleting one of its component segments, it is the "marked" segment that is deleted (e.g., /s/ is deleted from /s/ + stop clusters, but the liquids /r/ and /l/ are deleted from stop + liquid clusters). Other common modifications employed by children include weakening of stops, vowel epenthesis, and consonant metathesis (c.f. below).

Hawkins' (1973, 1979) longitudinal data on the durations of clustered *vs* unclustered consonants have also generated some very interesting theoretical notions. Because the progression of relative durations of /p,t,k/ in /s-r/ and /s-l/ clusters (e.g., /str/ in *struck*) was not a steadily decreasing one over a year's time for her children's speech, she postulated (Hawkins, 1979) a "replanning" strategy in which this interconsonantal stop serves as a kind of articulatory resting place, a transition point from the /st/ cluster to the /tr/ cluster in an /str/ sequence, for example. This hypothesis is consistent with action theory, discussed by MacNeilage (this volume), in that it suggests an ever expanding domain of the total action in speech production. Whereas in the adult this domain may be whole word or phrases, children may speak sequences of much shorter chunks, especially in unfamiliar words or as-yet-unpracticed segmental sequences (such as /str/ clusters).

2. GLOBAL SUPRASEGMENTAL EFFECTS ON SEGMENTAL REPRESENTATION

Syllables and clusters may be seen as rather local constraints on the segments, since the total span of their effects is usually not more than five or six segments and often less. We now turn to more global suprasegmental constraints on the segments, namely the effects of rate, rhythm, intonation, and discourse on segmental representation. These effects usually span whole phonological phrases or more.

Effects of changes in rate   The effects of variations in rate of speaking on characteristics of the produced speech has long been a topic of interest to phoneticians, and although some findings have withstood the test of time there remain a number of interesting questions. We shall address three of these, having to do with (1) the nature of rate changes, themselves, and (2) the reduction and (3) the reorganization of segments that result from increases in rate.

The nature of changes in speech rate   Although the physical characteristics of time suggest that there is logically no reason to consider slow, carefully articulated (lento) speech as more basic than fast (allegro) speech, most investigators have in fact done so by presenting their allegro data as various functions of lento "norms". Thus we wrote above of "reduction. . . of segments that results from increases in rate," rather than segmental expansion resulting from slower rate. There is, however, a practical reason for this basic preference, namely that it is much harder to predict the segmental composition of a lento form from a related allegro form which omits some segments (e.g., [ˈdʒi?ˈdʒɛ?] for *Did you eat yet?*) than vice versa.

Two types of rate variations must be distinguished, which for lack of a better name we shall call non-programmed *vs* programmed. Non-programmed variations were noted Allen (1973) to consist largely of gradual shifts of mean speech rate, over periods of minutes, and were hypothesized by him to be the result of changes in neural activation level in the speaker's brain. Although the absolute difference between the fastest and slowest rates exceed known difference limens for speech rate and/or segment duration, these extreme values are separated enough in time to go unnoticed. Likewise, the durational effect of these non-programmed changes is a statistically uniform shortening or lengthening of all segments in the utterance; i.e., no segment or class of segments changes proportionally more or less than any other, within the accuracy of the measurements so far performed.

Programmed shifts in speech rate are different, resulting from active conscious or subconscious choices by the speaker. Work by Gilbert and by Lass (e.g., Gilbert and Burk, 1969; Lass and Cain, 1972) suggests that subjects respond without difficulty, within limits, to instructions to speak x% faster or slower than some standard. There are some hints, however, that speech rate, unlike physical time, is not a continuously variable quantity. My reanalysis of Gay's (1968) data showed that each of his five subjects, when asked to speak more rapidly, shortened their diphthongs an average of 31%, and when asked to speak more slowly, they lengthened them by 33%. The fact that there were no statistical differences among speakers or diphthong types in this average effect suggests that "fast" and "slow" are (learned) categories rather than endpoints of a continuum.

Even if speech rate may be varied continuously, speeding up may involve different processes than slowing down. Goldman-Eisler (1970) was one of many to show that, whereas increases in speech rate involve a wide range of segmental allophonic changes (cf. below), speech is slowed as much by adding and lengthening pauses as by drawling the articulations. Along these lines, I should note that, in my reanalysis of Gay's (1968) data, the "fast" data showed a correlation between means and variances that the "slow" data did not, buttressing the notion that different psychomotor processes are involved. An hypothesis consistent with these data would be that increasing speech rate involves progressive "compression" of the standard (thereby reducing both mean and variance), whereas decreasing speech rate involves adding other material (such as pauses) to the standard.

Segment reduction resulting from increases in rate   A number of investigators have examined how various articulatory and durational features of vowels and consonants change as speech rate increases. Lindblom (1963), for example, showed that vowel formants take on more "centralized" values, which he attributed to articulatory "undershoot" of presumed "targets" for these vowels. With respect to duration, Kozhevnikov and Chistovich (1965) showed that vowels and consonants undergo proportionately different decreases in duration with increases in rate: they found consonants to shorten relatively less than vowels and to have a durational lower limit below which they could not shorten; vowels thus bore the greater share of the durational decreases in their data. Both of these effects have been verified across a wide range of languages, phonetic contexts, and physical and physiological measures: so long as the underlying articulatory program does not change, then an increase in rate results in articulatory undershoot and differential shortening in segment duration.

One important qualification of these characteristics of segmental reduction is that they are *not* accompanied by any decrease in articulatory precision. Although it was easy to hypothesize at first that articulatory undershoot and decreases in vowel duration are the result of an overall decrease in level of activation of the vocal tract, subsequent research (cf., Kent and Minifie, 1977, for a review) has shown that the reduced articulations are as precisely articulated as the full style segments, and they are often accompanied by local increases in muscle tension and speed of the associated articulator. In addition, the timing of the reduced articulations is no less (nor more) precise (Allen, 1973, 1975).

Segment reorganisation resulting from increases in rate   The processes involved in segment reorganisation from lento to allegro speech are many and fascinating. I shall restrict discussion here, however, to two examples which indicate the diversity, complexity, and importance of this topic. The first example involves changes in syllable boundaries, the second, discontinuous changes in the articulatory program.

The notion of where the syllable boundary may fall in a sequence of intervocalic consonants was discussed earlier; here we noted that, in many languages, as rate increases these consonant sequences change along with the position within that sequence of the syllable boundary. Two recent treatments of this process, from rather different points of view, are by Kahn (1976) and Bailey (1978). Kahn's work is phonologically oriented and seeks primarily to show the value of using the syllable as a basic unit of structure in descriptions of English phonology. Bailey *assumes* the importance of syllables, however, his goal being to describe how syllable structure changes with variations in rate or style. One interesting disagreement between them concerns the position of some syllable boundaries in allegro speech. Kahn claims, on phonetic grounds, that in a word like *hammer* the intervocalic /m/ is "ambisyllabic," that is, it both terminates the first syllable and initiates the second. Bailey (1978) claims, to the contrary, that Kahn overlooks relevant phonetic details and that the consonant can and should be assigned to one or the other syllable, but not both.

The functional load assigned to any such difference in syllable boundary location within English would probably be slight, and in fact there may not be enough contrasts to establish its existence. Nevertheless, the importance of such cues for signalling dialectal and language differences must not be ignored. As Bailey notes, one characteristic of such heavily tonic languages as English and German is that, as rate increases, consonants become more and more closely associated with the heavier of the two syllables they abut. These rate-dependent variations in the phonologically conditioned phonetic fine structure within and between syllables are known and therefore predictable to the adult native speaker; deviations from them impede communication, sometimes just at the social level, but often linguistically as well.

The other example of segment reorganization resulting from increases in rate to be discussed here concerns discontinuous changes in the articulatory program. It is not surprising that, within limits, durational shortening and formant target undershoot for vowels, discussed earlier, are smooth (even linear) functions of rate increase. Less convenient relationships are often found in the dynamic interconnections among consonants. Consider glottal strengthening or replacement in English, for example. Such a word as *mountain* ([ˈmæõn.tə̃n]), with a voiceless obstruent between two nasals, requires velar closure and glottal opening in order to build up oral pressure. As rate increases, however, the ability of the velum to move up and down quickly enough decreases to the point where, abruptly (?), the glottis takes over the responsibility for interrupting the air flow. The result is glottal replacement of the |t|: |ˈmæõ.ʔn]. If the nasal only follows the obstruent, the effect is still the same, for many dialects of English: lightning [ˈlaɪt?.nĩŋ]. For others, it is less complete, resulting in glottal strengthening of the [t]: [ˈlaɪ?.nĩŋ]. It is interesting to note, however, that at extremely fast rates, the nasalization will often spread even into the first vowel. Without the glottal stop, this velar lowering would result in nasal flow, which these dialects of English do not tolerate.

The point of these examples is that many such examples can be found where, as speech rate increases, the articulatory program suddenly changes substantially, for example by dropping out an articulation or substituting glottal for supraglottal gestures. These changes may be the result of physical or physiological constraints on the articulatory or perceptual mechanisms, but at least in adult speech they are as mental (learned) as any other phonological components of the speech process.

Before leaving the topic of speech rate, we should note here that, although the variations that result from changes in rate have caused problems for various theories of speech production and perception, it is an excellent example of the kind of issue approachable through studies of non-speech behavior. Most motor acts and most perceptual acts by most animals involve some form of temporal normalization; in highly repetitive acts, such as wing movements in bees, or song production and perception in some birds (e.g., chaffinches), this normalization is trivial and uninteresting. But coordinated, skilled, complex action, such as walking or catching flies (if you are a cat or a frog) *necessarily* requires temporal normalization. Let us look for answers to problems involving speech rate in such complex behaviors of other species (cf. Lubker, this volume).

Effects of Rhythm and Intonation on Segmental Representation   Phrase rhythm and intonation affect segmental structure primarily through their effects on syllable type. In English, for example, allophonic selection is heavily conditioned by syllabic weight (cf. above), which in turn is subject to at least two different kinds of rhythmic constraints toward heavy/light alternation (cf. Allen (1975) for a review). Lehiste's (1978) description of the morphophonemics of the Estonian disyllable is another example showing how phrase rhythm influences segmental representation.

Likewise, there are trade-offs between the use of pitch and duration as cues for marking heavy syllables in the English phrase, depending upon the position of that syllable relative to the so-called ''nuclear accented'' syllable. Heavy syllables preceding the nuclear accented syllable may use both pitch and durational cues, or either alone, whereas syllables after it may use only durational cues; allophonic selection is thereby constrained by phrase intonation.

In these examples it is possible to view the constraints in two stages, that is, the rhythm or intonation constrains the syllable type, which in turn constrains the segments. Although I cannot think of any good examples of more direct linkage of global prosody with segmental structure in adult speech, we have noticed some in our work on children's phrases. The best of these, described in Allen and Hawkins (1978), concerns the commonly observed metathesis of [s] and [ʃ] and perhaps all voiceless fricatives, from word-initial to -final position (e.g., *snow* [n̥os]). We argued there that the requirements for [s] and [ʃ] production (high airflow, long duration) and their resulting perceptual characteristics (high intensity, long duration) may make them seem more like weak syllables than consonants to the young speaker/listener. But since weak syllables are heavily constrained not to initiate these children's early words, these "syllabic consonants" are displaced to word-final position.

Effects of Discourse on Segmental Representation   In the ongoing ebb and flow of conversation we alter our style as the communicative needs of the situation dictate. For example, the first use of a new term will often be more precisely or completely articulated than later tokens of that word. As an example of this phenomenon, we turn once again to our phonological magnifying glass, the young child.
(Adult: What does your daddy like to eat?)
Eric: *Sandwiches*   [ˈsæ̃nwɪtʃɨz]
(Adult: What kind of sandwiches?)
Eric: Tuna *sandwiches* and . . .   [ˈtunə͵sæ̃nʃæ̃nː]
In reducing *sandwiches* to less than two syllables, Eric has done what we all do to greater or lesser extent (compare [ˈdʒiʔˈdʒɛʔ] above), constrained here semantically and pragmatically rather than phonologically. It is therefore not enough to know that a syllable is reduced in some environment; the degree of reduction may range from slight changes in the articulatory targets to rather extensive reprogramming of the output. The participants in the conversation process these changes smoothly, requiring only occasional restatement when too much information is omitted.

3. ON REDUCTION

The earlier sections of this paper contain references to a variety of processes to which we apply the term "reduction" or its related verb "reduce." A number of synonyms suggest themselves, viz. decrease, deteriorate (decay, atrophy), shorten, abbreviate, weaken, contract, condense, elide, relax, lower and many others. All of these can find their correlates in the processes we have reviewed above, and we should not be surprised to find that most of these specialized meanings can be generalized throughout behavior; that is, each kind of reduction is one of the ways we deal with our environment, linguistic, cognitive, and otherwise.

One other sense of "reduce", to "discount", has hopefully been adequately rejected in the earlier sections of this paper. In every instance to which "reduction" applies we find a number of characteristics or processes which appear as precise, as controlled, or as "strong" as the instances which are not reduced. Hence the reduction is always programmatic, i.e., part of the overall plan, and to "discount" it would be as much an impediment to our understanding of the entire program as would, say, the discounting of silence hinder our understanding the perception in noise. By incorporating the whole, with each part as important as every other, we may eventually "reduce" the problem in yet another way, that is overcome it, subdue it, and in all ways triumph over dark ignorance.

Discussion

Catherine P. Browman Both Nooteboom and Allen suggest that, while the suprasegmental aspect of speech is a global phenomenon, its effects are primarily on a local level. For example, Allen points out that, in production, increase in speech rate causes segmental allophonic changes, as well as differential shortening of vowels and consonants. Nooteboom reports on Summerfield's (1979) results showing that perception of /biz/ or /piz/ is dependent on the durations of only the immediately adjacent segments. This question of the global vs local effect of suprasegmentals is a major unsolved issued: is the overall pattern or the local perturbation more important in the perception and production of rhythm and pitch?

Both speakers also suggest that the effect of suprasegmentals is mediated via other levels. Nooteboom posits the word as the level in perception that can most profitably be studied, while Allen suggests that, in production, the syllable acts as the focus for suprasegmentals. The question of which level of organization is primary (and whether the notion of a primary level makes sense at all) has been and remains a widely debated issue. If, as the speakers suggest, production and perception are primarily organized on two different levels, then the problem of the interaction of the levels arises. Allen remarks that CV is the preferred syllable structure in children's productions (for at least certain C's). How does this syllable-initial bias in production relate to the apparent word-final perceptual bias for children?

In this session, production and perception have been treated as two separate systems, with different levels of organization. Ultimately, however, these systems are connected to each other through the lexicon. In thinking about the relationship between production and perception at the lexical level, it is important to remember that, just as perception and production are separate systems with independent structures, there may also be an independent structure to lexical memory that differs from both the perceptual and production systems. Language error data show that this is indeed the case.

Errors of production, perception, and lexical retrieval have been analyzed by various workers (see Browman, 1978; Fromkin, 1973), and the distribution of the errors within the word and with respect to stress determined. Each type of error shows a different distribution:

Error types

	perception	lexical retrieval	production
word effects	initial	initial and final	initial
stress effects	syllable	initial consonant	initial consonant

No single system shows the same distribution as another system; in particular the lexical retrieval errors cannot be described as simply a subset or combination of perceptual and production errors. Thus language errors provide evidence for three separate systems.

A. Cohen   On the whole it seems advisable to distinguish between structures and processes. So far we have heard a lot about processes; structures are mainly linguistic structures and the question then arises: do we think in terms of linguistic structures? Linguists certainly do, they intuit about them all the time. In phonetics we might as well face the fact that we have been thinking in terms of words: a phonetic alphabet, as any good alphabet, is based on words. Words can be broken up with some difficulty and abstract thinking into segments. How difficult this task is, any of our children will testify, no matter whether they learn English spelling, or any more phonetic type of orthography. How abstract it is, we all know, — particularly since Chomsky and Halle who discovered that all the barnacles of English spelling after all have given rise to a near perfect representation of structural relationships on a morphological basis.

We use words and we have to think ahead; normally in our own language words come pressing ahead in our minds and we therefore anticipate what is going to be expressed in words. All studies of speech errors show a bias for errors of anticipation; only due to fatigue, errors of perseveration come obtruding themselves.

So I am entirely in agreement with Sieb Nooteboom's plea for a shift of attention to the word as a unit of processing. George Allen's preoccupation with the effect of speech rate fits very well into this approach. We want to know what happens to words and their recognisability as a function of speech rate. The big issue as I see it, is: how do we as listeners segment the speech continuum into words and how do we recognise words, for words in speech do not come separated by blanks as they do in print. It would be a good thing if we took our cue from studies of visual word recognition, particularly in terms of so-called lexical decision tasks. This fits in nicely with some of the observations Dennis Klatt made yesterday about there being a limited number of candidates for rapid identification: you can only identify things (words) you know. It is jolly hard to "recognise" unknown names. Such a task would be to expose a listener to possible words including impossible ones and making him decide as quickly as possible whether they belong to his language.

Another approach would be through shadowing, a technique devised by Colin Cherry to illustrate the link between speaking and listening. By deliberately introducing errors the experimenter can check hypotheses about different stages of linguistic awareness and the possible suprasegmental factors influencing them, such as intonation, stress, place etc.

I throw out the challenge that this is a field as yet nearly untilled, the field of auditory word recognition. I hope some of you will take it up; if you do not, I can assure you we will!

Philip T. Smith   One of the most interesting observations in these papers was Nooteboom's demonstration that a pause in speech (that might indicate a syntactic boundary) can influence the perception of earlier phonemes. This is a good example of the sort of research I think we should be doing. What is surprising at a conference on cognitive representation is how little attention we are paying to the syntactic and semantic factors that influence production and perception; and prosodic variables, because they often have the property of linking groups of words, are likely to be central to any investigation of the interaction between high level linguistic factors and low level phonetic factors.

In some of my own work (Smith and Baker, 1976; Smith, in press; Groat, in press) I have demonstrated complex interactions between phonemic, prosodic and syntactic factors in speech production. Subjects read aloud nonsense words, embedded in otherwise normal English sentences, and we have found that subjects take into account phonemic information (whether the word ends in one or two consonants, whether the final vowel is lax or tense) and syntactic information (whether the word appears as a noun or a verb) in deciding where to locate primary stress in the nonsense word. This effect appears even with seven-year-old children. Moreover children trained to read with an alphabet that has more regular correspondences between graphemes and phonemes (the initial teaching alphabet) appear to be using a different set of phonological rules for their productions, in contrast with children taught with traditional orthography.

There are two theoretical implications I would like to stress on the basis of these results. First, these results set severe information-processing problems for adequate models of speech production: how can all the high level and low level influences on prosodic features be integrated in real time in a system with only limited working memory? Second, knowledge of spelling and writing may have a more profound influence than is currently imagined on our cognitive representations and prosodic outputs. In this context I would like to make a plea for more studies in speech perception that involve the listener's use of a fully fledged system of transcription: only such systems are likely to do justice to the listener's awareness of the many levels of linguistic information in the speech signal. Besides conventional orthographies, there exist simplified spelling systems for children, phonetic transcription systems such as I.P.A. alphabet and several shorthand systems, all of which have potential for tapping a wide range of the listener's linguistic perceptions.

Manjari Ohala Although I think the syllable is indeed an important unit of organization in phonology, it is not the case as G. Allen's paper seems to imply, that all phonotactic constraints can be stated in terms of syllable-structure constraints. There are many languages such as Hindi where the morpheme seems to be an indispensable unit in the statement of phonological rules and phonotactic constraints.

Chairman's Comments

Ilse Lehiste In the fifteen-minute discussion period that followed the presentations, counterarguments were presented to the claims made in both papers. Among others, Don Foss disagreed with Nooteboom's hypothesis that word recognition is not mediated by phoneme identification. Foss pointed out that reaction times can be affected by many variables, only one of which is the size of the unit to which the subjects are responding. Even though people may happen to respond more rapidly to syllables than to their initial phonological segments, this does not necessarily permit one to conclude that the syllable is the unit that is first available to the perceptual system. It is known that one of the important factors that affect the speed of lexical access is the frequency of the word. When one presents to listeners sentences such as "Yesterday afternoon the teacher borrowed an article from the library" versus "Yesterday afternoon the tutor borrowed an article from the library", there is a great deal of evidence that people are more rapid in accessing the more frequent word, *teacher*, than the word *tutor*. However, if listeners are asked to respond, in a reaction-time task, to the initial segment of *teacher* and *tutor*, the reaction times are identical. Foss interprets these results as supportive of the argument that the subjects are not having to retrieve the words that are carrying the initial segment. On the other hand, if the subjects are asked to respond to the word that follows the words *teacher* and *tutor*, in this case the word *borrowed*, the reaction times are about 40 msec longer. These data constitute a problem for a model that says that one goes directly from auditory representation to lexical representation, without some intermediate linguistic-phonetic representation.

Linday Shockey objected to Allen's characterization of the substitution of a glottal stop for /t/ as a function of speech rate. In working with conversational speech, Shockey has found that the glottal stop is perfectly free to occur at a slow speech rate. There is perhaps a distributional tendency for it to occur more frequently at fast rate, but the fully articulated /t/ is by no means precluded. Style influences production as well as rate. Shockey suggested that in order to solve the question whether certain processes are exclusively due to speech rate, one might look at a language like Spanish which has a tendency to articulate what is spelled *r* as a trill word-initially in slower rates and in a more formal style of speech, and as a flap at faster rates. This might be more of an all-or-none phenomenon; it also involves a different aerodynamic process.

Now some general comments. The announced topic of this seminar was "Suprasegmental constraints on segmental representation." I have the feeling that both the papers and the discussion contributions somehow drifted away from the specified focus. Traditionally, the term *suprasegmentals* refers to prosodic phenomena such as tone, stress and length (Lehiste 1970). The term does not signify higher-level units such as syllables, morphemes and words. Yet much of Nooteboom's very interesting paper was devoted to arguing for the importance of word-sized units in speech perception; a considerable part of Allen's thoughtful contribution dealt with syllable structure and phonotactics. To be sure, Allen's concern with speech rate relates directly to the topic of the seminar; Allen brings out the influence of speech tempo not only on the duration of individual segments, but also on their articulatory realization. But the time dimension is only one of the axes that define the multidimensional articulatory and perceptual space; and the other suprasegmental dimensions remained relatively undiscussed during the seminar.

The second half of the title, "segmental representation", likewise seemed to receive less attention than it deserved. No explicit consideration was given to the question what "segmental representation" really means in this context. Nooteboom's paper largely argued against setting up a segmental level in the first place; but it took Foss's comment to bring this into conscious focus. Is the "segmental representation" to be equated with the production and perception of phoneme-like segmental sounds (vowels and consonants)? Or does the term refer to the much more abstract level of representation in a mental lexicon?

Given the first interpretation, the topic of the seminar would have constrained the speakers to address themselves to the problem of the influence of suprasegmental factors on the production and perception of speech segments. We had some of that, but we also had a great deal of discussion of other things, especially of higher-level units. Now I am completely convinced that suprasegmentals play a part in establishing such higher-level units; likewise I have no doubt that the phonetic manifestation of segments is constrained by their location within higher-level units. As far as I am concerned, discussion of such constraints would have been even more interesting than the topic of the seminar; but I would have liked to see some awareness (apart from Allen's introductory remarks) that the constraints imposed by syllable/morpheme/word structure operate at a different level from suprasegmental constraints.

Potentially even more rewarding might have been a discussion of suprasegmental constraints on segmental representation at a purely theoretical level. This would have required confronting the issue of integrating suprasegmentals into phonological theory—a matter that has not been seriously attempted, much less accomplished, up to now. This, however, might have carried us too far from the immediate concerns of this conference.

While I thus expected to hear different things, I nevertheless liked what I did hear. The papers raised more questions than they solved—which is how it should be. Scholarship is advanced through a dialogue, and this seminar was a valuable contribution to this dialogue.

SESSION IV
REPRESENTATION AND PERFORMANCE

Seminar 7: Processing operations relating signal and representation

Chair   ANNE TREISMAN
Speakers   ROBERT CROWDER, DOMINIC MASSARO
Discussants   ALBERT BREGMAN, ANDREW ELLIS,
                 HIROYA FUJISAKI, QUENTIN SUMMERFIELD

Seminar 8: 'Higher-order' constraints on representation

Chair   PHILIP GOUGH
Speakers   DAVID SWINNEY, ERIC WANNER
Discussants   DON FOSS, JUREK KIRAKOWSKI,
                 PETER SIMPSON, ALISON ELLIOT

THE COGNITIVE REPRESENTATION OF SPEECH
T. Myers, J. Laver, J. Anderson (editors)
© *North-Holland Publishing Company, 1981*

The Role of Auditory Memory in Speech Perception and Discrimination

ROBERT G. CROWDER

Yale University and Haskins Laboratories

Abstract

Theoretical statements on the role of auditory short-term memory in speech perception and discrimination are reviewed. The significant empirical phenomena that fall within the domain of this review are categorical perception, the differences among phonetic classes in auditory persistence, contextual effects in phonetic labeling, and selective adaptation. Many of these observations can be organized by a theory of auditory representation in memory that draws on principles of recurrent lateral inhibition.

The operations for testing memory and perception in an experimental context are generally the same even though we often are smug enough to think we understand the difference between the two. In each case the person is asked to make some response on the basis of what he thought occurred in the past. The problem is very nicely illustrated in the discrimination procedure traditionally used for establishing the phenomenon of categorical perception (Liberman, Harris, Hoffman, & Griffith, 1957): the punch line in that demonstration, of course, is that people's discrimination of tokens from a synthetic /b, d, g/ continuum is no better than would be predicted on the basis of their phonetic labeling of those tokens. Items from within a phonetic category cannot be discriminated although physically equally close items that happen to cross a category boundary can.

THE DUAL CODING MODEL

It is when we examine the discrimination task used in the categorical perception experiment that we see the inseparability of perception and memory. The technique of choice for years was the ABX discrimination task, where the subject must decide whether a probe stimulus at the end of the presentation triad resembles more the first or the second in the triad. Formally, this procedure is a degenerate case of testing memory for temporal position. In a less degenerate case, the subject might be read lists of eight letters and be asked what position he heard a probe letter repeated at the end of the list—an A-B-C-D-E-F-G-H-X procedure. One might complain that the analogy is ridiculous because an eight-letter memory load is qualitatively different from a two-letter memory load. However, once it is realized that not only is memory for letters (or phonetic labels) involved but also memory for sounds, the characterization of the ABX task as a memory paradigm becomes quite serious.

This insight was the contribution of Fujisaki and Kawashima in a pair of brilliant technical reports in 1969 and 1970. Their model for the ABX task is shown in Figure 1 taken from Fujisaki and Kawashima 1969. A moment's study reveals that the model proposes a serial consultation of phonetic, then auditory memories during the task. The subject first decides whether the two initial stimuli (A & B) are different phonetic segments. If so, he classifies the probe X phonetically and compares its label with those stored for A and B. If A and B were given the same phonetic label, then the subject must rely on auditory short-term memory to decide which resembles X more.

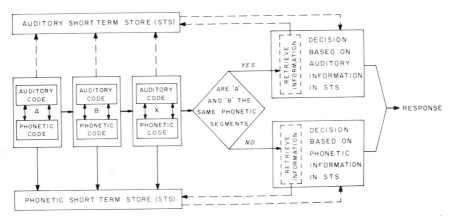

FIGURE 1   *The Fujisaki-Kawashima process model for auditory and phonetic memory in A-X discrimination.*

As these ideas are by now quite well known, I shall not pause to describe the independent evidence in their favor. Much of it is due to the experimental work of Pisoni (1971, 1973, 1975). The clear theoretical advance in Pisoni's work was to relate the "short-term memory" model of Figure 1 to the difference between stop consonants and vowels in categorical perception. (Fry, Abramson, Eimas, and Liberman, 1962, showed that unlike stop consonants, steady-state vowels can be discriminated well in the ABX paradigm even if they come from the same phonetic category.)

VOWELS AND CONSONANTS IN AUDITORY MEMORY

The notion advanced by Pisoni was that if speech discrimination depends on auditory and phonetic short-term memory a la Fujisaki and Kawashima, then the categorical perception result could be derived from a process model of discrimination In particular, obtaining categorical perception will depend on whether there is auditory short-term memory that survives until the comparisons of A, B, and X are made. If we assume that auditory memory for consonants is either absent or severely limited, it follows that they should be discriminated no better than they can be differentially labelled. If, on the other hand, vowels benefit from better or longer representation in auditory memory, then the subject should be able to supplement phonetic memory with auditory memory when A and B are from the same phonetic category.

Support from A-X (Same/Different) Discrimination This logic led to the prediction (Pisoni, 1973) that the time separating the to-be-discriminated sounds should affect performance. Pisoni switched to the simpler, A-X (same/different) discrimination task and varied the time interval between the two tokens from zero to two seconds. The stimuli were steady-state vowels or stop consonants. He found that the time separation of the two items had a large effect on within-category discrimination accuracy for vowels, with dramatic losses in performance betweeen the quarter-second and two-second intervals. However, within-category performance on the consonants was relatively unaffected by delay and uniformly poor. Between-category discrimination for the stops was quite high and not systematically affected by delay. These results make the case that it is the memory difference between vowels and consonants that underlies their classic differentiation in the categorical perception experiment.

Evidence from Immediate Memory Independent support for the memory difference between vowels and stops came from some immediate-memory experiments I reported a few years ago (Crowder, 1971, 1973a, 1973b). Morton and I (Crowder & Morton, 1969) had identified two experimental techniques for evaluating auditory memory in the context of list-memory experiments in which people had to repeat back series of memory-span items. We argued that the advantage of auditory over visual presentation, an advantage confined to the last positions within the list, could be understood as the consequence of a brief auditory short-term memory store not available in the visual-presentation condition. We showed that the addition of a redundant item, called a stimulus suffix, seemed to remove, or mask, this auditory advantage.

In one experiment (Crowder, 1971) I showed that the modality and suffix effects were absent when people have to remember lists of items distinguished only by stops (BAH BAH GAH DAH BAH DAH GAH) but that these effects showed up normally when comparable lists contained vowel distinctions (BEE BIH BIH BOO BEE BEE BOO). Subsequent experiments (Crowder, 1973a, 1973b) showed the following:

1) The result with stops does not depend on using initial stops because the outcome was the same with VC syllables (AHB, AHD, AHG, . . .).

2) Lists based on fricative contrasts give an intermediate result between the sizeable suffix and modality effects for steady-state vowels and the absence of these effects for stops.

3) The degree of auditory memory for vowels can be influenced by the particular tokens used. Long-duration (300 millisecond) vowels seem to allow better auditory-memory representation than short-duration vowels (50 milliseconds). This result matches findings by Fujisaki and Kawashima and Pisoni that vowels behave more like stops when their duration is sharply cut back.

My original interpretation of these results was in terms of a special speech processor (see also Liberman, Mattingly, and Turvey, 1972) that was selectively recruited for stop consonants; the idea was that the stop-vowel differentiation in memory could be understood in linguistic, rather than psychoacoustic, terms.

The Discriminability Hypothesis Darwin and Baddeley (1974) argued, on the contrary, that my results were better understood on the psychacoustic hypothesis of a universal auditory memory subject to degradation with the passage of time. They showed that other types of consonants besides stops did benefit from auditory memory representation in the suffix experiment, if they were drawn from a memory set with highly discriminable phonetic classes (including nasals and fricatives). Secondly, they showed that if vowels were selected from nearby locations in vowel space, so as to make them less easily discriminable than vowels from a wide set of locations, the auditory memory representation was reduced. Finally, they showed that diphthongs gave ample evidence of auditory memory even though they are based on transient, rather than steady-state, information.

Darwin and Baddeley concluded that auditory memory holds a crude representation of the signal, whatever speech sound it is, for a short period during which it is subject to increasing degradation. As they put it,

> The experiments reported here suggest that the result of this degradation is in some way to blur the information held in acoustic memory. After some degradation has taken place there may be sufficient information left to distinguish between a number of very different items, but perhaps not enough information left to distinguish between the same number of more similar ones. . . It may be that the different estimates of the duration of acoustic memory, that previous workers have found, are due to the different auditory resolution that their tasks required.

The psychoacoustic, degraded tape-recording, model is certainly the most parsimonious explanation for these results at present. My own thinking has come around to Darwin and Baddeley's on this point. In a recent theoretical paper (Crowder, 1978), I have made explicit that the form of an auditory memory is like a crude sound spectrogram or a crude Fourier analysis. This position will be explained in more detail below. For now, I want to continue with the line of reasoning based on Fujisaki and Kwashima's model because we have new reason to believe it is wrong.

PREDICTABILITY AND CONTEXT EFFECTS IN LABELING

A shortcoming of the Fujisaki-Kawashima-Pisoni position is that for any discrimination task, the contribution of auditory memory is assessed by measuring the difference between the discrimination performance predicted from phonetic labeling and the discrimination performance that is obtained. In other words, the extent to which performance exceeds a phonetic "categorical perception" baseline is the measure of how much auditory memory contribution there is. As MacMillan, Kaplan, and Creelman (1978) and others have commented, this is a dangerously circular way to define auditory memory; it is a sort of performance wastebasket.

Repp, Healy, and Crowder (1979) undertook to manipulate the availability of auditory-memory information for A-X vowel discrimination directly. They noted that Pisoni had shown that increasing the delay between the two stimuli to be discriminated reduces discrimination; this is presumably because of decay in the auditory short-term memory (since phonetic memory should not be affected by times on the order of a second). Also, Pisoni showed that interposition of a distractor sound between the AB pair and the X probe degrades discrimination performance, again, presumably through a masking of auditory memory not unlike the stimulus siffix effect. What Pisoni had not shown was that operations designed to affect the availability of auditory memory also affect the degree of fit between discrimination predicted from phonetic labeling and obtained discrimination.

Say that a sufficient delay and masking were introduced into the A-X task for vowels that no auditory memory at all remained for A at the time X occurred. We should then be able to predict exactly how successful the subject's "same-different" discrimination would be by knowing the probability that he assigned same or different phonetic labels to the two stimuli (which is measured separately). This prediction follows directly from the logic of Figure 1.

As Repp et al. put it,

> If accuracy of A-X discrimination can be predicted from phonetic labeling (identification), provided that both are better than chance, we may conclude that perception is categorical. The interesting possibility is that although discrimination shows a surplus over identification when auditory memory is present, vowel perception will be categorical when auditory memory has been removed.

In their first experiment, Repp et al. tested discrimination of steady-state vowels from the /i, ι, ε / continuum under four main conditions. The delay between the two A-X stimuli was about one-half second in two of the conditions and about two seconds in the other two conditions. Orthogonally, the delay interval was either left silent or was filled with a potentially interfering masking sound, /y/.

Both manipulations, increased delay and interference, reliably impaired discrimination performance. Furthermore, in the condition with both interference and the long delay, obtained discrimination was almost depressed to the level of discrimination predicted from a purely phonetic or "categorical perception" model. Repp et al. were not satisfied with this result at face value, however, for two reasons. First, the stimuli they used had not been chosen at equal spacings along the /i, ι, ε / continuum (for reasons that need not detain us here). Secondly, the data on phonetic labeling for their stimuli were taken from the conventional one-at-a-time or "out of context" identification test. Since vowel identification is known to be influenced by context (Eimas, 1963, for example), the fairer test would be to measure labeling (phonetic identification) of the sounds under exactly the circumstances the labels might be used in discrimination—that is, the context of the A-X discrimination tapes. In other words, the Fujisaki-Kawashima model assumes a covert phonetic process during discrimination; we wanted our *overt* phonetic process to be coming from the same discrimination context.

In the second experiment, there were only two main conditions, one with a short unfilled interval and another with a long filled interval; the delays and interference conditions were similar to those of the first study. But in this study there were two phonetic identification tasks from which to predict discrimination, one for the short unfilled interval and one for the long filled one.

As in the first experiment, the results showed that discrimination far exceeded predictions from the conventional (out-of-context) identification test in the short, unfilled condition, where there was presumed to be abundant auditory memory information. Discrimination in the long, filled condition was much worse, as in the earlier study; however, although discrimination approached single-item identification predictions here, we could not say performance was categorical by this criterion.

The main outcome concerned the identification data taken from the A-X discrimination tapes. In this measurement, subjects were asked to listen to both sounds in the pair and then respond with phonetic labels for each of the two stimuli. We were startled by the large, contrastive context effects that were evident in these data in the condition with a short unfilled interval between the two stimuli. In this condition, for example, the probability of labeling a stimulus as the sound (ε) in the interior of the 13-item continuum was .55 if the second stimulus of the pair came from opposite (/i/) side of the continuum. The probability dropped to a value of .27 when the second member of the pair was a more extreme example of / ε /.

The retroactive and proactive effects were not statistically distinguishable although the retroactive effects were numerically stronger. (Retroactive contrast is when the second of the items affects identification of the first item and proactive contrast is the reverse.) These contrast effects were much stronger in the short, unfilled condition than in the long, filled condition (although not completely absent in the latter). The fact that we got larger contrast effects at the short interval than at the long interval is important for it suggests a basis of the contrast effects in auditory memory. It will be proposed below that contrast should be expected to the degree that two vowels occupy auditory memory together.

The second main result of the Repp et al. experiment concerned the relation between obtained discrimination performance and predictions for discrimination based on ''in context'' labeling, where subjects listened to the same A-X discrimination tapes but tried to label each of the two sounds phonetically, rather than respond ''same'' or ''different.'' We took these identification data and then scored them as if subjects had been doing discrimination—if the two stimuli were assigned different labels we counted it as a ''same'' response, otherwise ''different.'' The finding was that these in-context identification data predicted obtained discrimination *very well but not perfectly*. The discrepancy between predicted and obtained discrimination was the same in the two delay conditions. Of course, since different phonetic identification was occurring in the two delay conditions (because of differential context effects) the predictability was measured separately for the two conditions. For stimuli from the mid-range of the thirteen-stimulus continuum, predictions were almost perfect—that is, subjects instructed to discriminate on the basis of physical identity did no better than when instructed to give the two items phonetic labels. At the extremes there were minor departures from categorical perception, particularly at the / ε / end of the scale.

Conclusions About Categorical Perception Whether one chooses to decide from these results that vowels are perceived categorically depends on which of two definitions of categorical perception one decides to embrace. By the traditional definition—whether discrimination on a physical criterion can be predicted from labeling on a phonetic criterion—vowels are perceived just about as categorically as consonants are. (There is quite typically a ''discrimination surplus'' in studies of stop consonants, too, although the surplus is not large, as it was not here.) Repp et al. observed that if one defines categorical as absolute, in the dictionary sense of the word, then vowels are not perceived categorically, since they are subject to such powerful context effects.

Conclusions About Auditory Memory in Speech Perception   Now it remains to carry these results back to our consideration of auditory memory and its role in speech perception. We think the Repp et al. results are decisive against the Fujisaki-Kawashima-Pisoni model: According to that model, discrimination is based on consultation of two short-term memory codes, first a phonetic code and then an auditory code. In our two interference conditions (short-unfilled versus long-filled) we demonstrably manipulated the integrity of the auditory memory. Therefore we should have found a much larger ''surplus'' of discrimination over identification in one condition than in the other. Instead, we found the discrepancies between discrimination and identification to be equal in the two conditions.

Repp et al. could not reach a firm conclusion about the basis for discrimination performance in their experiment; various mixtures of auditory and phonetic processing were proposed as alternatives. One possibility merits attention here because it is particularly novel and clear: The entire contribution of auditory memory may reside in context effects influencing application of phonetic labels and the actual discrimination may be entirely phonetic.

Why, then, do subjects bother to derive phonetic readings for the sounds in a physical A-X discrimination task? Repp et al. suggested that there might be an inherent priority for linguistic levels of analysis when stimuli include the potential for such analysis. The Stroop effect would be an example of such priority for linguistic analysis even when it is counterproductive. The modest discrepancy between the obtained discrimination and discrimination predicted on phonetic labeling just shows that this priority is not mandatory for all subjects on all trials.

RELATION TO SELECTIVE ADAPTATION

The hypothesis that auditory memory has a primary function in exerting contextual effects upon phonetic labeling is consistent with results that have been interpreted as evidence for selective adaptation of neural feature detectors in speech perception (Eimas & Corbit, 1973). We begin this argument with the comment that the formal operations are the same: In a selective adaptation experiment, the subject is played many repetitions of a token from one extreme of some continuum, say from the /ba/ end of the /ba-pa/ VOT continuum. The finding is that after such an experience, the /ba-pa/ boundary is shifted towards the adapting (/ba/) stimulus. In other words, an ambiguous item from near the boundary sounds more like /pa/ if the subject has been listening to unambiguous instances of /ba/. The Repp et al. result shows the same thing—a sound from the /i-ɩ/ boundary sounds less like the former if it is preceded immediately by a token from the left end of this continuum than otherwise.

There are two main differences between the selective adaptation paradigm and the phonetic contrast paradigm. First, the contrast effects most typically occur with vowels whereas the adaptation experiments typically use stops. However, we can dismiss this difference right away because Eimas (1963) showed that stops are subject to qualitatively the same contrast effects from neighboring identification targets as vowels are. The second difference is that the adaptation experiments use repeated presentation of the adaptation (context) stimulus whereas the contrast demonstrations are mainly interested in one prior or subsequent context item.

Selective Adaptation and Contrast   A recent article by Diehl, Elman, and McCusker (1978) suggests that the use of repeated adaptors may largely be a matter of superstition or faith in the fatigue metaphor. In their first experiment, these authors showed that a /b/-/d/ boundary shift could be obtained with a single adaptor separated by 1.5 seconds from the test item. They also showed that the effect depended on using extreme tokens as adapting stimuli rather than more ambiguous tokens, as is true in the selective adaptation literature. Diehl et al. showed in their second experiment that the "cross-series-adaptation" result could be simulated in the single-item context paradigm. Finally, their third experiment showed that substantial contrast effects still occurred when the "adapting" stimulus occured *after* the test stimulus. This result clearly is anomalous from the Eimas and Corbit (1973) feature detector perspective, but as we shall see below it is consistent with the contrast view. (Recall that Repp et al. found comparable forward and backward contrast effects in their experiment on steady-state vowels.)

Anchors, Contrast, and Selective Adaptation   Another recent publication, by Sawuch and Nusbaum (1979), adds weight to the contrastive interpretation of the selective adaptation result. These authors were interested in "anchor effects" and their possible relation to contrast. They used stimuli from the /i, ɩ, ɛ / continuum and presented either a balanced series for identification or a series in which a good examplar of one of the three phonetic categories occurred in an eight-to-one ratio to all the other 12 stimuli. There were four seconds between items. The finding was that boundaries shifted consistently toward the category chosen as anchor and accordingly over-represented in the test series. That is, in an identification series "heavy" with tokens of /i/, items from the /i/-/ι/ boundary would tend to be called /ι/ more than otherwise.

Sawuch and Nusbaum showed that these effects were symmetrical for the three different anchoring stimuli, /i, ι, ε /, and that the effect did not depend on the number of response categories available. In a final study, they instructed subjects that there would be many extra presentations of the anchoring vowel; however, this intended manipulation of response criterion had no effect on the boundary shift. The authors favor an interpretation based on the idea that a previous stimulus in auditory memory provides a "ground" against which new, ambiguous stimuli are heard in contrast.

The next section proposes a model that makes such an assumption explicit.

A MODEL FOR AUDITORY MEMORY AND CONTRAST

I have recently developed a theory of backward masking in auditory memory taking off from experiments using a list-memory technique (Crowder, 1978). Without reviewing that line of research here, I want to illustrate the major features of the theory in the event it might be useful in the present context. The major assumption is that auditory events are laid out on a two-dimensional array that encodes their time of arrival and the physical channel on which they came. The slightly novel feature of the assumption is that there might be a memory representation for time that is somehow neurally spatial. The simple-minded diagram of Figure 2 shows the hypothetical representation. Unfortunately it has not been possible for me to speak precisely about the second organizational dimension for this memory representation, called "Physical Channel" in Figure 2. I mean to capture with this dimension the traditional selective-attention sense of communication channel—the dimension on which two voices of the same sex are moderately discrepant, two voices of opposite sexes are more discrepant, and on which a speech signal and a noise are extremely discrepant. One might look to the experiments of Treisman and her collaborators in the 1960's (for example, Treisman & Geffen, 1967) for functional information on what distinctions can be called channel distinctions.

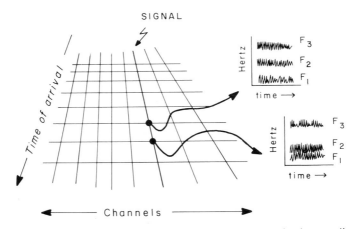

FIGURE 2   *A hypothetical representation for auditory memories in two-dimensional neural space. Entries are classified by channel of entry and time of arrival.*

The main process assumption that accompanies this representation assumption is borrowed wholesale from the retina of the Horseshoe Crab (see Cornsweet, 1970). I assumed that the memory representations defined by their locations on the time-by-channel array behaved as do units in the two-dimensional retinal array in the visual system, namely in accordance with the laws of *recurrent lateral inhibition*.

This accounts trivially for backward masking among auditory memory representations; if two activations are close enough together in time and similar or identical in channel of arrival, they will mutually inhibit one another. There are other facts in the list-memory setting which are nicely accommodated by the model, as can be verified in Crowder (1978). But my purpose now is to return with this model to problems addressed earlier in this paper.

Auditory Memory and Different Speech Sounds For example, there is the evidence that auditory memory is differentially rich for different sets of speech sounds. It will be recalled that this was a cornerstone of the Pisoni amplification of Fujisaki and Kawashima's model, that vowels are somehow better represented in auditory memory than stops. Independently, Crowder and Darwin and Baddeley turned in evidence directly relating auditory memory to "discriminability" of memory sets.

In the model of Figure 2, I made the assumption that the *contents* of the representations stored at intersections of the grid are some form of crude spectral analysis, perhaps comparable to a smudged sound spectrogram. This assumption was partly necessary because, in a masking situation, the level of activation of representational units by itself is not an informative event (unlike the state of affairs on the retinal mosaic, where degree of activation, rate of firing, is the important commodity.) It does little good to know that a particular channel was active at a particular moment; we need to know what happened there. Thus, the memory representation entered on the grid had to be something spectral. But it had to be only crudely accurate because a high fidelity representation would be too good: Remember the system of auditory memory has to be useful for highly distinct steady-state vowels but relatively useless for stop consonant distinctions. The best candidate seemed to be something like a sound spectrogram with a bit of perturbation—the sort of representation that would preserve long-term relations between formant frequencies, as can be used to cue steady-state vowels, but not subtle or transient formant changes, as are the cues for the less discriminable speech distinctions.

Contrast Effects As of this writing, there is one missing process assumption: It seems natural to assert that the lateral inhibitory influence of two representations that are close enough on the layout of Figure 2 should produce contrast in phonetic labeling. That is, if a representation for a good solid /i/ is close to a representation for a borderline /i/ or /ɪ/, the inhibitory influence of the first on the second might result in contrast. However, exactly why has not been clearly worked out. Only one rather wild conjecture has occurred to me:

The inhibition might be frequency specific in that memory representations that are close to one another on the grid inhibit *spectral components in common only*. It would be as if one took spectrograms of the two mutually inhibiting sounds and held them up together. Where they were identical in frequency, the intensity of both would decline. If the two sounds in question came from the same source channel, most of the energy would tend to be in overlapping frequency bands, hence the main backward masking result. With our two vowels /i/ and the ambiguous /i/-/ɪ/, however, although the high overlap in spectral energy would tend to weaken both, there would be specific changes from which we could derive contrast.

In this vowel continuum, it is F1 that is changing most informatively between /i/ and /ι/. Remember that the memory representation is a smudged spectrogram, which is the equivalent of a high bandwidth formant structure. Thus the prototype /i/ and the borderline /i/-/ι/ have considerable overlap in F1, though the latter will have an overall higher F1. The critical assumption is that the two stimuli cancel each other out to some extent in their common F1 "territory" and the *high F1 region of the latter stimulus is left relatively intact*. Thus, the surviving spectral information about the ambiguous token will, by virtue of the frequency-specific lateral inhibition, show a higher mean F1 and will accordingly be more confidently called /ι/ than when there was no contrasting sound in auditory memory.

Independent support for this conjecture must be sought; however, it does all fit together. The fact that Repp et al. observed symmetric forward and backward contrast effects is consistent with the general spirit of Figure 2, in which time has been transformed into a neurally-spatial dimension. The fact that selective adaptation and phonetic contrast effects are both larger when the adapting (context) stimulus is an acoustically "strong" contrast to the test stimuli than when it is only a "weak" contrast (see Diehl et al., 1978) is to be expected (although the application of these ideas to VOT has not yet been worked out). If the spectral overlap between adaptor and test stimulus were too high, there would be little information "escaping" lateral inhibition and forming the basis for contrast. That is, if our prototype /i/ were too close to the boundary itself, there would be little spectral information in the ambiguous /i/-/ι/ to form the basis for a functional elevation of the F1 in the latter.

In my judgment, the neural feature-detector interpretation of selective adaptation has been severely vexed by the finding (Ades, 1977a) that adaptation with one voice did not produce a boundary shift in a test stimulus presented by another voice. If it were a true phonetic feature detector in question, it should fire and get fatigued for, say, voiced stops, whoever happens to be saying them. On the other hand, the theory being sketched here anticipates this finding. If the two stimuli in question are separated in source channel, on Figure 2, we should expect no lateral inhibition and no contrast effect.

FURTHER EVIDENCE FOR THE MODEL

Although Pisoni and others have shown that increasing the time separation between two stimuli in the A-X discrimination paradigm leads to poorer performance, I made the conjecture above that A-X performance (in the Repp et al. study) might be based on phonetic and not auditory information. The Pisoni result would then have to be attributed to the following chain of events: The delay between A and X affects the amount of auditory contrast between them and hence the amount by which they tend to be given contrastive labels (if they are truly different). These phonetic labels are essentially serving to *sharpen differences* when the two are close together in auditory memory. These sharpened differences (like edge sharpening in vision) affect phonetic labeling, which is then subsequently used in responding "same" or "different."

By this account, it would be advisable to have some information on labeling behavior and its dependence on the interval between A and X when labeling is collected from A-X discrimination tapes. A recent unpublished experiment of mine provides such information.

Auditory Memory in Phonetic Labeling   In a recent experiment I played subjects pairs of steady-state vowels from a continuum ranging from /a/ to /æ/, which most subjects felt comfortable labeling with the vowel sounds from *cot, cut* and *cat*. In one half of the experiment I had them performing A-X discriminations; we shall not consider those results here. In another condition, I asked them to apply a phonetic label to the second member of each pair only. If one considers the 13 vowels on the continuum to be numbered from 1 (cot) to 13 (cat), the two items in a pair were always in ascending order. That is, the subject would hear stimuli paired 1-3, and 8-11, for example, but never 3-1, or 11-8. The items chosen for pairs were the 13 possible "same" pairs, all the 11 possible two-step discriminations, and all of the 10 possible three-step discriminations.

The stimuli were 300 milliseconds long and the main variable was the length of the silent interstimulus interval between A and X, which varied from .2 to 4.7 seconds in .5 second steps. The question was whether, on trials where the two stimuli were different, the boundaries would be shifted towards the first member of the pair and whether this influence would be stronger when the items of the pair were close together in time.

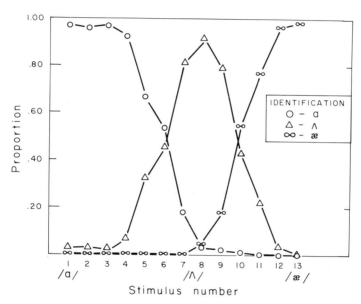

FIGURE 3 *Phonetic labeling on "same" trials, collapsed over interstimulus intervals.*

The labeling functions in Figure 3 show simply that subjects heard the 13 stimuli in three categories, as I had intended; these data are taken only from the trials in which the two stimuli were identical, the "same" trials. Notice that one category boundary occurs between items 6 and 7 and the other between items 9 and 10.

For purposes of examining boundary shifts, I collapsed the two boundaries as if there were only one, yielding an artifical average, boundary at between 7 and 8, for the data of Figure 3. For each interstimulus-interval condition, the combined boundary was estimated by linear regression using items 3 through 8 for the first boundary and items 8 through 11 for the second boundary. The ten interstimulus intervals were further collapsed into five to reduce variability.

The results are shown in Figure 4 which gives the combined boundary value separately for the "same" and "different" trials as a function of delay interval. As expected, the proximity of a prior context stimulus made no difference when it was identical to the subsequent, test stimulus. However, this was not the case when the two stimuli were different. At the shorter intervals, the boundary was shifted towards the left, that is towards the prior stimulus, in accordance with the contrast data under consideration here. At the longer interstimulus intervals, after about three seconds, the contrast disappeared and labeling was not different in the "same" and the "different" conditions.

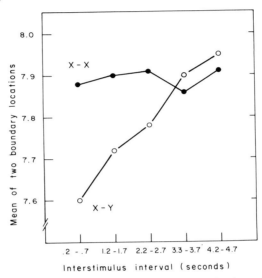

FIGURE 4 *Collapsed boundary values for "same" (x-x) and "different" (x-y) trials when subjects were labeling the second of two vowels separated by varying interstimulus intervals.*

The disappearance of contrast effects at about three seconds agrees perfectly with other evidence I have obtained with these and other stimuli, that a decay in *same-different discrimination performance* caused by increasing interstimulus interval is asymptotic at about three seconds.

CONCLUSIONS

Is it self-deception, or do the conclusions reached here make matters of theory a bit simpler than we thought before? Apparently, a theory of auditory memory developed within the context of verbal memory experiments can be carried, without gross distortion, into the speech-discrimination paradigm. In that new context, the theory permits a unified framework for considering categorical perception, the dual-coding hypothesis, contrast in phonetic identification, selective adaptation, and anchor effects. This theoretical framework is not yet clear of the rocks: One fundamental unsolved problem is whether the contrast effects of the sort observed in Figure 4, or in Repp. et al (1979), have an auditory or a phonetic basis. What if the person were *thinking of* the /i/ sound when he heard an ambiguous /i-ɪ/ token? Another problem is how to apply the contrast model based on lateral inhibition to the VOT continuum. Without that application we might as well give it up right at the beginning.

It is clear, in any case, that considerations of auditory memory are here to stay in speech perception research.

Note

Acknowledgement The preparation of this paper and the research in it were supported by NSF Grant BNS-77 07062. I appreciate the assistance of Virginia Walters in conducting the experiments reported here. Bruno Repp and Alice Healy were kind enough to comment on earlier versions of this paper but should not be held responsible for its faults.

THE COGNITIVE REPRESENTATION OF SPEECH
T. Myers, J. Laver, J. Anderson (editors)
© North-Holland Publishing Company, 1981

Sound to Representation:
An Information-Processing Analysis

DOMINIC W. MASSARO

University of Wisconsin

Whorf (1956) claimed that speech is the greatest show people put on and we are gathered here as part of our effort to gain some insights into a few acts of this great show. The information-processing approach provides a worthwhile analytic tool in the study of language processing. The goal is to dissect the complex show into its component parts. With this analysis, we hope to understand each of the parts and how they interact together in communication. The study of speech perception has been greatly influenced by the information processing approach in the last decade. According to the prototypical information-processing model, speech perception begins with the langauge stimulus and involves a sequence of internal processing stages before understanding occurs. The processing stages are logically successive although they overlap in time. Each stage of information processing operates on the information that is available to it and makes this transformed information available to the next stage of processing.

The speech stimulus consists of changes in the atmospheric pressure at the ear of the listener. The listener is able to experience the continuous changes in pressure as a set of discrete percepts and meanings. Our goal is to analyze the series of processing stages that allow this impressive transformation to take place. Figure 1 presents the model we have used to describe the temporal course of speech perception (Massaro, 1975a, 1975b, 1978, 1979, Oden & Massaro, 1978). At each

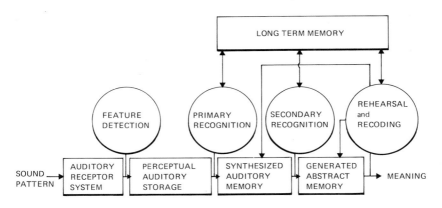

FIGURE 1   *Schematic diagram of the general auditory information processing model.*

stage the system contains structural and functional components. The structural component represents the information available at a particular stage of processing. The functional component specifies the procedures and processes that operate on the information held in the corresponding structural component. The model distinguishes four functional components; feature detection, primary recognition, secondary recognition, and rehearsal-recoding. The corresponding structural components represent the information available to each of these stages of processing. The present paper will provide a formal development of feature detection and primary recognition processes within this information-processing framework.

The changes in sound pressure set the eardrums in motion and these mechanical vibrations are transduced into a set of neural impulses. The neural impulses have a direct relationship to the changes in mechanical vibrations. We call the transformation from mechanical to neural information, feature detection and evaluation. The complex signal in the form of continuous changes in vibration pattern is transformed into a relatively small set of acoustic features. Features do not have to be relatively primitive such as the amount of energy in a particular frequency band, but they may include information about the duration of sound or silence, the rate of intensity change, and the rate of frequency change. It would be possible, for example, to have a feature detector that responds to the rising first formant transition that is characteristic of the class of stop consonants.

One traditional concern in speech research has been to determine the acoustic features that are utilized in perception. In terms of the model shown in Figure 1, the feature detection process places features in a brief temporary storage called preperceptual auditory storage, which holds information from the feature detection process for about 250 msec. The primary recognition process integrates these features into a synthesized percept which is placed in synthesized auditory memory. One critical question is what features are utilized and a second important question is how are all of the features integrated together. Does the listener only process the least ambiguous feature and ignore all others, or are the features given equal weight, and so on? Despite the overwhelming amount of research on acoustic features, very little is known about how the listener puts together the multitude of acoustic features in the signal in order to arrive at a synthesized percept.

The integration of acoustic features has not been extensively studied for two apparent reasons. The first is that research in this area was highly influenced by linguistic descriptions of binary all-or-none distinctive features (Jakobson, Fant, & Halle, 1951). Given the assumption of a binary representation of distinctive features the integration of information from two or more dimensions would be a trivial problem. Integrating binary features from voicing and place of articulation, for example, could be carried out by simple logical conjunction. If the consonant /b/ were represented as voiced and labial and /p/ were represented as voiceless and labial, the identification of voiced labial sound would be /b/ whereas the identification of a voiceless labial sound would be /p/. The simplicity of the logical conjunction of binary features may have discouraged psychologists and linguists from the study of the integration of acoustic featural information.

A second reason for the neglect of the integration problem is methodological. The primary method of study involved experiments in which the speech sound was varied along a single relevant dimension. For example, in a study of voicing all voicing cues were made neutral except one, such as voice onset time and then this dimension was varied through the relevant values. Similarly, place of articulation was studied by neutralizing all cues but one, and then varying the remaining dimension through the appropriate values. Very few experiments independently varied both voicing and place cues within a particular experiment. Those experiments that did (Hoffman, 1958) essentially reduced the data analyses to those of single dimension experiments. Therefore, little information was available about how these cues were integrated into a synthesized percept.

More recently, we have initiated a series of experiments that are aimed more directly at the study of the integration of acoustic features in speech perception (Massaro & Cohen, 1976, 1977; Oden & Massaro, 1978). In contrast to the traditional linguistic description, we assume that the acoustic features held in preperceptual auditory storage are continuous, so that a feature indicates the degree to which the quality is present in the speech sound. Rather than assuming that a feature is present or absent, it is necessary to describe a feature as a function of its degree of presence. This assumption is similar to Chomsky and Halle's (1968) distinction between the classificatory and phonetic function of distinctive features. The features are assumed to be binary in their classificatory function, but not in their phonetic or descriptive function. In the latter, features are multivalued representations that describe aspects of the speech sounds in the perceptual representation. Similarly, Ladefoged (1975) has also distinguished between the phonetic and phonemic level of feature description. A feature describing the phonetic quality of a sound has a value along a continuous scale whereas a feature classifying the phonemic composition is given a discrete value. In our framework, the continuous features in preperceptual storage are transformed into discrete percepts in synthesized memory by the primary recognition process.

There now appears to be some evidence that listeners can transmit information about the degree to which a given acoustic feature is present in a speech sound (Barclay, 1972; Pisoni & Tash, 1974). Miller (1977a) asked listeners to monitor one ear during a dichotic presentation of a voiced stop to the monitored ear and a voiceless stop to the unmonitored ear. The voice onset time (VOT) of the voiceless stop significantly affected the identification of the voiced stop to the monitored ear; the likelihood of a voiceless response increased systematically with increases in the VOT values of the stop presented to the unmonitored ear. In addition, adaptation with voiceless stops decreased voiceless responses as a direct function of the VOT of the adapting stimulus. Miller (1977a) interpreted these results to indicate that the output of the feature detector for VOT is a graded signal whose magnitude is a direct function of VOT.

Although Miller's results are consistent with the idea of continuous or multi-valued outputs of feature detectors, they do not disprove the possibility of all-or-none outputs. The findings of a relatively continuous identification function as a function of some stimulus property does not distinguish between the kinds of feature outputs. As assumed by the original categorical perception model (Liberman, Harris, Hoffman, & Griffith, 1957), identification probability can reflect the proportion of times the listener heard the stimulus as a given speech sound, not the degree to which the stimulus represented that speech sound. Accordingly, Miller's finding that the identification of a monitored sound was influenced by the VOT of the stop presented to the other ear might simply reflect the likelihood of the VOT detector firing in an all-or-none manner. Increasing the VOT of the non-monitored ear would change the probability of firing. Similarly, the effectiveness of an adapting stimulus as a function of its VOT value can simply reflect the probability that the stop is heard as completely voiced or completely voiceless on each successive presentation in the adapting series.

Asking listeners for continuous rather than discrete judgments provides a more direct method of assessing the nature of the output of feature detectors. If a stop consonant is consistently rated as being .6 voiced, we would have evidence for the availability of information about the degree to which a feature is represented in a sound. Since an average rating of .6 may also result from averaging across discrete judgments, it is necessary to evaluate the distribution of rating responses in differentiating between the possibilities of binary and continuous featural information. We have used rating responses to evaluate the nature of the featural information available to listeners in the perception of stops differing in VOT and F2-F3 formant transitions and vowels differing in their steady-state formant values (Massaro & Cohen, in preparation).

In these rating studies, subjects first listened to a stop consonant continuum changing in place (ba to da) or voicing (ba to pa) or a vowel continuum going from i to ι. The listeners were instructed about the nature of the continuum and were asked to rate the sounds according to where they fell on the continuum. The rating response was made by setting a pointer along a 5.5 cm scale. The ends of the scale were labeled with the two alternatives and subjects were told to place the pointer to the location that they think the sound belongs. The sounds were presented in random order and each subject rated each of the seven sounds on a given continuum 160 times. Figure 2 shows that the rating responses were a systematic function of the stimulus values for each of the three continua. The i-ι continuum was discriminated slightly better than the two stop continua as indexed by the larger range in ratings and the smaller standard deviations. However, we are confident that the vowel ratings could be made identical to the stops by either decreasing the stimulus range for the vowels or increasing the stimulus range for the stop consonants.

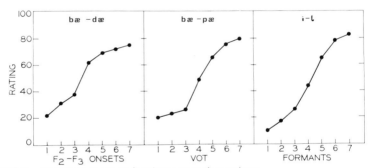

FIGURE 2   *Rating responses for three speech continua.*

The rating judgments demonstrate that listeners can transmit continuous information about acoustic properties of speech sounds. In the model developed by Oden and Massaro (1978), each acoustic feature is represented as a fuzzy predicate which describes the degree of presence or absence of the feature in the speech sound. The fuzzy predicate specifies the degree to which it is true that the sound has the acoustic feature. Truth values are expressed as continuous values between zero and one. For the dimension of VOT,

$$P \text{ (long VOT } (S_{ij})) = .60, \tag{1}$$

would represent the statement that it is .60 true that the sound S_{ij} has a long VOT. According to this idea, each unique value of VOT could take on a unique truth value. The rating judgments provide a relatively direct index of these truth values.

Once the idea of continuous features is accepted, the integration of information across two or more features becomes an important issue. In traditional all-or-none classificatory schemes, logical conjunction was sufficient to combine values across dimensions. Pluses and minuses in the feature matrix were sufficient to classify the speech sound. Many possible classificatory schemes can be developed to represent the integration of continuous featural information. Tests of models of featural integration require multifactor experiments rather than the more traditional single factor experiment. In a multifactor experiment, two or more acoustic dimensions are independently varied so that all combinations of the values of one dimension are paired with all combinations of the values of another property. The factorial design is optimal because it optimizes the number of data points relative to the number of parameters needed to test the various models of classification. Each level of each dimension requires a free parameter since the psychophysical function between the acoustic dimension and the truth value representing the feature is not usually known. However, Oden and Massaro (1978) and Derr and Massaro (submitted) have had some success in using an ogival relationship between the acoustic dimension and the truth values.

The ogival relationship predicts a reasonable relationship between changes in the acoustic dimension and changes in truth value. At extreme stimulus values, changes in the stimulus should have little consequence for the truth values. At intermediate stimulus values, however, small changes in the stimulus should produce relatively large changes in the truth values. A quantification of this relationship can be expressed as

$$t(x_i) = \frac{x_i^c}{x_i^c + (1 - x_i)^c} \qquad \text{where } y \geqslant 1 \qquad (2)$$

where the x_i values are a simple linear function of the integer value i of the stimulus factor

$$x_i = a_i + b \qquad (3)$$

except that values less than zero are set to zero and values greater than one are set to one. The form of the ogival function is specified by the three parameters a, b, and c. The values a and b allow the ogival function to shift along the stimulus dimension to position it at the optimal place. The exponent c determines the steepness of the ogival curve. Given that the ogival relationship requires 3 free parameters, a stimulus dimension of seven levels can be specified by just three rather than seven free parameters.

In order to illustrate how the present model is applied and tested, consider an experiment carried out by Massaro and Oden (submitted). Seven levels of voice onset time (VOT) were crossed with seven levels of the onsets of the F2-F3 transitions in stop consonant-vowel syllables. The VOT ranged from a completely voiced to a completely voiceless sound. The values were 10, 15, 20, 30, 25, and 40 msec. The seven levels of the F2-F3 onset frequencies ranged from 1345 to 1796 Hz for F2 and 2397 to 3200 Hz for F3 to give a continuum of sounds going from a labial to an alveolar place of articulation. Subjects made repeated identifications of the 49 unique syllables from the alternatives /bæ /, /dæ /, /pæ /, and /tæ /.

The four panels of Figure 3 present the percentage of /bæ /, /pæ /, /dæ /, and /tæ / identifications, respectively, as a function of the two independent variables. The levels along the abscissa are not equally spaced but rather have been adjusted to be proportional to the differences between the respective marginal means across the levels of the F2-F3 transitions. The differences were computed separately for each of the four response alternatives and then averaged over response types so that all four of the panels have the same spacing along the abscissa.

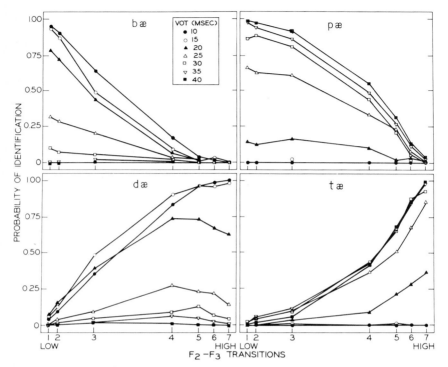

FIGURE 3 *Percentage of /bæ/, /pæ/, /dæ/, and /tæ/ identifications as a function of VOT and F2-F3 transitions.*

Evaluation of the results is facilitated by developing the basic model of featural integration given by Oden and Massaro (1978). Each of the four response alternatives is specified as a prototype corresponding to a proposition

/bæ/:	(short VOT) and (low F2-F3 onsets)	(4)
/pæ/:	(long VOT) and (low F2-F3 onsets)	(5)
/dæ/:	(short VOT) and (high F2-F3 onsets)	(6)
/tæ/:	(long VOT) and (high F2-F3 onsets)	(7)

The properties for the prototypes would also include other acoustic features characterizing stop consonants and the vowel /æ/. These are not included in the propositions since they are present in all of the four alternatives. These propositions specify the ideal values of each of the acoustic features for the particular speech sound.

Upon presentation of a speech sound, the feature detection process applies a truth value for each acoustic feature. The truth value specifies the degree to which it is true that the sound has the relevant acoustic feature. For example,

$$t[\text{short VOT } (S_{ij})] = .60 \qquad (8)$$

represents that it is .60 true that the speech sound S_{ij}, from the ith row and jth column of the factorial stimulus design, has a short VOT. To simplify the notation, let SV_i and LV_i correspond to short and long VOTs, respectively. The subscript i signifies that the values change only with changes in the row variable VOT. Similarly, LO_j and HO_j correspond to low and high F2-F3 onsets, respectively. The values change only with changes in the column j variable of the F2-F3 onset frequencies.

It is possible to simplify the descriptions of the prototypes by allowing each feature to be symmetrical along its acoustic dimension. In this case, a long VOT could be specified as the negation of the short VOT

$$\text{long VOT} = \text{NOT(short VOT)} \qquad (9)$$

It is also reasonable to define the truth of the negation of a feature as one minus the truth value of the feature. In this case, if .6 specifies the truth value of a short VOT, then $1 - .6 = .4$ would specify the truth value of a long VOT. In general, the value $LV_i = 1 - SV_i$. A similar symmetry could be assumed between high and low F2-F3 onsets

$$\text{low F2-F3 onsets} = \text{NOT (high F2-F3 onsets)} \qquad (10)$$

Following this logic, the value LO_j would be equal to $1 - HO_j$. Within limits, the assumption of symmetrical features in the prototypes leads to equivalent predictions as the more complex model given by Equations 4-7. Incorporating the assumption of symmetrical features in the prototype definitions gives Equations 11-14 in place of Equations 4-7.

/bæ/:	(short VOT) and NOT (high F2-F3 onsets)	(11)
/pæ/:	NOT (short VOT) and NOT (high F2-F3 onsets)	(12)
/dæ/:	(short VOT) and (high F2-F3 onsets)	(13)
/tæ/:	NOT (short VOT) and (high F2-F3 onsets)	(14)

At the prototype match stage, the truth values derived from feature detection are inserted in the prototypes. High truth values in the prototypes would represent a good match of the speech sound with the prototype alternative whereas low truth values would represent a poor match. However, a precise index of the degree to which the speech sound matches each prototype requires the conjunction of truth values across the acoustic features. Two possible conjunction rules are addition and multiplication. Given an additive conjunction rule, the degree to which the sound S_{ij} matches the prototype /b/ is given by the matching function

$$b\,æ\,(S_{ij}) = SV_i + LO_j \qquad (15)$$

The multiplicative rule gives the matching function

$$b\,æ\,(S_{ij}) = SV_i \times LO_j \qquad (16)$$

Given the matching functions for each of the alternative prototypes, the speech sound is identified on the basis of the *relative* degree of match. Following the rationale of Luce's (1959) choice model it is assumed that the probability of identifying a stimulus to be a particular syllable is equal to the *relative* degree to which that syllable matches the stimulus compared to the degree of match of the other syllables under consideration. In our example, the person must identify the speech sound as either /bæ/, /pæ/, /dæ/, or /tæ/.

The probability of a /bæ/ identification will, therefore, be given by

$$P(b\,æ\,|S_{ij}) = \frac{b\,æ\,(S_{ij})}{b\,æ\,(S_{ij}) + p\,æ\,(S_{ij}) + d\,æ\,(S_{ij}) + t\,æ\,(S_{ij})} \qquad (17)$$

where the variables in the ratio represent the matching functions for the four alternative speech sounds.

Returning to the results of the Massaro and Oden study shown in Figure 3, we can evaluate them in terms of the simple fuzzy logical model. The results provide a qualitative test between additive and multiplicative conjunction rules. An additive conjunction rule in the present model predicts a series of parallel lines within each of the panels. A multiplicative combination predicts a fan of diverging lines. For each response alternative, the pattern of results is that of a gradually diverging fan of curved lines. The fact that the lines come together at a point at zero percent and that the bottom curves are relatively flat near zero percent indicate that the information about the features associated with the two independent variables are combined in a multiplicative rather than additive or other fashion (see Massaro & Cohen, 1976; Oden, 1977) for each of the candidate phonemes.

The multiplicative combination rule has an appealing property not given by the additive rule. In the additive rule, a feature carries the same weight regardless of its value or the value of other features. The multiplicative rule, on the other hand, allows the least ambiguous feature to carry more weight with respect to the final truth value (see Massaro & Cohen, 1976).

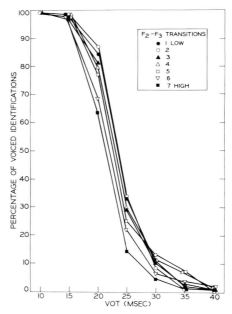

FIGURE 4   *Percentage of voiced identifications (/bæ / or /dæ /) as a function of VOT; the level of F2-F3 transitions is the curve parameter.*

Although the multiplicative combination rule does a better job than the additive rule, something in addition to a simple multiplication of the acoustic features of VOT and F2-F3 onsets must be involved. The simple model given by Equations 16 and 17 predicts straight lines when the abscissa is spaced in the manner of Figure

3. To better evaluate how the results deviate from the predictions of the simple fuzzy logical model, the responses can be replotted in terms of the percentage of voiced identifications on the one hand, and the percentage of labial identifications on the other.

Figure 4 presents the percentage of times the stimuli were identified to be voiced phonemes (/bæ/ or /dæ/) plotted as a function of VOT; F2-F3 transitions is the curve parameter. The results show that VOT is a sufficient cue for voicing; the data go from completely voiced at a 10 msec VOT to completely voiceless at a 40 msec VOT. Phoneme identifications were most ambiguous with respect to voicing at the 20 and 25 msec VOTs. Although VOT was a sufficient cue to voicing, Figure 4 shows that F2-F3 transitions also had a consistent influence on voicing: the percentage of voiced phoneme identifications increased as the onset frequencies of the F2-F3 transitions decreased. This result contrasts with our previous finding of no voicing boundary shift (Oden & Massaro, 1978) or the findings that the voicing boundary is at shorter values of VOT for labial stops than it is for alveolar stops (Lisker & Abramson, 1970; Miller, 1977)

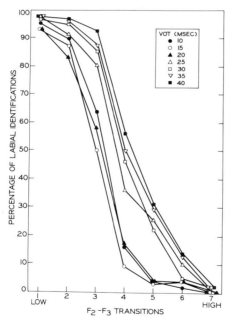

FIGURE 5   *Percentage of labial identifications (/pæ/ or /bæ/) as a function of F2-F3 transitions; VOT is the curve parameter.*

Figure 5 presents the percentage of times the stimuli were identified to be labial phonemes (/bæ/ or /pæ/) as a function of the F2-F3 transitions; VOT is the curve parameter. Replicating previous findings, phoneme identification with respect to place changed from labial to alveolar with increases in the onset frequencies of the F2-F3 transitions. Sounds with low F2-F3 onset frequencies were consistently heard as labial phonemes whereas those with high frequencies were heard as alveolar phonemes. Intermediate frequencies gave more ambiguous identifications. Although the F2-F3 transitions were sufficient cues to place, VOT also had a relatively large influence on place, especially at the intermediate levels of the F2-F3 transitions. Decreasing the VOT decreased the likelihood of a labial identification. The place boundary was at level 3 of the F2-F3 transitions for a VOT of 15 msec whereas it was at level 4 for a VOT of 35 msec. The decrease in the percentage of labial identifications with decreases in VOT was highly consistent except for an inversion with VOT of 10 msec. This general result agrees with those of Miller (1977b) and Repp (1977). Any possible explanations for the reversal at a VOT of 10 msec is secondary to the more important issue of the independence of labial identifications on VOT.

When the identification of a speech dimension such as voicing is also dependent on an acoustic feature for another dimension such as place, we called the outcome a boundary shift. That is to say, the transition from voiced to voiceless identifications as a function of VOT is shifted by the values of the F2-F3 onsets. We have distinguished three alternative explanations for the boundary shifts that have been observed. Although we are focusing on a specific result, the experiments have the promise of illuminating general processes in featural evaluation and integration in pattern recognition. The three explanations are (1) non-independence of feature evaluation, (2) multiple features, and (3) modifiers in long-term memory prototypes.

Feature Nonindependence   One possible type of feature nonindependence is that there are complex low-level auditory interactions so that, for example, the perceptual realization of VOT is modified by the F2-F3 transition frequencies. Analogously, the perceptual realization of the F2-F3 transitions could be modified by VOT. According to this view, VOT and F2-F3 transitions maintain their role as primary cues for voicing and place respectively, but the value of each acoustic cue is dependent on the stimulus value of the other. As an example of such an interaction in nonspeech stimuli, changing the perceived hue of a color from green to blue by changing the wavelength also changes the perceived brightness since we are less sensitive to wave-lengths in the blue than in the green part of the visible spectrum. An experiment in color perception which would be analogous to the present studies would independently vary the wavelength and intensity of the color and the results would presumably show that wavelength not only influences the perception of hue but also the perception of brightness.

Multiple Features   Tne second possible explanation for the boundary shifts is that changes in a single stimulus dimension may change more than one acoustic feature. Since any manipulation of an arbitrarily defined stimulus dimension will also produce changes along other dimensions, it may be that some of the co-varying changes are other acoustic features. When a given acoustic characteristic functions primarily as an acoustic feature for one distinction but also cues a second distinction, it is called a multiple feature. For example, increasing VOT not only increases the time between burst onset and vocal-chord vibration onset but also increases the total amount of aspiration noise. The quality of the aspiration may function as an independent acoustic feature for place of articulation. It is possible that the aspiration during the VOT period of most synthetic speech without bursts is more representative of the burst and aspiration of a voiceless labial (/p/) than a voicelss alveolar (/t/). The spectrograms in Figures 6 and 7 show that the aspiration during the VOT of our synthetic speech were more representative of the burst and aspiration of a natural /p/ than of a natural /t/. If this were the case, longer VOTs would have produced more aspiration which would have produced a more labial sound.

In terms of the formal model of Oden and Massaro (1978), both the F2-F3 transitions and the degree of aspiration during the VOT period contribute to perception of the place distinction. In this case, the prototype for /t/ would be defined as:

T:[NOT(aspiration)] and [high F2-F3 onsets] and [NOT(short VOT)]   (18)

where /t/ is now characterized by not having low-frequency aspiration.

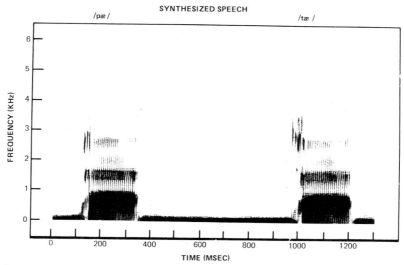

FIGURE 6   *Spectrograms of two synthesized speech sounds from the present Experiment 1.*

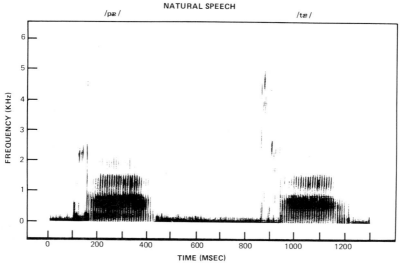

FIGURE 7   *Spectrograms of two naturally occurring speech sounds.*

Prototype Modifiers The third explanation of the boundary shifts is that the prototypes of the speech sounds in long-term memory include modifiers of the featural information. Rather than defining / t æ / as

$$/ \text{t æ} / : \text{(long VOT) and (high F2-F3 onsets)} \tag{19}$$

it could be assumed that /tae/ requires relatively extreme values of F2-F3 onsets

$$/ \text{t æ} / : \text{(long VOT) and quite (high F2-F3 onsets)} \tag{20}$$

where the modifier "quite" expresses the extremity of this feature in the prototype.

The central assumption of this explanation is that more extreme values of features are required for some phonemes. One way for this to come about could be through listener's experience with natural speech. For example, Fant (1973, Chapter 11) points out that, with most vowels, the locus of F2 at the instant of release is higher for /t/ than it is for /d/. Thus, since a high F2-locus is a cue to alveolarity, it would be reasonable for listeners to expect /t/ to be more strongly alveolar relative to /d/. If listeners use this information, then for a given level of F2-F3 transitions, they should make fewer /t/ identifications than they would if they did not have this expectation of higher F2 values for /t/. Producing fewer /t/ responses would mean that the place boundary would be shifted toward the alveolar end when the speech sounds are voiceless. This is exactly the result that was obtained in Figure 5.

The model has been developed and utilized to provide a framework for research in the identification of speech sounds varying on two or more dimensions. The model can also be extended to include other theoretical and empirical issues in speech perception research. In addition to a treatment of other multifactor experiments in speech, extensions of the model allow an account of auditory context effects, higher-order context effects, and normalization in speech perception. Auditory context sometimes produces contrast as in selective adaptation and anchor effects. Higher-order context is effective when information at a higher (more abstract) level influences lower-level decisions. Finally, normalization refers to the relative nature of featural information.

Summary In summary, we believe that the present framework offers a productive approach to the study of acoustic features in speech perception. Factorial designs have shown that a simple identification task of sounds differing on just a few dimensions produces relatively complex results. The results reject the idea of all-or-none binary features and, in addition, show that a single acoustic feature for a given articulatory distinction is probably not adequate. Furthermore, it seems likely that prototypes are defined in a more complex manner than might be expected from the binary assumption of linguistic features. We have not yet determined whether the descriptions of prototype speech sounds are relatively flexible and modifiable. Although other important issues remain unresolved, the present framework appears to offer a formal theoretical and empirical approach to the study of these issues.

Discussion

Albert S. Bregman We are faced with two questions: (1) What is the nature of the units (or schemas) that are used by the brain to analyze and represent speech; and (2) What is the nature of auditory memory? While these two questions may be stated separately, they are intimately connected.

Suppose, for example, that the recognition process employs "concepts" at various levels of abstraction operating at the same time and trying, as it were, to instantiate themselves in the mental representation of the signal. Each one would represent a regularity encountered in speech. Such regularities as the existence of independent acoustic streams, phones, phonemes, and phonetic transitions all the way up to words, syntactic forms, stress patterns, semantic concepts and emotional forms would be looked for simultaneously in the signal. Records of the actual or possible existence of each of these patterns would have to be held, for a greater or lesser time, by the brain. If recognition worked like this, our problem as memory theorists would be to conceive of a memory system which could hold all these concepts in registration with one another. I mean that each "concept" or "regularity processor" in such a system must know which piece of signal it encodes so that it can collaborate smoothly with other concepts to converge on the best description of the signal. Constraints must be free to run up, down and across the levels of the describing process. If, for example, a syllable is to be interpreted as belonging to a word in which that syllable is lexically unstressed, then the rise in intensity found in that syllable can be used to support a description involving a semantic stress. If, on the other hand, semantic stress is inconsistent with prior context, the data about increased intensity in the signal may be used to constrain the perceptual "choice" of lexical elements. Such a system requires a tight temporal coupling between descriptions at all levels and argues against separate "memory units" of the type employed by present-day computers.

A separate point I wish to make is that experimental efforts to divide memory into subsystems, each with a characteristic rate of decay, is made extremely difficult to interpret by the fact that one measure may show information to be absent while another demonstrates its presence. Kubovy and Howard have, for example, shown that when faced with a group of tones emanating simultaneously from different positions, a person cannot report anything but noise. Yet when perceptual sensitivity to movement of single components is used as a test, the listener demonstrates that information has been stored about the position of each tone. I conclude that a variety of measurement paradigms must be used to establish a decay rate for any proposed type of memory. Otherwise we are demonstrating only the presence or absence of *access* to the information by some particular response process.

Andrew A. Ellis It is possible, I believe, to discuss speech perception sensibly within a "dual-route" model of a sort familiar in the literature on visual rather than auditory word recognition. The model (Fig. 1) proposes that phonemes have psychological reality in speech production where they may be stored within a phonemic Response Buffer (Ellis, 1979), but that in normal speech perception, words may be accessed in the lexicon by a nonsegmental spectral analysis of the acoustic stimulus (Klatt, this volume). In such cases, phoneme identification will be post-lexical (Nooteboom, this volume). However, as Studdert-Kennedy (this volume) has reminded us, listeners possess the ability to mimic new words or nonwords, thus achieving a nonlexical acoustic-to-articulatory conversion. (Note that some acoustic analysis must, presumably, be common to both lexical and nonlexical routes).

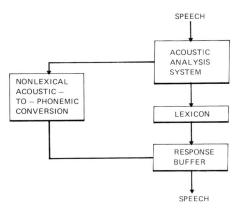

FIGURE 1   *'Dual-route' model of speech processing*

In many of the experiments reported here by Crowder and by Massaro, subjects are required to process nonword stimuli. In such experiments, subjects must initially resort to the nonlexical route if a spoken response or phonemic judgment is required, though it is possible that if particular stimuli are repeatedly presented, then lexical units will be set up to accommodate them. To the extent that auditory phenomena such as categorical perception, masking or contrast hold for both words and novel nonwords, they must be attributable to the common Acoustic Analysis System; to the extent that they are specific to either words or novel nonwords, then they must reflect properties unique to the lexical or nonlexical routes respectively.

Hiroya Fujisaki   Fujisaki and Kawashima (1968) showed experimentally that the so-called categorical and continuous modes of speech perception are not necessarily dichotomous, as originally suggested by Fry et al., (1962).

It was evident from the findings of Liberman et al. (1957) that the apparent non-uniformity of discriminability, along an acoustic continuum encompassing two or more adjacent phoneme regions, could not be explained on the basis of auditory information alone (i.e., an all-auditory model cannot explain the phenomenon). At the same time, the results of these and other studies could not be explained merely on the basis of phonemic information alone (i.e., an all-phonetic model also cannot explain the phenomenon). It was on the basis of these findings that Fujisaki and Kawashima (1970) proposed a model for the information processing conducted by a subject in the task of discrimination. The model assumes that both auditory and phonemic short-term memories are involved. The model has been referred to as the ''dual-coding model.''

Fujisaki and Kawashima (1971) further elaborated their model on the basis of a more rigorous formulation of various psychophysical factors involved, and showed that the decision noise (long-term random fluctuations of criteria for phoneme identification) and the memory noise (represented by short-term random disturbances to the signal retrieved from the short-term memory of timbre) are the dominant factors that give rise to the apparent enhancement of discriminability across a phoneme boundary. Their work also showed that, even within the framework of the "dual-coding model," the predicted performance could vary to a great extent depending on the assumptions made with respect to statistical properties of various noise sources contained in the model.

Crowder's criticism (also Repp et al., 1979) against the dual-coding model is based on the assertion that the discrimination performance can be predicted from the in-context performance equally well both in the case of short, unfilled interstimulus intervals and in the case of long, filled inter-stimulus intervals. However, the results shown in his paper do not justify rejection of the dual-coding model. For example, the agreement between measured and predicted values, which he claims to be excellent, is not good enough to support his strong conclusion.

Crowder also suggests various alternatives such as the all-auditory model, the all-phonetic model, and the mixed model (Repp et al. 1979). No quantitative formulations, however, are presented to allow comparison of their characteristics with those of the dual-coding model. Moreover, it is apparent that neither the all-auditory nor the all-phonetic model can explain the phenomenon. A mixed model, when it is more clearly formulated, will be quite similar to the dual-coding model which he denounces.

In spite of the criticism by Crowder, therefore, I believe that only the dual-coding model can give a plausible explanation of the categorical effect in discrimination.

Concerning Massaro's paper: It is true that linguistic performances such as phoneme identification, etc., can more sensibly be formulated on the perceptual continuum rather than on the physical/acoustic continuum. In order to construct such a perceptual space, however, the techniques adopted by Massaro may not necessarily be optimal. One may have to use, for instance, techniques of multi-dimensional scaling for a more rigorous derivation of the perceptual (feature) space.

Quentin Summerfield   Dominique Massaro's account of phonetic perception is a member of a class which posits an initial fractionation of the speech signal into elemental cues whose integration permits a phonetic decision. It is important to note that such accounts are based on a fundamental assumption. Our only definition of an acoustic cue is the operational pronouncement that a cue is a physical parameter of a speech signal whose manipulation can systematically influence the phonetic interpretation of the signal; it is an act of faith to ascribe to a cue the functional status of an ingredient in a perceptual process. However, if that assumption is allowed, such accounts must then resolve two problems. The first stems from the diversity of types of cue that are found to pertain to a single phonetic distinction; for stop voicing in initial position, for instance, increases in either the intensity of the release burst, the duration of the aspiration, or the frequency of the first formant at the onset of periodicity, amongst other parameters, all increase the likelihood of a voiceless percept. If these diverse measures are to be integrated, a common metric must be found in which they can be expressed. The second problem concerns the knowledge that a perceptual system must possess to be capable of appropriately integrating these measures. Successful integration requires a knowledge of the inter-relationships among the cues. Massaro resolves the first problem by converting the outputs of acoustic feature (cue)-detectors to probabilities. The second problem is overcome by expressing a knowledge of the interrelationships of the cues both in rules that combine the probabilistic outputs of feature-detectors and also in the specifications of canonical prototypes. These solutions allow the model to predict the observable consequences of manipulating acoustic cues but clearly do not rationalise them. That is so because the interrelationships among cues are not arbitrary. As perceivers, we are sensitive to precisely those acoustic variables that differentiate productions of phonetic categories, and, where trading relationships are observed to occur between cues in perceptual experiments, they can generally be related to similar relationships that occur in production. These observations have led some to suggest that the acoustics of speech are perceived as if the perceiver possessed a knowledge of how articulation structures sound. Results of experiments on audio-visual speech perception require that statement to be extended to include a knowledge of how articulation structures light. Herein, then, lies a paradox. For many forms of perception, including phonetic perception, feature-based accounts have been proposed because, while there is no apparent isomorphism between signal and percept, it is thought that features of the signal are more nearly invariant and can, therefore, serve as the detectable primitives for perception. Yet, the successful integration of these features appears to require mapping rules embodying a knowledge of precisely those higher-order constraints that we believe we cannot detect in the signal itself. Therefore, it is incumbent upon those who propose that phonetic perception entails the fractionation and integration of acoustic cues to explain how, either in ontogeny or evolution, perceivers have acquired the knowledge of articulatory constraints that is embodied in the mapping rules and in the specification of canonical prototypes. Without an answer to this question, an alternative expression of the information for phonetic perception should be sought, one that differs from the current inventory of acoustic cues and captures the commonality of structure that articulation imposes on both light and sound.

Chairman's Comments

Anne Treisman: Auditory Memory and Categorical Perception of Speech The aim of speech perception research is to account for the conversion of complex patterns of sound to the meanings and intention of the speaker. Two central questions which arise are the means by which we transform a linear, temporal sequence of sounds into an atemporal, probably hierarchical, linguistic structure, and the nature of the intermediate representations or stages of processing. Decisions about the syntax, meaning and prosody of whole phrases or clauses may require information to be stored and to be simultaneously available until the sequence is complete. The nature of the store (or stores) which makes these decisions possible is one of the main issues of concern in this symposium. The other, closely related question concerns the psychological reality of a level of representation at which the acoustic spectra are mapped into discrete phonetic features, which in turn are recombined into syllables and/or lexical entries.

Studies of short term verbal recall led to the theoretical separation of a pre-categorical and a post-categorical store, the former holding a temporary auditory record of the items to be recalled and the latter holding their perceived identities. Crowder elaborates this model to accommodate both the suffix effects in list recall and his new data on categorical perception and contrast effects with pairs of syllables. His auditory store holds only crude, spectral information. Its functions are to retain the speech sounds while they are categorized, and perhaps also to hold the auditory patterns which carry prosodic information. Its characteristics reflect these functions. For example, the decay time, of the order of three seconds, seems well adapted to holding stress and intonation for whole clauses or short sentences.

Bregman raises important but generally neglected questions about the relation of methodology to inference in the study of short term memory. For example, does the evidence for different pre- and post-categorical stores simply reflect different methods of accessing a single stored representation? If there are multiple stores for the different levels of representation (acoustic, phonetic and linguistic), how are they kept in temporal register so that we can integrate relevant information from each as required? We need converging evidence to justify the separation and concretisation of more than one store in models of speech perception. It is important, for example, that the precategorical store derived by Crowder and Morton (1969) from recency and suffix effects in list recall appears congruent in its properties with that inferred from the successive matching and identification of spoken syllables. It would add to our confidence if these properties also matched those of the buffer store in selective listening, which mediates the retrieval of initially unattended, and therefore precategorical, messages (e.g., Broadbent, 1958; Treisman, 1964; Parkinson & Hubbard, 1974). Agreement with the selective listening results is in fact quite good: the decay time for unattended words appears to be around 2 to 5 seconds (Treisman, 1964; Glucksberg and Cowan, 1970); retrieval from the unattended store is damaged in the same way by an irrelevant suffix (Parkinson & Hubbard, 1974); finally interference in both stores depends more on physical parameters (input channel) than on semantic ones. The early models put forward by Broadbent (1958) and by Crowder and Morton (1969) in fact ruled out the possibility that the two stores could be the same. Broadbent's 's' system preceded the selective filter, while Crowder and Morton's P.A.S. presumably followed it, since the reduction in interference from a suffix on a different input channel was explained by selective attention to the relevant channel only. However, Crowder now explains the reduced interference between items on different input channels by the suggestion that their representations are separated in the auditory store.

Crowder makes some further interesting suggestions about the structure of the auditory store. His model attributes both suffix interference in list recall, and contrast effects in the labelling of successive speech sounds, to a form of lateral inhibition between items which are temporally adjacent and on the same or neighbouring input channels. At this point his paper takes up another important issue in speech perception, relating to the existence of specialized feature detectors for phonetic categories. Shifts in phonetic boundaries resulting from selective adaptation offered some of the strongest support for the psychological reality of phonetic feature detectors. Thus Crowder's claim that selective adaptation may actually reflect not fatigue of specialized detectors but contrast effects due to lateral inhibition is both interesting and important. In discussion, Warren suggested that one explanation of the perceived contrast with isolated vowels might be the absence of the expected assimilation between adjacent sounds, which, in natural speech, results from co-articulation. Conversely, perhaps, one could argue that one function of contrast in the auditory store, if it occurs, might be to counteract the normal assimilation and sharpen the blurred differences between adjacent sounds.

An alternative account of Crowder's data may, however, be worth considering. Crowder presents two vowels, separated by a short or a long interval, and asks for both discrimination ("same-different") judgements and labelling responses to the same stimuli. At the short interval as well as the long, he finds 'categorical perception', in the sense that discrimination is hardly better than would be predicted from the labelling results. However, it is worth noting that (a) the predictions from labelling performance are much better in this condition than in the usual, single item labelling paradigm; (b) subjects could in fact be making relative rather than absolute judgements in the labelling as well as in the discrimination task. Thus, they might detect a difference between the two vowels and consequently label them differently, rather than, as Crowder suggests, labelling them differently and from the labels deriving a response of 'different' in the discrimination task. The change to relative from absolute judgements for the identification task would explain both the high level of performance on identification and its similarity to the discrimination results. The same account can be given of the study by Diehl, Elman and McCusker (1978).

If we accept this argument, it is no longer clear what is meant by contrast. The sounds in auditory memory could be quite unchanged by lateral inhibition; detection of differences between them may be much improved when both are present, simply because a relative judgement is possible, and relative judgements are consistently better than absolute judgements. When a difference *is* detected, subjects are more inclined to use different labels for the different sounds. On this view, we retain the idea that auditory memory holds a precategorical representation of speech sounds, but we no longer need to postulate frequency-specific lateral inhibition. Furthermore it may be premature to conclude that vowels are perceived categorically, that auditory memory plays no part in phoneme discrimination beyond inducing contextual contrasts, and that selective adaptation effects tell us nothing about the existence of specialized phonological feature detectors. There might have been other problems in accounting for *all* the selective adaptation findings in terms of contrast or lateral inhibition. Those experiments in which the adapting stimulus and the tested stimulus had nothing in common other than the phonetic feature on which they converged (e.g., Diehl, 1975) could not be explained by inhibition between spectrally overlapping auditory traces. There may, of course, be more than one level of feature detectors which are adapted by a repeated syllable. This means that evidence *for* an acoustic component in the adaptation effects (e.g., Tartter and Eimas, 1975) cannot count as evidence *against* the existence, in addition, of purely phonetic detectors; on the other hand evidence which cannot be explained acoustically is strong support for a level of phonetic feature analysis.

Some scepticism was expressed at the conference about the existence of such feature detectors. An alternative account assumes direct translation from sound spectra into lexical entries (e.g., Klatt, this volume). Ellis combines the two views in a dual access model, analogous to that proposed for reading (Coltheart, Davelaar, Jonasson and Besner, 1977). In normal speech perception, Ellis suggests the phonological level is bypassed; however, it can be used when we identify non-words or new words. He illustrated his claim with an example where the two routes give different outputs ('bamfer' out of context becomes 'banned for' in a sentence whose syntax and meaning constrain the lexical choices available). I wonder if this evidence for dual access is not equally well explained as a shift in the weight given to the top-down and bottom-up routes to speech perception. When no context is available, perception is determined entirely by the best fitting phonological match to the acoustic signal, whether it forms a word or not; in context, the constraints of meaning and syntax converge on candidate words in the lexicon, from which the phonological input selects the best match. The change may not be a switch of routes but a change in the balance of information from the context and from the physical signal.

Traditionally in speech research a link has been assumed between the finding of categorical perception and the inference of specialized phonetic detectors for speech sounds. Doubts about the link have been raised by the finding of categorical perception both for some non-speech sounds (e.g. Cutting & Rosner, 1974) and in non-human species (e.g. Morse & Snowden, 1975). Massaro's data reinforce these doubts by demonstrating the availability of continuous information about normally categorical speech sounds. However, his theory retains the idea of specialized feature detectors, and suggests how the graded information they register might be combined. His suggestion that fuzzy predicates specify the degree to which a particular sound instantiates a particular feature, offers a fruitful resolution of the apparent conflict between categorical judgements (the final decisions about the phoneme are categorical) and the availability of graded or probabilistic cues to those phonemes. Phonetic detectors would collect and keep available graded evidence from acoustic cues, and also pass it on to the prototypes for words or syllables to determine their particular categorical decision of presence or absence. The feature detectors themselves need not give a categorical output, although the range of continuous variation that they can signal may differ for different features (e.g., typically it is greater for vowels than for stop consonants).

In order to show, as Ellis claims, that a phonological representation is formed in one case and not the other, we would need converging diagnostics to characterize phonetic feature analysis. These are unfortunately hard to document. One piece of evidence which offers strong support for the psychological reality of features is the occurrence of errors in the form of illusory interchanges or recombinations of features (Treisman, 1979). These illusory conjunctions seem to occur primarily when attention is overloaded. Thus when two syllables are presented dichotically, subjects may report a new syllable which wrongly combines a feature from the syllable on one ear with the features of the syllable on the other ear (Studdert-Kennedy and Shankweiler, 1970; Cutting, 1976). 'Pa' and 'da' may interchange the features of place and voicing to give 'ba' and/or 'ta'. The fact that these interchanges occur at all seems good evidence that the features which wrongly recombine are initially registered as separate entities. Cross-series selective adaptation, particularly when the acoustic cues differ in adapting and test stimulus, is also important support for feature analysis, as mentioned earlier. Finally, the correlations between confusion errors (Miller, Heise and Lichten, 1951) or the detection of mispronunciations (Cole, 1973) and the number of shared features in the correct and erroneous items are consistent, though perhaps less compelling, arguments for a phonological representation.

The phonetic feature model is not without its problems, however. The complex context dependencies and trading relations shown for example, in the 'gray ship/ great ship' distinction (Repp, Liberman, Eccardt and Pesetzky, 1978) and the contingencies in selective adaptation between feature and source (Ades, 1977b) raise the spectre of an infinite multiplication of features to fit all possible contexts and contingencies. Massaro is well aware of these problems and adopts what I think is the most defensible solution. Instead of multiplying feature detectors, he introduces flexibility at a later stage in the prototypes against which the features are matched to mediate a decision about the word or syllable presented. Thus a wide variety of specific conjunctive or disjunctive sets of features, with different weightings and trading relations, can be selected as criterial for the detection of particular words in particular contexts, allowing the retention of a limited and manageable set of feature detectors at an earlier level. It is true that a large burden of explanation then migrates to this flexible decision level; however this burden seems no less daunting for models which reject a level of phonetic feature analysis. The use of measures from signal detection theory may help distinguish the top-down changes in decision criteria from changes in detectability at the feature level, such as those which Crowder attributes to contrast and lateral inhibition.

THE COGNITIVE REPRESENTATION OF SPEECH
T. Myers, J. Laver, J. Anderson (editors)
© North-Holland Publishing Company, 1981

Lexical Processing during Sentence Comprehension: Effects of Higher Order Constraints and Implications for Representation

DAVID A. SWINNEY

Tufts University

A fundamental problem in language comprehension is to obtain an accurate characterization of lexical processing and of the influence of contextual information upon that processing. This paper will examine evidence concerning the effects of so-called 'higher-order' constraints upon the various stages of lexical processing and will outline a model of the representation and processing of lexical material during sentence comprehension.

The conclusions that will result from this examination derive from a particular point of view about the general nature of cognitive processing and mental representation. Thus, some prelimary discussion of this view is important. In particular, I will take it as a basic tenet that questions of representation about speech and language can only be sensibly discussed in the context of a well defined performance model. In order to make meaningful (and testable) statements about the nature of representation in language, and to evaluate the relative role of the various representational 'facts' that have been garnered from theoretical linguistics and experimental psycholinguistics, the assumptions about the processes operating on those representations must be detailed. This position is certainly not novel to psycholinguistic inquiry. However, it appears to be overlooked far too often.

Thus, in order to begin at least a partial list of such assumptions, it can be noted that the domain of interest in this paper is that which I will call 'normal sentence comprehension'. This is intended to include those situations in which at least the following conditions prevail:

1. The materials of interest (words) do not occur in isolation, but are part of structured, fluent, utterances in which the goal of the listener is to understand the utterance.
2. The computation of a number of different types of linguistic information takes place (in either serial or parallel mode) during sentence comprehension. Among these informational types is (at least) acoustic, morpho-phonemic, lexical, syntactic, and semantic information. (No claims of independence or interactivity are being posited here.)
3. The speech signal is relatively intact and accessible despite a certain amount of noise in the signal. This is taken to be the most common situation in sentence comprehension even though it clearly does not always hold.

A brief discussion of the motivation behind these points may be helpful. It is reasonable to assume that the cognitive operations involved in different task situations will, themselves, differ. While some underlying operations are undoubtedly shared across different performance situations, it is not a trivial chore to determine which of the inferences that we make about cognitive processes are best attributable to 'underlying' representations and operations and which are attributable to superficial or task-related operations. Results from certain task situations may reflect more of how subjects *can* perform given certain requirements, than of what subjects normally do during language comprehension. Obviously, when sufficient evidence from different 'task' sources coincide, we have the basis for arguments about underlying representations. However, that situation is rare. Thus, because the task a subject sees himself as having — the *query* he poses to his/her cognitive system — may determine much of the cognitive strategies employed in that situation, a conservative position will be adopted here: we will not examine data about 'isolated' lexical tasks (such as isolated lexical decisions, same-different judgements to word pairs, category inclusion/exclusion decisions on single words) except when no other data is available. In doing so, some relevant evidence will undoubtedly be overlooked, but the model we sketch will also not be forced to account for irrelevant or inappropriate data.

The assumption that different types of information are generated *during* sentence comprehension follows at least in part from the extensive documentation of the existence, at some level, of these informational types (see, e.g. Fodor, Bever, and Garrett, 1974). Because the purpose of this paper is to examine evidence about effects of the "higher-level" information on lexical processing, no constraints on the availability of such information at any point in the processing scheme are being presupposed. (Note that this position is not always held in the literature; see Marslen-Wilson (1976) for a presentation of the arguments.)

Finally, the degree to which the signal is available for 'bottom-up' analysis deserves brief discussion. While much research exists on the conditions in which sufficient 'bottom-up' information is not available to provide unique identification for speech sounds or words, it is arguably the case that an adequate signal is available more often than not. Further, it is only in the presence of an adequate and available signal that the underlying roles of higher order information and bottom-up analysis can be examined definitively; if 'top down' information is only shown to operate following the failure of a 'bottom-up' analysis (due to insufficient low level information) then arguments for the predictivity of top down constraints are weak indeed. To follow this point a bit further, a number of the more important studies which have supported 'top down' constraints on processing (e.g., Marslen-Wilson and Welsh, 1978; Cole, 1973) have utilized tasks which encourage (and often require) these top-down processes to operate. While no one denies that such knowledge sources can have effects on interpretation, these tasks may not actually examine the normal comprehension process, and thus the value of these results to the issue at hand is uncertain.

Before turning to the evidence about lexical processing and processing constraints, it will be worthwhile to briefly consider some points about the general nature of lexical representation. The mental lexicon has been the major focus for theory and research about context effects (the interaction of higher and lower informational types) precisely because the representation for a word must contain 'low level' form (acoustic, phonetic) information, as well as 'high level' syntactic (distributional) and semantic (meaning) information (see, e.g., Garrett, 1978; Foss, In press; Marslen-Wilson & Welsh, 1978). Because these informational types are represented in some (presumably common) code for each word, it has been natural to posit the lexicon as the major point of interaction for these various information types. Whatever the nature of this interaction, it is almost universally assumed that there are identifiable 'stages' (or, depending on your theorist, 'systems' or 'levels' or 'modules') in sentence processing. One of the goals of this paper is, then, to attempt to establish the relative independence or interactivity of each of these stages. Such stages need not only distinguish the major informational types, but may also constitute definable processing subsystems within each informational level. We will examine the manner in which three such subsystems of lexical processing are constrained by higher order information: The process by which lexical candidates are segmented from (isolated in) the speech stream, the process by which lexical information is accessed, and the post-access processes which may be involved, for example, in the insertion of accessed lexical information into "higher" levels of sentence analysis. While different theorists have argued that these lexical processes operate on a number of different 'lower order' bases (such as the acoustic, **phonetic, phonological, or syllabic form of the word; see, e.g., Klatt, this volume; Foss, in press; Liberman and Studdert-Kennedy, 1978; Pisoni, 1978)**, any and all of these characterizations are sufficient to support the representations and operations that will be discussed. Thus, as questions about the nature of this base are neutral with respect to what follows, they will be largely ignored.

DEVELOPING THE MODEL

Overall, it is undeniable that higher order information exerts some effect on lexical interpretation; evidence abounds that semantic and syntactic information interacts with lexical processing. The question is one of where and how such information exerts its influence on lexical interpretation. There are two general (and extreme) models of this process — each with a large number of variations in the literature. One can be called the Contextually Predictive model and the other the Contextually Independent model. The Contextually Predictive model holds that higher order information acts to direct lexical processing. In the strong (and perhaps most common) version of this model, contextual information is used to predict subsequent information and, by doing so, to constrain and direct all stages of lexical processing. This is, then, a maximally interactive model in which semantic and syntactic information can each act to short-cut reliance on form alone in the retrieval and use of lexical information. The Contextually Independent model, on the other hand, holds that higher order constraints do not exist on all stages of lexical processing. Such constraints are seen as acting only on the output of the lexical retrieval process, following access. Thus, segmentation and access are viewed as independent and isolable subsystems that operate solely based on lower level information.

Examinations of the various forms of these models come from a number of sources. In the sentence comprehension domain, however, the overwhelming proportion of the evidence comes from studies which have examined the effects of contexts upon the interpretation of polysemous words (usually unsystematic lexical homographs/homophones). The reasons for this are straightforward. The meanings of lexical ambiguities can be differentiated rather easily, and thus the selective effects of higher order contextual constraints upon the functional activation of these meanings are relatively available to empirical examination. Further, not only are lexical ambiguities arguably as common as unambiguous words in language use, but nearly all words exhibit some type of indeterminancy in characterizations of their meanings anyway. Thus ambiguous words provide a useful and well founded vehicle for examining the effects of context upon lexical processing. Given a sufficiently sensitive task, one should be able to determine whether strongly predictive (higher order) contexts constrain the various stages of lexical processing by examining which meanings of the ambiguities are functional in the presence of these contexts.

LEXICAL ACCESS

The evidence from the large body of work in this area can be organized into a relatively coherent story. First, in the absence of any strongly biasing context it appears that all meanings of a lexical ambiguity are accessed. Such access is not available to conscious introspection and (typically) the listener eventually becomes aware of only one of the several meanings that was accessed for the ambiguity. More importantly, even in the presence of prior constraining semantic and syntactic contexts (contexts which strongly bias interpretation of the word toward just one of its meanings) all interpretations for an ambiguous word are accessed during sentence comprehension.

Most of the studies in this area have examined the effects of semantic contexts, and the majority of these have utilized the so-called 'ambiguity effect' in their investigations. The principle behind this effect is that the presence of a lexically ambiguous word causes increased processing difficulty (when compared to an unambiguous word) in sentence comprehension. The presence or absence of this 'effect' is thus taken as an indication of whether context is simplifying the access process. Use of the ambiguity effect has occurred in a number of experimental paradigms. Holmes, Arwas and Garrett (1977), for example, demonstrated that time to classify a sentence as meaningful is increased by the presence of a lexical ambiguity and, also, that the number of words recalled in a rapid serial visual presentation task is fewer in the presence of an ambiguity. Chodorow (1979) has shown that recall of materal under compressed speech presentation is poorer when lexical ambiguities are present. MacKay (1974) demonstrated that the presence of ambiguous words in sentence fragments causes sentence completion times to be slower. Foss and his colleagues (Foss, 1970; Foss and Jenkins, 1973; Cutler and Foss, Note 1) as well as Cairns and Kamerman (1975) and Cairns and Hsu (1979) have demonstrated that monitoring for a phoneme takes longer following an ambiguous word, even in the presence of a prior, biasing context.[1]

In addition to this work (which, overall, has argued in favor of the Contextually Independent model largely by virtue of failing to discover reductions in the 'ambiguity effect' in the presence of biasing semantic contexts) there is work that has reflected the access and activation of the several meanings of an ambiguity somewhat more directly. Lackner and Garrett (1972) provided such evidence using a task which combined dichotic presentation of sentences and a shadowing/paraphrasing task. Conrad (1974) also provided such evidence using a modified stroop task. She found interference for words related to each meaning of an ambiguity that appeared at the end of a sentence containing a biased semantic context. Similarly, Swinney (in press) and Swinney, Onifer and Hirshkowitz (Note 2) found that, even in the presence of strongly biasing semantic contexts, lexical decisions to visually presented words which were related to *each* meaning of an ambiguity were facilitated when presented immediately after the ambiguity was heard. Thus, in summary, there is a fair amount of evidence which argues that even in the presence of prior, strongly biasing, semantic contexts all meanings of an ambiguity are accessed, at least momentarily, during sentence comprehension.

Before examining this evidence in more detail, it is important to reconsider a methodological concern that was raised earlier. While we might hope that the tasks mentioned above (phoneme monitoring, paraphrasing, semantic priming, stroop interference, lexical decision and sentence completion) all reflect the same under-lying lexical (access) process, that assumption must be carefully examined because **each task clearly adds its own set of required strategies to those needed for sentence** comprehension. And, in addition, the tasks may be differentially sensitive to the lexical access process. While it is clear that we cannot have the ideal situation — one in which the task would add none of its characteristics to the basic sentence comprehension operation and would also be maximally sensitive to underlying processes — some of the tasks that have been used appear to approach that ideal more closely than others. One relevant factor appears to be the relative point of application of the experimental task to the comprehension process. Experimental techniques which examine lexical processing only following comprehension of the sentence containing the word of interest (such as occurs in some recall, paraphrase, and sentence classification tasks) appear to reflect different aspects of lexical processing than do tasks which occur temporally close to the critical word during comprehension of the sentence (such as in phoneme monitoring, lexical priming, and certain click detection and error detection tasks). Garrett (1970) was the first to point out this fact, and many others have since demonstrated its essential truth (see, e.g., Foss, 1970; Forster, 1979; Cutler and Norris, 1979, for discussion.). In all, it appears that the on-line or 'perceptual' tasks more accurately reflect the nature of the processes used to gain access to the representation of lexical items, and that the other 'post-perceptual' tasks appear to reflect only the final outcome of such processes. Another methodological concern is the degree to which subjects are presented with *predictable* experimental situations which allow and encourage the development of specialized processing strategies that may affect (change) the processes under investigation. In general, it is obvious that the less any experimental task permits such special strategies to develop, the more certain one can be that it is a 'normal', basic, process reflected in the data obtained with that task.

The point of this discussion is that a number of reviews exist which indict many of the experimental techniques discussed above for violations of these methodological considerations. At least partially for the reason that it appears to be one of the studies least susceptible to these methodological problems, the work reported by Swinney (in press) will thus be examined here in some detail. In this work, a cross modal lexical priming task was used. In this, subjects had two tasks. First, they were required to comprehend auditorily presented sentences which contained lexical ambiguities. In some conditions, a strongly biasing semantic context occurred prior to the ambiguity in these sentences. Subjects also performed a second task. They made lexical (word/nonword) decisions about visually presented letter strings. (In all cases, the relevant letter strings (words) appeared after the point at which the ambiguity was heard in the sentence.) This task employs use of the fact that automatic priming (facilitation) occurs for lexical decisions made to words that are related to material that has just been previously processed (Neeley, 1978; Swinney, Onifer, Prather, and Hirshkowitz, 1978). The rationale here is that such facilitation will only occur for lexical decisions made to words that are related to meanings of the ambiguity that were actually accessed and activated. That is, if strong semantic contexts constrain lexical access, one should only find priming for lexical decisions to words related to the contextually relevant meaning of the ambiguity; the contextually inappropriate meaning should never be accessed and thus will not provide a base for priming. It was found, however, that lexical decisions for visual words which were related to both the contextually relevant *and* the contextually inappropriate meanings of the ambiguity were facilitated (in comparison to unrelated control words) when they were presented *immediately* after the offset of the lexical ambigutiy. Sentence 1 provides a sample of one condition of these materials (that containing biasing semantic contexts). Lexical decisions were required for the words ANT, SPY, and SEW (which constitute the contextually relevant, contextually inappropriate, and unrelated control conditions, respectively). These words appeard (in different conditions, to different subjects) at the point indicated by ' △ ').

(1) The man was not surprised when he found several spiders, roaches, and other bugs in the corner of his room.
      △

The data from this study clearly support the Contextually Independent model of lexical access; all meanings are accessed for a word in spite of the presence of strong 'constraining' semantic contexts. (It is worth noting that there were sufficient 'foil' trials so that subjects could rarely report any relationship between material in the sentence and the visually presented words. In addition the task did not draw attention to the presence of ambiguities in the materials.)

Using this same task, Swinney, Onifer and Hirshkowitz (Note 2) have shown that these same effects hold even for sentences containing polarized ambiguous words (those ambiguities with one very likely meaning and one unlikely meaning). Thus, even in the most constraining situation where both frequency-of-use and strong semantic context predict that only a single, highly frequent meaning for a word will be appropriate, all meanings appear to be accessed. Lexical *access* is apparently an exhaustive process, unconstrained by higher order semantic information.

A related question — that of whether access proceeds by means of a direct form-addressable system or by a search procedure — can be examined with these data. The most popular of these models is the Terminating Ordered Search hypothesis, in which it is argued that candidate forms are compared against internal representations in order of frequency in a search which terminates once some entry is encountered (see, e.g., Forster, 1976, for a well developed presentation of this argument). However, much of the evidence for this model comes from isolated word processing paradigms and, while the conclusions are undoubtedly valid for that processing conditions, they are not supported in the sentence processing experiments of Swinney, Onifer and Hirshkowitz (Note 2). In fact, the Swinney et. al. results argue against any type of *terminating* search. This, in effect, leaves us with two models which will be very difficult to distinguish functionally: Access might occur via an exhaustive, form addressable system (an hypothesis compatible with, for example, the Morton (1969) logogen model) or it might be accomplished by means of an exhaustive search procedure (which could be an ordered serial, a random serial, or even a parallel process). However it is accomplished, the access routine that occurs during sentence comprehension appears to result in the exhaustive retrieval of information stored for a word.

While semantic information does not appear to constrain lexical access, other candidates for this role certainly exist. For example, it is fairly obvious that information about the grammatical class of a word *can* be used to access the lexicon. Given that this is so, it may well be that any higher order information which is able to predict the grammatical class of subsequent words can be used to constrain the access process for these words. Just such a role has been assigned to the closed class vocabulary (the words in the minor grammatical categories which are often the so-called 'function words'). It has been argued that these words are actively employed in the development of the structural description of a sentence, largely by virtue of facilitating the assignment of appropriate grammatical classifications to open class vocabulary (See, e.g., Bradly, 1979; Garrett, 1974.) For example, a context of 'the' can clearly aid the disambiguation of words with multiple grammatical class entries, such as 'watch'. Prather and Swinney (Note 3) utilized these facts in an experiment designed to determine whether the grammatical information provided by closed class materials could constrain lexical access. They presented sentences such as (2) and (3) which contained unsystematic categorial lexical ambiguities (e.g., watch, cross) which were themselves preceded in the sentence either by 'the' (or 'the + adj') or by 'to' (or 'to + adverb').

(2)   The seasoned old woodsman told the young boy the (battered) cross$_\triangle$ the indian gave him was made of silver.
(3)   The seasoned old woodsman told the young boy to (quickly) cross$_\triangle$ the stream above the beaver pond.

Again, employing the cross modal lexical priming technique, access and activation of the noun and the verb meanings for the ambiguity were examined in each of these biasing context conditions. Under all context conditions the evidence indicated that *all* meanings of an ambiguity are accessed, even if the grammatical class of some of the accessed meanings are inappropriate.

Finally, in somewhat related work both Swinney (unpublished) and Holmes (1979) have evidence indicating that selectional restrictions provide no apparent constraining effect on lexical access for either unambiguous or ambiguous words (respectively). While the research available does not exhaust the inventory of possible higher order constraints on the access process, that which is available strongly suggests that the access of lexical information is unconstrained by higher order information during sentence comprehension. Lexical access appears to be an independent subprocess in the sentence comprehension routine.

POST-ACCESS PROCESSING

It is clear, however, that higher order information does affect lexical interpretation. Thus, it seems reasonable to posit that the locus of higher order constraints on lexical processing will be in a post-access decision process, a process which will eventuate in the choice of a 'single' meaning of a word for insertion into the ongoing sentential analysis. A basic question about this process concerns the time course for the posited interaction of contextual information with the various accessed word meanings. Does such interaction immediately follow access of each word in a sentence, or must it wait until the end of a clause or sentoid (see, e.g., Foss, Bever, Silver, 1968; Fodor et. al., 1974, Bever, Garrett, and Hurtig, 1973)?

The study by Swinney (in press) also utilized the cross modal lexical priming technique to examine this question. In particular, the degree to which the several meanings for an ambiguity were (still) active at a point 3 syllables (about 900 msecs) following occurrence of the ambiguity was examined. It was found that only the contextually appropriate meaning of an ambiguity was active at this point. Apparently the time course of access, activation and post access processing is completed by the time that 3 additional syllables of information are processed. (Of course, this result most likely underestimates the speed of the post-access decision process; it may well have been completed before the point at which it was tested.) While these data do not allow us to determine the manner in which the contextually irrelevant meanings for a word are suppressed or discarded, they do support the conclusion that a post-access decision process occurs immediately following lexical access for each word, and does not wait for the conclusion of clausal processing. Further, it seems reasonable to suggest that this post-access decision mechanism may be a general process; only a subset of all the information stored and accessed for any word (whether it comprises a single 'sense' of an unambiguous word or a single 'meaning' of an ambiguity) will be selected by this process for integration into ongoing sentential analysis.

As a final comment about constraints on access and post-access lexical processing, it should be noted that there is recent work by Blank and Foss (1978) that has been interpreted as a demonstration that lexical access during sentence comprehension *is* facilitated by the occurrence of prior semantically related words. In this it was found that time to monitor for a phoneme target was faster when the word preceding the target was itself preceded by a semantically related word. However, as the phoneme monitoring task has been shown by Swinney (1979) to be relatively insensitive to access processes (due largely to the time-window involved in its application) it appears that the results could just as easily be attributed to the workings of the post-access decision process posited here, a process which is aided by semantic context. (Such an argument also applies to similar work by Morton and Long, 1976). Considering all the data available, this interpretation appears to be the more parsimonious one.

SEGMENTATION

While the access of information associated with any particular word may not be constrained once a 'sufficient' candidate form has initiated the process, it does not follow that the manner by which such lexical candidates are selected from the speech stream is also unconstrained. There are several types of constraining influences that might obtain. One of these has to do with the intrinsic ordering of the segmentation process. That is, there may be constraints on segmentation provided by the order in which potential lexical candidates are examined in the speech stream. For example, one possible model of the process could involve a minimal segmentation procedure in which the first encountered string of phonemes that constituted a word is accessed, followed by the access of the next string of phonemes that forms a word, etc. (Thus, all else being equal, the word "new" and then the word "display" would be accessed from the input / nudɪsple /[2].) Clearly, other possible order conditions on the segmentation process can be envisioned. There is evidence which examines possible order constraints on the segmentation of lexical candidates using the cross modal lexical priming technique. This work examines the processing of two types of complex lexical items — idioms and nominal compounds. Swinney and Cutler (in press) have demonstrated that idioms (such as 'kick the bucket') are represented in the lexicon in the same manner as is any other word. The cross modal priming task was used to examine the relative time course of segmentation (and access) of the idiomatic and literal meanings comprising such idiomatic word strings. Lexical decisions were obtained for visually presented words which were related to the literal words comprising the idiom string ('kick' and 'bucket') as well as for words related to the entire idiom (e.g., DIE). The related words were presented in two places. One test point was immediately following the first literal word in the idiom (kick) and the other followed the last literal word in the idiom (bucket). All idioms were heard in sentences. The results indicated that at the first test point the meaning for the literal word (kick), but *not* that for the entire idiom, had been accessed and activated. However, at the second test point, only the idiomatic meaning gave evidence of being activated; the literal word 'bucket' was apparently not accessed. A similar effect was found by Penny Prather and myself for certain nominal compounds (e.g. 'boycott') when examined in isolation. In all, it appears that the first potential word encountered in the speech stream is momentarily accessed, and that immediately subsequent potential words are not accessed *if* this subsequent information can combine with the originally accessed material to form a (large) word. This is the case for both nominal compounds and idioms.

To summarize the observations and conclusions that have been made about lexical processing:
1.   The segmentation of lexical candidates appears to be a modifiable left-to-right process that operates on what can be called a Minimal Accretion principle. By this, the first viable candidate (based on analysis of the underlying form) that is encountered is accessed. In addition, the form information for this accessed word is also conjoined with immediately subsequent information to determine whether the initial segment may be part of a larger word. The decision process which is posited to occur following access of any word seems likely to be involved in an evaluation of the viability of various accessed candidates in light of the contextual constraints which are incorporated in that decision process.
2.   Once a candidate form is determined, all information stored for that form is accessed and made available for evaluation and further processing; no higher order constraints appear to operate at this level.
3.   A rapid post-access decision process operates to evaluate the accessed information with respect to higher order contextual information. This process eventuates in selection of a subset of the available information (for further sentential processing) and in the suppression of inappropriate information.
4.   These observations hold for the domain of sentence comprehension in which an experienced (adult) listener comprehends a reasonably intact sentential signal.

The model sketched here makes some strong and, at least on the surface, inelegant claims about the nature of the processing and representation of lexical material. The apparent inelegance stems from the claim that potentially constraining higher order information is not used by the lexical access process. However, on closer examination there is an externally motivated consideration that makes this claim more parsimonious in the larger scheme of things. This consideration relates to summary point # 4, above. The sentence comprehension routine is a highly practiced ('over-learned') process for the adult listener. Much of what has been discovered about such processes indicates that they develop a degree of automaticity in which 'set' routines operate rapidly and without interruption (see, e.g., Neeley, 1977; Yates, 1978; Posner & Snyder, 1975; Shiffrin & Schneider, 1978). It may be that in the context of such routines, extremely rapid and automatic lexical recognition is best accomplished by an exhaustive retrieval of information which is then evaluated against all context. Evidence for such exhaustive routines in other practiced cognitive processes certainly exists in the literature (see, e.g., Sternberg, 1966). Further, it seems likely that when the lexical processing routine is removed from relatively 'normal' (automatic) processing conditions different operations may be brought to bear. The more that a task situation differs from the normal comprehension situation, the more one may find that (because they are neither as automatic nor as rapid) the access routines are constrained by contextual information.

In all, it may be that the variable of 'processing condition' represents the largest constraint on lexical processing. Because the perceived situational demands form the basis for what can be thought of as higher order pragmatic information, specification of the effects of such pragmatic constraints appear likely to form a necessary condition for the goal of specifying a complete model of lexical representation and processing.

Notes

1. Note that while recent papers by Newman and Dell (1979), Mehler, Segui & Carey (1978), and Cutler and Norris (1979) cast some doubt on the phoneme monitoring work due to the presence of confounding variables, it is not certain that the confounds are critical to the interpretation; see Swinney, 1979 and Cairns and Hsu, 1979, for related discussion.

2. Either: "new display" or "nudist play".

Reference Notes

1. Cutler, A. & Foss, D.J. Comprehension of ambiguous sentences. The locus of context effects. Paper presented at the Midwestern Psychological Association, Chicago, May 1974.

2. Swinney, D., Onifer, W. & Hirshkowitz, M. Accessing Lexical Ambiguities during Sentence Comprehension: Effects of Frequency-of-Meaning and Contextual Bias. Manuscript submitted for publication, 1979.

3. Prather, P. & Swinney, D. Some Effects of Syntactic Context Upon Lexical Access. Presented at a meeting of the American Psychological Association, San Francisco, California, August, 26, 1977.

4. Marslen-Wilson, W. Sequential decision processes during spoken word recognition. Paper presented at Psychonomic Society, San Antonio, 1979a.

THE COGNITIVE REPRESENTATION OF SPEECH
T. Myers, J. Laver, J. Anderson (editors)
© *North-Holland Publishing Company, 1981*

The Parser's Window

ERIC WANNER

Harvard University Press

However the human listener manages to parse sentences, we know that he or she must frequently manage to do so without ever having simultaneous access to the entire surface of the input sentence. This follows from two very simple and undisputed facts.

First, the physical speech signal fades extremely rapidly. The complex wave form which carries speech is damped almost immediately upon delivery. Mercifully perhaps, the air at the surface of the earth has no resonant properties by which to provide echoes of words, phrases, or sentences. With the exception of caves and canyons, the physical circumstances of speech ordinarily guarantee a highly transient life for the speech signal. To a certain extent, the human cognitive apparatus compensates for the rapid demise of the physical signal. Short term memory provides some of the resonant capacity that the speech environment lacks. But here the second fact intrudes for human short term memory is notoriously limited. Although exact estimates of short term memory capacity disagree (even to an extent which prompts serious questions about whether short term memory is a unitary psychological phenomenon), still there are no estimates of the capacity of immediate memory which would even remotely suggest that the human listener can hold in mind (say) the entire fifteen to twenty-five words of a modestly complicated spoken sentence. Perhaps the simplest way to appreciate this fact, is to notice that there are many sentences which we understand without difficulty in ordinary conversation but which we could not possibly repeat back word for word immediately upon hearing.

There are two consequences that follow directly from the fact that the human parser's simultaneous access to the surface of the sentence—it's ''window—is frequently too narrow to encompass a sentence which it nevertheless parses success-fully. These consequences take the form of constraints which any empirically adequate model of parsing must obey. The first such constraint might be called the *weak left-to-right constraint*. This constraint applies to the operation of the parsing model and it runs as follows: however the parsing model works, it must generally be able to complete its parse of the input elements which arrive early in a sentence before it completes its parse of the input elements which arrive late in a sentence. This constraint does *not* require parsing to run strictly from left to right in the sense that a given word can only be parsed once all words preceding it in the input sentence have already been parsed. But it does mean that the parsing model cannot require a buffer memory system which stores long stretches of unparsed input so that the analysis of the beginning of the sentence can be postponed until after the analysis of the end of the sentence.

The second constraint might be called the *left accessibility constraint*. Although this constraint is tightly related to the weak left-to-right constraint, it applies not to the process of parsing but to the form of the grammar which the parsing model employs. Assuming that such a grammar can be stated as a set of syntactic patterns which comprise the permissible forms of the language, and assuming also that the parser must be able to search through this set of patterns in order to determine which, if any, can be applied to the current input sentence, the left accessibility constraint specifies that the parser must be able to gain access to these patterns from their left edge rightward. It should be obvious without extended discussion why a parsing model requires a left accessible grammar in order to meet the weak left to right constraint. To take just one example, if the syntactic patterns in a grammar could only be accessed right edge first, then clearly any parser using such a grammar would be forced to postpone the analysis of the beginning of the sentence until its right most elements became available. It is just this sort of postponement which violates the weak left to right constraint.

Although these two constraints on the human parsing process seem beyond dispute, it is an entirely open question as to how models of parsing should be configured to meet them. At the risk of some over-simplification one can imagine a range of options arrayed along a continuum anchored at each end by idealized parsers which differ fundamentally in how they make use of short term memory. At one end, we have a class of parsers of the ''guess and back up'' variety. Such parsers are configured to make as many syntactic decisions as quickly as possible during the arrival of the input sentence. For example, such a parser might decide immediately after the arrival of each word what its contextually appropriate syntactic category might be and what position in the developing parse tree the categorized word might occupy. Because of the way sentences are structured, there is no way to guarantee that immediate decisions of this type will always be correct. Therefore, this class of parsers will uniformly require some sort of back-up procedure to rectify decisions which subsequently prove incorrect. Memory is employed to support back-up by storing the sequence of tentative decisions made during parsing. By examining the mnemonic record of previous decisions, it is possible to identify and correct an errant guess without restarting the entire parse.

At the other end of our imaginary continuum lies a class of parsers which might be called ''wait and see'' parsers. As befits their name, these parsers characteristically postpone parsing decisions past the point of the first possible guess just in order to avoid the process of correction required by guess and back up parsers. Short term memory is used by wait and see parsers in order to provide a ''buffer'' in which strings of unanalysed input words can be stored so that parsing decisions can be made contingent on the entire stored string.

All current parsing models can be located towards one end or the other of the idealized continuum just sketched. Kuno and Oettinger's (1962) Predictive Analyser and the Augmented Transition Network developed by Thorne, Bratley, and Dewar (1968), Bobrow and Fraser (1969), and Woods (1970) are parsers of the guess and back up variety. Both of these parsers assign as much structure as possible to each input word as it arrives and neither parser makes crucial use of an input buffer. On the other hand, Marcus's Parsifal (Marcus, 1978) and Fodor and Frazier's Sausage Machine (1978) both lie closer to the wait and see end of the continuum. Each of these parsers buffer the input sentence and postpone parsing decisions until several words have accumulated in the buffer.

A variety of claims has been made about the relative efficiency of buffered and unbuffered parsers (Marcus 1978). From a psychological standpoint, however, these claims are largely beside the point. There is no reason to expect that the most satisfactory model of human parsing will necessarily be the model that can be realized most efficiently on currently available computational facilities. What we require of a psychological model is that it provides the best explanation of reliable facts about how the listener parses sentences. The real question then is whether there are reliable facts about human parsing which can be better explained with a buffered parser or with an unbuffered parser. In a recent paper Lynn Frazier and Janet Fodor (1978) have claimed that there are such facts and that they favor buffered parsers in general and in particular a buffered parser of their own invention called the Sausage Machine.

One of the major results which Frazier and Fodor bring forward in support of their proposal concerns a parsing strategy which, following Kimball (1973), they call Right Association. The center-piece of their argument concerns an interaction between this parsing strategy and another one, which they call Minimal Attachment. Frazier and Fodor (henceforth FF) provide intersting evidence that the language user makes tacit use of both strategies to resolve temporary syntactic ambiguities that arise during parsing. FF then proceed to argue that the existence of these strategies, as well as the apparent interaction between them, can be fully explained if we assume that the language user's parsing system has an input buffer which limits its view of the sentence to approximately six words. FF further claim that parsing systems like the Augmented Transition Network (or ATN), which do not use memory to buffer input, cannot explain the interaction among parsing strategies that they have observed. According to FF's argument, it is impossible even to describe the two parsing strategies within the ATN framework. In effect then, FF are claiming that the Sausage Machine achieves explanatory adequacy in this case while the ATN fails to reach the level of descriptive adequacy.

These are strong and potentially important claims. If correct, they obviously provide grounds for pursuing parsing models built along the lines of the Sausage Machine rather than the ATN. However, when FF's arguments are examined at closer range, the comparison between parsing systems comes out rather differently than they claim. In particular, it appears that the Sausage Machine explanation of Right Association and its interaction with Minimal Attachment is empirically incorrect. Although the Sausage Machine's limited buffer does entail interesting predictions about the interaction among parsing strategies, these predictions can be shown to be wrong. Furthermore, an unbuffered parser, like an ATN, can be configured to describe FF's parsing strategies and when it is so configured, the interaction among strategies which FF observed can be explained as an automatic consequence of the left-to-right operation of the parser.

I want to claim then, that FF's results do not force us to conclude for a model of human parsing of the wait and see variety. But to support this claim in detail will require a bit of background.

THE SAUSAGE MACHINE

The Sausage Machine has two very distinct stages. According to Frazier and Fodor's proposal, ". . . . . the human sentence parsing device assigns phrase structure to word strings in two steps. The first stage parser (called the PPP) assigns lexical and phrasal nodes to substrings of roughly six words. The second stage parser (called the SSS) then adds higher nodes to link these phrasal packages together into a complete phrase marker" (p. 291). Although FF do not provide a detailed characterization of how the Sausage Machine works, they do supply the following sketch: the PPP has a "viewing window" which "shifts continuously through the sentence and accommodates perhaps half a dozen words" (p. 305). The PPP uses the rules of the grammar to assign each input string within the window "its lower lexical and phrasal nodes" (p. 296). It is important to understand that in making these structural assignments, the PPP can only take account of the six words within its current window plus any low level structure it may have already assigned to the words within the window. Given the severe "shortsightedness" of the PPP, the SSS "can survey the whole phrase marker for the sentence as it is computed, and it can keep track of dependencies between items that are widely separated in the sentence and of long term structural commitments which are acquired as the analysis proceeds" (p.292). The SSS works only on the output of the PPP. The low level phrasal packages assembled by the PPP are deposited "in the path of the SSS which is sweeping through the sentence behind it" (p.306). As it sweeps along, the SSS also uses the grammar to assemble the phrases left to it by the PPP into a complete phrase marker for the input sentence.

Although their description of the Sausage Machine is somewhat vague, it is precise enough for FF's purposes. According to their argument, there are only three features of the Sausage Machine which provide its explanatory power. These are also the features which most notably distinguish it from the ATN:
(A)   The existence of 2 separate stages of parsing.
(B)   The PPP's limitation to a six word viewing window.
(C)   The SSS's ability to appraise the whole phrase marker as it develops and therefore to make decisions contingent upon the geometry of the entire parse tree.

EVIDENCE FOR A LIMITED WINDOW

In FF's terms, a parsing strategy is a rule that governs situations in which the grammar permits the parser to attach a constituent in more than one possible way to the developing parse tree. So, for example, both sentence (1) and (2) are ambiguous because the final word in each can be attached at two possible points in the phrase marker:
(1)   Tom said that Bill had taken the cleaning out yesterday.
(2)   Joe called the friend who had smashed his new car up.
In (1), *yesterday* can be attached as an adverbial modifier either to the topmost S in the phrase marker (*Tom said. . . .*) or to the embedded S (*Bill had taken. . . .*). Similarly, in (2), *up* can be attached as a particle to the verb in the topmost S (*called*) or to the verb in the embedded S (*smashed*). In both sentences, the lower of the two possible attachments seems to be preferred by most people and Frazier (1978) has provided experimental evidence for the reliability of this preference.

According to FF, this type of bias can be adequately described by Kimball's principle of Right Association, which dictates that an ambiguous constituent should be "attached into the phrase marker as a right sister to existing constituents and as low in the tree as possible" (p.294). The Right Association strategy applies in the obvious way to make the correct predictions about the language user's preferences in sentences (1) and (2). But what explains the existence of this particular strategy? Why should the language user be uniformly biased toward low right attachment as opposed to (say) high right attachment? According to FF, the Sausage Machine can supply the answer. Their story begins with the observation that "the tendency towards low right association of an incoming constituent sets in only when the word is at some distance from the other daughter constituents of the higher node to which it might have been attached" (p.299). Sentences (3) and (4) provide the evidence for FF's claim that Right Association "sets in only. . . . . at some distance".
(3)   Joe bought the book that I had been trying to obtain for Susan.
(4)   Joe bought the book for Susan.
In (3) there are two possible attachments for the final prepositional phrase *for Susan:* it can be attached either to the object noun phrase (*the book that I had been trying to obtain for Susan*) or to the main clause verb phrase (*bought the book for Susan*). Right Association correctly predicts the preference for the first of these attachments, which is at the lower right margin of the phrase marker. Notice, however, that in

sentence (4), this preference seems to be reversed. The preferred attachment is to the verb phrase, not the noun phrase; and as phrase markers (5) and (6) demonstrate this is clearly the higher of the two possible attachments:

(5)

(6)

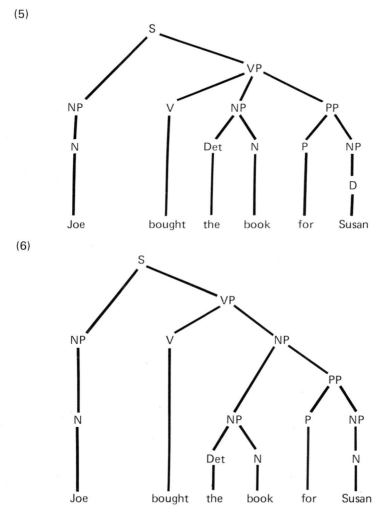

FF argue that the preference for (5) over (6) is a special case of the general parsing strategy they call Minimal Attachment. This strategy also governs situations where the grammar permits more than one possible attachment for a given constituent and it stipulates that the ambiguous item "is to be attached into the phrase marker with the fewest possible number of non-terminal nodes linking it with the nodes that are already present" (p.320). Comparison of (5) and (6) will show that noun phrase attachment involves one more non-terminal node than verb phrase attachment; hence the Minimal Attachment principle correctly predicts the language user's preference for (5). But why does Minimal Attachment prevail over Right Association in sentence (4)? And why does Right Association appear to set in only at a distance? Here FF offer an ingenious explanation based exclusively on the architecture of the Sausage Machine

> Let us suppose for the sake of argument that the first stage parser has the capacity to retain six words of the sentence, together with whatever lexical and phrasal nodes it has assigned to them. Then in processing (4), it will still be able to 'see' the verb when it encounters *for Susan*. It will know that there is a verb phrase node to which the prepositional phrase could be attached, and also that this particular verb is one which permits a *for*-phrase. But in sentence (3), where a long noun phrase follows the verb *bought*, the first stage parser will have lost access to *bought* by the time *for Susan* must be entered into the structure; the only possible attachment will be within the long noun phrase, as a modifier to *trying to obtain* (p.300)

Notice that according to this account, there need be no independent statement of Right Association anywhere in the Sausage Machine. The PPP simply makes whatever attachments it can. In long sentences like (3) the low right attachment of *for Susan* is the only attachment the PPP can make because its limited window prevents it from "seeing" the higher attachment possibility. Note also that this account automatically explains why Minimal Attachment prevails over Right Association in (4). Since there is no independent statement of Right Association in the parser there is no conflict to be explained. In short sentences like (1), the PPP will "see" both attachment possibilities. Therefore, there will be no bias towards low right attachment and the Minimal Attachment strategy prevails by default.[1] On the basis of this demonstration, FF claim to have achieved, at least in one important instance, their announced goal of showing that "the parser's decision preferences can be seen as an automatic consequence of its structure" (p.297).

There are, however, serious problems with this claim. If the preference for low right attachment "sets in only. . . at some distance" just because of the PPP's limitation to a six word window, then this limitation ought to operate uniformly in all cases. Just as the preference for low right attachment dissolves as sentence (3) is shortened into sentence (4), so it should also dissolve as sentences (1) and (2) are shortened. But it does not. Sentence sets (7) and (8) represent progressive shortenings of sentences (1) and (2):

(7) (a) Tom said that Bill had taken the cleaning out yesterday.
     (b) Tom said that Bill had taken it out yesterday.
     (c) Tom said that Bill had taken it yesterday.
     (d) Tom said that Bill took it yesterday.
     (e) Tom said that Bill died yesterday.
     (f) Tom said Bill died yesterday.
(8) (a) Joe called the friend who had smashed his new car up.
     (b) Joe called the friend who had smashed his car up.
     (c) Joe called the friend who had smashed it up.
     (d) Joe called the friend who smashed it up.
     (e) Joe called everyone who smashed it up.
     (f) Joe called everyone who smashed up.

Notice that as these sentences shrink, there is no noticeable tendency for the preference for low right attachment to diminish. Indeed, informants to whom I have given just the (f) versions uniformly report a preference in favor of the analysis in which the final word is attached to the lower of the two clauses.[2] But neither (f) version is more than six words long. Both (f) sentences can fit comfortably within the PPP's window. Hence the PPP could readily "see" both clauses as candidates for possible attachment. Therefore, the structure of the PPP cannot provide any explanation of the language user's continued preference for low right attachment in these short sentences. [3]

One might hope to save the Sausage Machine by somehow incorporating the Right Association strategy within the PPP itself. It might be possible to stipulate, for example, that the PPP try to fashion the longest possible phrases from the words within its window. But this move would leave us without an explanation of why Minimal Attachment appears to prevail over Right Association in sentence (4). Moreover, it would necessarily entail the abandonment of FF's goal of explaining Right Association exclusively in terms of Sausage Machine architecture. For as FF point out themselves, there is nothing about the division of labor between the PPP and SSS which might explain why the PPP should strive to build maximally long phrases:

> Trying to squeeze extra words into the current package could also be counter-productive, for it might happen that the limits of the PPP's capacity are reached at a point which is not a natural phrasal break in the sentence. In such circumstances it would have been better for the PPP to terminate the current package a word or two sooner, and start afresh with a new phrase as a new package. (p.312).

To summarize, it now appears that contrary to the Sausage Machine prediction, Right Association is not limited to cases of distant attachment. Moreover, the Sausage Machine offers no explanation of why the language user appears to follow the Right Association strategy in some short sentences (7f and 8f) but not others (4). Accordingly, it seems clear that the Sausage Machine's putative explanation of the behavior of Right Association strategy is simply incorrect. There is nothing about FF's observations which would require a parser with properties (A) and (B). However, it remains to be seen whether a parser like the ATN, which has neither two stages nor a limited input window, can give a satisfactory account of the behavior of Right Association and Minimal Attachment, as well as their somewhat puzzling interaction.

AN ATN ACCOUNT

According to FF, Minimal Attachment and Right Association cannot be described within the ATN framework. One problem, as they see it, is that the ATN lacks property (C) — the ability to make structural assignments contingent on the geometry of the developing phrase marker. In FF's words,

> An ATN parser could certainly be designed so that it would make exactly the same decisions at choice points as the Kimball parser. But because its decisions are determined by the ranking of arcs for specific word and phrase types, rather than in terms of concepts like 'lowest rightmost node in the phrase marker', the parser's structural preferences would have to be built in separately for each type of phrase and each sentence context in which it can appear. Evidence that the human sentence parser exhibits *general* preferences based on the geometric arrangement of nodes in the phrase marker indicates that its executive component does have access to the results of its prior computations. Its input at each choice point must consist of both the incoming lexical string and the phrase marker (or some portion thereof) which it has already assigned to previous lexical items. (p.294)

It is difficult to determine in general, whether the ATN will eventually require the addition of something like property (C). However, it is quite clear that no such property is required to give a perfectly general description of the two parsing strategies that FF have proposed. The structural preferences involved in these strategies would not have to be "built in separately for each type of phrase and each sentence context." On the contrary, it appears to be possible to formulate scheduling principles for the ATN that completely capture the structural preferences involved and that do so without explicit appeal to the geometry of the phrase marker. Moreover, when these principles are combined with an ATN grammar for FF's crucial sentences, the residual mysteries concerning the interaction between Right Association and Minimal Attachment are completely resolved.

To see this, recall first that a scheduling rule in an ATN, as described by Kaplan (1975, 1972) and by Wanner and Maratsos (1978), is essentially a specification of the order in which the ATN processor considers the arcs leaving a state in an ATN grammar network. Recall also that the ATN network includes at least 5 types of arcs:[4]

— WORD arcs that analyze specific grammatical morphemes such as *that* or *to;*
— CAT arcs that analyze grammatical categories such as Noun (N) or Verb (V);
— SEEK arcs that analyze whole phrases or clauses such as NP, VP, or S;
— SEND arcs which terminate a network;
— JUMP arcs which provide a free transition between states, thus expressing the optionality of certain sub-paths through a network.

Given this enumeration of arc types, we can formulate two general constraints on ATN scheduling rules which provide a general description of Right Association and Minimal Attachment:

(9) Right Association: Schedule all SEND arcs and all JUMP arcs after every other arc type. (Since SEND arcs and JUMP arcs never leave the same state, there is no ambiguity here with respect to the relative ordering of these two arc types.)

(10) Minimal Attachment: Schedule all CAT arcs and WORD arcs before all SEEK arcs.

Consider Minimal Attachment first. Basically this strategy stipulates that the parser should never add an additional non-terminal node to the parse tree unless it is forced to by the grammar. Scheduling rule (10) enforces this strategy by providing that any input element will be analysed as a category or a word of the current phrase before any SEEK to a lower phrase is attempted. Suppose, for example, that our ATN grammar includes the following network level that analyzes X phrases (XP):

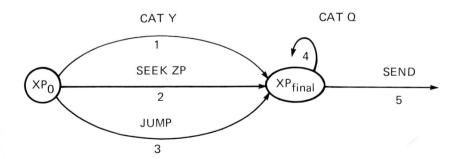

Note first that because CAT Y arc is ordered before SEEK ZP arc, the constituent XP will always be completed by means of categorical nodes rather than phrasal nodes, if such a completion is possible. This ordering guarantees Minimal Attachment. To see this, imagine our hypothetical ATN also includes a network for Z phrases (ZP), one path through which begins with a CAT Y arc, as in:

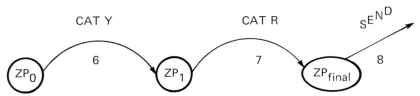

Suppose that the parser is in state XP_O at the moment that it encounters a word in the input string that belongs to the syntactic category Y. At this point, two analyses of Y are possible, roughly those corresponding to the following attachment possibilities:

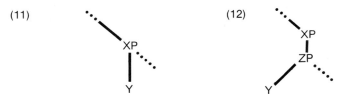

Obviously, (11) is the minimal attachment of Y to XP and it is just this possibility which will be tried first so long as arc 1 is ordered before arc 2.

Now consider *Right Association*. Basically, this strategy requires the parser to add as many nodes to the current constituent as possible. In an ATN this is enforced by postponing the network-final SEND arc as long as possible. To see this, suppose that the parser is in state XP final when it encounters a word in the input string that can be categorized as Q. So long as arc 4 is always ordered before arc 5 at this state, as it must be in order to obey the Right Association scheduling principle (10), the Q node will be attached as the right sister of the current constituent XP. To see how this guarantees Right Association, suppose our ATN also includes a network for U phrases (UP) which contains a path including a SEEK XP arc followed by a CAT Q arc, as in:

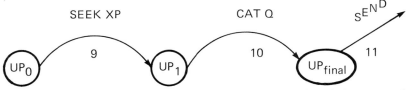

Suppose also that the SEEK XP on arc 9 has been issued and the parser has completed the partial path through the XP network to state XP final by finding a Y in the input. Now suppose the next word falls in the Q category. Here again, two attachments are possible. Either Q can be attached directly to the X constituent via arc 4 to yield (13) or Q can be attached to the UP constituent via arcs 5 and 10 to yield (14).

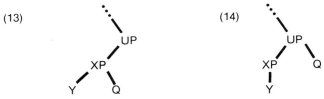

Obviously Right Association favors (13), and so long as arc 4 precedes arc 5, this is the analysis that the ATN will favor as well.

Finally, notice that the JUMP on arc 3 must be ordered last since it leads to the SEND on arc 5. If the JUMP were ordered earlier at state XP_0, it could lead the parser to violate Right Association by executing the SEND at arc 5 before trying the CAT and SEEK on arcs 1 and 2.

Given the ATN restatement of Right Association and Minimal Attachment provided by scheduling principles (9) and (10), we can now consider the way in which these principles apply to FF's crucial cases. Figure 1 presents an ATN grammar which will handle sentences (1), (4), and (7a - 7f). The grammar was constructed by restating in ATN terms all the phrase structure rules that FF implicitly used to construct the phrase markers given in their paper. Corresponding to every context free phrase structure rule in FF's generative grammar, there is a level of the ATN network which expresses the identical analysis of each phrase. [5] For simplicity,

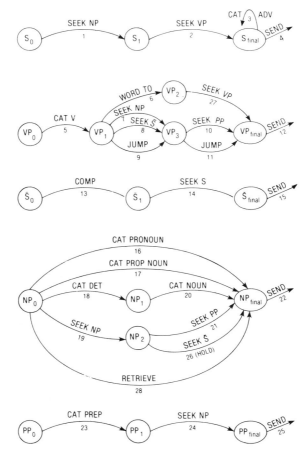

FIGURE 1   *An ATN grammar for sentences (3) ,(4) and (7).*

however, we have ignored irrelevant grammatical details pertaining to verbal auxillaries, verb particles, and deleted complementizers in the grammar of Figure 1. None of these omissions has any bearing upon the interesting aspects of the ATN analysis of FF's sentences.

To illustrate the way in which principle (9) captures Kimball's principle of Right Association, consider first the analysis of sentence (7e), repeated here alongside the arc sequence (15) which gives its analysis path through the grammar of Figure 1:

(7e) Tom said that Bill died yesterday.
(15) 1(17,22), 2(5, 8(13, 14(1, (17,22), 2(5, 9, 11, 12) 3, 4), 15), 11, 12), 4.

In constructing arc sequence (15), the arcs in the analysis sub-path that fulfill a SEEK have been listed in parenthesis after the number of the SEEK arc that caused the SEEK to be attempted. Thus the analysis of sentence (7e) begins with a SEEK for a NP on arc 1, which is completed when the proper noun "Tom" is analyzed on arc 17 and control returned to arc 1 by the SEND on arc 22. This arc sequence is represented in (15) as 1(17,22). Following the analysis from this point, we see that *said* is analyzed on arc 5, and a SEEK for the complement $\bar{S}$ is issued on arc 8. The complementizer *that* is analyzed on arc 13, followed by a SEEK S on arc 14. The SEEK S is pursued along arc 1 which analyzes the subject noun phrase *Bill* and arc 2 which analyzes the verb phrase *died*. At this point there is a choice between analyzing the adverb *yesterday* as a modifier of the complement clause on arc 3 or terminating the complement clause via the SEND on arc 4. However, since the SEND arc must be ordered after all other arcs according to principle (9), this choice must be resolved in favor of arc 3. Hence, *yesterday* is attached to the complement clause, thus insuring the low right attachment of the adverb. Notice also that this attachment will be preferred no matter how long or short the complement clause is[6] So long as the complement clause terminates at state S final, the fact that arc 3 precedes arc 4 will guarantee low right attachment. Since each complement clause in sentence set (7) terminates at just this state, the ATN successfully captures our intuitions that the lower attachment of *yesterday* is preferred throughout the entire set of sentences in (7). (Anyone with sufficient scepticism and stamina can prove this by tracing through the ATN analysis of the full set.)

Principle (9) also insures the low right attachment of *for Susan* (3), although here the principle applies at state VP3, where the JUMP on arc 11 must be ordered after the SEEK PP on arc 10. To see the effect of this ordering, consider the following analysis path for sentence (3) by the grammar of Figure 1:

(3) Joe bought the book that I had been trying to obtain for Susan.
(16) 1(17,22), 2(5, 7(19) (18,20,22), 26(13, 14) 1(16,22),
    2(5,6,27(5,7(28,22), 10(23,24(17,22),25), 12),12),4),15,22), 11,12),4.

The parser works its way to state VP3 by SEEKing an $\bar{S}$ at arc 26 in order to process the relative clause (*that I had been trying. . . . . . .*). As this SEEK is executed, the head noun phrase (*the book*) is put on HOLD in accordance with the ATN procedure for processing relative clauses (for details, see Wanner and Maratsos (1978). The relative clause is then processed as an ordinary declarative clause until the parser reaches state VP1, having just analyzed the infinitival complement *to obtain*. Since *obtain* requires an object noun phrase, *the book* will be removed from HOLD at this point and assigned as direct object on arc 7. Then, at state VP3, the parser must attempt to find a prepositional phrase on arc 10 to complete the complement clause. Since *for Susan* is available at this point in the input string, it is automatically attached as the indirect object of the complement clause. This is, of course, just the low right attachment that language users prefer in this case. The only way for the ATN to make the higher attachment would be to reverse the order of arcs 10 and 11 in violation of principle (9).

But now what about sentence (4)? Why doesn't Right Association operate there as well and come into conflict with Minimal Attachment? This is a natural question if one considers just the geometry of the alternative phrase markers for (4): in phrase marker (5), *for Susan* is minimally attached to the VP; in (6), *for Susan* is low right attached to the NP. However, the question disappears given the ATN formulation of the two parsing strategies. When the two parsing strategies are implemented by ordering arcs according to principles (9) and (10), the left-to-right operation of the ATN automatically establishes the priority of the Minimal Attachment analysis of sentence (4). One way to see this is to trace through the analysis of sentence (4) which is given below in arc sequence (17):

(4) Joe bought the book for Susan.
(17) 1(17,22), 2(5,7(18,20,22), 10(23,24(17,22), 25), 12), 4.

The subject noun phrase *Joe* is analyzed on arc 1, and the verb *bought* on arc 5, leaving the parser in state VP_1 where a noun phrase is sought on arc 7. This SEEK leads to state NP_O where the parser must decide whether to search for a simple noun phrase along the paths headed by CAT arcs 16, 16, and 18 or to search for a complex noun phrase along the path headed by the SEEK NP on arc 19. Since principle (10) requires that CAT arcs be tried before SEEK arcs, this decision is resolved in favor of attempting the simple NP analyses first. One of these succeeds when arcs 18 and 20 sucessfully apply to *the book*.[7] At this point, *the book* has been minimally attached to the verb phrase. In effect the CAT-before-SEEK arc ordering at state NP_O has selected partial structure (18) over structure (19):

(18)   (19)

Once this structure has been selected, there is only one possible attachment for the prepositional phrase *for Susan* and that is the direct attachment to the verb phrase. The ATN accomplishes this attachment on arc 10 once control returns to state VP_3 after the successful SEEK for an NP on arc 7. Notice that the conflict between the minimal attachment and the low right attachment *for Susan* never arises in the ATN analysis because the ATN never considers structure (19), and it is only in terms of *a comparision* between structures (18) and (19) that there appears to be a conflict between Minimal Attachment and Right Association. Therefore, it appears that the ATN resolves the apparent conflict in (4) between Minimal Attachment and Right Association in the psychologically appropriate way specifically because it does not appraise the geometry of the two possible parse trees. This is, of course, just the reverse of FF's claimed advantage for the Sausage Machine's ability to survey the structural details of the developing phrase marker.

To summarize, then, I hope to have shown, contrary to FF's claims, first that the ATN can provide a general statement of Minimal Attachment and Right Association; second, that the ATN can do so without explicit appeal to the geometry of the developing phrase marker; third, that a careful formulation of the two parsing strategies coupled with a detailed ATN grammar can account for the otherwise puzzling interactions between parsing strategies noted by FF simply by appeal to left-to-right processing and without any assumption of a limited input window.

Notes

A somewhat modified version of this paper appeared under the title ''The ATN or the Sausage Machine: which one is baloney?'' in *Cognition* 8 (1980), 209-25.

1. FF also offer a structural account for Minimal Attachment which is quite irrelevant to the interaction between the two strategies. Here it is sufficient to note that on FF's account, Minimal Attachment is insensitive to distance effects in the manner putatively characteristic of Right Association. Hence, Minimal Attachment continues to operate in contexts where Right Association does not.

2. Some informants find the higher attachment in (8f) ungrammatical, presumably because it requires an intransitive interpretation of ''smashed''. However, these informants all prefer the low right attachment in (8e) where there is no possible confounding from ungrammaticality of either attachment.

3. The same sort of argument can be brought to bear upon some of FF's other arguments for the explanatory power of the PPP's limited window. For example, FF argue that the multiply embedded sentence (a) is easier than the identically embedded sentence (b) because its major constituents (marked here by brackets) are approximately the length of the PPP's window:

    (a) [The very beautiful young woman] [the man the girl loved] [met on a cruise ship in Maine] [died of cholera in 1972].

    (b) The woman the man the girl loved met died.

    But again it is possible to construct an equivalent sentence which is short enough to fall entirely within the PPP's window yet is very difficult to comprehend:

    (c) Women men girls love meet die.

4. For a more detailed discussion of these arc types see the ATN sources cited above.

5. In adopting this principle for constructing the ATN grammar, I am following Bresnan's (1978) proposal for relating ATN and phrase structure grammars. ATN grammars according to this principle provide a well formed labelled bracketting of the input sentence directly by means of the sequence of transitions made in accepting the sentence. This avoids the use of LISP functions to build phrase markers thereby reducing the expressive power of the ATN. A limited set of additional actions is required to label grammatical functions and handle moved constituents. However, with one exception (the HOLD action) I have deleted these actions from the Figure 1 grammar since they play no part in the description of Minimal Attachment and Right Association.

6. I am indebted to Ronald Kaplan for pointing out this property of Right Association.

7. See Wanner, Kaplan and Shiner (1975) for evidence that garden paths have a measurable effect on comprehension time.

THE COGNITIVE REPRESENTATION OF SPEECH
T. Myers, J. Laver, J. Anderson (editors)
© *North-Holland Publishing Company, 1981*

On Some Continuous Properties in Language

T.G. BEVER and J.M. CARROLL

Columbia University and T.J. Watson Research Center I B M

1. INTRODUCTION

Many systematic phenomena in language are reflected in behavioral continua, rather than in discrete categories (Labov, 1972; Ross, 1974; Sankoff, 1978; Lakoff, 1973). This essay is concerned with the impact of such systematic statistical phenomena on the form of linguistic description. If linguistic grammars are allowed to exploit the descriptive power of non-categorical rules, more candidate grammars will be available for each set of facts: such proliferation of candidate descriptions reduces the empirical import of universal linguistic theory. Furthermore, if human language is defined in terms of a set of statistical principles (Greenberg, 1963), then the definition of "possible language" cannot be sharply drawn; rather, we can only describe a universally "likely" language.

In the present discussion we explore two examples of probabilistic properties of language, one a phenomenon of English and the other true of all languages. In each case we demonstrate that the phenomenon can be explained as the result of the interaction of categorical linguistic structures with a particular perceptual process, the processing of propositional relations. We also show that our explanation leads to the prediction of new facts.

Our considerations bear most directly on the nature of linguistic intuitions. We adopt the position that an acceptability intuition is the percept that results from an interaction of structural knowledge, behavioral processes, and the mechanisms of introspection. This interactive theory is distinct from the position that all reliable acceptability facts are pertinent to a "structural" linguistic description; and it is distinct from the position that all reliable facts are pertinent only to a processing description. Rather we seek to clarify the nature of language by distinguishing its impact on our intuitions from that of the behavioral systems that deploy it. In the course of our investigations we hope also to use linguistic and psycholinguistic theory as tools to clarify the nature of all introspective processes.

1.1 The Nouniness Squish in English.   Ross (1974) noticed that a large number of syntactic processes differ in their acceptability along a continuum of nominal structures, ranging from the lexical noun to the complex clause. Some of these processes yield highest acceptability with nouns, some highest with clauses. In each case, Ross showed that there is an acceptability continuum for nominal structures intermediate in complexity between nouns and clauses, e.g., degraded or tenseless clauses, nouns that are deverbal nominalizations (but cf. Gazdar and Klein, 1978).

The syntactic process of plural agreement, for example, applies best to "noun-like" arguments. Conjunctions of very noun-like initial sequences like *winning and losing*, as in (1e), are perfectly acceptable as compound subjects of plural verbs.

(1a) *That he will win and that you will lose
(1b) *For him to win and for you to lose
(1c) ?*Him winning and you losing
(1d) ??His winning and your losing
(1e) (The) winning and (the) losing

are inevitable.

More clause-like initial sequences, such as Poss-ing nominals in (1d), elicit increasing unacceptability, as indicated by Ross's ??-?*-* notational system.

The converse situation is illustrated by the process of extra-position. Very clause-like sequences like the sentential subject *that Max whistles* (2a) are perfectly acceptable as extraposed sentence-final sequences signaled by the dummy subject *it*.

(2) It appears to disturb Herbie

(a) that Max whistles.
(b) for Max to whistle.
(c) ?Max whistling.
(d) ?*Max's whistling.
(e) *(the) whistling.

However, more noun-like structures like the nominalization *Max whistling* (2c), are increasingly unacceptable in these frames.

Ross (1974) interpreted such data as proving the existence of structurally based "squishes" — in this case a squish from "noun" to "clause" with intermediate levels of nouniness/clausiness. Such empirical acceptability gradations between the extremes of noun-ness and clause-ness led Ross to claim that the categorial notions of "noun" and "clause" in linguistic theory must be given up in favor of a continuous gradient.

1.2 Upstairs Primacy Across Languages. Ross (1972) noted that optional reordering rules apply more freely within main clauses than within subordinate clauses. For example (3b) is an optional version of (3a), resulting from an adverb fronting process that applies to verb-phrase adverbs. (Note that the same acceptability phenomena are not true of "sentence" adverbs, e.g. "fortunately, certainly. . . .", at least because they are positioned by different rules)

(3a) John left quickly
(3b) Quickly John left.
(3c) After John left quickly, Mary became upset
(3d) *After quickly John left, Mary became upset

The same process cannot apply in (3c), as evidenced by the unacceptability of (3d). Ross also noted a difference in the strength of the main/subordinate asymmetry as a function of the surface order of the clauses — the effects are much weaker in final position. For example, (3e) is more acceptable than (3d).

(3e) ?Mary became upset after quickly John left.

Ross observed that such restrictions are generally true across languages, although some languages may exhibit isolated exceptions. The claim is that *if* there is an asymmetry in the range of application of a given rule it is in favor of broader application to main clauses than to subordinate clauses.

It is not immediately clear how to state such facts as part of universal grammar. Since *some* syntactic rules may be required specifically for subordinate clauses, we cannot simply require that all syntactic rules at least apply to main clauses. The difference in *relative* acceptability of sentence-initial and sentence-final subordinate clauses with such rules compounds this difficulty.

1.3 Explaining Statistical Regularities. The goal of studying linguistic structure is in part to isolate universals of language. Such universals are candidate universal properties of linguistic structure. Of course, certain universals, true of all known languages are not properties of universal grammar, but rather are due to nonlinguistic properties of human beings. For example, it is a universal of human languages that no language has a total lack of surface marking of deep structure relations. It is clear why such a property exists, namely to make the sentences in the language usable.

We can furthermore understand how the restriction would be naturally imposed on all existing human languages: children attempting to learn a language simply fail to master the use of linguistic rules or combinations of rules that would lead to intractable ambiguity (Bever 1970). However, to capture the relevant generalization as part of universal grammar would be unwieldy. The reason for this is that the notion of intractable ambiguity must be defined across the range of structurally possible devices which can signal deep structure relations, and that it refers to the sentence forms that are actually used in the language — not just to the *possible* sentence structures. (Bever and Langendoen, 1973; Carroll, 1980).

The same sorts of considerations arise in the description of language specific grammars. The acceptability of certain types of constructions, and the principles that these acceptability facts implicate, appear to be fundamentally behavioral — and not grammatical. The classic example is the unacceptability of multiply center embedded relative clauses (Miller and Chomsky, 1963) — which has defied a purely structural explanation (Bever, 1970; Carroll and Bever, 1976).

Clearly it is a theoretical advantage in interpreting the ontological and psychological status of grammar if its principles are categorical in nature, univocally governing the form of the rules and their procedures of application. However, there are many cases in which relative phenomena do not have behavioral explanations as obvious as those of intractable ambiguity and center embedding. In the following discussion we show that the primacy and nouniness phenomena are explicable as a function of experimentally and theoretically established principles of speech perception. Indeed, the same aspect of speech perception accounts for both phenomena, thus rendering them the result of an interaction of human speech behavior and linguistic structure.

2. SPEECH PERCEPTION

The listener is presented with an acoustic stimulus which can be analysed at a number of different levels, e.g. syllables, words, phrases, and so on. Sentence comprehension involves the perception of an integrated description of these different levels. The listener plays a relatively active role, formulating hypotheses about each level as he hears the sentence (Bever, 1975; Bever, Garrett, and Hurtig, 1973; Marslen-Wilson, 1973, 1975).

·*2.1 Segmentation Processes.* The processes of perception "segment" a heard sentence, recoding each segmented unit into an inner form. The teleology of segmentation processes is twofold: first, the listener must have some means of dividing sentences — which can be arbitrarily lengthly and/or complex — into smaller more manageable chunks (Miller, 1956); and second, by dividing the sentence into logical constituents, the listener can facilitate the perceptual reconstruction of the sentence into units that typically serve the goal of comprehension.

There are several typical behavioral indications of segmentation processing. Heightened processing load just prior to the ends of segmentation units is reflected in a decreased ability to carry out on-line ancillary tasks presented at that point (Abrams and Bever, 1969; Bever and Hurtig, 1975). Interruptions (e.g. clicks, tones, coughs) occurring during a sentence are subjectively heard at points between segmentation units (Fodor and Bever, 1965; Bever, Kirk and Lackner, 1969; Chapin, Smith & Abramson, 1972; Carroll and Tanenhaus, 1978; Warren and Warren, 1976).

Material that has been segmented is recoded into a more abstract representation. This is evidenced by an abrupt drop in verbatim recall and word recognition performance after segmentation boundaries (Caplan, 1972; Sachs, 1967; Carroll, 1978). Recoding also releases processing capacity, as indicated by an increased ability to perform memory tasks interpolated immediately after the point of segmentation (Wanner and Maratsos, 1978; Carroll, 1979a).

2.2 Segmentation Units. Several structural hypotheses have been advanced regarding the specification of units of sentence comprehension. Initially, it was suggested that surface phrase structure defined the relevant units (e.g., Fodor and Bever, 1965). Subsequently, it was shown that surface constituents are effective segmentation units just to the extent that they reflect deep structure clause organization (Bever, Lackner, and Kirk, 1969). This led to the hypothesis that deep clausal structure defines the relevant units of sentence processing — and that one of the fundamental goals in sentence perception is to isolate logically complete and coherent propositional sequences (e.g., subject - verb - object).

However, the surface realization of a deep clause is frequently degraded — often to a single word. In (4) the gerund *singing* corresponds to the deep structure clause GOALIE SING.

(4)   Singing was well known by all of the players on the local football squad to be the goalie's one passion in life.

However, isolating the word *singing* would not enable the listener to properly organize the propositional sequence to which it belongs — until 17 words later he encounters the subject noun *goalie*. Earlier we noted that processing load was one of the fundamental motivations for the construct of segmentation processing in the theory of sentence perception. But clearly a single word is an unlikely source of much processing load.

Accordingly, recent research has addressed the question of what cues in the surface sequence might inform the listener that a potentially propositional sequence may be isolated and recoded (Carroll, Tanenhaus, and Bever, 1978). Thus, instead of assuming that sentence segmentation units will find comprehensive definition at a particular level of syntactic structure, investigators have sought to define the ''functional clause'' as a compromise between the propositional structure of sentences and the perceptual processes which must reconstruct this structure during perception.

2.3 Functional Clauses. Functional clauses are optimally propositional, allowing listeners to recode them, and they are optimally long/complex, so as to utilize but not exceed the listener's segmentation processing capacity. Either or both of these properties may be compromised when necessary. A set of recoding strategies have been identified which are vehicles for this processing activity. The most well-studied of these recoding strategies is to listen for N-V-N sequences (Bever, 1970; Carroll, 1978). Given a noun-verb-noun sequence, the listener considers the possibility that some kind of a propositional subject-verb-object sequence has been isolated.

Carroll and Tanenhaus (1978) showed that brief tones interrupting sentences tended to be misheard as having occurred at or near a clause boundary more frequently when the preceding clause had the structure N-V-N. Carroll (1978) showed that immediate cued verbatim recall was slower if the cue originated in a prior N-V-N unit than the target, relative to cases in which no complete N-V-N unit separated the cue and the target. Carroll(1979a) found that performance on a memory task interpolated at the clause boundary was better when the initial clause was N-V-N than when it lacked either the subject or the object noun.

A second strategy is to isolate verb inflections (Carroll, 1976, 1978). In general, sequences with a tense-bearing verb stem also carry a complete set of propositional relations. "Deverbal" stems (e.g., gerunds) will often be embedded in propositionally incomplete sequences (as indeed was the case in example (4) above). But the verb inflection strategy operates even when it is not redundant with the N-V-N strategy. In the immediate cued recall task, response times were slower when the cue occurred in a tensed N-V-N sequence than when the cue originated in an N-V-N sequence that was not tensed (Carroll, 1978).

A third strategy involves subordinate marking: Clauses that are marked as subordinate must be integrated as modifiers of independent or main clauses. Carroll and Tanenhaus (1978) found that sentence initial main clauses attracted tones to the clause boundary region more than did sentence initial subordinate clauses. Tanenhaus and Carroll (1975) found greater release of processing capacity after main than subordinate clauses. Townsend and Bever (1978) found that sentence initial main clauses are semantically recoded more quickly than subordinate clauses: immediate meaning recognition was better for main clauses, but immediate verbatim recall was poorer for main clauses compared with subordinate clauses.

Townsend and Bever found that subordination effects differ according to how semantically "causal" and structurally "independent" a subordinate clause is from its main clause. Subordinate clauses introduced by *if* or *because* are behaviorally similar to main clauses, while a subordinate clause introduced by *although* shows the most different effects from main clauses. Townsend and Bever argued that the internal content of a causal *if*-clause can be semantically analysed without reference to the main clause, while this is specifically not true of an adversative *although*-clause. This coordinates with the fact that an *if*-clause sets up an explicit "cause-effect" sequence relation between the two clauses, while an *although*-clause specifically *denies* such a relation with respect to some part of the *although*-clause.

A non-structural influence on segmentation strategies is sequence length. In the absence of any other information, the mere length of a sequence provides some incentive for the listener to initiate segmentation. Carroll (1976) found latency differences in the immediate cued recall task between three word long and seven word long sentence-initial noun phrases. Response latencies were greater for longer noun phrases, indicating that they were treated perceptually as units more than were the shorter noun phrases.

In brief, a substantial body of experimental research supports the claim that there is a behaviorally-based set of considerations which govern the functional "goodness" of a sequence as a carrier of a clause-like propositional unit.

3. THE BEHAVIORAL BASIS OF NOUNINESS AND PRIMACY.

In this section we explain the two linguistic phenomena, the nouniness squish and primacy. Our account rests on the theory and research about the isolation of the major perceptual units in sentence perception. It is obvious that the processes of perception are involved to some extent in rendering acceptability intuitions, since a sentence must be apprehended in some sense in order to be adjudged acceptable, ambiguous, etc. We can expect there to be cases in which the perceptual processes themselves modify our apparent intuitions.

3.1 Primacy Explained   Since the theory of speech perception has an independent status in the theory of language, this approach is efficient: it rests on established concepts. For example, main/subordinate clause processing differences provide an explanation of the Primacy principle. Since subordinate clauses are retained in a more literal form, departures from canonical surface order would increase processing load more than in the case of main clauses. This asymmetry in processing load does not predict that there always will be fewer optional movement rules that can apply to subordinate clauses in a language. But it does predict that if there is an asymmetry in the range of application it will be in that direction. That prediction is exactly the Primacy principle (see Bever, 1975).

The behavioral explanation also accounts for why the principle holds more strongly for initial than for final clauses. The processing difference between main and subordinate clauses should matter less when the subordinate is sentence-final. Townsend and Bever (1978) found behavioral evidence that in final position the subordinate/main processing differences are attenuated in the predicted way.

3.2 Nouniness Explained. Recall now the nouniness acceptability squishes presented in (1) and (2) above. The various sequence types within these examples do appear to differ systematically with respect to the presence of verb tense and N-V-N sequences. All of the a, b, c, and d examples have N-V-N sequences. The a-cases are sentential subjects and have in addition tensed verbs. The b cases have infinitival verbs. The c and d examples have nominalized verbs, but the d cases in addition bear the subordinating element *'s*. Finally, the e cases consist of nominalizations without N-V-N sequences.

The most dramatic contrasts in Ross's data obtain between the a and e cases. The a cases, N-V-N and tensed, are far more potentially effective segmentation units than the e cases, which are neither N-V-N nor tensed. Between these extremes the sequences order themselves in terms of how deverbal the verb element of the sequence is: the infinitives of the b cases are more verbal than the nominalizations, and the nominalizations with the possessive inflection are even less verbal (cf. nouns are objects of possession) (See Tenenhaus and Carroll, 1975).

What seems to be going on is this: to the extent that the listener characteristically recodes a sequence as a coherent segmentation unit, that sequence will be more acceptable in syntactic environments that select clauses and less acceptable in syntactic environments that select nouns. Squish effects, thus, rest upon an internal confusion between the application of a process to a category (e.g., ''S'') and the typical behavioral reflex of that category (e.g., ''perceptual clause'').

4. NEW FACTS

The behavioral account of nouniness and primacy extends immediately to a range of other empirical domains — the two explanations in fact interact to provide an account of a set of complex and otherwise puzzling facts.

4.1 A New Nouniness Squish Fact The account of speech perception given in section 3 predicts new levels in the squish, ones not specifically analyzed by Ross, but rather predicted by the principle that coherent sentence processing units are bearers of propositional structures. The contrast in (b) is such a case.
(5a) *It bothers Herbie the whistling.
(5b) ??It bothers Herbie the whistling by Max.
Ross did not analyze such cases, but the speech perception theory predicts that the sequence *the whistling by Max* should be more coherent — and therefore more clause-like from the viewpoint of the process of extraposition — than the sequence *the whistling*. The reason is that the former sequence completely represents the proposition MAX WHISTLE, the latter fails to represent the subject relation *whistle*. This account follows the general account of the nouniness squish presented above.

4.2 The Primacy Squish The differences between subordinate clauses characterized by Townsend and Bever allow us to *predict* the possibility of an acceptability ordering of Primacy principle facts. "Causal" subordinates, like *if*, should show the weakest effects, while "adversative" clauses, like *although*, show the strongest effects. The sentences below seem to bear this out. It appears to us that the sentences from (6a) to (6c) are ordered in level of relative acceptability (just as they are ordered in level of relative causality and independence of the subordinate clause).

(6a) If quickly John left, everyone will be relieved.
(6b) ?When quickly John left, everyone was relieved.
(6c) ??Although quickly John left, everyone was relieved.

The primacy squish does *not* predict that *if*-clauses are less restrictive for all rules than *although*-clauses. For example the primacy squish predicts a pronominal command squish in which initial pronouns are *less* acceptable in initial *because*-clauses than *although*-clauses. This follows from the interpretation that a pronoun in a main clause cannot precede the first expression of the nounphrase it refers to. The more "like" a main clause the subordinate clause is, the less acceptable an initial pronoun in that clause should be. That is, such pronouns in *if*-clauses should be *less* acceptable than in *although*-clauses, as in (7). (We thank D. Townsend for calling these cases to our attention).

(7a) ?If he arrived late, something must have happened to Harry
(7b) Although he arrived early, something must have happened to Harry

4.3 Complex Compounds. Another area to which we have extended the account of nouniness is word formation. It is well known that in some cases noun *phrases* may participate in noun compounding.

(8a) a doll that is a little girl ⟶ a (little girl) doll
(8b) a doll that is a girl with a bike ⟶ a (girl with a bike) doll

Complex compound examples, like those in (8), become far less acceptable when the noun phrase to be inserted as the left-most constitutent contains tensed verbs and N-V-N sequences.

(9a) a doll that is a girl playing guitar ⟶ a (girl playing guitar) doll
(9b) a doll that is a girl that says "Mama" ⟶ a (girl that says "Mama") doll

When otherwise suitable segmentation sequences occur within a lexical structure, they may stimulate segmentation and recoding erroneously. Consider the plight of the listener, or intuiter, for sentence (10).

(10) For your birthday I will bring you a nice girl playing guitar/doll.

Notice first that the compound is hard to recognize, *girl* and *doll* are separated by the verb phrase *playing guitar*, which provides some processing loan encouragment of segmentation. Second, *girl playing guitar* can be (mis-)recognized as an N-V-N clausal unit. Finally, this mis-recognition is locally consistent with the rest of the information in the sentence — that is, the material prior to the slash constitutes a reasonable sentence by itself.

When complex compounds have less complete left-constituents, like *little girl doll*, these problems are mitigated, as in (11).

(11) For your birthday I will bring you a nice little girl/doll.

In this case, while the local information is still consistent with a segmentation at the slash position, nothing intervenes between *girl* and *doll,* and the suitability of *little girl* as an independent segmentation unit is low. (See Carroll, 1979b, for further discussion and report of related experimental research.)

4.3 The Nouniness-Primacy Squish. The behavioral explanation of the nouniness and primacy phenomena encourage behavioral consideration of their interaction. To examine this possibility, we embedded various structure types from the noun squish into subordinate constructions at different points in the Primacy squish. Consider (12), for example.

(12a) If it bothers Herbie that Max is whistling, that's too bad.
(12b) Although it bothers Herbie that Max is whistling, that's too bad.
(12c) ?if it bothers Herbie Max's whistling, that's too bad.
(12d) ?*Although it bothers Herbie Max's whistling, that's too bad.
(12e) ??If it bothers Herbie the whistling, that's too bad.
(12f) *Although it bothers Herbie the whistling, that's too bad.

The relevant generalization about these facts is that the effect of extraposition on the noun constituents is mitigated in *if*-clauses relative to *although*-clauses. These facts are predicted by the greater causality and independence of *if*-clauses. They occasion more segmentation following the object nounphrase *Herbie* which, in turn, isolates the extraposed nounphrase as a relatively independent perceptual clause. Conversely the more subordinate *although*-clause occasions less segmentation, leaving the extra-posed nounphrase to be incorporated as part of the preceding clause.

We have also isolated complementary cases, cases in which the fully acceptable sequence embeds the more noun-like constituent.

(13a) ?If that Max whistles bothers Herbie, that's too bad.
(13b) *Although that Max whistles bothers Herbie, that's too bad.
(13c) If Max's whistling bothers Herbie, that's too bad.
(13d) Although Max's whistling bothers Herbie, that's too bad.
(13e) If the whistling bothers Herbie, that's too bad.
(13f) Although the whistling bothers Herbie, that's too bad.

In these cases as well the acceptability is lower in the *although*-clauses, and particularily so at the most clause-like end of the noun-clause continuum. The explanation of these facts rests on the relative complexity of a complex subject embedded within a subordinate clause. During processing, subordinate clauses are retained in a relatively sequential form. This predicts that a complex non-canonical internal structure will cause greater processing load, than in main clauses.

Also consistent with our analysis of the primacy phenomenon, the unacceptability of the various subordinate types is mitigated when the critical clauses are postpositioned, as in (14).

(14a) That's too bad if it bothers Herbie the whistling.
(14b) ?That's too bad although it bothers Herbie the whistling.
(14c) That's too bad if that Max whistles bothers Herbie.
(14d) ?That's too bad although that Max whistles bothers Herbie.

5. THE REAL NATURE OF INTUITIONS.

The most basic linguistic facts reside in the personal intuitions rendered freely by native speakers of a language. Such data provide a simple and direct vehicle for testing theories of linguistic representation. Nevertheless, intuitions are not empirical primitives but complex behavioral performances in their own right. Methodological studies of intuitions have documented a range of relevant but extra-grammatical factors (Bever, 1970; Carroll, Bever, and Pollack, 1979; Gleitman and Gleitman, 1970; Spencer, 1973). The present essay also makes this point: in order to experience an acceptability intuition for a sentence, one characterically apprehends the sentence — and the processes that organize speech perception will contribute to the ultimate nature of the intuition.

There are three obvious options for dealing with the sort of data we have considered here. First, we may with Ross assume that non-discrete data directly imply non-discrete theories of grammar. This is not satisfactory: Non-discrete grammar offers no account of why the continua are the way they are. The correspondances between such grammatical analyses and the predictions of our behavioral account would have to be viewed as mere coincidence. And moreover, no distinction at all could be drawn between the squishy intuitions we have been concerned with here and the ineluctable intuitions upon which linguistic theory relies. A second option is to treat *all* acceptability phenomena as behavioral and non-structural (Clark and Haviland, 1974). This alternative also is inadequate: It cannot explain the categorical (un)acceptability of examples at either end of a continuum.

The third alternative is that examples with intermediate acceptability rest on an internal confusion by the informant between the application of a linguistic proces to a category (e.g., ''S'') and to the typical behavioral reflex of that category (e.g. ''perceptual clause''). This explanation explains a variety of acceptability facts as well as predicting hitherto unnoticed ones. However, it is important to specify what the general conditions are that will lead to an acceptability squish. We might expect such a confusion to arise because of the everyday behavioral importance of extracting propositions, even from degraded surface forms. A further source of difficulty may be that in English, ''S'' can dominate ''N'' as well as the reverse; this property of mutual dominability excludes any structural way of disentangling the two categories in intermediate cases.

An underlying theme of our proposal is that *all* grammatical properties are categorical and that all apparent departures from this have a general explanation in an interactionist framework — a totally discrete system of grammar interacting with behavioral processes.

Discussion

Don Foss: Counting, Computing, and Comprehending An important theoretical issue facing psycholinguistics in the 80's is the degree to which components of a viable comprehension model may be said to be independent. Both Wanner's and Swinney's papers bear, in different ways, on this issue. Because of space limitations, I will restrict my comments here to Wanner's interesting paper. These remarks will also address the issue Wanner raised of how one chooses among candidate parsing algorithms.

Wanner has proposed that the parsing problems identified by Frazier and Fodor (1978) can be handled within the framework of an ATN by appropriate scheduling algorithms (corresponding to Low Right Association and Minimal Attachment). In a related paper he justifies the choice of these algorithms by claiming that they both follow from the same principle, namely they both minimize computation during parsing. Thus, a theory of scheduling is itself dependent upon the principle of minimal computation. Importantly, he goes on to propose a metric for determining when computation is minimized: one counts the arcs that are traversed during the computation. Schedules that lead to low numbers of arcs are preferred over schedules that lead to high numbers. This is an important proposal. When investigators have tried to examine the psychological properties of ATNs it has not been clear what aspects of them count as contributing to comprehension difficulty. Wanner has taken a stand on this issue.

In evaluating Wanner's proposal we may first ask whether the arc counting metric is the only one that is relevant for determining psychological complexity. Since an ATN does not "look ahead", a property that Wanner is trying to save, it sometimes makes incorrect decisions—it goes down false paths. When it discovers that it is going down a blind alley, it then backs up and tries again. Backing up costs time when an ATN is implemented on a computer, and it is reasonable to suppose that it costs psychological resources when it happens during comprehension by human listeners. Thus, we may ask whether the total resources used by the listener are really less when we are restricted to a model that does not permit "look ahead." In order to answer this question, we must have a measure of complexity that measures the cost of backing up (counting total arcs traversed is surely one candidate). Wanner's proposal is a step in the right direction, but so far one cannot really tell whether it is sufficient grounds for rejecting models with the "look ahead" feature.

It would be useful if there were grounds for rejecting all "look ahead" models, for the task of constructing viable parsing theories would then be considerably simplified (though still enormously difficult). However, it is not yet clear whether or how much information is stored in a buffer before decisions about the parse are made. To the extent that a "parsing buffer" exists, we cannot reject all models with the "look ahead" feature, much as we would like to. (Discussions of parsing models, buffers, and the like should also include consideration of models using "beam search" techniques analogous to those of the HARPY speech understanding system [see Klatt, 1977, for a review], but space does not permit such discussion here.)

I would like to make one specific criticism of the Low Right Association scheduling principle since it brings into high relief the issue of whether or not two components of comprehension are independent. Consider sentences (1) and (2).

(1) The people to whom Tom spoke yesterday went shopping.
(2) The people to whom Tom will speak yesterday went shopping.

While the word "yesterday" can be attached to either verb in sentence (1), it clearly is attached to "spoke," following the principle of Low Right Association. However, in sentence (2) "yesterday" is not attached at that point. There is a conflict between tenses such that the future tense of "speak" precludes the modifier "yesterday". The latter word gets attached to the next clause, violating Low Right Association.

The point at issue concerns how this occurs. Is it the case that a later acting semantic system detects the discrepancy among the tenses and causes a backup and reparse? Or does the existence of the future tense marker affect the subsequent parsing of the clause? If the latter option is correct then we have a system in which the ongoing parse is affected by the semantic analysis tree that is developing as the sentence is processed. Devising a test to discriminate betweeen these two alternatives should have high priority since they exemplify two very different classes of comprehension theories.

Jurek Kirakowski   There are three recent developments in the field of speech perception which I would first like to draw together; two of these have already been touched upon during this symposium, the third has but recently appeared in print. From this synthesis I will make a few comments on the papers presented in our seminar.

The first comment concerns the important proposal that we may, after all, be able to design a model which takes us directly from the sound wave to the lexical representation; that our awareness of phonology may be a subsequent "top-down" process. This direct access approach was very clearly stated by Klatt. The second is the re-assessment of the role of prosody in speech perception: Kirakowski & Myers (1975, 1977) found evidence for the interdependence of prosody and grammar in perceptual processing. The third is Schlesinger's recent work in which he argues for a means of getting from strings of lexical items ("utterances") to a deeper representation ("I-markers") without passing through a stage of syntactic representation (Schlesinger, 1977).

Although one may disagree with Foss's remarks on the necessity for constraining the production of yet more models of speech perception (surely, non-viable models can be left to their own devices?), the ATN model as espoused by Wanner may nevertheless be questioned on two grounds. Firstly, it is difficult to see how prosodic information could be handled by the decision-making part of the program, simply because ATN works one word at a time and prosodic information almost by definition spans several words. But secondly, the perception of syntax itself may be handled in a top-down way, after the I-marker has been obtained.

Research reported in Kirakowski (1977) strongly supports the contention of there being a "time window" akin to that proposed by Frazier & Fodor—but defined in speech by the prosodic contour.

Turning now to Swinney's paper, we find that his data fit in very well with this synthesis. What is interesting to explore is the question of how much processing is done on each word immediately after input. One may speculate that only some classes of words are analysed so exhaustively and dramatically soon after presentation: those relating to the content of the utterance. Again, such words are usually differentiated from function words by prosodic means, and as Foss has shown, there are important immediate consequences after prosodically cued salient points have been perceived in speech.

SESSION V
BIOLOGICAL BASES OF REPRESENTATION

Seminar 9: Representation and the brain

Chair	DONALD MACKAY
Speakers	E. F. EVANS, SHEILA BLUMSTEIN
Discussants	KARL PRIBRAM, SHULI REICH,
	RUTH LESSER, ERIC KELLER

Seminar 10: Representation and evolution

Chair	JOHN MARSHALL
Speakers	GORDON HEWES, PHILIP LIEBERMAN
Discussants	IGNATIUS MATTINGLY,
	COLWYN TREVARTHEN, PETER MARLER

THE COGNITIVE REPRESENTATION OF SPEECH
T. Myers, J. Laver, J. Anderson (editors)
© North-Holland Publishing Company, 1981

Neural Encoding of Speech Signals at Peripheral and Central Levels of the Auditory System

E.F. EVANS

University of Keele

There have been very few systematic studies of the behaviour of single neurones in the mammalian auditory system in response to speech signals. A notable exception to this generalization are the studies of Young and Sachs summarized elsewhere in this volume, where the activity of large numbers of fibres in the cochlear nerve has been systematically mapped under conditions of stimulation by steady-state vowels. Most other studies have been conducted using steady tones, broad band noise or click stimuli (e.g. summarized in Kiang et al., 1965; Evans, 1975). In the last 10-20 years, however, more complex stimuli have been employed: amplitude and frequency-modulated tones (e.g. summarized in Moller, 1978; Evans, 1968, 1974a, 1975), multicomponent tone complexes and noise signals having comb-filtered noise spectra (e.g. summarized in Evans, 1975, 1978b), animal vocalizations themselves (e.g. summarized in Evans, 1974a; Bullock, 1977), and a limited set of human speech stimuli (e.g. Kiang and Moxon, 1972, 1974; Moore and Cashin, 1974; Hashimoto et al., 1975; Kiang, 1975; Rupert et al., 1977). From these studies, we have to infer the manner in which speech signals are processed and encoded by the auditory nervous sytem. A picture of this is most complete at the most peripheral level of the system, where we understand best the constraints put upon the neural representation of speech signals in what appears to be basically a short-term spectral representation. Here, the responses of auditory neurones are relatively homogeneous, stereotyped and straightforward to analyse. Yet even at this level, the exact nature of the representation is in doubt, particularly for speech presented at high sound levels. More centrally, in spite of the technical difficulties introduced by anaesthesia, and the variety and variability of neural response, it has been possible to identify mechanisms which serve to enhance the spectral and temporal contrast of encoded multicomponent and time-varying signals like speech, and to enhance features which appear likely to have salience to the animals themselves.

PERIPHERAL ENCODING: SHORT-TERM SPECTRAL ANALYSIS OF ACOUSTIC SIGNALS

Each of the fibres in the cochlear nerve can be considered, to a first approximation, to act as a narrow-band filter, the 30,000 or so fibres in the mammalian cochlear nerve thus constituting a filter bank. That is to say, the impulse activity of each fibre is increased by energy above a certain threshold value having a frequency falling within a relatively narrow band. Depending upon the centre (characteristic) frequency (CF) of the fibre (i.e. its origin along the cochlear partition), the cut-offs are steep, ranging (in cat and guinea pig) from 50-100 dB/oct at 1kHz to over 500 dB/oct at 10kHz. Their effective bandwidths (i.e. the half-power bandwidth) again depend on characteristic frequency, being about 100 Hz for CFs up to about

1kHz and 10% thereafter. Although there is systematic variation in these values from individual to individual, they are reasonably representative of measurements employing pure tone, broad-band and comb-filtered noise stimuli (Evans & Wilson, 1973; Evans, 1977b, 1978b). Cochlear fibres therefore act more like multiple pole band-pass than resonant filters, with a consequent optimization of the compromise between spectral and temporal resolution, the latter being of the order of 5-10 msecs.

This remarkably sharp cochlear filtering is manifest in the mean rates of discharge of fibres (within limits to be described later) and, for frequencies up to about 4-5kHz, in the temporal patterning of the discharges. That is to say, it is those frequencies which fall within the effective bandwidth of the filter that tend to dominate the mean discharge rate of the fibre and the time intervals between the spike discharges. Particularly for signals within 40 dB or so of the fibre's threshold, the filtering acts remarkably linearly, and the properties of cochlear fibres can be accurately simulated by simple electronic analogues (e.g. Evans, 1977c, 1980a; Kiang et al., 1979). This first approximation account ignores certain important cochlear non-linearities which are responsible for the generation of small levels of combination tones and of 'lateral suppression' phenomena, where the excitation generated by a stimulus at one frequency can be suppressed by that at another, nearby, frequency (see Evans, 1975 for review).

These considerations of physiological cochlear filtering are relevant because they are consistent with measurements of the human frequency selectivity obtained by psychophysical methods. Thus, the physiological effective bandwidths (obtained in cats) approximate to the values of the 'critical bands' in man, being somewhat smaller than the latter for frequencies above 1kHz (Evans & Wilson, 1973; see Evans, 1977a for review). The cut-off slopes and shapes of the frequency threshold ('tuning') curves of cochlear fibres are consistent with those determined by psychophysical masking techniques yielding the so-called 'psychoacoustic tuning curves' (e.g. Zwicker, 1974; Wightman et al., 1977). There is some difficulty in reconciling the filtering bandwidths derived from all the different types of psycho-acoustic and behavioural (e.g. Pickles, 1975; Moore, 1978; Johnson-Davies & Patterson, 1979) techniques of measurement (e.g. between simultaneous and non-simultaneous masking conditions), but an effective bandwidth of 10% (i.e. about 1/6 octave) for each element of the ear's peripheral filter bank would appear to be more appropriate than the value of 1/3 octave, commonly employed in modelling the "front end" of the auditory system.

This limited frequency resolution imparts important constraints on the first stages of processing by the auditory system. It sets limits on the closeness of the single frequency components that can be resolved; and conversely, it determines which harmonics of a complex sound will interact and dominate the fine temporal structure of discharge of the cochlear fibres (e.g. see Evans, 1978b, 1980b). Thus, animals such as chinchillas, with poor frequency selectivity compared with cats and man, cannot distinguish vowels having closely spaced formants (e.g. / æ / from /a/ but can others (e.g. /a/ from /i/; Miller, 1977). In hearing impairment due to cochlear pathology in man, where deterioration in peripheral selectivity is predicted from the animal physiology and confirmed psychophysically, impairment of intelligibility of the back vowels has been observed (see Evans, 1978a for review). Similar, but smaller deteriorations in cochlear frequency selectivity occur at high sound levels (about 70 dB SPL and above) as measured physiologically (see Evans, 1977b; Moller, 1977) and psychophysically (Pick, 1980).

The speech fundamental frequency is encoded at the cochlear nerve level in a number of ways. Fibres having characteristic frequencies corresponding to the fundamental frequency have relatively broad tuning, and 'place' representation is therefore likely to be poor. However, the time structure (phase-locking) of their discharges will reflect the fundamental frequency. Because of the limited frequency selectivity of cochlear fibres, it is doubtful that there will be sufficient resolution of the harmonic structure of the formants that pattern recognition pitch extraction type mechanisms (such as reviewed by Wilson, 1974, and de Boer, 1976) could operate on the place represented spectral information. On the other hand, for the same reason, interaction of harmonics within the cochlear nerve filters would produce significant modulation of discharge; and this can be 'followed' by cochlear nerve fibres and cochlear nucleus cells for frequencies up to several hundred Hz. This modulation of discharge is enhanced at the cochlear nucleus level by lateral inhibitory mechanisms to be described later.

THE PROBLEM OF THE LIMITED PERIPHERAL DYNAMIC RANGE

Like other receptors, cochlear nerve fibres have a limited dynamic range over which they can signal, in their rate of discharge, the level of a frequency component. This is limited in the great majority of cases to some 20-60 dB. Because the thresholds of normally tuned fibres occur within 20 dB or so of the audiometric threshold, this limited dynamic range constitutes a severe problem for auditory theory (see Evans, 1978a for review). For signals having resolvable components with energy below some 40-60 dB SPL, the profile of changes in mean discharge rate across the cochlear fibre array yields a spectrographic-like representation of the sound. This is the classical 'place' theory of the neural representation of signals. For higher sound levels, however, such as those encountered in moderately loud conversational speech, the discharge rates of the great majority of cochlear fibres are, in cat experiments, saturated, and are consequently unable to signal thereby the spectral distribution of energy in the stimulus. A very small proportion of fibres (10%) are not, however, completely saturated, but it is difficult to see how this small number can adequately convey the spectral information at these high stimulus levels (Palmer & Evans, 1979). (Interestingly, these fibres form a sub-population of cochlear nerve fibres having low spontaneous activity (Evans & Palmer, 1980)). The alternative possibility is that, because the fine time structure of the discharge patterns of cochlear fibres reflects their filtering (for frequencies up to 4-5kHz) for all sound levels regardless of saturation of their mean discharge rate (de Boer and de Jongh, 1978; Evans, 1977b, 1980b), this could be utilised to encode the 'place' information. If the higher levels of the auditory system could in fact extract this information, this would be a very robust 'place' representation of complex spectra such as those of speech, valid across a very wide dynamic range, as has been clearly demonstrated by Young and Sachs in their article in this volume.

It must be emphasised that these considerations depend upon the comparison between the behaviour of neurones in the anaesthetised cat and the psychophysics of the awake human ear. Such factors as the activity of the ear middle muscles, and of the efferent nervous system, are rendered inactive in physiological experiments, but may conceivably play a more crucial role than is apparent at present in extending the dynamic range of the peripheral auditory system.

Other factors which may be relevant, but which need more exploration, are the effects of adaptation resulting from long-term stimulation. On the one hand, there is evidence that the dynamic ranges of cochlear nerve fibres are even smaller with long-duration stimuli (of the order of seconds) than those referred to above, detemined with short-duration stimuli (about 50 msec); (see Evans, 1980b). Against this, is the finding that with *continuous background* noise stimulation of the order of minutes, the discharge rate dynamic ranges are shifted upwards in a manner somewhat analogous to, but much more restricted than, that occurring in vision (Evans, 1974b).

CENTRAL MECHANISMS: ENHANCEMENT OF SPECTRAL AND TEMPORAL
CONTRASTS

The spectral representation of acoustic signals in the cochlear fibre array projects
to several, apparently parallel processing, sub-systems or pathways, beginning in
the first auditory nucleus, the cochlear nucleus. In each division of the cochlear
nucleus, the 'place' representation of frequency is preserved, but each pathway
reflects different types of neural processing (Kiang et al., 1973, Evans & Nelson,
1973; see Evans, 1975 for review). Of the three main pathways which can be followed
through the brainstem, two are of most relevance for the present purposes, for they
both ascend separately to the collicular levels of the auditory nervous system and
beyond. The Ventral Pathway arises in the ventral division of the cochlear nucleus.
Its properties are not substantially different from those of the cochlear nerve.

The Dorsal Pathway however, arising in neurones in the dorsal cochlear nucleus
exhibits the powerful effects of neural lateral inhibition. This means that the
neurones receive in addition to their excitatory inputs, inhibitory inputs depending
upon frequency. Signal components having frequencies adjacent to the characteristic
frequency are able to inhibit the spontaneous and driven activity of the neurones.
This inhibition is very powerful (compared with lateral suppression at the cochlear
nerve level, for example). It serves to enhance the contrast between active and
non-active neural regions representing the spectral composition of the signal,
particularly under those conditions of high sound levels where the distribution of
activity in the cochlear nerve level is blurred out because of saturation of the
discharge rate. Here, in the dorsal cochlear nucleus, the adjacent frequency
components falling in the lateral inhibitory 'side-bands' of a neurone serve to 'bias'
the cell's discharge to below saturation levels so that it can signal intensity
differences over a very wide dynamic range (Evans & Palmer, 1975; Evans, 1977b).
It is less clear how these cells receive information on the level of the signal
components — whether from the small percentage of the cochlear nerve fibres not
completely saturated at high stimulus levels, or whether it is by virtue of some
decoding operation of the fine time-structure of the cochlear fibre discharges (see
Evans, 1978b for review).

Under dynamic conditions, the lateral inhibition serves to enhance temporal
contrasts. Under conditions of amplitude modulation, the inhibition 'biases' the
cell's resting discharge towards lower rates so that the neural signal-to-noise ratio
is enhanced (see Evans, 1975 for review). Under conditions of frequency modulation,
the frequency region of excitation becomes more sharply defined and narrower as a
result of the action of lateral inhibition (see Moller, 1978 for review).

Probably as a result of asymmetrical distributions of lateral inhibition with a
longer latency and time course than the excitation, we encounter in the dorsal
cochlear nucleus the first signs of an enhancement of the response to frequency
change and direction of frequency change, analogous to that encountered in the
retina and visual cortex (see Evans, 1975 for review).

Inhibition in the cochlear nucleus also serves to enhance the phenomenon of 'off-
suppression' evident at the cochlear nerve level: terminating a stimulus or reducing
its level is followed by a transient decrease in the neurone's spontaneous activity and
excitability. This means that at the termination of a spectrally-patterned stimulation
there will exist, for a period depending on the duration and level of the stimulus, a
'mirror-image' pattern of activity across the neural array representing frequency.
Thus, adaptation to sounds such as speech stimuli can produce adaptation contrast
effects without the necessary involvement of opponent-type mechanisms, although
at the level of the dorsal cochlear nucleus opponent-type cells do exist. These are
inhibited by tones and excited when the stimuli are terminated (see Evans & Nelson,

1973, Evans, 1975 for review). The adaptation effects at the cochlear nerve level have been described in detail by Young and Sachs (1973).

CENTRAL MECHANISMS: ENHANCEMENT OF BIOLOGICALLY RELEVANT STIMULUS FEATURES

At progressively higher levels of the auditory system, greater variety and multiplicity of response is encountered and this has made systematic collection of data difficult. Neurones are often difficult to drive consistently, and the search for the optimum stimulus may exhaust the ingenuity and patience of the physiologist. Cortical neurones, in comparison to those in the periphery, habituate readily when presented with the same stimulus repeatedly (see Evans, 1968). It is therefore likely that it is the upper levels of the auditory system that are primarily affected in psycho-physical experiments investigating the effects of 'adapting' stimuli. Thus, at the level of the primary auditory cortex a substantial contrast in response properties and stimulus representation exists compared with the auditory periphery. Only about three quarters of the neurones in the auditory cortex respond to pure tones and only then if the temporal characteristics of the tones are appropriate (see Suga, 1973; Evans, 1974a; Bullock, 1977; and Newman, 1978 for reviews). Many of these neurones have wide frequency response areas covering several octaves, and therefore they are in no sense comparable with peripheral auditory neurones in terms of frequency specificity. In spite of these broad frequency response areas, half of the primary auditory cortical neurones do not respond to broad-band stimuli, i.e. noise or clicks, again in contrast to the situation at the cochlear nerve level, where all fibres do so.

Cortical units are much more consistently stimulated by sounds, complex in their spectrum or dynamics. For neurones in the cat primary auditory cortex, for example, whispered sounds, keys, and bird-like sounds ('backdoor noises', see Evans, 1974a) are more effective than tonal stimuli. 85-90% of the cells studied in the squirrel-monkey auditory cortex respond to the complex vocalizations of that species (see Newman, 1978). It is the analysis of these non-linear responses to complex sounds which has led to the concept of feature sensitivity and selectivity in the upper levels of the auditory system.

Many cortical units 'prefer' certain features of a complex stimulus against steady-state tonal stimulation. Sensitivity to stimulus onsets, to change in frequency, or to changes in stimulus amplitude or to temporal patterning of stimuli, is commonly found in cortical units. Of more interest, are the selectivities shown by different minorities of cells for stimulus features, some of which are likely to be biologically relevant. Thus, about 10% of the cortical neurones responding to tones do so *only* if the frequency is changing and in many cases only if it is changing in a certain direction, within certain frequency and rate-of-change limits (see Evans, 1968, 1974a for reviews). In the bat, in addition, there is evidence of selectivities for the rate of rise of the stimulus amplitude (Suga, 1971).

These feature sensitivities and selectivities have been studied most meaningfully in the squirrel monkey with reference to the part that they may play in the neural analysis of these animals' particularly discrete and well characterised species-specific vocalisations (see Newman, 1978 for review). While nearly 30% of the cells in the squirrel monkey's auditory cortex responded to a wide variety of vocalisations, a large proportion responded preferentially to one or a few of the call-types. 8% responded only to certain classes of calls, i.e. either the atonal or the tonal vocalizations, but not to both. Of particular interest, however, is the finding of 5% of neurones which were unresponsive to all stimuli except a single vocalisation type, so called 'specialists'. 'Specialists' for nearly all of the major call types have been found. There is evidence that higher proportions of these highly specific cells may be found in the surrounding non-primary areas of cortex.

These selectivities are resistant to changes in behavioural state (Newman & Symmes, 1974) i.e. level of arousal, or to light anaesthesia (Winter & Funkenstein, 1973). There is therefore good reason to believe that they might be of importance in the recognition, at the neural level, of one socially meaningful call as distinct from another. Whether these 'selectivities' are 'wired in' and how they are achieved, still remains to be determined.

From another mammalian species having highly specialised vocalisations — the bat — comes clear evidence of cortical selectivities for simultaneously present formants (Suga *et al.,* 1979). These cells have a substantially lower threshold, and respond much more vigorously, to an appropriate combination of harmonics in the vocalisations used for echo-location, than to either harmonic alone.

While these findings of sensitivities and selectivities to specific features of complex cells are somewhat piecemeal, they are sufficient to indicate the presence of mechanisms in the higher neural centres of the auditory system which could serve the purposes of the abstraction of certain features of stimuli having biological relevance. Likewise, the contrast between the properties of central neurones with those of the periphery may be taken as some indication of serial processing mechanisms along the auditory pathway, analogous to those described in the visual system.

Further support for this view comes from the effects of ablating auditory cortex on auditory behaviour (see Neff, 1977, Evans, 1974a for reviews). As might be expected from the relative lack of responsiveness of cortical neurones to steady tones, and their relative lack of frequency specificity, loss of auditory cortex does not substantially affect an animal's ability to discriminate differences of intensity and frequency, and pitch generalizations can be made normally. What functions are impaired, are the ability to relearn discriminations between different directions of frequency modulation and to detect differences in the spectral and temporal patterning of sounds. Thus, bilateral ablation of the auditory cortex eliminated the ability of monkeys to relearn and retain discriminations between vowel sounds, whereas the animals could still discriminate tones from broad-band noise. Lesions to the temporal lobes in man have been reported to produce analogous sensory deficits.

There is also psychophysical evidence of frequency-modulation specific elements ('channels') in human audition, obtained from studies of the effects of 'adaptation' to sinusoidal frequency modulation and frequency sweeps (e.g. Kay & Matthews, 1972; Gardner & Wilson, 1979; Regan & Tansley, 1979).

THE COGNITIVE REPRESENTATION OF SPEECH
T. Myers, J. Laver, J. Anderson (editors)
© North-Holland Publishing Company, 1981

Perception of Speech in Aphasia: Its Relation to Language Comprehension, Auditory Processing, and Speech Production.

SHEILA E. BLUMSTEIN

Brown University
and
Boston Aphasic Research Center

Speech is the first order process in the language communication chain. Both at the level of production and perception, it serves as the primary interface with the linguistic code. In perception, the acoustic waveform is ultimately processed and perceived by the listener in terms of a grammatically, linguistically meaningful system. In production, these grammatical and meaningful attributes are transmitted in the final analysis by the speaker in terms of a set of physiological events.

In aphasia, we see the breakdown of the language communication process. However, what is not clear is why the patients may manifest a deficit in either comprehension or production of language. Many levels of language processing can be implicated in such disorders, i.e. speech, phonology, syntax, semantics, the lexicon. In the past five years, we have attempted to determine the extent to which a failure in either the speech perception or speech production mechanism contributes to the constellation of defects found in aphasia and to ascertain whether such failures can characterize the underlying basis of aphasic disorders.

To address this issue, we have focused on the ability of aphasics to perceive and produce the segmental properties of language. Specifically, we have attempted to address the following questions:

1. Do speech perception deficits underlie language comprehension deficits in aphasia? This question is based on the assumption that to process the higher levels of language, i.e. syntax, meaning, at least some ability to perceive the properties of speech is required.
2. To what extent do speech perception deficits reflect auditory processing deficits? That is, an inability to process speech might be due to a low-level auditory processing impairment. In this case, speech processing difficulties would result from an inability of the auditory system to handle certain types of acoustic events, and thus any language-speech impairment would be secondary to these auditory deficits.
3. How is speech production affected by speech perception deficits? That is, if a patient manifests a disorder in the perception of phonetic segments, will a similar deficit in production be shown? Such a relation suggests that perception and production are actually linked during ongoing linguisitc processing. A dissociation would suggest that the two systems are at least partially autonomous in the language processing mechanism.

The hypothesis that speech perception deficits may underlie language comprehension deficits was stated perhaps most strongly by A.R. Luria (1970). He argued that the severe comprehension deficit evidenced by Wernicke's aphasics is due to an impairment in phonemic hearing, i.e. in the ability to distinguish minimal phonological contrasts as 'pa' vs. 'ba' in contrast to 'pa' vs. 'la'. Evidence in support of this position was derived from patients' failure to repeat alternating syllables distinguished by a minimal number of features, to differentiate between two contrasts by making a response to one and not the other (Luria, 1970) or to match an auditorily presented word to its picture when presented in an array of phonemically similar test items (Goldblum and Albert, 1972; Schnell, Jenkins and Pabon, 1964).

It is noteworthy that all of these tasks require more than a simple discrimination of contrasts. Rather, they ask the S to make a linguistic judgement either by responding in a certain way to one type of stimulus and not the other, or by using the stimulus as a label for a particular concept. Thus, the patient's deficit might not necessarily reflect a ''. . . disturbance of auditory analysis and synthesis. . .'' (Luria, 1979, p.115, but a failure to use the sounds of language in a linguistically relevant way. There have been four studies conducted in our lab to address this issue. Each has focused on a particular aspect of the question — the first addressed the ability of aphasics to match phonemic contrasts, the second two tested the perception of acoustic parameters relevant to particular phonetic dimensions, and the fourth explored the effects of increasing semantic demands on the perception of phonetic contrasts.

In order to test asphasics' ability to make phonemic contrasts, a series of natural speech stimuli were paired such that they varied systematically in terms of the nature of the phonological contrasts (Blumstein, Baker and Goodglass, 1977). The contrasts were drawn from the set of stop consonants [p t k b d g]. Two tests were constructed. The first contrasted real words, e.g. 'pit' vs. 'kit', and the second contrasted nonsense syllables similar in their phonological structure to real words but containing no meaning, e.g. 'pib' vs. 'kib'. S's task was to press a button marked Yes if the stimuli were the same and a button marked No if they were different. The aphasic patients who participated in this study were assigned to one of four diagnostic groups based on the results of a composite aphasic exam including psychological, language, and neurological tests. Patients with anterior lesions were assigned to two groups: those with clinically good comprehension (Broca's aphasics), and those with impaired comprehension (mixed anterior group). Patients with posterior lesions were also divided into two groups: patients with poor comprehension in the context of fluent speech (Wernicke's aphasics) and another group of patients who represented several diagnostic categories. Language comprehension was assessed by performance on the auditory comprehension subtest of the Goodglass-Kaplan aphasia battery (Goodglass and Kaplan, 1972).

Results indicated that all groups showed some deficit on the phoneme discrimination task, with all groups showing better performances on the discrimination of real words than nonsense syllables. More importantly, the Wernicke aphasics, the group with the most severe comprehension deficit, were not the most impaired in phoneme discrimination. The mixed anterior patients showed a greater phonemic hearing deficit than did the Wernicke aphasics. These results suggest that phoneme discrimination is not selectively impaired in Wernicke's aphasics in comparison to other groups, nor does it seem to be the basis for the comprehension deficit of these patients.

Nevertheless, a failure to find a selective deficit in discrimination of speech sounds does not rule out the possibility that comprehension deficits in aphasia and Wernicke's aphasia in particular may be attributable, at least in part, to an inability to use phonological attributes in a linguistically meaningful way. That is, it is one thing to be able to ascertain the presence or absence of differences between speech sounds and quite another to use a particular phonological attribute to represent the meaning of a given word in contrast to another. A deficit in this latter case should result in difficulty in assigning a label to a particular speech sound or in the inability to point reliably to an appropriate picture given the test item auditorily.

To investigate this issue, two studies were conducted exploring aphasics' ability to label and discriminate acoustic continua which varied systematically along a particular phonetic dimension (e.g. voicing or place of articulation) Blumstein, Cooper, Zurif, and Caramazza, 1977; Blumstein, Nigro, Tartter, and Statlender, 1979). Perception studies with normal Ss have shown that the perception of speech continua is categorical (Liberman, Harris, Hoffman, and Griffin, 1957). That is, when asked to label these stimuli, Ss perceive them in terms of discrete phonetic categories, changing their label abruptly at a particular point along the continuum. When asked to discriminate differences between stimuli taken from the same continuum, Ss can only discriminate reliably those stimuli which belong to (were labelled as) different phonetic categories; those stimuli which were labelled as the same phonetic category are not discriminated reliably.

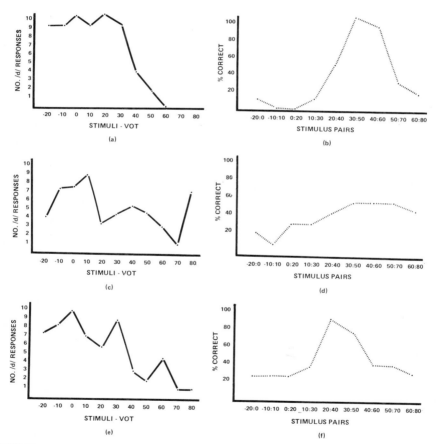

FIGURE 1   *The three patterns of labelling and discrimination of VOT shown by the aphasic patients. Each pattern (a,b), (c,d), (e,f) is represented by the performance of one aphasic patient. In (a), (c), (e), the abscissa represents the stimulus values of the continuum ranging from -20 to +80 VOT and the ordinate represents the total number of d-responses (maximum is 10). In (d), (b), (f), the abscissa represents the 'different' stimulus pairs; each pair was distinguished by a VOT of 20 msec. The ordinate represents the percent correct different responses.*

In the first study with aphasics (Blumstein, Cooper, Zurif, and Caramazza, 1977), the perception of voice-onset time as a cue to the voicing dimension, e.g. [d - t], was assessed. Voice-onset time or VOT can be defined as the timing relation between consonantal release and the onset of glottal pulsing. Voiced stops in English are characterized either by pre-voicing (glottal pulsing precedes consonantal release) or by a short lag (voice onset begins about 15 msec. after consonantal release). Voiceless consonants are characterized by a long lag of about 35 msec. An acoustic continuum was constructed ranging in VOT from -20 to +80 msec and two test tapes were made, an identification test and a discrimination test. In the identification test, Ss were required to identify each stimulus presented auditorily by pointing to the appropriate printed syllable, *da* or *ta.* In the discrimination test, they were asked to determine whether stimulus pairs presented were the same or different by pointing to a card marked *Yes* if the pair members were identical and *No* if they were not.

The performance of the aphasic patients on these tasks was characterized by three distinct patterns. These can be seen in Fig. 1. In the first pattern, patients performed normally on both identification and discrimination tasks. In the second, patients performed normally on the discrimination task, with appropriate boundary values, but were unable to identify the test stimuli reliably. In the third, patients could neither label nor discriminate the test stimuli.

These results demonstrate an important relation between identification and discrimination of a speech acoustic continuum. If a subject is able to identify reliably the stimuli, he is also able to make consistent discrimination judgements; no cases were found in which a patient was unable to discriminate but was able to label the stimuli. In addition, and perhaps of even greater significance, discrimination ability was reflected by peaks at the phoneme boundaries *even* for subjects who were unable to label the stimuli. Thus, it seems that discrimination ability underlies phoneme perception, and the use of linguisitc categories as discrete phonemic entities is based upon the system's ability to discriminate difficulties along a particular dimension.

The failure of some patients to both label and discriminate the stimuli, can be attributed to their inability to discriminate phonemic contrasts. More importantly, the impairment of those patients who can discriminate but cannot label the stimuli reflects an inability to maintain a stable configuration or category label — that is, there is a deficit in the relation between the sound and its linguistic usage or meaning. It is important to note here, that of four patients who evidenced the dissociation between labelling and discrimination, three of them were Wernicke's aphasics. These results indicate that Wernicke aphasics do not evidence a deficit in discriminating or perceiving phonemic contrasts, but rather seem to manifest an inability to relate sound structure to linguistic meaning.

Nevertheless, as in the previous study, the perception of VOT does not relate in any direct way to level of auditory comprehension. As Fig. 2 shows, some patients with excellent language comprehension fail to label or discriminate the stimuli, and perhaps more importantly, the S with the worst auditory language comprehension performed the perception tasks normally.

Similar results to those for the perception of VOT were found in a study of the perception of place of articulation (Blumstein, Nigro, Tartter and Statlender, 1979). Place of articulation is cued acoustically by the gross shape of the spectrum at consonantal release (Stevens and Blumstein, 1978) and is manipulated in acoustic continua by varying the onset frequency of the burst in relation to the onset frequency and direction and extent of the formant transitions. Ss were presented with two place of articulation continua varying along the phonetic dimension [b d g] for labelling and discrimination. The first continuum contained both burst and transition cues and the second continuum contained only transition cues. Results indicated that, as in the VOT study, labelling ability hinged crucially on discrimination ability. Further, there was no difference in performance depending on the particular acoustic cues used in the continuum (Blumstein et al, 1979). However, unlike the VOT results, Ss showed tremendous difficulty in perceiving place of articulation and many Ss failed to complete the tasks.

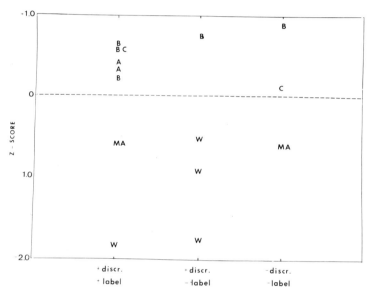

FIGURE 2 *Performance of aphasic subjects on the discrimination and labelling of a VOT continuum in relation to level of auditory comprehension. The aphasic subjects represented include Broca's (B), Mixed Anterior (MA), Conduction (C), Anomic (A) and Wernicke (W) aphasics. The abscissa represents performance on the discrimination and labelling tasks. A plus (+) indicates normal performance, a minus (—) impaired performance. The ordinate represents the aphasics' performance on the auditory comprehension subtest of the Goodglass-Kaplan Aphasic test battery converted to z-scores.*

Nevertheless, what is critical is that regardless of the phonetic dimension and the acoustic cues signalling that dimension, patients show a unique dissociation between labelling and discrimination ability. Thus, failure to label stimuli is not based on the apprehension of a particular acoustic dimension but rather on the "encoding" or classifying of that dimension into a linguistically relevant category.

The hypothesis that the association between sound-meaning correspondences accounts especially for the Wernicke aphasics' deficit was tested in a recent study (Baker, Blumstein, Goodglass, 1979). A series of three experiments was designed to test for the perception of phonological contrasts while systematically changing the semantic demands required of the subject to complete the task. If semantics or the sound-meaning relation is especially vulnerable in aphasia, then error rate should increase as the task requires more semantic processing. The first task was a replication of Blumstein et al. (1977) and simply required that the S discriminate (respond *Yes* or *No*) a pair of real words contrasting in a limited set of features (e.g. pear vs. bear). Results indicated that, as in the other experiment, Wernicke's aphasics are inferior to Broca's aphasics in making same-different judgements of phonemic contrasts. However, when subjects were required to make a same-different judgement given an auditory stimulus followed by a picture (e.g. auditorily presented 'pear', followed by a picture of a 'bear'), the performance spread between Broca's and Wernicke's aphasics widened. These results suggest that the deficit of the Wernicke aphasics can not be purely phonological, but rather meaning or semantic processing is implicated as well. This is supported further by the results of the third task which required subjects to point to the appropriate picture of an array of four, given the auditory presentation of its name. Results indicated that although Wernicke aphasics made errors based on phonemic contrasts (e.g. given 'bear', they pointed to 'pear'), they made a greater number of errors based on semantic contrasts (e.g. given 'bear', they pointed to 'wolf'). In contrast, Broca's aphasics made equal numbers of phonemic and semantic errors. Thus, semantic contrasts seemed to enhance the poor performance of Wernicke's aphasics.

Without question then the speech processing deficit of aphasic patients is not 'purely' phonological. Nevertheless, it is clear from the results of the studies reviewed, that there is some deficit in phonological processing, although not of the order or degree required to be the basis for the language comprehension abilities of aphasic patients. The failure of aphasic patients to perform normally in discriminating phonological contrasts, e.g. 'pear' vs 'bear', could reflect a speech processing deficit per se or an auditory processing deficit. It is to this question that we will now turn.

The hypothesis that language-speech deficits are a secondary consequence of low-level auditory processing deficits is not a new one. Efron (1963) and Swisher (1962), among others, have shown that left brain-damaged patients evidence deficits in tasks of temporal order judgement or intensity discrimination, and in addition require a considerably longer separation between two stimuli before they can judge them as two distinct events. Although these studies clearly demonstrate an auditory processing deficit in aphasic patients, they do not test directly the relation between such tasks and speech perception. The conclusion then that it is auditory processing deficits which cause speech-language problems is not inherent in the results obtained. More direct evidence however has been provided by Tallal and Piercy (1975). Working with a group of childhood aphasics, they showed that these children have difficulty discriminating transient acoustic events, i.e. rapid formant transitions important in speech as cues to place of articulation. In contrast, when the length of the transitions was increased while maintaining the phonetic percept, discrimination performance improved. These results suggest that speech processing deficits result from an inability of the *auditory* system to handle certain types of acoustic events, and any language problem is secondary to these deficits. Moreover, they suggest a principled explanation for the apparently great difficulty processing the phonetic dimension of place of articulation in aphasia.

Nevertheless, these results do not speak to the auditory processing abilities of adult aphasics as they effect speech-language processing. Tallal extended her work with lengthened transitions to residual adult aphasics and found a non-significant improvement in their discrimination abilities with lengthened transitions. Taking off from Tallal's findings, we decided to explore this issue in detail (Blumstein et al., 1979). First we asked whether systematically increased formant transitions from 45 to 65 to 85 msec for the stop consonants 'da' and 'ga' would show systematic increases in discrimination ability across a large group of aphasics. Second, we asked whether improved discrimination would result in improved labelling of the same stimuli. Third, we asked whether auditory stimuli, varying in the same parameters as the speech stimuli, would show parallel performance with the speech stimuli.

In this case, we used the third formant transitions of the 'da' and 'ga' stimuli at the three transition lengths. Results for the labelling and discrimination formant transitions and 'da' - 'ga' stimuli containing only formant transitions presented at the three transition rates are shown in Fig. 3. These data are derived from six anterior aphasics, seven posterior aphasics, and five non-brain-damaged control patients. Considering first discrimination, there is no consistent pattern for the group data or for individual Ss showing a systematic increase in performance as transition length is increased. Further, although there is a slight increase in performance in labelling 65 msec transitions compared to 45 msec transitions for anterior and posterior aphasics for burst and no burst conditions, the increase is non-significant. Perhaps more importantly, there was *no* systematic effect for *any* subject in either labelling or discrimination performance as transition length

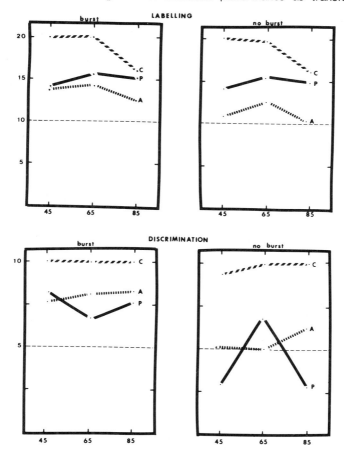

FIGURE 3 *Mean correct performance for labelling (20 observations) and discrimination (10 observations) of [d] and [g] varying in transition length for normal controls (C), Anterior (A), and posterior (P) aphasics. The abscissa represents the three transition lengths (45, 65, 85 msec.). The dotted line represents chance performance.*

increased. Finally, performance on the non-speech stimuli showed no effects of lengthened transitions, and indeed, there were several cases where there was a dissociation between the ability to discriminate speech and non-speech stimuli. Thus, there does not seem to be a direct relation between the ability to process acoustic dimensions in speech stimuli and analagous ones in non-speech stimuli. In sum, the results of this study do not support the general notion that tracking rapid acoustic events forms the basis of the speech processing deficit in aphasia, nor does it support the idea that auditory processing deficits underlie speech processing deficits in these patients.

The effects of phonological processing deficits as measured by segment perception and discussed in this paper, then, seem to be fairly elusive. On the one hand, they do not seem to correlate with level of auditory language comprehension and, on the other, they do not reflect, at least in a direct way, low-level auditory processing deficits. One possible effect of impaired phonological processing, however, might be on the production system. That is, if segment perception is impaired, it could ultimately affect segment production. Such effects could be manifested in an inability to maintain phonetic distinctions in production as a direct consequence of the fragility of the perceptual system in maintaining such distinctions.

This issue was addressed as a secondary question in the study investigating the perception of VOT in aphasia discussed above (Blumstein, Cooper, Zurif and Caramazza, 1979). The production of VOT can be assessed by means of an acoustic analysis of stop consonant productions. In particular, studies with normals have revealed that English-speaking subjects pronouncing words in citation form produce two distinct non-overlapping ranges of VOT responses for voiced and voiceless stop consonants sharing the same place of articulation, e.g. /d/-/t/ (Lisker and Abramson, 1964, 1967). The question then is whether aphasic patients show similar patterns of production of VOT as do normals and whether the patterns of production relate in any direct way to patterns of perception.

VOT analysis of the production of [d]-[t] was compared to the perception of this phonetic dimension in eight aphasic patients. Results can be summarized as follows — two patients (anomics) who showed normal discrimination and labelling functions in perception, also showed, as do normals, two clear-cut VOT production categories: two aphasics (one Broca and one Wernicke) who could discriminate but not label the stimuli in perception and one conduction aphasic who could neither label nor discriminate these stimuli, showed two clear-cut VOT production categories, but a number of target productions fell into the opposite phonetic category. These latter productions displayed phonemic substitution errors, e.g. 'dot' —» /tat/; finally, and most importantly three anterior aphasics who showed normal perception of VOT showed patterns of production evidenced by both overlap between the two phonetic categories and clean-cut substitutions across these categories. Thus, normal perception did not necessarily implicate normal production, nor did deficits in perception relate to type or severity of production errors. These results suggest that, at least for the adult, the perceptual and production systems are partially autonomous. This of course does not imply that the systems are wholly autonomous or that they are not inextricably linked during the language acquisition process. Rather, it suggests that with the internalizations of the language system, they become quasi-independent sub-systems.

In summary, this paper has attempted to delineate the nature of speech processing of phonetic segments in aphasics and its relation to language comprehension, auditory processing, and speech production. Taken together, the results of the studies reviewed suggest aphasics do evidence speech perception deficits. These deficits are linguistic and not auditory in nature and they seem to affect directly the nature of the link between sound-meaning correspondence, but have less of an impact on overall auditory language comprehension and on speech production abilities.

Note

Acknowledgement   This research was supported in part by Grants NS07615 to Clark University and NS06209 to Boston University School of Medicine.

Discussion

Karl Pribram: The papers by Ted Evans and (in Seminar 3) Eric Young brilliantly cover the essentials of our current knowledge and the leading edge of inquiry into the unknown. My own experience in auditory physiology is limited and so I will have to draw heavily on reasearch in the visual mode. But, as Dr. Evans has pointed out, the auditory and visual nervous systems are differently organized anatomically and so we might well expect differences in function. Nonetheless, some of the results of experiments in vision might have bearing on those obtained in audition.

First. In a set of experiments in which we began with one spot, went to two, and ended with many, we found that cells in the visual cortex respond to visual white noise by selecting to respond to an elongated set of the total of spots displayed. The aim of this experiment was to test the linearity of the visual system response by applying the Wiener equation. Unfortunately, we have not had sufficient funds to date to pursue the computations beyond the first Wiener Kernel — which seems to account for practically all, though not all, of the variance in some preliminary runs. [For a complete report of this experiment see Sutter, 1975.]

We have, however, pursued the "noise" technique in the auditory mode and showed it to be valid in describing the frequency selectivity of cells in the inferior colliculus as this is ordinarily determined. [For complete report, see Hosford, Thesis, 1977, Stanford University.] These results leave no doubt as to the inherent selectivity of the cells under investigation, even in the presence of white noise.

It is a different matter, however, when, as has been frequently stated in this conference, such cells are to be viewed as feature detectors. In the visual system, for instance, the same cell that demonstrates a spatially elongated receptive field is also selective of the direction of movement of lines, of the velocity of movement, the luminance of the visual stimulus, and in some instances, a particular *auditory* frequency (Spinelli et al, 1968). The definition of a detector would imply that the output of the cell be unique to a particular selectivity — some more complex concept that involves multiple selectivities must apply to the findings reported by Evans for the auditory system and those reviewed above for the visual system.

If a cortical cell is to be considered a detector of lines or edges and a response to a more complex figure is determined by a cell further along in a processing hierarchy, then presenting the complex figure should not change the response of the cell provided the line or edge elements within the figure remain unchanged (in length, width, orientation, etc.) If, on the other hand, the cell were selective of some more wholistic property of the entire figure — such as its spatial frequency — then the cell's response would change predictably according to the wholistic property involved.

DeValois et al. (1978) tested these possibilities by using gratings presented at optimal orientation which were then replaced by plaids that included the original gratings. In *every* case the shift predicted from consideration of the Fourier transform occurred.

Of course, as has been so elegantly demonstrated by Young and reviewed by Evans, the Fourier transform is insufficient to account for all of the complexity of the auditory analysis — the time domain must be considered in addition to the frequency. Similarly, in vision, the space domain is involved in locating a moving pattern — the receptive field subtends only 5° visual angle at most and it is the movement selectivity of cells across fields that is most likely involved in motion perception and the identification of locus (although this could be a function of encoding phase relations among fields).

What I would urge is that two dimensional Fourier analyses of auditory patterns be attempted to see how much of the variance of the response of cortical cells could be accounted for in this fashion. From all that Evans reported, of his own work and that of others, such an analysis will probably prove insufficient to deal with the entire spectrum of phonological productions. But it is possible that vowel sounds can be thus treated and that they can be thought to serve as carriers upon which consonants are modulated. The simplicity and power of the Fourier theorem or its derivative, time series analysis, makes it worthwhile to push the application as far as possible. In the visual mode we have been surprised at just how far this is.

Shuli S. Reich: In an interesting set of experiments, Blumstein explored the relationships between
   a)   speech perception and speech comprehension
   b)   auditory speech perception and auditory nonspeech perception
   c)   speech perception and speech production
         in different syndromes in dysphasia.

In connection with a), Blumstein asked whether the comprehension deficit that characterizes patients with posterior lesions, and who evince Wernicke's dysphasia, was caused by a disturbance of speech perception. The answer was negative. Although certain patients had severe perceptual difficulties in analysing speech, this was not related to their ability to understand speech.

I would like to suggest that, rather than perceptual factors, conceptual factors may be responsible for the deficit in comprehension. Disorders of speech such as dysphasia are often considered as though they occurred in isolation from thought. However, deliberate speech, unlike automatic cliché ridden speech, cannot be produced or comprehended without substantial cognitive activity (Jackson, 1932).

In order to examine the relationship between language and thought in dysphasia, I have conducted a series of experiments using classification tasks. Dysphasics and non brain damaged controls were required to sort sets of pictures of objects that belonged to various semantic categories such as fruit, animals, vehicles etc. On a separate occasion, the verbal labels (names) that referred to these objects were presented for classification.

Healthy subjects classified the pictures and their names in an hierarchical manner. Dogs were grouped with cats and other animals, and in a separate pile from the items that belonged to the other semantic categories. Dysphasics, however, used various systems of classification — from which three main groups were identified: —
1)   Pictures classified hierarchically, names not classified hierarchically.
2)   Pictures and names classified nonhierarchically, according to a single system of classification.
3)   Pictures and names classified nonhierarchically, but using two systems of classification.

Thus, in 1) language is disrupted but concepts remain intact. In 2) language is impaired and in a similar manner to thought, and in 3) language and thought are disrupted independently. Furthermore, whereas patterns 2) and 3) were most common in patients with comprehension disorders following lesions of the posterior regions of the left cerebral hemisphere, pattern 1) occurred most often in patients with dysphasia resulting from anterior lesions. Patients who failed to use an hierarchical system of classification grouped items according to their perceptual, functional or descriptive characteristics.

In short, our results indicate that comprehension disorders are often accompanied and influenced by disorders of thought. I would therefore like to argue that studies which examine speech in isolation from thought may be telling only half the story.

Ruth Lesser: Professor Blumstein's comprehensive paper summarises a series of illuminating experiments on the nature of the comprehension deficit in aphasia, a notoriously difficult area to study in which simplifying assumptions at present have to be made.

Amongst the findings reported, three important points emerge. First, the ability to perform perceptual tasks requiring phonological processing does not correlate with language comprehension ability, as measured by the Boston Diagnostic Aphasia Examination (Goodglass & Kaplan 1972). Since the latter's assessment of comprehension tests semantic choice and the understanding of sentences and paragraphs, this finding provides further evidence for the partial autonomy of levels of neurolinguistic organisation. Second, patients classified as Wernicke's aphasics (i.e. with poor comprehension but fluent speech) may be somewhat impaired in judging whether pairs of syllables like "da" and "ta", or "pit" and "kit" are the same or different, but they are always more impaired in associating speech sounds in such syllables with their labels (as syllable names or as referents for pictures like "pear" and "bear"). The key disorder in this category of aphasia would therefore seem to be in attaching linguistic input to meaning, rather than in phonological decoding, thus distinguishing Wernick's aphasia from word-deafness. Professor Blumstein's evidence could be used in support of the claim that there is a direct-access route to semantic comprehension by-passing phonological coding in the auditory modality, such as has been proposed for reading. Third, this paper reports that aphasics have considerably more difficulty in perceiving contrasts of place of articulation (e.g. b/d) than contrasts of voice-onset time (e.g. t/d). This is an interesting finding in view of the current discussion about the lateralisation of serial processing (see, for example, Divenyi & Efron's (1979) demonstration that there is a consistent right-ear advantage for the processing of temporal information in sounds, but that spectral cues can result in a right or left ear advantage). Aphasics appear to be impaired in the use of temporal information at other linguistic levels (e.g. in discriminating pairs of reversible words and sentences), and Professor Blumstein's finding should be a stimulus to further investigations of the possible role of deficits in time-tracking in aphasics' perception of language.

The paper unfortunately is not always clear about the distinctions amongst the three processes it associates with comprehension: e.g. low-level auditory processing, speech perception and overall language comprehension. Speech perception seems to be equated to linguistic processing at the phonological level, but contrasts are distinguished as "phonemic" (e.g. as between "pib" and "kib") or "phonetic" (e.g. as between "da" and "ta") in an unexplained way. The paper also has the advantages and disadvantages inherent in all studies which use clinical classifications of aphasia: not all members of a category always conform to prediction, owing to the approximate nature of present classifications. Examinations of patients' comprehension by techniques such as Professor Blumstein has used could make a valuable clinical contribution to a more exact definition of the nature of an individual patient's deficits.

Eric Keller: Language and the Brain I am very impressed with both contributions to this seminar, however my research experience forces me to limit my commentaries to the domain of the second address, that of aphasia. I would like to make two points, the first very briefly, and the second more in detail since it is of general interest to the psycholinguist considering data from neurogenic language disorders.

The first point is that research findings from a study I conducted with Ari Rothenberger and Michael Goepfert from the University of Ulm, Germany, are in accord with Sheila Blumstein's findings on differential impairment of productive and receptive phonological processing. We tested phonemic distinctiveness in production and perception by comparing patterns of breakdown on a minimal vowel pair perception test to that found in phonemic substitutions (Keller et al., 1980). On the basis of data from fifty German-speaking patients, sixteen French Canadian and five English Canadian patients, we determined that perceptual impairments affected preferentially distinctions between high vowels, while the productive impairments affected predominantly those between low vowels. It thus seems that even at the level of phonemic distinctiveness, speech production and auditory perception operate independently.

The second point concerns the question of whether aphasic speech errors are errors of performance alone, or errors of both competence and performance. The distinction between competence and performance, detached from its original theoretical framework (i.e. the Chomsky tradition (1965)), has in the last ten years proven to be a very useful notion in the psycholinguistic analysis of speech production. As measured against an "ideal delivery" (speech produced with utterances "executed in a single fluent speech train under one smooth intonation contour", Clark and Clark, 1977, p. 261), the speech errors of normal adult native speakers are mistakes at the processing or performance level, occurring independently of the speaker's knowledge concerning how an ideal delivery is to be achieved (i.e. his competence).[1] The study of performance independent of linguistic competence has recently led to the outlines of several variants of a psycholinguistic model of speech production (see e.g. Foss and Hakes, 1978, or Clark and Clark, 1977).

When attempting to assess the relevance of neurogenic speech pathology to such psycholinguistic models of speech production, we must investigate the similarities and differences between normal speech errors and pathological errors. Central to this effort is the question of whether data collected from patients with such pathology (i.e. aphasics, dysarthrics, and the rare case of stuttering due to a gross brain lesion) are reflections of disturbances of performance, of competence, or of both. Put another way, are errors of such patients irregular mistakes occurring during linguistic processing, or are they regularly occurring errors in the processing of linguistic structures, the accessing of information, or in the data base itself?

The question is not new. In 1970, Weigl and Bierwisch suggested that aphasic patients must be experiencing a loss of performance without attendant loss of competence because their performance varies greatly from one testing occasion to the next and from one testing modality (e.g. oral, written, etc.) to the next. Furthermore, they had found that a lack of success in one testing modality could be "deblocked", in their terminology, by success in another modality. Whitaker, 1971, in a spirited rebuttal, suggests on the other hand that "if brain damage cannot affect competence, then competence is not a property of the brain" (p. 16). Moreover, Goodglass and Blumstein, 1973, indicate that an alternative interpretation of Weigl and Bierwisch's generally valid observations is possible; according to them, "gaps in the aphasic's imperfectly retained competence may be temporarily restored by cuing or 'deblocking', with the result that adequate performance becomes possible" (p. 11). Also, it can be argued that the notion of an aphasic disorder itself is subject to constant updating, particularly in the patient's first few weeks after insult. A structure or a lexical item may suddenly be accessible to a patient after having been regularly inaccessible only a few days before. Nevertheless, if these items or structures are systematically unavailable at the time of testing, we must assume linguistic competence to be impaired at that time.

Empirical data from the particularly fertile research effort of the last ten years have consistently been in support of the notion that competence as well as performance can be impaired by aphasia, at least in cases of moderate to severe impairment. I shall exemplify this with one representative example from each of the major areas of impairments investigated, semantic, syntactic and phonological. Semantically, posterior fluent aphasic patients with anomia have been shown to suffer from a fairly severe deficit regarding the integrity of the boundaries between the semantic fields of lexical items (e.g. Zurif et al., 1974; Goodglass et al., 1976; Grossman, 1978; Whitehouse et al., 1978). In a typical experiment (Whitehouse et al., 1978), five Broca's (i.e. non-fluent) and five anomic patients were presented with a choice of several names for various prototypical and borderline drawings of a cup, based on a paradigm originally used with normal subjects by Labov (1973). (Labov had demonstrated that prototypical objects [a typical cup] are named consistently, but that borderline cases [objects which possess some properties of a cup, e.g. a handle, and certain properties of a bowl, e.g. width], are named inconsistently.) In a slightly modified procedure, Whitehouse et al. showed his patients 24 line drawings of food containers varying in such perceptual features as height, width, and the presence of a handle, as well as in functional context (pictorial contexts suggestive of a cup, glass, or a bowl). While Broca's aphasics chose prototypes consistently and borderline objects inconsistently, much as normals would, anomic aphasics did not establish a clear response pattern. Moreover, in borderline conditions, where the performance of normals and Broca's aphasics is improved by appropriate pictorial contexts, that of Wernick's aphasics remains nearly unaffected.

One may conclude from this and complementary evidence that anomic patients are lacking in the underlying semantic representation for the object to be picked, i.e. their semantic competence for lexical items. Though the alternate possibility of errors in the access to the underlying semantic representation has been investigated by a number of different strategems, such as naming, the tip-of-the-tongue phenomenon, and the the clustering of similar vs. dissimilar items, the result that consistently emerges is that fluent aphasics have simply less underlying semantic information to refer to than do comparatively impaired non-fluent aphasics or normals.

The study of aphasic syntax leads to a similar conclusion. It is useful to distinguish two types of syntactic impairment in aphasia, agrammatism (impoverished structure) and dys- or paragrammatism (incorrect structure). Agrammatic speech is typically seen in non-fluent (Broca's and conduction) aphasics, and is reminiscent of telegram style. (E.g. interviewer: "Why did you come to the hospital?" Patient: "Poozin' too much, poozin' too much." Int: "Pushing too much?" Pat: "Aldiholic." Int: "I, I have difficulties understanding." Pat: "Happyholic." Int: "Oh, 'alcoholic'" [Keller, 1975, p. 100]). Dysgrammatic speech, on the other hand, is typically seen with fluent (Wernicke's and anomic) aphasics. The following example is from Goodglass and Kaplan, 1972, p. 61. The patient is describing a picture showing a housewife at a sink that is overflowing and a boy and a girl in the background sneaking cookies from a cookie jar. "Well. . . this is. . . mother is away here working her work out o'here to get her better, but when she's looking, the two boys looking in the other part. One their small tile into her time here. She's working another time because she's getting, too." In such speech, individual phrases ("mother is away here", "out of here", "but when she's looking") are syntactically adequate, yet a correct integration into a complete syntactic string is lacking.

It is possible to interpret both of these forms of syntactic impairment without reference to competence. It is possible, for instance, that dysgrammatism is at least in part due to an occasional inability to retain in short-term memory the various phrases of a complete utterance string. Or it may be suggested that the agrammatism of some non-fluent aphasics is related to their lack of fluency, that their motor difficulties are reflected in a telegrammatic style.

Yet with respect to agrammatism at least, it is also possible to think of two indicators for impaired competence. The first is that lack of fluency can exist independent of agrammatic speech. Many patients who experience great difficulty in chaining syllables into an utterance, or in finding adequate phonemes to articulate a sentence, preserve their grammatical structure nearly perfectly. It is therefore unlikely that agrammatism is entirely due to an interference from the motor procesing (i.e. performance) problem of these patients. In addition, agrammatic patients show some adaptive strategies which they have apparently developed to circumvent a continuing problem, i.e. a competence impairment. Gleason et al., 1975, for instance, found that in completing sentences that unequivocally required a particular syntactic structure, patients tended to circumvent certain structures which posed particular problems. The future tense was for instance often circumvented by using an adverbial phrase; in places where the sentence completion ''he'll work'' was given by nearly all normals, agrammatic aphasics would often say ''he work again next week''. Even structures considered to be of exemplary theoretical simplicity were often circumvented by typical adverbial or agrammatic structures: ''The dog chases the cat'' was given as ''cat get running, and dog'', while ''she is taller'' and ''he is stronger'' were rendered as ''she's tall enough'' and ''he is strong enough''. The regularity of such adaptive strategies, in the speech of individual as well as of groups of patients, points to a true loss of grammatical competence, rather than to a temporary problem of access to a particular structure rule.

In phonological disorders of aphasia, some recent findings from our research group have led us to a similar conclusion. Yves Joanette, Roch Lecours and I have analyzed feature distances between 800 phonological targets (vowels and consonants) and the sequences of attempts at these targets given by five Brocas, eight conduction and three Wernicke's aphasics (Joanette, Keller and Lecours, in press). We divided our results according to patient groups, and in the case of conduction aphasics, according to tasks. Our over-all results confirmed a general clinical observation that patients get closer to the target as they perform repeated attempts to articulate a particular sound.

Yet there are two refinements to be noted to that general rule: first, conduction aphasics showed a fine gradation in the degree to which they improved their performance in the various tasks. They improved the most on successive attempts in the automatized sequences (reciting numbers, months of the year, etc.). They also showed excellent improvement on reading aloud, and good improvement on spontaneous speech. On the repetition tasks, however, they did not show any consistent tendency to improve, least of all in the repetition of nonsense words which actually showed decay over repeated attempts. It will be noted that a performance hypothesis invoking the impairment of short term memory could account for the difference between the result on the repetition tasks and the remaining tasks, but it fails to account for the fine gradation between tasks. Why should the recitation of automatized sequences for instance lead to a greater improvement than the production of spontaneous speech? The deficits seem more indicative of differences at the level of long-term rather than short-term storage. We were thus led to the hypothesis that the patient's underlying phonological representation might be differentially impaired, depending on the task. Automatized sequences might be particularly well represented in long-term memory through their frequent use, while the target can be continually refreshed in a reading task. In spontaneous speech, the target is of variable quality, while it is imposed from the outside in repetition tasks, and thus of particularly fleeting quality. Such systematic differential impairment of an underlying target would have to be within the domain of competence. It would not be indicative of performance mistakes in the processing of linguistic material, but of a systematic loss of strength of representation of the phonological target.

The second refinement to the general rule that patients improve their performance over repeated attempts provided us with the reason why we are more inclined to think that the underlying representation itself is impaired, rather than access to it (though either impairment would fall within the definition of a competence disorder). This is that Wernick's aphasics, in contrast to conduction and Broca's aphasics, showed no consistent over-all tendency to improve over successive attempts. As we have seen above, it seems that in at least the anomic type of fluent aphasics, it is the underlying semantic representation for vocabulary items which is impaired, rather than their access to such items. Since linguistic items must necessarily be stored in a phonological as well as in a semantic form, it was reasonable to assume that our results on the successive approximations of another type of fluent aphasic, the Wernicke type, were more indicative of a breakdown of the underlying representation itself than of access to it. Assuming on the basis of the considerable similarities between anomic and Wernicke's aphasics that we are dealing with the same basic disorder affecting lexical items, we could in this fashion extend the explanatory hypothesis for the semantic disorder of fluent aphasics to their phonological disorders.

In summary, it thus appears that while there may still be many aspects of aphasic disorders that need clarification, it now seems fairly certain that they are not analysable as a mere compounding of multiple performance mistakes. Rather, they give evidence of systematic competence disorders involving at least in part the underlying semantic and phonological representation of vocabulary items, and the underlying representation of, or access to, syntactic structures that serve to relate them within a complete utterance. This has three major implications for the use of aphasic data within a psycholinguistic theory of speech production and reception.

In the first place, it complicates the relationship between normal speech errors and those of neurogenic origin. It is not possible to say, as was common still a few years ago, that "aphasics do everything that normals do, only worse". As a conseqence, this realization imposes an extra caution on attempts at relating aphasic speech error data to psycholinguistic theories of performance which are extensively based on normal speech errors. Secondly, aphasic data are often less translucent than normal speech errors in their analysis. While data in favour of competence disorders have been cited here, it is also true that many findings from aphasia are indicative of a performance impairment. For instance both Blumstein (1973) and I (Keller, 1978) have found the sound inventory of aphasic patients to be complete even in cases where sound substitutions were the rule, rather than the exception. Since the sounds substituted for others vary greatly from one occasion to another, we must assume that the underlying representation is intact in at least a proportion of the data, and that the error is due to some fortuitous processing problem.

The third consequence, on the other hand, is a positive one. Aphasic data give us anatomical information about the areas involved in linguistic performance, which in turn can be related to larger neurophysiological theories of human motor and sensory processes. By relating our incomplete and occluded aphasic data on competence and performance breakdowns to findings from the recent blood flow studies (e.g. Lassen et al., 1978), to the greatly improved lesion information from computer tomography scans, and to laterality studies and to electrical stimulation of the brain, we can hope to come to congruent inferences concerning the processes involved in our use of language.

Notes

1.   In this context it may be noted that the handy distinction which English makes between "error" and "mistake" is unfortunately not exploited in our common use of the term "speech error". A "mistake" is akin to a "misinterpretation", while an error is a more serious "deviation from a code"; this distinction is commonly used with reference to the performance and competence deviations of second language learners (cf. Corder, 1967). Theoretically speaking, it would therefore be more felicitous to refer to spontaneous deviations from an ideal delivery as "speech mistakes". Yet in view of the well-known force of even recently established traditions, this need not be interpreted as a suggestion for a terminological change.

Acknowledgement   I would like to express my thanks to Nadine Lieberman, a student at the McGill School of Human Communications Disorders, Montreal, for her help in a review of the area of semantic impairments of aphasia.

Chairman's Comments

Donald M. MacKay: As Ted Evans has indicated, the cerebral representation of events and structures in the external world is still a matter of keen debate, in the field of auditory perception as elsewhere. I have little to add to the expert comments by Discussants, but would make one general point. The ultimate function of all neural analysers of sensory input is not mere description or classification, but the *shaping of conditional readiness to reckon with* the state of affairs betokened by that input. The main question to be answered by the sensory system is not 'What is it?' but 'What does it signify for me?', or if you like, 'So What?'. In our search for the primitives of the internal representation of speech, then, we should perhaps be guided not so much by the formal attractiveness of mathematical descriptors, whether in the frequency or time domains, as by the functional appropriateness of different categories to the purpose in hand — namely, the imposition of matching constraints on the conditional readinesses of the listener (MacKay, 1968, 1970). These constraints will doubtless operate at a hierarchy of levels from the most concrete of acoustic analysis to the most abstract of semantic interpretation; but at each level (if experience in other biological fields is any guide) we can expect to find the spectrum of primitive descriptors determined largely by the nature of the repertoire of internal matching responses upon which the input is required to exercise a selective function.

For this reason, I am less sanguine than Karl Pribram that Fourier transformation has much to offer that is not already exploited in the auditory domain. He does not make clear what 'second dimension' (in addition to time) he has in mind to give a 'two-dimensional Fourier analysis of auditory patterns'; but it should I think be stressed that even in the visual domain what Fourier analysis offers is a language in which to *describe* the selectivity of single units, rather than a theory to *explain* their function.

If, as I have been suggesting, that function is to categorise stimuli in associative terms which are (internally) action-oriented, we may have to adopt descriptors much less mathematically tidy than sine waves in order to make sense of the higher-level processing of auditory information by the nervous sytem. It would be a happy thing (and perhaps not beyond the bounds of present possibility) if the growing body of clinical material surveyed by Dr. Blumstein could provide us with pointers towards the selection of more realistic stimulus categories to this end.

THE COGNITIVE REPRESENTATION OF SPEECH
T. Myers, J. Laver, J. Anderson (editors)
© *North-Holland Publishing Company, 1981*

Pointing and Language

GORDON W. HEWES

University of Colorado

Pointing gestures probably played an important part in the origin of language. Pointing also seems to be a significant factor in the emergence of language in the human infant (Lock, 1978; Bruner, 1975, 1976). Evolutionary models for the development of language from gestural communication are handicapped by the fact that arm, hand, and finger signs are not prominent in the communicative behaviour of wild non-human primates, although visual signals based on gaze, facial expression, posture, and body movement seem to be at least as important as vocal calls. In captivity, apes can acquire humanlike gestures even for use in language or language-like codes (such as ASL, the American Sign Language of the deaf), although acquisition by apes of vocal signs not already part of their species-specific vocal call system is extraordinarily difficult and very limited (Laidler, 1978). For all higher primates, including man, it may be harder to establish noises as labels for environmental referents than visible signs.

Old World monkeys make great use of facial expressions — 19 different "faces" in the case of the pig-tailed macaque (Goosen & Kortmulder, 1979), indicating heavy reliance on visual signals, but without employment of manual gestures. Further, the behaviors involving the facial expressive code emerge in individual young monkeys in a fashion strikingly similar to the sensorimotor stages of Piaget's schema for human infants (Parker, 1977). "Pointing" has been studied in Old World monkeys (Taub, et al., 1975) involving laboratory training, in experiments to determine whether visual or proprioceptive feedback is necessary for accurate digital pointing or touching a target position. The results indicate that moving an arm or the digits into alignment with a visually perceived target is largely independent of either seeing the pointing arm or receiving kinaesthetic information from the movement. If this capability exists in monkeys, it presumably also exists in human beings, although we do not yet know how early it manifests itself, nor how much prior learning may be involved.

Anthropoid apes might be expected to exhibit pointing even without human training, given the success of the various manual sign-language experiments with chimpanzees, gorillas, and orang-utans (chiefly the two former). Vygotsky (1962:35) suggested that "By and large, these observations [of Köhler on chimpanzees in the Canary Island colony] confirm Wundt's opinion that pointing gestures, the first stage in the development of human speech, do not yet appear in animals but that some gestures of apes are a transitional form between grasping and pointing. We consider this transitional gesture a most important step from unadulterated affective expression toward objective language." Vygotsky went on to remind his readers that R.M. Yerkes had conjectured that chimpanzees might be trained to use manual gestures, rather than sounds, in an approximation of language (Vygotsky, 1963:38).

263

in detail change
it meaning the
ability of down
loping represen-
tative gesture ;
they are limited
to indicative
ones, and indi-
cation relies
not on gesture
quantity, but
on context
with a few
gestures

Field studies have failed to discover much gesticulation among chimpanzees in their natural habitats (Plooij, 1978). The roster of manual gestures in *Pan troglodytes* (the common chimpanzee) observed in the wild seems limited to a palm-up begging or solicitation gesture, and touching the mouth of another — both mainly for trying to obtain food; A. Kortlandt has added the use of a sole of the foot presentation gesture as an apparent halt signal on the trail. Menzel et al. suggest that gestures, in the strict sense of hand-arm signals, are unimportant in apes because, as quadrupeds, they can use their whole bodies to convey directional information (1978) Plooij's observations in the Gombe Stream area expand the gestural repertoire of Pan troglodytes to the "arm high" signal, seemingly serving as a request to be groomed, and secondarily as a signal of peaceable intent (Plooij, 1978:123).

but the di-
chotomy bet-
ween "natural"
and "instructed"
is not true :
there remains
among both
categories a
wide difference
full of mankey
ly developed
hours's in com-
tact with hum.
(which reminds
one of human
prelanguage de-
velopment, as
described by
Cair, 1980)

The rare pygmy chimpanzee, *Pan paniscus,* appears to have a richer manual gestural lexicon, which, if so far observed only in captivity, does not seem to be due to human instruction (D. Rumbaugh, S. Savage-Rumbaugh, & T. Gill, 1978). The life of Pan paniscus in its natural habitat is just beginning to be studied (Kuroda, 1979), and gestural behavior has not yet been reported. Pygmy chimpanzees live in large social groups, in varied ecological settings (though all within tropical rain forests) with what is described as "very flexible social behaviour". In captivity, a male pygmy chimpanzee used manual gestures to improve the posture or position of his two female companions for purposes of copulation. The first two gestural categories observed involved actual pushing or shoving of the other individual, or touching the other individual's body; only the third category, called by the investigators "completely iconic hand movements" were made at some distance from the body of the recipient of the signal. Out of 600 hours of observation, only 21 gestures of the third kind were recorded, including that of moving the extended hand toward another part of the enclosure, interpreted as a sign for the other individual to move there. This can be regarded as a *pointing gesture*, possibly spontaneous in *Pan paniscus*. It could still be argued that the sign was learned from human keepers, although the context (for positioning of sexual partners) suggests otherwise.

Data from pygmy chimpanzees living in the wild are obviously required to establish manual pointing as behaviour independent of human transmission. That *Pan paniscus* may stand closer than the common chimpanzee to the hominid line has been suggested by several anthropologists. Zihlman and Cramer (1978) observe that "A creature somewhat like the pygmy chimpanzee may very well have directly preceded the earliest hominids". Recent skeletal finds in Ethiopia make this more plausible (Johanson and White, 1979). If *Pan paniscus* uses as much gesture in the wild as it does in captivity, a small-bodied early hominid dwelling in open forest-savannah might be even more likely to employ arm and hand signals visible at a distance, especially since such early hominids are known to have been fully bipedal. The advantages for such a species in the ability to convey information about the environment would have been marked (Parker & Gibson, 1979; Shafton, 1973; Hewes, 1976). Menzel, Premack, and Woodruff (1978) show how much spatial information can be conveyed by chimpanzees to one another, in an experiment with closed-circuit televised black-and-white imagery. That manual pointing would enhance such exchanges of environmental information seems clear; we still rely to a considerable extent on such pointing gestures to find our way about in unfamiliar settings, despite the availability of spoken language, and modern road signs and similar directional aids in the visual mode can be regarded as extrapolations of hand and arm signals.

Wilhelm Wundt devoted several pages in *Völkerpsychologie* to demonstrative gesture (1921, 1973 reprint:74-77). He considered pointing to be "primary", the first to appear in infants, and there "most independently", that is, not dependent upon maternal example or teaching. This critical matter remains to be settled by well-designed experiments. Wundt recognized that pointing was "the surest way" to draw the attention of others to an object or event of interest to the baby or child. We now know that well before the appearance of pointing, mothers attend to the gaze-direction of their infants, and vice versa, although it remains to be seen just how gaze and pointing are related. Gazing or staring, in itself, is not necessarily a social behaviour, whereas pointing is more clearly social, even though young infants, left to themselves, may point to (or touch) objects. In modern cultures, such non-social pointing seems to occur mostly with illustrations in picture-books and the like. Finally, Wundt noted that where profoundly deaf children were brought up in isolation from other deaf persons, "pointing is practically the only gesture to occur initially".

Wundt knew that pointing is sometimes suppressed in some cultures, despite its protean character. In a few societies, pointing is taboo, or considered childish or boorish; in others, it may be forbidden to point to certain things — such as rainbows in several western North American groups. In Western Culture, it may be considered ill-mannered to point to crippled or handicapped persons. As Wundt notes, pointing may be avoided just because it is so easily deciphered. An occasional alternative to finger-pointing is to point with the pursed lips (Sherzer, 1973); its use may have something to do with its being less easily seen at a distance, and its diminished precision.

Wundt goes on to consider pointing to establish pronomial references, indicate directions (rather than specific objects), and even to indicate the functions of seeing, smelling, and, paradoxically, even hearing; a special pointing gesture is widely used to enjoin silence. Wundt, having reviewed studies on various sign languages, including those of the deaf and of the North American Plains Indians, realized that pointing can be used to denote past, present, and future time, name colors, and so on, and in the form of a moving point, draw "air pictures" of objects based on salient shapes or outlines. The step from such "air pictures" based on moving pointings, to drawing, engraving, and painting, is not in fact very great.

Wundt concluded (p. 127) that "pointing appears to be the very earliest [gesture] among human beings, and whose spontaneous origin may be observed in infants".

Another German psychologist of Wundt's day, Wilhelm Stern, had also noted the mediatory functions of gesture in establishing word-meanings, mentioning pointing in particular (Vygotsky, 1962:30-31). Wittgenstein devoted serious attention to ostension (i.e., pointing), although he argued that ostention in itself could never specify what it was that it was referring to, out of the complex welter of properties (Bruner, 1976:267). It is true that observation of another's pointing gesture — toward a third person, for example — might not make it clear whether what was being indicated was the entire individual, or one of his physical features, or articles of clothing, everday experience shows that such potential ambiguities are usually minimized in the context of actual situations. To return to pointing to rainbows, if I were to point toward the section of sky in which one were visible, the probability of my intention of calling attention to the rainbow would be vastly higher than, say, an intention to call attention to the colour of the sky.

Pointing gestures have been prominent in almost all formulations of the gestural theory of language origins, including Bernard Mandeville in his *Fable of the Bees* (1728), or in the work of Etienne de Condillac. St. Augustine recognized the importance of infantile pointing in his account of his own acquisition of language (*Confessions*, Book I). Trân Duc Thao, a modern Vietnamese philosopher, in his book on the origins of language and consciousness, stresses the creative role of pointing at great length (1973). He supposes that a gestural communication system arose among early hominid hunters, of Australopithecine grade, for use in coördinating the efforts of several hunters in locating and killing game animals. Trân completed his book before learning of the work of the Gardners or Premack with chimpanzees, but he did assemble much of what was then available on the possible language-acquisition abilities of anthropoid apes. After discussing the transition from ape to man with respect to proto-language, supposedly mainly gestural, he turned to language acquisition in the child, concluding that at 12 months, the human infant has about the same language capability as an adult chimpanzee. By 14 months, Trân equated human language ability to that of the adult fossil australopithecine hominids. Trân noted that 12 to 14 month old infants may use pointing gestures when alone, to focus their attention on objects of interest, such as pictures in a book. Apes trained to use manual gestures have recently been observed to do likewise. Trân joins Wundt, and the pioneer writer on North American Indian sign language, Mallery (1881) in accepting infantile gestures as intelligible long before the onset of speech. The most ingenious aspect of Trân's work is his derivation of all language from deictic gesture. While this probably goes too far, W. Stokoe's comments represent a more balanced judgment (1978:169-170):

> Communication in the human individual begins with gSigns [gestural signs], or gSigns in a behavioural matrix, not yet differentiated from touch. As well equipped as all human individuals are with a genetic propensity for language — even with an inborn ability to distinguish languages sounds — they begin communicating in a less specialized way than that of adult language, using gSigns at first. . . But it is not through the study of development in the usual and special individual only that we can see something like the phylogenetic development of sSign into speech-sign recapitulated. The gSign capabilities of chimpanzees and gorillas will tell us something more about languages and sign languages and what is verbal and non-verbal.

As we see, pointing behaviour has been recognized for a long time as a possible precursor of language, as far back as St. Augustine. Wundt, Stern, Wittgenstein, Vygotsky, de Laguna, and H. Werner and B. Kaplan (*Symbol Formation*, 1964) have dealt with pointing, although significant empirical data have been rare until the last two decades. As systematic studies of early infant behavior began on a large scale, especially with motion pictures and video-tape, pointing began to be regularly reported (cf. Bower, 1974: chap.6).

Meanwhile, some psychologists investigate pointing behaviour in adults, as a problem in perceptual and motor skill. This literature on the mechanics and optics of pointing focussed on the precision of the gesture under various experimental conditions. Lackner, for example, notes that normal adult subjects can point to a visible target to within 1/2° when they can see their pointing hand and finger; when hand and digit are not visible, accuracy diminishes, but not markedly. In monkeys, even when afferent sensory nerves have been cut, pointing accuracy is not drastically affected. Evidently, in habituated individuals, the spatial-motor schema is not greatly impaired by elimination of visual monitoring and kinaesthetic feedback.

G. de Laguna, in a well-known book on the function and development of speech, reported on pointing in one of her infant daughters (1927:70), suggesting that it led quickly on to speech. Vygotsky (quoted by Gray, 1978:160) observed:

> In the beginning, the pointing gesture is merely an unsuccessful grasping movement aimed at an object. . . the child tries to grasp too distant an object but its hand reaching for the object remains hanging in the air and the fingers make grasping movements. . . Here for the first time arises the pointing gesture in itself. . . . When the mother comes to the aid of the child and comprehends his movement as a pointing gesture the situation essentially changes. The pointing gesture becomes a gesture for others.

Gray adds that T.G.R. Bower suggested an alternative explanation: even at a few days of age, the infant's motor behaviour is already appropriate to the distance of an observed object. Even in five month old infants when an object is too far away to grasp, the shape of the infant's hand differs from an incipient grasping motion, and is more like a pointing gesture.

J.S. Bruner and his colleagues report on an impressive series of experiments relating to early infant cognition, including "what must be an early example of deixis" (Bruner, 1975:9). Well before pointing appears, there are "innately supported" exchanges of eye-to-eye attention between mother and infant. Scaife found, in Bruner's laboratory, that a 4-month old baby tended to follow the mother's glance more readily when she vocalized, saying "Oh, look!" or something similar. By 8 months Bruner adds that the infant is beginning to hold out his hand toward objects in non-grasping directional gestures (1976:271). Pointing is seen to be more of a signal of line of regard than as a frustrated grasp: "the extended hand becomes an external pointer for noting the line of regard".

Ninio and Bruner studied another aspect of pointing (1977): the civilized situation where infants examine pictures in books or magazines, and either point to or actually touch illustrated objects. As mentioned, this has now been reported in sign-language trained chimpanzees and gorillas. To be sure, quasi-realistic pictures cannot have played an important part in the development of pointing for the majority of past or even present mankind. In any case, Ninio and Bruner's subject exhibited "pure pointing" at 10 months, with referents which could not be manipulated, such as printed illustrations. K. Kaye (1977) observed 6-month-old infants held by their mothers close to a plexiglass barrier, behind which a desirable toy had been placed. The mothers used various strategies to encourage their children to reach for the toys around the barrier. Much pointing took place, and boys pointed significantly more often than girls. Collis and Schaffer (1975) investigated mother-infant communication, especially "visual co-orientation" between mother and child, which precedes pointing as a means of achieving similar co-orientation.

Blurton Jones (1972:273-274) notes that "pointing was a common response to novel events, and always involved looking at the mother". Anderson, a colleague of Blurton Jones, studied pointing in British toddlers and their mothers in public park settings. Pointing was the most reliable criterion for the mother-infant bond. Infants pointed to engage their mothers' attention, but not to attract the attention of other adults; until about 12 months, the infants did not follow their mothers' pointing, but gazed at their hands instead. Pointing was not ordinarily accompanied by emotional cries, screams, whimperings, or other sounds.

Catherine Murphy also examined pointing in infants (1978), reporting private, non-communicative pointing to nearby objects around 9 months. By 20 months, in Western cultures at any rate, most infants have been exposed to significant maternal efforts to enhance their speech, in which the mother points to things as she names them, and when the child has acquired some words, to elicit them. Most pointing in Murphy's account occurred in connexion with maternal elicitation of verbal responses. Anne Carter studied pointing in a single boy subject (1978) who was already producing some approximation of speech sounds. She comments, "The percentage of human communication that involves pointing out or drawing attention to an immediately perceptible object is undoubtedly extremely high". Unlike Anderson's quiet toddlers outdoors, Carter's subject vocalized while pointing, using alveolar consonant sounds.

Elizabeth Kordick devoted an entire doctoral dissertation (1975) to infant pointing, using the videotaped record of another single subject, a girl from 17 to 27 months. Kordick's data did not begin with this girl's first gestures, and the 272 pointing episodes analyzed included many with the subject's spoken accompaniment Kordick found that pointing served to "construct the child's world", accompanied actions such as giving or taking objects, to solicit information or services, as an adjunct to speech, clarifying meanings, counting, and to answer spoken questions, especially wh- questions. Adults use pointing for all of these purposes, including "world construction" broadly understood.

D. Givens studied finger extension movements in infants as young as one month (1978). The earliest finger movements were not seen by him as incipient points, nor abortive reaching movements, but as expressions of discomfort, aversion, or protest. Givens adopted a rigorous definition of pointing, in which index finger extension occurs to "direct the mother's attention toward something in the environment" (p.269), so that it is not surprising that he did not record it as starting until around 12 months of age.

Elizabeth Bates, et al., have been studying pre-speech cognitive and communicative behaviour, paying special attention to gestures. In both Italian and American infants, at 10 months, objects are displayed or extended toward adults, but not released; transfer of objects starts around 13 months, about the time that index-finger pointing appears. Before communicative pointing, however, Bates et al. report a phase of individual pointing, mostly in conjunction with picture-books, where pointing seems to help fix the infant's own orientation to novel stimuli. These observations suggest (as do some of the other studies surveyed) that pointing arises as an endogenous behaviour, later employed to elicit the attention of others.

Susan Goldin-Meadow, H. Feldman, and L. Gleitman, examined early gestural activity in congenitally deaf infants of hearing and speaking parents (1977, 1978, Feldman, 1978). Under strong professional pressures to avoid gestural communication with their babies (in keeping with a tenet of the proponents of the exclusively oral method of teaching the deaf), six children, aged 17 to 49 months were studied in an environment devoid of audible language, and of very restricted use of gesture. Despite sincere efforts, the parents did respond to some "home signs" made by their children, and may have inadvertently used such signs in communicating with them. Under these seemingly restricted conditions, one subject produced 4,854 pointings in the videotaped protocol, along with other gestures. For all six subjects, 51.3% of all gestures, on the average, aside from head noddings, were pointings — at things, people, and places. Some of the subjects even indicated colors by pointing. The investigators concluded that most of the signs used by the children were invented by them, and not learned from adults. Goldin-Meadow states (1977:303) that these subjects "reveal a natural inclination to develop a structured communication system". Significantly, much of that system seems to be based on pointing gestures.

Born-blind children, in contrast, do not point spontaneously, but then they also reveal a very limited tendency even to reach out for things (Bower, 1974: 167). We need not conclude from this that pointing must be wholly learned. The failure of blind babies, unassisted, to reach out or to point to visible objects presumably is due to the absence of visual input, which may trigger built-in motor responses.

The study of Meltzoff and Moore (1977), with neonate subjects, some as young as 60 minutes, and none older than 21 days, raises this question even more sharply. The experimenters report that neonates, exposed to adults making four "gestures" — tongue protrusion, mouth opening, lip protrusion, and "sequential finger movements", exhibit a statistically significant propensity to imitate such gestures. Despite various criticisms (cf. Anisfield, et al., 1979), the findings appear to be very important and germane to the topic of this paper. Meltzoff and Moore conclude (1979:78) that the infants in their study possess a "capacity to actively match visible behaviour of others" at an age presumably precluding opportunity for learning. It is remarkable that two of the gestures included in this study happen to be related to deictic gestures (sequential finger movements, and lip protusion), and that the gesture with the least ambiguity (that is, least likely to be erroneously imitated) was finger extension. Mouth-opening was the most ambiguous, although in Old World monkeys, mouth-opening happens to be a very frequent aggressive expression.

Finally, I have wondered whether indicative or pointing gestures are important constituents of established, formal sign-language systems. A cursory survey of four such sign-languages, not known to be recently related, namely: ASL (American Sign Language of the Deaf), Japanese Sign Language of the Deaf, the sign language used on Rennell Island in the South Pacific, and the sign language of the North American Plains Indians, reveals that pointing gestures or movements make up 29.3, 34.6, 19.3, and 28.8 percent of the total number of signs illustrated (O'Rourke, 1973; Zen Nihon Roa Remmei, 1977; Kuschel, 1974; Tomkins, 1969). That is, out of a grand total of 1,866 signs, 552 involve a pointing component, or 29.58%.

A neglected field for studies of gestural communication has to do with severely retarded individuals, including not only microcephalic subjects, but the much larger number of brain-damaged persons, children and adults, with whom basic communication is sometimes reduced to a few manual gestures, in which pointing is prominent (cf. Gainotto & Lemo, 1976). Still another line of research, neglected even more, relates to the employment of gesture between linguistically competent persons who do not share a common spoken language. To the extent that we have information about this, pointing would seem to play a very important rôle.

Beyond the Primate Order, various animals appear to possess limited human language receptive capabilities, so far very little investigated by psycholinguists. Moreover, some animal species exhibit "pointing behaviour" partly analogous to human deictic behaviour. Certain hunting dog breeds have long been selected for pointing at game — usually wildfowl, and their breeders and trainers seem convinced that the ability is inherited, although specialized training may perfect it. Such pointers have been bred for many centuries, and are referred to by Xenophon in a 4th c. B.C. treatise, *Cynegetica* (quoted in Davis, 1968:68). If bird-dogs, associated with man for not much more than 10,000 years at the most, can be shown to have built-in propensities to align themselves with external targets, is it far-fetched to suggest that sterotyped pointing behaviour could have been selected for in hominid evolution, in which hunting in open terrain was closely related to survival over much of the past three million years? Bruner's observation (1976:261) that "a long evolutionary history" has shaped human immaturity, leading to some invariant forms of mother-infant dependency based on innate predispositions, however much these may also require "priming by experience", appears quite plausible. Psycholinguists who, not long ago, were willing to accept Chomsky's innate "language acquisition device", ought not to reject the possibility of innate predisposition to perform simple deictic gestures (Shotter, 1978:57).

The ontogeny of speech and its cognitive representation appear to be related to the earlier employment of manual gestures by the infant, and of pointing in particular. Except for the so far quite inconclusive evidence of spontaneous pointing in the pygmy chimpanzee, manual pointing seems to be a peculiarly human behavioural specialization. To the extent that pointing rests on innate predisposition, it may have played an important rôle in the evolution of the human capacity for language.

THE COGNITIVE REPRESENTATION OF SPEECH
T. Myers, J. Laver, J. Anderson (editors)
© *North-Holland Publishing Company, 1981*

On The Evolution of Human Speech

PHILIP LIEBERMAN

Brown University

Recent years have seen the development of a theory that claims that human speech involves anatomical and neural specializations that form part of the pattern of hominid evolution. These specializations for human speech differentiate the linguistic ability of anatomically modern *Homo sapiens* from certain archaic, extinct hominids and from all other living animals. The theory, in brief, claims that the normal adult human supralaryngeal vocal tract has functional, physiologic, properties that yield speech sounds that are "better" signals for vocal communication than the sounds that are possible to make using the supralaryngeal vocal tract that other living animals have. (Lieberman, 1968; Lieberman and Crelin, 1971; Lieberman et al., 1972; Stevens, 1972; Crelin, 1973; Lieberman, 1973; 1975a,b; 1976a,b; 1977; 1978; 1979b; Laitman and Crelin, 1976; George, 1978; Laitman et al., 1978; 1979). The theory does *not* claim that speech is impossible without these supralaryngeal specializations nor does it claim that human speech is completely disjoint from the vocal communications of other animals. Evolution is as Darwin noted, a gradual process and human speech makes use of phonetic contrasts that can be produced by other animals. The theory likewise does not claim that human speech is the "key", i.e., the sole factor that differentiates human linguistic ability from that of other living animals or archaic hominids. Human speech however, is an integral part of human linguistic ability and it probably played an important role in channeling the course of human evolution.

The theory that I will review also provides a coherent framework for the coeval evolution of some of the neural property detectors that respond to the quantal acoustic signals that only the human supralaryngeal vocal tract can produce (Eimas, 1974; Cooper, 1974; Blumstein, Stevens, & Nigro, 1977). Recent data indicates that similar devices are present in non-human primates who appear to make use of neural "devices" tuned to conspecific vocalizations (Peterson et. al., 1978; 1979). Other property detectors respond to acoustic signals that can also be produced by other species (Eimas & Corbit, 1973; Kuhl & Miller, 1975). These property detectors provide a neural basis for the universal "distinctive features" that structure the phonology of all human languages (Jakobson, Fant, & Halle, 1951). They appear to be innately determined in *Homo sapiens* (Eimas, Siqueland, Jusczyk, & Vigorito, 1971; Morse, 1974; Kuhl, 1976). The presence of these detectors is consistent with a theory that claims that human linguistic ability developed gradually from hominids whose vocal communications were closer to those of present day nonhuman primates. Some of the sound contrasts that were present in these earlier, more primitive, hominids still play a role in human language and the presence of detectors tuned to respond to these signals in human beings represents a link to the past. On the other hand, the property detectors that respond to the sounds that only the human vocal tract can generate can be viewed as recent adaptions that hinge on the presence of the appropriate sound producing mechanisms. They are the result of a long evolutionary history in which the constraints of the human speech producing system, the vocal tract, have been matched with neural mechanisms (lieberman, 1970).

Anatomically modern *Homo sapiens* and chimpanzees, gorillas and orangutans, evolved over the past ten million years from a common ancestor. Although many of the anatomical features that structure the modes of behavior that differentiate humans from apes were present in some of the earliest hominids, other features were absent. Australopithecines who lived at least 4 million years ago, for example, have most of the anatomical specializations that are involved in human upright bipedal locomotion and traces of their footprints which have been preserved show that they walked upright (Leakey, 1979). Present day apes still lack the anatomical prerequisites for human-like bipedal locomotion. Australopithecines however, had much smaller brains than modern humans and had skulls that could not have supported a human-like supralaryngeal vocal tract. The total morphological pattern that characterizes modern human beings is thus not present in australopithecines. Australopithecines clearly are different from humans — though they also clearly share some of the anatomical complexes that are, at present, found only in human beings. They thus represent an intermediate step in the course of hominid evolution, i.e., the evolutionary process that resulted in modern *Homo sapiens*, because they had the anatomical prerequisites for human bipedal walking.

The process of human walking involves more than the anatomy of the hips, foot, etc. The muscular maneuvers involved in walking are extremely complex and it is apparent that human infants are innately equipped with the neural "devices" that control walking. The "walking reflex" is present in normal human infants shortly after birth before they can physically support their weight in an upright position or even sit up. The human "walking reflex" obviously developed in the course of hominid evolution after the presence of the specialized anatomy of the hip, foot, etc. We thus can infer that a fossil hominid that had the specialized anatomy for upright locomotion *might* have had a brain that included the neural "device" that specifies the walking reflex. In contrast, a hominid that lacked the anatomy for upright locomotion would probably have lacked the walk-reflex. Similar inferences can be made with respect to the neural devices that are involved in human speech and the anatomy of human speech production.

THE HUMAN SUPRALARYNGEAL VOCAL TRACT

The supralaryngeal vocal tracts of normal modern *Homo sapiens* after the age of three to nine months (George, 1978) differs from other primates and all other animals. In the human supralaryngeal vocal tract the pharynx and oral cavity are at a right angle and have approximately equal lengths (measured along their midlines). The tongue can move in the "space" defined by the back wall of the pharynx and the hard palate of the oral cavity in the "two-tube" human vocal tract. If the tongue is moved about in this space it is possible to produce "Quantal" sounds (Stevens, 1972) that other animals can not produce.

In Figure 1 illustrations of approximate midsagittal sections, cross-sectional area functions and acoustic transfer functions for the three quantal vowels [i], [u], and [ɑ] are presented. Articulatory and acoustic analyses have shown that these vowels are the limiting articulations of a vowel triangle that is language universal (Trubetskoy, 1939; Liljencrants & Lindblom, 1972). The body of the tongue is high and fronted in the production of [i] to form a constricted oral cavity and an expanded pharyngeal cavity. The tongue body is moved, as a whole, within the right angle geometry

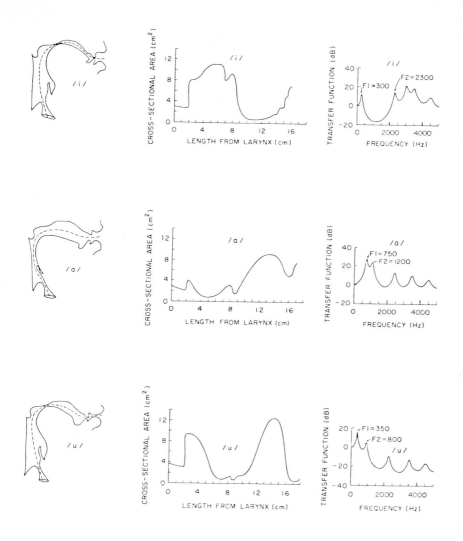

MIDSAGITTAL SECTION OF
THE VOCAL TRACT

CROSS-SECTION AREA
FUNCTION OF THE VOCAL TRACT

MAGNITUDE OF THE VOCAL
TRACT TRANSFER FUNCTION

FIGURE 1 *Approximate midsagittal sections, cross-sectional area functions and acoustic transfer functions for the three quantal vowels* [i], [u] *and* [ɑ].

defined by the intersection of the pharyngeal and oral cavities to form the area functions presented in Figure 1. Note that the cross sectional area function changes abruptly at the midpoint. Approximately 10 to 1 area functions are necessary to produce these vowels (Stevens & House, 1955). These area functions can be effected by simply shifting the tongue about in the human supralaryngeal vocal tract. It is not possible to produce similar area function discontinuities in nonhuman primate vocal tracts which lack a right angle bend (Lieberman et. al., 1972).

The quantal properties of these vowels involve both the spectral properties of the vowels' acoustic transfer functions and the acoustic stability of the cross-sectional area functions. These properties follow from the equal lengths of the pharyngeal and oral cavities. The acoustic transfer functions plotted in Figure 1 represent the filtering action of the supralaryngeal airways on the source of acoustic energy that is generated by the quasiperiodic "puffs" of air that issue from the larynx during phonation. The formant frequencies of the transfer function are the frequencies at which relative energy maxima will occur. The first and second formant frequencies, F1 and F2, are marked on Figure 1. Note that all three vowels have well defined spectral properties that are the result of the approximation of two formant frequencies. A central spectral peak occurs at about 1 kHz for [ɑ]. A low frequency peak occurs for [u], whereas a high frequency peak occurs for [i] because F2 and F3 approximate at high frequencies. These spectral peaks are resistant to articulatory perturbations.

There is a 2 cm range near the midpoint of the vocal tract within which the second formant varies only 50 Hz and the first formant even less (Stevens, 1972). These small changes are not perceptually significant because human listeners can not differentiate between formant frequencies that differ by less than 60 Hz (Flanagan, 1955). Note that all three of these vowels are produced by means of area functions that involve discontinuities at or near the midpoint of the vocal tract. The midpoint area function discontinuity thus has an important functional value. It allows human speakers to produce vowel signals that are acoustically distinct with relatively sloppy articulatory maneuvers.

The perceptual value of these vowels in human speech has been established by a number of independent psychoacoustic experiments. When phonetic and acoustic context are controlled so that listeners are either presented with short words that differ only with respect to their vowels [e.g., words like heed [i], hid [ɪ], had [æ] (Peterson & Barney, 1952) or isolated vowels (Fairbanks & Grubb, 1961; Bond, 1976) the vowels [i] and [u] are most readily identified. Bond (1976), for example, found that [i] was identified correctly 73% of the time when isolated from an oral context and [u] 64% whereas [ɑ] and [ɔ] (the words hood and hawed, respectively) were identified 22 and 28% of the time. Similar effects occur in the data of Peterson and Barney where [i] and [u] again are best identified. Nasalized vowels are also more difficult to perceive, the difference being 51% overall correct identification for oral, 35% correct identification for nasal vowels (Bond, 1976).

These articulatory and perceptual studies thus show that there is an advantage to having the vowels [i] and [u] in the phonetic repertoire. They are resistant to articulatory sloppiness and they are more readily identified. There obviously is a selective advantage to being able to use these vowels in vocal communication. There is also a selective advantage in being able to produce oral (i.e., non-nasal) sounds. As Charles Darwin noted:

> any variation, however slight and from whatever cause preceding, if it be in any degree profitable to an individual of any species, in its infinitely complex relations to other organic beings. . . is preserved. (1859, p. 610)

RELEVENT DATA, DISCUSSION AND IMPLICATIONS

I've sketched out the main points of the theory but I've omitted most of the data that were involved in developing and testing the theory. I will not discuss the topics of automatization and grammar, though these topics are important (Lieberman, 1975), since they warrant a fuller discussion than available space allows.

The Physiology of Speech Production Negus (1974) claimed that the larynges of many animals were adapted for vocal communication at the expense of respiratory efficiency. Negus's claim is consistent with recent studies, e.g., Wind (1970). Fink and Demarest (1978) claim that the human larynx differs from the larynges of other living primates but these differences would primarily affect respiration. There is general agreement that the supralaryngeal vocal tract of normal adult human beings differs from all other non-human primates and newborn human beings (Negus, 1949; Du Brul, 1958; Truby et al. 1965; Lieberman, 1968; Lieberman et al., 1969, 1972a, 1972b; Falk, 1975; Bosma, 1975; George, 1978; Laitman et al. 1978). There is, in effect, a "standard plan" for the supralaryngeal vocal tracts of non-human primates and human newborns. The larynx is positioned high, close to the base of the skull, and the tongue lies almost entirely within the oral cavity. The high position of the larynx in the non-human, "standard plan" airway permits the epiglottis to lock the larynx directly into the nasopharynx, allowing nose breathing during both normal respiration and while liquids are contained in the mouth (Negus, 1949; Laitman, et. al. 1978). Recent quantitative studies demonstrate that the airways of normal human infants change from the "standard plan" to the human "two tube" system. George (1978), for example, shows that the cranial base angle changes from a mean of 137° to 123° between the first month of life and age 5 years, 9 months. Most of the change in the sample of 26 children, in each of whom the base angle was measured by means of cephalometric x-rays taken at regular intervals, was completed by the 9th month of life when the mean cranial base angle fell to 125°, which is within the adult range. The pattern of maturation varies for different children and is quite advanced at one month for some and delayed at six months for others but all individuals followed the same pattern of decreasing angle size. Laitman, et. al. (1978) using quantitative procedures demonstrated that craniometric measures of the bony base-pharynx, derived from skulls, correlate with the presence of the "standard plan" airway in non-human primates and the development of the human "two tube" system which follows from the gradual development of the pharynx (King, 1952) in *Homo sapiens*. Although the sample of newborn human skulls used by Laitman et al. (1978) is relatively small, Begland (1965) demonstrated that the angulation of the nasopharynx is highly correlated with the cranial base angle measurements derived by George. There is no significant change in the base angle after age three (Bergland 1965; George, 1978).

Studies of the vocalizations of non-human primates and the development of speech in human infants show that a two-tube vocal tract is a necessary condition for the production of sounds like the human vowels [i], [u] and [ɑ]. The predictions of the computer modelling studies (Lieberman et al. 1969; 1972) of non-human primates have been confirmed. Richman (1976) and Andrew (1976) both derived formant frequency transitions for non-human primates that were predicted by the computer modelling experiments but not observed in earlier acoustic analyses of primate vocalizations. Geladas and Baboons produce [ɪ] and [æ] vowel sounds as well as various consonant sounds that also occur in human languages. Similar results have been noted for chimpanzees recorded at the Goombe Stream Reservation (Lieberman in preparation) who also produce some sound sequences that do not seem to occur in human speech. These sound sequences may have communicative value. Vowels like [i] and [u] do not occur. Vocalizations that appear to "sound" like [i]'s often occur but acoustic analysis consistently shows that these sounds spectrally are examples of

[ι] rather than [i], their first forman frequencies are too high while their second formant frequencies are too low.

Recent acoustic studies of the development of speech in human infants also demonstrate that the range of vowel production increases as the infant's supralaryngeal vocal tract restructures towards the adult two-tube system. The studies of Stark et al. (1976), Buhr (1976), George (1978), Lieberman (in press) all show the vowels [i], [u] or [ɑ] usually first occur about 24 to 28 weeks of life, never occur before 8 weeks, and always occur by 9 months. These studies also show that our ''ears'' play tricks when we attempt to identify the sounds produced by infants. As George (1978, p. 82) notes,

> There was the general inclination to perceive the limits of the infant's vowel space as larger than was actually the case. Thus [i] would be heard as [ι] before [ι] was produced and [ι] would often be heard as [i] before an [i] conforming to special specifications was produced.

The perceptual studies cited by Dingwall (1978, 1979), for example, which report a wider repertoire of sounds for various non-human primates probably involve errors of this sort since they lack any confirmatory acoustic analyses. Dingwall also appears to lack an elementary knowledge of the principles of acoustic analysis since he also accepts the claims of Jordan's (1971) acoustic analysis of chimpanzee vocalizations. Jordan used a technique that is appropriate for the spectral analysis of industrial noise; his interpretation of the output of the filter bank that he used is meaningless. Formant frequency bandwidths in excess of 1 kHz, for example, are reported. Dingwall also doesn't appear to understand the Source-Filter theory of speech production; he, for example, seems to believe that the presence of the larynx is necessary to generate the supralaryngeal filter function. Dingwall's critiques are typical of other comments that don't address the issues in question regarding the evolution of the supralaryngeal vocal tract, but instead reflect basic unfamiliarity with the principles of speech analysis, speech production, psychoacoustic tests and comparative anatomy.

Some additional relevant data are apparent in recent developmental studies of vowel production in infants and young children (Lieberman, in press). In the late babbling and early phonologic stages of development the ''Quantal'' vowels that children produce are not as ''well formed'' as adult vowels. If we take into consideration the higher formant frequencies of the child's vowels, which follow from their shorter supralaryngeal vocal tracts, we find that F1 of an [i] is, for example, higher than it should be relative to F2. This presumably is a consequence of the shorter length of the child's pharynx relative to the oral cavity (King, 1952). As the child matures F1 and F2 of the [i] come closer to the adult model. There is also a greater variability in the formant frequencies of all the child's vowels at earlier ages. This may be a consequence of the child's pharynx not being equal in length to the oral cavity, thus making vowels like [i] less ''quantal'' (Stevens, 1952) than adult [i]'s. The greater variation at earlier ages could also be the result of a lack of motor control. The relative importance of quantalness versus motor control can be assessed by using computer modeling studies like that in progress by Goldstein (1979).

The second point that emerges from the study of the development of vowels is that the child's vowel system is frequency scaled to the overall length of the child's vocal tract. The child hearing adult speech can not produce identical acoustic signals; the child instead produces equivalent signals scaled to the size of its supralaryngeal vocal tract. This argues for the presence of a formant frequency scaling device that allows the child to ''normalize'' incoming speech signals and the sounds that he or she produces. This normalizing device is consistent with the predictions of Nearey's

(1976) model of vowel production and perception in which among other things, [i] provides the ''best'' reference signal for vocal tract normalization.

Reconstructing The Supralaryngeal Vocal Tracts of Fossil Hominids   Two recent independent studies (George, 1978; Laitman et al., 1978, 1979) quantitatively replicate the procedures that have been used to reconstruct the supralaryngeal vocal tracts of fossil hominids (Lieberman and Crelin, 1971; Lieberman et al., 1972; Crelin, 1973). George, as I have noted, measured the cranial base angle using cephalometric x-rays of a sample of 26 children and correlated these measures with pharyngeal development and vowel development. Laitman and his colleagues measured the angulation of the bony nasopharynx from the skulls of non-human primates, human infants and adults and fossil hominids. Statistical techniques were then used to group these measures and compare them with the observed supralaryngeal vocal tracts and larynges of living primates. The bases for the reconstructions of the supralaryngeal airways of various fossil hominids are the similarities that exist between them and living primates. The procedure is neither startling or odd. It is, for example, analogous to the methods that have been used to reconstruct the musculature of dinosaurs. Dinosaurs are extinct but animals that have a similar skeletal morphology, lizards, are still with us. Though a lizard is not a dinosaur, the similarities provide a living model that relates skeletal morphology and soft tissue.

The basis for the reconstruction of the supralaryngeal airway of the ''classic'' La Chapelle aux Saints fossil thus consists of the similarities with newborn *Homo sapiens*. When one examines the La Chapelle fossil it is obvious that what LeGros Clark termed the ''total morphonological pattern'' of the base of the skull is similar to that of newborn human infants. It is unlikely that the soft tissue of the supralaryngeal vocal tract of the fossil could differ in any substantial way from that of the newborn human infant since the relationships that obtain between skeletal structure and soft tissue are uniform through the order of Primates. Applying the principles of comparative anatomy in the most conservative manner, the relationship between skeletal morphology and soft tissue in newborn infants and Neanderthal fossils must be virtually identical in these closely, though not directly related hominids.

Though there has been some debate about the precise position of the hyoid bone in primates (Falk, 1975; DuBrul, 1976, 1977), it is obvious that it would be bizarre to reconstruct an adult human supralaryngeal vocal tract on a Neanderthal, Australopithecine, a non-human primate, or a newborn human skull. The quantal nature of the human vowel [i], for example, follows from the two-tube supralaryngeal vocal tract in which the pharynx and oral cavity are at right angles and have equal lengths. If we were to ''put'' a pharynx into a human newborn that was equal in length to the newborn's comparatively long oral cavity the larynx would have to be positioned near or below the level of the newborn's sternum. Newborns also have relatively short necks which compounds the problem. The problem is further compounded in Neanderthal hominids who have much longer oral cavities than modern humans (Howells, 1970, 1974, 1976) and who also had shorter necks. We do not find *any* living primate whose larynx is positioned in the chest, so the claim that classic Neanderthal hominids or Australopithecines, whose skulls resemble female orangutan (Lieberman, 1975; Laitman et al., 1979), had functionally human supra-laryngeal vocal tracts can be sustained only if we're willing to accept a reconstruction that Dr. Frankenstein would probably have rejected.

Neanderthal hominids, though they lived to comparatively recent times, are quite different from anatomically modern Homo sapiens in many ways. They were not as well adapted for upright posture. They swallowed food, and opened their jaws like apes (Lieberman, 1979). Indeed two of the arguments advanced by Falk (1975) and DuBrul (1976, 1977) against the reconstruction of Lieberman and Crelin (1971) reinforce Boule's (1911-1913) view of the pongid-like character of many aspects of the morphology of classic Neanderthal hominids. Falk (1975) for example, argued that Neanderthals couldn't have a high largyngeal position because they wouldn't be able to swallow in upright position. DuBrul argued that they likewise couldn't open their jaws. However, chimpanzees and gorillas who have larynges that are also high and whose mandibular "hinges" are similar to the Neanderthal configuration regularly swallow food in an upright position and are able to open their jaws. The evidence seems to suggest that hominid evolution in the recent past (to 250,000 years before the present) has involved specializations for speech production and that the human supralaryngeal vocal tract is not simply a concomitant result of adaptations for upright posture (DuBrul, 1958, 1976, 1977). Australopithecines who walked with a fully upright bipedal gait at least 4 million years ago (Leakey, 1979) nonetheless retained the standard plan, non-human supralaryngeal vocal tract which was still present some 4 million years later in classic Neanderthal hominids.

The discussion of Neanderthal hominids can not be concluded without noting that there is a great deal of variation in the skeletal features of the Neanderthal population. Laitman et. al. (1979), for example, show that the angulation of the bony nasopharynx in some Neanderthal hominids approaches that of modern human adults. This suggests that at least some of the Neanderthal population may have been evolving towards the modern human supralaryngeal vocal tract. Laitman et. al. (1979) unfortunately, do not take into account the length of the palate in these Neanderthal fossils which would preclude a supralaryngeal vocal tract in which the length of the pharynx was equal to that of the oral cavity. However, it is obvious that there is variation in the Neanderthal fossil population in those skeletal features that are associated with the supralaryngeal vocal tract. In other words, these fossils may represent a population in which some intermediate stages in the evolution of the human supralaryngeal vocal tract were present. This may seem paradoxical; how could we have a population in which some people could produce speech sounds that others could not produce? The situation, however, is not paradoxical. It is exactly what we would expect to find if mutations that confer a selective advantage were diffusing through the gene pool. A mutation cannot spread instantly throughout an entire population. In the present human population, for example, some people are able to digest cow's milk better than other people. This reflects the fact that cows and other animals that can be milked, have been domesticated for less than ten thousand years. The mutations that allow some people to digest cow's milk thus have had a selective advantage for less than 10 thousand years and we're still in a transition period. The mutations that are responsible for the development of the modern human supralaryngeal vocal tract appear to have become characteristic of the entire human population only in the last 30,000 years with the emergence of anatomically modern Homo sapiens. Before that period some hominids were better adapted for chewing, swallowing and breathing while others were better adapted for speech production.

The Selective Advantages of the Speech of Modern Humans   In Lieberman et. al. (1972) we proposed that speech encoding would not be possible without the presence of the quantal vowels. This claim followed from data (Stevens and House, 1955; Russell, 1938, Perkell, 1969) that showed that other vowels could be produced with varying supralaryngeal vocal tract shapes so that it would be difficult for a listener to "normalize", i.e., adjust to the length of the supralaryngeal vocal tract that had produced the speech signal that was being "decoded". The data of Peterson and Barney (1952), furthermore, demonstrated that the vowels [i] and [u] were most readily perceived when listeners were presented with short words that differed only with respect to their vowels. More recent experiments demonstrated that speech encoding and decoding could make use of other "reference" signals and that the vocalizations of animals like chimpanzees could be encoded (Lieberman, 1975). A series of experiments initiated by Shankweiler and his colleagues, (Strange et. al. 1976; Fowler and Shankweiler 1978), moreover claimed that consonants furnished the necessary "reference" signals for vowel identification. In contrast, other studies like those of Nearey (1976) and Bond (1976) demonstrated that isolated vowels could be identified, with [i] and [u] being most consistently identified. Recent data seems to have resolved some of the paradoxes. The "consonontal" effects noted by Shankweiler and his associates for the most part, appear to be the result of transcription errors by their subjects (Assman, 1978; Kahn, 1978). The most recent data using synthetic speech stimuli (Pisoni et al., 1979) show that virtually no errors occur when listeners identify the vowels [i] and [u] in isolation whereas the error rate varies between 20 and 30 percent for other vowels. In other experimental situations using natural speech almost perfect identification occurs for all vowels (Assman, 1978; Kahn, 1978) though [i] and [u] still show a slight perceptual advantage. The best assessment of these data that I can make is that the quantal vowels [i] and [u] are the optimal vowels for speech communication with [i] being the "supervowel" for the reasons discussed in detail by Nearey (1976). The relative perceptual advantage of [i] and [u] appears to vary from about 5 percent to 40 percent (Bond, 1976). Nasalization, which inherently occurs for speech generated by the non-human single tube supralaryngeal vocal tract, also results in an additional 15 percent overall error rate.

Since selective advantages of 5 percent are sufficient for the effects of natural selection to become evident there is a basis for the claim that the human supralaryngeal vocal tract evolved, in part, for the enhancement of phonetic ability.

Matched Neural Property Detectors   One of the most interesting developments of the last 20 years of research on vocal communication in humans and other animals has been the discovery of neural mechanisms that are "matched" to respond to the acoustic signals that various species are able to produce. Bullfrogs, for example, have auditory mechanisms that respond selectively to the mating call of the species (Frishkopf & Goldstein, 1963). These neural mechanisms respond, if, and only if, the acoustic signal has the formant and fundamental frequencies characteristic of the bullfrogs' supralaryngeal airways and larynges (Capranica, 1965). The neural mechanisms that are involved in the bullfrog's perception of this call thus are "matched" to the constraints of the bullfrogs' sound producing anatomy. Indirect evidence for similar mechanisms exists for *Homo sapiens* and other primates (Peterson et. al., 1978, 1979; Eimas et. al. 1971; Eimas and Crobit, 1973; Kuhl, 1976): The classic Motor Theory of Speech Perception developed by Liberman and his associates indeed makes a similar claim, differing only with respect to the probable implementation of the match between production and perception. The neural implementation of the "match" is not the immediate concern of this paper and recent data indicate that human infants categorize vowels like [ɑ] and [i] and make consonantal distinctions like [d] vs [g] on the basis of the formant frequency patterns of these sounds in the first months of life (Morse, 1974; Kuhl, 1976). Innate mechanisms that respond selectively to the acoustic patterns that define human speech again seem to determine the infants' behavior. Psychoacoustic experiments with adult human listeners are consistent with the presence of neural property detectors that are matched to respond to the classes of acoustic signals that occur in human speech sounds like [b], [d] and [g] (Cooper, 1974; Blumstein et. al., 1977) as well as sounds that do not occur in English, but occur in other languages. The formant patterns that define the consonants that typically occur in human languages at labial ([b] and [p]), dental ([d] and [t]), velar ([g] and [k]), and pharyngeal "places of articulation'' follow from quantal properties of the human supralaryngeal vocal tract (Stevens, 1972). These quantal sounds don't all occur in every language, but in the languages of Homo sapiens as a whole, they occur more often than other consonantal sounds.

These data suggest that neural auditory mechanisms have evolved that match the quantal sounds of the human supralaryngeal vocal tract. It is possible that hominids, like Skhul V, who had human-like supralaryngeal vocal tracts also had matching neural mechanisms (Lieberman, 1975). It is likewise plausible that hominids who lacked the sound-producing anatomy that is necessary to produce quantal sounds like [g], and [k] also lacked the corresponding matched neural property detectors. Whatever special, innately determined perceptual mechanisms may be necessary to learn the sounds of any language, they are present in all normal human beings. There may be ''critical'' periods involved in learning a language, which lead to the presence of accents when people acquire a second language after their childhood. The situation however, is quite different than that which I propose for hominids who lacked the special neural mechanisms that are involved in the perception of the sounds that only the modern human supralaryngeal vocal tract can produce. It is possible that these hominids might have been able to learn to perceive these sounds, but they would have been using different perceptual mechanisms.

Discussion

Ignatius G. Mattingly The speakers at this session have offered two apparently conflicting accounts of the origin of human speech. Hewes argues that speech began with manual gestures; Lieberman argues that it began with anatomical changes in the supralaryngeal vocal tract that made it possible to produce distinguishable sounds with different vocal tract configurations.

For the Hewes account to be plausible, it has to be assumed that a neural system for producing manual gestures — in particular, pointing gestures — evolved into a system for producing articulatory gestures. Hewes offers evidence that an ontogenetic development of this sort actually occurs. His point of view is particularly attractive because articulatory gestures in speech production can be viewed as pointing gestures: an articulatory target is quite likely to be merely implied by the movement of an articulatory gesture in the direction of the target, rather than actually attained. But to complete Hewes' account, it is necessary to explain the shift from semantic pointing — that is, pointing to objects in the environment — to phonetic pointing, the environmental objects no longer being directly indicated, but represented by an arbitrary phonological coding of words in the lexicon. It is also necessary to explain how man developed the ability to infer the nature of the articulatory gestures, most of which are not directly observable, from the acoustic consequences of these gestures, that is, to explain the evolution of speech perception.

Lieberman offers a persuasive account of how the anatomy of the vocal tract evolved so as to provide distinctive acoustic signals. He then makes the more controversial argument that in speech perception, these signals serve as the input to acoustically-based neural "property detectors" that, according to Stevens (1972), are the basis of a universal phonetic-feature set. The evolution of these property detectors is said to be concomitant with the evolution of the vocal tract. On this view of speech perception, there is obviously no motivation for the recovery of articulatory gestures — these are seen as merely the means to an acoustic end — and therefore an account of the origin of speech from gesture has no particular appeal.

But it is still an open question whether phonetic features are best regarded as having an articulatory basis, as Liberman and his colleagues (1967) have argued; an acoustic basis, as Stevens argues; or a mixed basis, as Ladefoged (1971), and formerly Lieberman himself (1970), have argued. I do not wish to debate this question, but simply to point out that Lieberman's current view of speech perception is not necessarily entailed by Lieberman's account of vocal tract evolution. It could be that the vocal tract evolved as it did in support of a concomitantly evolving system for production and perception of articulatory gestures. If so, Hewes hypothesis and Lieberman's would be complementary rather than conflicting.

Colwyn Trevarthen: Antecedents of Speaking in Infant Behaviour While endorsing the approach which seeks to define special organs and behaviours which make human language possible, I would suggest to Professors Hewes and Lieberman that we cannot properly understand peripheral components, like the vocal mechanism or pointing gestures, without grasping the power of more central motivating structures that lead all humans to communicate with speech, or with other kinds of language like writing or A.S.L.

Research with infants has produced important evidence concerning highly specialized innate mental processes for perceiving the particular interests and intentions of other persons, and for cooperating with them in experience and action (Trevarthen, 1974; 1977; 1978; 1979a,b; Trevarthen & Hubley, 1978). The principal facts are as follows:

Immediately after the neonate period, in the second month, babies orient selectively and preferentially to persons, attending to their vocalizations, facial expressions, gestures and movements in discriminating ways. The imitation experiments cited and the demonstrations of motor synchronization between very young infants and others tend to lead to the idea that in neonates there is a set of fairly automatic responses to perception of others' expressive acts. However, more complete analysis of communicative interactions (op. cit.) shows that the baby is not just reacting reflexly, or with an I.R.M. for imitation, or performing conditioned responses. Temporally organized and well-patterned utterance-like emissions of a two-month-old to a sympathetic listener change radically if the listener fails to respond in the right time and with the right quality of friendliness. Experiments by Murray with this failure of interaction prove that the emotional quality, interpersonal value or mood of the infant's expression is organized to complement the personal expressions of an intimate caretaker, usually the mother. If treated with affection and happiness, they are happy and spontaneously expressive in facial expression, vocalization, gesture and postural attitude. If treated mysteriously or rudely by the same person, they become sad, depressed and, by grimace, gesture and vocalization emit a totally different communicative appeal. These activities are spontaneously patterned, not imitative.

In the above primary intersubjective behaviour, infants emit many gestures in close synchrony with their own facial expressions, which include rudimentary vocalizations (cooing) and a pattern of frequently silent lip and tongue movements crudely integrated with a basic breath control (prespeech[1]). Sylvester-Bradley has proved, by statistical analysis of occurrence of particular acts, that gestures above shoulder level and prespeech are coupled. Included in a wide repertoire of organized hand and arm movements, mostly undescribed, is index finger extension, and this is frequently synchronized with pursing of the lips and possibly with raised eyebrows. Index extension may not be oriented to a distal goal or target. It may be just a sign of a focal point or climax in the progress of the motive to express. However, in the first two months, infants also show highly coordinated cyclical reach and grasp movements which may be aimed to distal objects, though they rarely make contact. In these oriented prehensile movements (prereaching) frequently the index finger is extended at the climax, and the aim of the finger may be precise (within 10°). I see no reason to doubt that the adaptive purpose of this indexing is for communication. Therefore I reject the unsubstantiated theory that pointing develops out of grasping for objects. It is differentiated from the latter at the neonate stage.

The rich repertoire of expressions preadaptive to emotional and linguistic communication becomes organized into significant messages within the first year, before words are produced. We have traced the development of motives in the infant to combine object cognition with communication. Establishment of joint temporo-spatial reference and specification of the nature or meaning of an object both appear first in teasing games at about six months, after the infant has mastered efficient object prehension. Humorous interactions in play allow practice or coordinated and reciprocal intentions. Then at near ten months, infants usually, and sometimes quite suddenly, begin to deliberately seek to comply with the wishes, interests, instructions, actions and signs of feeling of a partner. Willingness to attend to and obey a request or to follow a lead appears at the same time as the emission of vocalizations signifying mutually acknowledged meanings (Halliday's proto-language).

The evidence clearly supports the idea that a central motivational structure for cooperative understanding of objects, actions, goals, etc., has reached a level of proficiency at this time. It is of great interest to me that this is the age at which the vocal tract begins to achieve a uniquely human configuration ready for speaking, and a time when the gestural and other expressive acts studied by Bates, Bruner and his colleagues and others appear in spontaneous communication between infants and their mothers.

I believe we are beginning to see the general nature of the morphogenetic process leading to human psychological cooperation and to the rich transmission of this cooperation in culturally perfected languages which are learned in childhood. Infants certainly support the theory that the motives for speaking to other persons about the shared world have elaborate organization before the act of speaking has developed.

Chairman's Comments

John C. Marshall: Language and Evolution   Despite (or perhaps because of) the numerous hedges that have been erected around discussion of the origins and evolution of language and speech, the topic continues to fascinate contemporary scholars to at least the extent that it did our intellectual ancestors. It is difficult to think of a major linguistic scholar from Epicurus to Humboldt who did not expound a theory of the origin of language. Yet by the middle of the nineteenth century many linguists were convinced that the effort devoted to this particular branch of speculative science considerably outweighed the gains in understanding that had been achieved. Whitney's (1870) summary is typically trenchant:

> No theme in linguistic science is more often and more voluminously treated than this, and by scholars of every grade and tendency; nor any, it may be added, with less profitable result in proportion to the labour expended.

The 'official' condemnation is to be found in the statutes of the Paris Société de Linguistique (1866). There we find the famous prohibition:

> "La Société n'admet aucune communication concernant. . . . l'origine du langage" (see Stam, 1976).

But in order to be at all effective the Society's ban had come at exactly the wrong time. Darwin's *The Origin of Species* had appeared in 1859; his *Descent of Man* was to be published in 1871. The most bitter arguments, both for and against the doctrines of descent and natural selection, were to take place over the plausibility of Darwin's theory in providing a naturalistic account of the origin and development of articulate language. Although Darwin's own writings on language were sparse, nowhere was his influence more keenly felt than in the rapidly developing disciplines of psycho- and neuro-linguistics. On the one hand, scholars such as Schleicher (1865) and Romanes (1888) were convinced that many topics in the ontogeny and phylogeny of language could be unified by Darwinian concepts; on the other hand, Tylor (1865) and Bateman (1877) remained unconvinced both of the existence of 'primitive' languages and of the plausibility of modelling an evolutionary history that would account for the apparently localized components of the language faculty that were being uncovered in the aphasia studies of Broca (1861) and Wernicke (1874).

To what extent have the undoubted advances of the last hundred years moved us closer to an understanding of language origins in the individual and species? As Mattingly notes in his comments on the session, our two main speakers *appear* to be proposing quite distinct hypotheses concerning the precursors of language and speech at the species level. Hewes sees a progression from pointing and other gestures to language, Lieberman from call-signs to speech. Hewes, then, is following the expositions of Wallace (1895) and Wundt (1900) in postulating that gesture-language preceded articulate language in the developmental stages of modern man, and he seems indeed to take the strongest of the classical positions in arguing that there is a functional and structural sense in which spoken language can 'grow out of' gesture language. It is clear, however, that if there is a genuine evolutionary linkage here, it is likely to be at the level of symbolic communication, not at the level of universal grammar. And even in the former case one has some difficulty in seeing precisely how pointing and 'iconic' gestures might lead the species (or the child) into an appreciation of communicative interactions involving displaced reference and conventional meaning: As Wittgenstein (1974) writes:

> The meaning of a name is not the thing we point to when we give an ostensive definition of the name: that is, it is not the bearer of the name.

Even more problematic is the relationship (if any) between 'natural' gestures and the formal constraints on rules and representations that constitute the biological matrix for the growth of grammar (Chomsky, 1980a). Anyone who has followed recent work on the structure and acquisition of American Sign Language (ASL) might be somewhat surprised by the stress that Hewes lays on the significance of pointing and iconicity (''air pictures'') in gestural languages (Klima and Bellugi, 1979). One only has to watch a sign-language poet (or a sign-language intellectual discussing linguistics) to realize that pointing in the service of ostensive definition and immediate reference bears little relationship to the structuring of sentences and discourse by constraints upon anaphora. One might also note in connection with arguments concerning the gestural abilities of extant species that whilst chimpanzees may interact, think, and solve problems in much the same way that we do (Woodruff and Premack, 1979), the evidence that they (or any other non-human species) possess *any* linguistic ability beyond simple naming is considerably less than compelling (Terrace, Petitto, Sanders and Bever, 1979; Petitto and Seidenberg, 1979; Seidenberg and Petitto, 1979). The issue of linguistic (in-) capacity in species other than ourselves is, of course, by no means closed (Marx, 1980), but it certainly seems that the day when a descendant of Kafka's ape will address a learned Academy on his transition from tool-use to fluent signing is some considerable way away.

None of this argues *directly* against the notion of 'simple' gestures as an evolutionary precursor of language, but it does emphasize the point that in any discussion of 'stages' one must postulate a *mechanism* that links the stages causally (Marshall, 1980). Otherwise we are left with mere temporal succession. That the human being demonstrates her capacity to scream before she demonstrates her capacity to learn quantum physics does not indicate that screaming is a functional precursor of intellectual achievement. The necessity to *show* the missing links (in terms of a formal model) remains even when one's intuitions would happily accept a connection. Thus Trevarthen in his commentary sees a ''morphological process'' that leads from 'prespeech' to ''human psychological cooperation and to the rich transmission of this cooperation in culturally perfected languages which are learned in childhood.'' One can see the intuitive plausibility of a connection between prespeech exchanges and adult social interactions, although one might be happier about the link if one was given a theory of the relevent ''morphological process''. Be that as it may, the peculiarly human *form* of linguistic expression remains, I think, opaque to explanation in terms of socialization practices and constraints on inter-personal communication (Blank, Gessner, and Exposito, 1979).

Lieberman's paper addresses itself to what seems like a more immediately tractable (sic) problem — the evolution of human vocalization and the comparative study of the noise-making properties of the vocal tracts of living primates and extinct hominids. One does not have to deny the beauty and power of sign-languages to see that a vocal language may have conferred an evolutionary advantage upon its users. It is, after all, quite difficult to either wash up or aim a spear whilst conversing in ASL. It is thus of very considerable interest to discover what kinds of peripheral adaptations are required if a rich and effective system of vocal signals is to be produced. Although technical problems abound with some of the fossil reconstructions, Lieberman is obviously correct in arguing that some supralaryngeal tracts can and others cannot produce the full range of highly modulated signals upon which human phonetic and phonological systems are based. But he is careful to note that his theory "does *not* claim that speech is impossible without [the particular] supralaryngeal specializations [that he documents], nor does it claim that human speech is completely disjoint from the vocal communications of other animals".

In order to be acted upon by natural selection, any peripheral modifications must presumably go hand-in-hand with the development of the central brain-organs that control the input and output systems. (Who would have guessed what canaries can sing and 'say' solely on the basis of dissecting a syrinx?). Once again we recapitulate the preoccupations of the nineteenth century. Keane (1895) writes:

> "For the evolutionist, who necessarily traces man back to a speechless precursor, speech is a function which perfects itself hand in hand with the growth of the organ [of the brain].
> Hence the faculty starts from a germ, and its history is one of continuous upward evolution from slowly accumulating crude utterances. Such utterances, vague at first in sound and sense, are to be regarded as the imperfect expression of inward emotion and feelings, of outward things and actions, differing from the accompanying gesture-language only in this, that the one appeals to the sense of vision, the other to that of hearing.
> Primitive man, always a social being congregating in family groups, expressed his thoughts by speech and gesture, and as speech expanded with the infinite capabilities of the vocal organs, gesture fell more and more into abeyance, now surviving only amongst the lower and some of the more emotional higher races (American Aborigines, Neapolitans)."

What kinds of central mechanisms and adaptations are required for the emergence of language abilities? Much interest has recently been aroused by demonstrations of anatomical and functional specialisation of the hemispheres in non-human species. Although the data are still rather crude, there do seem to be anatomical asymmetries favouring the left temporal lobe in some of the great apes and other higher primates (LeMay & Geschwind, 1975; Yeni-Komshian & Benson, 1976). Such asymmetries, that are in areas approximately homologous to human auditory association cortex, may have functional significance. Thus Dewson (1977) has reported left-hemisphere specialization for delayed selective response to tones in the Irus Macaque; Petersen, Beecher, Zoloth, Moody and Stebbins (1978) have shown left-hemisphere superiorities in the discrimination of species-specific vocalizations by the Japanese Macaque. (It should be noted, however, that evidence of analogous *anatomical* asymmetry in monkeys is currently lacking.) These observations complement the earlier studies of Nottebohm (1979) on a marked left-hemisphere dominance for the vocal control of full song in birds such as canaries. Whilst humans are descended from neither macaques nor canaries, one does nonetheless, wonder whether nature made a number of related efforts at producing a language-using organism before finally succeeding somewhere along the hominid line.

Although we are far from understanding the biological matrix that underlies hemispheric specialization in man, evidence does appear to be converging on the critical role of neural mechanisms that can respond to and produce rapid rates of change. The right-ear advantage in dichotic listening is maximal when the elements of complexly patterned signals are of short duration (Mills and Rollman, 1979), and when, for example, the formant transitions of CV syllables are brief (Schwartz and Tallal, 1980). The analysis of temporal order and rhythm are likewise grist to the left hemisphere's mill (Papcun, Krashen, Terbeek, Remington, and Harshman, 1974; Craig, 1979). Although auditory stimuli "are sensory prototypes of higher codes that emphasize . . . . . temporal processing" (Grossberg, 1980), the types of pattern that preferentially engage the left-hemisphere are not modality-specific. To a first approximation, the perception and comprehension of sign-language draw upon the same central neurological substrate that is implicated in the acquisition and use of audio-vocal language (Poizner and Battison, 1979).

On the production side there is also evidence that the left-hemisphere is the primary locus of ". . . . . a system for accurate internal representation of moving body parts, important for the control of changes in the position of both oral and branchial articulators" (Kimura, 1979). In support of this localization, Kimura notes the frequent association of limb apraxias with aphasia following left-hamisphere lesions. And she claims that the relevant apraxias (those illustrated by tasks that depend upon the accurate representation and control of fast moving parts) occur more frequently with the symptom-complex of Wernicke's aphasia than they do with Broca's aphasia. The anatomic specialization of the left posterior peri-Sylvian region may thus range over both language and praxic skills that demand rapid changes from one target position to another (but see Basso, Luzzatti, and Spinnler, 1980, and De Renzi, Motti, and Nichelli, 1980).

It seems likely, then, that there have been central pre-adaptations for language at both the input (analysis of fast-changing signals) and the output (control of rapid, sequential movements) side. But the basic mysteries remain: A molecular analysis of these adaptations at the level of cell, synapse, and circuit physiology continues to elude us (but see Grossberg, 1980). Similarly, we have no models for the 'evolution' of the schematism of universal grammar with free parameters to be filled in by exposure to the linguistic environment (Chomsky, 1975; 1980b). We know, however, from studies of early hemispherectomy, that syntactic (Dennis and Whitaker, 1976) and morphological capacities (Day and Ulatowska, 1979) are most effectively mediated by a left-hemisphere substrate. One might accordingly, raise the issue of whether this lateralized grammatical specialization is 'intrinsic' or is rather induced by adaptations underlying the reception and control of the physical signs and signals that mediate language.

Note

1. By 'prespeech' I mean a particular form of infant expressive behaviour which the evidence suggests is developmentally related to the act of articulating speech. It is an embryonic or rudimentary speaking not learned by imitating. I am not referring to babyhood before speech, or to any physiological activity immediately before the act of speaking.

SESSION VI
DEVELOPMENT OF REPRESENTATION

Seminar 11: Representation of speech in infancy

Chair	ADRIAN FOURCIN
Speakers	JEAN BERKO GLEASON,
	JACQUES MEHLER
Discussants	BENEDICTE de BOYSSON-BARDIES,
	JACQUELINE SACHS
	EVELYN ABBERTON, JOHN GILBERT

Seminar 12: The development of representation

Chair	HAZEL FRANCIS
Speakers	NEIL SMITH, NATALIE WATERSON
Discussants	BARBARA DODD, MICHAEL GARMAN,
	HARRY McGURK, WALBURGA von
	RAFFLER-ENGEL, PiNTIP TUAYCHAROEN

THE COGNITIVE REPRESENTATION OF SPEECH
T. Myers, J. Laver, J. Anderson (editors)
© North-Holland Publishing Company, 1981

Phonological Modifications in Adults' Speech to Infants: Some Implications for Theories of Language Acquisition

JEAN BERKO GLEASON

Boston University

In studying the infant's representation of speech, most research has concentrated on attempting to delineate the special cognitive and perceptual mechanisms that infants bring to the task. By contrast, there has been very little discussion of the special nature of the speech that infants actually hear in their everyday lives. Even if it is true that infants enter the world equipped with hard-wired perceptual and hypothesis-generating equipment, they still must attend to a sample of actual language in order to begin to acquire language, and the nature of the corpus of speech that the infant hears should provide some insight into the degree of sophistication required by whatever inborn mechanisms there may be. Discriminations that infants are called upon to make in the laboratory may not be illustrative of the kinds of discriminations they have to make when learning language; and the assumption that the rapid and frequently slurred speech that is common in adult conversations is also the corpus that infants must somehow segment and decode is misleading. Rather, infants must decode the specially modified speech that is directed to them.

It is probably safe to say that infants do not, and perhaps could not, acquire language simply by overhearing adults in discourse with one another. The notion that mere *exposure* to language is all that the infant needs in order to acquire language is not upheld by any evidence that this ever happens: in every community that has thus far been studied adults not only speak to children, they speak to them in specially modified ways. Children acquire langauge through *interaction*, rather than exposure. During the past few years a great deal of research has been concentrated on specifying the features and describing the characteristics of speech to infants and young children from this interactional perspective. It has long been recognized that adults provide modifications when speaking to children, and before the present epoch such speech was labeled *baby talk*; it is now generally referred to as *input language,* and the new terminology reflects our expectation that the input language will have some effect on the output, that is on the language subsequently developed by the child.

In very general terms, input language has been shown to differ from adult-to-adult language at all levels: it is lexically, semantically, syntactically, and phonologically simpler than adult-adult speech. At the same time, it contains some features that are not found in speech to adults. Moreover, it changes over time; speech to newborns is not the same as speech to one year olds, which, in turn, differs from speech to two year olds, and so on. Just what causes adults to speak as they do to change their speech over time is not known. Adults speak as they do at least in part because they have preconceived notions about how to talk to infants: for instance, Catherine Snow (1972) asked adult subjects to talk on the telephone to two year olds who did not actually exist. Nonetheless, the speech of these adults contained the same set of features typically found in home samples of mothers talking to their actual children. On the other hand, signals from infants themselves can cause dramatic modifications in adult speech: Bohannon (1977) brought graduate students into the laboratory to talk to a young child who had been trained to give signals of non-comprehension at specified points in the interaction. After receiving these signals, the adults quite unconsciously produced much shorter and simpler utterances. Adults, therefore, appear not only to modify their speech when addressing young children, but to do so sensitively, so that the input language may be adjusted to the particular level of the child at any given moment. While these are general statements, they also apply to modifications in the phonological input that children receive.

PHONOLOGICAL MODIFICATIONS TO PRELINGUISTIC INFANTS

There are a great many phonological modifications that adults employ when talking to infants. In addition to features that we can all agree are essentially phonological in nature, there are some that serve a phonological function: for instance, repetition. Many studies in English and other languages have reported that parents repeat themselves. They say things like, *Give me the ball. That's right, give me the ball. Give me the ball.* (Frequently with a rising terminal, as well). Since the acoustic signal fades rapidly, repetition is one device that adults use that can help to give the infant time to decode the message. Repetition prolongs the signal.

Speech to infants typically exhibits great intonational variety and a high, sometimes very high, fundamental frequency. Adults also use some specialized baby talk vocabulary to young infants (e.g. *tum-tum* for *stomach* in English or *dodo* for *dormir* in French.) These words are characterized by an additional set of phonological features, such as gemination, reduplication, and consonant cluster reduction, and such features are found in baby talk lexicons around the world, (Ferguson 1977). Not all speakers use the baby talk lexicon however, and a discussion of these baby talk words is beyond the scope of this paper.

The high fundamental frequency and the intonational variety may serve several important functions. Jacqueline Sachs (1977) has argued that adult speech to prelinguistic infants is a:

> species typical pattern whose evolution has been determined by the sensory capacities of infants and by the infant's requirements for normal communication with its social world. (p. 51)

Sachs indicates that speech to prelinguistic infants exhibits higher pitch, special intonational patterns, rythmic and temporal patterning, and the use of special sounds. Her research further shows that infants, when given the choice, prefer to listen to voices that have these features. Moreover, it is just this set of adult input features that infants gain control of in their earliest months. Prelinguistic babies, for instance, can frequently produce speech-like jargon with all the intonational patterns of the adult language around them. Early input features appear to be tuned to the sensory capacities of infants, and to their developing productive ability.

The very common phenomenon of the high fundamental frequency has attracted the attention of a number of researchers, who have noted, for instance, that an adult speaking to several young children uses a higher pitch to the youngest child. This has led to the claim that there may be some sort of pitch-matching strategy in operation here, with adults trying to sound like the child they are addressing. Pitch-matching, however, does not appear to be the case in experimental studies of adults speaking to one another (Bernstein and Jeje 1978). In the Bernstein and Jeje study, male and female university students were interviewed twice, once with a same sex—and once with an opposite-sex interviewer. Their fundamental frequencies were analyzed with the MIT pitch-extraction program. A pitch matching strategy would have led the males to raise their fundamental frequency when speaking to females, and the females to lower theirs when talking to males. This was not the case, however, since both sexes lowered their voices in the mixed sex dyads while at the same time restricting their intonational range. The speakers were apparently attempting to approximate a model of what is supposed to be sexually attractive in our society, and these considerations overrode any tendency there may be for pitch matching. In speaking to infants, the rise in fundamental frequency may be associated with the expression of affection and may also be the result of some sort of empathizing with the infant's smallness. The high pitch may also result from the adult's unconscious desire to appear nonthreatening to the infant.

Speech to infants thus has both affective and attention-getting qualities. The phonological modifications serve to mark the speech as *for* the infant, and they have characteristics that convey affection and appear to fit with the infant's sensory capacities. These features help lay the motivational base for acquiring language; they also enable infants to engage in early vocal interpersonal communication, since during this period adults and babies engage in babbled conversations that are sustained by these phonological modifications.

MODIFICATIONS IN SPEECH TO INFANTS LEARNING LANGUAGE

As infants enter the second half of the first year, and begin to comprehend speech, tne nature of the adult modifications changes markedly. While the high fundamental frequency remains, the adult speech now becomes slower—half the rate of adult-adult speech. The speech also becomes louder, and pauses are placed external to clause boundaries. In a study comparing adult-adult and adult-child speech, Garnica (1977) found, in addition to the above: rising speech terminals where adult-adult has falling terminals; whispered speech; longer duration on content words; and many instances of double primary stress in sentences that to an adult would have a single primary stress. Some of these prosodic and paralinguistic modifications go beyond the affective and attention-giving functions mentioned earlier; they also help to segment the stream of speech, emphasize important words, and, in general, make the task of breaking the code easier.

An examination of phonological modifications on a much narrower level has been carried out by Moslin and Nigro (1976) at Brown University. These researchers sought to determine if adults tailor their speech on the phonetic level. They chose to look at voice onset time (VOT) for initial English voiced and voiceless stop consonants. Their subjects were mothers of infants of varying ages. Moslin and Nigro found that among the mothers in their sample there was considerable overlap in VOT in pairs like *p* and *b* when they were talking to another adult, but when speaking to their language-learning infants, the mothers made clean distinctions. For instance, one mother's mean VOT value for *p* when talking to an adult was 35 msec; but her mean VOT value for *p* produced to her infant was 52 msec. This kind of distinction was found especially in speech to infants just learning to talk, and was not found in speech either to very young prelinguistic infants who presumably could not benefit from such clarification or in speech to older children who could already make the distinctions. Moslin (1976) concludes:

. . the mothers under study are very sensitive language teachers, and appear to be clarifying for their children the phonological distinction of voicing along the phonetic dimension of VOT.

This gives additional weight to the claim that speech to language-learning children has special phonological characteristics that make the code easier to crack than might otherwise be the case. Laboratory studies of speech perception in infants are valuable because they indicate the limits of the infant's capabilities; studies of input language suggest that infants are not called upon to exercise all of their potential, and that adult modifications themselves provide some of the categorizations that have been imputed to infants.

SPEECH TO OLDER CHILDREN

Even after children have acquired language, adults continue to provide some kinds of phonological modifications in their speech to them. These modifications no longer appear to be specifically designed for clarification, but, rather, serve other functions. Some researchers (e.g. Blount 1976) have recorded many phonological features used by adults when speaking with children, but not with one another. Some of these include: creaky voice, whisper (where quiet is not required, as in reading stories), falsetto, breathy voice, and so on.

As Blount noted, these modifications make the word *harder*, rather than easier, to distinguish phonetically. He raised the question of how they can in any sense be appropriate if this is the case. In our own laboratory, Lise Menn has been working on this question. Menn has examined recordings we have made of fathers and mothers interacting with their two and three year old children. She has found many instances of falsetto (more for fathers than mothers), marked high, singing voice, glottalized creaky voice. She also found some instances of soft, whisper, nasal, shriek, marked low, breathy, and hoarse voice in the speech of these adults, who were engaged in such things as playing store with their children, reading books, and taking apart and putting back together a toy automobile. The features that appear to obscure rather than clarify phonology were, however, not evenly distributed in the parents' speech. When Menn examined specific teaching episodes, that is, those many cases where the adult was introducing a new word to the child, these markers were not used; there was no apparent interference. New words might be presented with extra stress or greater duration, but adults do not introduce new words in a whisper, or a shriek, for that matter. The marked voice quality in this speech to somewhat older children is used for affect and attention getting, and also for contextual purposes. In the latter instance, it might be used to mark the role of a character in a story, for example. The same feature can be used for a variety of purposes, depending on the situation: Menn found that in some cases falsetto was used as an affect marker of disbelief, and in others as the voice of a character.

CONCLUSION

If we characterize the phonological modifications found in adult speech to children during their first three or four years, we find a change in both the features used and their major functions over time. Speech to very young infants contains modifications that are primarily affective and tuned to infants' perceptual preferences in such a way that they help establish preverbal communication. As infants begin to comprehend speech, adults switch on a modification program that cleans up fuzzy phonetic distinctions, segments the stream of speech into short clauses, highlights important words, and, in general, makes the system cleaner and clearer. Still later, after children have acquired the basic phonological and grammatical distinctions of the language, these language-teaching modifications drop out, and adults use marked voice quality to convey information about the social world.

The information we now have about input to children has obvious implications for linguistic theory. Every language that has thus far been studies has a special register for speaking to infants. To what extent there might be universals in the modifications used by adults is not known. Some of these modifications seem, on an intuitive basis, to be rather likely candidates for universal status: high fundamental frequency, for instance, may have a biologically determined origin—that is, from an ethological perspective one can speculate that infants, perhaps infants of all species, *release* this particular kind of vocal behavior on the part of adults. Other features might be in complementary distribution or free variation. Harkness (1976), for instance, found that in Guatemala mothers did not use slow rate in speaking to their language-learning children, but that they did repeat themselves very frequently, in fact as often as necessary for the child to understand. American mothers do not repeat as much as Guatemalan mothers, but they use slow rate as well, thus distributing the clarifying processes more broadly.

None of the information we now have on input language has led us to believe that infants are *tabulae rasae*; clearly, they are born with highly specialized perceptual, cognitive, and language learning capacities. It does appear, however, that adults provide environmental assistance in the form of modified input. It is likely that some modifications serve adult needs, while others are essential to the infant. Linguistic theory will be well served if, and when, we can discover which phonological modifications are necessary and sufficient in order for the infant to be able to acquire language.

Note

Jean Berko Gleason's research, and the research of Lise Menn reported in this paper, are supported by a grant from the National Science Foundation, no. BNS 75-21909 A01.

THE COGNITIVE REPRESENTATION OF SPEECH
T. Myers, J. Laver, J. Anderson (editors)
© *North-Holland Publishing Company, 1981*

The Role of the Syllable in Language Acquisition and Perception

JACQUES MEHLER, JUAN SEGUI and ULI FRAUENFELDER

C.N.R.S. and E.H.E.S.S., Paris

Work in developmental psycholinguistics can generally be classified according to one of the following two approaches. The first aims at discovering the ways in which language is learned; the second attempts to identify the universal dispositions for language present at birth in the human infant. Unfortunately, psychologists working along only one of these two lines rarely feel concerned by the results gathered by anyone working along the other. Such a state of affairs seems to reflect a strong epistemological parti pris attached to a philosophical position. It is the nativists who search for universals while the empiricists look for learning processes. Unfortunately both approaches have, to some extent, yet to yield results. Consequently, both approaches should be brought to task if anything is to be understood about the way in which language is acquired, elaborated, represented and used.

In the coming pages we will present some aspects of the acquisition of speech processing and in doing so some of the major problems encountered by the nativists and the empiricists. In our presentation we will review some of the data from adults and children that suggest that the syllable is one of the basic unanlyzed initial structures the child uses. In the course of development such basic initial structures are analyzed and in so doing some of the more primitive linguistic entities like phonemes and distinctive features acquire classificatory status and may even be used in speech processing.

In the past few years a number of investigations have explicitly revealed the phenomenal abilities that allow the very young infant to discriminate minimally differing syllables. Eimas (1971) among others, have demonstrated this fact in a persuasive fashion. His results lead him to postulate the existence of specialized feature detectors that respond only to certain complex acoustic patterns. Furthermore, infants have also displayed abilities for discriminating syllables according to rising or falling intonations (Jusczyck and Thompson, 1978), differentiating speakers voices (Mehler *et al.*, 1978) and discriminating pitch and rhythmic sequences Mehler and Bertoncini 1979)

Thus, there is no denying that studies of the initial state have yielded many important results. However, they have hitherto failed to unveil a plausible set of functional universals that can account for the way in which languages acquire the phonological and supra-segmental structures that they all share. We have to acknowledge that in spite of its richness the data gathered about initial states is striking given a certain degree of poverty as to the hypotheses that exist about the universal dispositions that may yield the universal phonological structure of natural languages. As mentioned, there is Eimas' hypothesis maintaining that humans have a number of specialized detectors or analyzers corresponding roughly to the matrix of distinctive features underlying natural language. Such devices are, of course, specialized in the processing of speech sounds. However, several interesting problems have arisen in relation to this hypothesis which is still undergoing careful scrutiny and re-elaboration. Nonetheless, at this time it seems fair to assert that the data is largely unfavorable to Eimas' hypothesis. Furthermore, it seems unlikely that the descriptive simplicity inherent in the claim that part of our innate disposition for speech resides in the feature matrix, can account for a process which is as complex and context sensitive as speech perception and production. A certain number of alternative proposals concerning the nature of the universal endowment with which humans come equipped do exist, but most have the same limitations as the ones we have mentioned in connection with this proposal. We shall come back to another proposal later that though less precise seems to hold some promise.

Insofar as the learning approach is concerned, it has followed a research program mostly concerned with detailed descriptions of typical behaviors of children in the process of learning language. Good accounts are found in Brown (1973) and Bloom (1970). However, after a certain number of years of research of this kind, it is becoming apparent that no theory of language acquisition or of language learning has become available. In retrospect, this learning approach can be described as having relied upon the implicit belief that *since the child learns to speak, a continuous description of the behaviors at all times during learning must contain the clue to our understanding of how the child learns to speak*. The belief in this parable is so strong in certain quarters, that blind measurement and description of everything involved in the ontogenesis of behavior has automatically been looked on as justified. Though developmental psycholinguistics is not the only area of psychology where this has occurred, it does not make the attitude more warranted.

The outcome of the past decade of language acquisition research is that no cogent theory of language learning is available. Nonetheless, we have to recognize that some of the investigations that have looked upon the acquisition of syntax in a cross linguistic fashion have unveiled some mechanisms that may not only be of general interest but which are also somewhat related to the ones that we will postulate by the end of this chapter. Indeed Slobin (1975) argues that in the acquisition of syntax children strive towards order. Thus they tend to impose structure upon all the inputs they receive. This eventually results in the children having stronger and more rigid structures than their parents. Furthermore, as Slobin has argued, when the semantics are transparent the form may be relaxed whereas when the semantics remain partially opaque the form becomes very rigid. This proposal is not unrelated to the one that Werner advanced many years ago when he claimed that children go from syncretic-holistic structures to a form that becomes increasingly analytic and over which further generalizations may be predicated. Mehler and Bertoncini make a similar claim for speech perception as we shall see below.

PHONEMES AND SYLLABLES

Historically, the notion of the *phoneme* has played an important role for a long time even though the term itself was coined by Baudoin de Courtenay just over a century ago. However, even nowadays the status of the phoneme as a processing unit is still unclear and a source of heated debate in many quarters. After decades of intense and interesting investigation, the physical counterpart to the psychological invariance of the phoneme is still to be found. In the course of these investigations many related issues have been cleared and much of what is believed to constitute critical data for the elaboration of a theory of speech perception has resulted from this search for invariances. But, not only have these invariances not been found but what is more, some of the findings about speech allow us to be sceptical as to the processing role of the phoneme. To this end, we will review a part of existing evidence.

Some years ago, Savin and Bever (1970) asked Ss to respond either to a phoneme, or to a syllable in a sequence of nonsense syllables. Thus, for instance, the Ss had to respond either to the phoneme /b/ or to the syllable *bap* in the target. The apparently paradoxical result that Savin and Bever obtained was that the authors assumed that for a chunk x (making up a larger chunk X) to have the status of a perceptual unit, it must be identifiable before X. Since this was not the case for phonemes, Savin and Bever claimed that phonemes are "neither perceptual nor articulatory entities"; perceptual status was given to the syllable.

Several other authors have argued that the results of Savin and Bever were misinterpreted or artifactual and therefore not a true reflection of the processing underlying speech perception. McNeill and Lindig (1973) claimed that:

. . . . the results reported by Savin and Bever arose from the "difficulty" subjects experience when there is a mismatch between linguistic level of the target and the level of the search list. Since the level where the target and the list match, and thus the RT's are entirely determined by the experimental design, there is no possibility that such monitoring experiments can reveal the perceptual units of speech. Depending on the levels being compared, the level of producing the minimal RT can equally be the phoneme, syllable, word or sentence. (p. 428)

While the results that McNeill and Lindig obtained were consistent with their claim, there was an important experimental artifact for the phoneme monitoring conditions. As the authors themselves admit, subjects when given targets specified as syllables are unable to disregard the accompanying vowel. In fact, Wood and Day (1975) have shown this experimentally. Thus the conditions that the authors defined as phoneme monitoring are in reality syllable monitoring.

Another somewhat paradoxical result obtained by McNeill and Lindig was the fact that the shortest RT's were obtained on the so-called phoneme monitoring in the phoneme list condition. However, this result can be attributed to the type of list used by McNeill and Lindig in this condition; they apparently used the same constant vowel environment for all items in the list.

The problem of defining an adequate phoneme monitoring condition is not just limited to this study, but indeed plagues many others. Swinney and Prather (1980) compared a CV syllable monitoring condition to different C monitoring conditions in which the V environment was varied to different degrees. On the basis of their results in which syllables and phonemes with a constant vowel showed no RT differences, the authors conclude that there is not necessarily syllable superiority. However, they failed to note that the subjects in the phoneme condition most likely elaborated a syllabic representation of the target after a few trials. Similar criticisms can be made of another study (Mills, 1980) in which target stimulus match and mismatch conditions for phonemes were compared with syllable monitoring. The fact that there was no difference between the phoneme target stimulus match condition and the syllable monitoring one is hardly surprising, since the subjects are again looking for Syllable targets in both cases. Thus, as Segui, Frauenfelder and Mehler claim (unpub) ". . . the experiments using a target-stimulus match with constant vowel environment (McNeill and Lindig, 1973; Swinney and Prather, 1980; Mills, 1980) confuse syllable and phoneme monitoring". Indeed, it is likely that in both conditions, subjects elaborate some syllabic representation of the target even if from an experimental point of view different targets (phoneme/syllable) are given. The important fact given is that the target-stimulus mismatch paradigm constitutes a *necessary condition* for a phoneme monitoring condition.

Finally, in an experiment conducted by Healy and Cutting (1976), the authors claim that they compared phoneme and syllable monitoring directly. They used short lists of synthetic speech sequences in which isolated vowels were defined as phoneme targets and VC sequences were considered syllable targets. However, since it is usually accepted that vowels in isolation are syllables (or even words), the materials used by these authors are not really adequate for comparing the perception of phonemes and syllables.

Given the methodological and procedural failures of the attempts to counter Savin and Bever, we can uphold the position favoured by these authors. However, the fact that the phoneme cannot be taken as a "realistic" unit for speech processing is not sufficient to promote the syllable into the role the phoneme was supposed to be playing. Rather, we have to grant that there seem to be problems as serious with syllables as there have been with phonemes. For instance, Liberman and Studdert-Kennedy (1978) have stated that:

> . . . Ss would not be able to assign the syllables to their appropriate morphemes without analyzing them into their phonetic segments. For example, syllabification of the simple phrase 'he' is a repeated offender' will yield eight CV syllables. In other words, syllable boundaries in fluent speech are frequently random with respect to words or morphemes. (p. 173)

The point made above is quite damning to a putative segmentation of speech into syllables as basic units for further processing, if and only if the only information the speech processing device gets is the phonetic transcription of the sequence going from one peak to the next peak in the speech wave. If, however, the information for the speech processing device, as we will see below, is richer, then this objection may be weakened. We will thus present some results that are necessary if we are to propose that the output of the speech signal parser is something quite close to the syllable.

In order to postulate for the syllable the special status corresponding to that of being a basic processing unit, only empirical facts will provide any satisfaction. The case favouring the syllable as a processing unit is thus not closed. For the time being, we can present a few results that argue strongly for the syllable's having such a processing status. One piece of evidence concerns the speed with which Ss respond to phonemes and syllables both in word and non-word contexts. On the basis of the evidence presented, we will evaluate comparatively the status of syllables and words in speech processing. Furthermore, if we ask Ss to respond to a given sequence corresponding to the first phonetic items of a word or to the first syllable of a word, will the times be different if the phonetic sequence is either smaller or longer than the actual first syllable of the word? If results could be gathered indicating that the syllable is marked as a surface or acoustic unit, an important empirical addition to the elaboration of the theory of speech perception would become available.

On the basis of an experiment on phoneme, syllable and word monitoring, Foss and Swinney (1973) concluded that the smaller units are identified by fractionating larger ones. Furthermore, Foss and Swinney claim that phonemes and syllables are available only after lexical access. Indeed, Rubin, Turvey and Van Gelder (1976) found that when Ss were asked to detect phonemes in a list made up of words and pronounceable non-words (the phoneme to be monitored was always in first position for all target items) they would respond faster when the phoneme was in word initial position than when it was in non-word initial position. In their experiment these authors utilized only monosyllabic items. Furthermore, their reported times are much longer than the ones obtained in this kind of investigation. It would not be an exaggeration to claim that their times are about twice as long as what is generally the case. Rubin et al., interpret their results as indicating that phoneme detection follows lexical access. Our belief is that this may be true in their experiment but it is not typical of all other similar experiments. In fact, given that the items used are monosyllables and that we believe that syllables are the segmentation units, it is quite likely that Ss will respond to the target phoneme after having accessed the item itself. Furthermore, if the syllable is a word, the word will automatically have been accessed by the time the phoneme has been responded to. The word and non-word difference may thus, reflect several artifacts e.g. the fact that lexical access is inevitable in the case of monosyllables. But what is the case with multisyllabic words when a classical target monitoring task is used? Segui, Frauenfelder and Mehler (unpub) in a recent experiment have raised a similar issue using bisyllabic word lists. All the experimental words began with /pi/, /ba/, or /de/, and for each such experimental word a matched non-word was constructed by changing the consonant in the second syllable, making sure that such a change preserved the pronunciability of the item. All experimental word items were matched for frequency of usage. Ss were required to respond to an item per list. There were thirty six such lists. Results are presented in Table 1.

	Word	Nonword
Phoneme	347	346
Syllable	285	281

TABLE 1   *Mean RT (msec) as a function of lexical status (word/nonword) and target type (phoneme/syllable)*

It emerges very clearly from the results that there is no difference in the RT with which Ss respond to a phoneme in a word or a non word. Neither did we find any effect when the Ss were instructed to monitor for a syllable rather than for a phoneme. Another result of our experiment is that the syllabic instructions lead to faster results than the phoneme ones. Interestingly, there was a very marked correlation between the time taken to respond to a syllable and the time taken to detect the syllable's first phoneme. This correlation is highly significant and can be taken as indicating that phonemes are detected after syllables have been accessed. Again, we take this result to mean that the syllable is a basic product of the device responsible for the parsing of speech into processing chunks.

Once we had considered the possibility of having the syllable be the output of the segmentation device, we were still left with the riddle that we mentioned above in the passage from Liberman and Studdert-Kennedy (1978). It should be noted that Liberman and Studdert-Kennedy were considering a quite crude device with very little proceeding along many levels at once. However, it seems improbable that man comes equipped with a device as crude as the one they proposed. It may be that the device functions by going from peak to peak and that at each such point it checks to see whether it is at the end of a linguistically motivated unit. But this is almost begging the question. Namely, a device that segments a continuous flow of speech into processing units in a blind fashion but which also has information about the nature of the chunk it has secured, and that for each CV, seems unlikely. Dommergues, Segui and Mehler (unpub) designed an experiment in order to explore such an a priori, dubious possibility. Consider the French words *carotte* and *cartable.* Even though both words share the first three phonemes, the word *carotte* has CA as its first syllable while the word *cartable* has CAR as its first syllable. If the segmenting device does, in fact, go blindly from peak to peak, it ought not to differentiate beteen the CAs corresponding to these two words. But if the segmenting device has a built in sensitivity to syllabicity or to some parameter that correlates with syllabicity, then it ought to treat the CAs corresponding to the two words differently. In order to explore the problem, we asked Ss to respond to an initial sequence in a word and we presented the target visually. The words were presented in lists and the target carrying word was always the last item on a list. The target occupied positions two to five in a list. The Ss did not know that these were the only positions since dummy items were introduced in positions one and six. There were five controlled pairs of items all having the same properties as *carotte* and *cartable*, namely sharing the initial three phonemes, CV being syllabic for one word and CVC for the other. The results show that Ss responded faster to a CV in a CV+ . . . word than they did to the same word when operating with a CVC instruction (obviously CV+ . . . represents a word whose first syllable is CV while CVC+ . . . represents a word whose first syllable is a CVC). Likewise, when responding to a CVC+ . . . word with a CVC instuction, Ss tend to respond faster than when responding to the same word with a CV target instruction.

		Words	
		CV +	CVC +
Targets	CV	352	378
	CVC	371	356

TABLE 2   *Mean RT (msec) as a function of word syllabic structure (CV+ / CVC+) and target type (CV/CVC)*

In brief, then, the results in the experiment described above tend to demonstrate that an initial phoneme sequence in a word can be responded to more or less rapidly as a function of the syllabic value of the sequence in the word. In our experiment, reaction times to syllables are roughly on the order of the duration of the syllables themselves. There are several ways in which this result may be interpreted. Apparently, any interpretation must postulate that the signal has cues indicating the syllabic structure of the word or at least of the first syllable of the word. Thus Ss given a phoneme sequence can know whether it functions as a syllable or not. More recent results tend to show that Ss respond differently to a VC as a function of whether the phonemes belong to the same syllable or to two syllables in the target word. Furthermore, given the unpublished results cited by Mills (1980), it would appear that Ss are sensitive to the end of a syllabic segment in item terminal position.

The rather involved procedures that Ss appear to follow in order to retrieve structural information about syllables from the available surface acoustic information, severely weakens the thrust of Liberman and Studdert-Kennedy's argument. Their point is based on a hypothetical segmenting device that isolates chunks from peak to peak and attributes these to strict phonological transcriptions that are segment-concatenated thereafter. Morphological segments thus cannot coincide with syllabic chunks. But if as we proposed, the segmenting device uses richer acoustic information about syllabic structure and also functions interactively, syllables may be dynamically used during lexical access and syntactic processing. In return, both lexical and syntactic parameters may considerably modulate the way in which the segmenting device operates from peak to peak. Thus, a more adequate compatibility between syllabic and morphemic segments may result.

Having gotten this far in our claim that adults tend to segment speech sequences into syllables and that syllables mesh with left to right decision making about the lexical and syntactic structure of the sentence being heard, it is now necessary to inspect the litterature available on the units that infancts use spontaneously in listening to speech.

In the past decade, considerable efforts have been made to investigate dispositions for speech in the very young infant. Research in this area, however, has largely tended to stress the discriminative abilities of the very young child. This is probably due to the fact that methods, namely non-nutritive sucking, habituation, etc., were all conceived in order to investigate discriminative performance in the infant. As we pointed out in the first section of this chapter, Eimas' hypothesis assuming that infants come equipped with innate feature-detectors that insure discrimination between pairs of stop consonants, underlies much of the research that has been carried out over the last few years. Although his research initially gathered substantial evidence about discriminative abilities in young infants, there is some question today as to whether such performance is necessarily a reflection of the specialized innate detectors that were originally postulated. Indeed, some researchers claim that mere acoustic detectors may mediate the infant's behavior. Even though more data is needed to resolve this issue, what concerns us is the infant's ability to discriminate syllables that differ only with respect to the initial stop consonant. Results on this particular topic are neutral in terms of whether infants analyze the speech signal in terms of a syllabic or phonemic segmenting device. There is, however, some recent evidence that suggests that it is the syllable that plays the more significant role in determining infant behavior.

Bertoncini and Mehler (1981) have presented the hypothesis that infants analyze the continuous speech signal into segments that go roughly from peak to peak in the speech wave. Hence the chunks obtained generally contain both consonantal and vocalic information, although the infant may not analyze the parts that make up the chunk. Presumably, the chunk is dealt with as a whole. If this is so, then it may well be that any speech sound that is made up of a few phonemes but which has alternations of vowels and consonants is treated as a potentially interesting item that is stored for futher processing. Non alternating sequences of phonemes do not yield such behavior. Consequently, when the child is asked to make a number of discriminations, he performs better on potential syllables than on impossible ones. Let us explain what is meant by an impossible syllable. As was stated by Jakobson and Waugh (1979) ". . . it is the mutual sequential contiguity of consonants and vowels which plays the main role in their interrelation within any given language" (p.86). Now, suppose that we present a speaker with a sequence like /pst/, this pseudo word could most probably be considered a linguistically impossible syllable. Jakobson and Waugh give some examples of Korlak dysyllabic words such as ktkt 'frozen snow crust' or vtvt. The issue with these rather exceptional cases (others exist as well in Shilha, or in Bella Cool) is that they are extreme, very rare and their status is rather poorly understood. Jakobson supposes that there is an ultra-brief glottal release in Korlak and that in most cases the problem is one of phoneme/ grapheme transcription. He quotes Alan Bell, who claims "we always find that phonetically there is a release of transitional vocoid present. The question that must be asked is 'how should such syllables be specified in phonetic representation?'".

We believe that sequences of phonemes must contain at least one alternation between consonant and vowel in order to be acceptable as syllables. Given this assumption, we conceived of an experiment in which we familiarized infants with either $C_1V_XC_2$ or $C_1C_XC_2$ syllabic or non-syllabic sequences respectively. After the habituation period, infants were tested with stimuli for discrimination that contained the same phonemes as those used during the habituation period only with the phonemes in reverse order, namely, $C_2V_XC_1$ or $C_2C_XC_1$ respectively (which would be like changing *pat* into *tap* and *tsp* into *pst* respectively). In both cases the physical change in the sequence was the same. Adults who listen to our stimuli usually claim that changing the syllable /tap/ into the syllable /pat/ results in a completely different acoustic image and that the insight that the two are made of the same phonemes is not immediate. When they listen to the non-syllabic change, the *Ss* report a modification of the ensuing auditory image that is less salient than in the previous case. If infants process speech more or less as adults do, then they ought to discriminate syllabic-like stimuli better than non-syllabic-like stimuli. As a corollary of such a statement, we hypothesize that if infants are habituated with one syllable they should demonstrate considerable dishabituation if they are presented with the other syllable in the mentioned pair. The same would not be the case when they are habituated with one of the non-syllables and tested with the other one. In

Groups	Mean sucking rate before change	Mean sucking rate after change	Student t (DF)
CVC	36.5	50.1	4.82 (14) ° ° °
CCC	44.5	50.5	2.47 (14) °
VCCCV	45.6	62.4	3.52 (9) ° °
Control.	37.8	44.1	1.39 (9)

° p < .05; ° ° p < .01; ° ° °p < .001

TABLE 3   *Mean sucking rates for the minute preceding and that following stimulus change*

the experiment by Bertoncini and Mehler (1981), we found that a group of 4-week-old infants who had to make a CVC discrimination show more than a forty per cent increase in their sucking rate after stimulus change, while subjects in the CCC group show only a change of about eighteen per cent. This result is congruent with our prediction.

Although this isolated result is in line with what we expected, several interpretations are possible. It could well be that for unknown acoustic reasons CVCs are intrinsically simpler to discriminate than CCCs, without there being linguistic dispositions in the *Ss* making the discrimination. Ideally, we would like to know whether the child is more asymmetrical in his discrimination than, say, a chimp or a chinchilla might be. Since no such experiment has ever yet been carried out, we were obliged to effect a control experiment.

If our hypothesis was correct, CCC's are not only hard to discriminate for acoustic reasons, but also because they are syllables. If they are placed within a vocalic context, however, matters should change. For instance with $VC_1C_XC_2V$ the stimulus should be easy to discriminate from $VC_2C_XC_1V$. One reason for this prediction resides in the hypothetical functioning of the segmenting device. Indeed, this putative device splices the cluster into two syllables each serving for the purposes of discrimination. Natural language offers many examples of such clusters and they do not result in overwhelming processing difficulty. To recapitulate, although CCCs are very difficult to discriminate, this difficulty is reduced when the order of the phonemes is reversed and the same sequence is presented in a vocalic context. Figure 1 presents dishabituation ratios for each group.

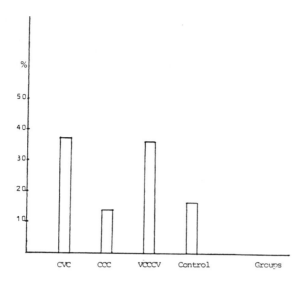

FIGURE 1 *Dishabituation ratios*

The control carried out by Bertoncini and Mehler is interesting in that the level of dishabituation was again on the order of forty per cent which is much higher than that in a control group (fourteen per cent). Of course, the control group infants received the same stimulus before and after criterion, shifting from habituation to test stimuli. Although the data reported are not particularly strong and must still be replicated, we think that infants may well have a "linguistic" notion of what constitutes a speech sequence. This notion is probably close to that of the syllable, namely, any stimulus having an alternation between vowel and consonant. Notice that for the time being, we have very little data on whether vowels are the only elements valid for alternation purposes or not.

These results, in themselves, do not allow us to claim that the infant comes equipped with syllable templates or analyzers. Neither does this investigation allow us to say anything concerning the validity of the notion that infants come equipped with a segmenting device if, indeed, there is one. The only thing that may be said at this point is that infants distinguish between two possible syllables but not between two impossible ones (even though the phonetic change is equivalent in both cases). Fortunately, there are some other studies that may be invoked in favour of the syllable as a basic segmenting unit.

Shankweiler, Fisher and Carter (1974) showed that young children could not perform a tapping game according to a phoneme segmentation rule but could master it easily if instead of being given a phoneme they were given the syllable in which the phoneme appeared. Naturally, older children performed well under both instructions. However, why this should be so remains elusive. Morais et al. (1979) have helped to solve this problem. These authors gathered data on the way in which a simple segmentation task was performed by a population of adult Portuguese illiterates. The results show that these subjects could neither delete the initial phoneme from a word nor add one to it. The same subjects had no difficulty whatsoever when asked to add or delete one syllable to a word. Of course, adults who have mastered the alphabetic system do not encounter any difficulty with either of the tasks. Bertoncini and Mehler interpreted these results by saying that ''the syllable is the natural speech processing unit, while the phoneme is the classificatory unit available to speakers who have mastered the alphabetic system of reading and writing''. When we say this, the issue that comes immediately to mind is as follows:suppose that we accept that alphabetic systems are the result of our awareness of phonemes, then how have the alphabetic systems themselves developed? Though it is not easy to give a knowledgeable response to this question, there is a plausible one. In the course of human evolution not only does man concern himself with the perception of speech, but also with the production of speech. It may well be that the way in which speech sequences are programmed implies a notion of invariance close to that of the phoneme. It is perhaps not a coincidence that most of the theories about phoneme perception are heavily grounded in an articulatory definition of invariance.

CONCLUSION

In the first part of this article, we have reviewed some evidence from monitoring studies testing the functional validity of the phoneme, the syllable and the word during speech processing. From this study, we have been led to a position in which the syllable has the status of a processing unit for speech perception. Indeed, we have concluded that many of the studies that have attempted to show that the syllable is not a priviledged processing unit generally suffer from substantial artifacts.

We have presented several studies that tend to show that the syllable operates as the basic speech processing device. If this assertion turns out to be true it could have important implications. Some recent theories of lexical access, such as Marslen wilson's (1980) cohort theory, generally assume that left to right phoneme sequences determine not only how but also when the listener can make an access to his lexicon. In our view, the syllable will turn out to be a much better device for computing cohort sizes than the left to right sequence of phonemes. Future work can test the different predictions that can be made on issues in lexical access.

In the second part of our article we have considered the relative status of the phoneme and of the syllable in the course of language acquisition. It appears that most of the evidence currently available is favourable to the syllable as the basic processing unit during speech acquisition. However, given that the infant segments speech into syllables going from peak to peak in the acoustic signal (a time sampling constant may be added to such a mechanism) one can ask how it can make decisions as to which syllables in the language require a new template and which are just tokens of prior types. Suppose that an infant hears a syllable like *big* and then one like *pig* and forms a template for both, how will it then decide that another template is unnecessary when it hears *pig* again but produced by a speaker of a different age or sex? Perhaps something closely resembling phonemes or even distinctive features will be required to do this. However, for the time being, we do not yet have an answer to these questions.

One way in which the view that we have been defending in this paper can be tested is by looking at natural languages. Our position obliges us to predict that there will never be a natural language in which a productive morphological rule can be expressed in terms of a single phonetic change (a stop consonant going from voiced to voiceless or vice versa) independently of the syllabic context in which such a phoneme appears. The existence of such languages implies that very young children who master such morphological rules are operating upon the phoneme or even upon some sub-phonetic components. If this were the case, then clearly the syllable could no longer be a credible unit in language acquisition. Empirical studies will clarify whether such rules exist in infant language and if so how they are learned.

If syllables are initially segmented into syncretic wholes, then in the course of development they probably will be analyzed and classified on the basis of their phonetic constituents. Thus this achievement may, in part, be due to the contrast between speech perception and speech production. Although for the perception process, the syllable may well be the syncretic whole, we are postulating that this cannot be so during the first phases of production.

Discussion

Bénédicte de Boysson-Bardies We have observed the functioning of a non-segmental level of representation in a child's late babbling stage.

—There are signs of linguistic organization. Not only does intonation transform sequences of sounds into functionally significant units related to the intonation contours of questions, statements, etc., but it gives them an internal sentence-like structure (i.e. comment-topic type contours).

—At the level of temporal organization. Initially, sequence durations are approximately constant for a given number of syllables. The child's strategy could be described as the filling of places in an intonation contour with CV syllables. (See Figure 1). Later, 2-3 syllable utterances become longer and syllable lengths vary with their position in the sequence and their nature. This change is linked to a change in syllabic structure: syllables of type CV are often replaced by syllables of type V and there is an increase in high vowels. The variations in duration are primarily due to increased length of the vocalic nucleus of final syllables.

The asymmetry between young children's and babies' speech production and recognition raises the question of how these two capacities are linked. The proposed solution postulates the existence of a representation of linguistic structure which is relatively independent of the strategies used by subjects. This point of view does not prevent us doing behavioral studies to try to clarify this relation. But two points must nevertheless be stressed.

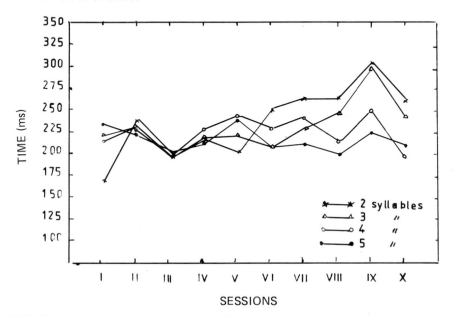

FIGURE 1 *Mean values of syllable duration*

307

First, identification of natural behavioral processes and speech production requires a theoretical approach that allows their relations to fundamental points such as universals or the status of rules to be defined.

Second, observed behavior is not simply an instantiation of theoretical propositions about the structure of representation but rather it may lead to propositions about the way this structure can function. Given the choices that subjects can make, there is no reason to postulate fixed patterns in production. The diversity found in the way speech is acquired, and the variation in the forms produced and routes of development in early speech, can reflect the choices children make in exploring their knowledge and their capacities (central and peripheral).

In this respect, the type of late babbling we have described is not always found. In fact, many children quickly abandon pitch variation as their principal means of communicating. Instead, they try to use short, phonetically adequate forms. In this case, structured prosodic patterns are not found.

Jacqueline Sachs: Geason has provided an excellent summary of the ways that linguistic input to young children may form the basis for the child's developing representation of speech. In this discussion, I wish to comment on one similarity in the theoretical development in child language research and other areas of speech research. In several papers in this volume, the concept of a "prototype" has been discussed, usually with reference to the relative merits of a prototype (or template) versus feature description of some aspect of speech. I will suggest that a number of the characteristics of input described in Gleason's paper can be usefully viewed as providing prototypes for the child.

The concept of prototype was first used in child language research in the area of semantics. Traditionally, semantic categories were viewed as made up of exemplars that shared criterial features. Rosch (1973) questioned this characterization, suggesting instead that categories are built up around an ideal representative of the set, with other members related to the prototype by various attributes that create a "family resemblance." Thus, no one set of features may characterize the entire category. Following this model, a number of researchers in language acquisition have suggested that the child may acquire a semantic category by first attaching a name to a representative instantiation and then gradually increasing the semantic domain. Anglin (1977) has shown that adults tend to provide new labels for young children only when a very good example of the category is at hand.

The concept of prototype has also been applied to the acquisition of syntax. De Villiers (in press) argues that there are also prototypical forms of grammatical structures (for example, that agents are the prototypical subjects of sentences.) In some cases, the prototypical form may be the one that is most salient for the child on nonlinguistic grounds. The existence of the prototype serves as a focal point for the learning of the new form. In input, Sachs (1979) found that the adults in one family introduced syntactic marking for past tense in a situation in which something had just occurred (e.g., *you dropped it*). Thus the child was first exposed to a prototypical form for past with clear semantic intent, providing a basis for the later acquisition of the more abstract uses of past tense.

Similarly, in the area of phonological development, it has been found that adults produce more prototypical articulations to young children. In Moslin and Nigro (1976), the voice onset time of apical stops was measured in adults' speech to children. VOT in the speech of adult to adult varies considerably from the values for the best examplars of the phonemic contrast, but in speech to children there were few tokens that were ambiguous in terms of measured VOT. Thus, the notion of prototype nicely captures the fact that a linguistic form may exist with considerable permissable variation, yet be best represented by a particular form. The fact that adults often supply that form for the young child may help to explain the internal organization of our cognitive representation of speech.

Evelyn Abberton My remarks relate to the almost entirely unexplored notion of normalisation in the development of speech perceptual ability, concerning particularly the role of fundamental frequency, the major physical correlate of intonation.

Normalisation is the cognitive skill that enables a listener to map differing physical outputs from vocal tracts of various sizes onto common phonetic and phonological units. It involves pattern recognition and, in the case of a young child learner, his subsequent speech production shows that imitation in normal speech acquisition is never a matter of simple direct copying of physical forms.

The term *intonation* is used to refer to the patterns of speech, fundamental frequency variation, rhythm and voice quality, that play both linguistic and paralinguistic roles in speech communication. For the infant his mother's intonation not only attracts his attention and gives affective information but also:
1)   gradually leads to speaker identification (Mills and Melhuish, 1974); absolute values as well as patterns contribute here;
2)   provides the correct phonatory framework for later integration of *segmental* articulatory and phonological skills — the child imitates the patterns of fundamental frequency he hears, not the absolute values;
3)   gradually leads to the acquisition of a linguistic system of contrasts, carried by pitch changes;
4)   develops the discourse skills necessary in conversation, e.g. turn taking.

It is frequently remarked that mothers use either very high fundamental frequency or unusually extended fundamental frequency range when talking to small children. We may speculate that this is not simply an attention-getting device, but that she is matching her output as nearly as possible to the child's to make his normalisation task easy in the very early period of speech development, aiding cognitive and linguistic development as well as social and emotional. Fourcin (in Snow and Waterson, 1978) shows a particular example of a mother adjusting her larygeal output to match that of her baby.

In this context, it is worth noting the great normalisation problem for infants in a tone language environment.

We may also speculate on what could go wrong if a child is unable to normalise. The lack of this ability may contribute to the speech problems of those children with apparently normal hearing as measured by pure tone audiometry but grossly disordered speech comprehension and production. The same cognitive disability may also be at work in the autistic child with an obsession for absolute sameness, even to the extent of attempting to imitate the low fundamental frequency of her father, to whom she related better than her mother.

Chairman's Comments

Adrian Fourcin The five contributions to this session are distributed in some respects in a complementary fashion. Jacques Mehler and Benedicte Boysson-Bardies are both primarily concerned with the speech processing behaviour of the infants themselves. Jean Berko-Gleason and Jacqueline Sachs concentrate on the input to infants from the speaking adult environment. Evelyn Abberton is concerned with the sensory-perceptual bridge that allows intercommunication between infant and adult. A common theme is that an increased knowledge of the processes underlying the earliest stages of speech and language acquisition will necessarily lead to a greater knowledge of the linguistic structure of the most developed forms of adult language.

An early objection to this idea came from a contribution to the general discussion. The speaker implied that only epiphenomena were involved in Sach's discussion of prototypic forms and Gleason's examples of language modification in the speech of adults to infants. In a sense the proposition that it is not helpful for adults to modify their spoken input to children is allied with what Mehler refers to as the 'nativist' approach. And this in turn is compatible with the holistic views of speech contrasts which are implicit in articulatory phonetics, distinctive feature theory, the Motor Theory, and the experimental attempts which have been made to show that the suckling child categorises phonemically. In short, if the bases of speech perception are innately available either because speech is too complex to be learnt from experience, or because experiment shows that this is the way things are anyway, then the work of this session is futile.

I find myself in agreement with our five speakers — in the spirit if not in the letter of their arguments. My own experiments (Fourcin '75) have shown me that the new born baby may cry with an apparent paresis of the vocal folds that comes only from the lack of the skill that he has mastered when six weeks of outer life have passed. His mother is indeed likely to use a voice pitch in the onset of her speech to him which matches that of his range. The expedient would certainly simplify his normalization task, (and my student, Teresa Ching, and I have found that even 8 - 9 year Cantonese children cannot normalize lexical tones as well as adults). Similarly, with increasing age and more complex contrasts. Claude Simon and I (Simon and Fourcin '78) have found that English children may take until past the age of ten before they have mastered the auditory pattern complexities of the voiced-voiceless initial consonant opposition. Experimental results of this type, in which non-speech stimuli which cannot be produced by a human vocal tract (because a large fundamental frequency range is used, or because flat F1 onset stimuli were synthesised), are easily explicable in terms of an auditory pattern theory of speech perception. They provide the basis for an analytic account of speech processing in adult and child, and give a framework for the representation of speech processing ability in infancy in which different stages of development are related to the relative simplicity and sensory dominance of the acoustic pattern elements from which speech can be constructed. Physically, the most important element of speech is associated with the quasi-regular spectral line structure of its voiced components, and voice pitch provides the basis for the baby's first communication. Pitch is mediated by two auditory mechanisms, place and time, and this provides a powerful basis for its auditory salience. In consequence, since fundamental frequency may be both physically and perceptually dominant, and voicing must precede other productive skills, we must expect that all normal babies in all language environments acquire skill in voice, laryngeal, processing before all the other pattern components of speech. Similarly, we must expect that the adult world which supports the child in other ways, will also help in the acquisition of this essential speaking ability. We are involved with a phenomenon which is central, not peripheral, to language and speech. The argument is capable of fruitful extension to all of the child's speech development and eventually we find that the adult uses, develops even, his vocal tract to serve auditory ends.

When Mehler in his thoughtful contribution, considers the possibility that the syllable may be dominant in the early stages of speech organisation in the child, and that at later stages more elementary components are likely to be utilised, he is not likely to provoke undue dissension. This is an example of the flow from the use of simple to more complex forms that characterises development and in acoustic terms it would accompany the use of more elements and element combinations patterned in time with increasingly elaborate combinations of Fx, F1 F2, F3 and voiceless excitation. On the other hand, the power of this auditory processing makes it necessary to beware of acoustic artefacts— for example, in the carotte-cartable experiment, mere vowel duration could explain the response strategy, not syllable structure difference. Gleason's interesting discussion can, I believe, be viewed similarly from an auditory point of view, and then the role of high Fx appears not only affective but also as a vital aid to the development of normalization ability discussed by Abberton.

It is not possible to do justice to the extended general discussion which followed the main contributions, and the following points are perhaps chosen with a slight bias.

First, Studdert-Kennedy criticised the work done by investigators running speech response experiments on neonates, and made what perhaps is now beginning to be a generally accepted point, that it seems wrong to postulate any innate disposition to particular phonemic categorisation in the process of development, contrary to the interpretation given by Eimas to experiments of this type, since this would require a course of development going from the particular to the general. McGurk accepting the initial importance of adult fundamental frequency modification, wondered if similar phenomena could be observed to develop in the speech output of the previously unique sibling in communication with a new baby. Fujimura, in discussing Abberton's contribution, was concerned to know whether poor normalization ability as a possible cause for language retardation might not in fact be due merely to poor hearing, in the sense that whilst intensity sensitivity was normal, frequency discrimination was poor. (Pathologically, this is a condition which would be very rare, and not difficult to detect, in the sense that it would give rise to markedly aberrant speech productive patterns). Marshall's comment in regard to adult modification being an epiphenomenon was partly answered by Gleason, and discussed by others from the floor — in respect of the particular case of normally hearing children born to profoundly deaf parents (in the U.S.A.), who had been exposed to television-broadcast speech but hardly any other spoken input. These children invariably had many language problems. Gilbert commented on the importance of individual differences between children in respect of output and growth of language ability, and the interruption which may result from the direction of cognitive attention to the development of different skills ("walking stops talking")

THE COGNITIVE REPRESENTATION OF SPEECH
T. Myers, J. Laver, J. Anderson (editors)
© North-Holland Publishing Company, 1981

On The Cognitive Representation of Developing Phonology [1]

N.V. SMITH

University College London

Given that the young child's pronunciation of forms in his[2] nascent language diverges regularly from the of adult models, as illustrated in (1): [3]

(1) duck - gʌk   blue   - buː
     pin - bin   bottle - bɔkəl

we are confronted with two major problems: first to discover the causes of this divergence and then to establish the extent to which his performance is a faithful reflection of his competence. We therefore need to determine: i) the precise nature of the input to the child; ii) the role of perception in the child's interpretation of that input and his setting up of a phonological representation; iii) the role of motor immaturity in the child's transformation of that representation to his output; iv) the existence and role of any other, non-perceptual, non-productional, factors in this mapping. We also have such second-order problems as determining: v) the relevant units (phonetic or phonological, distinctive features or phonemes, etc.) in terms of which the child is operating at each stage; vi) the extent to which the strategies he adopts are innately determined; vii) how he progresses over time: i.e. the stages through which a child goes from etymological "infancy" to mastery of the language; viii) how this progression differs in pathological conditions from normal development.

As a minimal model for child phonology then we have a diagram such as figure 1, with an input, an output and a number — conceivably zero — of intermediate levels of representation, linked by a set, or set of sets, of rules.

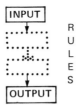

FIG. 1.

The major disagreements in the literature revolve around the number and status of these intermediate boxes and the nature of the rule blocks relating them. In many cases these disagreements can be obviated if a clear demarcation is made between those parts of the model which are taken to represent the child's knowlege and those parts which are taken to represent how he comes by that knowledge and how he uses it in communication. I will attempt to distinguish these in what follows.

The nature of the input is uncontroversial, at least in comparison with the situation in syntax, where the "degeneracy" or otherwise of the input signal has been a matter of contention for a decade. Adults' speech to young children tends to be slower, clearer and more laconic than their speech to other adults (cf. Garnica, 1977, for a review), and there seems to be no serious problem in accepting that a correct representation of the input is something like a traditional phonemic transcription. Problems begin when we try to decide what the child does with this "phonemic" input.

Given that there exist physically distinct signals that the adult perceives as the same, is it the case that the child can make the parallel discrimination and perceive all the minimal distinctions in the language he is exposed to, or is his perception to some degree defective? To see what is at issue, let us take a single simple example: the pronunciation [bɔkəl] for *bottle*. Is this mispronunciation due to the child's failure to hear /bɔtəl/ correctly, i.e. a perceptual problem; inability to pronounce [bɔtəl] even though he can perceive the sounds adequately; or what? The answer to this question is presumably different at different ages. For the first few months of life it is likely that the child is largely incapable of successfully perceiving the totality of sounds in a word as complex as *bottle*, even if he has developed discriminative ability for a few gestalts such as his own name. *A fortiori* he is unable to reproduce something he has been unable to store. By the age of two years there is good evidence that the child's perception is near perfect and that he can perceive most of the contrasts made by the adults around him. Three representative pieces of evidence for this claim are summarised here. First, the child could successfully discriminate in decontextualised situations pairs of words such as those in (2) which he produced as homophones:

(2)   bad, bat   → bæt
      teddy, Daddy → dædiː
      mouth, mouse → maus

Second, he typically implemented changes to his system "across-the-board" as indicated in (3). That is, having learned to produce a particular configuration for one word: e.g. [bluː] for *blue* in place of the earlier [buː], this new-found ability was immediately generalised to all and only those words containing a post-consonantal liquid in the adult language, indicating that these words must have been correctly stored, and hence correctly perceived.

(3)
t1	t2	*ti
blue → buː	blue → bluː	blue → bluː
play → bei	play → plei	play → bei

Crucially there was no stage ti where some of these words changed and some did not. Third, he formed plurals differentially for words which ended in different segments in the adult language but the same segment in his speech. Thus the examples in (4):

(4)   cloth   → klɔt   cloths   → klɔtid
      cat   → kæt   cats   → kæt
      horse → ɔːt   horses → ɔːtid

indicate that his lexical representation for these words could not be the same as his output, and that he perceived the differences in the adult words on the basis of which these contrasts are predictable.

Even at the age of two years or more, however, there is evidence that children's perception, while impressive, is not perfect. Thus Barton (1976) has noted that the two-year-old's perceptual ability is dependent on the familiarity of the word heard: so *coat* and *goat* might be discriminated but *coast* and *ghost* might not be; and Macken (1978) has demonstrated that "the child does have (in some cases) a unique, non-adult underlying representation. . .one that is, moreover, based on a perceptual error". Her argument is based on a difference between two kinds of free variation:

intra-word free variation of the sort exemplified by the alternative pronunciations of a single word, as in (5):

(5) frog → wɔg, flɔg, wlɔg, βrɔg

and inter-word free variation of the sort exemplified in (6):

(6)

bottle	→ bɔkəl		cuddle	→ kʌdəl
puddle	→ pʌgəl		beetle	→ biːtəl
kennel	→ kɛŋəl			

where a wide-spread rule which applies regularly in some words to velarise a coronal stop before a dark [ɫ], has apparently arbitrary exceptions. Whereas the former kind of free variation can be satisfactorily accounted for on the assumption that the child has the adult form as his lexical representation and mangles it by rules some of which are optional, no such explanation can account for the latter type (inter-word free variation) where the pronunciation of each word is self-consistent. In this case the variation presumably derives precisely from a difference in the child's lexical representation. But if the cause of the variation is a difference in lexical representation between the two items (e.g. *puddle* and *cuddle*) then it cannot be the case that both of them are represented in terms of the adult surface form — the putative input. This establishes that the child does not always internalise the adult form, that the cause of the difference is perceptual follows from two further observations; the piece-meal nature of the changes over time in such exceptional items, and the fact that when the perceptual encoding rule is changed it is applied incorrectly to some items. Whereas the vast majority of mapping rules were virtually exceptionless, some 20% of those items which should have undergone the velarisation rule converting *puddle* to [pʌgəl] failed to do so. More importantly, some items, exemplified in (7), acquired their correct pronunciation in a gradual piece-meal fashion rather than simultaneously across-the-board; indicating that the child was getting things right word by word and not by phonological generalisation.

(7)

t1		t2		t3	
bottle	→ bɔkəl	bottle	→ bɔkəl	bottle	→ bɔtəl
puddle	→ pʌgəl	puddle	→ pʌgəl	puddle	→ pʌdəl
cuddle	→ kʌdəl	cuddle	→ kʌdəl	cuddle	→ kʌdəl
beetle	→ biːkəl	beetle	→ biːtəl	beetle	→ biːtəl

More significantly still, there were some adult words, listed in (8),

(8)

t1		t2		t3	
circle	→ təːkəl	circle	→ səːkəl	circle	→ səːtəl
pickle	→ pikəl	pickle	→ pikəl	pickle	→ pitəl
winkle	→ wiŋkəl	winkle	→ wiŋkəl	winkle	→ vintəl

with an original velar, which were incorrectly given an alveolar at the time the examples in (7) were changing. That is, after being correctly pronounced as, for instance, [təːkəl] for many months, *circle* and similar words acquired an anomalous incorrect pronunciation with [t]. This is a clear indication that the child's lexical representation was vacillating: as a result of not discriminating perceptually between /t/ and /k/ in this environment, he had to learn piece meal which sound went with which word after he had made the relevant perceptual progress.

Both Barton's and Macken's work indicate that we need crucially to distinguish the perceptible from the perceived. That is, it may well be the case that children *can* perceive all possible contrasts in the adult language virtually *ab ovo*, but that some of the more difficult ones such as f/θ, t/k before dark [ɫ], voicing in some environments, etc. are often not perceived systematically. More experimental research is needed to determine precisely which contrasts are difficult and how general the difficulty is. Unfortunately, children below the age of two years are so recalcitrant to systematic experimentation that it is virtually impossible to establish unequivocally the extent to which defects in their output are attributable to their (lack of) perceptual ability and how much to other factors.

Comparable remarks obtain with regard to production except that here it is relatively clear that there are sounds and sequences that are truly unpronounceable for the child over a considerable time: not even two-year-olds are very good at tongue-twisters, and the control of fricatives and affricates probably represents an insuperable problem initially for the child. Thus the neutralisation of the four items in (9):

(9)   mat, mass, mash, match   →   mæt

is probably due mainly, if not exclusively, to the child's inability to articulate the sounds concerned. This phenomenon is of little interest at a symposium on the cognitive representation of speech provided that it is truly a motor difficulty that accounts for the pronunciation. That it is, is indicated by the kind of perceptual evidence given in (2).

It seems then that we have minimally to complicate the model in figure 1 to that given in figure 2.

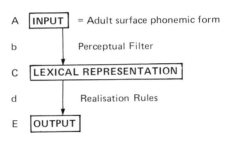

FIG. 2.

Ex hypothesi only the levels C and E and the rules d represent the child's internalised knowledge; the rest of the diagram models part of the basis on which he acquires this knowledge. The set of realisation rules d is then a reflection of the uncontroversial claim that perception, while not infallible, is ahead of production. These rules convert the lexical representation, based on what the child perceives, into something he can pronounce. In the unmarked case these rules are constrained both formally and functionally by universal principles (cf. Smith, 1973). Specifically, any rule has to implement one or more of the strategies serving to maximise the phenomena illustrated in (10):

10 a)   *Consonant or vowel harmony*, as in the pronunciation[gʌk]for *duck*;
   b)   *Cluster reduction*, as in the pronunciation [buː] for *blue*;
   c)   *Systemic simplification*, as in the neutralisation in (9);
   d)   *Grammatical simplification*, as in the pronunciation [ai] for both the singular *eye* and the plural *eyes*.

Differences between various children are then ascribable to the differential implementation of these four strategies: thus one child might implement consonant harmony by changing *duck* to[gʌk], another by changing it to[dʌt] and so on.

Apparent exceptions to the strategies here: e.g. "idiosyncratic strategies" of the sort discussed by Ferguson & Farwell (1975) or Priestley (1977) where the set of forms undergoing a process do not constitute a phonologically well-defined class, are attributable either to perceptual factors (cf. Smith, 1979), or are explicable in terms of a theory of markedness along the lines of Chomsky (1977). For general discussion, cf. Smith & Wilson (1979, ch. 12).

I consider the strategies listed in (10) to be a universal set of necessary and sufficient conditions on mapping rules which the child, as part of his innate endowment, brings to bear on the task of language learning. An alternative interpretation of the complex relationship between adult and child forms is that, intermediate between the lexical representation and the output are one or more further levels of representation idiosyncratic to the child. Typical examples in the literature are provided by Ingram (1974, 1976a), Waterson (1971, 1980), and by the morpheme structure conditions in Smith (1973) which I in fact argued against. Ingram (op. cit.) suggests three levels of representation: perceptual, organisational and productional, such that the pronunciation of a word like *duck* as [ɡʌk] may be due to perceptual problems: the child does not hear the difference between [dʌk] and [ɡʌk]; to productional difficulties: he cannot pronounce [dʌk]; or to organisational constraints: he produces all words with consonant harmony for independent reasons. Now there is clearly a difference between providing a teleology for the constraints that exist and setting up a linguistic level for each kind of explanation. I agree that the divergencies between adult and child forms are ultimately explicable in terms of the parameters Ingram suggests, what I deny is that there is evidence for setting up a further level of representation. Given general constraints on realisation rules of the sort seen in (10), the level is superfluous.

On the same lines as Ingram, Menn (1978) suggests that many though not all "rules are best seen in terms of the satisfaction of output constraints" of the kind "no consonant clusters are allowed". That is, Menn is claiming that the absence of clusters of consonants is to be attributed not (or not only) to the operation of a strategy defined over the adult input, but wholly or in part to the child's conforming to a template peculiar to his own system. It is then a clear instance of a claim that the child does have his own system.

Before attempting to evaluate this claim two points need to be made: first, that realisation rules (i.e. mapping rules parasitic on the adult language) are necessary anyway so that the correct output is associated with the correct lexical representation second, that in many, perhaps most, instances realisation rules and output constraints make equivalent predictions. Accordingly, Occam makes it incumbent on a defender of output constraints to justify invoking the extra construct.

To justify the claim that output constraints are redundant, I will first give a case where a realisation rule can handle the data but an output constraint is unable to describe what is going on. The example will also help to indicate the unimportance in general of production difficulty for the child in that he deforms adult words in a way that superficially appears to run counter to an increase in ease of articulation.

For somewhat over a year A had a rule converting adult sequences of the form CwVC to the form CVp, resulting *inter alia* in the examples in (11):
(11) quick → kip
      quite → kaip
      twice → taip
Given that there was another rule reducing clusters of a consonant followed by a sonorant to the consonant, as exemplified in (12):
(12) green → giːn
      black → bæk
      new   → nuː
the expected output of forms with post-consonantal /w/ would be CVC.
Given further that CVC forms with all consonants in position C2 were allowed, as exemplified in (13):
(13) skip → kip
      kiss → kit
      kick → kik

then the forms given in (11) can clearly not be accounted for by an output constraint. However, a strategy of consonant harmony, assimilating the final consonant to the point of articulation of the labial /w/, accounts for the facts simply and explains the apparent avoidance of consonant harmony in the change of the final /k/ to [p] in *quick*. Realisation rules are then clearly necessary to achieve observational adequacy. Further, the relation between the segments in the underlying representation and the segments in the child's surface forms is a many : many one — a situation which output constraints are unable to handle. Although the neutralisation of an adult contrast by the child (as in 10c) can be described by either output constraints or realisation rules, the reverse situation where a single segment in the adult language is realised alternatively as two or more different segments by the child (as in 5) is captured very simply by means of an optional rule, but cannot be handled by output constraints.

Consider also the longitudinal development of certain forms in A's speech, as illustrated in (14):

(14)

	t1			t2			t3	
slip	-	lip	slip	-	lip	slip	-	ɬip
bit	-	b̥it	bit	-	bit	bit	-	bit
pit	-	b̥it	pit	-	pit	pit	-	pit
spit	-	b̥it	spit	-	pit	spit	-	pit

At time t1 there were two relevant rules operative: one deleting pre-consonantal /s/, the other neutralising the adult voicing contrast. At t2 the rule neutralising voicing disappeared and the child correctly contrasted *pit* and *bit*. As *spit* still fell together with *pit* rather than *bit* at this stage, I assume that the child had a rule devoicing non-sonorant consonants after /s/, which applied before /s/ deletion, cf. (15):

(15)
$$\begin{bmatrix} C \\ -son \end{bmatrix} \rightarrow \quad [\text{-voiced}] \quad / \quad s\_\_\_\_$$

At t3 the child suddenly acquired a series of so-called voiceless sonorants, as illustrated in (16):

(16) **Smith** - m̥it
      snail - n̥eil
      slip   - ɬip

It is hard to see what account of the acquisition of "un-English" sounds could be given by output constraints, but these data are an automatic consequence of a process of realisation rule simplification: the structural description of the rule (15) has been simplified by the omission of the feature [sonorant] to give the rule in (17):

(17)   C   →   [-voiced]   /   s____

In an interesting recent paper Menn (1979) has clarified her position on output constraints, describing them as "levels of processing" (p.12) not as levels of grammar. While they define "what constitutes articulatory capacity" (p.13) they are themselves "epiphenomena" (p.15). Seen in this light they bear a close resemblance to the constraints in (10) above and are clearly well motivated. On this interpretation, however, there is little justification for setting up, as Menn does, a further linguistic level designated the "output lexicon" or "production store" intermediate between the "Lexical representation" and the "Output" in figure 2. I take a linguistic level to be defined by a set of linguistic rules having formal properties in common (cf. Smith & Wilson, p. 279), but if output constraints are not part of the grammar then they cannot justify a level of representation in that grammar. The only specific argument that Menn gives for the existence of the level "Output lexicon" is the "survival" of forms of the child's speech after the rules producing them are dead (p. 7). But at the survival stage the relevant output constraints will, by definition, not in fact be operative; rather they will now characterise only the residual forms themselves. Accordingly "survivals" provide evidence only that a rule was once operative but is so no longer; they do not permit the conclusion that there are two different representations for them: one underlying and one "output". I suspect that my earlier assumption (Smith, 1973: 143ff.) that the child's underlying lexical representation of such items has been "restructured" is correct, but perceptual experimentation on a child with survival forms should choose between the two positions. Specifically, children do not in general accept repetitions or tape-recordings of their own mispronunciations as appropriate for adult lexical items (cf. Dodd, 1975). If their lexical representation is indeed restructured, they should accept their deformations in precisely those cases and only those.

The claim that there is no output lexicon implies that the rules to which it is the input are themselves suspect as part of a model of the child's knowledge. That is, the "production rules" of Menn's "elaborated model" (op. cit. fig. 2) are themselves epiphenomenal, although she claims categorically that these "output programs" are "what the child has" (p.15). One can agree that certain of the rules linking the lexical representation to the output act as triggers for performance synergisms. However, the fact that a particular configuration of phonetic features or segments calls into play a particular synergism of motor operations does not justify the claim that parts of what is synergised are cognitively redundant and should therefore be omitted from the lexical representation, or indeed from any other level of grammar. Once again it is necessary to distinguish what constitutes linguistic knowledge and how this knowledge is translated into speech. Output programs, synergisms and the like clearly come in the latter category.

Even if there is no such level as the output lexicon, there may more plausibly be argued to be a further level between the lexical representation and the phonetic output in figure 2; specifically, a level of phonemic representation. At the perception end of the speech chain the child can clearly convert a phonetic signal into a phonemic representation. Although it is not self-evident that this must be the case, the fact that the child can identify as equivalent and in some cases reproduce physically different tokens of the same type, not only from a single speaker but across speakers as different as men and little girls, indicates phonological not just phonetic perception. Given also that young infants have, at least in part, categorial perception, and the fact that in some cases all and only the allophones of one adult phoneme change their realisation simultaneously as the child develops, it would be perverse to assume that the child's lexical representation was not in some form of phonemic code. Grounds for doubt that this is always the case arise from the fact that certain adult contrasts — e.g. of voice — may be acquired at different times with different allophones; indicating possibly, but not necessarily, that the child has not made the usual identification of the allophones involved.

It is much harder to provide independent evidence for a phonemic level in the child's speech distinct from the phonetic representation of his output. If the child's system is parasitic on the adult system, as has been suggested here, then even though standard criteria of complementary distribution and phonetic similarity can be adduced to set up classical phonemic and allophonic statements, it is not clear what the psychological status of these statements is. In order to determine whether the realisation rules linking the underlying representation to the phonetic surface should be divided into a phonemic and a phonetic set, we need to carry out experiments on the child's categorial perception of his own edited articulations. Little work appears to have been done on this.

I suggested earlier that the constraints on realisation rules given in (10) are universal. If true, the most plausible, albeit not necessary, assumption is that this universality reflects innateness: it is biologically determined. Kiparsky & Menn (1977) have argued convincingly that the rules typical of child phonology are all invented by the child as solutions to specific problems, rather than being innately specified. While I accept this in one sense — it is fully compatible with the position in Smith (1973) — and take it as a partial rebuttal of Stampe's (1969) position, it still seems necessary to account in more general terms for the rather limited range of solutions that children do come up with. It is at this level of abstractness that it makes sense to talk about innateness. Since the term "innate" has been given a number of different interpretations, we can — following Aslin & Pisoni (1978) — distinguish among:

1. an ability which is fully developed at birth but which may be lost if external stimulation is absent. A typical example is provided by vision;
2. an ability which is partially developed at birth, such as birdsong;
3. an ability which is undeveloped at birth but which is triggered off by some external stimulus, either immediately — as in imprinting — or after further maturation.

It seems clear that the ability to invent phonological rules is an instance of this final sub-type. The ability is not present at birth; indeed, it may not operate fully in the earliest stages of language acquisition, as witness the existence of "phonological" idioms" which by-pass the rules: e.g. the early (about 11 months) pronunciation [priti] for *pretty* reported by Leopold (1939 - 1947), and it is obviously dependent on external stimulation. This is not a claim for empiricist inductivism; rather it is a claim that the hypotheses the child can come up with to solve his problems belong to a limited set constrained by the strategies discussed above.

A final question in language acquisition studies concerns the status of the "stages" set up in describing the child's development. It is clearly necessary to break up a two-year (or even shorter) period into more manageable chunks if one is not to be overwhelmed with disparate kinds of data; but it seems that all such divisions of what is a continuum are arbitrary. Although Piaget's stages of cognitive development form a useful background framework, most phonological development takes place within the "preconceptual" sub-period part of the period of concrete operations, and some finer delimitation is clearly desirable. An arbitrary delimitation may not matter in studying the normal development of the phonological system, but there are two areas where the division into distinct stages is more crucial: first, whether it is sensible to talk about a pre-phonological stage; second, in the comparison with abnormal development. At the transition from babbling to the development of a phonological system proper there may be a pre-phonological stage (cf. Ingram, 1976b; Ferguson & Farwell, 1975) when words often appear to be learned as complete gestalts on an imitative basis rather than as composites of phonological elements. Accordingly, the tight phonological constraints discussed here can be violated on a limited scale with impunity, and one might expect to see phonological idioms of the sort mentioned above.

On the contrast between normal and abnormal development and the question at what stage one decides that a child falls outside normal limits, matters are more vexed. Given that all stages except perhaps "pre-phonological" and "equivalent to adult" are arbitrary, that variation among children and even within one child is considerable, and that the distinction between delayed and deviant phonology is tenuous, it is hard to give specific differentiating criteria. However, to take one parameter only, a prime characteristic of normal development is the steady change of the child's output over time in accordance with specifiable rules. For instance, A who was impressionistically slow in his phonological development, made an average of one change to his sytem every five days for a period of two years. (There were 132 documented changes over some 30 stages each of which averaged 22 days). Although one would not expect such figures to be repeated from case to case very closely, one would expect a normal system to remain dynamic, and a system static over some months can be interpreted as the first sign of one kind of abnormality. This would of course tell us nothing about the abnormality of a child whose disability lay for instance in the grossness of the substitutions made rather than in the variation among such substitutions over time, but it affords one possible index.

There are many areas I have skirted too briefly or have completely ignored: the importance of syntagmatic rather than paradigmatic relations in phonological acquisition, emphasized in a recent interesting paper by Chiat (1979); the problem of variation as highlighted in the work of Olmsted (1971) and others; the coherency hypothesis of Stampe (1969); the competing claims of prosodic, autosegmental and more standard analyses, etc. All of these presuppose that we have a clear idea of what we are investigating, hence the present paper's emphasis on the most fundamental distinction between the child's knowledge and the sources and uses of that knowledge.

Notes

1. This article is in part an abbreviation and modification of Smith (1979). It was prepared while I was in receipt of Grant No. HR 5393 from the Social Science Research Council, to whom I am extremely grateful.

2. The apparent sexism in this pronominal usage is explained, if not justified, by the fact that I have two sons and no daughters. Substitute ''she'' if you wish.

3. Examples throughout are taken from the analysis of A in Smith (1973).

THE COGNITIVE REPRESENTATION OF SPEECH
T. Myers, J. Laver, J. Anderson (editors)
© North-Holland Publishing Company, 1981

A Tentative Developmental Model of Phonological Representation

NATALIE WATERSON

S.O.A.S., University of London

In the present state of knowledge, the postulating of an underlying representation for speech can only be very tentative but such attempts are justified as they raise issues which provide new bases for discussion and research. It is hoped that the model proposed in this paper will serve such a function. The writer sees its main contribution as offering an alternative theoretical approach for work on speech perception and interpretation, namely that of pattern recognition and pattern matching as opposed to phoneme segment identification. What is put forward is not purely speculative but is firmly data-based. It arises from naturalistic case studies of the acquisition of the phonological system of English.

It is now widely accepted that the phoneme is not a useful concept for the study of speech perception. This has emerged particularly clearly in several contributions to this Symposium and also at the Ninth International Congress of Phonetic Sciences in Copenhagen (Fischer-Jorgensen, 1979). It is also widely recognized that speech interpretation is not normally dependent solely and primarily on the use of auditory cues but is greatly assisted by factors such as knowledge of the language, gestures, knowledge of the subject matter, context, cultural backgrounds of speaker and hearer, and so on. These produce expectations and at the same time constrain the probabilities. A speech processing model must be compatible with this and should not place too heavy dependence on phonetic and phonological cues. In the model presented here, speech recognition depends on a minimum of auditory cues (which comprise the 'pattern' of the word or larger unit) and leans heavily on knowledge of the language and the kind of non-verbal cues listed above. A developmental model needs to be universal in principle, that is to say, the principles must be applicable to speech processing in general, but it must also be able to handle the data of specific languages, that is, the acquisition of the phonological system of a particular language. It is claimed that the model presented in this paper fulfils these conditions.

As the acquisition of the phonological system is gradual (Waterson, 1978) a model needs to account for the development of levels of representation, whatever these may be, and changes in the form of a child's word in process of acquisition should be relatable to changes in the levels of representation. The developmental model proposed in this paper takes this into account.

The proposed model is grounded in Prosodic Phonology which places an emphasis on whole units in speech and on the syntagmatic relations within and between the units. The theory thus takes into account coarticulations and overlapping which are essential features of speech. Because of this syntagmatic character, there is a greater correlation between findings made in acoustic studies and the phonological elements of this theory than with those of phoneme-based theories.[1]

Those proposing models of underlying phonological representation in relation to child language are much concerned with the question of how many levels of representation are required and what their nature is, cf. Ingram, 1976; Macken, 1980; Menn, 1979a, 1979b; Smith, this volume. In this paper a case is made for two levels: a phonetic level, Underlying Representation I (URI) for speech reception and recognition, and a lexical-phonological level (the lexicon), Underlying Representation II (URII) which is concerned with interpretation and production.

A phonetic level of representation is necessary in order to relate the physical (acoustic) form of the utterance to its interpretation as a word or sentence of the language. From the rapidity with which utterances are interpreted, it is clear that the whole of the acoustic signal cannot be processed and that there can be no one-to-one relation between the input and its interpretation (Denes, 1963). Segment by segment processing is, of course, quite out of the question. It seems that there must be some kind of analysis involving a restricted number of cues, and evidence from first language acquisition of learning by auditory pattern recognition (Waterson, 1971a, 1976, 1978) suggests the likelihood of serial scanning for word and sentence patterns as an essential part of the processing of an utterance.

If then, as suggested above, only a limited number of acoustic cues in the form of an auditory pattern is used for word recognition, this is added confirmation of there being no direct access from the auditory input to the word in the lexicon and a further justification for a phonetic level of representation. It is suggested that the acoustic signal is filtered so that only the essential cues remain: these, it is proposed, are mainly the auditorily salient features (Waterson, 1976). It is proposed that they are then synthesized into possible phonetic patterns of the language and are matched with the phonological patterns in the lexicon for interpretation.

There is less controversy about a lexical level of representation. No one disputes that every speaker has a lexicon, that is to say, that there is a large number of words known to him which are recognized when heard and most of which are used by him. There is thus a stock of words stored in some form in the memory. The phonological system at word level (leaving aside the phonology of larger units like word-group, clause, sentence) is part of the lexicon in that the latter incorporates the total set of different word structures with their different distributions of a limited set of sounds. The lexicon and phonological system are thus inextricably linked, hence URII being labelled 'lexical-phonological'. As *whole* words are known and remembered (it appears in auditory form) it may be deduced that each word in the lexicon has its full phonetic specification. It is suggested that the phonetic specifications may be organized in a 'network' such as shown in Fig. 2, in order that pattern matching between URI and URII can take place in the most economical way.

For ease of exposition, the final stage of the proposed developmental model is considered first. Fig. 1 shows the functions of URI and URII in relation to input and output as suggested for the fluent speaker/hearer. The model applies to the monolingual speaker but it can also apply to the bilingual and multilingual speaker, in which cases each language will have its own section in URI and a separate URII. As the title of the paper indicates, the model is tentative, and as all will appreciate, it is oversimple. It deals only with phonetics and phonology and hence must be seen as part of a larger processing system. Among other things, it should be linked to a component in which ideas are formulated for expression as speech. A syntactic component is also essential. This would be comprised of syntactic patterns. In fact, multi-word utterances can be handled by the model if phrase, clause, and sentence patterns are included in URI and URII. A semantic component is also necessary to link together words of similar meanings. The scope of this paper is restricted to the representation of phonology, so syntactic and semantic components are not considered.

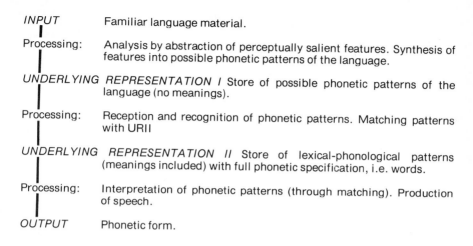

INPUT   Familiar language material.

Processing: Analysis by abstraction of perceptually salient features. Synthesis of
               features into possible phonetic patterns of the language.

UNDERLYING REPRESENTATION I Store of possible phonetic patterns of the
               language (no meanings).

Processing: Reception and recognition of phonetic patterns. Matching patterns
               with URII

UNDERLYING REPRESENTATION II Store of lexical-phonological patterns
               (meanings included) with full phonetic specification, i.e. words.

Processing: Interpretation of phonetic patterns (through matching). Production
               of speech.

OUTPUT   Phonetic form.

FIG. 1. *Phonological processing model: fluent monolingual speaker / hearer*

The model functions in the following way. The first analysis of the input is to distinguish between speech and non-speech (not shown in Fig. 1); the latter includes birdsong, music, animal calls, thunder, noise of machines, etc., etc., and will be further analysed under a different heading from speech. Speech will be divided into known language(s), and other possibilities, for example unknown language(s), phonetic 'nonsense', and so on (also not shown). Fig. 1 shows the processing of familiar language material. Utterances are scanned and broken up into chunks, say, into phrase, clause, sentence, on the basis of intonation patterns. Each chunk is scanned further for salient areas on which attention is then focused, for instance on areas of stress and accent which mark the high information points; these are generally carried by content words. Auditorily salient features at these points are abstracted and synthesized into possible phonetic patterns of the language which are stored in URI. These patterns have no lexical meaning. The synthesis of each pattern is constrained by the set of salient features abstracted at the particular points in the chunk. Many non-salient, redundant features are ignored. The synthesized patterns are then matched with the lexical-phonological patterns in URII, which include meanings (that is to say, they represent words). This is done with the aid of the semantics and pragmatics of what the utterance is predicted most likely to mean from the sequence of content words and the non-verbal cues. The scanning and the matching of patterns within the chunk is carried on simultaneously so that the interpretation of the words is considered together, and the scanning of the following chunk starts before the interpretation of the first is complete so that that too influences the interpretation.

Salient auditory cues in certain arrangements comprise the phonetic patterns of words. These patterns are schemas only, not the full acoustic spectra, and are sufficient to enable known words to be recognized with the aid of non-verbal cues. The recognition of content words in a particular sequence in an utterance provides enough information to constrain the probabilities of how they relate to each other and to enable the unstressed, non-salient function words to be filled in to fit the rhythmic pattern of the utterance, in other words, the syntactic pattern can be reconstructed, and the whole utterance can thus be interpreted. (For confirmation of this kind of interpretation from hearing errors see Waterson, 1971b). The function words do not need to be given much attention in speech processing in the normal course of events as they are limited in number, and the contexts in which they occur are often predictable from the sequence in which the high information content words appear. That words should be recognized by only part of their acoustic make-up is not surprising if there is a parallel between visual and auditory perception, as it seems there must be (Neisser, 1966). The visual image of a familiar object can be reconstructed mentally from a viewing of a part of it. For instance, if one sees a corner of a tape recorder showing from under a pile of papers, one has no difficulty in recognizing it as a whole tape recorder, that is, reconstructing a mental image of the whole. Similarly, it is highly probable that one needs only an auditory pattern or even part of a pattern of a familiar word in order to be able to recognize it, that is to say, to reconstruct the full phonetic form. That familiarity aids speech processing is well known.

As already indicated, URII is concerned with the storage of words in their full phonetic form and provides for the identification of the input by pattern matching. It is also the basis for production. The way words and their phonetic specifications are organized (that is, the phonological system) is obviously crucial to the model as it must be possible, for whole or part phonetic patterns to be matched very rapidly with the appropriate phonological patterns. A possible organization of phonological patterns in the form of a network is illustrated from child language in Fig. 2. In the early stages a child's URI and URII are considered to differ considerably from those of an adult. As all who have studied the language development of very young children know, children's vocabulary for comprehension and production is very small at first and great use is made of contextual cues; adult speech has to be adapted in various ways to their level of comprehension (Snow and Ferguson, 1977). Children's limited experience of langauge at the start means that they do not control a sufficient number of different word structures to cover all the patterns and functional sound contrasts of the adult language, nor do they necessarily pay attention to and recognize all the sounds of the adult language when first beginning to speak (Waterson, 1976; Fourcin, 1978). They therefore cannot have the adult phonological representation at the time when speech begins, unless of course they are late starters. As learning progresses, they pay attention to more of what is functional in the adult phonological system (Waterson, 1976, 1978) so eventually their representation matches the adult's.

The examples used for illustrating the possible organization of phonological patterns are taken from a stage in language development when there was a sudden expansion in the vocabulary. At this time the child had mostly CV, VC, CVC, and CVCV words. As the intention is to illustrate the principle, only CVC examples are considered and the network for only one particular pattern is given. The child had the following patterns:
1. Plosive-vowel plosive, e.g. [bʌp], cup, [bɪp] bib, [gek] cake, [gɔk] clock, [gɪk] stick, [gʌk] duck, [dɔp] stop. In URII these are organized under PVP.
2. Plosive-vowel-nasal, e.g. [gɔn] gone, [daɔn] down, [dʌn] stone. These are organized under PVN.
3. Nasal-vowel-nasal, e.g. [muːm]moon, [mæm]man, organized under NVN.
PVP, which has the largest number of examples, is selected for illustration.

The symbols A, E, I, are used to represent the three functional contrasts at the V place of PVP and relate to open, middle, and close vowel grades respectively. These function in conjunction with contrasting syllable prosodies which are represented by the symbols, y, w, and ə , the phonetic exponents of which are frontness and non-rounding, backness and rounding, and neutrality as regards these features, respectively. P stands for the plosive system which has the possibility of a contrast of three terms: p (labial), t (alveolar), and k (velar). A fuller account of child English Phonology in terms of Prosodic theory is available in Waterson, 1980b.

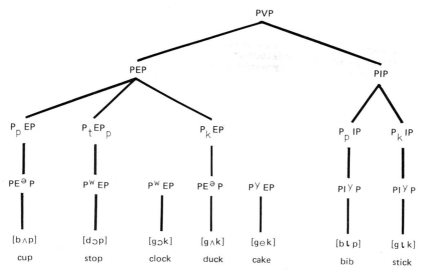

FIG. 2. *Organization (network) of phonological patterns in URII*

The organization of the child's PVP words shows a division by grade into PEP and PIP. Under each of these headings further subdivisions are made by the terms at the onset, namely p, t, and k, and by the prosodies y, w, and ə (see Fig. 2). There are certain redundancies that can be by-passed in processing. Suppose a phonetic pattern is matched with PVP — PEP — P_pEP: the contrast of ə and w of PE^əP and P^wEP is redundant, so can be by-passed, to go directly from P_pEP to [bʌp] cup. However, if the match is with F_kEP, the w, ə, y contrast is important as it carries the main distinction between [gɔk] clock, [gʌk] duck, and [gek] cake. If the match is with PIP, the contrast of p and k carries the main distinction, and y is redundant.

If the child next acquires 'cat' as [gæk], he will have a new V contrast in the PVP network, that of A:

If he then acquires 'cart' as [gɑk], he will have a new prosodic contrast of y and w, and the network will expand again:

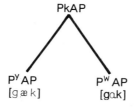

Suppose the child then acquires 'cook' as [gɔk]. This will result in a new contrast of y and w with PIP:

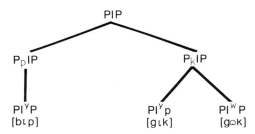

In these ways the PVP network will expand and become more differentiated. When the child begins to make a contrast of place of articulation between onset and ending, for instance velar-labial, in 'cup', and alveolar-velar in 'duck', and so on, his network will become even more complex.

Only a very small sample of a very simple system has been shown. If one thinks of the adult system, with many thousands of words in the lexicon, the adult network must be extremely complex. However, this does not invalidate the model as the network of the human brain is very complex and it is not impossible that it could handle such a processing system.

An example of how the interpretation of speech takes place in relation to the suggested network is given below.

Context: The child is out with his mother. She draws his attention to a dog carrying a stick by saying 'look, doggie got stick.' Stick has the strongest accent and is thus the most salient, and is also salient by recency. The child has the word 'stick' as [gɪk]. He sees the dog carrying the stick. He pays attention to the most salient part of the utterance, which is 'stick' but as [s] of [stɪk] is not auditorily salient, he identifies the phonetic pattern as plosive-vowel-plosive; this is probably by the sudden increase in acoustic energy on the release of the articulatory closure of the first plosive; the peak of intensity during the production of the syllabic element, which indicates a vowel, and the sudden cutting off of the syllabic phase which indicates a final plosive. The position of F 1 (first formant) shows a close vowel.[2] This restricted information enables him to make a match with PVP and on to PIP (see Fig. 2). No further matching is necessary: the contrast of p and k is redundant as the context, the presence of the stick, provides enough information to identify what the child has heard as [gɪk], his 'stick', and not [bɪp], his 'bib'. Thus the few acoustic cues by which he recognizes a plosive-close vowel-plosive pattern, together with the visual cues of the context, are sufficient for the recognition of the word as 'stick'. The context can assist in rapid speech processing without the necessity for detailed auditory analysis and matching.

In the case of PEP words: [bʌp], [dɔp], [gɔk], [gʌk], [gek], the hearer's knowledge that there is a wide range of possibilities will no doubt ensure that more acoustic information will be included in the scanning. The presence of the relevant object will of course constrain the probabilities very considerably. More processing will be needed in a situation where, for instance, a toy cup, clock, and duck are all present and the child is asked for one of them. In that event more scanning of the acoustic signal is needed (as in the learning of new words, see below) to include, for example, F 2 transitions to identify whether matching should be with p, t, or k.

At the stage of development of the network in Fig. 2, the child's URI and URII patterns are unlike the adult's, and so is his pronunciation. At later stages, the child's URI patterns become like the adult's but his URII patterns may differ, depending on the constraints of his production ability and the level of development of the network. Later still his URI and URII patterns will be like the adult's but his production may differ for a time. Of course not all the patterns are at the same stage of development at the same time. Some progress faster than others, and some may match the adult's long before others. Eventually URI, URII, and production all match the adult's.

The processing involved in learning a new word must differ from that of recognizing a familiar one. Having looked at how familiar words may be recognized and interpreted in accordance with the model, consideration will now be given to the way a new word is learnt, that is, how the patterns of URI and URII are constructed. In the case of a child learning his first language, the patterns of URI and URII are constructed and reconstructed as perceptual and production skills develop. When a new word is being learnt, a great deal of analysis needs to be made in order to arrive at a phonetic specificiation for URII. This means that there must be more detailed scanning of the acoustic signal in learning than in the recognition of a familiar word for which only the pattern or part of the pattern suffices.

The progress of a child's forms of the word 'pudding' in relation to URI and URII will now be considered. This particular example has been selected because several very different forms were recorded for it which provide an interesting case for trying to relate changes in form to changes in underlying representation. The forms are: age 1;6 [pɒpɒ]; early 1;7 [bɒbaʧ] and [bɒbʊʧn]; later 1;7 [pɒpəɲ] and [bɒpəɲ]; 1;8 [bɒdɒn]; then [pɒdɒn] and finally [p ɒdʊ ɲ].

The child's productions are assumed to follow his perception, so as URII is constructed on the basis of URI, URII is considered to change before there is a change in production.[3]

Age 1;6 [pɒpɒ] the child's production suggests that most attention is given to the auditorily salient features of pudding [ˈpɒdʊŋ], namely the whole of the accented first syllable, and the plosive and close vowel grade of the second. The final nasal is short and weakly articulated and is non-salient and is not produced by the child, nor are the features of frontness and spreading which are associated with F2 and F3. The salient features listed above are considered to be the input.

The analysis for the construction of the URI pattern would involve the following:
1. Number of syllables;
2. Type of syllable, that is, open or closed onset and ending; breathy or non-breathy onset and ending;
3. Type of closure: stop or continuant;
4. Place of closure: labial or non-labial.
5. Type of syllabic phase: open, mid, or close vowel grade; long or short;
6. Syllable features: backness and rounding; frontness and spreading, or neutrality as to those features.

Synthesis would follow the analysis and a pattern would be constructed on the basis of the features abstracted. In this case there are two open syllables, the first with a breathy onset; both syllables with initial stop, the first with labial place, and both syllables with mid vowels; the first syllable with backness and rounding. The place of the stop, the type of onset, and the syllable features of the second syllable are left unspecified. The URI pattern is thus unlike the adult's but it is the pattern by which the child will recognize adults' 'pudding'. The pattern in URII is based on the URI pattern but with the added constraints of what the child is able to produce and the degree of development of the network of URII. The specification for the second syllable is incomplete so that all the child can construct on the bases of his URI pattern is PVPV → ^{h}PI $^?$PI → $P_p I^w P_p I^?$. However, as the URII pattern is the basis for production, the specification must be completed. The problem is overcome by using the same term, namely p, and the same prosodies, namely h and w, as in the first syllable: $^hPl^hPl \rightarrow P_pl^wP_pl^w$. This then is the basis for the form [pɔpɔ] a reduplicated form, the latter being the usual structure of the child's two-syllable words at this time. The form [pɔpɔ] was used for some time before it underwent a change.

The child's recognition of adult's 'pudding' [pɔdιŋ], as mentioned earlier, will be on the basis of his URI pattern which differs from his URII pattern. In [pɔpɔ] both syllables are salient, the first is accented, the second is stressed. In [pɔdιŋ] the first is accented and salient but the second is unstressed with only a few features salient, as already noted. Thus [pɔpɔ] would require a different URI pattern from that of [pɔdιŋ]. In fact the child does not have a URI pattern for [pɔpɔ] as it is his production based on his URII pattern for [pɔdιŋ]. Therefore, if an adult used [pɔpɔ] for 'pudding' instead of [pɔdιŋ], it would be a different word for the child because it would not match his URI pattern for 'pudding' and so could not be matched with the URII pattern. This offers a possible explanation for children's non-recognition of their own forms either current or past when used by adults.

Age: early 1;7 [bɔbaιŋ] and [bɔbuιɲ]. These forms suggest that the child has become aware of features that he had not noted before, either now or a little earlier, and he is attempting to produce them. He is aware of the final nasal and may or may not be aware of the velar place of closure.[4] He is also aware of the frontness and spreading of the second syllable as opposed to the backness and rounding of the first. The URI pattern will now include the frontness and spreading of the second syllable and a final nasal, with place of closure possibly unspecified. The onset of the first syllable will be breathy as before and that of the second may still be unspecified. As a result of the changes in the URI pattern, a new URII pattern is constructed. This incorporates the newly acquired features; it has final N, and a w-y contrast between the two syllables, thus getting closer to the adult URII pattern: PVPVN $\rightarrow$ $^hPl^hPIN$ — $P_pl^wP_pl^YN$. It lacks only the h-*h* contrast at the onsets of the syllables, and the p, t, and k contrasts of P-P-N. In the URII pattern onsets of both syllables are *h* (non-breathy) as was more usual in the child's sytem at this time. These were apparently easier to produce through familiarity so what was less easy was reduced when attempting the new and unfamiliar. The attempts at frontness in the second syllable are conducive to the production of palatal (nasal) closure in final position. The points at which frontness starts in the two forms is probably related to production difficulties.

Age: later 1;7 [pɔpəɲ] and [bɔpəɲ] the two forms show greater skill in production: the child is now using breathy onsets with the recently acquired contrasts between the syllables. He has also begun to make a contrast of non-breathy and breathy onset. In view of the rapid progress of his forms at 1;8 (the changes took place within three days) it is likely that he is already aware of the contrast of breathy onset versus non-breathy onset of the two syllables of [pɔdιŋ], and of the different places at which the closures are made, namely labial, alveolar and velar. In this case, his URI pattern will have these features but production difficulties mean that his URII pattern will still differ from the adult's and will be as at early 1;7 but with the possibility of h and *h* contrast at the onset of the first syllable, and h onset of the second syllable: $^h/^hPl^hPIN$.

Age: 1;8 [bɔdɔɲ], followed by [pɔdɔɲ] and then [pɔdιŋ] within three days. The child first attempts the labial-aveolar place contrast and while doing so, uses the familiar non-breathy syllable onsets and no contrast of syllable features; the final nasal is alveolar and harmonizes with the alveolar plosive. These articulatory simplifications make the production of the new contrast of labial and alveolar place easier to handle. In the second form, [pɔdɔɲ], the new labial-alveolar contrast is used with the contrast of breathy and non-breathy syllable onsets. Finally, these contrasts are used with the earlier acquired contrast of backness and rounding of the first syllable and frontness and spreading of the second, together with the new contrast of labial, alveolar, and velar places. The child's production is now like the adult's and this means that his URII pattern is also like the adult's, that is: PVPVN → ^{h}PI^{h}PIN → P$_p$l ^{w}P$_t$l^{y}N$_k$ The progress to the adult form within three days and by the use of articulatory simplification suggests that the child's URII pattern was like the adult's at the start of 1;8 but that he still had production difficulties. At this time the child would certainly reject [bɔdɔn] for 'pudding' from an adult, being well aware that this form is not correct, and may well say, 'not budun, budun'.

The child's changing forms have been considered in relation to changes in URI and URII patterns. It now remains to outline the developmental model and show how URI and URII gradually develop, starting in the early pre-verbal period.

It is proposed that a child starts with no URI and no URII but with an innate ability to recognize human vocalizations as different from other sounds, and with an ability to recognize auditory samenesses and differences. As the function of URI and URII are now known to the reader, the account of the developmental model can be brief. The period from three weeks to 18 months is described; after 18 months development is as shown for 'pudding'.

Non-crying vocalizations start at around three weeks and from this time to about four months the vocalizations take the form of grunting, murmuring, cooing, shrieking, and unstructured babbling. There appears to be no voluntary production of same vocalizations so it may be deduced that there is no recognition by the child of his own vocalizations nor probably those of adults though there may be direct imitation.

From approximately four months to ten months, vocalizations include structured babbling, that is repetitive strings. The fact that the same repetitive strings are repeated on different occasions suggest that the child is able to recognize his own babbling patterns and hence that URI begins to develop. At this time the child also seems to recognize adult imitations of his patterns and imitates back. This production of same patterns means that there may well be storage, that is to say, the start of URII. The child's output is still random in the main, but some is on the bases of URII. URI and URII are not yet linguistically functional and at this time are universal. Some time at around eight months, a 'proto-language' begins to be used, that is a limited set of simple functional vocalizations supplemented by gestures (Halliday, 1975). These are the first phonological patterns and are language specific, so URII now has rudimentary linguistic function.

Somewhere between 10 and 18 months the first words appear while babbling and the proto-language continue, so phonetic patterns of the specific language begin to be stored in URI, and lexical-phonological patterns in URII. The network is very simple at this time, each individual word having its own fully specified pattern, as yet there being only one word per pattern. URI and URII now develop linguistic function and are language specific. When the vocabulary begins to expand by way of pattern recognition, the network in URII begins to be organized by pattern in addition to by individual item. Progress of child's forms to adult forms takes place in a similar way to that shown for 'pudding'.

The implications of this model are that the development of URI and URII is universal up to the proto-language stage and acts as a preparation for the language specific development which starts with the proto-language. Thus a very simple non-linguistic network develops first; this changes to a more complex network for the proto-language which is a necessary precursor for the more elaborate lexical-phonological network of language.

Conclusions

The proposed model can handle the phonetic and phonological processing of the adult speaker/hearer whether monolingual, bilingual, or multilingual, as well as the acquisition of the phonological system of a language. It is universal in that the principles apply to speech processing in general and it is language specific in that the patterns are the patterns of the language of the environment. The model therefore fulfils the two essential conditions required of a theory of speech processing.

The theory behind the model, that of pattern recognition and pattern matching, is compatible with what is known at other levels of human perception. The phonetic patterns and the phonetic features used to describe them are compatible with much of the acoustic information available in relation to speech.

The model takes into account the importance of non-verbal cues and of the redundancy of speech, and shows why only a small part of the acoustic signal is sufficient for speech interpretation.

On the above grounds alone it seems that the model is worthy of further consideration and development. There are, however, certain further advantages, and these are given below.

As mentioned above, the processing of speech by pattern allows for a great deal of redundancy. As it is a pattern that is recognized, variation in the form of segments within it is unimportant since segments do not need to be identified; any such variation does not interfere with recognition and interpretation. This explains why normalization from one speaker to another across boundaries of dialect, age, sex, rate of speaking, and so on, is so easy and why speech can be understood under noisy conditions.

The model has a place for acceptable phonetic and phonological forms of words which do not happen to occur in the language, e.g. 'blick' and 'shreep' in English, but excludes forms that are not acceptable, e.g. 'fsog' and 'ngalt'.

Familiar words are shown to be processed differently from the new and unfamiliar.

The model can account for continuous development of speech processing from the pre-verbal stage to fluent speech, and allows for the growth and extension of the phonological system with the expansion of the vocabulary throughout adulthood.

Children's early simplified forms can be explained by limited linguistic perceptual discrimination, restricted articulatory skills, and the constraints of the developing phonological system in the form of a storage network. The network is organized by pattern and as it is being constructed on limited material, it must perforce be very simple at first. There may be some items which are relatively complex, for instance [ʔə vm̩] for 'Heaven', which have individual entries, but the majority have to fit into networks if speech processing is to be efficient and economical. Patterns change gradually as perceptual and articulatory skills develop, and the whole phonological system and its storage network (a network of networks) changes and becomes more complex. Such a view makes it plain why children do not have consonant clusters at first and why mostly one syllable words are used and few two and three syllable words. It also becomes clear why there is a minimum of consonant contrasts in their speech and why consonants in CVC words tend to harmonize, as in [g ʌk], and two syllable words are reduplicated, as in [mama], especially at the time when the vocabulary begins to expand rapidly. Learning by pattern recognition can also explain many early forms that differ widely from the adult forms, there being individual differences in the way children create their patterns (for instance; Menn, 1971; Waterson, 1971a; Priestley, 1977; Macken, 1978).

It has been noted in the literature that a child's direct imitation of an adult form is often more correct than his everyday usage. The model can explain this as the by-passing of URII. In imitation, the adult form is given detailed analysis as in the learning of a new word and is then synthesized as for URII with its full phonetic specification but it is produced directly as phonetic nonsense, that is to say, it does not have a place in the network.

Finally, the model can account for a child's failure to recognize his own form of a word when used by an adult, and also earlier forms that have gone out of use. It can account too for a child's annoyance at an adult's use of his incorrect form, the fis phenomenon.

The phoneme based approach has held sway in phonetic research for several decades but results in terms of insights into speech processing have proved disappointing. An alternative is offered in this paper which can explain aspects of speech processing for which answers have not been found previously. This suggests that it could provide a promising new line of research.

Notes

1. For Prosodic Phonology see Fischer-Jorgensen, 1975; Palmer, 1970; Robins, 1964; Waterson, 1980a, 1980b.

2. F1 is of a lower frequency and greater intensity than F2 and F3, and children pay greater attention to the lower frequencies at first (Waterson, 1976; Fourcin, 1978).

3. For the relation between perception and production see Waterson, 1976.

4. The description is now given in articulatory terms instead of the acoustic for reasons of simplicity.

Discussion

Barbara Dodd There seems to be some agreement that children's phonological abilities are limited by perceptual, cognitive and output constraints. The problem is to measure the effect of each of these constraints on children's representations of words. Obviously, simply examining normal children's productive data has its drawbacks.

Another approach is to examine factors on which normal development might be dependent. The two most obvious factors are intelligence and hearing, since it is well known that severely subnormal (SSN) and prelingually profoundly deaf children have a high incidence of phonological disorders.

Studies with SSN subjects indicate that there is a link between general cognitive development and phonological development. That is, a twelve years old SSN child who has a mental age of three years, used the same phonological rules as a normal three year old. The exceptions to this are Down's Syndrome children who have inconsistent speech errors, and are better in imitation than spontaneous production.

Studies with deaf subjects indicate that prelingually profoundly deaf children, who have been educated in the oral tradition, can develop extensive phoneme repertoires and their speech is at least partially rule governed by phonological rules that are similar to those described by Neil Smith. They can also, on information derived primarily from lip reading identify rhymes, match homophones, convert lip-read nonsense words into graphemes, and recode a written nonsense word into a phonological code for short term storage. Thus, despite their lack of an auditory input, they can derive and use what is usually called a phonological code.

Since the deaf can develop an at least partially rule-governed phonological system without being able to monitor their output auditorily, it raises the question of how closely young normally hearing children monitor their output, i.e. do they store their own phonological forms for recognition?

Experimental investigation of this question revealed that 2 to 4 year old children were significantly better at understanding adult forms of words than they were at understanding their own. Further, the extent to which they could understand their own speech was related to the degree to which their own deviant forms resembled the adult forms, e.g. [brɛlʌ] for umbrella was correctly identified but [beʲʌ] for umbrella was not correctly identified. The results indicate that children do not store their own phonological forms for recognition, but perceptually appear to be dependent upon the adult form of words.

The finding that they can recognize those of their own forms which closely resemble the adult forms might indicate that the fit between the input and the internal representation does not have to be exact. Like adults, children try to make sense of what they hear.

Mike Garman The papers by Smith and Waterson illustrate clearly divergent paths of enquiry into phonological development. It seems to me that our ignorance in this area is so great that both paths may be equally necessary. Smith's arguments proceed in part from a concern with theoretical parsimony, and this is wholly appropriate; but there is a need also to consider what distinctions should be made among the possible levels of processing which might be involved in phonological

335

development. Each approach, of course, has its problems: we *can* establish a single level of abstract phonological representation common to both perception and production, but this involves throwing a heavier burden on realisation rules interpreting that level, and it is not clear why we *should* do so; equally, though, we may find it very hard to discover crucial data which unequivocally support a distinction (e.g. between the child's representation and the adult's) which we may not wish to rule out of consideration at the outset.

It seems quite clear now, at any rate, that the child's underlying phonological system is not totally adultlike from the start (whenever that is taken to be). That leaves us facing tricky questions involving matters of degree, such as (i) What do we mean by *partially* adultlike? and (ii) How *aberrant* are misperceptions on the part of the child? Even if we could answer these questions, of course, we should still be far from knowing the answers to such other questions as (iii) What are the relative effects of perceptual and production constraints in the child's speech?, (iv) What is the organisation of the underlying system? and (v) Is the development of the system to be described as occurring through stages or along a continuum?

Our ignorance must be attacked on two levels, both experimentally and through naturalistic studies. On the level of *input*, we need more refined investigations of early speech discriminative abilities (to mention just one of a host of problems in this area, take that suggested in Menyuk & Menn 1979 — some perceptual discriminations may be available to the young child only with difficulty, i.e. available in (nearly) minimal contrast, but not otherwise); on the level of *output*, more instrumental analyses are required (e.g. Macken & Barton's 1978 study of how children from 1;6 develop the English VOT contrast for voiced and voiceless stops in initial position — a study which nicely illustrates, incidentally, the difficulty of stage vs. continuum interpretations). And of course, we have to take the two levels together, and ask about the relative ease or difficulty of certain speech contrasts at each of them. Clumeck (1979) documents what may be a pattern of 'easy input, easy output' in order to account for labial dominance over velar with reference to certain labiovelar targets: and possibly the pattern 'easy input, hard output' holds for English /s/ vs. / ʃ / at the level of development where the 'fiss-phenomenon' may be reported. And we ought also to consider the pattern 'hard input, easy output' in cases such as the occurrence of alveolar or velar stop plus lateral clusters in certain environments in English: if they illustrate a regular pattern of misperception, they may not be properly characterised as 'mistakes'.

Harry McGurk: Listening with Eye and Ear   Both Smith and Waterson regard speech perception as a purely auditory process. Consequently they address the issue of constraints on phonological development in purely auditory terms. Phonology is largely acquired in the context of conversation, and in this context speech perception is at least a bimodal process; the individual listens with ear and with eye.

In an earlier presentation, Lubker (this volume) illustrated, from EMG recordings, how anticipatory lip movements for the articulation of an utterance occur some 400 - 600 m sec. before the voicing of the utterance. In our laboratory we have recently demonstrated how this kind of visually available information from lip and face movements can be used by listeners to decode utterances. For example, reaction time data reveal that CV syllables are identified on the basis of lip movement information prior to their being perceived auditorily. Thus, for mature listeners, the visual information gets into the system earlier than the auditory information and may operate to set constraints on what the listener expects to hear.

More profoundly, we have demonstrated how, from early childhood onwards, vision and audition interact in the speech perception process. In one experiment involving natural speech, voicing for the syllable /ba/ was dubbed onto lip movements for /ga/; under this condition subjects regularly report hearing /da/. Similarly, when the utterance "My bab pope me poo brive" is dubbed onto lip movements for "My gag koke me koo grive" the percept is "My dad taught me to drive"! These are robust phenomena and have been replicated many times. They clearly demonstrate a role for vision in the perception of speech by normally hearing listeners. Incidentally, they cast serious doubt on any theory of speech perception which allocates a significant role to putative primitive auditory feature detectors.

A substantial body of data, some from our laboratory, some contributed by Dodd, testifies to the important role which vision plays in the perception of speech by young children. There is every reason to believe that visual processes signify in the development of phonology. The acquisition of phonological representation is based upon exposure to speech stimuli in a conversational, audio-visual context. Visual as well as auditory processes must feature in our thinking on perceptual constraints upon the development of phonology. For example, many common articulatory errors of the type classified as cluster reductions would yield to analysis in terms of lip reading confusability between an adult's model and the child's output.

Pintip Tuaycharoen: The Acquisition of Tones in Thai Before the writer is going to discuss whether the proposed models could take into account the development of Thai tones, she would like to present some data to give the picture of how tones develop.

In Thai, there are 5 distinctive tones, i.e. Mid, Low (phonetically, low with a slight drop at the end), Falling (high-falling), High (high with a slight rising at the end), and Rising (low-rising). From the writer's study on the speech development of a Thai child, aged 13-18 months old (Tuaycharoen, 1979), it was found that tones were developed from pitch. That is to say pitch appeared in the early stages, and its levels varied greatly; later, pitch became less variable and appeared to be more patterned. During this period certain levels of pitch were used constantly in the child vocalization, i.e. in his proto-language to show his intentions and to acknowledge what has been said to him. At the age of 11 months old when a few first words appeared, it was found that the mid and the low pitch levels first appeared at the lexical level. These two levels of tones were used spontaneously in various contexts. Then the Rising tone appeared, and these 3 tones, i.e. Mid, Low, and Rising, were used consistently from about 11 months old onwards. The Falling and the High tones appeared when the child was about 17 months old, but these two tones were inconsistently used at that time.

With reference to responses to adult models, it was found that at the beginning, the child responded correctly to words which have Mid and Low tones, and in response to words with High and Rising tones, the child used either Mid or Low tone. The interesting thing is that at the stage when Falling tone had not been acquired, words with Falling tone were responded to as Low tone.

This seems possible since the Falling and the Low tones have a falling component, i.e. from high to low for Falling, and from low to lower for Low. The child at this stage seems to pay more attention to the lower frequency of these two tones, and as his phonological system was limited he produced Falling-tone words as Low-tone words. For example,

\ m ɛ :	'mother'	as __m ɛ :
\ p h ɔ :	'father'	as __p ɔ :
\ p a :	'aunt'	as __p a :

Later when the child developed the Rising tone in his phonological system, he still used Low tone for Falling tone, but at this time he used any one of the Low, Mid, and Rising tones in response to the High tone. Such a response continued for a long time until the child was about 17 months old when he began to acquire the High and the Falling tones.

The development of pitch or tones in the present study seems to fit in well with the Waterson model, starting with pitch which is non-language-specific, and gradually developing linguistic function. Apart from pitch, consonantal and vowel elements as well as other language specific features, i.e. aspiration, glottalization, are acquired in the similar way. That is from non-language-specific to language-specific when the phonological system is gradually built up.

According to the writer's study, she does not think that it is valid to treat the production of tones of her subject as similar to that of adult tonemes. Thus, what is needed is a model which can take into account phonetic features as well as some phonological representations.

Walburga Von Raffler-Engel: On Some Missing Ingredients at Our Symposium
In general, I have two basic objections to the underlying forms proposed throughout this symposium. My first reservation is that they isolate the auditory image from the visual image and here I will not even discuss the conceptual image of the referent in Paivio's sense (1974). What I plan to talk about is the kinesic component of human communication. Children hear and see people talking.

The fact that infants imitate lip movements at two weeks of age was demonstrated in 1957 (Zazzo, 1957) and has been fairly well accepted. The perception and production of gestural behavior, on the other hand, has received general attention only lately. According to the theory of language acquisition which I formulated in 1960 (Von Raffler-Engel, 1964, 1970, 1976, 1977) language development follows an interactionist model. In the beginning, language, paralanguage, and kinesis are not clearly separate. Gesture does not precede vocalization but accompanies it from the start in a rhythmic motion involving the whole body. The six subjects which I observed at the time manifested a *carrier-sound*, an articulatory constant with variations in pitch contour to signify differences in meaning, and which was accompanied by a pointing gesture. In one subject which I studied in depth the first ''word'' was the leave-taking formula uttered together with the hand waving motion at seven months.

The early appearance of the leave-taking formula may be explained by its consistent occurrence in its combined verbal and nonverbal expression(von Raffler-Engel, 1975) The information is thus highly redundant, a factor similar to what Waterson eventually (1976) called *salient*.

During the period of transformational-generative grammar my theory was not accepted and even termed a non-theory (Kessler, 1971). Later it was translated verbatim without reference to the original (Bates, 1976). Almost twenty years later I am equally convinced that the study of communication from a purely verbal perspective is not only incomplete but erroneous because it attributes to languages that which pertains to kinesics, giving rise to theories of language which are too powerful.

The co-occurrence of language and kinesics may be obligatory or optional but it is well defined. It is optional whether one says *no* with or without nodding, or one may simply nod. Bowing always accompanies the Japanese greeting formula. I have shown (von Raffler-Engel, 1974) that the child acquires the concept of conversational dominance verbally and nonverbally. The nine year old girl in my study copied her father's question-initiating behavior as well as his dominant posture when she in turn talked with a smaller, three year old child.

The three basic communicative functions can each be expressed linguistically, paralinguistically, and/or kinesically. The referential, regulatory, and affective functions are not correctly separated, if separated at all, by the small child. If the expressions for these functions are stored in different parts of the brain, and if auditory and visual images are processed in opposite hemispheres, I am at considerable loss to explain the universals and culture-specifics of perception, storage, retrieval, and production in language acquisition. The speakers at this symposium appear considerably less troubled.

My second and most fundamental reservation about the proposed underlying forms is that they treat language as if it occurred out of situation and without context. They take absolutely no account of the conversation partner. The few participants who mentioned monitoring and feedback treated these terms as if they were synonymous. To my mind, their analysis is inadequate even within the simplest of models of communication (von Raffler-Engel, 1979).

Hoping to gain some insight into the mechanism of perception and production I videotaped adults while talking about the behavior of children which they had previously watched on videotape (von Raffler-Engel and von Steven Weinstein, 1977). The comparison of the original movements of the children with those made by the adults when describing the same produced the following chart.

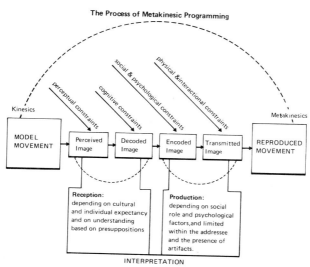

The Process of Metakinesic Programming

The internal and external constraints operating on perception and production in nonverbal behavior are probably applicable as well to verbal behavior.

Chairman's Comments

Hazel Francis The essential topic of this seminar is the characterisation of what the developing child knows about words as he hears them and as he speaks them. The speakers deal with the development of phonology.

Smith argues that, apart from some minor limitations on perception, the child is able to discriminate all the phonetic forms in the adult language and therefore is able to store full or nearly-full, systematically related, phonetic representations of such words as he grasps. This accumulated store is termed the underlying representation. At least by the end of his second year the child shows evidence of phonemic organisation of phonetic elements and therefore of a phonemic system which can be related to the underlying lexical system through realisation rules. Moreover this system can also be related to his speaking via phonetic rules which map it to articulation. While he acknowledges that development implies change with age in the model of the child's phonemic knowledge and that aspects of realisation rules might be explained by such factors as motor inability or idiosyncratic output constraints, Smith maintains that the *same* systematic representation underlies the perception and production of words at any one stage, and that certain aspects of realisation rules are universal. In other words there is no need to posit a level of the child's word organisation which is different from the adult's; and only this one level of cognitive representation has 'psychological reality'. Differences between child and adult lie in the development of realisation rules.

Waterson, however, develops the idea of two levels of representation to meet the data she has from a younger child than the boy with whom Smith has been accustomed to working. Unlike Smith she does not suggest phonetically full or nearly full lexical storage from the child's hearing of words, but rather a partial representation. Moreover this is not seen as the underlying system for articulation, but as one for recognition which also acts as a feeder for the child's own productive system. This latter draws from the recognition level whatever is permitted by current articulatory skill. The recognition level can also be informed from the productive system, reception of adult speech thus being influenced by the latter.

What are the advantages and shortcomings of these very different accounts? Smith's, of course, is set up with a claim to the virtue of parsimony, but then it risks the criticism of being over-simplified. This could be avoided if other accounts such as Waterson's could be subsumed within it by some non-objectionable translation of terms, but in this case the obstacles seem too great. Paramount are Waterson's claim that, at the stage she treats, the child does not carry anything like the full phonetic representation of 'words' he recognises, and her reference to a child's phonetic pattern system, rather than a phonemic system, behind articulation. This has the virtue of claiming less abstract knowledge in the child, and is supported by other data such as that presented by Tuaycharoen, but the disadvantage of lack of evidence to clinch the argument that the child does not perceive or know more. With such differences between the theorists in two respects it is necessary to ask whether in each case both can be right in some sense, whether one position is to be preferred, or whether both seriously fall short.

As to the question of the knowledge the child has of the phonetic form of 'adult words' the evidence suggests that the capacity for categorical phonetic discrimination is an attribute of the human species which is present in the very, very young and may even be found in other mammalian species (Kuhl, 1978). But certain phonetic discriminations in human speech appear to depend on maturation and/or experience. Moreover discrimination of phonetically patterned syllables has been shown to improve during the first year of life (Eilers, 1978). These findings rest, however, on particular experimental paradigms which, simply stated, depend on testing a rather bored infant with a novel stimulus. Small wonder differences can be detected! While these may inform us as to the 'ceiling' discrimination powers of the infants, they do not tell us what the infant actually notices in the course of everyday contact with speaking adults. Attention in such natural circumstances is spread over much information through non-auditory as well as auditory channels, and what is perceived of adult phonetic forms may therefore be less than maximal. The experience of having a young child painstakingly produce a careful imitation, and then revert to his usual activity-related form as soon as the demand disappears, suggests that not only may he produce less but he may also hear less in the normal course of events. It seems possible that Smith's claim for the perceptual skills of the child should be restricted, and that only further exploration will establish the developmental patterns in different situations. Waterson may be near the mark for her data. Thus both theorists may be correct about the child's grasp of the phonetic structuring of the words he hears, but Smith's marginal concession to perceptual difficulties may have to be extended increasingly down the age scale.

As to the question of phonemic representations, the problem does not appear to be one of difference of degree but of kind. Although he seems not to consider it as a level of representation, Smith's characterisation of a phonemic system derived by realisation rules from the level of underlying lexical representation seems open to description as the 'child's own system' as distinct from the adult system involved in full lexical phonetic forms. But even if it is possible to compare this with Waterson's productive phonological system, neither receptive nor productive representation is characterised by her as 'phonemic', but both are so described, directly or inferentially by Smith. How then can a move be made from phonetic pattern to phonemic system, not in terms of linguistic theory, but in terms of the child's knowledge? In a sense here Waterson has the edge, for phonemic implies phonetic but is not implied by it. The onus is therefore on Smith to make a case for his stronger position. I shall return to this, but meanwhile join with Garman in emphasising the need for an empirical attack on our ignorance.

In the light of my earlier comment on the way auditory perception may be supplemented via other channels, it is interesting that the discussants very sensibly remind us that speech is not only heard, but words are also seen to be spoken, and are spoken in a context of informative gestures and actions. On McGurk's showing, visual information seems to be part and parcel of the normal perception of speech at the level of decision about phonetic word structure. Not only may it confirm an auditory percept, but it may also bias a mis-hearing or partial hearing towards what is said rather than what is heard. If we also consider Dodd's discussion of the evidence of the ability of the deaf to lip-read and of phonological structuring in their speech comprehension and articulation, we must conclude that any account of the development of phonology which rests on the auditory channel alone is too limited.

Von Raffler-Engel's discussion reinforces this awareness with its setting of speech within total communicative acts. It serves also to point to other features of lexical storage than the phonetic or phonemic forms of words. The whole point of making phonetic discriminations is to discriminate between words carrying different meanings, and lexical storage also implies meaningful verbal memory. The young child's differential attention to phonetic detail in the production of words from different form classes with correspondingly different syntactic and semantic functions is evidence that phonological coding in production operates within a wider framework. The question of word identification and storage in relation to multiple sources of information is interestingly treated by Morton in his logogen theory (Morton, 1969), while the complexity of lexical organisation is discussed in depth by Miller (1978). If we consider the implications of the relationships between the various perceptual channels, and the interdependence of the different aspects of language in speech, a question that must be asked is whether our theoretical representations, be they psychological or linguistic, do justice to the reality. An important criterion for choosing between theories of phonological knowledge must therefore be their 'goodness of fit' in a more comprehensive model of linguistic and communicative competence. It is difficult to see how Smith's deliberately isolated model might fit a larger one, whereas tentative suggestions could be made about Waterson's. Neither, however, is particularly useful in this respect.

Besides the criterion of having a place in the larger scheme of things, that of lack of ambiguity might also be used. The main speakers view their positions as dissimilar to an extent which suggests attention should be paid to the meanings of the terms used.

'Cognitive representations' seems in general to be used to cover the notions of ideas and knowledge of a systematic nature, but, when it is applied to all aspects of the use of speech including hearing, talking and understanding, the sheer complexity of what is involved demands some very clear thinking. As a psychologist I find myself asking what kind of ideas or knowledge are being attributed, and to whom, when terminology based on linguistic theory is being used. Both Smith and Waterson speak of underlying phonological and lexical representations implying that the child has some, albeit unconscious, knowledge of linguistic structure in at least two domains. Smith also sees the speech which is attended to by the child as a surface (i.e. spoken) representation of the phonemic structure of words. He is therefore using the notion of representation in two ways. In one the product of articulation is a physical representation of the phonological and lexical knowledge of the speaker (adult), and in the other the child's understanding of what is spoken is achieved in his mental representations (at the levels of phonological and lexical knowledge) of what he hears. The speaker, it seems, samples his own knowledge while the hearer relates the sampling to his. This is true whether the child or adult be the speaker or hearer, and for each only one level of phonological knowledge is required. Waterson looks at the child as speaker and hearer and finds that the process of hearing and understanding seems to suggest a rather different phonological knowledge from that suggested by the production of speech. It is as though what the child knows about the words he hears is not quite the same as what he knows about those he produces.

It seems to me that in this very simplified account there are several problems. First, what is the nature and status of the kind of knowledge being talked about? Both speakers use examples of child speech to infer some sort of systematic knowledge in the child, but the first step in their inferences is to use their own ideas of linguistic structure to seek systematic descriptions of the children's performances. But what sort of knowledge or cognitive representation is appropriately attributed to children, and, indeed, to non-linguist adults and to linguists when they are simply listening and talking?

One usage of the term is an application to different degrees or levels of abstraction; and it is not always clear whether theoretical abstraction is meant, and whether child or linguist is the relevant theorist. I shall return to this point. But another use occurs when different levels or stages of mental processing are being attributed to the speaker/hearer. When suggestions of the latter kind are made there is an implicit idea of a sequential analysis of speech, moving from auditory analysis of the acoustic form to phonetic to phonemic to lexical levels of analysis, each with their own representation, and related somehow to levels of syntactic and semantic representation. In other words, all the systems of acoustic and linguistic representations of theory are somehow located or represented in the mental processes, each being referred to as a level. It is only too easy for the unwary to slip into thinking of this as a description of actual sensory and brain processes in understanding and producing speech. There is an appealing economy in keeping the number of levels as small as theory and data will allow, each level encompassing a complex category and rule system. We need to remember, however, that descriptions of designs in nature may not accord with the structure of theory of their products. Brain processes may entail a large number of levels, each with a simple rule system. So very many cells and connections are available for use in spatial as well as temporal organisation and coordination.

It is perhaps helpful, then, to consider that the term 'representation' may be used in different theoretical domains — those of description of brain, sensory and motor function, of mental processes, of linguistic knowledge, and of speech sound patterns. The term 'cognitive representation' might only properly be applied to those where 'thinking' or 'knowing' are appropriate terms, that is to the domains of descriptions of mental processes and of linguistic knowledge. An important difference between Smith's and Waterson's accounts is that Waterson tends towards usage in the former domain while Smith tends towards the latter. Neither seems entirely clear, but the difference suggests that comparison between the two positions should be made at least with caution and at most not at all. It also suggests that for Smith to make his strong case for the child's abstract phonemic knowledge necessitates a different argument from that of evidence for the organisation of phonetic distinctions in the course of understanding and producing speech. Waterson's argument for phonetic pattern knowledge in the child can rest on such evidence, though neither argument nor evidence are yet adequate for a firm theory. But Smith's discussion needs some explanation of what he means by children's knowledge of abstract phonemic structure, and whether indeed the notion can have any meaning in relation to young children beyond being a linguist's own cognitive representation of the structure of their linguistic abilities.

SESSION VII
REPRESENTATION AND PHONOLOGY

Seminar 13: Cognitive reality of segmental phonology

Chair	BRUCE DERWING
Speakers	JOAN BYBEE HOOPER, TERRANCE NEAREY
Discussants	MANJARI OHALA, NEIL SMITH,
	JOHN OHALA, RONNIE WILBUR,
	NATALIE WATERSON

Seminar 14: Cognitive reality of suprasegmental phonology

Chair	VICTORIA FROMKIN
Speakers	ELISABETH SELKIRK, ROBERT LADD, Jr.
Discussants	ANNE CUTLER, JOHN OHALA,
	PHILIP LIEBERMAN, LINDA SHOCKEY

THE COGNITIVE REPRESENTATION OF SPEECH
T. Myers, J. Laver, J. Anderson (editors)
© *North-Holland Publishing Company, 1981*

The Empirical Determination of Phonological Representations

JOAN BYBEE HOOPER

SUNY Buffalo

PHONOLOGICAL REPRESENTATION

This report concentrates on the nature of lexical representations with respect to their segmental phonology. In particular, this paper questions the empirical validity of lexical representations in terms of minimal contrastive units, or phonemes. There are several types of phonemes — autonomous phonemes, classical phonemes, systematic phonemes — and phonemes have a number of defining properties that could be examined critically. We will focus here on a single property, the central property that all types of phonemes have in common, i.e., that phonemes are discrete phonological units which contain no information which is predicted by rule. This is the essence of the phoneme as a descriptive device, and it is a very good descriptive device. There are, however, some facts about language that have been discussed in the literature in the last few years that are quite incompatible with this traditional descriptive notion. In the following, I discuss this evidence and its implications for phonological theory.

There are at least three types of phonological representations argued for in recent literature:

I   Fully-specified phonemic representation of SPE phonology and natural phonology (Stanley 1967, Chomsky and Halle 1968, Stampe 1973, Donegan and Stampe 1979)

II Redundancy-free archi-segmental representation (Hooper 1975, 1976, Rudes 1976).

III Fully-specified phonetic representation (Vennemann 1974, 1978, Leben and Robinson 1977).

In Hooper 1975, I argued against a model which has a phonemic representation with different feature values from the phonetic representation, on the grounds that such a model required conflicting generalizations at the underlying and surface levels, and required an arbitrary and unparsimonious division of rules into two types that apply at two levels. On the other hand, archi-segmental representations and fully-specified phonetic representation have identical consequences for the system of rules. I decided on the archi-segmental representation because it allows a lexicon of morphemes, while the other proposal required a lexicon of words.

It was noted at the time that all the arguments were formal, and that empirical evidence concerning underlying forms was simply not available. Most issues concerning underlying representations, especially in generative phonology, are decided on the basis of the rules posited. A typical argument goes as follows: since we have an independently motivated rule of English which devoices an obstruent following a voiceless obstruent, the underlying form of the plural morpheme must be

347

/z/ rather than /s/, which would require a voicing rule. More extreme instances of the same type of argument lead Chomsky and Halle 1968 to the postulation of an underlying low front rounded vowel in English as the representation of the diphthong in *boy*. This relation between rules and underlying forms, however, is not a necessary one, as shown by Vennemann's (1974) model in which rules apply vacuously to underlying forms. Thus, if there is any empirical evidence concerning the nature of underlying forms, it must be independent of the rules the linguist posits. Such evidence would seem very difficult, if not impossible to obtain, since underlying forms are not directly accessible to the native speaker or linguist.

It turns out, however, that much of the evidence we need is indeed available, if we turn our attention again to the study of phonological changes in progress. In the following sections we will examine evidence that suggests that restructuring of underlying forms is gradual both phonetically and lexically. The implication for synchronic phonology is that underlying representations cannot be composed exclusively of discrete contrastive structural units.

GRADUAL RESTRUCTURING

Labov begins his 1972b article on "The internal evolution of linguistic rules" by quoting Hockett on the necessarily abrupt nature of phonemic change.

A phonemic restructuring . . . must in a sense be absolutely sudden. No matter how gradual was the approach of EME / æ: / and /ɔ: / towards each other, we cannot imagine the actual coalescence of the two other than a sudden event: on such-and-such a day . . . the two fell together as /aː/ and the whole system of stressed nuclei . . . was restructured. Yet there is no reason to think that we would ever be able to detect this kind of event by direct observation. (1958: 456-57)

Labov approaches the problem of reconciling the gradualness of sound change with the notion of a discrete and non-variable linguistic structure. But for Labov, too, changes in underlying forms must be abrupt. His rules are variable and account for some of the gradualness of sound change, but these rules always apply to underlying forms that remain unchanged.

In any theory in which underlying representations consist only of contrastive structural units, a change in underlying representations must be abrupt. Yet the facts of sound change as observed at close range show that all instances of a given "phoneme" do not change at the same time, nor do they change at the same rate. A sound change that has progressed to a certain extent in one lexical item could be at a more advanced stage in another lexical item, and at a less advanced stage in a third. As Ferguson and Farwell (1975) point out, this phenomenon cannot be accounted for if one maintains a strict separation of phonetic and phonological levels, it can only be accounted for by assuming that lexical items have their own particular phonetic shape. Let us briefly consider some examples of lexical diffusion.

Some recent discussions of lexical diffusion have unfortunately lumped together as "sound change" three very different types of change: phoneme substitution, morpho-phonemic change and phonetically-motivated change (Chen and Wang 1975, Leben and Robinson 1977, Krishnamurti 1978). One very accessible example from Chen and Wang will illustrate: they point to the steady growth of the class of diatones (N-V pairs differentiated only by stress, e.g. *abstract*, *addict*, *accent*) as a case of lexical diffusion, which it is. It is not, however, lexical diffusion of a sound change, but rather lexical diffusion of a morphological rule.

It is the lexical diffusion of a gradual phonetic change that bears directly on the issue of the phonological representation of lexical items. Sub-phonemic distinctions consistently associated with particular lexical items are common during periods of variability or change in progress, indeed, at all stages. Consider, for example, the gradual loss of syllabicity in post-tonic syllables in American English (Zwicky, 1972; Hooper, 1976b, 1978).[1] This process takes place when schwa is followed by a liquid or nasal and another unstressed syllable: *every, camera, memory, scenery, nursery, family,* etc. We can distinguish at least three stages in the phonetic development: (1) total loss of syllabicity, as in *every* and *camera* (where the pronunciations with schwa would be unacceptable), (2) variable pronunciation between syllabic [r̩] and loss, as in *memory* or *family*, and (3) variation between [ər] and [r̩], as in *cursory* or *mammary* (where the pronunciation without syllabicity is unacceptable).[2] Ordinarily, one does not recognize for English phonemic syllabic liquids, since in most cases these syllabics are predictable from a schwa plus a liquid. Further, one hesitates to regard pairs such as *nursery, cursory,* and *memory, mammary* as instances of contrast. Nevertheless, there are phonetic differences associated with these particular words and many others, which are not "phonemic" differences.

If we view the lexicon as the component of the grammar that contains all the information that is idiosyncratic to particular lexical items, then some phonetic information (although it is not clear how much) must be included in lexical representations.[3] This does not mean that the productive process that produces the phonetic differences in question does not also exist in the grammar. More evidence is necessary, however, to determine precisely how a given lexical item and a productive process interact in any given utterance.

Another example of a phonetic change in progress is the aspiration (weakening to [h]) and deletion of final /s/ in various dialects of Spanish (Terrell, 1975, 1977; Hooper, 1977a). Following Terrell, we use three phonetic categories, although many more are recognizable. We will refer to [s], to [h], which results from the weakening of the lingual articulation of /s/, and to ϕ, which results from the loss of the glottal articulation of /s/.[4] The original phonetic change is the loss or assimilation of lingual articulation to a following consonant. Inside a word in Cuban Spanish the appearance of [h] is almost categorical before a C.

(1) Cuban Spanish

	s	h	ϕ	Number
__C	2%	97%	1%	1567
__## C	2%	75%	23%	2949
__## V	16%	50%	34%	1145
__/ /	63%	13%	24%	1488
				5582

The following are examples of /s/ in the environments shown in (1):

a. __C: word-internally before a C

   Examples: feli*h*mente   'happily'
              e*h*tilo   'type'
              dentista   'dentist'

b. __ ## C : word-finally before a C

   Examples: o se traen animale*h* finos
              "or fine animals are brought"
              haya muchos temas
              "there were many themes"
              suϕ detalle*h*
              "his details"

c.   ___ ## V: word-finally before a V

> y mientra*h* esa sonoridad asi
> "and during this voicing thus"
> no va*s* a encontrar
> "you are not going to find"

d.   ___/ /: before a pause

> en momento*s* / / libre*h* / /
> "in moments" "free"

The situation when /s/ is word-final is much more complex, for here /s/ sometimes occurs before a C, sometimes before a V and sometimes before a pause. It is in these positions that deletion becomes a possibility, and aspiration becomes variable. We will return in section 3 to a discussion of the reasons for this, but for now it is enough to note that some lexical items behave very differently with respect to aspiration and deletion across a word boundary.

We will compare four sets of figures for different lexical items to get an idea of the range of variation. We will be interested primarily in the different phonetic realizations before V's, because the proportions in the other environments tend to remain steadier. Compare (2), which shows the percentage of [s], [h] and ϕ for *pues*, a common interjection, to the overall figures for the dialect:

(2) *pues* "well"   tokens: 92

	s	h	ϕ
___ ## C	0%	68%	32%
___ ## V	6%	41%	53%
___/ /	75%	11%	14%

Note that *pues* shows fewer instances of [s] before ## V than the average and more instances of ϕ.

The numerals present quite a different picture, for here the percentage of [s] before a vowel is very high and the percentage of deletion is very low.

(3) numerals, *dos, tres, seis, diez*   tokens: 190

	s	h	ϕ
___ ## C	3%	86%	11%
___ ## V	42%	42%	16%
___/ /	80%	14%	6%

The third person singular present indicative of the copula shows very high aspiration before a V, but low deletion and s-retention:

(4) *es*

	s	h	ϕ	
___ ## C	3%	94%	3%	tokens: 466
___ ## V	9%	83%	8%	
___/ /	74%	17%	9%	

Finally, *entonces* 'then' shows very high deletion before a C and before a V.

(5) *entonces* 'then'   tokens: 209

	s	h	ϕ
__ ## C	1%	9%	90%
__ ## V	6%	6%	88%
__ / /	55%	6%	39%

Just considering these pre-vocalic figures we find variation for *pues* ranging from [h] to ϕ, for the numerals from [s] to [h], for *es* a more consistent [h] and for *entonces* a more consistent ϕ. These could be taken as their respective lexical forms, but the following factors must be taken into consideration.

First, the occurrence of [s] before a pause might argue that [s] may still be taken as underlying. The interesting point about the realizations before pause is that realizations in this position are the most consistent across lexical items. In every case the occurrence of [s] before pause is higher than anywhere else, and the favored realization before pause is consistently [s]. This consistency should be compared to the wild variability of realization before ## V. It should also be noted that *entonces* which has 90% deletion before ## C, has 55% [s] before pause. All this consistency is indicative of rule-governed behavior, while the variability before ## V is indicative of lexicalized differences. It seems that the phonetic vestige of /s/ is allowed to reach an [s]-like articulation before pause, because here no following articulations are exerting any influence on it.

Assuming that the pre-vocalic realizations are indicative of the lexical realization (for which the strongest argument is yet to come), we will have to make a number of phonetic distinctions lexically: at least the four mentioned above, corresponding to (2) - (5), and these will have to be distinguished from words that end in vowels, for words that end etymologically in vowels never have aspiration or [s] prepausally. Thus *entonces* cannot be represented as /entonse/, but rather must have an underlying final C, a very weak version of [h]. *Pues* will have a slightly stronger [h], *es* will have an [h] which is stronger still, and the numerals could have underlying [s] or a weakened [s].

Any structuralist theory (in which I include SPE-style generative phonology) would have an underlying final /s/ for all of these words, for [s] and [h] are, after all, complementary distribution. The full [s] occurs at the beginnings of syllables, [h] occurs syllable-finally before a C, and there is variation in other environments. Only one structural unit needs to be recognized to account for the phonology. Such a theory cannot, however, account for the lexical variation.

GRADUAL CHANGE IN THE LOCUS OF CONTRAST.

There are other types of evidence that lexical restructuring is gradual and that a distributional analysis will not necessarily yield a psychologically valid lexical representation. Hyman (1977a) discusses the gradual replacement of one phonemic distinction with another. We can take as one example a change that English seems to be undergoing at present concerning the contrastive status of obstruent voicing and vowel length. As is well known, English vowels (especially in monosyllables) are longer before voiced obstruents than before voiceless ones. Such a vowel length difference is found in many languages, but in English, the difference between the short and long vowels is much greater than in other languages where this difference is predictable (Chen, 1970). In casual speech in many dialects, the final obstruent is devoiced. Thus a phonemic distinction between *pat* /p æ t/ and *pad* /p æ d/ becomes a distinction betwen /p æ t/ and /p æ :t/. Hyman points out that such a change is gradual and necessarily involves a stage at which the phonetic representation is the same, [p æ t] and [p æ :d], but the vowel length distinction has been analyzed as the contrastive feature and the obstruent voicing has become redundant, for only then can the voicing distinction be lost without losing the contrast between the two words.

This means that there are some cases in which phonetic features which are in perfect complementary distribution must nonetheless be considered contrastive. Since the change from predictable to constrastive for vowel length is a covert change, not reflected initially by a change in the surface forms, one might conclude that such a change can never be deteted. But this isn't so. There are a number of ways to determine contrastiveness other than by examining distributional patterns. In the case at hand, a number of perceptual experiments, beginning with Deneš (1955), have shown vowel length to be an important cue for distinguishing words with voiced and voiceless final consonants. Other evidence that vowel length is contrastive in English is presented in Hooper (1977b).

In cases such as this one, there is no necessity for even the covert change from one contrast to another to be abrupt. There is no reason, other than consideration of structural economy, for the speakers to choose one contrast over the other. It is possible that a group of two or more features may together supply the contrast, which means, again, that lexical representations must contain considerably more phonetic information than a phonemic representation.

Another example of a change in contrast from one feature to another is discussed in Hooper (1974, 1976a). Here it is seen that the new contrast is fully established while vestiges of the old contrast still appear in phonetic representation. This case involves the aspiration and loss of final /s/ in Andalusian Spanish (the Granada dialect, Alonso et al., 1950). The vowel in a syllable closed by /s/ was slightly lower than in a free syllable. As /s/ weakens, the vowel opens more.

The loss of final /s/ in Spanish means the loss of the plural marker in nouns and adjectives. In the Granada dialect, the height of the vowel takes on the function of signalling the singular/plural distinction. This is reinforced by a vowel harmony process that makes *all* the vowels of a plural noun or adjective more open than the vowels of the corresponding singular.[5]

Orthography	Singular	Plural	Gloss
pedazo	[peðáθo]	[pệðạθǫ]	'piece'
alto	[álto]	[ậltǫʰ]	'tall'
cabeza	[kaβéθa]	[kaβẹ́θậ]	'head'
selva	[sélva]	[sẹ́lvạ]	'forest'
lobo	[lóβo]	[lǫ́βǫʰ]	'wolf'
tonto	[tónto]	[tǫ́ntǫ]	'stupid'
piso	[piso]	[pịsǫʰ]	'floor'
fin	[fiŋ]	[fịnẹʰ]	'end'
grupo	[grúpo]	[grụ́pǫʰ]	'group'

Notice that in these transcriptions the aspiration that is the vestige of the plural /s/ is still present in most cases. Note also that [h] is in complementary distribution and alternates with [s], as in [boʰ] 'voice' [boseʰ] 'voices'. Despite this, we must conclude that final /s/ has been restructured as [h], or else there would be no reason for the vowel harmony system to have developed.

BOUNDARY PHENOMENA

The interaction of phonological processes with word boundaries, whether the boundary conditions or blocks the process, is an indication of restructuring. In either case the boundaries serve to indicate that the segments inside of them are behaving as though they belong to a particular word, which is equivalent to saying that the phonetic features in question are an inherent part of the word (Hooper, 1977a; Leben and Robinson, 1977).

As an example of a process that appears to be conditioned partially by word boundaries, let us consider again the data presented above from Cuban Spanish. The table showing the percentage of occurrence of [s], [h] and ϕ in the form environments is repeated here, with a similar table for Argentinian Spanish.

(6) CUBAN

		s	h	ϕ	# of tokens
_C	A	2%	97%	1%	1567
_## C		2%	75%	23%	2949
_## V					
	B	16%	50%	34%	1145
_//		63%	13%	24%	1488

(7) ARGENTINIAN

		s	h	ϕ	# of tokens
_C	A	12%	80%	8%	4150
_## C		11%	69%	20%	5475
_## V	B	88%	7%	5%	2649
		78%	11%	11%	2407

As I mentioned above, the original phonetic environment for the aspiration of /s/ is pre-consonantal position. This is evident from the fact that the degree of aspiration pre-consonantally is quite consistent whether or not the /s/ is word-final (whether or not a word-boundary intervenes). Comparing the A boxes in (6) and (7), it can be seen that although the process is less advanced in Argentinian, the lowest percentages of [s] occur before a C.

Now consider the development of aspiration before ## V. Note that aspiration never occurs before a V inside of a word in these dialects. Therefore, when aspiration occurs before ## V, it is occurring outside of its phonetic environment. It can be seen from the tables that this is a secondary development. In Cuban, where the process is well advanced, only 16% of the occurrences before ## V are [s], but in Argentinian there is still a high occurrence of [s] before ## V. In a traditional rule format we would have to say that the rule of aspiration had "generalized" from (8a) to (8b):

(8) a. $s \rightarrow h / \underline{\quad} (\ \#\# \ )\, C$
    b. $s \rightarrow h / \underline{\quad} \Bigl\{ {(\ \#\# \ )\, C \atop \#\# \ V} \Bigr.$

The problem with this description is that what appears to be a generalization of the process to more environments must be expressed as a complication of the rule. The fact that the expression of the rule cannot be improved upon suggests that this is not a rule generalization at all.

Note that (8a) has strictly phonetic conditioning, and that the parenthesized ## merely indicates that word boundaries are *not* relevant to the application of the process. In (8b), however, the obligatory ## indicate that the environment is non-phonetic, or lexical. The weakening of the /s/ is due to that C's position in the word. This fact is expressed very awkwardly by (8b) but very naturally by registering the aspiration as a part of the lexical representation of the word. That is, the reason [h] now shows up word-finally outside of its phonetic environment is that the [h] has become an inherent part of the word.

The difference between the Cuban and the Argentinian dialects is that restructuring is well along in Cuba but only just beginning in Argentina. It is interesting to note, also, the basis of the restructured form is the pre-consonantal form of the word (as opposed to the pre-pausal form as predicted by Vennemann 1974). The reason for this could be the greater frequency of the pre-consonantal environment. Compare the number of tokens for each word-final environment: the pre-consonantal position is more frequent that the pre-vocalic and pre-pausal positions combined.

I am suggesting, then, that all phonetic variation conditioned by the presence of word boundaries must be represented lexically. This would include the famous distinction between *nitrate* and *night rate*. The difference between these two sequences is in the position of the syllable boundary (e.g. [nay $t^{h}reyt] vs. [nayt $reyt]), but the syllabication is based on the syntactic constituency, i.e. the fact that *night rate* is made up of two existing words. Thus when *night* occurs in the compound *night rate* it has a lenis [t] that is syllable-final, because the word *night* always has a syllable-final lenis [t]. This particular phonetic configuration is always associated with the word *night* and should be considered an inherent part of the lexical representation for *night*.

Does this mean that the difference between *nitrate* and *night rate,* this phonetic difference between the /t/ and the /r/, is phonemic? It does, if the criterion for phonemic status is the ability to distinguish between words, because it is this phonetic difference that distinguishes the two words. But if phonemic status implies that they are structural units with an existence independent of the words they occur in, then these different [t]'s and [r]'s are not phonemes. The reason that examples such as these have troubled linguists for so long is that the phonetic building blocks of a language — the phonemes — are *not* independent of the words they occur in.

The blocking effect of syntactic boundaries on phonological processes also leads to conclusions regarding lexical restructuring. To state the case very briefly, phonetic features positioned contiguous to a word boundary are always in an alternating environment. That is, the phonetic features on the other side of the boundary can vary considerably depending on the syntactic environment. Timberlake (1978) has shown that sound change progresses more slowly in alternating environments than in non-alternating environments. This is because restructuring occurs more readily in cases where the phonetic realization is more consistent. On the view that sound change *is* lexical change, the blocking effect of syntactic boundaries is easily explained.

To summarize, a process that makes reference to word boundaries, either as conditioning or blocking the process, should be represented as a process whose output is being lexicalized. There is a particularly clear argument concerning word boundaries as conditioning in Vennemann (1978). Here it is shown that certain sandhi phenomena in Sanskrit can be understood only as a rule inversion based on a restructuring of a phonetic variant that occurs word-finally.

PERIPHERAL PHONEMES

Peripheral phonemes — phonemes with defective distribution or low functional load — serve to illustrate the point that sounds are not totally independent of the words they occur in. Consider as an example the case of the German velar and palatal spirants. Their distribution is for the most part predictable: the velar occurs after back and central vowels and glides; the palatal occurs elsewhere, which amounts to positions after front vowels and glides and after /r, n, l/. The process involved is usually described as an assimilation of the velar to a preceding palatal environment. However, in a few cases the palatal occurs outside of its phonetic environment. The diminutive suffix *-chen* always begins with the palatal spirant, even when it occurs after a back vowel, as in *Tauchen* [ç] "small rope" and *Pfauchen* [ç] "little peacock" which contrast with *tauchen* "to dive" and *fauchen* "to spit" which have the velar spirant. Further, certain loan words contain [ç] in initial position, and after a back vowel: *China* [ç] and *Photochemie* [ç].

This case has been the subject of some controversy (Moulton 1947; Leopold, 1948). Since [ç] has such a limited distribution, the analyst is reluctant to regard it as a full-fledged phoneme of German. Its distinctive function as part of the diminutive suffix cannot be denied, however. The only way around phonemic status for [ç] is to use a boundary (open juncture in Moulton's terms) to predict the occurrence of [c]. This is tantamount to saying that [ç] belongs in the diminutive suffix, which is the same as saying that [ç] belongs in the lexical representation of *-chen*. Furthermore, for the current situation, in which [ç] occurs after back vowels and glides, to have arisen, *-chen* must have had a lexical representation with [ç] *before* it ever began to appear after back vowels and glides. That is, *-chen* had restructured while the palatal was still predictable from the phonetic environment.

In general, cases of peripheral phonemes develop because words have *phonetic* representations consistently associated with them. New marginal phonemes such as [ç] could not develop if words had only phonemic representation.

CONCLUSIONS

In the foregoing, I have assembled several different types of evidence that all converge on a single conclusion, that lexical representations must contain a significant amount of phonetic material, or that there is immediate lexical restructuring of the output of productive phonetically-conditioned processes. I have drawn primarily on evidence from change in progress, but evidence from child language, particularly that of Ferguson and Farwell (1975), should also be mentioned. It is sometimes asked whether this type of evidence is more important than distributional evidence. The answer to that question is affirmative, because it has never been shown that *speakers* use distributional evidence, we only know that linguists find it useful in description.

The evidence presented here is known to most phonologists, but I'm not sure that its full import has been appreciated. In particular I would like to emphasize that this evidence shows that for phonetically-conditioned processes the issues of what's a rule and what's an underlying form are totally distinct issues and must be decided separately. This means that questions of parsimony — economy in the lexicon or economy in the rules (an issue that could never be decided anyway) — is totally irrelevant.

This evidence argues for the dialectologists' old motto "every word has its own history." But certainly this dictum is too strong. The words of a language do not differ from one another in an infinite number of ways. The phonetic shapes of words are restricted by the phonological processes and constraints whose existence is amply demonstrated by the way speakers treat new words. So what we have is a system somewhere in between one in which every word has its own history and one in which "tout se tient." In this system the function of a lexical entry is to record what is idiosyncratic about a particular item, which, as we have seen, may include some phonetic detail. The function of a phonological rule is to specify a range of phonetic realizations for a particular configuration of features.

Vennemann's (1974, 1978) model is the one that comes closest to accounting for the facts discussed here. Vennemann proposes that a lexicon consists of a list of the words of a language in their "systematic phonetic" representation, citing Chomsky and Halle (1968) for a definition of "systematic phonetics."

Vennemann says:

> . . . a single kind of phonological structure is specified by a single set of phonological constraints, constraints which specify what is and what is not pronounceable in the language. (Note that 'pronounceable' must here be understood in the sense of what Chomsky and Halle call a 'systematic phonetic representation'; i.e. 'fast speech' rules and other kinds of 'variable' rules are assumed to apply to 'systematic phonetic representations' and are not considered here. This is not to deny the systematicity of such rules, but rather to distinguish between 'phonological rules (proper)' and 'variable rules', and between a 'systematic phonetic representation' on the other hand and a 'phonetic realization' in a given cultural, situational, and textual context on the other.)

Unfortunately, Chomsky and Halle (1968) do not define "systematic phonetic" representation. Chomsky (1964) says that the level of systematic phonetics is "the representation in terms of phones (and, possibly, phonetic junctures) that constitutes the output of the phonological component." (p 87). This definition, which presupposes a different theory, will not do to specify lexical representations.

Ladefoged (1977) presents a very clear definition of "systematic phonetic." For Ladefoged a systematic phonetic representation must contain enough information to distinguish an utterance from all other non-homophonous utterances in other dialects, and it must show the differences between languages, but not contain any universally predictable information, or any information due to individual differences among speakers.

Ladefoged is also referring to the output of a grammar here, but this characterization could fit into Vennemann's model. The problem is, as Vennemann realizes, that there may be more than one phonetic realization of a single lexical item, and for this reason Vennemann excludes variation that is the output of "fast speech" and "variable" rules. It is reasonable to assume that rules such as these apply to a very explicit, careful speech representation (Rudes, 1976; Hooper, 1976a).

The evidence we have examined in the section concerned with Gradual Restructuring, however, suggests that a systematic phonetic representation does not contain enough information. The difficulty lies with the phonetic differences between lexical items, such as between English *nursery* and *cursory*, Spanish *pues* and *es.* The differences between these items occur in a single dialect and do not solely distinguish non-homophonous utterances. Furthermore, it doesn't seem right to choose a single, perhaps most careful, representation for each of these items when they exhibit individual differences not just in their careful forms, but also in the degree or reduction allowed in their casual forms.

It seems, rather, that if we are to adopt a model such as Vennemann's, we must modify our notions of lexical representations and our notions of rule. A lexical item may not have a discrete representation, but rather consist of a specification of ranges of variation for features that comprise it. Rules may not specify absolute constraints on pronounceability, but rather they may specify possible ranges of variation. It is important to note here that all phonetically-conditioned rules or processes create variable output, so that a division of rule into variable and non-variable is not possible anyway.

In this paper I have examined a number of ways that the determination of underlying representation can be made an empirical rather than a formal matter. Work of this type needs to be extended considerably in order to determine exactly how much phonetic information is coded in lexical representations and how much should be considered predictable. A possible hypothesis is that intrinsic variation is not represented lexically but extrinsic variation is (Hyman, 1977a). Further, while I have argued that restructuring is both lexically and phonetically gradual, it is still possible that some abrupt lexical changes occur also, especially in the language acquisition process. More detailed studies of lexical and phonetic change in progress will reveal the interaction of gradual and abrupt changes in restructuring.

Notes

1. Other examples of this type of lexical diffusion phenomena are found in Fidelholtz, 1975, and in Gerritsen and Jensen, 1979.

2. It is probably arbitrary to distinguish only three stages along this continuum of phonetic development. I have restricted the discussion to three stages in order to simplify it.

3. Generative formalism provides two devices that make it possible to avoid including subphonemic contrasts in underlying representations. One is a rule feature analysis, in which lexical terms are marked with a diacritic which triggers a schwa deletion rule. This is just a more complex way of marking the phonetic differences in the lexical item. A second method (brought up by M. Ohala during the symposium) allows the listing, in the rule, of the particular lexical items that undergo it. This is also a complex notational variant of including phonetic information in lexical entries, and has the further undesireable consequence of destroying the concept of a rule as a generalization that is superior to a list.

4. Terrell and his associates used taped interviews made with Cubans a few months after their arrival in Miami, and with Argentinians in Buenos Aires. In transcribing the tapes, Terrell and his associates found numberous allophones of /s/ occurring pre-consonantally: some voiced, some voiceless, some velar, some palatal, and so on, depending on the particular environment. These variants were divided into three categories in order to make the data manageable. The variant was transcribed as [s] if significant sibilance was detected, as [h] if the presence of a fricative consonant was detected, but without sibilance, and as ϕ if no consonant seemed to be present. This impressionistic method is not as reliable as an instrumental one, but the large number of tokens recorded makes the general figures reliable.

5. The tail under the vowel ([ę]) indicates an open vowel. In the case of /a/ the more open variant is slightly fronted.

THE COGNITIVE REPRESENTATION OF SPEECH
T. Myers, J. Laver, J. Anderson (editors)
© North-Holland Publishing Company, 1981

The Psychological Reality of Phonological Representations:
Experimental Evidence

TERRANCE M. NEAREY

Dept. of Linguistics, University of Albert

LEVELS OF REPRESENTATION AND TYPES OF EVIDENCE

Four levels of representation have been generally recognized as being of potential relevance to linguistic theory (Chomsky, 1964): (i) physical phonetics, (ii) systematic phonetics (narrow transcription), (iii) taxonomic phonemics and (iv) systematic phonemics (morphophonemics). In this paper, I will discuss four types of evidence that have a bearing on the psychological reality of phonological representations. These are:

1. Synchronic distributional data, i.e. the distribution of forms within a single language.

2. Facts about 'typological predominance'. Certain phonological situations are 'more expected' typologically across languages and certain types of diachronic change are more expected than others.

3. 'Naturalistic' or 'ecological' observation, where the investigator observes behavior without disturbing the environment. Types of data include acquisition speech errors, language games, borrowing and interference phenomena.

4. Controlled experimentation and other situations in which the observer affects the environment of the subject, e.g., second language teaching situations.

FORMAL EVIDENCE AND MODES OF ARGUMENTATION

The first two types of evidence may be referred to together as 'formal evidence', in that they concern linguistic forms. They are also sometimes referred to as 'internal evidence'. This kind of evidence can be obtained solely from the examination of texts and transcriptions of linguistic data, though it is not necessarily limited to these sources. Synchronic distributional evidence has been the most basic concern of modern linguistics. In the case of taxonomic phonemics, this was virtually the only evidence considered relevant to an analysis. Any theory of language would have to be responsible to this type of data.

The term 'generative phonology' will be used to refer to the model of phology set forth by Chomsky and Halle (1968) in the first eight chapters of *The Sound Pattern of English* (henceforth SPE). A major new source of evidence to generative phonology is typological predominance or 'expectedness'. In fact, I believe that this is the only additional realm of evidence or 'field of application' (Popper, 1965: 126-130, and appendix i) for which generative phonology assumes direct empirical responsibility.

Many of the early arguments against taxonomic phonemics were based on its failure to distinguish between 'expected' and 'unexpected' situations. The basic mode of argumentation for or against particular types of representation and formal devices revolves about the 'differential expectedness argument'.

The basic elements of the differential simplicity argument are:

1. We are presented with two language situations A & B such that the expectedness of situation A is greater than the expectedness of B: $E(A) > E(B)$

2. For each language situation we are given two distinct descriptions: for A, D1(A) versus D2(A) and for B, D1(B) versus D2(B). Ordinarily, D1 and D2 are equivalent, except that D2 contains a proposed new convention or abbreviatory device not included in D1.

3. We are given a fixed evaluation criteron V.

4. We accept description D2 over D1 if and only if: $V((D2(A)) > V(D2(B))$ while $V(D1(A)) \leq V(D1(B))$. That is, D2 is preferred if its valuation reflects the differential expectedness of the two situations, while D1 does not.

The task of phonology is seen as largely a matter of constructing a set of descriptive devices (as an *evaluation metric* — though this has been essentially held constant) such that the proper differential evaluations are given to all clear cases of differential expectedness. The particular evaluation metric of generative phonology is based on the inverse of the feature count of a set of rules when it is reduced to minimal form consistent with the set of abbreviations and devices in the theory.

With one reservation, I believe that the differential simplicity argument represents a true advance in phonology. I view it as an advance because it has expanded the empirical content of phonology. Phonology must account not only for distributional facts within a language, but also for the relative expectedness of different types of phonological situations. My one reservation involves the relatively loose definition of 'differential expectedness' — usually in such arguments the 'empirical' data appealed to is the 'professional intuition' of the linguist. In spite of this advance, I feel strongly that the theoretical superstructure of generative phonology rests on an overly narrow data base. The number of 'clear cases' upon which theoretical developments hinges seems to be rather limited.

Argumentation concerning the validity of new conventions is often very subtle and even the most brilliant analysts overlook the consequences of their own examples. Consider the case of the Greek variable conventions of Chapter 8 of SPE. The introduction of these 'alpha' conventions is a paradigm case of the differential simplicity argument. We are asked, in effect, to consider two versions of phonological theory, one without Greek variable coefficients and one with. We are also asked to consider two phonological situations, one based on Southern Paiute illustrating a 'familiar' process of place of articulation assimilation. The description of this situation under the set of conventions D1, without the variable coefficients, is given in Rule 1.

$$
\text{Rule 1:} \quad [+\text{cons}] \longrightarrow
\left\{
\begin{array}{l}
\begin{bmatrix} +\text{ant} \\ -\text{cor} \\ -\text{high} \\ -\text{back} \end{bmatrix} \Big/ \underline{\quad} + \begin{bmatrix} +\text{ant} \\ -\text{cor} \\ -\text{high} \\ -\text{back} \end{bmatrix} \\[2em]
\begin{bmatrix} +\text{ant} \\ +\text{cor} \\ -\text{high} \\ -\text{back} \end{bmatrix} \Big/ \underline{\quad} + \begin{bmatrix} +\text{ant} \\ +\text{cor} \\ -\text{high} \\ -\text{back} \end{bmatrix} \\[2em]
\begin{bmatrix} -\text{ant} \\ -\text{cor} \\ +\text{high} \\ +\text{back} \end{bmatrix} \Big/ \underline{\quad} + \begin{bmatrix} -\text{ant} \\ -\text{cor} \\ +\text{high} \\ +\text{back} \end{bmatrix}
\end{array}
\right\}
$$

The second situation is described as 'totally implausible' and its description under D1 is given in Rule 2, which might be characterized as a 'feature salad'. One of the subrules of Rule 2 says that consonants become labial in the environment of velarized retroflexes. Note that under D1, both the familiar place of articulation

$$
\text{Rule 2:} \qquad [+\text{cons}] \longrightarrow
\left\{
\begin{array}{l}
\begin{bmatrix} +\text{ant} \\ -\text{cor} \\ -\text{high} \\ -\text{back} \end{bmatrix} \Big/ \underline{\quad} + \begin{bmatrix} -\text{ant} \\ +\text{cor} \\ -\text{high} \\ +\text{back} \end{bmatrix} \\[2.5em]
\begin{bmatrix} +\text{ant} \\ +\text{cor} \\ -\text{high} \\ -\text{back} \end{bmatrix} \Big/ \underline{\quad} + \begin{bmatrix} +\text{ant} \\ -\text{cor} \\ +\text{high} \\ +\text{back} \end{bmatrix} \\[2.5em]
\begin{bmatrix} -\text{ant} \\ -\text{cor} \\ +\text{high} \\ +\text{back} \end{bmatrix} \Big/ \underline{\quad} + \begin{bmatrix} -\text{ant} \\ +\text{cor} \\ +\text{high} \\ -\text{back} \end{bmatrix}
\end{array}
\right\}
$$

assimilation situation and the 'totally implausible situation' have the same valuation. We are then asked to consider the two situations under the proposed revised set of conventions, D2, which includes variable feature coefficients. D2 allows the abbreviation of Rule 1 to Rule 3, while Rule 2 cannot be so abbreviated. Consequently, the descriptive framework that includes variable coefficients correctly reflects the relative expectedness of the two situations and D2 is accepted as representing an additional linguistically significant generalization that D1 misses.

$$
\text{Rule 3:} \qquad [+\text{cons}] \longrightarrow
\begin{bmatrix} \alpha\ \text{ant} \\ \beta\ \text{cor} \\ \gamma\ \text{high} \\ \delta\ \text{back} \end{bmatrix} \Big/ \underline{\quad} +
\begin{bmatrix} +\text{cons} \\ \alpha\ \text{ant} \\ \beta\ \text{cor} \\ \gamma\ \text{high} \\ \delta\ \text{back} \end{bmatrix}
$$

Note at this point that Greek letter variables are restricted essentially to assimilation processes — a variable in the 'output' is matched with a variable in the environment portion of the rule on the same feature. In the next few pages of SPE, some additional 'clear cases' are introduced to motivate the generalization of variable coefficients to allow for dissimilation effects and other phenomena. With this liberalization, we find that the content of Rule 2 can be included in a generalized Rule 4, where the features [high] and [coronal] have been eliminated from the environment as redundant. Rule 4 is a very peculiar consonant harmony rule that says among other things that consonants become velar in the environment of palatals and that consonants become labial in the environment of velars. Thus reducing these conventions to minimal form, we find that the 'totally implausible' situation is actually 'more highly valued' than the place of articulation assimilation. Hence the original differential expectedness argument is reversed. Thus a counter-example for the liberalized use of variable coefficients has been introduced prior to its motivating examples!

$$
\text{Rule 4:} \qquad [+\text{cons}] \longrightarrow
\begin{bmatrix} \alpha\ \text{ant} \\ \beta\ \text{cor} \\ -\alpha\ \text{high} \\ -\alpha\ \text{back} \end{bmatrix} \Big/ \underline{\quad} +
\begin{bmatrix} \beta\ \text{ant} \\ \alpha\ \text{back} \end{bmatrix}
$$

In my view, the paucity of clear cases, the subtlety of argumentation, and the failure to adequately test the full range of implications of proposed conventions against even the textbook examples must result in painfully slow progress in purely formal phonology. But this is not my main reason for appealing for a more broadly based phonology. It is possible that generative phonological arguments will eventually be constructed that are so compelling that there is a broad consensus on what must be psychologically real. Even so we would demand some independent *extrinsic* testing of the hypotheses in question. The degree to which generative phonology actually does successfully predict typological expectedness is not clear. Even if it were enormously successful at this, the assumption of a close correspondence between specific constructs of the theory and psychological entities would require independent testing. In fact, this is precisely the type of thing that Kiparsky (1968) had in mind when he proposed that, e.g., rules collapsed by braces must act as a unit in historical change and that failure for them to do so would constitute '. . . prima facie evidence that . . [braces are] a spurious notation (p. 179).' In effect, this amounts to the claim that braces are more than an arbitrary notational device in a calculus of differential expectedness. But if specific constructs of generative phonology have psychological reality, then we may expect them to have testable empirical consequences beyond (or 'external to') the patterns of synchronic, diachronic and typological distributions of linguistic forms.

The fact is that even now there has been some movement among 'main line' generative phonologists to include at least the third kind of evidence mentioned above, 'ecological observation', within the realm of relevant evidence. Perhaps the most notable among the recent suggestions are Kiparsky's (1973) proposals to 'add clauses' to the feature-counting evaluation metric so as to reflect facts of acquisition. Though I expect that revisions more radical than 'patching up' the evaluation metric will be necessary to account for this type of data, I welcome this and all other attempts to include 'ecological observation' of non-distributional but language-related evidence within the range of *empirical responsibility* of linguistic theory. The only drawback to this type of evidence is that we have no control over the quantity or quality of observations relevant to crucial theoretical questions.

Generative linguists have been disturbingly reluctant to deal with the fourth source of evidence mentioned above, experimentation. For many there seems to be a pathological fear that all experiments are fraught with performance effects that will totally obscure 'what is really going on.' Others take what I believe is a methodologically indefensible position that only evidence that corroborates formal linguistic hypotheses is admissable from the experimental domain, while falsifying evidence may be freely ignored. A small but increasing number of linguists have rejected both these views. Instead, we feel that the greatest potential for rapid progress in phonological theory is to be found in the time-honored technique of testing theoretical predictions directly with experiments. It is well recognized that artifacts may crop up in experiments; however, the advantage of experimental artifacts over other 'accidents of observation' is that they are experiment-specific. A fruitful approach in experimentation is to use different experimental paradigms to get at the same phenomena. It is to be expected that the basic characteristics that underly language use will remain nearly invariant to our experimental manipulation and artifactual effects will tend to cancel each other out. In what follows, I will try to show the kinds of questions that have been addressed in phonology through experimentation, with special attention to results obtained by my colleagues at the University of Alberta.

EXPERIMENTAL EVIDENCE FOR 'AUTONOMOUS' CONTRASTIVE UNITS

First, let us consider experimental evidence bearing on the level of 'systematic phonetics' or 'narrow transcription'. Lieberman (1979a) has recently rejected this level, at least as a set of discrete elements. A more appropriate model is, in his view, that of quasi-continuous universal phonetic space within which languages of the world are relatively free to set up language-specific nodes, representing phonological categories. (Certain positions in the space may be preferred because of such factors as stability in production and perception.) I would emphasize that these units are phonological (rather than phonetic) precisely because they are language-specific.   The existence of such language specific nodes is strongly supported by experimental phonetics. Typically, when relevant acoustic control variables are manipulated systematically, listeners' judgements are characterized by continuous categorization curves. Results have shown that the categorization of the same synthetic continua by speakers of different languages reflects differences in the phonological systems of the languages in question (Abramson and Lisker, 1970). Furthermore, even the more basic perceptual task of discrimination shows the influence of linguistically determined categories.

These phenomena are not new. However, I think that their implications for phonology have been largely overlooked. The presence of well-defined 'tuning curves' on physical continua for linguistic categories provides strong evidence for psychologically real units of perception that are effectively 'autonomous' (from the point of view of higher grammatico-semantic considerations). These perceptual units are similar to taxonomic phonemes in that they are less abstract than morphophonemes and are more closely related to phonetic dimensions, and they are related to lexically relevant contrasts. More precisely, these units would seem to correspond to contrasting allophones in specific environments. This evidence strongly suggests that a psychologically real model of language should explicitly contain such a level of representation — perhaps a set of neural detectors, perhaps the output of some other identification process.

THE PHONEMIC MEMBERSHIP OF ALLOPHONES

While the above techniques provide strong support for the existence of units corresponding to contrastive allophones, these experimental phonetic techniques do not indicate how (or if) such units occurring in different environments are to be 'combined' into phonemic or morphophonemic units. However, a number of experimental techniques show promise of shedding some light on this issue. One that I have been developing in coloboration with B. Derwing is based on a similarity-rating technique of Vitz and Winkler (1973).

The basic procedure is to present subjects with pairs of words and ask for similarity ratings. Vitz and Winkler's experiments showed that similarity judgements were strongly related to the simple proportion of phoneme matches across the two strings. We have recently been running small scale experiments to attempt to clarify the procedure for use in an experimental probe of phoneme identity. Our results show that the presence of the same phoneme in two strings always shows increased similarity to control cases: hence the pair *gill* and *grill* would always be rated closer than *gill* and *spill*.

The way in which this technique may be used to shed light on phonemic membership may be illustrated as follows:
Traditionally, three allophones of stop consonants have been considered important: (1) 'voiceless aspirated' as in *pill*, (2) 'voiceless' unaspirated' as in *spill*, (3) 'voiced' as in *bill* — Allophone (2) is in complementary distribution with both (1) and (3) — Experimental research has indicated that allophone (3) in *bill* is only rarely voiced during the consonantal closure in initial position in English and that it is in fact frequently very similar to voiceless unaspirates in other languages, at least from the point of view of voice onset time. Furthermore, perceptual experiments indicate that when the /s/ is gated from words like *spill*, English listeners classify the resulting

syllable as *bill*. From the point of view of phonetic similarity, there is some reason to link allophone (2) with allophone (3) rather than allophone (1). What do phoneme similarity judgements have to say about this?

Table 1 shows the results of a pilot study using 9 subjects. All were linguistically naive university students and native speakers of English. They were asked to rate the word pairs on a scale of 1 to 9. Previous experiments we had run indicated that subjects found greater similarity between [p ^{h}]-[sp] pairs than between [b]-[sp] pairs, as most traditional phonemicizations would indicate. However, orthographic interference is an important potential source of artifacts in all phonological experiments involving literate subjects. The present experiment was designed to control at least in part for this. Note that the first two pairs in Table 1 have 'spelling support' of a closer link between [ph]-[sp] items. The next three pairs are not supported by spelling. The sixth pair has ambiguous spelling support (*cool* and *school* share *c*, while *ghoul* and *school* share *h*). The last pair involves only nonsense words.

TABLE I

STIMULUS PAIRS	NUMBER OF CASES	MEAN	DIFFERENCE MEAN	ST. DEV.
(SPELLING SUPPORTED)				
'pill'-'spill'		6.4444		
	9		1.2222	2.048
'bill'-'spill'		5.2222		
'skill'-'kill'		6.4444		
	9		0.8889	1.833
'skill'-'gill'		5.5556		
(NON-SUPPORTED)				
'skull'-'cull'		6.1111		
	9		0.2222	1.481
'skull'-'gull'		5.8889		
'skein'-'cane'		6.2222		
	9		0.6667	1.323
'skein'-'gain'		5.5556		
'cot'-'squat'		5.0000		
	9		1.4444	2.744
'got'-'squat'		3.5556		
(OTHER)				
'cool'-'school'		5.4444		
	9		0.1111	1.616
'ghoul'-'school'		5.3333		
/spif/-/pif/		5.7500		
	8		0.2500	0.886
/spif/-/bif/		5.5000		

All of the means are higher for the [p ^{h}]-[sp] comparisons than for [b]-[sp]. A correlated means t test shows this to be highly significant (t (62) = 3.71, p < .001). If we consider only the spelling-supported items, the differences are again significant in the predicted direction (t (17) = 3.75 p < .001). The difference is also significant for the non-spelling-supported words (t (26) = 2.14, p < .025). Though the average difference for the matched pairs across subjects between the spelling-supported items and non-supported items is significant only at the .10 level, it is nonetheless sufficient to indicate that orthographic interference may be a real factor in these judgements. Any conclusion drawn from these experiments should be subject to confirmation by 'preliterate' subjects.

On the whole, however, we are very encouraged with results from these 'string similarity' experiments and we believe that the technique has great potential as a probe in exploring phonological questions. Derwing (1976) has provided evidence that orthographic interference is at least not an overwhelming factor in these experiments, since partial correlation analysis of orthographic versus phoneme-based similarity metrics showed that orthographic similarity was not significantly correlated with listeners' similarity judgments when phoneme similarity was controlled for. The phoneme-based measure of similarity, on the other hand, was significantly correlated with judgments even after controlling for orthographic similarity. Furthermore, the word list used in Derwing (1976) has subsequently been given to another group of subjects with an auditory presentation mode, rather than a written questionaire, with rather remarkable results. The correlation between the means of the two groups for each of the items was better than .95.

Jeri Jaeger (1979) at Berkeley has used two quite different probes to address the 'membership of allophones' problem. One was a classical conditioning (shock — galvonic skin response) experiment. The second was a 'category formation' paradigm in which subjects were 'trained' to push a button on all occurrences of *aspirated* [k] on a training set. This training set does not contain any other allophones of /k/. When the subject had reached a certain criterion of performance, he was presented with a new list which contained 'suspicious items'. Thus far, these results also support the traditional assignment of stop allophones. Subjects generally said 'yes' to [sk] items, but 'no' to [g] items. A parallel experiment has been suggested, though not run, in which the subjects are trained to say 'yes' to [g] items. This would be a more direct test of the allophone membership question than is the similarity experiment discussed earlier.

EVIDENCE FOR MORPHOPHONEMIC RULES

There is also experimental evidence bearing on somewhat more abstract phonological problems. Morphophonemics generally involves three elements: (1) invariant meaning units (morphemes), (2) which are realized in variable phonetic shapes, (3) by a system of rules. A straightforward interpretation of the systematic phonemics of generative phonology implies that morphemes should be represented in the internal lexicon in a single invariant shape (except for cases of suppletion). Though direct experimental evidence concerning the exact shape of lexical storage may never be available, recent research has provided some evidence for the existence of some types of morphophonemic rules. Derwing (1979; cf. also Derwing and Baker, 1977) has evaluated a number of hypotheses concerning speakers' knowledge of English plurals in light of evidence elicited from 112 children ranging in age from three to nine. Let us consider four, given in Rules 5-8. The first (Rule 5) is really a list of arbitrary associations: it assumes that children learn the plural form of each word individually. Thus, *cats* must be memorized as the plural of *cat* just as *feet* must be memorized as the plural of *foot*.

This hypothesis may be rejected on the basis of a Berko-type test (Berko, 1958) in which new (nonsense forms) lexical items are provided by the experimenter and the child is asked to finish a sentence frame that requires the plural form of the new item. (Certain productive derivational suffixes, and certain real irregular plural

Rule 5:

$$(Pl) = \left\{ \begin{array}{lll} \text{—əz} & / & \{ \text{fes, glas, roz, dɪš̌, wɪč̌, stuǰ, etc. . .} \} \quad \text{——} \\ \text{—s} & / & \{ \text{payp, bɪt, kæt, kɔk, sak, etc. . . . . .} \} \quad \text{——} \\ \text{—z} & / & \{ \begin{array}{l} \text{təb, pɪg, stov, krəm, gən, wɔl,} \\ \text{pɪl, pay, kaw, tɔy, etc. . . . .} \end{array} \} \quad \text{——} \end{array} \right\}$$

forms were presented in a similar manner with similar results.) If, in acquisition, there were no generalization of plural formation on the basis of some analysis of the stems, it would be impossible for children to produce new plural items. This is clearly not the case, except for the youngest subjects.

A more subtle problem exists when one considers the evaluation of the next two alternatives (Rules 6 and 7). Rule 6 says that the generalization for pluralization

Rule 6:

$$(Pl) = \left\{ \begin{array}{lll} \text{—əz} & / & \{ \text{s, z, š̌, ž̌, č̌, ǰ} \} \quad \text{——} \\ \text{—s} & / & \{ \text{p, t, k, f, θ} \} \quad \text{——} \\ \text{—z} & / & \{ \begin{array}{l} \text{b, d, g, v, ð̌, m, n, ŋ, r, l,} \\ \text{y, w, i, e, u, o, a, ɔ, ər} \end{array} \} \quad \text{——} \end{array} \right\}$$

involves the association of a set of allomorphs that are selected on the basis of an arbitrary list of stem-final consonants. Rule 7 says that the allomorphs are selected on the basis of a feature analysis of the stem-final consonant. Note that both of these have exactly the same set of predictions for the pluralization of new lexical items. If language acquisition were instantaneous (as in the SPE model), the experiment would provide no evidence to select between these models. However, thanks to 'performance limitations', we are able to reject the arbitrary list hypothesis. The reason for this is that children show four distinct stages in their mastery of adult forms. The groups with the lowest performance is unable to pluralize correctly at all. The next best group pluralizes correctly all English stems except those ending in fricatives. The third group pluralizes all forms correctly except sibilants. Finally the sibilants are learned. This order of acquisition clearly shows that children are generalizing on the basis of 'natural classes' rather than individual stem-final sounds, although these particular natural classes are not necessarily those predicted by generative phonology.

Rule 7:

$$(Pl) = \left\{ \begin{array}{lll} \text{—əz} & / & \left[\text{+ sibilant} \right] \quad \text{——} \\ \text{—s} & / & \left[\begin{array}{l} \text{- sibilant} \\ \text{- voiced} \end{array} \right] \quad \text{——} \\ \text{—z} & / & \left[\begin{array}{l} \text{- sibilant} \\ \text{+ voiced} \end{array} \right] \quad \text{——} \end{array} \right\}$$

Note that the above observations deal only with respect to the stems. The usual generative phonological analysis (Rule 8) also supposes that generalization has taken place with respect to the ending as well. Can this be tested? We think so. We have designed an experiment that involves the learning of what is in effect a new derivational suffix in English in the context of a learning game. I will describe it briefly.

Rule 8:

A. $\phi \rightarrow \partial$ / [+sibilant] _____ [+sibilant] ##

B. [+obstruent] $\rightarrow$ [α voiced] / $\begin{bmatrix} +\text{obstruent} \\ \alpha \text{ voiced} \end{bmatrix}$ _____ ##

Subjects are first given a small booklet that has the pictures and names of a set of creatures from a new planet. The experimenter has a set of cards with these pictures. The subject is asked the name of a particular creature: at first, he is given access to his guide book to assist in learning. After reaching criterion in learning the names, the subject is shown an expanded deck of cards which includes certain of the creatures in their pre-adult state. The young creatures are all blue, while the adults are white. The names of the young creatures are identical to those of the adults, except that the new 'diminutive' suffix /-ž/ is added. In this first trial run, only creatures whose base form names end in resonants are included, so that the predicted form (by Rule 8) involves only a pure agglutination (concatenation) of the suffix. When the subject has had practice in this task (which so far has produced little difficulty, except for a slight tendency for subjects to add the more common /ǰ/ in place of /ž/), additional items ending in voiceless consonants and sibilants are added to the list. Preliminary results indicate that most subjects spontaneously devoice the suffix without any hesitation in the environment of voiceless non-sibilants. Note that some hypotheses concerning the acquisition of allomorphs can be rejected in this case — subjects never heard the voiceless allomorphs and yet were able to produce them unhesitatingly. In the case of sibilant stem, however, subjects appear to have a great deal of difficulty. None of the six subjects studied thus far spontaneously produced the predicted form, /- z/, on the first trial for sibilant stems. We plan to run a full-scale version of this experiment in which the period of exposure to the non-problematic resonant stems is prolonged to increase the chances that the suffix is 'internalized' by the subjects before they are required to manipulate it in novel environments.

WHEN IS A 'RULE' A REAL GENERALIZATION?

The experiments just described deal with relatively 'close to the surface' morphological alternations. Experimental techniques have also been used to investigate more abstract morphological rules, including the controversial 'vowel shift' rules in English. Cena (1978) has used a paired associate learning paradigm to test for the psychological reality of the vowel alternations embodied in this rule. His experiments show that (1) it is easier for subjects to learn pairs of items showing 'correct' English alternations and (2) the English alternation patterns tended to interfere with the learning of non-English pairings. Thus in case (2), subjects who were 'taught' a pair like /ɪnsnayp/-ɪnsnɛpɪti/ tended to 'correct' the latter with /ɪnsnɪpɪti/. Other experiments (Moskowitz, 1973; Myerson, 1976) have also provided some support for the 'psychological reality' of the vowel-shift alternations.

However, it should be pointed out that there are strong experimental indications of differences between fully productive, relatively 'shallow' rules, such as English

Plural formation, and 'minor rules' such as vowel shift which apply to a more restricted set of lexical items. Indeed, there is some doubt as to whether such 'minor rules' are really 'rules' at all.

Direct approaches, such as that of Steinberg and Krohn (1975), involve asking subjects to add suffixes such as *-ic*, *-ity* to stems on which they do not ordinarily occur — e.g. *snide*. These experiments generally show that subjects are unable to provide spontaneously the predicted English form. Such behavior is to be contrasted with the unhesitantly correct response of very young children to the novel pluralization task.

A further, somewhat more subtle difference should be mentioned. McCawley (1979) in his comments on Cena's data has emphasized some of the differences in response among items that are parallel from the point of view of the vowel shift rule as it is formulated in SPE, for example. One interesting point that Cena himself makes is that the vowel alternation pair /ʌ - aw/ behaves quite differently from the others — it is more difficult to learn than other real English alternatives and it is less likely to interfere with the learning of arbitrary non-English alternations. In fact, the non-occurring /ɔ - aw/ alternation shows a stronger influence than /ʌ - aw/.

McCawley believes that this provides evidence concerning the 'individuation' (as opposed to 'generalization') of the vowel shift rule. The /ʌ - aw/ alternation in English is exceedingly rare. Yet formally, from the point of view of the SPE vowel shift rule, it is treated totally parallel to the considerably more frequent /ɪ - ay/ alternation (*divine-divinity*). In Cena's experiment, the latter alternation had a considerable influence on subjects' learning patterns while the former did not. Yet, excluding the /ʌ - aw/ alternation from the SPE vowel shift rules would require a formally unmotivated complication of the rule.

The sensitivity of a particular alternation to frequency of existing items may turn out to provide evidence as to the nature of the generalization (or lack of it) in question. Some additional results reported by Derwing (1979) are suggestive in this regard. Derwing found that the frequency of the *individual* stem ending had very little to do with childrens' ability to pluralize correctly. Once frequent vowel stems such as /i/ were pluralized correctly, infrequent vowel stems such as those ending in /ɔ/ were also pluralized correctly. However, when results for *irregular* English plurals were studied, frequency of occurrence appeared to play a much greater role. In general, more correct responses were given to more frequent irregular items. A possible interpretation of this result is that the vowel shift rule in English is more like a list of individual vowel alternations that must be learned separately rather than as a generalization.

Experimental evidence suggests that more abstract morphophonemic alternations may have some role in organizing the lexicon and in facilitating learning of new items. Nevertheless, the experimentally confirmed differences between such patterns and fully productive rules require an explanation in a psychologically adequate phonology. Another area in which experimental research shows promise is in setting limits on the degree of phonetic and semantic deviation that pairs of items can display and still be felt to be related by linguistically naive subjects. Derwing (1976) has addressed this question of morpheme recognition. Derwing presented a list of words, ranging from words with 'clear' morphological relationships (e.g. *teach - teacher*) to those with none (e.g. *carpenter - wagon*) to two different groups of subjects. One was asked to judge the similarity of sound between the pairs, ignoring meaning. The other was asked to judge the similarity of meaning, ignoring sound. The average scores on the sound and meaning similarity experiments were then compared with results of a morpheme recognition task on a third group of subjects. In general, only items that scored high similarity ratings on both the semantic and phonetic indices were likely to be judged as containing the same 'meaning unit' by this third group. Most such items involved highly productive elements of English derivational morphology.

Eventually, converging experimental techniques in conjunction with more traditional linguistic evidence, including the typological predominance for certain morphophonemic patterns, may lead to a well-motivated distinction between types of morphophonemic (and perhaps other) rules.

CONCLUSION

Although phonological experimentation is still in its infancy, I believe that the results reviewed here are highly encouraging. With Ohala and Ohala (1975), I believe that all that is necessary '. . . to make any experimental technique useful is to formulate our hypotheses in explicit enough fashion to render them testable.' Although a strong argument for the relevance of experimental research to linguistic theory can be made on purely methodological grounds, the success of the experimental approach will be assured only if we continue to get interesting and consistent results from our experiments. Thus far, I believe we are off to a splendid start.

Discussion

Manjari Ohala I support Bybee's call for empirical evidence rather than simply formal arguments in deciding on issues in phonological theory. However, there are problems with some of the details of the evidence she cites such that it does not unambiguosly support her position on phonological representations.

First, as mentioned by J. Ohala (this volume) part of the variation one finds in a language is due to 'down-stream' factors, i.e. not centrally programmed. Thus the variation in the perception of the 'syllabicity' of the liquid in forms such as *cursory* that Bybee reports on could be of this origin (and thus not what one would want to attribute to the speaker's mental lexicon). It has recently been shown that the duration of the liquid is the primary cue of the 'syllabicity' in such words (Semiloff 1976). And we also know from other investigations that the duration of segments can be expected to vary considerably in fluent speech, and thus it is possible that such durational variation would affect the perception of syllabicity.

In the case of the variation she reports for the Spanish /s/, I wonder if it might not be in the perception of these sounds on the part of the linguist rather than in the production of the speaker. In particular, differentiating [h] and ϕ, and even more so degrees of [h], would seem to be a very chancy thing even if one had spectrographic records.

A more substantive point, however, is that even if we accept the variation data, it does not unambiguosly support the position Bybee argues for. It is compatible with other positions. For example, investigators such as Sankoff have also noticed such variation. But they posit a single underlying form stated in terms of phonemes and then have variable rules apply to these forms. A variable rule would say that the change specified in it would have some given probability of applying in a given environment, which may include specific lexical items.

Thus both of these positions would account for the variation. However, from experiments such as those of Jaeger (1979; referred to in Nearey's paper) and Nearey's (discussed in his paper) there is evidence that native speakers of English put phonetically distinct sounds such as [k], [k^h], etc. into the same psychological category (i.e. phoneme-sized units seem to be psychologically real). And extrapolating from such experiments it seems reasonable to assume that the Spanish speaker also would consider these different [h]'s to be members of one unit. Now Sankoff would of course be able to account for this by having one underlying form (as mentioned above), but it is not at all clear how Bybee would. She might posit a rule along with these non-phonemic underlying forms and claim that the rule would somehow reflect the unity of the phonetic variants, but it is unclear to me what the input to such a rule could be.

Let us for the sake of argument even allow for these two competing positions. What we need is crucial data to decide between them. Bybee's argument, like those that she criticizes, uses mostly naturalistic evidence (or what Nearey calls ecological evidence). Such evidence is seldom conclusive, as Nearey has indicated, because it can not be gathered under sufficiently well-controlled circumstances. To decide on these and other issues in phonology what we need are more experiments. It is true that experimental results can often be interpreted in different ways, but at least then one has the opportunity to re-do the experiment and introduce whatever additional controls are necessary to make the results less ambiguous.

N. V. Smith   Ad Hooper: A psychologically real grammar is the construct of a single individual. Accordingly, arguments based on group data, esp. those derived from a comparison of disjoint dialects, are invalid. Even on the assumption that variation precisely comparable to that described for groups occurs within each individual, it is not clear that Hooper's arguments for the inclusion of sub-phonemic (phonetic) information in lexical representations succeed. Concerning the gradual phonetic change reflected in the different pronunciations of *every, memory* and *mammary*, I see no reason to ''hesitate'' in characterising the three classes described in terms of the absence or optional presence of a phonemic schwa. The phonological **representations would be respectively:** /evri:/, /mem(ə)ri:/, /mæməri:/. There is little objection to the claim that /ə/ is a phoneme of English, so the only matter of contention is the possibility of using optional elements in representations. This seems unexceptional and widespread: e.g. in my speech *deftly* is always [deftli:] but *softly* is either [softli:] or [sofli:]. Postulating an optional /t/ in *softly* accounts simply for these facts. That the distribution of /ə/ may differ from person to person is irrelevant for psychological reality. The examples of *s* aspiration in Cuban Spanish seem equally unproblematic as regards phonological representation: in all cases /s/ is underlying. If individuals show systematically different lexical sensitivity to particular rules this can be handled à la Labov.

Hyman's example of the contrast [pæt-pæ:ɖ] being reanalysed from /pæt-pæd/ to /pæt-pæ:t/ is not a problem unless one makes the unnecessary assumption that all the variation in the community is psychologically real for each member of the community at all times. The examples of boundary phenomena are equally unconvincing. Using syntactic information to predict the difference in pronunciation of *night-rate* and *nitrate* is *not* ''equivalent to saying that the phonetic features. . . are an inherent part of the word''. The syntactic information is independently necessary elsewhere in the grammar and does not allow the encoding of phonetic information except at word-boundaries. Peripheral phonemes are still *phonemes*, despite Hooper's ''reluctance'' to treat them as such. /ç/ in German, just like /ã/ in English *restaurant, fiancèe*, is phonemically contrastive. That its functional load is slight, its origin recent, its distribution from speaker to speaker different and its prognosis perhaps poor do not affect its status in the grammar of the individual using it.

It would be foolish to deny that Hooper's proposals for including phonetic information in lexical representations are possible; they may even be right. This conclusion, however, does not follow from her arguments.

Ad Nearey: Just as group data are unable to support Hooper's suggestions, so are *typological* facts irrelevant to establishing psychological reality unless one assumes that typological naturalness corresponds fairly directly to innate properties of markedness: a position Nearey doesn't mention. Without such an assumption strictly typological generalisations raise severe problems for theories seeking psychological reality, in that they express something which is not universal, and hence is unlikely to be innate, but which also belongs to no single language and hence is not obviously learnable. Something neither innate nor learned is unlikely to be psychologically real. Evidence from ''pre-literate'' subjects for the phonemic identification of the ''p'' in *spill* with the ''p'' in *pill* rather than the ''b'' in *bill*, already exists: cf. Smith (1973:58) where I give the example of the early neutral-isation of *spin, pin* and *bin* as [ɓin], but with subsequent differentiation of *spin* and *pin* as [pin] and *bin* as [bin][8]

For the rest I find myself in agreement with Nearey except that I see no reason to accept the implication that we should assign priority to experimental as opposed to formal evidence. We hardly needed experiments to confirm our feelings that *gill* is closer to *grill* than to *spill*. The wheel does not need reinventing.

John J. Ohala The concept of psychological reality and how to discover what is psychologically real has been made out to be a very subtle and/or complicated issue. I think this has been overdone and would like to attempt to simplify it by means of an extended analogy. Many of us are teachers. One of the tasks required of teachers is certification that students know certain academic material in order that they may receive a grade, a diploma, or a degree. In these cases, the teacher must, in effect, assess the psychological reality of students' knowledge or mental ability. How is this done? By obtaining some behavioral evidence, e.g., performance on a test, presentation of an original scholarly paper, etc., which evidence is consistent with the students having the knowledge or ability attributed to them. Conscientious teachers do not usually take the mere fact that the students have been exposed to the academic material as sufficient evidence that they know and understand the material. Of course, it is not easy to devise good tests and most of us therefore spend much time refining our tests. Nevertheless, I am not aware thay anyone in academia rejects, in principle, the need for such overt behavioral evidence in assessing students' knowledge and mental ability. The same practice should apply when we seek to verify the psychological reality of posited phonological constructs.

This analogy also permits us to evaluate a claim made by Fromkin at this symposium: that it is only necessary to use external evidence, including experimental evidence, to ascertain what a possible psychologically real phonological construct might be and that it is therefore not necessary to justify positing such constructs for each and every language whose sound pattern suggests the need for such constructs. If we were to apply this practice in education, which Fromkin advocates for phonology, it would mean that all we would have to do is find *one* student who demonstrated via test performance or papers that he knew the academic material and we could then assume without the necessity of behavioral evidence that all other students exposed to the same kind of material had likewise mastered it!

R. Wilbur. This discussion will focus primarily on the implications of the argumentation in Nearey's paper. It is Nearey's contention that only a model of phonology which is based on broad "empirical" data is appropriate as a linguistic model. In his summary, Nearey indicates his agreement with a quote from Ohala and Ohala (1975) that '. . . to make any experimental technique useful is to formulate our hypotheses in explicit enough fashion to render them testable.'

There is little argument that Ohala and Ohala's guideline provides the most direct route for deriving the greatest gain from an experimental endeavor. What Nearey has failed to recognize is that he is seeking answers to questions which are different from those addressed by the generative phonologists which he attacks. The aims of generative phonology include providing a model in which it is possible to address such questions as:
  a) What are the constraints on possible phonological generalizations?
  b) What is an allowable phonological rule?
  c) What do the formational characteristics of spoken and signed languages have in common?
  d) How does the phonology of one language compare to another?
  e) How do two dialects of the same language differ?
  f) What historical changes have occurred and why? What can be predicted about future changes?
The answers to such questions certainly require explicit formulation of hypotheses, but the relevant data are not that of people in a laboratory situation. The crucial data could derive from a survey of all known phonological processes, of synchronic or diachronic cross-linguistics comparisons.

The types of studies which Nearey is suggesting address themselves to how languages are processed by humans. Perception, production, acquisition, and metalinguistic judgments are things people do with language; they are not *language* itself. The aims of the models and theories are different. Language is a system. Perception, production, acquisition, and judgments are interactions with the sytem. The English language exists; a child must acquire it. No child acquires the entire language, nor do two children end up with identical knowledge of the language. The resulting knowledge depends on numerous factors, including interaction with care-givers, peers, educators, etc. Furthermore, the metalinguistic judgments which will be rendered by these children when they become adults will likely vary, for similar reasons. Why, then, should a theory of the phonology of English (or any other language) explain how a child learns it? The end result of what the child learns is a subset of the total English language. It is there where expectedness enters. Certain things the child is expected to learn (plurals, tenses) while the acquisition of other things may depend on education (learning to read, learning Latin, studying grammar). I have argued elsewhere (Wilbur, 1979) that caution is required when attempting to use child data as an argument for or against a model of adult phonology. Child data does not automatically constitute an empirical test of the adult model.

It appears that Nearey interprets "productivity" as the criterion for 'psycho-logically real.' This raises the general question of the definitions of 'psychological reality' and 'cognition' that are being used. In Wilbur and Menn (1974, 1975) we attempted to describe a model of psychological reality. This model includes four factors, each of which is a continuum itself: a) productivity, b) semantic transparency c) morphological paradigmaticity, d) phonological coherence. Notice that in this model, psychological reality is not equivalent to productivity. Thus, the absence of productivity in a laboratory situation would not be taken as conclusive evidence for the lack of psychological reality, since high salience on one of the other factors could contribute to significant psychological reality. The point is that until an explicit formulation is given to the hypothesis of psychological reality, there will be arguments as to what constitutes acceptable data or convincing tests.

Finally, as Fromkin has pointed out more recently (Keynote Presentation, Fourth Annual Boston University Conference on Language Development), before the experimental hypotheses can be formulated explicitly, one must know what phonological processes are to be tested and what would provide the crucial evidence. For that, one must start with the phonological analyses generated by the theoretical phonologist.

Chairman's Comments

Bruce L. Derwing The two papers presented in this session complement one another nicely. Both are concerned with the question of segmental phonological representations in a cognitively valid theory of language and with problems associated with the empirical justification of such a theory. Both authors are also convinced of the need to go beyond the traditional "primary" or "internal" data sources of formal descriptive linguistics in order to resolve important theoretical controversies in this area. They differ, then, primarily in the nature of the methods they employ in their quest for new, "external" data which bear on these controversies. Bybee Hooper emphasizes evidence from such underexploited sources as language change and language variation, still accessible by means of the more familiar "naturalistic" data-gathering procedures of traditional linguistic inquiry; Nearey, on the other hand (without denying the value of any of the prior data sources or methods), is more concerned with whatever relevant new kinds of evidence can be uncovered with the aid of controlled experimental techniques. There seems to be no controversy at all here regarding the "empirical" status of either brand of new evidence: both are concerned with matters of fact and may provide potentially useful barometers against which to measure the propriety of fluctuations in "received" linguistic opinion, just as both are subject to potentially devastating errors of observation, interpretation, etc. (As O. Fujimura brought out from the floor, one of the most serious of these problems is the question of how — or whether — any particular sample of data, however gathered, relates to any particular linguistic or psychological claim. See Derwing (1979) on the "interpretation problem" and Botha (1973) on the general issue of "qualitative relevance.")

As already indicated by the remarks of the other commentators, however, there are two important factors which do distinguish the former, naturalistic (or "ecological") approach and its data-product from that of the latter, or experimental. The first, of course, relates to the matter of *control*. As J. Ohala, in particular, points out in his comments, a chief advantage of the experimental approach is that it permits the investigator to focus immediately and directly onto the theoretical issue at hand: if we seek to know whether a language user knows one thing rather than (or in addition to) another, it is usually more expedient to ask him (by means of some suitable experimental design) than to wait around until he may chance to give us some relevant tidbit of spontaneous "natural" evidence. By the same token (i.e., almost as a corollary of this first point), as M. Ohala has argued, the controlled experimental evidence tends to be "crucial" or "decisive" in ways that the more haphazard, ecological evidence ordinarily cannot be. This is because the experimenter attempts to select out precisely those data which *are* crucial to a theory, rather than settling for more readily accessible, but usually far more ambiguous, "natural" data. So in the long tradition of linguistic debate based on the more "casual" and "handy" forms of data, as Smith quite correctly observes, Bybee Hooper's proposals on the question of lexical representations "are possible" and "may even be right," but this conclusion does not necessarily "follow from her arguments." This is no isolated case; the problem is endemic.

I can also sympathize with Smith on the matter of the apparent obscurity of the relationship between typological evidence (or what Nearey calls arguments of "differential expectedness") and the question of psychological reality. (This is a special case of the general "relevance" issue discussed above.) Such evidence and arguments thus provide only a very limited empirical advance, at best (just as Nearey suggests), and very tenuous support indeed for the full notational machinery associated with the so-called "simplicity" or "evaluation" metric in generative phonology (cf. Chomsky & Halle, 1968, pp. 330-399).

Smith can be strongly challenged, however, on some of his other statements. True enough, "a psychologically real grammar is the construct of a single individual." (The same, note, is true of an individual *linguist's* grammar, but with no guarantee that the latter is *psychologically* real for anybody!) From this it does not follow, however, that "arguments based on group data. . .are invalid" insofar as questions of psychological reality are concerned. Suppose that we were to discover, for example, using a variety of different experimental tests on a broad sample of typical (i.e., normal, native, adult, monolingual, linguistically naive, etc.) English speakers, that virtually all saw a clear morphological connection between such words as *teacher* and *teach*, or *quietly* and *quiet,* but only a small minority were able to do the same for a pair of words like *fabulous* and *fable* (say around 15-20%, about the same number who related *heavy* with *heave.*). On the basis of such data it would be (and is, since such experiments have, in fact, been carried out, with the results indicated; see Derwing & Nearey, in press) quite legitimate to conclude that any linguistic theory or claim based on the assumption that the latter examples need not be distinguished from the former would not likely reflect a "psychologically real" state of affairs for the vast majority of such speakers. Such "extrapolated" reasoning (i.e., from a representative sample of subjects to the population as a whole) is quite consonant with the way in which research is ordinarily carried out in psychology, since that discipline, too, is interested mainly in establishing general principles (or learning, knowledge, perception, etc.), rather than merely cataloguing isolated facts about specific individuals. It is not clear, therefore, why *linguistic psychology* (i.e. linguistics) should not do likewise.

Finally, on the matter of Smith's pooh-poohing of Nearey's and my experiments on "the phonemic membership of allophones," these are certainly not vitiated by his prior evidence from " 'pre-literate' subjects," since the data in question consist exclusively of observations by *one investigator* (himself) of the developmental behavior of *one subject* of very *suspect representativeness* (the child "of an English father and an Indian mother" who was, moreover, "exposed to a considerable amount of American English at a stage when he was gaining an at least latent knowledge of the [sic] language"). No finding from such a source, obviously, can be taken as the last word on anything. I must also dispute Smith's glib claim that we "hardly needed experiments to confirm our feeling that *gill* is closer to *grill* than to *spill*." How does Smith know, first of all, that *his* feeling is the same as "ours" (i.e., everybody else's)? Experiments could conveniently and usefully clarify this. Second, to what extent might his — and perhaps even our — judgements on such matters be influenced by the orthography of our language, rather than by its "sound system" and/or the acoustic input? (We could no doubt all have been quite easily persuaded that *truck* began with a /č/ rather than a /t/, were the conventional spelling *chruck*. See Read, 1975, for some suggestive experimental evidence that bears on this question.) Third, with the foregoing in mind, we must surely take seriously the possibility that the viable candidates for a "psychologically real" phonemicization for English may not be limited to those which appear in the "standard" linguistics texts. (Perhaps, for example, consonant clusters should all be treated as single units, rather than as sequences of separate phonemes — or perhaps entire syllables would make better feature receptacles than either segments or clusters.) We may *believe* what we like, but we won't *know* the answers until the requisite background experimental work has been carried out, controlling for factors like orthographic interference (not to mention many others which, at this very early stage in the game, we may not even have imagined as yet). Finally, to show how far, in fact, Smith really misses the point, even if we did know for sure that his personal "feeling" was quite reliable and valid in the particular case at hand, there are plenty of other cases available where controversy is rife (What is the "underlying vowel system of English," for example; should the *ng* of *sing* or the *ai* of *pain* be treated as single phonemes or as clusters — or might not quite different representations be countenanced at different "levels" or for different functions etc., etc.) and where further (psychological) evidence would surely be welcome. But if our (or any other) technique is to provide any of this evidence, the procedures involved will have to be first validated against some set of less controversial ("clear") cases, will they not? This, in fact, was our main purpose at this stage, and we must confess to making some pre-experimental (but suitably tentative) assumptions very much along the lines that Smith prescribes. (On this last issue, Smith seems to be a rather hard man to please. He can accept his own intuitions about the likely outcome of an experiment, but finds it an "insult to the intelligence" for others to do likewise. See Smith, 1975: 269, where he also rails against the adoption of certain, again quite tentative, pre-experimental assumptions about homogeneity of stimuli.)

All in all, then, there seem to be several quite good grounds here for disputing Smith's last and most important claim, namely, that there is "no reason to accept the implication that we should assign priority to experimental as opposed to formal evidence.'' The reasons are many — and all quite compelling.

THE COGNITIVE REPRESENTATION OF SPEECH
T. Myers, J. Laver, J. Anderson (editors)
© *North-Holland Publishing Company, 1981*

On the Nature of
Phonological Representation

ELISABETH O. SELKIRK

University of Massachusetts,
Amherst

What units of analysis have a place in the description of language? This question is an absolutely fundamental one in the study of language, for no research can proceed without a theory of the combinatorial building blocks out of which the utterance is built. Linguists have long debated this question, and at present still agree (in their vast majority) that a unit the size of the segment or phoneme must be posited. Perhaps less universally accepted, but nonetheless prevalent, is the notion that segments decompose into an (unordered) set of *distinctive features*. As for phonological units *above* the level of the segment, the one which has most often enjoyed some status in linguistic theory is the *syllable*, and currently it, too, is acquiring increasingly wide acceptance (overcoming its demise in American structuralist and early generative phonological theories). In each case, such units of phonological analysis are given a place in linguistic theory on the grounds that, without them, significant linguistic generalizations cannot be captured.

Units such as the feature, the segment (or phoneme), and the syllable have figured in models of speech production and perception as well. Though it is not obviously true that units of linguistic theory, a theory of competence, should necessarily have a role in theories of performance, clearly such units stand as the foremost and most serious candidates for units of performance theories. Thus much research in speech production and perception has either assumed the existence of these units, or has directly sought evidence for their existence, in models of the processing of speech.

Recent work in linguistics has focussed attention on units larger than the segment, and, while giving additional support for the syllable, has furthermore shown the necessity of positing an even richer array of types above the level of the syllable. The postulation of a rather richly structured phonological representation, such as that illustrated in Figures 1 and 2, represents a radical departure from standard approaches to phonology (e.g. Chomsky and Halle (1968)). It is justified insofar as it permits a more insightful explanation of phonological phenomena than was available in terms of the more impoverished, and restrictive, theories which do not impute a hierarchical structuring to the phonological representation. And indeed, as

 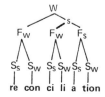

Figure 1

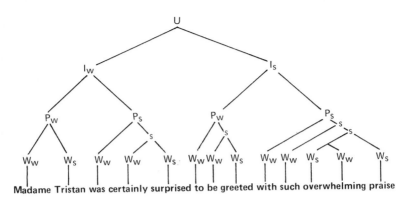

Figure 2

will be seen below, the theory of suprasegmental phonological structure being proposed here does permit a far more satisfactory treatment of a number of important areas of phonology, e.g. those concerning phonotactics, stress and prominence relations, and the characterization of the domains of phonological rules, among others.

This work on the units of phonological representation incorporates and develops an extremely important idea concerning the representation of stress or prominence put forth by Liberman (1975), and elaborated in numerous publications since (cf. especially Liberman and Prince (1977); also Kiparsky, 1979; McCarthy, 1979; Selkirk, 1980; Prince, 1980; Selkirk, forthcoming; Vergnaud and Halle, in preparation). Liberman argued that stress — at both the word and phrasal levels — must be represented as a relation *between* elements, rather than as a property *of* an element, as had been the case in standard treatments (cf. Chomsky and Halle 1968), which saw stress uniquely as a feature of individual vowels. Specifically, it was proposed that a phonological representation be thought of as consisting of a binary-branching tree (dominating the "terminal" sequence of segments) wherein one sister node is always strong (s) with respect to the other (labelled w for weak). A representation such as this represents prominence relations directly, not in terms of a feature [n stress]. (See Rischel (1961) and Fisher-Jørgenson (1948) for slightly different articulations of this same fundamental idea.) This idea, argued for at length and for a wide variety of cases, in the works cited, is adopted here, but in somewhat modified form. The modification consists essentially in the postulation of units or levels of analysis which provide a rather richer and more specific articulation of the phonological representation. (See Pike (1967) and Lehiste (1970) for some development of a not dissimilar notion of hierarchically arranged phonological units.) It has been shown that the postulation of such units is necessary for, among other things, a completely suprasegmental representation of the prominence relations which Liberman's system seeks to describe (cf. Selkirk, 1980; Selkirk, forthcoming; Vergnaud and Halle, in preparation; Prince, 1980).

The examination of stress, vowel quantity relations and other phonological phenomena within the word in a wide variety of languages has led to the positing of a unit of analysis, properly phonological (i.e. not syntactic) in character, that one might call the *prosodic* (or accentual) *word* (symbolized W), and to the postulation of a unit of analysis intermediary between the syllable (symbolized S) and the prosodic word which has been referred to as the *foot* or *stress foot* (symbolized F). (Cf. Selkirk, 1978, 1980, forthcoming; Vergnaud and Halle, in preparation; Prince, 1980. [Note that this term *foot* is not to be confused with the Abercrombian foot (cf. Abercrombie (1964)), which has its place in the description of rhythm, rather than stress patterns.] The examples of Figure 1 illustrate the place of such higher order units in the underlying representation of English words. (For the sake of expediency, I will not be considering, or attempting to represent, suprasegmental structure internal to the syllable, such as the grouping of segments into onset and rime, and nucleus and coda. (See Selkirk, (forthcoming); Fujimura and Lovins (1978), Fudge (1969), for some treatment of this question.) The examination of phrasal stress, rhythm, and intonation, as well as the operation of rules of segmental phonology beyond the level of the word (external sandhi), has led to the postulation of a certain number of yet higher-order units in phonology, such as the phonological phrase (symbolized *P*), the intonational phrase (symbolized *I*), and the utterance (symbolized *U*) (Selkirk, forthcoming; Bing, 1979; Mitchell, 1979). The example of Figure 2 illustrates one of several possible (underlying) representations of this English sentence in terms of these units.

What role (if any) do these newly established linguistic units have in the processing of speech? Are some or all of them units of planning and production, or of perception? Do the units of word level and below come into play in lexical access? Do those above the word come into play in the parsing of sentences? These are the obvious questions to ask at this point. It is not my place to attempt some sort of answer to them. Rather, my purpose in this paper is merely to present in its grand outlines this developing conception of suprasegmental phonological representation in linguistic theory.

The phonological units alluded to here will be referred to as *prosodic categories*, and the hierarchically arranged suprasegmental portion of phonological representation will be referred to as *prosodic structure*. The term ''category'' is chosen consciously in order to evoke a very apt analogy to the categories of syntax. The notion ''category'' is central to syntactic analysis. In defining a set of syntactic categories, e.g. Noun Phrase (NP), Sentence (S), Adjective (Adj.), etc. . . (cf. Chomsky, 1965; Jackendoff, 1977), and the relations between these, basic generalizations about what constitutes a syntactically well-formed sentence of a language may be stated. (In a generative grammar, these statements about phrase structure take the form of context free rewriting rules; these are said to generate the underlying syntactic representation of a sentence (i.e., its deep structure).) And these categories themselves are constitutive of the syntactic representation of a particular sentence: a syntactic representation is hypothesized to be a (hierarchically arranged) tree structure whose nodes are labelled in terms of syntactic categories, e.g. NP, N, S, etc. Evidence that this categorial information must be available in a syntactic representation comes from the operation of rules of the grammar which ''look at'' syntactic representation — transformations, rules of semantic interpretation, and so on. These rules must ''know'' about the categorial composition of a sentence; they must ''know'', for example, that some string of phonemes constitutes a noun phrase and not a verb phrase. A phonological representation, I am arguing here, is no different from a syntactic representation on that score. Information about the analysis of a sentence into prosodic categories must form part of that representation, for rules of the phonological component require it. This includes familiar rules of segmental phonology, whose characteristic domains of application are defined in terms of this prosodic structure, as well as what may be called rules of phonetic interpretation. Moreover, prosodic categories can be shown to be necessary for expressing generalizations in the grammar about the phonological well-formedness of utterances of a language. It is through defining the prosodic categories and the relations that may obtain between them that statements can be made (a) about the phonotactics of an utterance, e.g. the distribution of possible sequences of segments, and (b) about the stress or prominence relations within an utterance.

The combinatorial possibilities of prosodic categories are far more restricted than those of syntactic categories. Suppose the prosodic categories were identified with integers, with *1* being assigned to the segment, *2* to the syllable, *3* to the stress foot, *4* to the prosodic word, *5* to the phonological phrase, *6* to the intonational phrase and *7* to the utterance. In general, it is true that a prosodic category of level *n* is defined as consisting of categories of level *n-1*. For example, a syllable is constituted of segments, a stress foot of syllables, a prosodic word of stress feet, and so on, as in Figures 1 and 2. Languages will differ in details concerning what sub-types of categories of level *n-1* go into making up categories of level *n*, e.g., what types of segments in what order may constitute a syllable, or what types of syllables in what order may constitute stress feet. For example, an English syllable-initial consonant cluster may contain two obstruents only if the first is an *s*. And the English stress foot may consist of a single heavy syllable, while in other languages this is not allowed. Clearly, the grammar of English must contain statements to this effect. Furthermore, languages will differ in details concerning the relations between the categories of type *n-1* dominated by the category of *n*. It has been argued that when more than two constituents of level *n-1* are contained within a *n* category they group into a left branching structure, e.g., C_n [[C_{n-1} C_{n-1}] C $_{n-1}$] C_n or a right branching structure, e.g., C_n [C_{n-1} [C_{n-1} C_{n-1}]] C_n, depending on the particular category, and on the particular language. (See especially Vergnaud and Halle (in preparation).) In English, according to Liberman (1975), Liberman and Prince (1977), and Selkirk (1980), a tri-syllabic stress foot is left-branching, while a prosodic word groups feet in a right branching structure. So the grammar of English, or of any language, must include statements governing the proper branching relations within the various prosodic categories. These statements and the sort mentioned just before will be referred to as *principles of structure*. They may be thought of as well-formedness conditions on *underlying* phonological representation.)

Intimately connected to principles of structure are a second type of well-formedness conditions which will be referred to as *principles of prominence*. These concern the strong/weak relations among the nodes of the tree. Within the English prosodic word, for example, a righthand node is labelled *s* just in case it branches (cf. Liberman (1975), Liberman and Prince (1977)), where the branching internal to the foot "counts" with respect to this principle (compare the two examples of Figure 1). Like in English, the prosodic word in French is right-branching, but in French, a righthand node in *W* will always be labelled *s*, regardless of whether it branches or not (cf. Selkirk (1979, forthcoming)). (The effect of this principle in French is to assure final stress.) The principles for assigning s and w are in large part predictable given the branching properties of the tree (cf. Vergnaud and Halle, in preparation), but, as the differences between English and French show, certain details must nonetheless be stated in the grammars of individual languages.

It would undoubtedly be useful to examine in somewhat more detail some examples of how this theory is put into practice. The examples will be drawn from English. We will first look at how the phonotactics (i.e. possible distributions of segment and syllable types) and the stress patterns of words can be treated in a unified and explanatory fashion by this theory. Then we will touch on the treatment afforded of stress and intonational phenomena above the level of the word, a treatment which at the same time offers a characterization of what one might call the phonotactics of the utterance.

The necessity of giving the category syllable a role in phonological description is by now amply demonstrated (see Bell and Hooper (1978) and the references cited therein; on English, see especially Fudge (1969), Kahn (1976) and Selkirk (1979, forthcoming)). Assume that the word (where here I use the term loosely) is a sequence of syllables. Clearly, then, by defining what sequences of segments may constitute a syllable we have a definition of what sequences of segments may constitute a word. It is predicted that the sequences permitted word-initially are those permitted syllable-initially, those permitted word-finally are the possible syllable-final ones, and word-medial sequences are only those made possible by the juxtaposition of syllables. In general, this prediction is borne out. We see, then, that by positing a combinatorial unit syllable one can considerably simplify the statements a grammar makes about the phonotactics of the word, which in this case is to say that the grammar is able to capture real generalizations about it. Further justification for positing the syllable, in English and other languages, comes from the operation of phonological rules, which apply to a representation, and must "know" what the analysis of a word into syllables is. It is known, for example, that the rule in English governing the aspiration of voiceless stops applies only to those stops in syllable-initial position (cf. Hoard (1971), Kahn (1976), and references therein). Another well-known example comes from German, where syllable-final consonants are devoiced (cf. Venneman, 1972). Additional examples of phonological rules which are sensitive to the composition of the utterance in terms of syllables abound. The conclusion that must be drawn is that the unit syllable has a place *in the phonological representation*: *Syllable* must "label" the appropriate nodes in the hierarchy. Here, then, is an instance of the convergence mentioned above between units of distribution (phonotactics) and units serving as characteristic domains for phonological rules. This convergence is explained by assuming that the units of phonotactics form part of the representation and are thus made available to processes which "look at" or interpret that representation.

Next I will briefly describe the well-formedness conditions on stress feet in English. The analysis presented here is developed at greater length in Selkirk (1980, forthcoming). First of all, one must distinguish the three basic syllable types of the language. One type, symbolized CV, consists of a lax vowel in an open syllable; a second type, symbolized CVC, contains a lax vowel and is closed by one or more consonants; the third type, symbolized $C\bar{V}$, consists of a tense (long) vowel (and may also be closed by one or more consonants). Stress feet in English fall into essentially three types, depending in part on their composition in terms of these syllable types:

   (i) $F = [[CVC]_S]$ or $[[C\bar{V}]_S]$
  (ii) $F = [[S]_S [CV(C)]_W]$
 (iii) $F = [[[S]_S [CV]_W]_S [CV(C)]_W]$

The first is monosyllabic, consisting of either sort of heavy syllable, CVC or $C\bar{V}$. The second is bisyllabic, with a syllable (S) of any type (CV, $C\bar{V}$, or CVC) as its first strong element, and a lax vowel syllable, open or closed, as its second weak element. The third type is trisyllabic, with a syllable of any type as its first, strong, element, a CV as its second and a CV or CVC as its third. My claim is that a syllable of English is "stressed" if it is the strong, i.e. *s*, element of a stress foot. There is only one strong syllable per F, i.e. one "stressed" syllable per F. (In (i), the lone syllable is considered to be *s*; this follows from a general convention according to which one prosodic category exhaustively dominated by another is always interpreted as a strong within it (cf. Selkirk (1980, forthcoming)).) (i) through (iii) are well-formedness conditions. Note that they embody both principles of structure, specifying what syllable types fit where and what their branching relations are (the F is left branching in English, cf. (iii)), as well as principles of prominence, according to which constituents of F are in a s-w relation. The function of (i) - (iii) is to contribute to a definition of what constitutes a well-formed (underlying) phonological representation in English. In essence, they allow for the expression of generalizations about the distribution of stressed and unstressed syllables within the word. Specifically, the claim is that a word in English is to be analyzed as a sequence of stress feet in underlying representation; in other words, all syllables of a word belong to some stress foot. Put another way, a possible word of English is claimed to consist of a sequence of syllables which is parsable into come combination of stress feet as defined in (i) - (iii).

The following generalizations about the stress patterns of English words are captured in a straightforward way by this theory. (a) A CV syllable is always stressed, eg. *dáta, rótàte, éulogìze*, etc. (Note that tense vowels produced by phonological rule, and hence not present in underlying representation, are not subject to this generalization. These include certain word-final tense vowels, eg. *ágency*, and those in prevocalic position, eg. *álien*, See Chomsky and Halle (1968) for some discussion of this matter.) This follows from the fact that (in this theory) CV̄ is either a F on its own, and therefore strong, or it occupies the strong position of a polysyllabic F. It is never in a weak position in a F. (b) A CVC may be stressed, under any circumstance. This is because it may be a F on its own, as in *cónvìct, cátamaràn, angína, detéct, gýmnàst*, or the strong element of a polysyllabic F, eg. *áctress, wínter, mándarin, éxercìze*. (c) A CVC may be stressless, eg. *vérdict, rēcompènse, ánecdòte, hýmnal, dígital, cátalyst*, for it may be in a weak position in a F as well. (Note that, according to (iii), it is claimed that no CVC ever occupies second position in a trisyllabic foot, which is to say that no stressless CVC may be followed in turn by another stressless syllable in English. This seems to be a correct prediction). (d) As for the CV syllable type, the generalization is that it may be stressed only if followed by at least one stressless syllable, eg. *Àlabáma, América, inítial, Cánada, mètricálity*. This is because a CV is claimed not to be a F on its own, and so is only strong with respect to a following syllable within a polysyllabic F. It is correctly predicted, therefore, that no stressed CV is possible word-finally (eg. **Senecá*), or within a word immediately before another stressed syllable (eg. **Japánèse* vs *Jápanèse*). There are two circumstances, however, where stressed CV are found without a following stressless syllable and these are not yet explained, given the theory laid out so far. One is the case of monosyllabic words such as *spá*. The other is the case of stressed initial CV, as in *sátìre, Wábàsh, ràccóon*. Given our approach these are all instances of a F constituted of a lone CV, something not allowed by (i) - (iii). I would claim that the grammar of English need not explicitly mention the possibility of a CV stress foot in these circumstances but rather that the existence of them follows from two other principles. The first principle is that well-formedness conditions may have a directionality, i.e. may be thought of as "applying" either from left to right or right to left. Given this, it is the word-initial syllable that might be left over, "unfootable" with respect to (i) - (iii). The second principle requires that all syllables belong to a stress foot in underlying representation. This second principle assures that the "left over" initial CV syllable or the CV monosyllable will be "footed" regardless of whether it is provided for explicitly by the well-formedness conditions of the language. We see, then, that (i) - (iii) in addition to two additional general principles correctly predict the patterns of stressing CV. (e) CV may be stressless, e.g. *Cánada*, for it may occupy the weak position of a stress foot. (Note that there is so far no way of accounting for an initial stressless CV followed by a stressed syllable, as in *América*. I would claim that in underlying representation that syllable is a F, as in *sàtíre*; it is "defooted", i.e. "destressed", in the course of the derivation of phonetic representation (cf. Selkirk, 1980). (f) At most two stressless syllables may be found at the end of a word, and at most two stressless syllables intervene between two stressed syllables. This follows from the fact that a F has at most two weak syllables following the strong one.

Obviously there is more to be said about English word stress. With this overbrief discussion I hope merely to have shown that by positing a combinatorial unit stress foot one can neatly capture the generalizations concerning the patterns of stressed and unstressed syllables in English. One can also do away with a segmental feature [n stress]: syllable stress in this sytem is entirely a matter of the prosodic hierarchy, of whether a syllable is *s* within a stress foot.

The *relative* prominence of stressed syllables within a word is to be seen as following from the relations of the stress feet (F) to which they belong within the prosodic word (W). As can be seen in Figure 2, F are grouped into a right branching structure in W: this is the principle of structure for W. The principle of prominence, as first set out by Liberman and Prince (1977), is (roughly) that within W a righthand node (of the level of F or above) will be strong just in case it branches. Compare *cátamaràn*, whose righthand F does not branch and is hence, *w*, to *rèconcìliátion*, where the righthand F branches, as does the node directly above it. In this system, then, the syllable which has the primary stress of a word is that one which is dominated only by *s* nodes within W.

Evidence that these units F and W, which are crucial to describing patterns of stress, do actually form part of (i.e., "label" the nodes of) a phonological representation comes again from the rules of the phonology. It can be argued, for example, that the F is crucial as a domain for processes involved in the converting of the phonemes /t/ or /d/ to the flap [D] in English. (cf. Kiparsky 1979, Selkirk forthcoming.) As for the W, it is in terms of this unit that any processes said to apply "word-finally" or "word-initially" apply. In English, this includes word-final lengthening, word-final tensing of non-low vowels, etc. See Selkirk (forthcoming) for more discussion of these matters.

To sum up thus far, we have seen that by positing the units of linguistic analysis syllable, stress foot and prosodic word, and specifying well-formedness conditions for each type, one is able to express in eminently simple fashion generalizations about the distribution of segments, the distribution of stress vs. stressless syllables and the position of the primary-stressed syllable within the word. Prosodic categories such as these are the linchpins of phonology. Essential to a description of suprasegmental phenomena such as stress, they are also just those units which allow for a correct characterization of the domains of rules of segmental phonology. Only given a phonological representation of the type proposed here can this convergence between the suprasegmental and the segmental be explained.

There is unfortunately not the space here to elaborate in any detail on the other higher order prosodic categories which, I would argue, must be posited in order to describe both the suprasegmental and the segmental phonology of words in combination. So I will simply review them and some of their more interesting features. The existence of a unit which will be called the utterance (U) will simply be taken for granted. It will normally correspond to a single "highest" sentence (which may include embedded sentences), and may sometimes include more than one. The utterance is a unit of phonological representation, of prosodic structure. We know so far that it must be seen as consisting of a sequence of prosodic words. Do these prosodic words show any tendency to group together in particular ways? If so, according to what principles? The answer to the first question is yes. It can be shown that the utterance manifests a rather complex internal phonologically-related phrasing, and that this phrasing can be explained in terms of two additional types of prosodic categories—which will be called the intonational phrase (I) and the phonological phrase (P). The claim is that suprasegmental phenomena such as intonation, phrase stress and rhythm, and segmental phenomena such as external sandhi, rely crucially on the parsing of the utterance into these phrase types.

Briefly, then, the utterance is to be seen as consisting of one or more intonational phrases. The intonational phrase is the unit with which an intonational melody, which has at most one nuclear tone, is associated. In particular, the nuclear tone is associated with the primary-stressed element of I. (See Liberman (1975), Ladd (1978), Bing (1979) on the analysis of intonational melodies and their relation to stress. Other phenomena, like final lengthening, certain rhythmic effects, and even inter-word segmental rules such as voicing assimilation may be associated with the intonational phrase domain (cf. Selkirk (forthcoming)). The following sentences of

English are U consisting of more than one I (an I is parenthesized): (a) (*Some of us think that Jáne*), (*who wórks too hard*), (*should take more vacátions*). (b) (*After five months awáy,*) (*Jane returned to work much refréshed.*) (c) (*Mme. Tristan was certainly surprísed*) (*to be greeted with such overwhelming práise.*) In (a) and (b), the phrasing is obligatory: non-restrictive relatives and preposed adverbials seem to always be I on their own, thereby imposing a parsing into I on either side of them. (in (c), this phrasing is optional: there need not be a nuclear tone on *surprised*). The entire sentence could be uttered as a single I. With certain sentences, then, options are available. In Figure 2, we see the sentence of (c) parsed into the two I. The second I is labelled *s*, the first *w*. At this level, this labelling is taken to reflect the greater prominence (= pitch range) manifested by the final nuclear tone (a fall or rise) in the sentence. In keeping with the general approach (cf. Liberman, 1975; Vergnaud and Halle, in preparation), I will assume that with three or more I, there is a right branching structure (though one needn't insist on this). The rightmost I (and any nodes dominating it) will be *s*.

It can be argued that the intonational phrase itself has a complex internal structure, and, in particular, that it is constituted of units of a level intermediate between it and prosodic word. These are the phonological phrases. The existence of such an intermediary level is pointed to be a variety of phenomena (cf. Selkirk, forthcoming). Most important, perhaps, is the fact that there exist local stress prominences within the I. In the sentence (c), for example, the words *Tristan, surprised, greeted* and *praise* are prominent with respect to their (weaker) neighbors. In the framework being developed here, these locally prominent W are construed as being the ''main-stressed'' elements of phonological phrases, those W labelled *s* and dominated only by *s* in P (cf. Figure 2). Were the I not to be seen as consisting of some such phrasing, the existence of local stress prominences, and their regular correspondences to constituents of syntactic structure (to which we turn below), would go unexplained. So the I consists of P. The rightmost of the P will (in general) be the strongest (i.e. labelled *s*) and as a consequence it is the ''main-stressed'' W of that strongest P which bears the nuclear tone of the intonational melody. (It will be assumed that when an I consists of more than one P, it groups them in a right-branching structure, the righthand nodes of which are labelled *s* (the others *w*).) Finally, the phonological phrase consists of W, grouped essentially into a right-branching tree with, in the case of ''neutral stress'', the righthand nodes labelled *s* (cf. Figure 2). (Divergences from ''neutral stress'' are divergences from final primary stress, which in this framework means the *s* labelling of some non-righthand node.) The P serves as well as the characteristic domain of a variety of phonological processes, in English and other languages, including the rule of Rhythmic Reversal (cf. Liberman and Prince (1977), which produces *thírteèn mén* from *thìrteén mén*, or *óverwhèlming práise* from *òverwhélming práise*, or the rules involved in *liaison* in French, (cf. Selkirk, 1979, forthcoming).

In sum, the picture of a phonological representation that emerges here is one that is not so radically different in character from a syntactic representation. The key elements are the categories, which are hierarchically arranged. For each category the grammar specifies some set of well-formedness conditions. And, finally, these categories figure in the formulation of processes which apply to the representation. Of course this phonological representation is not identical to a syntactic representation. What, then, *is* the relation between the prosodic structure of a sentence and its syntactic structure? It is to this question that we now turn.

In a generative grammar, the output of the syntactic component provides the basis for the input to the phonological component. That is, the phonological component is seen as interpretive of the syntax. More precisely, a relation is defined in the grammar between a syntactic representation s_n and a phonological representation p_1. s_n is the *surface structure* of a sentence and p_1 is the *underlying phonological* representation, which is related to a representation p_n, the *phonetic* representation, by rules of the phonological component. Clearly, the syntactic representation s_n cannot be seen as isomorphic to the phonological representation p_1. What is a syntactic representation? It is a well-formed labelled tree, or bracketing, such as that in Figure 3. The phonological representation, too, is a well-formed labelled bracketing or tree, as illustrated in Figure 2. (The structure below the level of W, which has the general characteristics illustrated in Figure 1, has been omitted, for simplicity's sake, from Figure 2.) But the differences are considerable. First and most obviously, the categories of the syntax are not the same as the categories of the phonology. And, moreover, there are no syntactic analogues to the strong / weak relations of the phonology, which are represented as annotations of nodes in a representation. The second important difference is that there is no direct correspondence between the constituents (the words and phrases) of the syntax and those of the phonology. For example, there is no word internal syntactic branching to a monomorphemic word like *catamaran*, yet it has an elaborate structuring in terms of syllables and stress feet. Or, consider the fact that where there *is* syntactic branching, as above the level of the word, the branching of the prosodic structure will not necessarily correspond to it. Compare Figure 2, where the phonological phrases are *Mme. Tristan, was certainly surprised, to be greeted,* and *with such overwhelming praise.* None of these sequences, except the first, form constituents in syntactic representation. What this non-isomorphism attests to is the fact that the relation, or mapping, which must be defined between syntactic representation and phonological representation is not a trivial one.

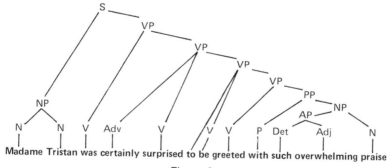

Figure 3

In what terms is this mapping to be defined? A reasonable answer is that the well-formedness conditions for prosodic categories, made specific to designated syntactic domains, *are* the mapping. Speaking loosely, the well-formedness conditions could be seen as taking as input the terminal string of segments of syntactic representation and giving as output a well-formed prosodic structure. With this conception of things, then, the well-formedness conditions must be seen as conditions on *underlying* phonological representation. (In this view, they are not necessarily directly relevant to characterizing possible prosodic structures of the phonetic representation, p_n. Clearly, phonological rules bring about changes in prosodic structure, especially in the area of syllable structure, and it is not at all obvious that the output of these rules always conforms to the well-formedness conditions.) It should be noted that one undoubtedly controversial claim being made by considering the prosodic well-formedness conditions to characterize underlying phonological representation is that stress or prominence relations are defined at the outset, not by rules in the course of a phonological derivation.

The final point to understand about the mapping is that the well-formedness conditions apply in such a way as to respect, or take note of, certain features of syntactic representation. A phonological phrase, for example, always ends with the head of a major syntactic phrase. As for the intonational phrase, though it is extremely variable in its composition, its limits will nonetheless always correspond to the limits of certain types of syntactic phrases, such as parentheticals or non-restrictive relative clauses. As for the prosodic word, it may include more than a single syntactic word, as is the case in French or Arabic, where pronouns form part of the same accentual unit as the verb or noun to which they attach, or it may include less than the syntactic word, as in English, where the so-called neutral affixes are not part of the prosodic word. In the grammar of each language, the syntactic domain over which the well-formedness of a prosodic category is defined must be stipulated. Languages may differ significantly in this respect. (See Selkirk (forthcoming) for a full examination of the relation between syntax and phonology in a generative grammar.)

A last claim that I wish to make is that phonological rules are sensitive to prosodic structure, but not to syntactic structure. This would follow if, as has been suggested, syntactic structure does not form part of phonological representation. What this means is that phonetic effects such as rhythm, or final lengthening, or the realization of intonation contours, cannot be seen as depending directly on syntactic structure (contrary to what many scholars, such as Cooper (1975) or Klatt (1975) have assumed). Rather, in this theory, prosodic structure mediates between syntax and phonetic realization, and it is in terms of it that all aspects of phonetic interpretation are to be explained. Time will tell whether the predications of this theory, a far more restrictive and hence more interesting theory of phonology and its relation to syntax than the standard variety, continue to be borne out in fact. The implications of this theory for a theory of sentence processing should be clear.

THE COGNITIVE REPRESENTATION OF SPEECH
T. Myers, J. Laver, J. Anderson (editors)
© *North-Holland Publishing Company, 1981*

On Intonational Universals

D. ROBERT LADD, JR.

Cornell University

TWO HYPOTHESES

This paper discusses two opposing views on the analysis of intonation and its place in language, views which I will refer to as the "Strong Universalist Hypothesis (SUH)" and the "Nuclear Tone Hypothesis (NTH)". I hope to show that the SUH, for all its attractiveness and its apparent power and simplicity, is excessively Procrustean in the way it treats individual langauages, and that the NTH, though superficially less ambitious in the claims it makes about intonational universals, is nonetheless far superior in the analysis of individual languages and more revealing about the features that languages share.

Three questions are central to the debate, and they are appropriate questions to the theme of this symposium. First, to what extent is intonational function innately specified or physiologically natural? Second, to what extent do the primitives "Rise" and "Fall" permit adequate description or representation of the intonational systems of the world's languages? And third, to what extent is "accent" or "prominence" perceptually and cognitively associated with pitch peaks and pitch obtrusions?

The Strong Universalist Hypothesis   These three questions are actually logically independent, but in practice those who strongly support universality or innateness generally base their arguments on similarities in the use of rises and falls in different languages and on the frequent association of perceived accent with a substantial pitch jump or prominence. That is, the SUH makes the following claims:
— The linguisitc functions of intonation are innately specified and/or respond to natural physiological states of the speaker.
— There are two primary functions, which are formally separate and to some extent unrelated, namely, the signalling of accent (prominence, emphasis, etc.) and the signalling of phrase boundaries, questions, statements, etc.
— Accent is signalled primarily by pitch peak or pitch obtrusion, resulting from increased muscular tension which reflects the speaker's insistence on (or perhaps special interest in) the accented word or syllable.
— Phrasing and sentence-types are signalled primarily by high or rising pitch at the end of incomplete or unresolved phrases or utterances, and low or falling pitch at the end of complete or final ones, resulting from either sustained or reduced muscular tension which again reflect the speaker's intention either to continue or to stop. The use of high or rising terminals for "question intonation" signals incompleteness or lack of resolution at the discourse level, with one speaker inviting resolution (i.e. response) from the other speaker.
While this statement of the SUH is an abstraction or idealization, its elements

are found in such works as Lieberman (1967), Bolinger (1949, 1962, 1964, and esp. 1978), Gardiner (1977) and Cruttenden (1979).

The Nuclear Tone Hypothesis   The most explicit statement of the NTH is presented for English in my dissertation (Ladd, 1980), but as I show there, it represents a synthesis of a good deal of past work, and as I hope to show here, it can be applied to languages other than English and provides a universally-applicable basis for understanding the relationship between pitch contour and accent. The NTH makes the following claims:
— Stress and intonation are assumed to be cognitively and functionally separate but perceptually and phonetically interdependent, like rhythm and melody in music. Stress patterns, including the major prominences or accents, are seen as abstract relations among syllables in an utterance, relations that determine (among other things) the alignment or association of the syllables with the pitch contour of the utterance. This "alignment" does not mean, as in the universalist's straight phonetic approach to accent, that the accented syllable occurs with a pitch peak or pitch obtrusion. For example, in English

(1)   ⌒◞

   Wonderful

the accent is signalled by the association of the (lexically) stressed syllable *won-* with the *nucleus* (not the pitch peak) of a particular nuclear tone, in this instance a "scooped" falling tone ⌒◞. Such cases are difficult to handle if accent is seen as a function of pitch prominence. (For details see Ladd, 1980 Ch. 2.)
— The pitch contour centered on the nuclear syllable is assumed to include the pitch movements that follow that syllable, up to the next such syllable or tone group boundary. Thus the pitch peaks and phrase-final contours that are kept separate in the universalist view are combined, which means a wider variety of basic units than just prominence, rise, and fall. The nuclear tone anlysis of English, for example, includes at least Fall, Fall-Rise, High-Rise, and Low-Rise, with others such as the scooped fall just mentioned perhaps representing modifications of the basic units.

— Languages may have different inventories of nuclear tones just as they have different segmental inventories, and the function of "the same" tone in different languages may be different. This is not to claim that there are no universals, but simply that there *are* conventional, language-specific contours. What is universal, or at least widespread, is that many languages have the same *kind* of unit—the nuclear tone. This conception of the universal and the language-specific is well expressed by Trim in the introduction to his nuclear-tone analysis of German:

> "in [German], too, relevance attaches to choices made in connection with certain stressed syllables. It is not, of course, a question of transferring the system, complete with symbols and conventions *en bloc*, but rather of applying the same principles of representation to a body of bahavior which is rather differently organized" (Trim, 1964: 374).

The universal traits emphasized by proponents of the SUH—common symbolic themes in rises and falls, highs and lows—are taken by the NTH to represent sound symbolism of the sort found in segmental phonology in e.g. the relation between high vowels and words denoting smallness; the sound symbolism is in some sense present along with the conventional meaning of a given unit.

The NTH view of the relation between stress and intonation is related to the autosegmental concept of "tune-text association" (Goldsmith, 1976), and is compatible with the rhythmic view of stress proposed by Martin (1972), Liberman and Prince (1977), and Selkirk (this volume).The nuclear tone analysis of English intonation is based specifically on the British tradition (e.g. Palmer, 1922; Kingdon, 1958; Crystal 1969), but the general notion of different meaningful contours associated with accented syllables is found in such otherwise incompatible analyses as Liberman (1978) and Bolinger's accent analysis (1958).

Testing the Two Hypotheses One would think that the disagreement between the two approaches just sketched should be relatively simply resolved with recourse to actual language data—either languages do use intonation the same way, or they don't; either prominence, rise, and fall are enough to describe intonation systems, or they aren't. Unfortunately, there is a recurring difficulty in comparing analyses, which seems to doom our deliberations to inconclusiveness, namely the supposed dichotomy between "grammatical" and "affective" uses of intonation. The problem is as follows.

Consider what we might call "comma intonation" in English as compared to many other languages of Europe. In French, German, and Rumanian, to name only a few, comma pauses are generally preceded by a high and/or rising contour, while in English they are normally preceded by a fall-rise. Thus:

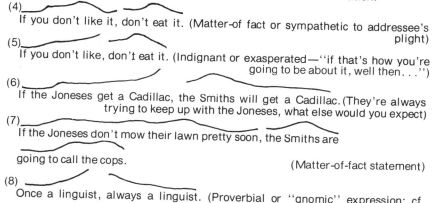

(2)
In English, before commas, we find a fall-rise.

whereas

(3)
En francais, devant les virgules, on trouve une intonation ascendante.

This difference is a well-known problem in foreign language teaching (cf. Delattre, 1963; Bolinger 1964, 1978), and from the non-universalist point of view looks like pretty good evidence that English and French use intonation differently. From the universalist standpoint, however, the terminal rise of the English fall-rise can be treated separately, and the claim that "rises" are used before comma pauses in both languages is thereby confirmed. (An alternate version of this analysis is simply that "Fall-rise is a type of rise.")

Additional data get us no farther. The French-style high-rise does occur before comma pauses in English, in a variety of contexts whose common theme seems to be that what follows is somehow expected or formulaic—lists, proverbs, and sentences where the constituent following the comma contains little new information:

(4)
If you don't like it, don't eat it. (Matter-of fact or sympathetic to addressee's plight)

(5)
If you don't like, don't eat it. (Indignant or exasperated—"if that's how you're going to be about it, well then. . .")

(6)
If the Joneses get a Cadillac, the Smiths will get a Cadillac. (They're always trying to keep up with the Joneses, what else would you expect)

(7)
If the Joneses don't mow their lawn pretty soon, the Smiths are

going to call the cops. (Matter-of-fact statement)

(8)
Once a linguist, always a linguist. (Proverbial or "gnomic" expression; cf. Bolinger, 1964: 295).

The NTH takes this as evidence against the view that fall-rise is simply a variant on the universal theme "rise", and treats fall-rise and high-rise as two distinct units in the intonational system of English. The universalist view does not deny the existence of the intonational nuance involved in (4) through (8), but argues instead that it is not relevant to the analysis of the intonation system on the grounds that it is an "affective" distinction rather than a "grammatical" one. (Cf. for example Lieberman's dismissal of the British nuclear tone tradition 1967: 174-5.)

In the absence of any clear definition of "grammatical" and "affective", then, arguments about the analysis of intonation are essentially arguments about *what data to account for.* (For a full discussion of this problem see Ladd, 1980: Ch. 5.) With regard to the specific issues under discussion here, we see that as long as the grammatical-affective dichotomy can be invoked, universalist analyses can generally ignore certain data that are taken into account in nuclear-tone analyses, and the latter can be recast in universalist terms. What this means is that the only conclusive way for the NTH to refute the SUH is on the basis of data in which the function of the intonational contrasts is uncontroversially grammatical. It is for this reason that the rest of the paper is based on a discussion of yes/no question intonation in Rumanian and Hungarian.

YES/NO QUESTIONS IN RUMANIAN AND HUNGARIAN

This section is based both on my own recent observations and on numerous published descriptions (see list of references). Data are presented both from the "standard" or capital-city varieties of Rumanian and Hungarian and from the speech of educated speakers of both languages in Transylvania. For those to whom Transylvania is only the mythical home of Dracula, a bit of geographical and sociolinguistic background may be in order. The region is currently part of Rumania, but for at least eight or nine centuries there have been large populations of both Rumanians and Hungarians living there, and until 1918 the area was ruled to one extent or another by Hungarian noblemen. Today most Hungarians speak Rumanian but a good many Rumanians also speak at least some Hungarian, and Hungarian language and culture continue to flourish. The main point here is that the two languages have been in extensive contact for a long time. The other relevant point of background for what follows is that Hungarian has fixed first-syllable word stress, while Rumanian has phonemic stress that is approximately as predictable as in English.

Standard Hungarian The typical description of yes/no question intonation in standard Hungarian states that the penultimate syllable of the utterance has high pitch, followed by a steep fall and low pitch on the final syllable. The placement of the high pitch peak is said not to depend on word stress. Thus:

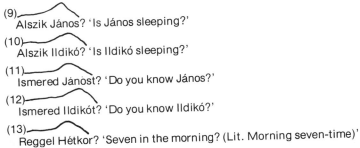

(9) Alszik János? 'Is János sleeping?'

(10) Alszik Ildikó? 'Is Ildikó sleeping?'

(11) Ismered Jánost? 'Do you know János?'

(12) Ismered Ildikót? 'Do you know Ildikó?'

(13) Reggel Hétkor? 'Seven in the morning? (Lit. Morning seven-time)'

This contour is said to require at least three syllables for its full realization, since a two-syllable utterance that began high and ended low would be interpreted as a statement. That is, a question

(14)
Ildikó?

is readily distinguished from a statement

(15)
Ildikó

but if the penultimate-peak rule applied to two syllable utterances as well, there would be no way to determine whether

(16)
János

was a statement or a question. Hence if question intonation is to be applied to a two-syllable word, the high pitch is on the second (i.e. final) syllable, though it often falls slightly or even considerably, creating something that sounds to English ears rather like a stress on the second syllable, e.g.

(17)
János?

Monosyllabic questions are pronounced on a high, slightly rising pitch:

(18)
Pál? 'Paul?'

Some descriptions (e.g. DeSivers, Ginter and Tarnói, Koski and Mihalyfy) take note of a further phenomenon, namely that the placement of the high pitch depends in some contexts on the focus of the question. For example,

(19)
János alszik? 'Is János sleeping?'

with pitch assigned according to the rule just given, has focus or emphasis on *János* (i.e. is it János or someone else), while

(20)
János alszik?

with pitch assigned as if *alszik* were a two-syllable question, asks whether János is or is not sleeping; that is, this might be considered the "normal" intonation for this sentence. (However, it is interesting to note that this intonation is felt by native speakers to focus on the verb in the same way that (19) focuses on János, and indeed, can be used for the meaning 'is he sleeping or doing something else?' In the same way—and even more interesting from the English point of view—the intonation in (11) and (12) is also felt to focus on the verb, though again this is the "normal" intonation for these questions). As a final example, note that the intonation in (13) asks whether the hearer intends seven in the morning or the evening; the other possibility,

(21)
Reggel Hétkor?

asks about the hour (i.e. seven as opposed to nine).

Standard Rumanian There are only a few descriptions of Rumanian question intonation that go beyond vague references to "rises" (notably Kallioinen, 1967; and Dascălu, various dates). These few speak of a phenomenon which is similar to that just described for Hungarian; the intonation contour at the end of the sentence seems to depend on the focus of the question. Dascălu (1975) gives the clearest description. The focused word of the question, or at least its stressed syllable, is pronounced on low pitch; the stressed syllable of the final word is then pronounced on high pitch, and any following syllables on a lower pitch. If the focused word is also the final word, then the stressed syllable is pronounced low, followed by a rise. If the final word has stress on its final syllable, then regardless of focus it is pronounced high. Thus we have:

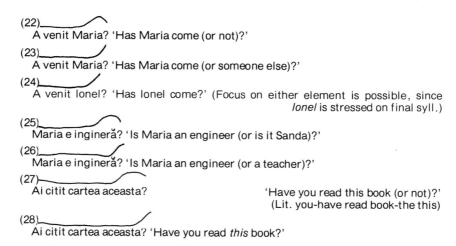

(22) A venit Maria? 'Has Maria come (or not)?'

(23) A venit Maria? 'Has Maria come (or someone else)?'

(24) A venit Ionel? 'Has Ionel come?' (Focus on either element is possible, since *Ionel* is stressed on final syll.)

(25) Maria e inginerǎ? 'Is Maria an engineer (or is it Sanda)?'

(26) Maria e inginerǎ? 'Is Maria an engineer (or a teacher)?'

(27) Ai citit cartea aceasta?   'Have you read this book (or not)?'
                                                 (Lit. you-have read book-the this)

(28) Ai citit cartea aceasta? 'Have you read *this* book?'

Transylvanian varieties In the Transylvanian varieties of both Hungarian and Rumanian, the intonation patterns in which the focus occurs earlier in the sentence (e.g. 9 - 13 and 22, 25, 27) are generally replaced by a different contour, which has a steep rise on the stressed syllable of the focused word, followed by a fall at the end of the sentence (this is the contour described by Makarenko, 1979). In Rumanian the final fall occurs on the last stressed syllable of the last word, while in Hungarian it occurs on the penultimate syllable of the utterance. (The exact placement of the rise and fall with respect to their relevant syllables is a matter for further phonetic investigation; the description here is sufficiently detailed for our purposes). Thus in Transylvanian Rumanian, in place of (27), we find something like

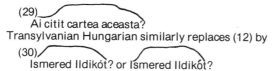

(29) Ai citit cartea aceasta?

Transylvanian Hungarian similarly replaces (12) by

(30) Ismered Ildikót? or Ismered Ildikót?

The intonations used to signal focus late in the sentence (e.g. 20, 21, 23, 26) remain unchanged in the Transylvanian varieties.

The Transylvanian intonation does occur in standard Rumanian under restricted circumstances that are not clear; in some contexts it seems to involve extra affective messages of politeness, interest, or curiosity. I have not yet been able to determine if the Transylvanian intonation also occurs in standard Hungarian, but it is definitely interpreted as a question by standard speakers.

IMPLICATIONS FOR THE SUH

While the foregoing brief description obviously leaves most of the intonational systems of the two languages untouched, several conclusions can nevertheless be drawn just from the data presented so far. Light is shed on all three of the issues raised at the beginning of the paper—innateness, representation, and prominence.

Innateness The most obvious point to an English speaker is that many of these sentences do not sound very much like questions. This is particularly true of the

Transylvanian intonation, with its initial rise and final fall. In fact, that intonation is nearly identical to one used in German for a kind of topic/comment statement, with a rising "accent" on a fronted topic and a fall on the last accented word of the sentence, as in

(31) Herrn Schmidt kenne ich nicht. 'I don't know Mr. S' (but implied 'I may know someone else you're interested in.')

This similarity between the Transylvanian question intonation and the German topic/comment statement intonation is prima facie something of a problem for any straightforward theory of intonational universals in which the contours that distinguish questions and statements are said to be natural or innate.

The second argument against innateness comes from the fact that the Transylvanian intonation occurs in both Hungarian and Rumanian. The fact that varieties of two unrelated languages that have been in extensive contact for centuries share the same intonational peculiarity can hardly be explained, it seems to me, except by assuming some kind of borrowing or mutual influence. This also presents problems for any universalist view, since it means that the supposedly natural or innate question intonation has been replaced by something else under the influence of another language. This suggests that intonation in general is more conventional and less natural than the SUH claims, and that intonation contours are subject to borrowing just as other features of langauge are.

Representation All the data just presented argue for a representation of intonation capable of making more distinctions than simply fall vs. rise. I will briefly mention two points. First, if we do assume that the similarity between Hungarian and Rumanian is due to mutual influence, then we must have a description of intonational form fine-grained enough that it permits us to distinguish the Transylvanian question intonation from other possible question intonations, including those of the standard varieties. That is, in order to state how the Transylvanian varieties have diverged from the standard varieties, we must be able to say that Contour X has been replaced by Contour Y, which we obviously cannot do if both contours are simply seen as insignificant variations on some universal theme.

Second, it is important to note that in both Rumanian and Hungarian certain of the question intonations discussed above contrast with statement intonations that are phonetically quite similar. Thus in standard Rumanian there is a contrast between

(32) Maria e inginerǎ 'Maria is an *engineer.*

and

(33) Maria e inginerǎ 'Is *Maria* an engineer?'

In Transylvanian Hungarian there is a contrast between

(34) János alszik 'János is sleeping'

and

(35) János alszik? 'Is János sleeping?'

In both cases, especially in the Rumanian case, the overall shapes of the two contours are quite similar, but the contrast of meaning is sharp and clear. This is exactly the sort of situation that led Bolinger (1958) to formulate his system of pitch accents for English: he treated certain contrasting but superficially similar contours by suggesting that their systematic difference lies in the position of stressed syllables relative to certain significant pitch movements or prominences. (As we noted above, this aspect of Bolinger's work is very close to the premises of the NTH.) I believe that the solution to the Hungarian and Rumanian data is to be found along those lines; this brings us to the subject of prominence, which is treated briefly in the next section.

Prominence   The universalist conception of intonation and prominence runs into serious trouble in both standard Hungarian and standard Rumanian with the pitch obtrusion at the end of the "normal" question intonation. That is, in Rumanian

(27)
        Ai citit cartea aceasta?
the only obvious pitch obtrusion is the one on *aceasta*, but native speakers agree that the focus is on *citit*. To focus on *aceasta*, as we saw, we need a *different kind* of pitch movement, namely

(28)
        Ai citit cartea aceasta?

In Hungarian, the problem is even worse; not only is the pitch obtrusion not on the focused word, but, in contrast to the Rumanian example just given, it need not even fall on the stressed syllable of the word. Thus, in

(12)
        Ismered Ildikót?
the pitch obtrusion is on -*di*-, but (as we saw above) *ismered* is the focused word, and *Il*- is the stressed syllable of *Ildikót*.

A Nuclear Tone Analysis   All the Hungarian and Rumanian question and focus data surveyed above can be accounted for if we assume that the single intonation involved in all cases is a Low-Rise-Fall nuclear tone. In Hungarian, in a three-syllable question, the stressed syllable of the focused word is aligned with the nucleus— i.e. low pitch—and the rise and fall are realized over the following two syllables. In a longer question, the low pitch of the nucleus is maintained more or less steady (there may be a slight gradual rise) until the penultimate syllable of the utterance, at which point the rise-fall movement takes place. In one and two-syllable questions, the pitch movement is compressed, especially in one-syllable ones; these are, in effect, "allophonic" differences. Given these allophonic differences, the focus distinctions are readily explainable as different nucleus placements. Thus, in

(19)
        János alszik? 'Is János sleeping?'
the nucleus is on the stressed syllable *Ján*- and the contour continues over the remaining syllables of the utterance. In

(20)
        János alszik?
on the other hand, the nucleus is on *al*- and the contour is compressed onto the single following syllable. This analysis of nucleus placement corresponds with native speaker intuitions about focus, and makes focus appear as a function of nucleus placement. Since focus is a function of nucleus placement in many other languages, and in statements in Hungarian, the NTH makes the focus intuitions in Hungarian questions, which seem quite capricious in a universalist/phonetic analysis, appear to fit a very widespread pattern after all. The NTH analysis is also applicable to Transylvanian Hungarian, the chief difference being that the low pitch *and the rise* occur at the nucleus, and only the fall is left for the penultimate syllable. In longer

questions this yields the characteristic initial-rise-plus-final-fall intonation; in a two or three syllable question no difference results. In summary, all the apparent complexities of Hungarian question intonation are accounted for as geographical or contextual variation of a single basic unit, the Low-Rise-Fall nuclear tone. Furthermore, no additional statement need be made concerning the relation of intonation, focus, and prominence beyond the already widely-applicable assumptions of the NTH.

A similar analysis can be given for Rumanian, but because of space limitations the details must be omitted here. Before concluding, however, mention should be made of further confirmation of the analysis in another neighboring language: the Low-Rise-Fall as I have described it corresponds in detail to the "reverse pattern" described for Serbo-Croatian by Lehiste and Ivić (cf. also Leed, 1968; Nakić and Browne, 1975). In Serbo-Croatian the accented syllable of the focused word in a question (often the final word) is pronounced on low pitch, followed by much higher pitch and then a fall; as in Rumanian and Hungarian, three syllables are required for full realization. Also as in Rumanian and Hungarian, if the final syllable of the question bears the nucleus, it is pronounced rather high and slightly rising. All three languages thus share the Low-Rise-Fall nuclear tone for yes/no questions, and share some (but not all) details about the phonetic realization of the tone as well.

Lehiste and Ivić speculate that the use of low pitch for focus in questions may constitute a new Balkanism. I would agree that mutual influence is the best explanation for the similarities these three languages exhibit, but as I have shown, the nuclear tone analysis reveals similarities far more detailed than merely the association of low pitch and focus. That is, the nuclear tone analysis makes it possible to talk of intonational borrowing with a clear notion of just what is being borrowed—in this case, the Low-Rise-Fall—and it does not seem unreasonable to assume that if we have found something that can be borrowed, we have found something psychologically real. In short, the NTH, while recognizing intonational differences among languages, nevertheless makes claims about the nature of the cognitive representation and universal aspects of intonation that are just as strong and, in their own way, just as simplifying as those made by the SUH. My goal in this paper has been to show that, in addition, the NTH is in substantially better agreement with the facts.

Note

Acknowledgements Most of the work for this paper was done during a year (1978-79) spent in Cluj, Rumania, on a visiting lectureship under the Fulbright-Hays Educational Exchange Program. I am grateful to Wayles Browne for comments and discussion, and for making it possible for me to present a working version of this paper to the Zagreb Linguistics Circle in May 1979.

Discussion

Anne Cutler As the lone psychologist on this panel, I shall emphasise the "cognitive reality" part of our title by citing some psycholinguistic evidence that prosodic *structure* is psychologically real. In this limited discussion I shall confine my remarks to the temporal structure of English. English is said to exhibit a tendency towards isochrony, in that speakers adjust the duration of unstressed syllables so that stressed syllables occur at roughly equal intervals. There is very little evidence that English is in fact *physically* isochronous; however, the case for the *psychological* reality of isochrony is much stronger.

Firstly, English speakers certainly *perceive* their language as isochronous. In a recent study Donovan and Darwin (1979) presented listeners with sentences in which all stressed syllables began with the same sound, e.g. /t/, and asked them to adjust a sequence of noise bursts to coincide temporally with the /t/ sounds in the sentence. They could hear both sentence and burst sequence as often as they liked, but not together. Donovan and Darwin found that the noise bursts were always adjusted so that the intervals between them were more nearly equal than the intervals between the stressed syllables in the actual sentence — i.e., the listeners heard the sentences as more isochronous than they really were.

Secondly, there is the role of rhythm in syntactic disambiguation. Lehiste (1977) argues that speakers trade on listener expectations by breaking the rhythm of utterances to signify the presence of a syntactic boundary. Durational cues certainly seem to be the most effective at resolving syntactic ambiguities(see, e.g., Streeter, 1978); and recent work by Scott (forthcoming) has demonstrated that boundaries are indicated not merely by a pause or by phrase-final syllabic lengthening, but crucially by the rhythm — the fact that the foot (inter-stress interval) containing the boundary is lengthened with respect to the other feet in the utterance. Moreover, in a further study of syntactically ambiguous sentences (Cutler & Isard, in press), it was found that speakers tended to lengthen the foot containing the boundary to an integral multiple of the length of the other feet, i.e. "skip a beat" and thus *maintain* the rhythm.

Finally, there is relevant speech error evidence (Cutler, in press): when an error alters the rhythm of an utterance (a syllable is dropped or added, or stress shifts to a different syllable), it is almost always the case that the error has a more regular rhythm than the intended utterance would have had. In the following examples (syllable omission and stress error), each foot (marked by /) begins with a stressed syllable:

(1) /opering /out of a /front room in /Walthamstow
     (Target: /operating /out of a /front room in /Walthamstow)
(2) We /do think in /specific /terms
     (Target: We /do think in spe/cific /terms)

The number of unstressed syllables between the stressed syllables is more equal in the errors than in the target utterances. The consistent pattern of such errors supports the notion that isochrony in English is psychologically real: the speakers have adjusted the rhythm of their utterances to what they feel it ought to be.

John J. Ohala Selkirk reports on a very interesting attempt to unify prosodic (sentence-level) and syllabic phonology using rather abstract, almost mathematical constructs. But if this is to be taken as something real, cognitively or otherwise, I would ask what recommends it over the dozens of other schemes offered to account for the same or similar data? Have the other schemes been disproved? In fact, none of them, including Selkirk's, have been the subject of empirical verification. As far as I can determine, none of the data cited, including that mentioned by Cutler in her remarks, unambiguously supports this model over any other.

I grant that the attempt to unify some of the phonological processes at the word and the phrase level is ingenious, but I wonder if all this machinery at the word level is necessary? A lexicon containing the pronunciation (including stress) of all existing words, both stems and derivations, can account for the data as well. The pronunciation of new words can be done by analogy (Ohala, 1974).

One of the examples mentioned in Selkirk's (pre-circulated) paper deserves careful examination. She notes that the word *rhythm* [rιðm̩] with a syllabic [m̩] yields the derived forms *rhythmy* [rιðmi] with the syllabic [m̩] retained, and *rhythmic* [rιðmιk] with the syllabicity of the [m] lost. The explanation offered for the different treatment of [m] is that the suffix -y [i] is a morphologically neutral suffix, and thus does not interact phonologically with the stem, whereas -ic [ιk], being morphologically active, can affect the syllable structure of the stem. This explanation could be tested. We could examine speakers' pronunciation of new derivations of e.g., *prism* [prιzm]: *prismy* and *prismic*. I can't say what the results will be but I feel I would render both with syllabic [m̩], i.e., [prιzm̩i] and [prιzm̩ιk]. The pronunciation that would be predicted according to Selkirk, [prιzmιk], I would reject because I would doubt that my listeners could recover the stem *prism* from it. Only after extensive usage and long familiarity with such a form would I risk the pronunciation [prιzmιk] and then by the process of analogy, the models being *rhythmic, orgasmic, cataclysmic, logarithmic,* etc. There being no existing models (that I know of) for a pronunciation such as *[prιzmi], i.e., with non-syllabic [m]. I would expect that *prismy* would always remain [prιzm̩i] in spite of familiarity and long usage.

I find Ladd's paper well reasoned and, on the whole, quite convincing. Further evidence supporting his view that intonational contours tend to be language-specific and conventional comes from recent work by Larry Hyman and Jean-Marie Hombart on Cameroonian languages where, in some cases, they have found downdrift to be eliminated or constrained due to certain language-specific tonal traits (Hyman and Hombert, personal communication).

Nevertheless, it is still tempting to think that there is some kind of universal substrate on which language-specific uses of fundamental frequency are superimposed. Although it may not be an obsolute universal, it seems very common that uncertainty and lack of self-assurance is signalled with a generally high Fo whereas certainty, self-assurance, even agression, is signalled with low Fo. It is interesting to note (as I did in Ohala, 1970) that much the same use of Fo is found in the animal kingdom as well, e.g., among dogs, raccoons, etc. That is, in an encounter between individuals, a low-pitched growl signals self-assurance and aggression whereas a high-pitched squeal is used to signal appeasement, surrender, lack of assuredness. Being an amateur ethologist, I would speculate that in emitting a high-pitched sound, the animal is trying to imitate the necessarily high-pitched sound of the young of the species in order, perhaps, to elicit some kind of maternal or paternal response from his antagonist. I say 'necessarily high-pitched' because younger individuals, being physically smaller, will have less massive vocal cords (or syringeal flaps in the case of birds) and consequently higher Fo. If we are carrying this type of innate programming around inside of us, it would not be surprising if some of it manifested itself in our linguistic use of Fo. Unfortunately, I can't think of any simple way to test these speculations.

SESSION VIII
MACHINE REPRESENTATION OF SPEECH

Seminar 15: Speech synthesis programs as models of speech production

Chair	JOHN HOLMES
Speakers	RENE CARRE, IGNATIUS MATTINGLY
Discussants	W. A. AINSWORTH, STEPHEN ISARD,
	CELIA SCULLY, SHINJI MAEDA

Seminar 16: Speech recognition programs as models of speech perception

Chair	CHRISTOPHER LONGUET-HIGGINS
Speakers	ROGER MOORE, JACQUELINE VAISSIERE
Discussants	JOHN BRIDLE, DENNIS KLATT,
	ALAN HENDRIKSON

THE COGNITIVE REPRESENTATION OF SPEECH
T. Myers, J. Laver, J. Anderson (editors)
© *North-Holland Publishing Company, 1981*

Vocal Tract Modelling and Speech Synthesis:
its Use for Improving Knowledge on Speech Production

R. CARRE

Laboratoire de la Communication
Parlée, E.N.S.E.R.G., Grenoble

During the last 20 years, significant progress in speech synthesis can be associated with better vocal-tract modeling. A model is constructed from all available data coming from acoustical, physiological and neurophysiological studies. Such a model can be improved by using analysis by synthesis techniques. The differences between behaviors of the original system and the model being detected, new problems can be formalized and, perhaps, solved. Many back and forth motions will be needed to postulate a reasonable model of the speech production, i.e. a model quite usable for speech synthesis. Obviously, with a correct model, better knowledge about speech production can be obtained. For example, the function and the importance of any element of the model can be studied much more easily than in the human system. At first, a direct simulation of the vocal tract as an acoustic tube (transmission-line analogs of the vocal tract) was studied. After that, formant synthesizers (terminal analog synthesizers) which are much easier to control, were used for numerous studies on speech synthesis, synthesis by rules and for perception tests. At the present time, research using analogs of the vocal tract are again being undertaken, since this kind of model is more adapted for basic research : on losses along the vocal tract, on the coupling effects between vocal tract and the source, that between vocal tract and nasal tract, etc. In other respects, it is also necessary to have a right model of the vocal cords, the voice source seeming to be responsible in part for the quality of the synthesized speech.

Generally speaking, the search for high quality speech has motivated this work, and, for that, we try to obtain the best agreement between the original system and the model in terms of the acoustical aspects which are also observed through the physiological aspects.

The first electrical speech production model consisted of, only, a source connected to a filter bank, i.e. channel vocoder. Formant synthesizers are much closer to the physical reality. This modeling approach is an attempt to specify the transfer function of the tract by its resonance frequencies and bandwidths. But, in order to study the coupling effects, the noise source excitations, the compensatory effects. . ., direct analogs of the vocal tract seem most useful, at least in the basic research field where real-time operation is not essential.

Speech production procedures may be modeled on different levels : a higher command level, an articulatory level, and an acoustic level.
—*At the higher level* : input phonetic strings are transformed into sequences of articulatory commands.
—*At the articulatory level* : these models take into account spatial and motional constraints on the human articulatory system. When moving from one stated shape to another, realistic intermediate shapes may be interpolated. At the output of the model, a time-varying vocal tract area function is given.

—*At the acoustical level* : a modeling can be obtained with formant synthesizers, predictive coding synthesizers and vocal tract analogs. They are controlled by different corresponding sets of parameters : respectively formant frequencies, predictive or reflection coefficients and area function.

It is not my intention to cover all the work done on the far ranging problem of speech production modeling but only to point out major results obtained in the last 20 years on acoustical vocal-tract modeling and on the relations between area function parameters and the formant-pattern (F-pattern).

GENERALITIES ON SPEECH PRODUCTION THEORY
(Fant, 1960 — Flanagan, 1972)

Speech signals can be considered as the result of an air flow source acting on the vocal tract and the nasal tract. There are three different kinds of sources.
—*Glottal source*— The volume flow waveform of air through the glottis (slitlike orifice between the cords) as a function of time is roughly triangular in shape. The fundamental frequency range of vibration (or pitch) is 50-450 Hz (mean value for a male voice: 120 Hz; female voice: 220 Hz; child's voice: 300 Hz). The source signal spectrum decreases in amplitude to the higher frequency components at about 12 dB/octave (Figure 1a). The internal impedance is generally considered as very high compared with the vocal tract impedance.
—*Noise source* — A turbulent flow of air is created at the place of a constriction in the tract when certain conditions on pressure and constriction area are met. Unvoiced continuant sounds are formed from this source. Acting simultaneously with the glottal source, voiced fricative sounds can be obtained.
—*Transient source*— An impulse source is created by a pressure build up at some point of closure followed by an abrupt release. The transient excitation can be used with or without vocal cord vibrations to produce voiced or unvoiced plosives.

The vocal tract is a non uniform acoustical tube. It can be considered as consisting of one or generally two main coupled cavities : the pharynx and the mouth cavities,

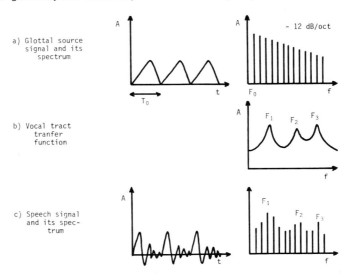

a) Glottal source signal and its spectrum

b) Vocal tract tranfer function

c) Speech signal and its spectrum

FIGURE 1   *Aspects of the speech signal*

separated by the tongue constriction. The resonance frequencies F1, F2, F3. . . of such a system are called formants (Fig. 1b) and correspond to the maxima of the transfer function. B1, B2, B3. . . are the formant bandwidths.

The output signal and its spectrum is represented in Figure 1c. This spectral representation of the speech signal is very useful, the frequencies of the first two or three formants being considered pertinent to a perceptual point of view. When the tract is coupled with the nasal tract, complex zeros and extra formants due to shunt effects appear.

VOCAL TRACT MODELING

A rather good vocal tract model has been obtained thanks to studies on wave propagation patterns, energy dissipation along the vocal tract, boundary effects related to the subglottal system, the glottal source, the cavity walls and the lip termination — Fant, 1960; Flanagan, 1965; Fant & Pauli, 1974; Mrayati & Guerin, 1976; Mrayati & Carre, 1976; Flanagan, Ishizaka & Shipley, 1975; Wakita & Fant, 1978; Descout et al 1976.

Such a model can be helpful in bringing together our fragmentary data on the vocal tract and in verifying the exactness of the overall relation. It can also be used to analyse the relation of the vocal tract parameters to formant frequencies and bandwidths and to point out the acoustically important parts of the vocal tract.

Vocal tract losses The formulation of the losses inside the vocal tract due to air viscosity and heat conduction seems now well admitted. It is not quite the same for the wall vibration losses. Several recent studies (Fant, 1972; Sondhi, 1974; Ishizaka, French & Flanagan, 1976; Mrayati & Guerin, 1976; Fant, Nord & Branderud, 1976; Wakita & Fant, 1978) show the important effects of the wall vibration losses at low frequencies i.e. for the first formant frequency and bandwidth. Because of the lack of precise vocal tract shape and the corresponding sweep-tone measurements of vocal tract characteristics at closed glottis, it is not easy to point out the best modeling of the wall vibration lossess. Ishizaka et al (1976) made direct measurements of the vocal tract wall impedance of the cheek and the neck under different conditions, i.e. tensed and relaxed conditions. The compliance of the wall is often neglected. Mrayati & Guerin (1976) using vocal tract modeling for 11 French vowels with a

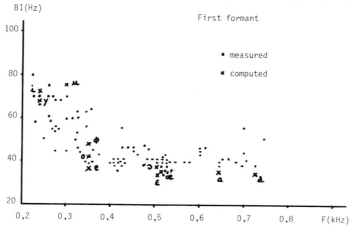

FIGURE 2: *Computed bandwidths for II French vowels and measured bandwidths (Fujimura and Lindqvist 1971)*

uniform distribution of the losses tried, for different wall impedance values to get the best fit with the Fujimura & Lindqvist (1971) data on the formant bandwidths at closed glottis (Figure 2).

There is an increase of the formant frequencies and bandwidths when wall losses are taken into account. Formant frequencies and partial bandwidths corresponding to the different losses are given in Table 1 (Mrayati & Guerin 1976).

			Bandwidth (Hz) Heat + Viscosity	Bandwidth (Hz) Wall	Bandwidth (Hz) Radiation	Bandwidth (Hz) Total
	F1 = 725 Hz	B1	6	18	11	35
[a]	F2 = 1300	B2	10	4	49	63
	F3 = 2640	B3	17	2	61	30
	F1 = 240	B1	3	65	4	72
[i]	F2 = 2500	B2	12	2	5	19
	F3 = 3140	B3	35	2	215	252
	F1 = 240	B1	8	66	1	75
[u]	F2 = 750	B2	10	10	0	20
	F3 = 2200	B3	16	2	0	18

TABLE 1: *Bandwidths due to different losses for 3 French vowels*

Spatial distribution of the losses is given in Figure 3. The curves are normalized with respect to the maximum ordinate. Such curves help towards a better understanding of the loss phenomenon. For example, in the case of the vowel [a], the back part of the vocal tract is responsible for the damping mainly because of the wall losses. The first formant bandwidth is not very much associated with the mouth cavity. Viscosity losses are important at the place of constrictions mainly if constrictions coincide with a maximum pressure.

Spatial characteristics of vocal tract resonance   Cavity-formant affiliations (Fant, 1960) represent an important aspect of the phonetic description. This knowledge is also very useful in vocal tract modeling. A resonance mode is mainly associated with the part of the vocal tract where a constriction and a maximum volume flow (maximum kinetic energy) occur together, or where a cavity coincides with a maximum pressure (maximum potential energy). Thus, as a measure of the cavity formant affiliation, Fant (1960) suggested the density of kinetic and potential energy, i.e. the density of total reactive energy. Spatial distribution of the total reactive energy is represented in Figure 4 for 3 French vowels (Mrayati & Carre, 1976).

Using these curves for formant cavity affiliation, it follows that, for example:— for the [a] vowel, F1 and F2 depends on both cavities but F1 is rather associated with the front cavity and the tongue constriction. F3 is rather associated with the back cavity. — for the [u] vowel, F1 depends first on the lip aperture then on the back cavity then the front cavity; F2 depends on the back cavity and the front cavity and the tongue constriction. — for the [i] vowel, F1 and F2 are rather associated with the back cavity, while F3 is associated with the front cavity. A vowel formant associated with the front cavity is perturbed by lip radiation. Energy distribution can be interpreted as a sensitivity function for the variations of the length of the sectional area. Another way to study the formant cavity affiliation is to consider the sensitivity to local perturbations in area. The maxima of such perturbations are also important for a correct articulatory

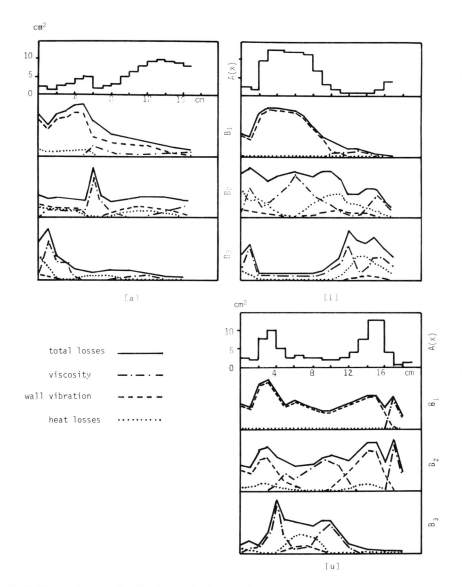

FIGURE 3 *Spatial distribution of the losses along the vocal tract*

modeling. (Fant & Pauli, 1974, Mrayati & Carre; 1976). The results can be compared with the energy distributions of the vocal tract. Generally, all the resonance modes are affected by area perturbations, but special modifications affecting only one mode can be found.

If, on the one hand, all the spatial distribution curves can be used to know the

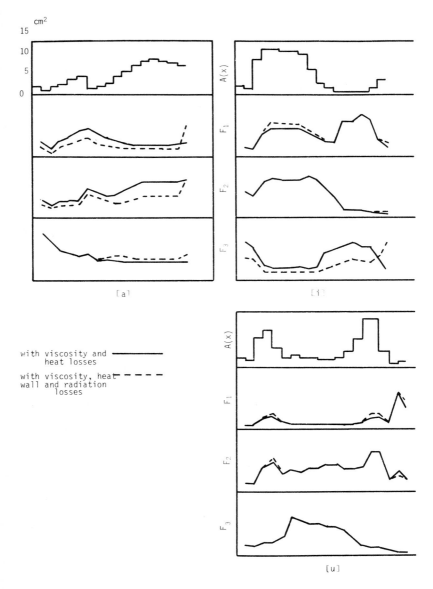

FIGURE 4 *Spatial distribution of the total reactive energy for 3 French vowels*

sensitive parts of the vocal tract, on the other hand, the acoustical stability elements can also be localized, for example, to study the quantal nature of speech proposed by Stevens (1972). Such spatial distributions were used to calculate the change in area function from one F-pattern to another in order to get plausible area functions for French vowels on the basis of their derivation from Russian vowels (Fant, 1960).

Dynamic acoustical modeling of the vocal tract In the case of variation of the vocal tract configuration, the speed of variation of the vocal tract area function is generally considered small enough to allow point-by-point calculations of the static behavior. In fact, according to results obtained by Jospa (1977), formant frequencies are not very much affected, but more important increases or decreases of formant bandwidths have to be considered. These are probably less significant perceptually than the rapidly varying formant frequencies but when using inverse transformations to get area functions during transitions, a model taking into account such corrections probably has to be used.

This bandwidth effect, closely related to the dynamic nature of the vocal tract deformations, is very sensitive to the position of the constriction. Experimental results confirm the theory, taking into account the mode analysed and the direction of the effect (Bd < 0, Bd ≃ Bd > 0). In these experiments the corresponding theoretical bandwidth range is −20 to +20 Hz.

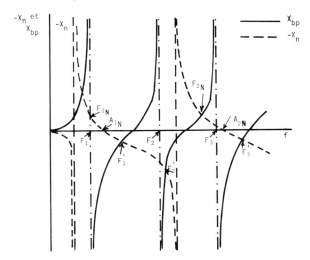

FIGURE 5   *Reactances Xbp and -Xn at the driving point*

Vocal tract-nasal tract coupling Some results on nasal and nasalized vowels were obtained by Fant (1960) with a nasal cavity system coupled with a vocal tract. Such a nasal tract model was used for studying French nasal vowels (Mrayati & Carre, 1975) At the driving point, if X_{bp} is the resulting reactance for the vocal tract and X_n the reactive part of the impedance of the nasal tract, we obtain (Fujimura, 1962) the formant frequencies of the whole system (Figure 5) when:

$$- X_n = X_{bp} .$$

F1, F2, F3 are the formant frequencies when the coupling coefficient is zero
F1', F2', F3'are the new formant frequencies when coupling occurs,
$A1_N$, $A2_N$ are the zeros due to the nasal tract. With this approach to coupling phenomena, characteristics of the French nasal vowels have been pointed out:
— the first nasal formant $F1_N$ and the second nasal zero $A2_N$ are quasi-stable with various coupling coefficients and depend upon the nasal tract configuration.
— the first oral formant F1'is related with the coupling coefficient and is higher than

the one without coupling.
— the first nasal zero is put between F1$_N$ and F1′. It is nearer F1′when the coupling coefficient is increased. In that case, the amplitude of F1′is decreased.
— the second formant F2′is generally very near F2 but its amplitude can be different. All these general characteristics have been verified on natural nasal vowels. Again the sensitivity functions provide more quantitative information.

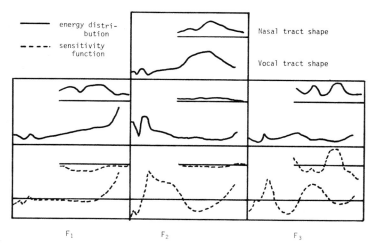

FIGURE 6   *Total energy distributions and sensitivity functions for the French vowel [ɑ̃]*

Figure 6 represents the spatial distribution of the total reactive energy distribution (French vowel [ɑ̃]). As we can see, the nasal tract area perturbation sensitivity of the second formant is hardly modified by the lowering of the velum for this nasal vowel (the same results are obtained with other nasal vowels). Unfortunately, there are not enough data on a supposed volume adjustment of the pharyngeal cavity when nasal vowel production occurs for improving the modeling of the nasal tract-vocal tract coupling. But, the loss problems are not solved. Without new oral and nasal tract shapes during phonation, it is impossible to study in detail the complex coupling effects.

Determination of the area function of the vocal tract   There is a lack of reliable data on the vocal tract shapes for studying details of the vocal tract and differences between males, females and children. To avoid exposures to X-ray radiations, two main techniques have been proposed (Mermelstein, 1967; Sondhi & Gopinath, 1971; Wakita, 1973; Wakita & Descout, 1977; Ladefoged et al 1978; Atal et al 1978; Fant, 1979b). By a direct method, the area function is calculated either from speech waveform or from acoustic data such as formant frequencies. By an indirect method, it is obtained from external acoustic measurements such as lip impedance or impulse response at the lips. I shall not go into the details of these different techniques.

I would just like to point out that:
— to support most such methods, a very accurate model of the vocal tract has to be known, taking into account all kinds of losses and sometimes, vocal source characteristics, and/or the vocal tract length;
— the validity of these methods is limited to non nasal, non constricted articulations;
— these methods have to prove their validity in the case of transitions from one configuration to another;

— the same set of formant frequencies and bandwidths can be produced from an infinite number of different shapes and of different lengths of the vocal tract. Thus, many "pseudo-area functions" can be obtained by methods which are usable for synthetic speech but unusable for real area functions. Different articulatory constraints can be used to obtain optimal evaluation (Ladefoged et al 1978). Although these techniques are not very apt to provide reference material, they are useful for gaining insight into the functional aspect of a vocal tract model. If the consequences of small changes in area functions on the speech spectrum (mainly on formant frequencies) can be studied with the sensitivity functions, conversely, with the help of inverse transformations, a lot of area functions obtained from a same set of formant frequencies and bandwidths (Atal et al 1978), permit compensatory effects to be studied. Small frequency variations can be related to many different sets of area functions providing information for working out articulatory modeling in relation to spatial and temporal constraints.

VOCAL SOURCE MODELING AND SOURCE TRACT COUPLING

A two mass model of the vocal cords (Ishizaka & Flanagan, 1972) seems to be a relatively good approximation of the vocal cord vibrations (Figures 7 and 8). Now most of the research is focused on the evaluation of its validity. With correct values of parameters, the shape of the volume flow $U_g(t)$ is generally in agreement with the experimental data. But, also, vowel intrinsic pitch, glottal losses can be studied with such a model when there is coupling with a vocal tract.

Control parameters of the model Characteristics of the vocal cord vibrations are related to the following parameters : subglottal pressure, mass and stiffness of the

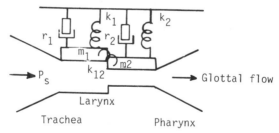

FIGURE 7   *Two mass model of the vocal cords*

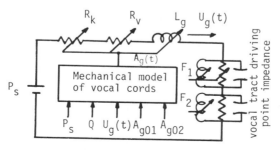

FIGURE 8   *Glottal source model loaded by an equivalent circuit of the vocal impedance*

vocal cords. A simplified control of a two mass model was proposed (Guerin & Boe, 1977). The fundamental frequency F0 is mainly dependent on the stiffness. The sound pressure level is well correlated with the subglottal pressure.

Vowel intrinsic pitch   It is well known that high vowels have a higher intrinsic pitch than low vowels. Such a phenomenon could be explained by the variable acoustic load of the source. But, the variations of the fundamental frequency of the model with different loadings corresponding to different vowel configurations are opposite and small compared to the intrinsic pitch differences (Delos et al 1976). Such behavior was verified on a real vocal tract (Ishizaka & Flanagan, 1972). Thus, intrinsic pitch phenomena can only be explained by larynx movements according to supraglottal configurations.

Glottal losses   The main formant excitation normally occurs at glottal closure (Holmes, 1976) which explains the large glottal losses when the glottis is open. Recent studies of Wakita & Fant (1978) indicate that the instantaneous bandwidth component from the glottal resistance is roughly proportional to the glottal area and is inversely proportional to the particle velocity of the glottal flow and also inversely proportional to the cross-sectional area of the lower part of the pharynx. These effects are more sensitive for the vowel [a] where the glottal impedance is of the order of the vocal tract impedance (for F1). Such behavior has still to be studied on Ishizaka and Flanagan's model of the vibration of the vocal cords.

SPEECH SYNTHESIZERS

Two major kinds of speech synthesizers have been studied as a result of vocal tract modeling. Formant synthesizers duplicate the transmission properties of the tract represented by its transfer function. Formant frequencies and bandwidths are the main parameters of such a synthesizer. Transmission-line analogs of the vocal tract are a representation of the shape of the vocal tract by its area function. The non-uniform tract is approximated by numerous cylindrical elements. Predictive coding synthesizers duplicate also the transmission properties of the vocal tract (with some spectral characteristics of the source). But the nature of the prediction coefficients does not permit easy interpretation of the production phenomena at the level of losses. These synthesizers are used in vocoders for telecommunications.

Formant synthesizers   Formant synthesizers, of the parallel and cascade types,

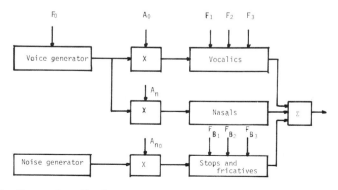

FIGURE 9   *Formant synthesiser*

have been constructed and operated — (Fant 1959. . .) They are controlled by about 10 parameters (for example Figure 9). Natural speech is analysed to obtain these parameters. These data, when controlling a synthesizer produce synthetic speech similar to the original utterance. Formant bandwidths representing all the different kinds of losses involved during production can also be used as variable parameters. Such a synthesizer was first built to verify the general theory of speech production. It can now mainly be used as an audio response unit or for perception test purposes. This type of synthesizer is very easy to use because most of speech analysis research uses easily interpretable formant data. But, this kind of synthesizer does not take into account the problem of vocal tract-vocal sound coupling. Guerin et al (1976) propose, as a vocal source, a two-mass model of the vocal cords loaded by an equivalent of the tract impedance, this impedance being controlled by F1 and F2. The interest of such a source has not been proved by perception tests.

Transmission line analogs of the vocal tract   The difficulties involved in modeling all relevant factors in the acoustic production process explain the small number of vocal tract analog synthesizers.

The most successful attempt to construct a complete model is that of Flanagan et al (1975). Vocal cords and vocal tract behavior are simulated. The control parameters are subglottal lung pressure, vocal cord tension and glottis opening at rest, vocal tract shape, and nasal coupling. Thus, inherent properties of the model duplicate phenomena observed in human speech : source-tract acoustic interaction, cord vibration, tract wall radiation during occlusion, voicing onset-offset behavior.

Simulation of such a model in the frequency domain is relatively easy. This is not the case for the time domain, for synthesis purposes, where frequency dependent elements have to be included.

CONCLUSIONS

It is now possible to obtain good synthetic speech with formant synthesizers, predictive coding synthesizers or the vocal tract analogs. They are used for man-machine dialog as audio response units, or for phonetic research : to study, for example, the relevant features of production of any kind of speech sounds in connection with perception tests. Otherwise, transmission lines as vocal tract models are used to improve our knowledge about speech production phenomena inside the vocal tract and also to improve the exactness of the modeling.

Important new results have been obtained during recent years, but many problems remain to be studied. To develop high quality synthesis, we lack physiological data especially with respect to consonants. More information about area functions will have to be obtained from X-ray but also completed with frontal sections (obtained by scanner). Corresponding sweep-tone measurements of the vocal tract characteristics at closed glottis have to be made at the same time. The model has to be improved especially for stops, laterals, unvoiced continuants and nasals. The noise source characteristics have to be investigated further. The nasal cavity system generally adopted is not sufficient to explain the formant patterns of nasal vowels, especially as far as the bandwidths is concerned. The distribution of wall losses along the vocal tract will require further study as well. Similarly, the impedance of a two mass model of the vocal cords will have to be investigated and compared with the recent results obtained by Fant (1978a) on the glottis impedance.

Finally, the initial work of Jospa (1977) on dynamic aspects of deformations of the vocal tract has to be pursued.

We still have a long way to go in speech modeling research before obtaining a very accurate model of the vocal tract which would also be usable for high quality speech synthesis.

THE COGNITIVE REPRESENTATION OF SPEECH
T. Myers, J. Laver, J. Anderson (editors)
© *North-Holland Publishing Company, 1981*

Phonetic Representation and Speech Synthesis by Rule

IGNATIUS G. MATTINGLY

University of Connecticut and Haskins Laboratories

While a computer model of performance in speech production is certainly conceivable, the title of this seminar, "Speech Synthesis Programs as Models of Speech Production," seems incorrect as a characterization of existing systems for synthesis of speech by rule. Insofar as these systems have had more than the purely pragmatic goal of converting written utterances into spoken utterances, the objective has been a more modest one, but one that is nonetheless directly related to the theme of this Symposium, "The Cognitive Representation of Speech." The objective has been to elucidate the nature of the phonetic representation shared by speaker and hearer (and recorded, after a fashion, in a conventional phonetic transcription) and the relationship of this representation to physical events. A simulation of the mental activity underlying actual speech production would be a far more ambitious project, though one well worth attempting.

Synthesis-by-rule has also, of course, considered other interesting questions: the relationship of the conventional orthography to the phonemic representation, and the relationship of the latter to phonetic representation. But its central concern, surely, has been to relate the phonetic representation either to the articulatory or to the acoustic parameters of continuous speech. The practitioner of synthesis-by-rule cannot avoid this concern, for his rules must somehow specify the physical correlates of the elements of the phonetic representation, and his program must necessarily include some kind of algorithm for getting from one phonetic element to the next.

The simplest conceivable synthesis-by-rule system would be one in which each phonetic element is associated with an articulatory or acoustic segment of specified duation (or of a sequence of such segments). Since the inventory would be small, prerecorded segments of natural speech rather than parametrically-specified synthetic segments could be used. This system would have only one "rule": concatenate segments corresponding to successive phonetic elements. Such schemes have indeed been proposed (Harris, 1953), but it was appreciated quite early by practitioners of speech synthesis by rule that the acoustic record (and *a fortiori* the articulatory record) contained intervals that could not reasonably be viewed as steady-state segments correlated with single phonetic elements, and that these intervals (which were regarded as "transitions" connecting "true" steady-state segments) were perceptually extremely important (Liberman, Ingemann, Lisker, Delattre & Cooper, 1959).

Thus, the synthesis-by-rule systems developed in the 60's (see Mattingly, 1974, for a review), though differing in detail, had in common the requirement that transitions, as well as steady states, had to be described in the synthesis rules. In the synthesis-by-rule system described by Holmes, Mattingly & Shearme (1964), for example, each "phoneme table" specifies, for each parameter, not only a steady-state value but also a contribution to a "boundary value," and the moment-by-moment values during a transition are calculated by linear interpolation from the steady-state value for the current phonetic element to the boundary value, and from the boundary value to the steady-state value for the following element. The interpretation of the phonetic representation implicit in these systems was thus consistent with the concept of segmentation proposed by Pike (1943): speech consists of "level segments," during which one or more articulatory "crests or troughs of stricture" are maintained, connected by "glide" segments, during which one or more strictures are being applied or released. Successive elements of the phonetic representation referred to successive level segments, from which the glides could be predicted.

This approach to synthesis-by-rule, though demonstrably capable of producing speech that was by conventional measures intelligible (Nye and Gaitenby, 1973; Pisoni, 1979), ran into three related sorts of difficulty. First, it can be observed in natural speech that the acoustic "steady-state" segment associated with a particular phonetic element, and likewise the transitions from the preceding and to the following segments, vary according to the immediate phonetic context in ways that are clearly of perceptual importance. For practical purposes, this variation could be dealt with by writing allophone rules to modify the phonetic specification according to context, or by allowing the transition from the preceding steady-state segment and the transition to the following steady-state segment to overlap, eliminating the current steady-state segment (Holmes, et al., 1964). Either approach was an admission of a deficiency in the Pikean view of phonetic representation (from an articulatory standpoint, the deficiencies of the Pikean view are even more glaring since the simultaneous maintenance of several constrictions over a period of time — an articulatory "steady-state" — is quite unusual).

Variations that depended on non-adjacent phonetic context were less easily dealt with. Since the algorithms used in these systems considered only two consecutive phonetic elements at a time, this kind of contextual variation could be handled only by frankly *ad hoc* procedures. Though it was generally assumed that such variation was on the whole of little perceptual importance, its very existence posed further problems for the Pikean view.

The final, and theoretically most damning, difficulty with the Pikean approach was that the durations of steady-state and transitional segments are subject to extensive contextual variation and had to be assigned completely *ad hoc.* Even these *adhoc* assignments were notoriously unsuccessful in producing realistic speech-timing patterns. But what is at issue is not just whether the durations for phonetic elements could be adequately specified within a segment-by-segment framework (or even by a more elaborate framework involving higher-order prosodic units), but whether the elements of a phonetic representation can be said to have durations at all.

The fact that some synthesis-by-rule systems have respectable intelligibility scores should not lead anyone to suppose that these problems are of no practical importance. It is clear that the speech produced by these systems, though intelligible places a much greater load on short-term memory than does natural speech. Nye and Gaitenby (1974) investigated the ability of listeners to recall immediately after presentation semantically anomalous but syntactically acceptable sentences (e.g., "The wrong shot led the farm") under two conditions. In one condition, listeners heard naturally-spoken sentences; in the other, sentences synthesized with the Haskins Laboratories synthesis-by-rule system. Pisoni (1979) later used the same test in an evaluation of Klatt's (1976) synthesis-by-rule system. The percentages of words correctly reported were for natural speech, 95%; for the Haskins system (Mattingly, 1968; Kuhn, 1973), 78%; and for the Klatt system, 78.7%.

Though both synthesis-by-rule systems have conventional intelligibility scores close to natural speech, it would seem that the unnaturalness of synthetic speech, in particular, perhaps, the failure to represent coarticulatory variation adequately and the unnaturalness of the timing of acoustic events, seriously interferes with short-term memory coding.

The objections to segmental models have often been pointed out, and it is rather surprising that practitioners of synthesis-by-rule have paid so little attention. Menzerath & Lacerda (1933), Joos (1948), Fant (1962), Liberman, Cooper, Shankweiler & Studdert-Kennedy (1967) and many others have made it clear that a many-to-many relationship between phonetic elements and acoustic segments, however defined, is the norm rather than the exception in speech, and that — in Fant's words — ''several adjacent sounds [i.e., acoustic segments] may carry information on one and the same phoneme, and there is overlapping insofar as one and the same sound segment carries information on several adjacent phonemes'' (1962:9). Nor is it the case that the many-to-many relationship is to be attributed solely to the merging into a single acoustic stream of effects due to several articulators, for multiple phonetic influences simultaneously affect the movements of an individual articulator (MacNeilage & Scholes, 1964; MacNeilage & DeClerk, 1969).

In other words, information in speech is transmitted in parallel, and it is this fact that makes possible higher information rates for speech than would be possible in a truly segmental process. But parallel transmission appears to present no difficulty for the speech-perception mechanism. On the contrary this mechanism seems to be specialized for decomposing an encoded period of speech into the component phonetic influences, and is rather less at home with isolated consonants or isolated vowels (Liberman, et al., 1967).

Both acoustic and articulatory models to account for the many-to-many relationship between phonetic elements and acoustic events have been proposed. Joos regarded phonetic elements as ''overlapping innervation waves'' and showed that the formant trajectory for a C_1VC_2 syllable could be decomposed into a vowel ''layer'', an initial-consonant layer and a final-consonant layer (Joos, 1948:109,125). In the model proposed by Ohman (1967) to account for observed dynamic changes in vocal-tract shape in V,CV_2 syllables, the predicted shape depends on a time function, a vowel-shape function, a consonant-shape function, and a coarticulation function associated with the consonant. Even for values of the time function where the consonant-shape function predominates, the predicted shape function depends also on the vowel function, to the extent determined by the value of the coarticulation function. Moreover, if the vowel-shape function is not constant but varies depending on the time-varying values of phonetic features, that is, if $V_1 \neq V_2$, the predicted shape at any point in the $V_1 CV_2$ sequence depends on these feature-value time functions as well as on the consonant-shape and coarticulation functions. An observed vocal-tract shape during a VCV utterance is thus interpreted as the result of superimposition of a consonant shape tolerating a certain degree of coarticulation upon a changing vowel shape.

It is worth noting that the Joos and Ohman models are essentially ''prosodic.'' That is, they treat elements of the so-called segmental sequence in the way that prosodic features are conventionally treated. The overlapping and layering of prosodic features is usually taken for granted: it would be quite unconventional to propose a division of the signal into stress and intonation segments. These models are also quite consistent with earlier attempts by phoneticians and phonologists to treat one or another ''segmental'' element as if it were a prosodic feature (see, for example, Hockett's discussion of ''componential analysis'', 1955: 129ff).

However, it is not sufficient to regard the sounds of speech merely as an inventory of "innervation functions" or (as we prefer to call them) "phonetic-influence functions" that may overlap with one another freely and to an indefinite extent. Phonetic elements are perceived as ordered, and if this ordering is not to be attributed to the existence of successive segments, some other explanation is required. Moreover, there are obvious restrictions on the co-occurrence of overlapping patterns, and corresponding restrictions on the perceived ordering of phonetic elements.

The basis for these restrictions becomes obvious if we consider what combinations of phonetic influences can in fact be effectively transmitted in parallel. If, in the utterance [pla], the onset, constriction and release for [l] were to occur entirely during the period of closure for [p], the [l] would have no acoustic correlates. But if the [l] release is delayed until after the [p] release is well advanced, information about [l] (as well as about [p] and [a]) is available both before and after the [l] release. There has to be some means of guaranteeing that this second pattern will in fact be the one that is used. Again, in stop sequences of the form $V_1 S_1 \ldots S_n V_2$, information about stops $S_2 \ldots S_{n-1}$ will be present if the release of S_j is delayed relative to that of S_{j-1}. But the period of constriction for S_j, because the constriction is maximally close, will convey only manner information, and the burst will convey place information about S_j itself, but little, or no information about any other phonetic element. Hence there will be no effective parallel transmission except for the periods when the S_1 constriction is being applied during the constriction for V_1 and the S_n constriction is being released during the constriction for V_2. Thus length of stop sequences has to be severely limited, as is the case in all languages.

The general articulatory prerequisite for parallel transmission would appear to be that the constrictions for one or more closer articulations must be in the process of being released or applied in the presence of constrictions for one or more less close articulations. In terms of this formulation, the conventional ranking of manner classes according to degree of closeness (obstruents, nasals, liquids, glides, vowels) corresponds to a ranking according to the degree to which information can be encoded during the release or application of the constriction, and the inverse of this ordering, to the degree to which information can be encoded during the period of maximal constriction (Holmes et al. (1964) exploited this ranking of the manner classes to a limited extent in their synthesis-by-rule system). If parallel transmission is to be maximized, then the articulations of speech must be scheduled so that periods during which constrictions are released in rank order alternate with periods during which constrictions are applied in inverse rank order. This is of course exactly what is accomplished by the syllabic organization of speech. It would seem, therefore, that the syllable has more than a phonological or prosodic role: it is the means by which phonetic influences are scheduled so as to maximize parallel transmission.

The perception that phonetic elements are ordered now has an obvious explanation. This perception does not arise from the detection of successive segments, or even of the successive releases or applications of constrictions. It is rather the ranking of the manner classes itself that governs the percept. That is, the listener interprets the available acoustic data in terms of a framework of expectations about the structure of the syllable based on the ranking of manner classes.

Interpreting syllable structure in terms of the manner-class ranking is in itself hardly novel: Jespersen (1926) proposed such a ranking, based on "sonority," as the basis for an account of the syllable. But the argument here is that if segments are to be replaced in a phonetic model by phonetic-influence functions, syllable structure is essential for efficient speech communication and not simply a concomitant linguistic structure.

At Haskins Laboratories, we are developing a new synthesis-by-rule system in which acoustic parameters depend on the interaction of overlapping phonetic influences, and the timing of these influences is determined by the structure of phonetic syllables. For various practical reasons, we have chosen to use the acoustic parameters of a terminal-analog synthesizer rather than articulatory ones, but an essentially similar approach could be used with an articulatory synthesizer.

The phonetic elements that are considered to influence the acoustic character of the syllable in our system are the vowels of the current, preceding and following syllables, the initial consonants of the current and following syllables, and the final consonants of the current and preceding syllables (higher-level prosodic elements have not as yet been taken into consideration). With each such phonetic influence is associated a rank that depends upon the manner class of the element, and within manner class, upon temporal order; a set of target parameter values; and a time-function, ranging in value between 0 and 1, that represents the weight of the influence relative to the combined weight of all lower-ranking influences.

A phonetic-influence function is defined from the beginning of the preceding syllable to the end of the current syllable, in the case of syllable-initial articulations, or from the beginning of the current syllable to the end of the following syllable, in the case of syllable-final articulations (in this way, intersyllabic influences are taken care of). An influence function has a growth period, during which it has the form $I_t = k e^{\beta t}$ (cf. Lindblom, 1963), a possible steady-state period of duration h during which $I_t = 1$, and a declining period during which $I_t = k e^{-\gamma(t-h)}$. The rate at which an influence grows (or declines) depends on β (or γ), its effective onset time on k. Syllables may vary in duration according to their phonetic structure and the value of k is adjusted accordingly.

Given $I_{i,t}$, the strength of the ith-ranking influence at time t, and $T_{i,j}$, the target value for the jth parameter associated with this influence, the parameter value reflecting the ith and lower-ranking influences is

$$V_{i,t,j} = V_{i-1,t,j} + I_{i,t}(T_{i,j} - V_{i-1,t,j})$$

Taking as $T_{0,j}$ the target value for the vowel of the previous syllable, the parameter value reflecting all influences can be calculated iteratively. At any particular instant, the weight of most possible influences will be zero or near zero, and computation is speeded by neglecting these influences.

The variables of this algorithm that are associated with influences of elements of each manner class are defined by an ordered set of rules. These variables include the target parameter values, the increment to syllable duration attributable to the element, the duration of the steady-state period, the times relative to the notional beginning (or end) of a syllable, when the strength of an initial (or final) influence equals .5, 1, and .5 again (β, γ and k are determined from these time-values). The definitions of these variables in the rules are conditional upon particular patterns of feature-values that might be specified in the phonetic description of the syllable. Before the parameter values are computed, the pattern of feature-values in each rule is compared with the actual phonetic description. If the rule applies, the algorithmic variables mentioned are defined according to the rules. Since the rules are ordered, a variable may well be redefined by one or more subsequent rules.

We feel that this scheme reflects more clearly the essential character of the relationship between the phonetic representation and acoustic events than our earlier synthesis-by-rule system, or other systems in which a Pikean segmentation was assumed. We hope that it will make possible the production of at least equally intelligible and more natural and more understandable synthetic speech.

Acknowledgement   Support from the National Institutes of Health (NICHD) and the University of Connecticut Research Foundation is gratefully acknowledged.

Discussion

W.A. Ainsworth: As well as the programs for the synthesis of speech from a model of the vocal tract and by synthesis-by-rule which the speakers have discussed, there is another class of programs known as synthesis-from-text which provide a more comprehensive model of speech production. These, typically, consist of a number of sequential operations. In one which I built a few years ago (Ainsworth, 1973), the text was first segmented into breath groups, then the orthographic spelling was translated into a phonemic string by means of context-dependent rules. Next stress marks were inserted, from which the intonation and rhythm were derived. These processes generated the input to a synthesis-by-rule program which in turn produced the parameters for a formant synthesiser.

Much more advanced synthesis-from-text schemes have been developed since, notably by Allen at M.I.T. and Granstrom and Carlson in Stockholm (Allen et al., 1979). The main advances have been to introduce a feature-based synthesis-by-rule system, to improve the prosodic component by incorporating a parsing element, and to carry out the orthographic-to-phonetic translation partly by rule and partly by an exceptions dictionary.

An alternative, and in many ways more appropriate, model of speech production is the speech synthesis-from-concept system developed by Fallside and Young (1978). In this system the data from which the message is to be derived is stored in a data base, rather than as text. The application described involves a computer-controlled water-supply network consisting of reservoirs and pumping stations located over a wide area. Maintenance engineers working on the system need to know past and present values of water levels and flow rates which they obtain by phoning the computer and interrogating its data base by means of auditory tone generators. The computer replies with synthesised speech.

The speech is generated in the following manner. The sequence of tones indicates the question which has been asked, and this determines the structure of the answer. This is essentially the deep structure of the utterance to be generated. The content of the data base determines the substance of the answer. The deep structure is transformed by a set of rules to produce the surface structure of a well-formed sentence. Another set of rules uses this structure to determine the rhythm and intonation of the utterance. The acoustic form of the words in the sentence is provided by a lexicon containing linear predictive coefficients for each entry. These are concatenated in the appropriate order then sent, with the appropriate intonation, to an LPC synthesiser.

It is programs of this type which currently provide the most realistic models of the speech production process. Such programs also provide excellent systems for testing the consequences of linguistic rules.

S.D. Isard: Throughout this conference there has been a certain tension between what have been called the "physical" and "programming" approaches. That is, between attempts to explain various properties of speech as following directly from the physics of the vocal mechanism, and attempts to explain them in terms of the mental programs which cause us to use the vocal mechanism in one way rather than another.

I take it that we would all expect some facts to require one sort of explanation, some the other, and some both. However, given a particular fact in need of explanation, it may not be obvious in advance which form the explanation ought to take, and we have heard both approaches tried here on the phenomena associated with lip-rounding and fast speech.

My own interest and competence lie very much on the programming side. As I have listened to the talks, I have formed a sort of visual metaphor of the research questions under discussion as a number of ducks bobbing about on the surface of a lake, with physical explanations as some sort of dark primitive forces — snapping turtles, perhaps — trying to seize them from below and drag them under, never to be seen again.

From this point of view, I think the role of a good vocal tract model is to get the carnage over with, and leave us to study whatever remains of the decimated duck population. Put less dramatically, it should tell us what restriction of the class of sounds we might possibly make, to the class we actually do make in speech, needs to be accounted for by a theory of how we plan our utterances.

A really good model should also assist us by specifying through its input parameters what the planning program needs to give as its output. This leads us, finally, back to the question of cognitive representation. Given an accurate model, we will want to know what aspects of it are represented within the cognitive program. (Do the ducks know about the turtles?) The many compensatory articulation studies mentioned at this conference make it clear that we have some model of the input-output characteristics of the vocal system. It remains an open question how much more of the vocal tract is mentally represented.

I would like to end with one isolated question about Ignatius Mattingly's paper. As I understand his model, phonemes do not exist as temporal segments, but rather as "articulatory influences" overlaid on one another, with higher ranking influences on top. Our intuition of "phoneme order" is explained as really being an intuition of rank. I find this appealing, but I don't see how it can explain intuitions of phoneme order within consonant clusters, e.g., the difference between "lest" and "lets", since the ranks of phonemes are supposed to be fixed. How is this to be accounted for?

C. Scully: The problem posed is to define the aims — the tasks — of speech production. I assume that a speaker's task is to generate, with a high degree of reliability, broadly defined sequences of sound patterns that contrast with each other in the particular phonological system used. Acoustic-based synthesis, using terminal -analog synthesizers, investigates the acoustic structures achieved and their significance for the listener; articulatory synthesis may help us to learn something about the means of achieving those acoustic ends. Real speech gives information about successfully organized speech production; articulatory synthesis allows the possibility of generating 'wrong' sound patterns by combining articulatory components in unsuitable ways — and then asking why these are wrong.

Even if acoustically more stable vocal tract target shapes are preferred, it is important to recall that acoustic stability must be multi-dimensional. It seems unlikely that all acoustic features associated with a particular phonological contrast will be equally stable with respect to perturbations along each of the articulatory dimensions. More stable acoustic features are likely to carry greater weight as perceptual cues and articulatory modelling should have predictive power here. A computer model, which includes the aerodynamic and sound source stages, has been used to investigate regions of stability for plosives and fricatives (Scully 1977, 1979). Simple patterns of vocal fold action and different coordinations between vocal fold and supraglottal articulators created a wide range of fricative and plosive structures.

A model must display the same kind of dependence of sound sources on articulator coordination and perturbation as that of real speech. Sources must not be inserted arbitrarily, but must be defined by vocal tract shapes and aerodynamic conditions. Much modelling in the frequency domain is needed to indicate the approximations that may be justified in the time domain.

To what extent does the speaker make fine adjustments to the articulatory programs in order to create particular sound sequences? To what extent does the speaker tailor the sounds to fit within a rather simple articulatory control system? Articulatory synthesis can explore the full implications of a limited set of specific articulatory component gestures.

Problem solving in preliminary work (supported by the Science Research Council) with a model which generates speechlike sounds suggests possible analogous approaches for real speech. Trial and error to determine successful coordinations seems appropriate. In the model, phoneme boundaries do not have to be defined or considered. Different problems of precision arise in modelling plosives and fricatives. Unsuccessful attempts to achieve female-sounding speech from articulatory patterns similar to those of men reinforce the view that sounds, not gestures, are the aims of speech production.

Chairman's Comments

J.N. Holmes: There are very many levels at which speech synthesis systems could be considered as models of speech production. At the lowest level the only require-ment is to produce an acoustic signal perceptually more or less equivalent to human speech from a parameterized acoustic description. At the highest level the input signal to the system might be some cognitive representation of the semantics of the message. Between these two extremes there are many possible intermediate levels. Some of these levels are concerned with the accurate modelling of the acoustic processes of sound production, and others with articulator control, taking into account physical effects such as inertia. At a somewhat higher level there are systems for conversion from phonemic to phonetic levels, and for converting a general set of prosodic features to detailed fundamental frequency and timing information. Detailed modelling of human processes at any of these levels can be accompanied by merely functional models at higher or lower levels to make a complete system for generating speech signals to listen to. Although at the purely acoustic level no cognitive processing is involved and thus it could be argued that such modelling is outside the scope of this symposium, acoustic models have not been excluded from this seminar. Their inclusion can, perhaps, be justified by the fact that the cognitive level of speech generation presumably has to be sufficiently aware of the acoustic processes to be able to work out how to control them.

With the notable exception of certain aids for the deaf, very few synthesis models have dealt with the visual aspects of speech production, in spite of the fact that it is well established that in face-to-face or TV communication the visual path is made considerable use of by normal hearing people. These non-visual speech synthesis models can therefore only be regarded specifically as models of telephonic or recorded speech production.

René Carré's paper has considered in detail various aspects of articulatory modelling, such as is used in the Flanagan, Ishizaka and Shipley (1975) model of the speech production system. Although the main physiological features of the human system are reasonably well represented in this model, so far the speech produced by it has been appreciably less natural-sounding than the better attempts using resonance synthesizers to copy acoustic features of human speech. Is this because we do not yet have sufficiently accurate physiological data and control information for such a model, or is it that the model is still too simple to model important acoustic properties? It may be easier to answer this question by study of resonance synthesizers to evaluate which of the features of the signal are necessary, and then to consider whether the articulatory models can produce those features.

The paper by Ignatius Mattingly describes a syllable-based set of rules for controlling a synthesizer, in which there is a hierarchy of layers of control of the synthesis process. The various segments are ranked in a way somewhat analogous to that of Holmes, Mattingly and Shearme (1964). In Mattingly's system vowel segments define underlying gestures, and successive overlays modify these gestures, until the obstruents, in the top layer, control the more rapid timing of closure gestures. A major point of this model is that the relative timing of events is determined essentially by the composition of the syllables, and thus co-articulation is dealt with in an elegant way. However, as Stephen Isard points out in his comments, such an approach does not satisfactorily deal with contrasts such as "lest" and "lets", and *ad hoc* additions to the model to deal with order variations in consonant clusters detract considerably from its appeal. In the face of such examples, I find it difficult to believe that the timing of consonantal gestures is an automatic consequence of syllable composition, rather than an explicit, if not very precisely defined, cognitive function.

Written contributions from three of the four discussants precede these comments. In fact, the discussants covered wider aspects of modelling speech production than were dealt with in the two papers. In particular, Bill Ainsworth pointed out that synthesis from text could be regarded as a model of reading aloud, but that attempts to model normal question and answer communication require some way of converting through a conventional orthographic form, and the "speech synthesis from concept" system of Young and Fallside (1979) is a step in this direction. However, the Young and Fallside system illustrates another feature of speech production modelling: it is possible to experiment with modelling the higher cognitive levels, while completely ignoring the rules determining how the articulatory and acoustic levels behave. In the Young and Fallside case the sound generation was achieved by concatenating words previously spoken by a human talker and stored in the form of linear prediction coefficients. This approach enables the fundamental frequency and timing to be specified by rule in a sensible way, related to the message structure, but cannot deal effectively with coarticulation across word boundaries, and other context-dependent articulatory changes.

In her comments, Celia Scully emphasized that an articulatory model is a valuable tool for investigating speech production, but she suggests that trial and error, with acoustic analysis of the resultant sounds, is a very satisfactory way of learning to control such a model. She pointed out that the almost direct auditory feedback of the child learning to speak is likely to be even more effective in the acquisition of articulatory control than the much slower auditory feedback which was successful for her computer model.

The main point made by Stephen Isard was the contrast between physical effects and the cognitive processes which try to keep them in control. I myself am strongly of the opinion that the higher cognitive levels are subconsciously well aware of the effects of constraints of the physical system, as exemplified by the vowel articulatory compensation shown in bite-block experiments of Lindblom, McAllister and Lubker (1977).

An important comment by Shinji Maeda was that in any model of speech production, successful speech generation was not sufficient to justify a claim to be modelling the cognitive process. The most that could be claimed would be that such a model should be considered as a candidate.

There were many useful contributions from members of the audience, concluding with a comment by Peter Ladefoged that for the present the best way to understand how the articulators behave is by articulatory analysis rather than by articulatory synthesis. He also expressed doubt about the value of studying muscle behaviour, rather than articulator movement.

THE COGNITIVE REPRESENTATION OF SPEECH
T. Myers, J. Laver, J. Anderson (editors)
© *North-Holland Publishing Company, 1981*

Speech Recognition Systems and Theories of Speech Perception

ROGER K. MOORE

University College London

Abstract

Until 1970 work in speech perception was in many ways superior to contemporary speech recognition programs. At this time, however, significant advances were made as speech recognition systems became based on a structure consisting of a number of interactive processing levels. The creators of these systems, which were complete in the sense that they attempted to perform some defined task in response to a connected speech utterance, did not claim them to be models of human speech perception. Nevertheless, the fact that they have performed with some success does provide valuable insights into such behaviour. One in particular, the HARPY system, has outstripped all others in performance and hence has been the object of some scrutiny. Its principle of compiling phonetic, syntactic and semantic knowledge into a network containing all possible utterances which is searched using a dynamic programming algorithm, although shallow, does exhibit some of the behaviour found in human speech perception and attempts have been made to understand its psychological implications. There are, however, many aspects of speech perception which HARPY does not utilize: the ability to normalize from one speaker to another over sex, accent and dialect differences, the use of prosodic features of stress and intonation, and the general use of speech pattern contrast information. Whilst there is work in progress aimed at these areas, it seems that speech recognition should now, more than ever, pay attention to perceptual models, as well as vice versa.

INTRODUCTION

Since the author has little authority to comment on matters of speech perception, it is tempting, in this paper, merely to review the wide range of automatic speech recognition machines and techniques that have been developed over the past few years. Judgements on questions of psychological reality can then be left to the reader. However, there are two reasons for not following this line of approach. Firstly, there are already some excellent reviews in the literature (Reddy 1976, White 1976 Klatt 1977), and secondly, there has been some recent work which directly addresses the question: can an automatic speech recognition program reveal anything about human speech perception? As a result, this paper is mainly concerned with the structure of just one automatic speech recognition system, called HARPY (Lowerre 1976).

The reason for this seemingly narrow approach will be made clear by posing the question: what contributions to speech perception research would workers in that field like from automatic speech recognition? A possible answer might be, that they would like to see a working recogniser that suggests a model of speech perception of sufficient stature to stand alongside established models, such as the motor theory Liberman et al., 1962), analysis by synthesis (Stevens, 1960), or multistage hierarchical models (Bondarko, 1970; Pisoni, 1975). What, therefore, have automatic speech recognition programs got to offer?

Although the field of automatic speech recognition is some twenty seven years old, it was not until 1970 that it possessed anything significant in the way of a methodology for building recognisers. Up to that date most research work had been directed towards recognising single words spoken in isolation. No-one had much of an idea how to overcome all the difficulties encountered with continuous speech in which words become joined together and their beginnings and ends are lost. Then a change occurred. A new philosophy spread into automatic speech recognition research from ideas floating about in the field of artificial intelligence.

It was felt that an effort could be made to build machines which performed some task in response to a connected speech utterance. The emphasis was to be on correct responses to spoken commands, rather than correct recognition of each word. The goal was to be achieved by using high level information, such as syntax and semantics, to overcome the deficiencies arising from poor quality acoustic data (Newell et al., 1973).

This new view of an automatic recognition system led to a number of five year projects being set up in the U.S.A., in 1971, funded by the Advanced Projects Research Agency (ARPA). The projects were based at Carnegie-Mellon University, Bolt, Beranek & Newman Inc., Stanford Research Institute, and Systems Development Corporation. The specifications for each of the projects are shown in Figure 1.

THE SYSTEM SHOULD:

- ACCEPT CONTINUOUS SPEECH
- FROM MANY
- COOPERATIVE SPEAKERS
- IN A QUIET ROOM
- USING A GOOD MICROPHONE
- WITH SLIGHT TUNING/SPEAKER
- ACCEPTING 1000 WORDS
- USING AN ARTIFICIAL SYNTAX
- IN A CONSTRAINING TASK
- YIELDING LESS THAN 10% SEMANTIC ERROR
- IN A FEW TIMES REAL TIME
- ON A 100 MIPS MACHINE

FIGURE 1   *Specifications for the ARPA speech recognition systems.*

From this new impetus in speech recognition came the first methodological models. Components such as acoustics, phonetics, morphemics, syntactic semantics and pragmatics became known as 'knowledge sources' and their cooperative interaction became the object of research. Figure 2 shows some of the models evolved by automatic speech recognition research (Reddy, 1975).

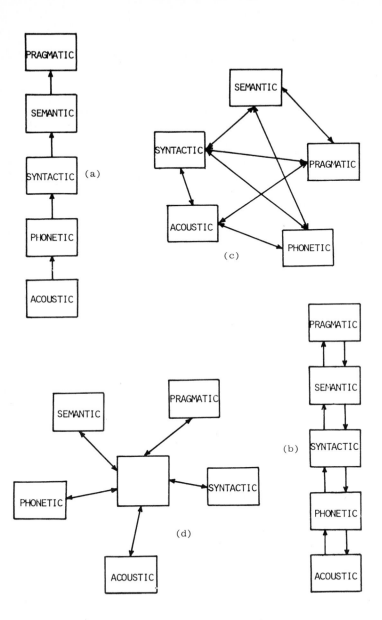

FIGURE 2   *Models for speech recognition systems: (a) hierarchical, (b) generative, (c) heterarchical and (d) blackboard.*

The hierarchical, or bottom-up, model reflects the simplest organisation. Speech data is subjected to higher and higher levels of abstraction until the meaning of an utterance is obtained. In practice such an arrangement is very inefficient since the variability of speech requires that a large amount of data be transferred from level to level to ensure that the correct answer is not excluded. The generative, or top-down, model is essentially analysis-by-synthesis at all levels. It is popular because most linguistic rules are easier to express generatively, but the space of behaviour recognisable is constrained by those rules. The heterarchical model allows communication between any knowledge sources. The problem here is to discover the conventions that should be used to enable high level knowledge to interact satisfactorily with low level knowledge. Finally, the blackboard model suggests an organisation analogous to a committee of experts posting notes to each other on a common notice board.

The rest of the paper is devoted to describing two particular automatic speech recognition systems, one very briefly, and the other in depth. The first system (HWIM) was the result of one of the ARPA projects and its structure is a practical demonstration of many of the concepts outlined above, as well as being a candidate for a model of speech perception. However, after five years research it performed poorly! The second system (HARPY) has a provocative structure, it satisfies *all* of the specifications in Figure 1, and it was the result of only one man-year of research effort!

HWIM

HWIM (Hear What I Mean) is the name given to the speech recognition system developed by BBN Inc. (Woods et al., 1976). Its structure is shown in Figure 3. Essentially it conforms to a generative model, although the word verification strategy almost renders it heterarchical. Its task was to recognise utterances pertaining to the management of a travel budget. A typical utterance might be; ''What is the plane fare to Ottowa?''.

HWIM operates by first digitizing the incoming speech and then performing a low level acoustic analysis. The utterance is then segmented and labelled phonetically, a process which results in the segment lattice. This is simply a matrix of alternative segmentations and labellings along the length of the utterance. The accuracy of this stage has been measured as 52% correct phonetic labelling.

Recognition proceeds by searching the segment lattice for a high scoring 'seed' word. This may be found anywhere in the utterance. The technique reflects HWIM's philosophy of working from 'islands of reliability'. A strict left to right policy will be confused if the first word in an utterance is badly articulated. Whereas, stressed information bearing words will tend to be well articulated and hence should act as good anchor points. The best seed words are sent to the word verifier.

The word verification component checks the presence of the seed words by synthesising a spectral representation for each one which is matched against the low level acoustic data. The resulting scores are combined with the lexical matching scores and the word which comes out with the highest score is sent to the syntactic component.

The syntax, in HWIM, is expressed in terms of an augmented transition network (ATN) grammar. When it receives an hypothesised word, it predicts words to the left and right of it. Scores for the predicted words are then obtained via the lexical network (which incorporates word juncture rules). The best scoring two-word hypotheses are verified and sent back to the syntax, which predicts more words to the left and right.

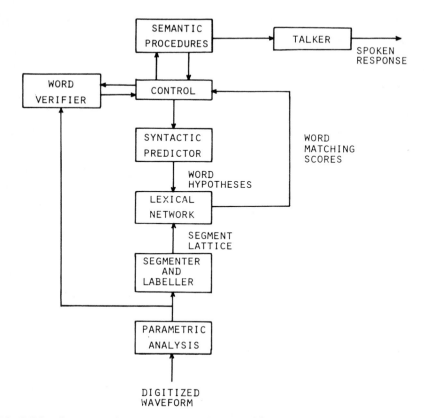

FIGURE 3   *Structure of the HWIM speech recognition system.*

The predict, score, verify cycle continues until a complete sentence is found. Semantic procedures (in practice, embedded in the ATN grammar) are then applied to perform whatever action is required and a verbal response is synthesised.

HWIM operated in one-thousand times real time and, as a result, it was very difficult to optimise. A measure of its linguistic complexity is given by the grammar branching factor of 195. This means that, on average, there were 195 possible words which could legally follow any particular word. HWIM's performance was poor. The utterance recognition rate was only 44% correct.

It can be appreciated from the above description that HWIM tries to recognise utterances in a fairly sensible way. Its structure conforms to a possible model of speech perception, and it uses sophisticated strategies to concentrate its attention on the most likely hypotheses. The fact that its performance is poor is disappointing, and it is not obvious why this is the case. The purpose behind describing HWIM here is to provide a feel for how a conventional speech recognition system works in order to put HARPY into context.

HARPY

Figure 4 shows the structure of the HARPY speech recognition system. Basically it consists of two entirely separate procedures. Prior to any attempt to recognise an utterance, HARPY compiles all its grammatical, lexical and phonetic knowledge into a single huge network. This network contains a representation of *all possible utterances* in the task domain. The compilation phase is a one-off top-down process. To recognise an incoming utterance, it is first subjected to some simple bottom-up analysis and then it is matched against the network. The result of this match determines the identity of the utterance and hence the words within it.

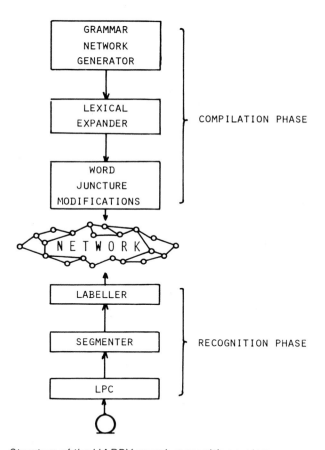

FIGURE 4   *Structure of the HARPY speech recognition system.*

At first sight HARPY appears a rather shallow approach to the speech recognition problem. In fact it has been called an engineering solution. However, it has several redeeming factors. The main one is that it achieved *every single one* of the specifications set out in Figure 1. HARPY could accept continuous speech from three male and two female speakers, in a document retrieval task which had a vocabulary of over one thousand words, and with an utterance recognition rate of 95%. Also, it has a number of interesting properties which seem to relate to behaviour observed in human speech perception. But before discussing these, it is necessary to describe in detail the two phases of HARPY's operation.

Compilation Phase In the compilation phase, HARPY starts out with a definition of its document retrieval grammar as a set of rewrite rules which express the sequential relationships between the words of the task. The HARPY grammar could generate 108 possible sentences up to eight words in length. From the rewrite rules a grammar network is generated. In this network a state corresponds to a word in the grammar, and paths leading from a state indicate allowable words to follow the first word. Figure 5 shows a fragment of the HARPY grammar network. The branching factor was 33.

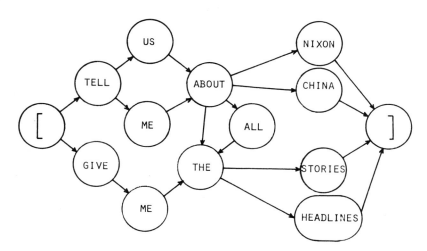

FIGURE 5 *A fragment of the HARPY grammar network.*

The HARPY lexicon contains 1011 words. Each entry in the lexicon represents a number of alternative pronunciations of a particular word. Figure 6 shows the phonetic network that is generated by the lexical entry for the word "into". The next stage of the compilation phase is to expand each state in the grammar network by substituting the appropriate phonetic network for each word. This gives rise to a very large network containing about 15000 states.

The final step is to run through the network applying word juncture rules which modify some of the phonetic states at word boundaries. In practice, HARPY had very few of these rules. The resultant network might look something like Figure 7. This depicts the expansion of the grammar network shown in Figure 5.

Recognition Phase In the recognition phase, incoming speech is segmented into 'chunks' of data which are spectrally stable. The average segment length is 35 ms. Each segment is then labelled phonetically by matching against ninety-eight speaker specific spectral templates. The network is then searched to find which path through it best corresponds to the input utterance. The search is performed using a dynamic programming algorithm:

$$P_{i,t} = A_{i,t} \times \underset{j}{\text{Max}} \left[P_{j,\,t-l} \right]$$

where $P_{i,t}$ is the probability of being in state i at time t, $A_{i,t}$ is the acoustic match probability between the template at state i and the data at time t, and j is restricted to states connected to state i.

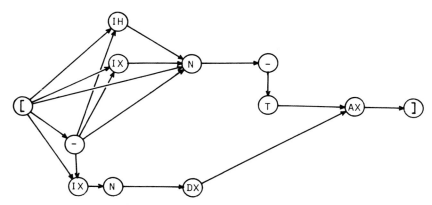

FIGURE 6   *The phonetic network for the word "into".*

In effect, the dynamic programming algorithm considers every possible path through the network. Hence, the best solution is guaranteed. Unfortunately, this results in a large amount of calculation. For an utterance with L segments (say 800) and a network of size N (15000), then N × L (12000000) probabilities must be calculated. HARPY's solution is to keep the 'best few' probabilities within a threshold of the highest state probability at a given point in time. This 'beam search' reduces the amount of calculation to 1% of the total possible. Of course, the reduction means that HARPY can no longer guarantee to find the best solution every time.

Having calculated the probability beam through the network, the words are found by tracing back from the final state along the optimum path. As the backtrace proceeds, so words are read out from the network until the start state is reached. Figure 8 demonstrates this process.

HARPY AS A MODEL OF HUMAN SPEECH PERCEPTION

Despite its provocative structure, HARPY is currently the best automatic speech recognition system available. Consequently, it might be constructive to look at the possibility of considering it as a model of speech perception. Newell has attempted this using a technique known as 'sufficiency analysis' (Newell 1978):

> Important confirming evidence for a psychological theory is whether a system designed according to the theory is sufficient to perform the intellectual functions the theory purports to explain, providing that the mechanisms involved are reasonable according to general knowledge of human capabilities.

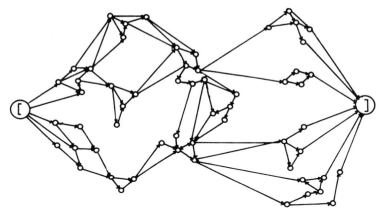

FIGURE 7 *Final network obtained by substituting phonetic networks into the grammar network of figure 5.*

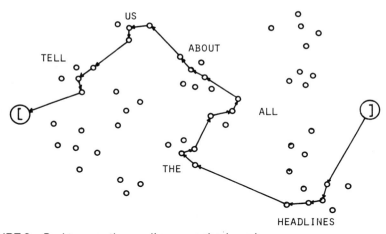

FIGURE 8 *Backtrace path revealing recognised words.*

HARPY is sufficient to recognise speech in its limited task domain, so Newell's idea was to compare its mechanisms with data relating to human speech perception. However, before doing so, Newell mapped HARPY into a general model of human cognition. That is, HARPY's mechanisms are effectively reprogrammed into a machine which already reflects a great deal of human cognitive behaviour. In this way HARPY's mechanisms are easier to discuss. Also, if HARPY can be mapped satisfactorily into such a model, then that alone is an indication of its plausibility as a model of speech perception.

Newell's Model of Human Cognition   Newell's general model of human cognition is based on a production system called HPSA77 (Human Production System Architecture 1977). Figure 9 shows the basic idea. A production memory (long term memory) contains a large number of productions of the form shown. Each production has some conditions associated with it, and if they become satisfied, then the production fires and the prescribed actions are taken. The condition and action elements of a production refer to data elements in the working memory (short term memory).

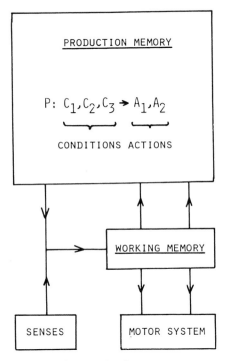

FIGURE 9   *Structure of HPSA77 production system.*

The fundamental behaviour of HPSA77 is the 'recognition-act' cycle. All productions are matched against the contents of the working memory to determine those productions which are satisfied: the 'conflict set'. Productions are then selected from the conflict set on the basis of various priority conditions. A limited number of the actions of the selected production are then activated causing new elements to be placed in the working memory. The recognition-act cycle is then repeated.

In order that HPSA77 might account, both qualitatively and quantitatively, for what Newell called "Sternberg" phenomena in human behaviour, a number of assumptions had to be made. For example, productions could contain variables, but it was necessary to hypothesise a single mechanism for using variables. This imposes some serial behaviour on HPSA77. Another assumption was that elements already established in the production memory have relatively long resident times in working memory, of the order of seconds. Conversely, elements not established in the production memory have relatively short residence times, about ¼ second. Also, to account for some human recall behaviour, HPSA77 assumes that productions themselves remain in a state of activation for many seconds after execution. This means that an activated production may become satisfied again if an element enters working memory that satisfies a single one of its conditions. Finally, to account for the obvious parallelism in human behaviour, productions that do not have variables are free to execute asynchronously and concurrently (subject to some restrictions).

Mapping HARPY into HPSA77 In turning HARPY into a production system, Newell considers only the network and the recognition phase. States in the network correspond to symbols or data elements in the production system. Transitions between states thus become productions. The parametric representation of an incoming utterance arises in the working memory as data elements. The template comparison is performed by the recognition match (although questions of a suitable metric were avoided). Lastly, the probability associated with a point on a path becomes the level of activation of a state data element.

After a considerable amount of discussion, Newell arrives at the production system shown in Figure 10. The network defines the set of productions P. Each P_{ij} generates a transition from State S_i to state S_j without regard for acoustic data. The level of activation of the new state is related to the activation L of the old state, decreased by a factor K_{ij}. This allows states which are not supported by acoustic data to decay. Hence, productions which are off the 'beam' are not activated. To enable the backtrace to be performed, each state element contains an encoding of the identity of the previous state. The " = " symbol in the condition state element causes this backtrace data to be ignored during the operation of a P production. The set of productions Q increases activation d for states supported by acoustic data. This is equivalent to the main function of HARPY's recognition phase.

$$P_{i,j}: \quad (\text{STATE } S_i=)\left[=L\right] \rightarrow (\text{STATE } S_j \ S_i)\left[=L-K_{ij}\right]$$

$$Q_i: \quad (\text{STATE } S_i=)(\text{DATA } A_{i1}\ldots A_{im})\left[=d\right] \rightarrow (\text{STATE } S_i=)\left[+=d\right]$$

$$R_k: \quad D_1D_2\ldots D_m \rightarrow (\text{DATA } D_1D_2\ldots D_m)$$

$$U_1: \quad (\text{STATE }=S=)(\text{DATA } A_S) \rightarrow (\text{UTTERANCE } S_{\text{END}}=S)$$

$$U_2: \quad (\text{UTTERANCE } ==S)(\text{STATE }=S'=S'') \rightarrow (\text{TEST }=S=S'=S'')$$

$$U_3: \quad (\text{TEST }=S=S'=S'') \rightarrow (\text{UTTERANCE }=S=S')$$

$$W_i: \quad (\text{UTTERANCE } S_i=) \rightarrow (\text{WORD } W_x)$$

$$V_k: \quad (\text{DATA } A_k) \rightarrow (\text{STATE } S_j \ S_{\text{START}})\left[L_k\right]$$

FIGURE 10 *Production system for HARPY*

Thus the production sets P and Q perform the HARPY forward search. The P productions generate the network just ahead of the Q productions which boost states which might be on the path. States not on the beam simply die away. The whole process is started by the productions V_k. These use some predefined start signal to generate the first state element which will trigger off the P and Q productions. R_k segments the acoustic representation and causes the description to occur in working memory.

The backtrace is triggered by U, which recognises a long silence (Data A_s) as the end of an utterance. The final state is selected as the state with the highest activation. U_1 uses the variable $=S$ to transfer the identity of the final state of working memory, and this triggers U_2 and U_3 to perform the backtrace. These two productions also use variables, so the backtrace becomes an essentially serial operation. Words are recovered from the backtrace path by the productions W_i.

Sufficiency Analysis   It can be seen from the above that HARPY maps fairly easily into Newell's model of human cognition. Hence, it does seem to be worthy of consideration as a model of speech perception. Newell further pursued his analysis by extending the production system version of HARPY (P.S.HARPY) to cover full speech, that is, a much less restricted domain than used by HARPY. This extension was based on many assumptions about the linguistic complexity of an unrestricted domain, but Newell felt that such a step was necessary if P.S. HARPY was to be compared with data on human speech perception. The result was a set of statistics that seemed to rule out P.S. HARPY as a model. For example, with a grammar branching factor of only 160, P.S.HARPY would require over 1012 productions; obviously out of the question.

However, Newell discovered that by modifying the basic HARPY algorithm in two simple ways, the P.S. HARPY statistics became more reasonable. Figure 11 shows the statistics for P.S.HARPY if the beam width is reduced by a factor of ten, and if the depth before backtrace is reduced by a factor of two. It can be seen that even though, for a branching factor of 320, some of the numbers are very large, they are not inconceivable.

GRAMMAR BRANCHING	20	40	80	160	320
GRAMMAR STATES	200	$2*10^3$	10^4	10^5	$9*10^5$
HARPY STATES	$2*10^3$	10^4	10^5	$9*10^5$	$7*10^6$
BRANCHING FACTOR	3.5	4.2	4.8	5.5	6.3
PRODUCTIONS	$2*10^4$	$9*10^4$	$7*10^5$	$6*10^6$	$5*10^7$
FIRINGS PER SEC	200	10^3	10^4	$9*10^4$	$8*10^5$
W.M. LOAD	30	200	$2*10^3$	10^4	10^5

FIGURE 11   *Statistics for the extension of P.S. HARPY.*

To complete the sufficiency analysis, Newell posed some specific questions. Can P.S.HARPY recognise speech, can it be extended to full speech, and can it recognise full speech quickly enough? Does P.S.HARPY require too much immediate memory? How does it cope with creativity and variability in speech, especially speaker variability? Is language aquisition possible? The answers to some of these questions are contained in the statistics of Figure 11. As to whether it can recognise speech, the basic P.S. HARPY should recognise speech as well as the original, but it is difficult to know what effect the extension might have. Although the grammar branching factor increases, the actual branching factor of the network increases only very slightly, so it is possible that recognition might not be drastically reduced. Newell calculated that P.S. HARPY could recognise speech in four to six times real time, and he postulated some changes in the timing of the recognition-act cycle which might bring this figure down. On the question of P.S.HARPY's response to ungrammatical utterances, it is likely that in such a situation fragments of the network would be activated and it would be up to the, as yet unspecified, semantic component to make sense of the result. The speaker variability problem is the same for P.S.HARPY as for HARPY. Finally, if it is assumed that it takes about ten seconds to learn a new production, then it would take approximately 300 hours to learn a reasonable sized network. This is not an unreasonable length of time.

Newell's conclusion was that despite the many issues left unresolved, P.S.HARPY *did not* seem to be rejectable on sufficiency grounds.

Speech Phenomena Having completed the investigation into the mechanisms of P.S.HARPY, Newell went on to observe some parallels between its behaviour and human behaviour. The first phenomenon is that of automatic extrapolation. It has been shown that, in many different situations, a listener naturally and automatically predicts what the speaker is about to say. This can also occur in P.S.HARPY since the network productions P_{ij} are always activated ahead (and independently) of the search productions Q_i. Consequently, if a break in an utterance occurs, a backtrace will be initiated and states will be retrieved which were generated by P_j but which were not yet supported by Q_i.

A second phenomenon is the phoneme restoration effect. If a noise replaces a phoneme in an utterance, the phoneme is perceived as being present. The noise is heard but it cannot be precisely located in the utterance. In P.S.HARPY, the P_{ij} productions would pass over noise and there would be no evidence remaining to show that the recovered path had been momentarily unsupported. Recognition of noise as noise would require different mechanisms and hence the time localisation of such an event could not be made with respect to the speech events of an utterance. In P.S.HARPY, only speech events are heard in order.

Another phenomenon of speech perception is the apparent absence of active parsing. A listener generally arrives at the syntactic and semantic structure of an utterance without any conscious effort. Further, the listener cannot discover how he worked out such structures. P.S.HARPY exhibits this behaviour (at least syntactically) in as much as the precompiled network avoids the need to parse an utterance. The simple forward and backward passes reveal the syntactic structure directly.

In the situation where there is ambiguity in an utterance, the human can get, at best, a few alternative readings. P.S.HARPY selects the single best path through the network, but it could find alternative paths (many of which would be alternative pronunciations rather than alternative readings). However, P.S. HARPY would also be limited to just a few alternative paths since the paths would be decaying at a rate comparable to the time taken to perform each new backtrace.

The tendency for humans to perceive speech categorically is also reflected by P.S.HARPY. If it is assumed that the P_{ij} productions are acquired in order to discriminate one utterance from another, then the states in the network which develop will reflect syntactic and semantic distinctions in the language. This means that there will be few intermediate states between minimal linguistic distinctions, and the network will behave categorically.

One more phenomenon in perception is the faster recognition time for higher level linguistic units. For example, subjects are able to respond to a word faster than to a letter in the word. Similarly in speech, a word can be recognised faster than one of its syllables, and a syllable can be recognised faster than one of its phonemes. P.S.HARPY might demonstrate this effect since the search reveals the identity of the utterance (the high level data), then tracing the path reveals the words (low level data). Phonemes could be found by a more detailed examination of the path.

Finally, the last phenomenon is the word frequency effect. Common words tend to be more quickly recognised than unfamiliar words. Newell suggests that in P.S.HARPY the decay factor K_{ij} might be a function of frequency of use. Thus, common paths would race ahead to completion. The backtrace could then be triggered early and recognition would follow.

Discussion   There are a number of important areas of speech perception into which P.S.HARPY does not provide any insights. Both HARPY and P.S.HARPY cope with different speakers by having interchangeable sets of speaker specific spectral templates. Obviously, this is not a satisfactory mechanism for speaker normalisation. Also P.S.HARPY does not incorporate any prosodic information. It may be possible to include timing information into the network, but it is not obvious how intonation could be integrated. This reflects on the problem of how semantic structures are organised. P.S.HARPY is basically a recognition strategy, it gives no indication of how the meaning of an utterance might be accessed. The other aspect of perception which P.S.HARPY says little about is learning and adaptation. Is the compilation phase a suitable mechanism for network generation, or is an incremental development more likely? P.S.HARPY does not show how a new situation can be recognised prior to the generation of new productions and states.

It is possible to see some further extensions to P.S.HARPY which would make its structure less controversial. A major problem is the backtrace occuring at the end of an utterance. This does not seem correct psychologically and indeed the statistics Newell calculated showed that it must occur earlier. Newell suggests it could be triggered by silence. Alternatively, perhaps it could be initiated by reliable acoustic cues, for example, syllabic events. This could allow the network to fold back on itself, thus providing the ideal structure in which to apply phonotactic constraints to new words and sentences. Folding back the network at a sub-word level introduces the need for a separate network for words. Otherwise only syllables could be recognised. Following the same arguments, the word network could fold back on itself, thus providing a structure which could apply word juncture rules to new word sequences (in effect, this is the HWIM lexical network). One can therefore imagine a hierarchy of HARPY like networks, each containing a complete inventory of the units at a particular level. In terms of P.S.HARPY, this extension need not alter the P or Q productions, but merely introduces a hierarchy of backtrace mechanisms.

CONCLUSIONS

In 1969 Pierce, at Bell Laboratories, likened the building of automatic speech recognisers to attempting to turn water into gold (Pierce 1969). It might invite similar criticism if it were claimed here that P.S.HARPY is a model of human speech perception. However, in the light of the analysis reported here, it is certain that HARPY should not be simply written off.

Referring back to the question posed in the introduction; can an automatic speech recognition program reveal anything about human speech perception? The answer is an unqualified *yes*, for two reasons: Firstly, this paper has shown how an actual speech recogniser has led to some interesting insights into some aspects of human behaviour. Secondly, the field of speech perception does have a new model to put alongside the motor theory etc. The LAFS model (Klatt, this conference) *has come directly from the work in automatic speech recognition*. In fact, it turns out that this paper has been a tutorial on the background of the LAFS model.

From an automatic speech recognition point of view, HARPY is simply the best system that currently exists. It represents a remarkable solution to the phonetic-syntactic interface. Nevertheless, for any progress to be made in using such a model to build more complex systems, which tackle tasks the size of the one HWIM attempted, there must be an immense improvement in the understanding and implementation of acoustic-phonetic mechanisms. Consequently, it is probably more important that workers in speech recognition pay strict attention to the work in speech perception, rather than the other way round.

THE COGNITIVE REPRESENTATION OF SPEECH
T. Myers, J. Laver, J. Anderson (editors)
© *North-Holland Publishing Company, 1981*

Speech Recognition Programs as Models of Speech Perception

JACQUELINE VAISSIERE

Centre National d'Etudes des Télécommunications, Lannion

INTRODUCTION

Computer scientists have, in recent years, turned their attention increasingly to programs for the computer recognition of spoken sentences. The work has not only brought to light some fundamental questions concerning the way the acoustic signal has to be processed in order that words embedded in sentences may be recognised automatically, it has also, indirectly, stimulated research on the cognitive aspects of sentence perception.

Although there is no clear consensus at present concerning an ideal system organisation for a speech recognition system (SRS), and although the performance of existing SRSs is still a long way from matching the level of human performance, the solutions reached in this area may make a valuable contribution to the effort to construct models of the way humans perceive speech. For comprehensive reviews of speaker recognition systems in the United States see Reddy (1976), Klatt (1977) and De Mori (1979).

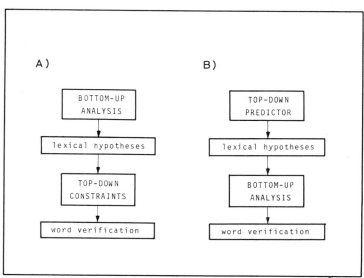

FIGURE 1   *Bottom-up and top-down components of an SRS*

As Klatt observed, an SRS may be thought to consist of two main components: a *bottom-up* component that converts acoustic data into lexical hypotheses and a *top-down* component that attempts to predict the words most likely to have been spoken (see Figure 1).

The first part of this paper concerns the problem of determining how much information (segmental and suprasegmental) can be derived automatically by direct analysis of the input signal. It will be shown that not enough information can be extracted from the acoustic input to decode the spoken sentence into a unique string of words. A bottom-up analysis of the speech signal results in multiple lexical hypotheses (candidates). One is led to ask whether, in the processing of the same sentence by a human listener, a strictly bottom-up analysis would be sufficient to derive a unique representation of the sentence.

The second part of this paper deals with the use of other sources of prestored knowledge about the sentences in a particular language, knowledge of syntactic, semantic, and pragmatic constraints. Such top-down constraints are used in an SRS to select, from the lexical hypotheses proposed by the bottom-up analysis, the most likely sequence of words corresponding to the spoken input. Such a strategy is discussed in relation to human perception of speech.

PART ONE: BOTTOM-UP ANALYSIS OF THE SPEECH SIGNAL

The ultimate purpose of an SRS is to recognize the successive *words* in the spoken sentence. The word is the major point of interaction, in an SRS, between the acoustic input, the lexicon (which contains the list of possible words), and the available top-down constraints. We shall first review the two basic problems associated with the word as an acoustic entity, that the word is embedded in a sentence, and that the sentence is pronounced differently by different speakers. The first problem concerns the segmentation of the spoken sentence into a discrete sequence of words. The second concerns the identification of each word in the sequence.

Segmental and Suprasegmental Cues to Word-Boundaries   One of the strategies that might be incorporated into an automatic sentence recognition system is first to detect where individual words start and end, and then to "translate" the portion of the acoustic continuum corresponding to each word into its orthographic form, using some kind of acoustic-orthographic lexicon (a word-template matching technique).

In fact, the speech signal contains some known segmental and suprasegmental cues to word boundaries:
— the *segmental cues* can be distinct syllable-initial allophones (/l/ and /r/, for example, in English, see Nakatani et al, 1977), burst, aspiration, glottal stops, laryngealisation, etc. . . (see for example, Lehiste, 1976).
— the *suprasegmental cues* are duration and fundamental frequency (Fo), which contrast the initial and the final syllable of a word against the surrounding syllables, A *word-final syllable lengthening* has been observed for a number of languages, including French (Delattre, 1938), Swedish (Lindblom, 1968), and English (Oller, 1973). *Word-initial consonants* are lengthened relative to the word-medial consonants (Lehiste, 1960; Oller, 1973; Klatt, 1974; Umeda, 1977). Fo contours may also be cues to word-boundaries. In French, the word-demarcating function of the Fo contours seems to be more apparent than in other languages, because the Fo fluctuations in this particular language are primarily dependent on the location of word boundaries (Vaissière, 1975), while in other languages, like English and Swedish, they are related to the lexical stress position. However, it is interesting to note that segmental lengthening as a word-boundary marker is a common characteristic for French, English and Swedish.

The first question to be asked is whether it is possible, in an SRS, to divide the sentence into word-like segments prior to word recognition. The answer is rather negative for the following three reasons. First, the boundaries of successive words may not necessarily have clear acoustic correlates (segmental or suprasegmental), at least not in sentences that are pronounced none too carefully. Second, even when such cues exist, there are difficulties in identifying them uniquely as boundary markers: the segmental cues to word boundary (such as word-initial allophones) are of the same nature as other segmental cues. The acoustic-phonetic analyzer in an SRS, as we will see later, is not able to assign just one label to each segment, and a fortiori, to distinguish the segmental cues to word boundary from other segmental cues. The suprasegmental cues are less ambiguous, but a durational or Fo contrast can often receive more than a single interpretation in terms of word-boundaries. Thirdly, the segmental and suprasegmental cues are not invariant: they vary quantitatively (and we may say also qualitatively) from one sentence to another, and from one speaker to another. The durations and the Fo values have to be interpreted relative to a baseline, and the baseline varies also with the rate of speaking. Consequently, none of the existing SRSs starts the analysis of the input sentence by segmentating it into word-like segments.

The situation is probably very different for a human listener. The segmental and the suprasegmental cues may help to recover many of the word boundaries. It is difficult to evaluate the exact contribution of such cues in the sentence recognition process. However, some experiments indicate that prosodic features must play a large role in sentence processing. They are transmitted even when the speech is unrecognizable, provided that enough of the segmental information remains for the syllabicity to be perceived (Blesser, 1969). They are the parts of the speech signal most resistant to distortion. Carlson (1973) used reiterant speech to show that listeners could transcribe the stress pattern and also hear word boundaries (see also Nakatani and Schaffer, 1978; Liberman and Streeter, 1978). It is probably feasible to formalize the way listeners use the information contained in reiterant speech, and to transfer such a capabiliiy to a computer. However, none of the existing SRSs is able to extract information from reiterant speech, because the prosodic characteristics of the sentence are with few exceptions, not used. The exceptions are considered later.

Variability in Word Pronunciation The second problem arises from variability in pronounciation. A given word does not just have one acoustic image, either on the segmental or on the suprasegmental levels. The factors influencing the acoustic realisation of a word in a sentence are numerous: the identity of the speaker (inter-speaker variations); the pronounciation rate; the speaking style; the sentence the word is embedded in; the prior context (the less predicatable a word the more carefully is it pronounced (Liberman, 1963)), etc. . . The quality obtained by synthesis-by-rule programs for a number of languages demonstrates that, despite high intelligibility, we do not yet have a complete model of how to control for the variability in pronounciation of a word on either the segmental (especially since there is a lack of rules for word-to-word coarticulation) or on the suprasegmental levels. However, it has to be noted that some of the variations can be captured by so-called "phonological rules".

It is known that some of the variation occurring in natural, continuous speech, that assocated with palatalisation, vowel reduction, alveolar flapping, assimilation, etc... (see for example, Schane, 1973 and Selkirk, 1972) is governed by phonological environment. Many of these systematic variations can be captured as general phonological rules and incorporated explicitly or implicitly in an SRS (Oshika et al, 1975). Such rules consist essentially of relabeling segmental units (insertion, deletion, or allophonic variations). The rules have proved very useful in SRSs, not only for predicting alternative pronounciations for a given word, but for indicating also invariant characteristics of the word. In a word like "médecin"[me dœs ɛ̃],in French, for example, the intermediate /ʲe/ may be suppressed, the voiced /d/ may consequently be devoiced (/t/) in contact with the voiceless fricative /s/ (assimilation rule) and the close vowel /e/ may become more open /ɛ/). But the initial consonant /m/ and the final syllable /s ɛ̃/ are not altered by the phonological rules. The initial consonant and the final syllable may be considered as relatively precise targets for that word, while the other intermediate sounds have to be represented by an incomplete set of distinctive features.

Further, none of the existing systems has solved the problem of speaker adaptation: recognition scores drop considerably when a sentence is pronounced by a speaker unknown to the system. A system such as Harpy (Lowerre, 1976), which is the only existing speaker-adaptable sentence recognition system, requires first to analyse about twenty known sentences pronounced by the speaker, in order to derive talker-specific templates. The main problem is the lack of a valid and formalized theory on how human listeners adapt to a new talker. Relatively little research has been done on automatic speaker adaptation, and only ad-hoc solutions, such as that adopted in Harpy, are presently available.

Because of the intra- and interspeaker variabilities in pronunciation, it is impossible to decode all of the words in a sentence by using only a word pattern-matching technique (Klatt, 1977). A more complicated access to the lexicon is needed and an intermediate representation of the acoustic input necessary, in order to match the speech signal against the lexicon. Human listeners, by contrast, adapt very well to word variability in pronunciation, though, as noted earlier, little is known about how they adapt. Moreover, the acoustic information embodying a word is sometimes insufficient to specify its identity as may be demonstrated by excerpting the word from its sentence context (Pollack and Picket, 1953). This is particularly the case when the sentence is pronounced rapidly, as in every-day conversation. Miller et al (1951) showed that for a given signal-to-noise ratio, intelligibility is greater for words heard in sentence context than for words heard in isolation. The fact that the speech signal may not contain enough information for an immediate decision concerning the word, plays an important role in speech perception models. This problem will be reviewed later, together with a discussion of the different strategies simulated in those SRSs for recognizing words embedded in sentences.

The Segmental Representation of Words We have noted that a word cannot be represented in the lexicon as an acoustic invariant because it cannot be found as such in sentences. The problem of prestoring the representation of a word is twofold. First, the representation has to be sufficiently abstract to be adequate for any spoken occurrence of the word. Second, the representation has to be concrete enough that it may be compared with the input acoustic signal. Any solution of the representation problem will therefore, be a compromise between the two contradictory requirements. So far no conscensus has been reached concerning the optimum representation of a word in the lexicon. But let us examine briefly problems associated with the choice of a unit of representation smaller than the word.

One kind of abstract representation for a word that springs immediately to mind is, of course, that of a sequence of phonemes, or at least, some kind of phonetic transcription (with the assumption that for each word there may correspond more than one phonetic transcription). Such an approach has been adopted in most SRSs. There are, however, basically two problems associated with the phoneme as a unit for the bottom-up analysis of a speech signal: the first is that of segmentation (due to the fact that the signal is continuously varying); the second concerns the labeling of the phoneme-sized segments (due to the variability in the acoustic realisation of a phoneme).

Automatic segmentation of the continuum into phoneme-like segments works, in fact, much better than one might expect. Some boundaries between certain phonemes are indeed difficult to locate, particularly when the variations are not rapid enough (such as for the consonants /l/ and /r'/, and the dipthongs). In general, the automatic procedure "misses" some boundaries, "creates" extra-boundaries, and some boundaries are shifted. Segmentation obtained automatically is comparable with the results obtained by visual inspection of spectrograms. The details of the segmentation procedure vary from one system to another: for example, in a system like Hearsay I (Reddy et al, 1976), a partial identification may precede segmentation. A spectral template sampled every 10 msec is labeled and then the templates with the same labels are grouped together into a phoneme-sized unit. The segmentation into phoneme-sized units may be preceded by a segmentation into syllable-like units, etc. . . The general philosophy underlying the segmentation is that a boundary is accompanied by a rapid spectral change, and that the nucleus of the vocalic part of the syllable corresponds to a peak in amplitude (in a voiced portion) where the acoustic properties are changing relatively slowly over time.

The phoneme-like segment may be labeled by direct spectral matching (particularly if the speaker is known by the system), or by matching a certain number of parameters extracted from the speech signal. These parameters vary from one system to another: formant frequencies, formant transitions, fundamental frequency gross spectral shape, burst onsets, zero crossing counts, linear prediction coefficients, energy as a function of time in several frequency passbands, etc. . . Generally, the number of labels is higher than the number of phonemes, and it includes a certain number of allophones. Further, a single label may correspond to multiple reference patterns.

Depending on the system strategy chosen to deal with the problem of errors, ambiguities and omissions, a number of possible labels is assigned with a probability score. None of the systems is able to assign one label only to each of the successive segments. As will be seen later, the speech signal does not contain enough information for immediate decisions about the identity of each successive phoneme.

One of the sources of indecision in the labeling of segments arises from coarticulation: the production of a phoneme is partially influenced by the identity of the surrounding phonemes. Because of coarticulation (Ohman, 1966), some researchers do not agree that a phoneme-like segment is the optimum size of unit in an SRS. Considering environmental assimilation, Fujimura (1975) has proposed the syllable as a better unit. Many of the systems actually perform, with relative success, a segmentation of the continuum into syllable-like segments (such a segmentation is essentially based on local maxima and minima in the overall amplitude function of the utterance). In fact, syllables are easier to locate than phonemes (Mermelstein, 1975; Gresser and Mercier, 1975). There are however, some problems in assigning syllable-boundaries (it is not always clear if a consonant belongs to the preceding or to the following syllable; the consonant clusters pose a particular problem). The properties of a given syllable are partially influenced both by the position of the syllable in the sentence and by the surrounding syllables. The number of syllables in a language is much larger than the number of phonemes (between one and ten thousand for a language like French or English). However, there seem to be clear advantages in using the syllable or the demisyllable as a unit (Fujimura, 1976c). The inventory size for demisyllables is relatively small (less than one thousand for English, compared with ten thousand for syllables: see Lovins et al, 1979). Some work is in progress using the syllable as a unit (Mermelstein, 1975; De Mori et al, 1976; Ruske and Schotola, 1978).

Perhaps motivated by the success of a system like Harpy (Lowerre, 1976), which is rather simple conceptually in comparison with other systems, Klatt proposes an acoustic-phonetic regognizer whereby the transitions are represented by sequences of a few static spectra (Klatt, 1979). Just as in Harpy the acoustic units are steady-state portions of the speech signal, and the problem of segmentation is avoided to some extent, so in Klatt's system the transition from say, the consonant /t/ to the vowel /a/ in a word like "top", is represented by four static spectra, corresponding to the silence, the burst, the aspiration and the voicing onset, respectively. Klatt hopes to discover the appropriate measurements to compare the input spectra of the signal to be identified (sampled every 10 msec) with spectral templates in a network. The system is not realised as yet.

Klatt's approach has some aspects in common with Gestalt theory as applied to the perception of speech. In the Gestalt approach, the unit of recognition, whether phoneme, syllable or word is treated as a configurational whole. It is not analysed into smaller elements. Accordingly, the word is both an acoustic entity and a unit of perception; it is recognized as a whole and there is no intermediate recognition of the speech sounds (or phonemes) that constitute it. If the phoneme (instead of the word) is taken as the primary unit of recognition, it also is recognized as a whole (or a Gestalt), and there is no prior detection of a set of subphonemic units. Dynamic programming, which is a method currently used for the automatic recognition of isolated words pronounced by a known speaker, simulates the Gestalt approach. Although Klatt's approach is probably of theoretical interest for automatic recognition, it is not convincingly superior to Gestalt theory in providing a model of speech perception by humans.

Because of the progress made between 1965 and 1975 in research on the physiology and psychophysics of the auditory system, new acoustic-phonetic analyzers have been built, which incorporate essential psychoacoustic principles (Caelen, 1979; Searle et al, 1979; Zwicker et al, 1979). Whether such developments represent a promising advance toward the recognition of syllables and phonemes, they do permit better simulation of speech processing at the level of the peripheral auditory system by enabling the discriminative capabilities of the receptors to be taken into account. At higher levels, speech seems to be perceived categorically (Liberman et al, 1967). Consider in particular, the perception of consonants.

There is no a priori reason why a machine has to identify the units of segmentation, whether phoneme-sized, syllable-sized, or steady-state portions of the acoustic continuum, in the way that human listeners do. Machines are probably better than the human ear in certain tasks, such as pattern matching, while the human brain is better at identification based on the integration of decisions based on a large number of cues. Research in speech perception has been concerned with determining the relevant acoustic cues necessary for the perception of phonetic contrasts in natural language, and it has tended to follow the analytic approach, concentrating on the simplest possible stimuli, such as monosyllabic pairs presented in isolation (Pisoni, 1978). It is not obvious that the results can be applied directly to real-life communication. It is still a matter of controversy whether speech perception by human listeners involves at a preliminary stage, or even at a later stage, the identification of an ordered series of units, such as phonemes. Fant (1962) noted that the identification of phonemes in a sentence is probably not strictly sequential, but of arbitrary order, within a time-window that spans a number of syllables. Morton and Broadbent (1967) speculated that under certain circumstances (low signal-to-noise ratios) the perception of speech sounds may be processed by an indirect, constructive or inferential route (cf, Neisser, 1967). It may be hypothesized that some words are recognized without identifying every phoneme. A few segmental cues, together with suprasegmental characteristics, could be sufficient to recognize most of the words occurring in every-day speech, due to the redundancy of the message, the prior context, etc. . . (see the discussion on recognition strategies below).

Compared to machines, human listeners are generally very good at deriving directly from the auditory signal a phonetic transcription (at least a rough phonetic transcription), even if the words are nonsense words, provided they are composed of plausible strings of phonemes for the particular language, and that they are pronounced carefully (listeners are sensitive to the phonotactic structure of their language). The perceptual skill that underlies phonetic transcription has never been well enough explained that an algorithm could be derived to transmit such a capability to a machine. Here too, formal models are lacking. Existing programs are unable to give a unique representation of clearly pronounced syllables or isolated phonemes.

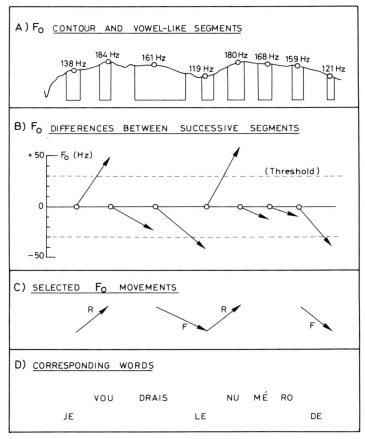

FIGURE 2   *Segment lattice, Fo analysis and lexical match* [2]

Figure 2A illustrates the output from an acoustic-phonetic analyzer in one recognition system, the KEAL system (for the French language). The segmentation into syllables involves an error of less than 5% (including insertions and missing syllables). To each phoneme-like segment are assigned automatically a number of alternative labels, arranged in their order of probability. Analysis of the results shows that speaker-independent detection of the manner of articulation by a set of "features" (voicing "detector", frication "detector", etc. . .) is relatively successful while identification of the place of articulation, though less successful, is better than might have been expected, except by specialists in automatic speech recognition. In a system like KEAL, which is not yet speaker-adaptable, the "ideal" phoneme is one of the first labels proposed in more than 75% of those instances that the speaker is not the reference speaker (see Mercier, 1979, for more details). Some of the segments represented in Figure 2 are superimposed with a prosodic mark, derived directly from the anlysis of the input signal in the manner we will now briefly describe.

The Suprasegmental Representation of a Sentence   A system can construct a prosodic representation of the sentence to be recognized directly from the speech signal, and prior to phoneme recognition. The prosodic component records the duration of the successive syllables, on the one hand, and selects the Fo value corresponding to the steady-state portion of each vocalic part, on the other. The longest syllables are then selected (using a speaker-dependent threshold), and the large Fo movements between two successive vowels are located (using two speaker-dependent thresholds, for the Fo rises and the Fo falls, respectively). The prosodic markers are superimposed on the segmental representation (Figure 2B). See Vaissière (1976), Vivès et al (1977) for the Fo markers, and Vaissière (1977), for the duration markers, for the French system; see Lea (1973, 1976) for English.

Only the French system KEAL, uses the suprasegmental representation of the sentence for narrowing down the number of lexical hypotheses. Lea has proposed to use the existence of fall-rise valleys in Fo to score the likelihood of major syntactic boundaries. Both approaches are complementary. The way prosodic markers may be used to narrow down the number of lexical hypotheses will be discussed, after the different strategies for accessing the lexicon have been presented.

Access to the Segmental Lexicon   Without going into detail, we may note that there are at least four different strategies for accessing the lexicon.
(1)— the words can be arranged in the lexicon according to their acoustic similarities from left to right, as in the alphabetic order of a dictionary. The recognition of the first acoustic segment in a word constrains the range of possible acoustic segments which may follow.
(2)— the entire parametric representation of the words is taken into consideration for comparison with the hypothesized labels from the speech input. The ordering of the words in the lexicon is not important in such an access strategy.
(3)— the access to the lexicon can be hierarchical: the words are first grouped according to their gross syllable structure, in particular, the number of syllables and the presence of a stop or a fricative. An advantage of such an arrangement comes from the fact that the acoustic-phonetic analyzers perform better at identifying the manner-of-articulation (vowels versus consonants, fricatives, stops, etc. . .) than the place of articulation. A finer phonetic transcription is then carried out on words with the same gross syllable structure.
(4)— the words are arranged in the lexicon according to acoustic similarities in their stressed syllables. Such an arrangement is based on the fact that the stressed syllable in a word is likely to be more carefully pronounced by the speaker, and consequently to contain better acoustic correlates for a fine acoustic transcription. The problem with such an access to the lexicon is that the location of every word's lexical stress has to be automatically detected in the continuum, prior to recognition. No such algorithm seems to exist.

We should note that it is possible, theoretically, for there to be more than one way to access the lexicon. However, SRSs generally employ a single means of access.

Figure 3 illustrates the results obtained after the lexical search has taken place: the segment lattice representation of the sentence has been replaced by a word lattice representation. Every lexical hypothesis is assigned a probability score. The lexicon, in this example, has been accessed using the second method. The system accepts some missing segments, extra segments and errors in matching the lexicon against the input in the segment lattice representation of the sentence.

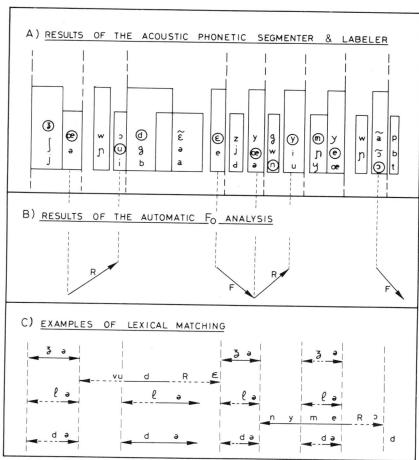

FIGURE 3   *Automatic detection of Fo markers* [3]

The lexical hypotheses can now undergo two kinds of verification: a segmental verification and a suprasegmental one.

Verification by analysis-by-synthesis The results of the Klatt-Stevens spectrograms experiments (Klatt and Stevens, 1973), suggest that an ability to verify word hypotheses against acoustic evidence could be useful in an SRS for scoring the likelihood of the hypotheses. Given a word hypothesized at a given position in a sentence, a verification component looks up the pronounciation of the word in a dictionary, then generates an acoustic representation of the word by a synthesis-by-rule program. The parameters of the hypothesized word, which are derived from the synthesis-by-rule program, and the parameters of the portion of utterance corresponding to the hypothesized word are then compared. A distance measure is interpreted as the likelihood of the word having actually occurred over the given portion of the utterance (Woods et al, 1976). Such a strategy is used in the BBN system. The problem with such an approach is that it is impossible adequately to synthesize by-rule the speaker-dependent segmental and suprasegmental parameters corresponding to a given word in a given position (demisyllabic patterns may afford a better approach than a strictly synthesis-by-rule approach). As noted before, the problem of automatic speech synthesis is itself only partially solved.

Suprasegmental verification The general philosophy underlying the prosodic component of the KEAL system is that a word can be represented not only by a phonetic transcription, but also by a network of expected suprasegmental characteristics.

The use of prosody in the KEAL system is still rather experimental. An extensive analysis of Fo contours demonstrates that a large Fo movement between two syllables (that is a rise or a fall), may be superimposed only on specific syllables in a word. For example, only the first or the last syllable of a word may be accompanied by a large rise. The prosodic component verifies that the lexical hypotheses do not contradict such prosodic constraints. The verification procedure in KEAL indicates that the prosodic component is more powerful in eliminating long words (where there are more prosodic constraints) than short words.

The relative duration of the syllables in the word may also be included in the lexicon as an intrinsic characteristic of the word (for example, in French, the last syllable, is, ceteris paribus, the longest). Unfortunately, the part of the prosodic component based on duration has not yet been included in the general system, because the module is very sensitive to errors in segmentation by the acoustic-phonetic analyzer (Vaissière, 1977). This idea should be tested in a system where the phonetic transcription is given a priori, but it has not as yet been done.

A prosodic component has also been developed for one of the SRSs for English. Its function is to score the likelihood of major syntactic boundaries, by reference to features of the Fo contour of the utterance. It is based on the fact that boundaries between major constituents are often marked by fall-rise valleys in Fo. One of the problems in using intonationally-detected phrase boundaries is that the position of the detected boundary may not line up with the exact location of the boundary between phrases. Unfortunately, this component was not sufficiently tested to be included in the final version of the BBN (Bolt, Beranek, and Newman) SRS. In fact, the systems developed for English have usually ignored the suprasegmental aspect of the input signal. Their theoretical orientation tends to exclude the consideration of prosody.

We have noted that the different SRSs use disparate strategies for access to the lexicon. The arrangement of the lexical items in the mental lexicon is not well known either, though there are various hypotheses. Cutler (1976) notes that several kinds of adjacency for words in the lexicon are possible. She speculates, however, that the primary principle by which a word is classified is the nature of its stressed syllable. When a stressed syllable is identified, the sentence processor can begin at once to locate in the mental lexicon the word of which it is a part, using information about the stressed syllable and the number of unstressed syllables immediately before and after it. A number of possible matches might be found and compared with the (incomplete) information about the phonetic structure of the unstressed syllables before a choice is made. Cutler argues that a part of the sentence comprehension process is the prediction of sentence accents. In an instance of the "tip-of-the-tongue" phenomenon, a speaker may produce a word which, while unrelated in meaning to the target word, reproduces correctly its stress pattern and the nature of its stressed syllable (Brown and McNeill, 1966, reported by Cutler, 1976). Such an approach seems very reasonable for English.

Another approach to mental lexicon access assumes that words are arranged according to similarities in their beginnings. The sounds which begin a word are used to access word candidates (Cole and Jakimik, 1979; Marslen-Wilson, 1978). Accordingly, reaction times to mispronounced second syllables are about 180 msec faster than mispronunciations in word-initial syllables. Cole and Jakimik found that the faster reaction time to mispronounced second syllables is largely independent of syllable stress.

Prosodic analysis of the speech signal argues in favor of both approaches (which are contradictory, if we assume that there is only one access to the mental lexicon): the stressed syllable is made more prominent relative to the surrounding syllables by both Fo and durational contrasts; the word beginnings are also prosodically marked (particularly in French), by consonant lengthening, syllable-initial allophones, and the Fo contour.

There are other more complex representations of the mental lexicon, as in, for example, the logogen model (each word in the lexicon has a corresponding logogen, which contains a specification of the word's defining characteristics along various perceptual and semantic dimensions; see Morton, 1969) and the autonomous search model (information about words are stored in a master file, and access to the entries in this file is only possible through a number of different access files (see Forster, 1976)). See Marslen-Wilson and Welsch (1978) for a discussion of different models.

We may conclude that there is more than one possible access to the lexion in an SRS, and none of the methods adopted has proved superior to any other. Likewise, more than one model has been proposed for access to the mental lexicon in human speech processing. Concerning the representation of words in the mental lexicon, we do not know to what extent this is acoustic (with invariant segmental features). Moreover, the possible role of prosodic cues in the identification of a particular word in such a lexicon, though potentially of great interest, remains largely unexplored.

Conclusion to Part One: We have seen that segmental and suprasegmental information conveyed by the speech signal cannot provide for a unique solution to the bottom-up analysis of spoken sentences, even when the lexical inventory is extremely limited. General purpose SRSs, therefore, must also take account of the structural properties of the speech signal, those that are specific to the language in question. Accordingly, knowledge of the phonology, syntax and semantics of the language has to be prestored in the SRS. Pragmatic knowledge also must be stored for particular tasks. Using these linguistic and pragmatic constraints, the amount of acoustic information necessary for an SRS to recognize a sentence is reduced.

PART TWO: TOP-DOWN CONSTRAINTS

Since it is impossible to uniquely decode the sentence to be recognized by a bottom-up analysis, with an acoustic-phonetic analyzer and a lexicon (together with some phonological rules describing systematic variations in the pronunciations of the words, and with some suprasegmental constraints on the words), other sources of knowledge are needed. Let us then, briefly review the different types of top-down constraints used in SRSs.

Top-down Sources of Knowledge   The top-down knowledge included in existing SRSs is more or less task-dependent. This knowledge can be phonological, syntactic, semantic, pragmatic or prosodic. The meaning of words like "phonology", "syntax", "semantics" or "pragmatics" has little in common with the linguistic competence of a native speaker to recognize a sentence as syntactically, semantically or pragmatically incorrect or prosodically inadequate.

Phonology may include statistics on the occurrence of a particular phoneme, or of a sequence of phonemes, or statistics on stressed syllables (Rossi, 1975). The phonological rules implemented in the BBN system are an instance of this use of the term "phonology" (Oshika et al, 1975). Phonology consists essentially of a description of the restrictions on sequential combinations of segments in a particular language. None of the systems is able to decide if a syllable pronounced in isolation may or may not belong to the language in question.

Syntax, semantics and pragmatics provide a description of the restrictions on word combinations in a particular language. They provide a mechanism for reducing search by restricting the number of acceptable alternatives. Such knowledge can be used either for the selection of words proposed by the bottom-up analysis (as verifiers), or it can be used to predict (and propose) a list of candidates for a word occurring in the spoken sentence. Such predictions are then compared with the parametric representation of the sentence (see Figure 2). A relatively task-independent syntax has been included in most of the systems, because syntax is somehow an already formalized concept. The semantic and the pragmatic components included in the systems are strictly task-dependent.

The problem with the use of prosody is that the suprasegmental features are intimately integrated with a number of other sources of knowledge, such as syntax (the hierarchical groupings of the words into larger and larger units often have prosodic correlates), semantics (the "prosodic word" (Vaissière, 1975) may be viewed as a unit of meaning, and the prosodic features contribute to put into relief the more important units of meaning in a sentence), and pragmatics (focusing on a word or a sequence of words, depending on the prior context). One of these three sources of influence may dominate in a sentence, and the same sentence may be pronounced very differently from one speaker to another. Such a fact may explain why prosody has been of reduced use in existing SRSs, and why it has been used only in verification tasks at the level of the word (Vaissière, 1976) or at the level of the syntax (Lea, 1976).

The Different Strategies Employed in SRSs.   All of the systems use top-down constraints, but the philosophies for using them differ. The computer can store an entire phonetic representation of speech in memory. It is technically possible to start from any place in the sentence. Strictly left-to-right sentence analysis is, however, more often used. Such a strategy allows for wider use of the syntactic constraints: fewer local syntactic constraints can be applied to a segment in the middle of an utterance (Reddy, 1976). The syntax can predict the possible right extensions of a hypothesized word sequence. A problem may arise if the beginning of the sentence has not been clearly pronounced, or is not well scored.

Middle-out strategies are based on the fact that some words can show a high score and represent "safety islands" or "seeds". For some "seeds", it is possible to predict what words could appear to both the left and right of them (syntactic, semantic, or pragmatic predictions). Each of the predicted words is matched against the unmatched symbols, and an acceptable word sequence generated. This process is repeated until an acceptable word sequence has been determined for the whole sentence. It may also extend all sequences in parallel (see Reddy, 1976, for a review).

A hybrid strategy can also be used (Wolf and Woods, 1979): the system jumps over the initial first few segments to find a seed word, and then works strictly left-to-right.

Independently of the fact that the sentence may be recognized by a left-to-right or by a middle-out strategy, is the problem of having all available sources of knowledge communicate and collaborate in the presence of errors and uncertainties. The simplest organisation is that illustrated by a system like Harpy (Lowerre, 1976): the different sources of knowledge are precompiled into a uniform network representation at the level of the spectrum (the sentence is strictly processed from left to right, as well as the words). In a simple system like Hearsay II (Lesser et al, 1975), the system configuration consists of a set of parallel asynchronous processes that stimulate each of the component knowledge sources of an SRS, and the knowledge sources communicate via a blackboard (see Klatt, 1977, for a review). The block diagrams and the organisational philosophies differ from one system to another. Some configurations, such as in Harpy, can only be used if the task domain and the syntax are very restricted.

What is the strategy used by human listeners to recognize sentences? Pisoni (1975) notes that current theories of speech perception are ''quite general and vague, and for the most part, not terribly well developed, at least by the standards in other areas of experimental psychology. Indeed, it is not unreasonable to characterize these theories as only preliminary attempts at specifying what a possible model of human speech perception might entail.'' (Pisoni, 1978, pp 217).

Hierarchical organization of levels of processing in speech perception has been assumed by some investigators (Liberman, 1970). The levels of processing may be the following: the auditory level, the phonetic level, the phonological level, the syntax and semantics. The number and the ordering of these levels are still a matter of controversy. In a serial process, the direction of information is serial so that, whatever the later interactions between levels, the initial input to a given level requires a preliminary analysis at least, at the level just below (Miller, 1962).

A fully interactive parallel process has been proposed also: each word, as it is heard in the context of normal discourse, is immediately entered into the processing system at all levels (phonetic, lexical, syntactic and semantic) of description and is simultaneously analyzed at all these levels in the light of whatever information is available in the processing of the sentence (Marslen-Wilson, 1975).

The word is often proposed as a decision unit. Miller (1962) suggests that the phrase —usually two or three words at a time— is probably the natural decision unit for speech. He assumes that people have available a relatively slow, single-channel mechanism for making decisions, so that it is necessary to store some of the input information and to process it as a unit. Decisions, therefore, occur at discrete points in time and serve to mark the boundaries for the units involved. The larger decisions are pursued first, and details are pursued only in so far as they are necessary to serve our immediate purpose. Such a delayed-decision strategy provides an opportunity to take advantage of the redundancy of the message. In word-by-word processing, as proposed by Marslen-Wilson (1975) and others, the listener takes advantage of the prior context and of early intervention from top-down decisions. In contrast to Miller's theory, these decisions can be made before sufficient bottom-up information could have accumulated to allow a single word-candidate to be selected on the basis of bottom-up information alone (in other words, a word may be recognized before being completely uttered).

Unfortunately, SRSs are not flexible enough to verify hypotheses about the possible strategies used by human listeners in processing speech. They are far from simulating the various sources of knowledge that a human being may use. The acoustic and prosodic cues, and the semantic, syntactic, and circumstantial cues are not well defined. Moreover, there is probably more than one valid model for speech perception. Aaranson (1976) demonstrates that the task demands (essentially memory and comprehension demands) influence the listener's coding procedure and also the resultant linguistic representation of the stimulus. The memory and comprehension demands influence the direction of coding, the structural units involved, and the coding time over the sentence. These task demands also influence the linguistic level and the amount and classes of stimulus information that are preserved by the subject. Aaranson notes that while the human being is tremendously flexible in his coding strategies, all too often the psycholinguist is unconcerned with the cognitive requirements of the experimental task, and the cognitive psychologist does not vary the linguistic properties of the stimulus material.

CONCLUDING REMARKS:

There is no clear agreement about choice of segmentation unit in an SRS; access to the lexicon; the representation of words in the lexicon, or the strategies for using sources of knowledge higher than the input signal. Nor is there any clear agreement about how speech is processed by humans, although more and more is known about the capabilities of human listeners in certain circumscribed tasks. The problem in the human case, is to integrate knowledge about the diverse abilities of listeners into a single speech perception model. Such a model does not as yet exist, and speech recognition systems are of no help in building such a model because their performance is too modest in comparison with human performance.

The fact that the research in speech recognition systems aims to build more and more specialized machines should not make one too optimistic about the future scientific contribution that such systems could provide in other fields. However, both research domains, of speech perception and of speech recognition systems, are, in some respects, complementary. Speech perception research concerns essentially how the spoken input is processed by humans, while research in speech recognition systems focuses attention on what kind of information (segmental and suprasegmental) is actually contained in the speech signal itself.

Notes

1. Figure 1A illustrates the general philosophy used in the SRS's: the bottom-up analysis of the input sentence results in a number of lexical hypotheses. The top-down constraints are used to select the possible string of words representing the input sentence, from the lexical hypotheses proposed by the bottom-up analysis. In fact, the lexical hypotheses can be issued not only from the bottom-up analysis of the input sentence, but the top-down constraints can act as a word predictor, as illustrated in Figure 1B.

2. Figure 2A illustrates the segment lattice corresponding to the beginning of a sentence "Je voudrais le numèro de téléphone. . ." (/ʒœvudrɛlœnymerodœtelefɔn/). Some phoneme boundaries are missing (/r/ in /vudrɛ/), some are added (the vowel /ɛ/ has been divided into two vowels), and there is one uncertainty in segmenting the 6th segment. The "right" phoneme is circled.

Overall, segmentation into phoneme-like segments works better than one might expect, although there are problems in identifying the place of articulation.

Figure 2B indicates the Fo markers (rises and falls) detected by the prosodic component (see also Figure 3).

Figure 2C shows some of the word matchings found by the lexical search. The number of lexical hypotheses depends on the complexity of the segment lattice, and on the threshold accepted for word likelihood. Some phonemes of the word may be missing, and some may be added (see Vivès, 1979).

3. The Fo value corresponding to the steady-portion of the vocalic part of each syllable is entered into the prosodic component. The Fo variation from one syllable to another is then calculated. Those Fo rises and falls, for which amplitude is greater than a certain speaker-dependent threshold (30 Hz for the speaker in Fig. 2 and Fig. 3) are selected for further interpretation.

Note that an Fo rise marks the beginnings of both "voudrais" and "numéro", and a fall signals their endings.

Acknowledgement The author would like to thank Dr. O. Fujimura of the Bell Laboratories at Murray Hill for his helpful suggestions and valuable comments for revising the presentation of the manuscript. The author is also very grateful to the Speech Communication Group at M.I.T. for encouragement and fruitful discussions.

Discussion

John S. Bridle The automatic speech recognition system, Harpy, should be of considerable interest to students of speech perception, and not just because it appeared to work better than the other ARPA 'Speech Understanding' systems. As we have just heard, Newell has shown that it is conceivable that a similar method could be used by humans. We must look for predictions which could be tested in speech perception experiments.

Dr Vaissière has given us an excellent review of current attempts to build speech recognition systems incorporating segmentation, labelling, lexical retreival etc. I would like to add that syllables and consonant clusters are being used by some groups as units which are segmented out and recognised.

In the rest of this symposium I have been struck by the importance which has been given to the word as a unit in speech perception. You will be interesetd to know that all commercially available speech recognition machines that I know of use words as the only recognition unit. Admittedly these machines are primitive, and typically can accept only words or short phrases from a known talker who has previously spoken all the vocabulary utterances in a "training session'. It is often assumed that such an approach is a dead end, but we have recently seen a commercial machine, still based on whole-word pattern matching, which copes very well with short connected sequences of words.

I agree with Dr Vaissière that we have made very little headway with the problems of dealing with the differences between the speech of different persons. There are several apparently related problems concerning 'adaptation' and 'normalisation' but the main message that I get from the difficulties that automatic speech recognition has is that we must deal not with absolute measurements but with contrasts and rather high order patterns in the acoustic signal. We do not even know how to adjust our analysis to speech-rate changes, although there have been some relevant perceptual experiments.

Automatic Speech Recognition needs results from auditory neurophysiology and perceptual psychology. At present we represent the speech signal in terms of a short-term spectrum, then immediately start comparing patterns or segmenting and labelling. I believe we need to use a lot more processing of the acoustic signal before any form of recognition. We probably need several representations which make explicit different kinds of features and relationships in the raw pattern. The neurophysiology results we have heard about at this symposium are very relevant.

Finally, I would like to mention a subject which has had only a brief mention so far at the symposium, and which I think is important for the future of Automatic Speech Recognition. In speech communication between two persons each seems to have a 'model' of the other, which includes his knowledge of the subject being discussed, linguistic background, and listening situation. Such information alters the way we talk, and during the conversation the model gets updated. I suggest that when a person uses a speech recognition machine he also has assumptions about the 'other person', and that they may be rather pathological. For instance, some people tend to shout at the machine when it has difficulty in recognising the words. The designers of man machine communication systems incorporating automatic speech recognition need to be able to use the dialogue to constrain and manipulate that model of the machine that the man has. This will probably mean that the machine needs to have a model of some aspects of the user.

459

Dennis H. Klatt: Speech Understanding Systems as Models of Speech Perception
Let me begin by expressing the feeling that the attempts to build speech understanding computer systems constitute perhaps the most fascinating research topic of this entire conference. This is particularly true with respect to potential implications for models of speech perception and cognition. These systems constitute concrete implementations of theories that would otherwise remain only partially specified in the back of one's head. The requirement for fully specified algorithms can lead to important advances in the identification of the real issues remaining to be confronted before advances are made in our understanding of *human* information processing. In fact, it seems that efforts to build speech understanding systems are having a profound impact on the nature of the questions being asked in psychology, and I think this is a very good situation.

The two papers presented in this session are excellent examples of just this point. Roger Moore presented an insightful summary of the Harpy speech recognition system and its theoretical extension as a ''production system'' perceptual model by Alan Newell. Harpy engenders strong emotional reactions. Some people say ''wow, it is really interesting that a machine can understand spoken sentences that well'', while others dismiss Harpy out of hand as a possible psychological model because of its obvious finiteness, crude phonetic discrimination capabilities, and remote connections to conventional perceptual models. Newell took Harpy seriously as a potential psychological model and argued that a production systems version of extended Harpy is computationally within the capabilities of the human brain. I took Harpy seriously, tried to remove the finite-grammar limitation, and tried to augment the power of the acoustic-phonetic decoding strategies — resulting in the LAFS perceptual model that was described in Seminar 1.

Jacqueline Vaissière emphasized prosodic cues to the decoding of spoken sentences in the written version of her paper. This point cannot be overemphasized. For example, durations of individual segments are lengthened at the ends of syntactic units in English and many other languages. Lengthening is a useful perceptual cue to syntactic structure, constraining our expectations during speech perception.

One of the most serious problems in the design of a speech understanding system is to limit the number of lexical alternatives each time a decision must be made. Syntactic expectations can constrain the alternatives that must be considered. Experience with the speech understanding systems constructed during the ARPA project (Lea, 1979; Klatt, 1977) indicates that more than syntactic constraint is needed to limit lexical choices sufficiently for good system performance. On the average, the BBN system had to select between 195 words at each position in an unknown utterance, and the acoustic-phonetic processor simply was incapable of resolving this amount of ambiguity all of the time. CMU Harpy and Hearsay-II entertained far fewer lexical alternatives at each position in the grammer. However, the syntactic/semantic constraints used to achieve a lower ''grammatical branching factor'' were unrealistic and the resulting grammar was not habitable. What is the average number of words that we choose from while listening to speech? Is the entire 10,000 to 15,000 morpheme lexicon searched all of the time, or are only 100 or so likely words entertained? Whatever the answer, it is important for the development of future speech understanding systems to find realistic ways to limit the search.

Perhaps a word should be devoted to the other speech understanding systems that were developed during the ARPA project. Some of the systems failed to meet the stated goals of the project for reasons that don't have anything to do with the strategies adopted, and these strategies seem worthy of future attention. One idea is to focus on portions of the incoming speech that are stressed and therefore somewhat better articulated. Both Hearsay-II and the BBN HWIM system abandoned a strict left-to-right processing strategy in favor of an ability to skip to the seemingly most reliable portion of an utterance as a focus for further processing to both the left and right. Working in both directions turned out to result in serious bookkeeping problems and reduced syntactic constraint. Not only does there seem to be a computational advantage to straight left-to-right processing, but is seems likely that people must perceive speech in this way to overcome memory limitations by recoding the input into lexical units.

The second strategy that strikes me as psychologically interesting is the blackboard used in the CMU Hearsay-II system. The blackboard is employed as a means for several autonomous modules (acoustic, phonetic, syntactic, semantic) to communicate intermediate results of sentence analysis by a well-defined and simple interface. Such a modular view of perception is attractive to a number of psychologists who have defended the view of an autonomous syntax (Garrett, 1979) and autonomous lexical access. The alternative is a highly interactive system that might take the form of a logogen specifying expected acoustic, syntactic, and semantic properties for each word (Morton, 1970). Future competition between these views is sure to be intensive and productive.

What have we learned from the efforts to build speech understanding systems, aside from the obvious need to expand our views on possible models of the speech perception process? What strategies and models can be dismissed at this point? My view is perhaps strongly biased, but I can't get over the feeling that the computational advantages of precompilation of acoustic-phonetic and phonological knowledge, as in Harpy and LAFS, i.e. putting knowledge in a form that is optimal for direct bottom-up recognition, are so overwhelming that a special-purpose lexical hypothesizer is a part of the perceptual apparatus. This implies that the analysis-by-synthesis model and a literal realization of the motor theory of speech perception are suboptimal variants of a precompiled knowledge network structure. Secondly, I believe that left-to-right processing, with some ability to get started again when e.g. noise makes a portion of the input, is the normal method of speech processing, and middle-out strategies such as exemplified by the BBN system can be dismissed.

How good do the phonetic recognition capabilities of a system have to be in order for the system to perform well, or in order to mimic human abilities? Two answers have come from recent work. Victor Zue has learned to read broadband sound spectrograms, i.e. produce a broad phonetic transcription, with an accuracy of 85 to 90 percent correct (Cole *et al.*, 1979). And Liberman and Nakatani found informally that naive listeners can be trained to transcribe nonsense English names embedded in a spoken sentence with an accuracy of 90 to 95 percent correct.

How does this compare with the performance of the speech understanding systems? Harpy is correct phonetically only about 40% of the time, and achieves its high sentence recognition performance because alternative sentences are so different acoustically. The best performance, about 65% correct phonetic recognition, has been attained by the BBN system and by an IBM system (Klatt, 1977). Why isn't performance better? It turns out to be surprisingly difficult to put into algorithmic form all of the acoustic-phonetic details that one knows to be true of speech. This is especially true of computer programs that take the form of an initial preliminary segmentation and labeling followed by refinements to the phonetic transcription that is produced. Portions of the program interact in complex ways, so that it is rare that the program behaves exactly as the programmer intended. And, of course, there is much yet to be learned about the acoustic-phonetic characteristics of sentences. One advantage of LAFS is that relations between acoustics and lexical items are memorized in a direct form, so that multi-leveled decision tree structures are avoided. Not only is this desirable from a programming viewpoint, it is also probably an advantage given whatever constraints there may be on general cognitive abilities.

REFERENCES

AARANSON, D. 1976 Performance theories for sentence coding: some qualitative observations JOURNAL OF EXPERIMENTAL PSYCHOLOGY 2: 42-55

ABBAS, P.J. & SACHS, M.B. 1976 Two-tone suppression in auditory-nerve fibers: extension of a stimulus-response relationship JOURNAL OF THE ACOUSTICAL SOCIETY OF AMERICA 59: 112-122

ABBS, J.H. 1979 Speech motor equivalence: The need for a multi-level control system PROCEEDINGS OF THE NINTH INTERNATIONAL CONGRESS OF PHONETIC SCIENCES, VOL 2: 318-324 INSTITUTE OF PHONETICS, UNIVERSITY OF COPENHAGEN

ABBS, J.H. & EILENBERG, G.R. 1976 Peripheral mechanisms of speech motor control IN N.J. LASS (ED), CONTEMPORARY ISSUES IN EXPERIMENTAL PHONETICS, 139-168, ACADEMIC PRESS, NEW YORK

ABERCROMBIE, D. 1964 Syllable quantity and enclitics in English IN D. ABERCROMBIE, ET AL (EDS) IN HONOUR OF DANIEL JONES, LONGMANS, LONDON

ABRAMS, K. & BEVER, T.G. 1969 Syntactic structure modifies attention during speech perception and recognition QUARTERLY JOURNAL OF EXPERIMENTAL PSYCHOLOGY 21: 280-290

ABRAMSON, A. & LISKER, L. 1970 Discriminability along the voicing continuum: cross-language tests PROCEEDINGS OF THE SIXTH INTERNATIONAL CONGRESS OF PHONETIC SCIENCES, 569- , ACADEMIA, PRAGUE

ADES, A.E. 1977A Vowels, consonants, speech and nonspeech PSYCHOLOGICAL REVIEW 84: 524-530

ADES, A.E. 1977B Source assignment and feature extraction in speech JOURNAL OF EXPERIMENTAL PSYCHOLOGY 3 : 673-685

AINSWORTH, W.A. 1972 Duration as a cue in the recognition of synthetic vowels JOURNAL OF THE ACOUSTICAL SOCIETY OF AMERICA 51: 648-651

AINSWORTH, W.A. 1973 A system for converting English text into speech IEEE TRANSACTIONS, AU-21: 288-290

AINSWORTH, W.A. 1974 The influence of precursive sentences on the perception of synthesized vowels LANGUAGE AND SPEECH 17: 103-109

ALLEN, G.D. 1973 Segmental timing control in speech production JOURNAL OF PHONETICS 1: 219-237

ALLEN, G.D. 1975 Speech rhythm: its relation to performance universals and articulatory timing JOURNAL OF PHONETICS 3: 91-102

ALLEN, G.D. & HAWKINS, S. 1978 The development of phonological rhythm IN A. BELL AND J.B. HOOPER (EDS) SYLLABLES AND SEGMENTS, 173-185, NORTH-HOLLAND, AMSTERDAM

ALLEN, G.I. & TSUKAHARA, N. 1974 Cerebrocerebellar communications systems PHYSIOLOGICAL REVIEWS 54: 957-1006

ALLEN, J., HUNNICUTT, S., CARLSON, R. & GRANSTROM, B. 1979 MITALK-79: the 1979 MIT text-to-speech system JOURNAL OF THE ACOUSTICAL SOCIETY OF AMERICA 65: S130

ALONSO, D., ALONSO, Z.M. & CANELLADA DE ZAMORA, M.J. 1950 Vocales andaluzas NUEVA REVISTA DE FILOLOGIA HISPANICA 4.3: 209-230

ANDERSON, J.W. 1972 Attachment out of doors IN N. BLURTON JONES (ED) ETHOLOGICAL STUDIES OF CHILD BEHAVIOUR, 199-215, CAMBRIDGE UNIVERSITY PRESS

ANDERSON, R.M., HUNT, S.C. VAN DER STOEP, A. & PRIBRAM, K.H. 1976 Object permanency and delayed response as spatial context in monkeys with frontal lesions NEUROPSYCHOLOGIA 14: 481-490

ANDREW, R.J. 1976 Use of formants in the grunts of baboons and other nonhuman primates IN S.R. HARNAD, H.D. STEKLIS AND J. LANCASTER (EDS) ORIGINS AND EVOLUTION OF LANGUAGE AND SPEECH, ANNALS OF THE NEW YORK ACADEMY OF SCIENCES 280: 673-693

ANGLIN, J.M. 1977 Word, Object, and Conceptual Development NORTON, NEW YORK

ANISFIELD, M., MASTERS, J.C., JACOBSON, S., KAGAN, J., MELTZOFF, A.N. & MOORE, M.K. 1979 Interpreting 'imitative' responses in early infancy SCIENCE 205: 214-219

ARTHUR, R.M. 1976 Harmonic analysis of two-tone discharge patterns in cochlear nerve fibers BIOLOGICAL CYBERNETICS 22: 21-31

ASLIN, R. & PISONI, D. 1978 Some developmental processes in speech perception PAPER PRESENTED AT THE CONFERENCE ON CHILD PHONOLOGY, BETHESDA

ASSMAN, R.A. 1978 Identification of vowels UNIVERSITY OF ALBERTA WORKING PAPERS, EDMONTON

BAILEY, C.-J.N. 1978 Gradience in English Syllabization and a Revised Concept of Unmarked Syllabication INDIANA UNIVERSITY LINGUISTICS CLUB, BLOOMINGTON

BAKER, E., BLUMSTEIN, S.E. & GOODGLASS, H. 1979 Phonemic discrimination as a factor in the auditory comprehension of Broca's and Wernicke's aphasia UNPUBLISHED MANUSCRIPT

BARCLAY, J.R. 1972 Non-categorical perception of a voiced stop: a replication PERCEPTION AND PSYCHOPHYSICS 11: 269-273

BARTON, D. 1976 The role of perception in the acquisition of phonology UNIVERSITY OF LONDON PH.D. DISSERTATION (AVAILABLE FROM INDIANA UNIVERSITY LINGUISTICS CLUB)

BASSO, A., LUZZATTI, C. & SPINNLER, H. 1980 Is ideomotor apraxia the outcome of damage to well-defined regions of the left hemisphere? JOURNAL OF NEUROLOGY, NEUROSURGERY, AND PSYCHIATRY 43: 118-126

BASTIAN, J., DELATTRE, & LIBERMAN, A.M. 1959 Silent interval as a cue for the distinction between stops and semi-vowels in medial position JOURNAL OF THE ACOUSTICAL SOCIETY OF AMERICA 31: 1568(A)

BATEMAN, F. 1877 Darwinism Tested by Language RIVINGTON, LONDON

BATES, E. 1976 Language and Context: The Acquisition of Pragmatics ACADEMIC PRESS, NEW YORK

BATES, E., BENIGNI, L., BRETHERTON, I. & VOLTERRA, V. 1977 From gesture to the first word: on cognitive and social prerequisites IN M. LEWIS AND L.A. ROSENBLUM (EDS) INTERACTION, CONVERSATION AND THE DEVELOPMENT OF LANGUAGE, CHAPTER 11, WILEY, NEW YORK

BATES, E., CAMAIONI, L. & VOLTERRA, V. 1975 The acquisition of performatives prior to speech MERRILL-PALMER QUARTERLY 21: 205-226

BEKESY, G. VON 1960 Experiments in Hearing ACADEMIC PRESS, LONDON

BELL, A. & HOOPER, J.B. (EDS) 1978A Syllables and Segments NORTH-HOLLAND, AMSTERDAM

BELL, A. & HOOPER, J.B. 1978B Issues and evidence in syllabic phonology IN A. BELL AND J.B. HOOPER (EDS) SYLLABLES AND SEGMENTS, 3-22, NORTH-HOLLAND, AMSTERDAM

BELL-BERTI, F. & HARRIS, K.S. 1979 Anticipatory coarticulation: some implications from a study of lip rounding JOURNAL OF THE ACOUSTICAL SOCIETY OF AMERICA 65: 1268-1270

BENGUEREL, A.-P. & COWAN, H. 1974 Coarticulation of upper lip protrusion in French PHONETICA 30: 41-55

BENGUEREL, A.-P. & ADELMAN, S. 1976 Perception of coarticulated lip rounding PHONETICA 33: 113-126

BERGKABDM O. 1963 The bony nasopharynx, a roentgen-craniometric study ACTA ODONTOLOGICA SCANDINAVICA 21: SUPPLEMENT 35

BERKO GLEASON, J. GOODGLASS, H., GREEN, E., ACKERMAN, N. & HYDE, M.R. 1975 The retrieval of syntax in Broca's aphasia BRAIN AND LANGUAGE 2: 451-471

BERKO, J. 1958 The child's learning of English morphology WORD 14, 150-177

BERMAN, N. & JEJE, S. 1978 Higher pitch in babytalk: are these trix just for kids PAPER PRESENTED AT THE THIRD ANNUAL BOSTON UNIVERSITY CONFERENCE ON LANGUAGE DEVELOPMENT

BERNSTEIN, N.A. 1967 The Coordination and Regulation of Movements PERGAMON PRESS, OXFORD

BERTONCINI, J. & MEHLER, J. (1981) Syllables as units in infants' speech perception INFANT BEHAVIOR AND DEVELOPMENT 4: 1

BEST, C.T., MORONGIELLO, B. & ROBSON, R. 1980 Phonetic specificity of speech cue equivalence STATUS REPORT 62, HASKINS LABORATORIES, NEW HAVEN, CONNECTICUT

BEVER, T.G. 1970 The cognitive basis for linguistic structures IN J. HAYES (ED) COGNITION AND THE DEVELOPMENT OF LANGUAGE, WILEY, NEW YORK

BEVER, T.G. & HURTIG, R. 1975 Detectability of a non-linguistic stimulus is poorest at the end of a clause JOURNAL OF PSYCHOLINGUISTIC RESEARCH 4: 1-7

BEVER, T.G. & LANGENDOEN, D.T. 1971 A dynamic model for the evolution of language LINGUISTIC INQUIRY 2: 433-463

BEVER, T.G., GARRETT, M.F. & HURTIG, R. 1973 The interaction of perceptual processes and ambiguous sentences MEMORY & COGNITION 1: 227-286

BEVER, T.G., LACKNER, J. & KIRK, R. 1969 The underlying structures of sentences are the primary units of immediate speech processing PERCEPTION AND PSYCHOPHYSICS 5: 225-234

BING, J.M. 1979 Aspects of English prosody PH.D. DISSERTATION, UNIVERSITY OF MASSACHUSETTS, AMHERST

BIZZI, E. 1975 Motor coordination: central and peripheral control during eye-head movement IN M.S. GAZZANIGA AND C. BLAKEMORE (EDS), HANDBOOK OF PSYCHOBIOLOGY, ACADEMIC PRESS, NEW YORK

BLANK, M., GESSNER, M. & EXPOSITO, A. 1979 Language without communication: a case study JOURNAL OF CHILD LANGUAGE 6: 329-352

BLANK, M.A. & FOSS, D.F. 1978 Semantic facilitation and lexical access during sentence processing MEMORY & COGNITION 6: 664-652

BLESSER, B. 1969 Perception of spectrally rotated speech PH.D. DISSERTATION, MASSACHUSETTS INSTITUTE OF TECHNOLOGY

BLOOM, L. 1970 Language Development MASSACHUSETTS INSTITUTE OF TECHNOLOGY PRESS

BLOOM, L. 1976 Child language and the origin of language IN S. HARNAD, H. STEKLIS AND J. LANCASTER (EDS) ORIGINS AND EVOLUTION OF LANGUAGE AND SPEECH, ANNALS OF THE NEW YORK ACADEMY OF SCIENCES 280: 170-172

BLOUNT, B.G. & PADGUG, E.J. 1976 Mother and father speech: distribution of parental speech features in English and Spanish PAPERS AND REPORTS IN CHILD LANGUAGE DEVELOPMENT, DEPARTMENT OF LINGUISTICS, STANFORD UNIVERSITY, CALIFORNIA

BLUMSTEIN, S.E. 1973 A Phonological Investigation of Aphasic Speech MOUTON, THE HAGUE

BLUMSTEIN, S.E., BAKER, E. & GOODGLASS, H. 1977 Phonological factors in auditory comprehension in aphasia NEUROPSYCHOLOGIA 15: 19-30

BLUMSTEIN, S.E., COOPER, W.E., ZURIF & CARAMAZZA, A. 1977 The perception and production of voice-onset time in aphasia NEUROPSYCHOLOGIA 15: 371-384

BLUMSTEIN, S.E., NIGRO, G., TARTTER, V. & STATLENDER, S 1979 The acoustic-auditory basis for the perception of place of articulation in aphasia (IN PREPARATION)

BLUMSTEIN, S.E. & STEVENS, K.N. 1979 Acoustic invariance in speech production: evidence from measurements of the spectral characteristics of stop consonants JOURNAL OF THE ACOUSTICAL SOCIETY OF AMERICA 66: 1001-1017

BLUMSTEIN, S.E. & STEVENS, K.N. 1980 Perceptual invariance and onset spectra for stop consonants in different vowel environments JOURNAL OF THE ACOUSTICAL SOCIETY OF AMERICA 67: 648-662

BLUMSTEIN, S.E., STEVENS, K.N. & NIGRO, G.N. 1977 Property detectors for bursts and transitions in speech perception JOURNAL OF THE ACOUSTICAL SOCIETY OF AMERICA 61: 1301-1313

BLURTON JONES, N.G. 1972 Non-verbal communication in children IN R. HINDE (ED) NON-VERBAL COMMUNICATION, 271-296, CAMBRIDGE UNIVERSITY PRESS

BOBROW, D. & FRASER, B. 1969 An augmented state transition network analysis procedure IN D. WALKER AND L. NORTON (EDS) PROCEEDINGS OF THE INTERNATIONAL JOINT CONFERENCE ON ARTIFICIAL INTELLIGENCE, WASHINGTON, D.C.

BOE, L.J., R. DESCOUT AND B. GUERIN (EDS) 1979 Proceedings of the Seminar: Larynx et Parole G.A.L.F., GRENOBLE

BOHANNON, J.N. III & MARQUIS, A.L. 1977 Children's control of adult speech CHILD DEVELOPMENT 48: 1002-1008

BOLINGER, D.L. 1949 Intonation and analysis WORD 5: 248-254

BOLINGER, D.L. 1958 A theory of pitch accent in English WORD 14: 109-149

BOLINGER, D.L. 1962 Intonation as a universal IN H.G. LUNT (ED) PROCEEDINGS OF THE NINTH INTERNATIONAL CONGRESS OF LINGUISTS, MOUTON, THE HAGUE

BOLINGER, D.L. 1964 Around the edge of language: intonation HARVARD EDUCATIONAL REVIEW 34: 282-296

BOLINGER, D.L. 1978 Intonation across languages IN J. GREENBERG ET AL (EDS) UNIVERSALS OF HUMAN LANGUAGE, VOL 2 (PHONOLOGY), STANFORD UNIVERSITY PRESS

BOND, Z.S. 1976 Identification of vowels excerpted from neutral and nasal contexts JOURNAL OF THE ACOUSTICAL SOCIETY OF AMERICA 59: 1229-1232

BONDARKO, L.V. 1970 A model of speech perception in humans WORKING PAPERS IN LINGUISTICS NO. 6, COMPUTER AND INFORMATION RESEARCH CENTER, OHIO STATE UNIVERSITY

BOOMER, D.S. & LAVER, J.D.M. 1968 Slips of the tongue BRIT. J. DIS. COMM., 3: 2-12

BORDEN, G. 1979 An interpretation of research on feedback interruption in speech BRAIN AND LANGUAGE 7: 307-319

BORG, E. 1978 A quantitative study of the effect of the acoustic reflex on sound transmission through the middle ear of man ACTA OTOLARYNGOLOGICA 66: 461-472

BORG, E. & ZAKRISSON, J. 1973 Stapedius reflex and speech features JOURNAL OF THE ACOUSTICAL SOCIETY OF AMERICA 54: 525-527

BOSMA, J.F. 1975 Anatomic and physiologic development of the speech apparatus IN D.B. TOWERS, (ED) HUMAN COMMUNICATION AND ITS DISORDERS, 469-481, RAVEN, NEW YORK

BOTHA, R. 1973 The Justification of Linguistic Hypotheses MOUTON, THE HAGUE

BOULE, M. 1911-1913 L'homme fosille de la Chapelle-aux-Saints ANN. PALEONTAL. 6: 109; 7,21,85,8,1

BOWER, T.R.G. 1974 Development in Infancy FREEMAN, SAN FRANCISCO

BRADLEY, D.C. 1978 Computational distinction of vocabulary type PH.D. DISSERTATION, MASSACHUSETTS INSTITUTE OF TECHNOLOGY

BRADY, S.A. & DARWIN, C.J. 1978 Range effect in the perception of voicing JOURNAL OF THE ACOUSTICAL SOCIETY OF AMERICA 63: 1556-1558

BRAINE, M. 1976 Review of: Smith (1973) LANGUAGE 52: 489-498

BRESNAN, J. 1978 A realistic transformational grammer IN M. HALLE, J. BRESNAN AND G.A. MILLER (EDS) LINGUISTIC THEORY AND PSYCHOLOGICAL REALITY, MASSACHUSETTS INSTITUTE OF TECHNOLOGY PRESS

BROADBENT, D.E. 1958 Perception and Communication PERGAMON PRESS, NEW YORK

BROCA, P. 1861 Remarques sur le siège de la faculté du langage articulé, suivies d'une observation d'aphémie BULLETIN DE LA SOCIETE ANATOMIQUE 6: 330-357

BRODY, B.A. & PRIBRAM, K.H. 1978 The role of frontal and parietal cortex in cognitive processing: tests of spatial and sequence functions BRAIN 101: 607-633

BROEN, P. 1972 The verbal environment of the language learning child MONOGRAPH OF THE AMERICAN SPEECH AND HEARING ASSOCIATION, NO. 17

BROKX, J.P.L. 1979 Waargenomen continuiteit in spraak DOCTORAL DISSERTATION, EINDHOVEN UNIVERSITY OF TECHNOLOGY

BROWMAN, CATHERINE P. 1978 Tip of the tongue and slip of the ear: implications for language processing WORKING PAPERS IN PHONETICS 42, UNIVERSITY OF CALIFORNIA AT LOS ANGELES

BROWN, R. 1973 A First Language: The Early Stages HARVARD UNIVERSITY PRESS, CAMBRIDGE, MASSACHUSETTS

BROWN, R. & MCNEILL, D. 1966 The 'tip-of-the-tongue' phenomenon JOURNAL OF VERBAL LEARNING AND VERBAL BEHAVIOR 5: 325-337

BRUGGE, J.F., ANDERSON, D.J., HIND, J.E. & ROSE, J.E. 1969 Time structure of discharges in single auditory nerve fibers of the squirrel monkey in response to complex periodic sounds JOURNAL OF NEUROPHYSIOLOGY 32: 386-401

BRUNER, J.S. 1975 The ontogenesis of speech acts JOURNAL OF CHILD LANGUAGE 2: 1-19

BRUNER, J.S. 1976 From communication to language - a psychological perspective COGNITION 3: 255-287

BUHR, R.D. 1976 The emergence of vowels in infants: a progress report M.A. THESIS, BROWN UNIVERSITY, PROVIDENCE, R.I.

BULLOCK, T.H. (ED) 1977 Recognition of Complex Acoustic Signals DAHLEM KONFERENZEN, BERLIN

CAELEN, J. 1979 Modèle d'Oreille et Application à la Reconnaisance THESE D'ETAT, TOULOUSE

CAIRNS, H.S. & HSU, J.R. 1979 Effects of prior context upon lexical access during sentence comprehension: a replication and reinterpretation JOURNAL OF PSYCHOLINGUISTIC RESEARCH (IN PRESS)

CAIRNS, H.S. & KAMERMAN, J. 1975 Lexical information processing during sentence comprehension JOURNAL OF VERBAL LEARNING AND VERBAL BEHAVIOR 14: 170-179

CAPLAN, D. 1972 Clause boundaries and recognition latencies for words in sentences PERCEPTION AND PSYCHOPHYSICS 12: 73-76

CAPRANICA, R.R. 1965 The Evoked Vocal Response of the Bullfrog MASSACHUSETTS INSTITUTE OF TECHNOLOGY

CARLSON, R., FANT, G. & GRANSTROM, B. 1975 Two-formant models, pitch and vowel perception IN G. FANT AND M.A.A. TATHAM (EDS) AUDITORY ANALYSIS AND PERCEPTION OF SPEECH, 55-82, ACADEMIC PRESS, LONDON

CARLSON, R., GRANSTROM, B., & KLATT, D.H. 1979 Vowel perception: the relative perceptual salience of selected acoustic manipulations IN SPEECH COMMUNICATION PAPERS PRESENTED AT THE 97TH MEETING OF THE ACOUSTICAL SOCIETY OF AMERICA, J.J. WOLF & D.H. KLATT (EDS) PUBLISHED BY THE ACOUSTICAL SOCIETY OF AMERICA, NEW YORK

CARLSON, R., GRANSTROM, B., LINDBLOM, B. & RAPP, K. 1973 Some timing and fundamental frequency characteristics of Swedish sentences: data, rules and perceptual evaluation QUARTERLY STATUS AND PROGRESS REPORT 1, SPEECH TRANSMISSION LABORATORY, ROYAL INSTITUTE OF TECHNOLOGY, STOCKHOLM

CARRE, R. DESCOUT AND M. WAJSKOP (EDS) 1977 Proceedings of the Symposium on Articulatory Modeling G.A.L.F., GRENOBLE

CARROLL, J.M. 1976 The interaction of structural and functional variables in sentence perception PH.D. DISSERTATION, COLUMBIA UNIVERSITY

CARROLL, J.M. 1978 Sentence perception units and levels of syntactic structure PERCEPTION AND PSYCHOPHYSICS 23: 506-514

CARROLL, J.M. 1979A Functional completeness as a determinant of processing load during sentence comprehension LANGUAGE AND SPEECH (IN PRESS)

CARROLL, J.M. 1979B Complex compounds: phrasal embedding in lexical structures IBM RESEARCH REPORT

CARROLL, J.M. 1980 Creative analogy and language evolution JOURNAL OF PSYCHOLINGUISTIC RESEARCH (IN PRESS)

CARROLL, J.M. & BEVER, T.G. 1976 Sentence comprehension: a case study in the relation of knowledge to perception IN E. CARTERETTE AND M. FRIEDMAN (EDS) THE HANDBOOK OF PERCEPTION, VOL 7, SPEECH AND HEARING, ACADEMIC PRESS, NEW YORK

CARROLL, J.M., BEVER, T.G. & POLLACK, C. 1979 The non-uniqueness of linguistic intuitions

CARROLL, J.M. & TANENHAUS, M.K. 1978 Functional completeness and sentence segmentation JOURNAL OF SPEECH AND HEARING RESEARCH 21: 793-808

CARROLL, J.M., TANENHAUS, M.K. & BEVER, T.G. 1978 The perception of relations: the interaction of structural, functional, and contextual factors in the segmentation of sentences IN W. LEVELT AND G. FLORES D'ARCAIS (EDS) STUDIES IN PERCEPTION OF LANGUAGE, WILEY, LONDON

CARTER, A.L. 1978 From sensory-motor vocalizations to words: a case study of the evolution of attention-directing communication in the second year IN A. LOCK (ED) ACTION, GESTURE AND SYMBOL: THE EMERGENCE OF LANGUAGE, 309-349, ACADEMIC PRESS, LONDON

CATFORD, J.C. & KRIEG, L.J. 1979 Distinctive features of sibilants; a closer look JOURNAL OF THE ACOUSTICAL SOCIETY OF AMERICA 66 SUPPLEMENT I, S88 (A)

CENA, R. 1978 When is a Phonological Generalization Psychologically Real? INDIANA LINGUISTICS CLUB, BLOOMINGTON

CHAO, Y.-R. 1934 The non-uniqueness of phonemic solutions of phonetic systems BULLETIN OF THE INSTITUTE OF HISTORY AND PHILOLOGY, ACADEMIA SINICA 4: 363-397

CHAPIN, P., SMITH, T. & ABRAMSOM, A. 1972 Two factors in the segmentation of speech JOURNAL OF VERBAL LEARNING AND VERBAL BEHAVIOR 11: 164-173

CHEN, M. 1970 Vowel length variation as a function of voicing of the consonant environment PHONETICA 22: 129-159

CHEN, M. & WANG, S.-Y. W. 1975 Sound change: actuation and implementation LANGUAGE 51: 255-281

CHIAT, S. 1979 The role of the word in phonological development MIMEO, LONDON SCHOOL OF ECONOMICS

CHISTOVICH, J.A., GROSTREM, M.P., KOZHEVNIKOV, V.A., LESEGOR, L.W., SHUPLJAKOV, V.S., TALJASIN, P.A. & TJULKOF, W.A. 1974 A Functional model of signal processing in the peripheral auditory system ACOUSTICA 31: 349-353

CHODOROW, M. 1979 Time compressed speech and the study of lexical and syntactic processing IN W. COOPER AND E.C.T. WALKER (EDS) SENTENCE PROCESSING: PSYCHOLINGUISTIC STUDIES PRESENTED TO MERRILL GARRETT, ERLBAUM, HILLSDALE, NEW JERSEY

CHOMSKY, N. 1965 Aspects of the Theory of Syntax MASSACHUSETTS INSTITUTE OF TECHNOLOGY PRESS

CHOMSKY, N. 1969 Current Issues in Linguistic Theory MOUTON, THE HAGUE

CHOMSKY, N. 1970 Remarks on nominalization IN R. JACOBS AND P. ROSENBAUM (EDS) READINGS IN ENGLISH TRANSFORMATIONAL GRAMMAR, GINN, WALTHAM, MASSACHUSETTS

CHOMSKY, N. 1975 Reflections on Language PANTHEON, NEW YORK

CHOMSKY, N. 1977 On wh-movement IN P. CULICOVER ET AL (EDS) FORMAL SYNTAX, 71-132, ACADEMIC PRESS, NEW YORK

CHOMSKY, N. 1980A Rules and Representations COLUMBIA UNIVERSITY PRESS, NEW YORK

CHOMSKY, N. 1980B Principles and parameters IN N. HORNSTEIN AND D. LIGHTFOOT (EDS) EXPLANATION IN LINGUISTICS LONGMANS, LONDON

CHOMSKY, N. & HALLE, M. 1968 The Sound Pattern of English HARPER & ROW, NEW YORK

CLARK, H.H. & CLARK, E.V. 1977 Psychology and Language HARCOURT BRACE JOVANOVICH, NEW YORK

CLARK, H.H. & HAVILAND, S.E. 1977 Comprehension and the given-new contract IN R.O. FREEDLE (ED) DISCOURSE PRODUCTION AND COMPREHENSION VOL.1: 1-40, ABLEX PUBLISHING, NORWOOD, NEW JERSEY

CLOPTON, B.M., WINFIELD, J.A. & FLAMMINO, F.J. 1974 Tonotopic organization: review and analysis BRAIN RESEARCH 76: 1-20

CLUMECK, H. 1976 Patterns of soft palate movements in six languages JOURNAL OF PHONETICS 4: 337-351

CLUMECK, H. 1979 A parallel between child and adult language: a study in the phonetic explanation of sound patterns JOURNAL OF CHILD LANGUAGE 6: 595-600

COHEN, P.S. & MERCER, R.L. 1975 The phonological component of a speech recognition system IN SPEECH RECOGNITION: INVITED PAPERS PRESENTED AT THE 1974 IEEE SYMPOSIUM, D.R. REDDY (ED), 275-320, ACADEMIC PRESS, NEW YORK

COLE, R.A. 1973 Listening for mispronunciations: a measure of what we hear during speech PERCEPTION & PSYCHOPHYSICS 1: 153-156

COLE, R.A. & JAKIMIK, J. 1978 Understanding speech: how words are heard IN G. UNDERWOOD (ED) STRATEGIES OF INFORMATION PROCESSING, ACADEMIC PRESS, NEW YORK

COLE, R.A. & JAKIMIK, J. 1979 A model of speech perception IN R.A. COLE (ED) PERCEPTION AND PRODUCTION OF FLUENT SPEECH, ERLBAUM, HILLSDALE, NEW JERSEY

COLE, R.A., RUDNICKY, A., ZUE, V. & REDDY, D.R. 1979 Speech as patterns on paper IN R.A. COLE (ED) PERCEPTION AND PRODUCTION OF FLUENT SPEECH, ERLBAUM, HILLSDALE, NEW JERSEY

COLLIER, R. & 'T HART, J. 1975 The role of intonation in speech perception IN A. COHEN AND S.G. NOOTEBOOM (EDS) STRUCTURE AND PROCESS IN SPEECH PERCEPTION, SPRINGER-VERLAG, NEW YORK

COLLIS, G.M. & SCHAFFER, H.R. 1975 Synchronization of visual attention in mother-infant pairs JOURNAL OF CHILD PSYCHIATRY 16: 315-320

CONRAD, B. & SCHONLE, P. 1979 Speech and respiration, ARCHIV FUR PSYCHIATRIE UND NERVENKRANKHEIT 226: 251-268

CONRAD, C. 1974 Context effects in sentence comprehension: a study of the subjective lexicon MEMORY & COGNITION 2, NO. 1A: 130-138

CONRAD, R. 1965 Order error in immediate recall of sequences JOURNAL OF VERBAL LEARNING AND VERBAL BEHAVIOUR 4: 101-109

COOPER, F.S. 1966 Describing the speech process in motor command terms STATUS REPORTS ON SPEECH RESEARCH 5/6: 2.1-2.27, HASKINS LABORATORIES, NEW HAVEN

COOPER, W.A. 1974 Adaption of phonetic feature analyzers for place articulation JOURNAL OF THE ACOUSTICAL SOCIETY OF AMERICA 56: 617-627

COOPER, W.E. 1975 Syntactic control of speech timing PH.D. DISSERTATION, MASSACHUSETTS INSTITUTE OF TECHNOLOGY, CAMBRIDGE

COOPER, W.E., SORENSEN, J.M. & PACCIA, J.M. 1977 Correlations of duration for nonadjacent segments in speech: aspects of grammatical coding JOURNAL OF THE ACOUSTICAL SOCIETY OF AMERICA 61: 1046-1050

COOPER, W.E. & WALKER, E.T.C. 1979 PSYCHOLINGUISTIC STUDIES PRESENTED TO MERRILL GARRETT, ERLBAUM, HILLSDALE, NEW JERSEY

CORDER, S.P. 1967 The significance of learners' errors INTERNATIONAL REVIEW OF APPLIED LINGUISTICS 5 (REPRINTED IN J.C. RICHARDS (ED) ERROR ANALYSIS: PERSPECTIVES ON SECOND LANGUAGE ACQUISITION, 19-27, LONGMAN, LONDON)

CORNSWEET, T.N. 1970 Visual Perception ACADEMIC PRESS, NEW YORK

CRAIG, J.D. 1979 Asymmetries in processing auditory nonverbal stimuli PSYCHOLOGICAL BULLETIN 86: 1339-1349

CRITCHLEY, M. & KUBIK, C.S. 1925 The mechanism of speech and deglutition in progressive bulbar palsy BRAIN 48: 492-534

CROWDER, R.G. 1971 The sound of vowels and consonants in immediate memory JOURNAL OF VERBAL LEARNING AND VERBAL BEHAVIOR 10: 587

CROWDER, R.G. 1973A The sounds of speech in immediate memory JOURNAL OF EXPERIMENTAL PSYCHOLOGY 98: 14-24

CROWDER, R.G. 1973B Precategorical acoustic storage for vowels of short and long duration PERCEPTION AND PSYCHOPHYSICS 13: 502-506 (B)

CROWDER, R.G. 1978 Mechanisms of auditory backward masking in the stimulus suffix effect PSYCHOLOGICAL REVIEW 85: 502-524

CROWDER, R.G. 1979 CONTRIBUTION TO THIS SYMPOSIUM

CROWDER, R.G. & MORTON, J. 1969 Precategorical acoustic storage (PAS) PERCEPTION AND PSYCHOPHYSICS 5: 365-373

CRUTTENDEN, A. 1979 Falls and rises: meanings and universals PAPER PRESENTED AT 9TH INTERNATIONAL CONGRESS OF PHONETIC SCIENCES, INSTITUTE OF PHONETICS, UNIVERSITY OF COPENHAGEN

CRYSTAL, D. 1969 Prosodic Systems and Intonation in English CAMBRIDGE UNIVERSITY PRESS

CUTLER, A. 1976 Phoneme-monitoring reaction time as a function of the preceding intonation contour PERCEPTION AND PSYCHOPHYSICS 20: 55-60

CUTLER, A. 1979 Queering the pitch: errors of stress and intonation IN SLIPS OF THE TONGUE, EAR, PEN, AND HAND, V. FROMKIN (ED) ACADEMIC PRESS, NEW YORK

CUTLER, A. (IN PRESS) Syllable omission errors and isochrony IN H.W. DECHERT AND M. RAUPACH (EDS) TEMPORAL VARIABLES IN SPEECH: STUDIES IN HONOUR OF FRIEDA GOLDMAN-EISLER, MOUTON, THE HAGUE

CUTLER, A. & FOSS, D.J. 1974 Comprehension of ambiguous sentences: the locus of context effects PAPER PRESENTED AT THE MIDWESTERN PSYCHOLOGICAL ASSOCIATION, CHICAGO

CUTLER, A. & ISARD, S.D. (IN PRESS) The production of prosody IN B. BUTTERWORTH (ED) LANGUAGE PRODUCTION, ACADEMIC PRESS, LONDON

CUTLER, A. & NORRIS, D. 1979 Monitoring sentence comprehension IN W.E. COOPER & E.C.T. WALKER (EDS) SENTENCE PROCESSING: PSYCHOLINGUISTIC STUDIES PRESENTED TO MERRILL GARRETT, ERLBAUM, HILLSDALE, NEW JERSEY

CUTTING, J.E. 1976 Auditory and linguistic processes in speech perception: inferences from six fusions in dichotic listening PSYCHOLOGICAL REVIEW 83: 114-140

CUTTING, J.E. 1977 There may be nothing peculiar to perceiving in speech mode IN P. RABBITT AND S. DORNIC (EDS) ATTENTION AND PERFORMANCE, VOL. 7, ACADEMIC PRESS, LONDON

CUTTING, J.E. & ROSNER, B.S. 1974 Categories and boundaries in speech and music PERCEPTION AND PSYCHOPHYSICS 16: 564-570

DANILOFF, R. & MOLL, K. 1968 Coarticulation of lip rounding JOURNAL OF SPEECH AND HEARING RESEARCH 11: 707-721

DANILOFF, R.G. & HAMMARBERG, R.E. 1973 On defining co-articulation JOURNAL OF PHONETICS 1: 239-248

DARWIN, C. 1859 The Origin of Species MURRAY, LONDON

DARWIN, C. 1871 The Descent of Man MURRAY, LONDON

DARWIN, C.J. & BADDELEY, A.D. 1974 Acoustic memory and the perception of speech COGNITIVE PSYCHOLOGY 6: 41-60

DASCALU, L. 1975 What are you asking about (on the intonation of emphasis in "yes-no" questions) REVUE ROUMAINE DE LINGUISTIQUE 20: 477-480

DASCALU, L. 1979 Teste de perceptie asupra intonatiei in limba romana STUDII SI CERCETARI LINGVISTICE 2: 125-139

DAVIS, H.P. 1969 Training Your Own Bird Dog PUTNAM, NEW YORK

DAY, P.S. & ULATOWSKA, H.K. 1979 Perceptual, cognitive, and linguistic development after early hemispherectomy: two case studies BRAIN AND LANGUAGE 7: 17-33

DE BOER, E. 1976 On the 'residue' and auditory pitch perception IN W.D. KEIDEL AND W.D. NEFF (EDS) HANDBOOK OF SENSORY PHYSIOLOGY, VOL 5/3: 479-583, SPRINGER-VERLAG, BERLIN

DE BOER, E. & DE JONGH, H.R. 1978 On cochlear coding: potentialities and limitations of the reverse correlation technique JOURNAL OF THE ACOUSTICAL SOCIETY OF AMERICA 63: 115-135

DE LAGUNA, G.A. 1927 Speech, its Function and Development YALE UNIVERSITY PRESS, NEW HAVEN

DE MORI, R. 1979 Recent advances in automatic speech recognition SIGNAL PROCESSING 1: 95-123

DE MORI, R., LAFACE, P. & PICCOLO, E. 1976 Automatic detection and description of syllabic features in continuous speech IEEE TRANSACTIONS, ASSP-24: 365-379

DE RENZI, E., MOTTI, F. & NICHELLI, P. 1980 Imitating gestures: a quantitative approach to ideomotor apraxia ARCHIVES OF NEUROLOGY 37: 6-10

DE ROOIJ, J.J. 1979 Speech punctuation DOCTORAL DISSERTATION, UTRECHT UNIVERSITY

DE SIVERS, F. 1965 L'unité intonationelle d'interrogation en hongrois LA LINGUISTIQUE 1: 75-112

DE VILLIERS, J.G. The process of rule learning in child speech: a new look IN K.E. NELSON (ED) CHILD LANGUAGE, VOLUME 2 (IN PRESS)

DELATTRE, P. 1938 L'accent final en Français : accent d'intensité, accent de hauteur, accent de durée FRENCH REVIEW 12: 141-145

DELATTRE, P. 1963 Comparing the prosodic features of English, German, Spanish and French INTERNATIONAL REVIEW OF APPLIED LINGUISTICS 1: 193-210

DELATTRE, P. 1966 A comparison of syllable length conditioning among languages INTERNATIONAL REVIEW OF APPLIED LINGUISTICS 4(3) 183-

DELATTRE, P.C., LIBERMAN, A.M. & COOPER, F.S. 1955 Acoustic loci and transitional cues for consonants JOURNAL OF THE ACOUSTICAL SOCIETY OF AMERICA 27: 769-773

DELGUTTE, B. 1978 Codage des changements rapides d'intensité dans le nerf auditive: Expériences avec des sons pures NEUVIEME JOURNEES D'ETUDE SUR LA PAROLE, LANNION, FRANCE

DELL, G.S. & REICH, P.A. 1979 Toward a unified model of slips of the tongue IN SLIPS OF THE TONGUE, EAR, PEN, AND HAND, V. FROMKIN (ED) ACADEMIC PRESS, NEW YORK

DELOS M., GUERIN, B., MRAYATI, M. & CARRE, R. 1976 Study of intrinsic pitch of vowels JOURNAL OF THE ACOUSTICAL SOCIETY OF AMERICA 59: S 72

DENES, P. 1955 Effect of duration on the perception of voicing JOURNAL OF THE ACOUSTICAL SOCIETY OF AMERICA 27: 761-764

DENES, P. 1963 On the statistics of spoken English JOURNAL OF THE ACOUSTICAL SOCIETY OF AMERICA 35: 892-904

DENNIS, M. & WHITAKER, H.A. 1976 Language acquisition following hemidecortication: linguistic superiority of the left over the right hemisphere BRAIN AND LANGUAGE 3: 404-433

DERR, M.A. & MASSARO, D.W. The contribution of vowel duration, F0 contour, and frication duration as cues to the /juz/-/jus/ distinction PERCEPTION AND PSYCHOPHYSICS (SUBMITTED)

DERWING, B. 1976 Morpheme recognition and the learning of rules for derivational morphology CANADIAN JOURNAL OF LINGUISTICS, 1973, 12: 38-66

DERWING, B. 1979 English pluralization: a testing ground for rule evaluation IN G.D. PRIDEAUX, B.L. DERWING AND W.J. BAKER (EDS) EXPERIMENTAL LINGUISTICS: INTEGRATION OF THEORIES AND APPLICATIONS, E. STORY-SCIENTIA, GHENT

DERWING, B. & BAKER, W. 1979 The psychological basis for morphological rules IN J. MACNAMARA (ED) LANGUAGE LEARNING AND THOUGHT, PLENUM PRESS, NEW YORK

DERWING, B. & NEAREY, T.M. A decade of experimental phonology at the University of Alberta PAPER PRESENTED TO THE CONFERENCE ON EXPERIMENTAL PHONOLOGY, BERKELEY

DESCOUT, R., COURBON, J.L., ROUMIGUIERE, J.P. & BOE, L.J. 1976 Evaluation des performances d'un simulateur du conduit vocal RECHERCHES ACOUSTIQUES 3, CNET LANNION

DEVALOIS, R.L., ALBRECHT, D.G. & THORELL, L.G. 1978 Spatial tuning of lgn and cortical cells in monkey visual system IN H. SPEKREIJSE (ED) SPATIAL CONTRAST, MONOGRAPH SERIES, ROYAL NETHERLANDS ACADEMY OF SCIENCES

DEWSON, J.H. 1977 Preliminary evidence of hemispheric asymmetry of auditory function in monkeys IN S. HARNAD, R.W. DOTY, L. GOLDSTEIN, J. JAYNES AND G. KRAUTHAMMER (EDS) LATERALIZATION IN THE NERVOUS SYSTEM, ACADEMIC PRESS, NEW YORK

DIEHL, R.L. 1975 The effect of adaptation on the identification of speech sounds PERCEPTION AND PSYCHOPHYSICS 17: 68-72

DIEHL, R.L., ELMAN, J.L. & MCCUSKER, S.B. 1978 Contrast effects in stop consonant identification JOURNAL OF EXPERIMENTAL PSYCHOLOGY 4: 599-609

DINGWALL, W.O. 1979 The evolution of human communication systems IN H. AND H.A. WHITAKER (EDS) STUDIES IN NEUROLINGUISTICS, 4, ACADEMIC PRESS, NEW YORK

DIVENYI, P.L. & EFRON, R. 1979 Spectral versus temporal features in dichotic listening BRAIN AND LANGUAGE 7: 375-386

DODD, B. 1975 Children's understanding of their own phonological forms QUARTERLY JOURNAL OF EXPERIMENTAL PSYCHOLOGY 27: 165-172

DODD, B. 1977 The role of vision in the perception of speech PERCEPTION 6: 31-40

DOLMAZON, J.M., BASTET, L., & SCHUPLJAKOF, V.S. 1977 A Functional model of the peripheral model of the peripheral auditory system in speech processing CONFERENCE RECORD OF THE IEEE ACOUSTICS, SPEECH, AND SIGNAL PROCESSING MEETING

DOMMERGUES, J.Y., SEGUI, J. & MEHLER, J. The syllabic structure of words UNPUBLISHED MANUSCRIPT

DONEGAN, P.D. & STAMPE, D. 1979 The study of natural phonology IN D.A. DINNSEN (ED) CURRENT APPROACHES TO PHONOLOGICAL THEORY, 126-173, INDIANA UNIVERSITY PRESS, BLOOMINGTON

DONOVAN, A. & DARWIN, C.J. 1979 The perceived rhythm of speech PROCEEDINGS OF THE NINTH INTERNATIONAL CONGRESS OF PHONETIC SCIENCES, VOL II, 268-274, INSTITUTE OF PHONETICS, UNIVERSITY OF COPENHAGEN

DU BRUL, E.L. 1958 Evolution of the Speech Apparatus THOMAS, SPRINGFIELD, ILLINOIS

DU BRUL, E.L. 1976 Biomechanics of speech sounds ANNALS OF THE NEW YORK ACADEMY OF SCIENCES 280: 631-642

DU BRUL, E.L. 1977 Origin of the speech apparatus and its reconstruction in fossils BRAIN AND LANGUAGE 4: 365-381

DUBNER, R., SESSLE, B.J., & STOREY, A.T. 1978 The Neural Basis of Oral and Facial Function PLENUM PRESS, NEW YORK

EFRON, R. 1963 Temporal perception aphasia and déja vu BRAIN 86: 403-424

EILERS, R.E. 1978 Discussion summary: development of phonology IN F.D. MINIFIE AND L.L. LLOYD (EDS) COMMUNICATIVE AND COGNITIVE ABILITIES - EARLY BEHAVIORAL ASSESSMENT, UNIVERSITY PARK PRESS, BALTIMORE

EIMAS, P.D. 1963 The relation between identification and discrimination along speech and nonspeech continua LANGUAGE AND SPEECH 6: 206-217

EIMAS, P.D. 1971 Speech perception in early infancy IN L. COHEN AND P. SALAPATEK (EDS) INFANT PERCEPTION FROM SENSATION TO COGNITION, VOLUME II, ACADEMIC PRESS, NEW YORK

EIMAS, P.D. 1974 Auditory and linguistic processing of cues for place of articulation by infants PERCEPTION AND PSYCHOLOGY 16: 513-521

EIMAS, P.D. & CORBIT, J.D. 1973 Selective adaptation of linguistic feature detectors COGNITIVE PSYCHOLOGY 4: 99-109

EIMAS, P.D., SIQUELAND, E.R., JUSCZYK, P. & VIGORITO, J. 1971 Speech perception in infants SCIENCE 171: 303-306

ELLIS, A.W. 1979 Speech production and short-term memory IN J. MORTON AND J.C. MARSHALL (EDS) PSYCHOLINGUISTICS SERIES VOL 2: STRUCTURES AND PROCESSES, ELEK SCIENCE, LONDON

EVANS, E.F. 1968 Cortical representation IN A.V.S. DE REUCK AND J. KNIGHT (EDS) HEARING MECHANISMS IN VERTEBRATES, 272-287, CHURCHILL, LONDON

EVANS, E.F. 1974A Neural processes for the detection of acoustic patterns and for sound localization IN F.G. WORDEN AND F.O. SCHMITT (EDS) THE NEUROSCIENCES: THIRD STUDY PROGRAM, 131-145, MASSACHUCHUSETTS INSTITUTE OF TECHNOLOGY, CAMBRIDGE

EVANS, E.F. 1974B Auditory frequency selectivity and the cochlear nerve IN E. ZWICKER AND E. TERHARDT (EDS) FACTS AND MODELS IN HEARING, 118-129, SPRINGER-VERLAG, HEIDELBERG

EVANS. E.F. 1975 The cochlear nerve and cochlear nucleus IN W.D. KEIDEL AND W.D. NEFF (EDS) HANDBOOK OF SENSORY PHYSIOLOGY, VOL 5/2: 1-108, SPRINGER-VERLAG, HEIDELBERG

EVANS, E.F. 1977A Some interactions between physiology and psychophysics in acoustics IN PROCEEDINGS OF THE NINTH INTERNATIONAL CONGRESS ON ACOUSTICS, REVIEW LECTURES, 55-65, SPANISH ACOUSTICAL SOCIETY,MADRID

EVANS, E.F. 1977B Frequency selectivity at high signal levels of single units in cochlear nerve and nucleus IN E.F. EVANS AND J.P. WILSON (EDS) PSYCHOPHYSICS AND PHYSIOLOGY OF HEARING, 185-192, ACADEMIC PRESS, LONDON

EVANS, E.F. 1977C Peripheral processing of complex sounds IN T.H. BULLOCK (ED) RECOGNITION OF COMPLEX ACOUSTIC SIGNALS, 145-159, DAHLEM KONFERENZEN, BERLIN

EVANS, E.F. 1978A Peripheral auditory processing in normal and abormal ears: physiological considerations for attempts to compensate for auditory deficits by acoustics and electrical prostheses IN C. LUDVIGSEN AND J. BARFOD (EDS) SENSORINEURAL HEARING IMPAIRMENT AND HEARING AIDS, 9-44, SCANDINAVIAN AUDIOLOGY, SUPPLEMENTUM 6

EVANS, E.F. 1978B Place and time coding of frequency in the peripheral auditory system: some physiological pros and cons AUDIOLOGY 17: 369-420

EVANS, E.F. 1980A An electronic analogue of single unit recording from the cochlear nerve for teaching and research JOURNAL OF PHYSIOLOGY 298: 6-7

EVANS, E.F. 1980B 'Phase-locking' of cochlear fibres and the problem of dynamic range IN G.V.D. BRINK AND F. BILSEN (EDS) INTERNATIONAL SYMPOSIUM ON PSYCHOPHYSICAL, PHYSIOLOGICAL AND BEHAVIOURAL STUDIES IN HEARING, 300-309, DELFT UNIVERSITY PRESS, DELFT

EVANS, E.F. & NELSON, P.G. 1973 The responses of single neurones in the cochlear nucleus of the cat as a function of their location and the anaesthetic state EXPERIMENTAL BRAIN RESEARCH 17: 402-427

EVANS, E.F. & PALMER, A.R. 1975 Responses of units in the cochlear nerve and nucleus of the cat to signals in the presence of bandstop noise JOURNAL OF PHYSIOLOGY 252: 60-62

EVANS, E.F. & PALMER, A.R. 1980 Relationship between the dynamic range of cochlear nerve fibres and their spontaneous activity EXPERIMENTAL BRAIN RESEARCH 40: 115-118

EVANS, E.F. & WILSON, J.P. 1973 The frequency selectivity of the cochlea IN A.R. MØLLER (ED) BASIC MECHANISMS IN HEARING, 519-551, ACADEMIC PRESS, NEW YORK

EVARTS, E.V., BIZZI, E., BURKE, R.E. DELONG, M. & THACH, W.T.(EDS) 1971 Central control of movement NEUROSCIENCES RESEARCH PROGRAM BULLETIN 9, 1

FAIRBANKS, G., & GRUBB, P. 1961 A psychological investigation of vowel formants JOURNAL OF SPEECH AND HEARING RESEARCH 4: 203-219

FALK, D. 1975 Comparative anatomy of the larynx in man and the chimpanzee: implications for language in neanderthal AMERICAN JOURNAL OF PHYSICAL ANTHROPOLOGY 43: 123-132

FALLSIDE, F. & YOUNG, S.J. 1978 Speech output from a computer-controlled water-supply network IEEE PROCEEDINGS 125: 157-161

FANT, G. 1959 Acoustic analysis and synthesis of speech with application to Swedish ERICSSON TECHNICS 15: 3-109

FANT, G. 1960 Acoustic Theory of Speech Production MOUTON, THE HAGUE

FANT, G. 1962A Descriptive analysis of the acoustic aspects of speech LOGOS 5: 3-17

FANT, G. 1962B Automatic recognition and speech research QUARTERLY PROGRESS AND STATUS REPORT 1, SPEECH TRANSMISSION LABORATORY, ROYAL INSTITUTE OF TECHNOLOGY, STOCKHOLM

FANT, G. 1969 Stops in CV syllables QUARTERLY PROGRESS AND STATUS REPORT 4: 1-25, SPEECH TRANSMISSION LABORATORY, ROYAL INSTITUTE OF TECHNOLOGY, STOCKHOLM

FANT, G. 1970 Automatic recognition and speech research SPEECH TRANSMISSION LABORATORY QUARTERLY PROGRESS AND STATUS REPORT, NO. 1, ROYAL INSTITUTE OF TECHNOLOGY, STOCKHOLM

FANT, G. 1972 Vocal tract wall effects, losses and resonance bandwidth QUARTERLY PROGRESS AND STATUS REPORT 2-3: 28-52, SPEECH TRANSMISSION LABORATORY, ROYAL INSTITUTE OF TECHNOLOGY, STOCKHOLM

FANT, G. 1979A Temporal fine structure of formant damping and excitation 50TH ANNIVERSARY MEETING OF THE ACOUSTICAL SOCIETY OF AMERICA, BOSTON

FANT, G. 1979B The relations between area functions and the acoustical signal INTERNATIONAL CONGRESS OF PHONETIC SCIENCES, INSTITUTE OF PHONETICS, UNIVERSITY OF COPENHAGEN

FANT, G., LILJENCRANTS, J., MALAC, V. & BOROVICKOVA, B. 1970 Perceptual evaluation of coarticulation effects QUARTERLY PROGRESS AND STATUS REPORTS 1: 10-13, SPEECH TRANSMISSION LABORATORY, ROYAL INSTITUTE OF TECHNOLOGY, STOCKHOLM

FANT, G., NORD, L. & BRANDERUD, P. 1976 A note on the vocal tract wall impedance QUARTERLY PROGRESS AND STATUS REPORT 4: 13-20, SPEECH TRANSMISSION LABORATORY, ROYAL INSTITUTE OF TECHNOLOGY, STOCKHOLM

FANT, G. & PAULI, S. 1975 Spatial characteristics of vocal tract resonance modes SPEECH COMMUNICATION 2 ALSO IN G. FANT (ED) SPEECH PRODUCTION AND SYNTHESIS BY RULES, ALMQVIST & WIKSELL, STOCKHOLM

FAY, D. 1979 Performing transformations IN R. COLE (ED) THE PERCEPTION AND PRODUCTION OF FLUENT SPEECH, ERLBAUM, HILLSDALE, NEW JERSEY

FAY, D. & CUTLER, A. 1977 Malapropisms and the structure of the mental lexicon LINGUISTIC INQUIRY (IN PRESS)

FELDMAN, H., GOLDIN-MEADOW, S. & GLEITMAN, L. 1978 Beyond Herodotus: the creation of language by linguistically deprived deaf children IN A. LOCK (ED) ACTION, GESTURE AND SYMBOL, 351-414, ACADEMIC PRESS, LONDON

FERGUSON, C & FARWELL, C. 1975 Words and sounds in early language acquisition LANGUAGE 51: 419-439

FERGUSON, C.A. 1977 Babytalk as a simplified register IN C. SNOW AND C.A. FERGUSON (EDS) TALKING TO CHILDREN: LANGUAGE INPUT AND ACQUISITION, 209-235, CAMBRIDGE UNIVERSITY PRESS

FIDELHOLTZ, J.L. 1975 Word frequency and vowel reduction in English PAPERS FROM THE ELEVENTH MEETING OF THE CHICAGO LINGUISTIC SOCIETY

FINK, B.R. & DEMAREST, R.J. 1978 Laryngeal Biomechanics HARVARD UNIVERSITY PRESS

FISCHER-JØRGENSEN, E. 1948 Some remarks on the function of stress with special reference to the Germanic languages INTERNATIONAL CONGRESS OF THE ANTHROPOLOGICAL SCIENCES, 86-88, BRUSSELS

FISCHER-JØRGENSEN, E. 1975 Trends in Phonological Theory AKADEMISK, COPENHAGEN

FISCHER-JØRGENSEN, E., RISCHEL, J. & THORSEN, N. (EDS) 1979 Proceedings of the Ninth International Congress of Phonetic Sciences INSTITUTE OF PHONETICS, UNIVERSITY OF COPENHAGEN

FLANAGAN, J.L. 1955 A difference limen for vowel formant frequency JOURNAL OF THE ACOUSTICAL SOCIETY OF AMERICA 27: 613-617

FLANAGAN, J.L. 1972 Speech Analysis, Synthesis and Perception SPRINGER-VERLAG, NEW YORK

FLANAGAN, J.L., ISHIZAKA, K. & SHIPLEY, K.L. 1975 Synthesis of speech from a dynamic model of the vocal cords and vocal tract BELL SYSTEM TECHNICAL JOURNAL 54: 485-506

FLISBERG, K & LINDHOLM, T. 1970 Electrical stimulation of the human recurrent laryngeal nerve during thyroid operation ACTA OTOLARYNGOLOGICA 263: 63-67

FODOR, J.A. & BEVER, T.G. 1965 The psychological reality of linguistic segments JOURNAL OF VERBAL LEARNING AND VERBAL BEHAVIOR 4: 414-420

FODOR, J.A., BEVER, T.G. & GARRETT, M.F. 1974 The Psychology of Language: An Introduction to Psycholinguistics and Generative Grammar MCGRAW-HILL, NEW YORK

FOLKINS, J.W. 1979 Masseter, temporalis, and medial pterygoid activity with the mandible free and fixed PROCEEDINGS OF THE NINTH INTERNATIONAL CONGRESS OF PHONETIC SCIENCES, VOL 2: 337-343, INSTITUTE OF PHONETICS, UNIVERSITY OF COPENHAGEN

FOLKINS, J.W. & ABBS J.H. 1975 Lip and jaw motor control during speech: responses to resistive loading of the jaw JOURNAL OF SPEECH AND HEARING RESEARCH 18: 207-220

FOLKINS, J.W. & ABBS, J.H. 1976 Additional observations on responses to resistive loading of the jaw JOURNAL OF SPEECH AND HEARING RESEARCH 19: 820-821

FORSTER, K.I. 1976 Accessing the mental lexicon IN R.J. WALES AND E. WALKER (EDS) NEW APPROACHES TO LANGUAGE MECHANISMS, NORTH-HOLLAND, AMSTERDAM

FORSTER, K.I. 1979 Levels of processing and the structure of the language processor IN W.E. COOPER AND E. WALKER (EDS) SENTENCE PROCESSING: PSYCHOLINGUISTIC STUDIES PRESENTED TO MERRILL GARRETT, ERLBAUM, HILLSDALE, NEW JERSEY

FOSS, D.J. 1970 Some effects of ambiguity upon sentence comprehension JOURNAL OF VERBAL LEARNING AND VERBAL BEHAVIOR 9: 699-706

FOSS, D.J. 1979 Deciphering decoding decisions: data and devices IN R.A. COLE (ED) PERCEPTION AND PRODUCTION OF FLUENT SPEECH, ERLBAUM, HILLSDALE, NEW JERSEY

FOSS, D.J. & HAKES, D.T. 1978 Psycholinguistics: an Introduction to the Psychology of Language PRENTICE-HALL, ENGLEWOOD CLIFFS, NEW JERSEY

FOSS,D.J. & JENKINS, C. 1973 Some effects of context on the comprehension of ambiguous sentences JOURNAL OF VERBAL LEARNING AND VERBAL BEHAVIOR 12: 577-589

FOSS, D.J. & SWINNEY, D.A. 1973 On the psychological reality of the phoneme: perception, identification and consciousness JOURNAL OF VERBAL LEARNING AND VERBAL BEHAVIOR 12: 246-257

FOSS, D.J., BEVER, T.G. & SILVER, M. 1968 The comprehension and verification of ambiguous sentences PERCEPTION & PSYCHOPHYSICS 4: 304-306

FOURCIN, A.J. 1972 Perceptual mechanisms at the first level of speech perception IN A. RIGAULT (ED) PROCEEDINGS OF THE EIGHTH INTERNATIONAL CONGRESS OF PHONETIC SCIENCES, 48-62, MOUTON, THE HAGUE

FOURCIN, A.J. 1978 Acoustic patterns and speech acquisition IN N. WATERSON AND C.E. SNOW (EDS) THE DEVELOPMENT OF COMMUNICATION, 47-72, WILEY, NEW YORK

FOWLER, C.A. 1977 Timing Control in Speech Production INDIANA UNIVERSITY LINGUISTICS CLUB, BLOOMINGTON, INDIANA

FOWLER, C.A., RUBIN, P., REMEZ, R.E., & TURVEY, M.T. 1978 Implications for speech production of a general theory of action IN B. BUTTERWORTH (ED) LANGUAGE PRODUCTION, ACADEMIC PRESS, NEW YORK

FOWLER, C.A. & SHANKWEILER, D.P. 1978 Identification of vowels in speech and nonspeech contexts JOURNAL OF THE ACOUSTICAL SOCIETY OF AMERICA 63, SUPPLEMENT 1, S4 (A)

FOWLER, C.A. & TURVEY, M.T. 1977 Skill acquisition: an event approach with special reference to searching for the optimum of a function several variables PAPER PRESENTED AT CIC SYMPOSIUM ON INFORMATION PROCESSING IN MOTOR CONTROL AND LEARNING, MADISON, WISCONSIN, APRIL 1977

FRAZIER, L. 1978 On comprehending sentences: syntactic parsing strategies PH.D. DISSERTATION, UNIVERSITY OF CONNECTICUT

FRAZIER, L. & FODOR, J.D. 1978 The sausage machine: a new two-stage parsing model COGNITION 6: 291-325

FRISHKOPF, L.A. & GOLDSTEIN, M.H. JR 1963 Response to acoustic stimuli from single units in the eighth nerve of the bullfrog JOURNAL OF THE ACOUSTICAL SOCIETY OF AMERICA 35: 1219-1228

FRITZELL, B. 1969 The velopharyngeal muscles in speech ACTA OTOLARYNGOLOGICA SUPPLEMENT 250

FROMKIN, V. 1971 The non-anomolous nature of anomolous utterances LANGUAGE 47: 27-52

FROMKIN, V.A. (ED) 1973 Speech Errors as Linguistic Evidence MOUTON, THE HAGUE

FROMKIN, V.A. 1976 Putting the emphasis on the wrong syllable PAPER PRESENTED TO STRESSFEST, USC, FEB. 28-29

FRY, D.B. 1969 The linguistic evidence of speech errors BRNO STUDIES IN ENGLISH

FRY, D.B., ABRAMSON, A.S., EIMAS, P.D. & LIBERMAN, A.M. 1962 The identification and discrimination of synthetic vowels LANGUAGE AND SPEECH 5: 171-189

FUDGE, E.C. 1969 Syllables JOURNAL OF LINGUISTICS 5: 253-286

FUJIMURA, O. (IN PRESS) An analysis of English syllables as cores and affixes ZEITSCHRIFT FUER PHONETIK, SPRACHWISSENSCHAFT UND KOMMUNIKATIONSFORSCHUNG

FUJIMURA, O. 1962 Analysis of nasal consonants JOURNAL OF THE ACOUSTICAL SOCIETY OF AMERICA 49: 541-558

FUJIMURA, O. 1975 Syllable as a unit of speech recognition IEEE TRANSACTIONS, ASSP-23: 82-86

FUJIMURA, O. 1976A Speech production - observation and modeling of the articulatory gestures IN S. SAHA (ED) PROCEEDINGS OF THE FOURTH ANNUAL BIOENGINEERING CONFERENCE, YALE UNIVERSITY, 469-474 PERGAMON PRESS, NEW YORK

FUJIMURA, O. 1976B Syllable as concatenated demisyllables and affixes PAPER PRESENTED AT THE 91ST MEETING OF THE ACOUSTICAL SOCIETY OF AMERICA, APRIL 1976, (UNPUBLISHED PAPER, BELL LABORATORIES)

FUJIMURA, O. 1977 Recent findings on articulatory processes - velum and tongue movements as syllable features IN R. CARRE, R. DESCOUT AND M. WAJSKOP (EDS) PROCEEDINGS OF THE SYMPOSIUM ON ARTICULATORY MODELLING, 115-126, G.A.L.F., GRENOBLE

FUJIMURA, O. & KAKITA, Y. 1979 Remarks on quantitative description of the lingual articulation IN B. LINDBLOM AND S. OHMAN (EDS) FRONTIERS OF SPEECH COMMUNICATION RESEARCH, 17-24, ACADEMIC PRESS, LONDON

FUJIMURA, O., KIRITANI, S. & ISHIDA, H. 1973 Computer controlled radiography for observation of movements of articulatory and other human organs COMPUTERS IN BIOLOGY AND MEDICINE 3: 371-384

FUJIMURA, O. & LINDQVIST, J. 1971 Sweep-tone measurements of vocal-tract characteristics JOURNAL OF THE ACOUSTICAL SOCIETY OF AMERICA 49: 541-558

FUJIMURA, O. & LOVINS, J.B. 1978 Syllables as concatenative phonetic units IN A. BELL AND J.B. HOOPER (EDS) SYLLABLES AND SEGMENTS, 107-120, NORTH-HOLLAND, AMSTERDAM

FUJIMURA, O. & MILLER, J.E. 1975 An x-ray observation of movements of the velum and the tongue REVISED VERSION OF A PAPER PRESENTED AT THE 90TH MEETING OF THE ACOUSTICAL SOCIETY OF AMERICA, NOVEMBER 1975 (UNPUBLISHED PAPER, BELL LABORATORIES)

FUJIMURA, O. & MILLER, J.E. 1977 A computer-controlled x-ray microbeam study of articulatory characteristics of nasal consonants in English and Japanese PROCEEDINGS OF THE NINTH INTERNATIONAL CONGRESS OF ACOUSTICS, MADRID

FUJIMURA, O. & MILLER, J.E. (IN PRESS) Mandible height and syllable-final tenseness PHONETICA

FUJISAKI, H. 1979 On the modes and mechanisms of speech perception - analysis and interpretation of categorical effects in discrimination IN B. LINDBLOM AND S. OHMAN (EDS) FRONTIERS OF SPEECH COMMUNICATION RESEARCH, 177-189, ACADEMIC PRESS, LONDON

FUJISAKI, H. & KAWASHIMA, T. 1968 The influence of various factors on the identification and discrimination of synthetic speech sounds REPORTS OF THE SIXTH INTERNATIONAL CONGRESS ON ACOUSTICS, B-3-6, TOKYO

FUJISAKI, H. & KAWASHIMA, T. 1969 On the modes and mechanisms of speech perception ANNUAL REPORT OF THE ENGINEERING RESEARCH INSTITUTE 28: 67-73, FACULTY OF ENGINEERING, UNIVERSITY OF TOKYO

FUJISAKI, H. & KAWASHIMA, T. 1970 Some experiments on speech perception and a model for the perceptual mechanisms, ANNUAL REPORT OF THE ENGINEERING RESEARCH INSTITUTE 29: 207-214, FACULTY OF ENGINEERING, UNIVERSITY OF TOKYO

FUJISAKI, H. & KAWASHIMA, T. 1971 A model of the mechanisms for speech perception - quantitative analysis of categorical effects in discrimination ANNUAL REPORT OF THE ENGINEERING RESEARCH INSTITUTE 30: 59-60, FACULTY OF ENGINEERING, UNIVERSITY OF TOKYO;

FUJISAKI, H., NAKAMURA, K. & IMOTO, T. 1975 Auditory perception of duration of speech and non-speech stimuli IN G. FANT AND M.A.A. TATHAM (EDS) AUDITORY ANALYSIS AND PERCEPTION OF SPEECH, ACADEMIC PRESS, LONDON

GAGNOULET, C., MERCIER, G., VIVES, R., VAISSIERE, J. & QUINTON, P. 1977 A multipurpose speech understanding system IEEE PROCEEDINGS, 815-818, ASSP CONFERENCE, HARTFORD, CONNECTICUT

GAINOTTI, G. & LEMMO, M.A. 1976 Comprehension of symbolic gestures in aphasia BRAIN AND LANGUAGE 3: 451-460

GANONG, W.F. III 1978 A word advantage in phoneme boundary experiments JOURNAL OF THE ACOUSTICAL SOCIETY OF AMERICA 63, SUPPLEMENT 1, S20

GARDINER, D. 1977 Two assumptions in the study of intonation PAPER READ AT LINGUISTIC SOCIETY OF AMERICA, CHICAGO

GARDNER, R.B. & WILSON, J.P. 1979 Evidence for direction-specific channels in the processing of frequency modulation JOURNAL OF THE ACOUSTICAL SOCIETY OF AMERICA 66: 704-709

GARNICA, O. 1977 Some prosodic and paralinguistic features of speech to young children IN C. SNOW AND C. FERGUSON (EDS) TALKING TO CHILDREN: LANGUAGE INPUT AND ACQUISITION, 63-88, CAMBRIDGE UNIVERSITY PRESS

GARRETT, M. 1970 Does ambiguity complicate the perception of sentences? IN G. FLORES D'ARCAIS AND W.J. LEVELT (EDS) ADVANCES IN PSYCHOLINGUISTICS, NORTH-HOLLAND, AMSTERDAM

GARRETT, M. 1975 The analysis of sentence production IN G. BOWER (ED) THE PSYCHOLOGY OF LEARNING AND MOTIVATION: ADVANCES IN RESEARCH AND THEORY, VOL 9, ACADEMIC PRESS, NEW YORK

GARRETT, M. 1976 Syntactic processes in sentence production IN R.J. WALES AND E.C.T. WALKER (EDS) NEW APPROACHES TO LANGUAGE MECHANISMS, NORTH-HOLLAND, AMSTERDAM

GARRETT, M. 1978 Word and sentence perception IN R. HELD, H.W. LIEBOWITZ AND H.L. TEUBER (EDS) HANDBOOK OF SENSORY PHYSIOLOGY VOL VIII: PERCEPTION, SPRINGER-VERLAG, BERLIN

GAY, T. 1968 Effect of speaking rate on diphthong formant movements JOURNAL OF THE ACOUSTICAL SOCIETY OF AMERICA 44: 1570-1573

GAY, T. 1974 A cinefluorographic study of vowel production JOURNAL OF PHONETICS 2: 255-266

GAY, T. 1976 Some electromyographic measures of coarticulation in VCV utterances IN M.A.A. TATHAM (ED), PROCEEDINGS OF THE FIFTH PHONETICS SYMPOSIUM, 115-119, UNIVERSITY OF ESSEX

GAY, T. 1977 Articulatory movements in VCV sequences JOURNAL OF THE ACOUSTICAL SOCIETY OF AMERICA 62: 183-193

GAY, T. 1978 Articulatory studies of segment organization IN A. BELL AND J. HOOPER (EDS) SEGMENTS AND SYLLABLES, 121-132, NORTH-HOLLAND, AMSTERDAM

GAY, T. 1979 Coarticulation in some consonant-vowel and consonant cluster-vowel syllables IN B. LINDBLOM AND S. OHMAN (EDS) FRONTIERS OF SPEECH COMMUNICATION, 69-76, ACADEMIC PRESS, LONDON

GAY, T. & TURVEY, M. 1979 Effects of afferent and efferent interference on speech production: implications for a generative theory of speech control PROCEEDINGS OF THE NINTH INTERNATIONAL CONGRESS OF PHONETIC SCIENCES, VOL 2: 344-350, INSTITUTE OF PHONETICS, UNIVERSITY OF COPENHAGEN

GAY, T., LINDBLOM, B. & LUBKER, J. 1979 An x-ray analysis of compensatory vowel production JOURNAL OF THE ACOUSTICAL SOCIETY OF AMERICA, SUBMITTED FOR PUBLICATION

GAZDAR, G. & KLEIN, E. 1978 Review of Keenan 'Formal Semantics of Natural Language' LANGUAGE 54: 666

GEL'FAND, I.M., GURFINKEL, V.S., TSETLIN, H.L. & SHIK, M.L. 1971 Some problems in the analysis of movements IN I.M. GEL'FAND, V.S. FOMIN AND M.T. TSETLIN (EDS) MODELS OF THE STRUCTURAL-FUNCTIONAL ORGANIZATION OF CERTAIN BIOLOGICAL SYSTEMS, 329-345, MASSACHUSETTS INSTITUTE OF TECHNOLOGY PRESS, CAMBRIDGE

GEORGE, S.L. 1978 The relationship between cranial base angle morphology and infant vocalizations PH.D. DISSERTATION, UNIVERSITY OF CONNECTICUT

GERRITSEN, M. & JANSEN, F. 1978 Word frequency and lexical diffusion in dialect borrowing and phonological change TO APPEAR IN ROBINSON, VAN COETSEM AND ZONNEVELD (EDS) DUTCH STUDIES IV: STUDIES IN DUTCH PHONOLOGY, AMSTERDAM

GHAZELI, S. 1977 Back consonants and backing coarticulation in Arabic PH.D. DISSERTATION, UNIVERSITY OF TEXAS

GILBERT, J.H.V. & BURK, K.W. 1969 Rate alterations in oral reading LANGUAGE AND SPEECH 12: 192-201

GINTER, K. & TARNOI, L. 1974 Ungarisch fur Auslander AKADEMIAI TANKONYVKIADO, BUDAPEST

GIVENS, D. 1978 Social expressivity during the first year of life SIGN LANGUAGE STUDIES 20: 251-274

GLEITMAN, L. & GLEITMAN, H. 1970 Phrase and Paraphrase NORTON, NEW YORK

GLUCKSBERG, S. & COWAN, G.C. 1970 Memory for nonattended auditory material COGNITIVE PSYCHOLOGY 1: 149-156

GOLDBLUM, M.D. & ALBERT, M. 1972 Phonemic discrimination in sensory aphasia INTERNATIONAL JOURNAL OF MENTAL HEALTH 1: 25-29

GOLDIN-MEADOW, S. 1978 Structure in a manual communication system developed without a conventional language model: language without a helping hand IN H. WHITAKER AND H.A. WHITAKER (EDS) STUDIES IN NEUROLINGUISTICS 4, ACADEMIC PRESS, NEW YORK

GOLDIN-MEADOW, S. & FELDMAN, H. 1977 The development of language-like communication without a language model SCIENCE 197: 401-403

GOLDMAN-EISLER, F. 1970 Psycholinguistics: Experiments in Spontaneous speech ACADEMIC PRESS, NEW YORK

GOLDSMITH, J. 1976 Autosegmental phonology PH.D. DISSERTATION, MASSACHUSETTS INSTITUTE OF TECHNOLOGY, (AVAILABLE FROM INDIANA LINGUISTICS CLUB)

GOLDSTEIN, J.L. 1972 Neural phase locking to combination tones predicted by simple transducer models JOURNAL OF THE ACOUSTICAL SOCIETY OF AMERICA 52: 142 (A)

GOLDSTEIN, J.L. 1973 An optimum processor theory for the central formation of the pitch of complex tones JOURNAL OF THE ACOUSTICAL SOCIETY OF AMERICA 54: 1496-1516

GOLDSTEIN, J.L. & SRULOVICZ, P. 1977 Auditory-nerve spike intervals as an adequate basis for aural frequency measurement IN E.F. EVANS AND J.P. WILSON (EDS) PSYCHOPHYSICS AND PHYSIOLOGY OF HEARING, 337-346, ACADEMIC PRESS, LONDON

GOLDSTEIN, L. 1978 Perceptual salience of stressed syllables THREE STUDIES IN SPEECH PERCEPTION: FEATURES, RELATIVE SALIENCE AND BIAS, WORKING PAPERS IN PHONETICS 39, CHAPTER II, UNIVERSITY OF CALIFORNIA AT LOS ANGELES

GOLDSTEIN, L. 1979 Categorical features in perception and production JOURNAL OF THE ACOUSTICAL SOCIETY OF AMERICA (IN PRESS)

GOLDSTEIN, U.G. 1979 Modelling children's vocal tracts SPEECH COMMUNICATION PAPERS PRESENTED AT THE 97TH MEETING OF THE ACOUSTICAL SOCIETY OF AMERICA, 139-142

GOODGLASS, H. & BLUMSTEIN, S.E. (EDS) 1973 Psycholinguistics and Aphasia THE JOHNS HOPKINS UNIVERSITY PRESS, BALTIMORE

GOODGLASS, H. & KAPLAN, E. 1972 The Assessment of Aphasia and Related Disorders LEA AND FEBIGER, PHILADELPHIA

GOODGLASS, H., KAPLAN, E., WEINTRAUB, S. & ACKERMAN, N. 1976 The "tip-of-the-tongue" phenomenon in aphasia CORTEX 12: 145-153

GOOSEN, C. & KORTMULDER, K. 1979 Relationships between faces and body motor patterns in a group of captive pigtailed macaques (macaca nemestrina) PRIMATES 20: 221-236

GRAMMONT, M. 1939 Traité de Phonétique (SECOND EDITION) DELAGRAVE, PARIS

GRANDGENT, C.H. 1896 Warmpth PUBLICATIONS OF THE MODERN LANGUAGE ASSOCIATION 11 (NEW SERIES) 4: 63-75

GRAY, H. 1978 Learning to take an object from the mother IN A. LOCK (ED) ACTION, GESTURE AND SYMBOL, CHAPTER 8, ACADEMIC PRESS, LONDON

GREENBERG, J. (ED) 1963 Universals of Language MASSACHUSETTS INSTITUTE OF TECHNOLOGY, CAMBRIDGE

GREENLEE, M. 1974 Interacting processes in the child's acquisition of stop-liquid clusters PAPERS AND REPORTS ON CHILD LANGUAGE DEVELOPMENT 7: 85-100, DEPARTMENT OF LINGUISTICS, STANFORD UNIVERSITY

GRESSER, J.Y. & MERCIER, G. 1975 Automatic segmentation of speech into syllable and phonetic units IN G. FANT AND M.A.A. TATHAM (EDS) AUDITORY ANALYSIS AND PERCEPTION OF SPEECH, 349-359, ACADEMIC PRESS, LONDON

GROAT, A. The use of English stress assignment rules by children taught either with traditional orthography or with the Initial Teaching Alphabet JOURNAL OF EXPERIMENTAL CHILD PSYCHOLOGY (IN PRESS)

GROSSBER, S. 1980 How does the brain build a cognitive code? PSYCHOLOGICAL REVIEW 87: 1-51

GROSSMAN, M. 1978 The game of the name: an examination of linguistic reference after brain damage BRAIN AND LANGUAGE 6: 112-119

GUERIN, B. & BOE, L.J. 1977 A two-mass model of the vocal cords: determination of control parameters and their respective consequences IEEE CONFERENCE ON ACOUSTICS, SPEECH AND SIGNAL PROCESSING, 583-586, HARTFORD

HAGGARD, M. 1974 Perceptual processing of coarticulation - a case study of /l/ JOURNAL OF PHONETICS 2: 117-123

HAGGARD, M.P., SUMMERFIELD, A.Q. & ROBERTS, M. 1980 Psychoacoustical and cultural determinants of phoneme boundaries JOURNAL OF PHONETICS (IN PRESS)

HALLE, M. 1964 On the bases of phonology IN THE STRUCTURE OF LANGUAGE: READINGS IN THE PHILOSOPHY OF LANGUAGE, J. FODOR & J. KATZ (EDS), PRENTICE-HALL, ENGLEWOOD CLIFFS, NEW JERSEY

HALLE, M., HUGHES, G.W. & RADLEY J.-P.A.1957 Acoustic properties of stop consonants JOURNAL OF THE ACOUSTICAL SOCIETY OF AMERICA 29: 107-116

HALLE, M. & SMITH, C.P. 1952 Distinctive features of voiceless stop consonants QUARTERLY PROGRESS REPORT 27: 48-53, RESEARCH LABORATORY OF ELECTRONICS, MASSACHUSETTS INSTITUTE OF TECHNOLOGY

HALLE, M. & STEVENS, K.N. 1979 Some reflections on the theoretical bases of phonetics IN B. LINDBLOM AND S. OHMAN (EDS) FRONTIERS OF SPEECH COMMUNCATION RESEARCH, 335-349, ACADEMIC PRESS, LONDON

HALLIDAY, M.A.K. 1975 Learning How to Mean : Explorations in the Development of Language ARNOLD, LONDON

HAMLET, S.L. & STONE, M. 1976 Compensatory vowel characteristics resulting from the presence of different types of experimental dental prostheses JOURNAL OF PHONETICS 4: 199-218

HAMLET, S.L. & STONE, M. 1978 Compensatory alveolar consonant production induced by wearing a dental prosthesis JOURNAL OF PHONETICS 6: 227-248

HARKNESS, S. 1971 Cultural variation in mothers' language IN W. VON RAFFLER-ENGEL (ED) CHILD LANGUAGE-1975, 495-8, SPECIAL ISSUE OF WORD 27: 1-3 (PUBLISHED IN 1976)

HARMS, R.T. 1973 Some Non-Rules of English INDIANA LINGUISTICS CLUB

HARRIS, C.M. 1953 A study of the building blocks of speech JOURNAL OF THE ACOUSTICAL SOCIETY OF AMERICA 25: 962-969

HASHIMOTO, T., KATAYAMA, Y., MURATA K. & TANIGUCHI, I. 1975 Pitch synchronous response of cat cochlear nerve fibers to speech sounds JAPANESE JOURNAL OF PHYSIOLOGY 25: 633

HAWKINS, S. 1973 Temporal coordination of consonants in the speech of children: preliminary data JOURNAL OF PHONETICS 1: 181-217

HAWKINS, S. 1979 Temporal coordination of consonants in the speech of children: further data JOURNAL OF PHONETICS 7 (IN PRESS)

HEALY, A.F. & CUTTING, J.E. 1976 Units of speech perception: phoneme and syllable JOURNAL OF VERBAL LEARNING AND VERBAL BEHAVIOR 15: 73-83

HEBB, D.O. 1949 The Organization of Behavior: a Neuropsychological Theory WILEY, NEW YORK

HELMHOLTZ, H.L.F. VON 1863 On the Sensations of Tone ENGLISH TRANSLATION BY A.J. ELLIS 1885, DOVER, NEW YORK 1954

HENKE, W.L. 1966 Dynamic articulatory model of speech production using computer simulation PH.D. DISSERTATION, MASSACHUSETTS INSTITUTE OF TECHNOLOGY

HENNEMAN, E. 1974 Spinal reflexes and the control of movement IN V.B. MOUNTCASTLE (ED) MEDICAL PHYSIOLOGY, MOSBY, SAINT LOUIS

HEWES, G.W. 1976 The current status of the gestural theory of language origins IN S. HARNAD, H. STEKLIS AND J. LANCASTER (EDS) ORIGINS AND EVOLUTION OF LANGUAGE AND SPEECH, ANNALS OF THE NEW YORK ACADEMY OF SCIENCES 280: 482-504

HIND, J.E., ANDERSON, D.J., BRUGGE, J.F. & ROSE, J.E. 1967 Coding of information pertaining to paired low-frequency tones in single auditory nerve fibers of the squirrel monkey JOURNAL OF NEUROPHYSIOLOGY 30: 794-816

HIROSE, H., USHIJIMA, T. & SAWASHIMA, M. 1969 An experimental study of the contraction properties of the laryngeal muscles in the cat ANNALS OF OTOLARYNGOLOGY 78: 297-307

HIRSH, I.J. 1959 Auditory perception of temporal order JOURNAL OF THE ACOUSTICAL SOCIETY OF AMERICA 31: 759-767

HIXON, T.J. 1973 Respiratory function in speech IN F.D. MINIFIE, T.J. HIXON & F. WILLIAMS (EDS): NORMAL ASPECTS OF SPEECH, HEARING AND LANGUAGE, 73-126, PRENTICE-HALL, ENGLEWOOD CLIFFS, NEW JERSEY

HOARD, J.E. 1971 Aspiration, tenseness and syllabicization in English LANGUAGE 47: 133-140

HOCKETT, C.F. 1955 A Manual of Phonology MEMOIR 11, INTERNATIONAL JOURNAL OF AMERICAN LINGUISTICS, 21, NO. 4, PART 1

HOCKETT, C.F. 1958 A Course in Modern Linguistics MACMILLAN, NEW YORK

HOCKETT, C.F. 1967 Where the tongue slips, there slip I. IN TO HONOR ROMAN JAKOBSON, MOUTON, THE HAGUE

HOFFMAN, H.S. 1958 Studies of some cues in the perception of the voiced stop consonants JOURNAL OF THE ACOUSTICAL SOCIETY OF AMERICA 30: 1035-1041

HOLMES, J.N. 1976 Formant excitation before and after glottal closure IEEE CONFERENCE ON ACOUSTICS, SPEECH AND SIGNAL PROCESSING, PHILADELPHIA

HOLMES, J.N., MATTINGLY, I.G. & SHEARME, J.N. 1964 Speech synthesis by rule LANGUAGE AND SPEECH 7: 127-143

HOLMES, V.M. 1979 Accessing ambiguous words during sentence comprehension QUARTERLY JOURNAL OF EXPERIMENTAL PSYCHOLOGY (IN PRESS)

HOLMES, V.M., ARWAS, R. & GARRETT, M.F. 1977 Prior context and the perception of lexically ambiguous sentences MEMORY & COGNITION 5: 103-110

HOMBERT, J.M. 1976 Word games; some implications for analysis of tone and other phonological processes WORKING PAPERS IN PHONETICS 33: 67-80, UNIVERSITY OF CALIFORNIA AT LOS ANGELES

HOMBERT, J.M., OHALA, J.J. & EWAN, W.G. 1979 Phonetic explanations for the development of tones LANGUAGE 55: 37-58

HOOPER, J.B. 1975 The archisegment in natural generative phonology LANGUAGE 51: 536-560

HOOPER J.B. 1976A Introduction to Natural Generative Phonology ACADEMIC PRESS, NEW YORK

HOOPER, J.B. 1976B Word frequency in lexical diffusion and the source of morpho-phonological change IN W. CHRISTIE (ED) CURRENT PROGRESS IN HISTORICAL LINGUISTICS, 95-105, NORTH-HOLLAND, AMSTERDAM

HOOPER, J.B. 1977A Rule death and restructuring PAPER PRESENTED AT THE THIRD INTERNATIONAL CONFERENCE ON HISTORICAL LINGUISTICS, HAMBURG, GERMANY, AND IN BUFFALO WORKING PAPERS ON LINGUISTICS, VOL I

HOOPER, J.B. 1977B Substantive evidence for linearity: vowel length and nasality in English IN W. BEACH ET AL (EDS) PAPERS FROM THE THIRTEENTH REGIONAL CHICAGO MEETING, 152-164, CHICAGO LINGUISTIC SOCIETY

HOOPER, J.B. 1978 Constraints on schwa-deletion in American English IN J. FISIAK (ED) RECENT DEVELOPMENTS IN HISTORICAL PHONOLOGY, 183-207, DE GRUYTER, BERLIN

HOSFORD, H.L. 1977 Binaural waveform coding in the inferior colliculus of the cat: single unit responses to simple and complex stimuli PH.D. DISSERTATION, STANFORD UNIVERSITY, CALIFORNIA

HOUDE, R.A. 1968 A study of tongue body motion during speech sounds SPEECH COMMUNICATIONS RESEARCH LABORATORY MONOGRAPH 2, SANTA BARBARA, CALIFORNIA

HOUK, J.C. 1979 Regulation of stiffness by skeletomotor reflexes ANNUAL REVIEW OF PHYSIOLOGY 41: 99-114

HOUTGAST, R. 1974 Auditory analysis of vowel-like sounds ACUSTICA 31: 320-324

HOWELLS, W.W. 1970 Mount Carmel man: morphological relationships PROCEEDINGS OF THE EIGHTH INTERNATIONAL CONGRESS OF ANTHROPOLOGICAL AND ETHNOLOGICAL SCIENCES, VOL 1, 269-272, TOKYO AND KYOTO

HOWELLS, W.W. 1974 Neanderthals: names, hypotheses and scientific method AMERICAN ANTHROPOLOGY 76: 24-38

HOWELLS, W.W. 1976 Neanderthal man: facts and figures PROCEEDINGS OF THE NINTH INTERNATIONAL CONGRESS OF ANTHROPOLOGICAL AND ETHNOLOGICAL SCIENCES, CHICAGO

HUGHES, G.W. & HALLE, M. 1956 Spectral properties of fricative consonants JOURNAL OF THE ACOUSTICAL SOCIETY OF AMERICA 28: 303-310

HUGHES, O.M. & ABBS, J.H. 1976 Labial-mandibular coordination in the production of speech; implications for the operation of motor equivalence PHONETICA 33: 199-201

HYMAN, L.M. 1977A Phonologization IN J. ALPHONSE (ED) LINGUISTIC STUDIES OFFERED TO JOSEPH GREENBERG, 407-418, ANMA LIBRI., SARATOGA, CALIFORNIA

HYMAN, L.M. 1977B On the nature of linguistic stress IN L. HYMAN (ED) STUDIES IN STRESS AND ACCENT, 37-82 LINGUISTICS DEPARTMENT, UNIVERSITY OF SOUTHERN CALIFORNIA

HYMAN, L.M. & SCHUH, R. 1974 Universals of tone rules: evidence from West Africa LINGUISTIC INQUIRY 5: 81-115

INGRAM, D. 1974 Phonological rules in young children JOURNAL OF CHILD LANGUAGE 1: 49-64

INGRAM, D. 1976A Phonological analysis of a child GLOSSA 10: 3-27

INGRAM, D. 1976B Phonological Disability in Children ARNOLD, LONDON

ISHIZAKA, K. & FLANAGAN, J.L. 1972 Synthesis of voiced sounds from a two-mass model of the vocal cords BELL SYSTEM TECHNICAL JOURNAL 51: 1233-1268

ISKHIZAKA, K., FRENCH, J.C. & FLANAGAN, J.L. 1975 Direct determination of vocal tract wall impedance IEEE TRANSACTIONS, ASSP-23: 370-373

JACKENDOFF, R. 1978 $\bar{X}$ syntax: a study of phrase structure LINGUISTIC INQUIRY MONOGRAPH NO. 2

JACKSON, J.H. 1932 Selected writings of J.H. Jackson, Vol.2, (J. Taylor, Ed.) HODDER AND STOUGHTON, LONDON

JAEGER, J. 1979 Phonological experiments using the concept formation paradigm PAPER PRESENTED TO THE CONFERENCE ON EXPERIMENTAL PHONOLOGY, BERKELEY

JAKOBSON, R. 1968 Child Language, Aphasia, and Phonological Universals MOUTON, THE HAGUE

JAKOBSON, R., FANT, C.G.M. & HALLE, M. 1951 Preliminaries to Speech Analysis: The Distinctive Features and their Correlates MASSACHUSETTS INSTITUTE OF TECHNOLOGY PRESS

JAKOBSON, R. & WAUGH, L.R. 1979 The Sound Shape of Language MOUTON, THE HAGUE

JESPERSEN, O. 1926 Lehrbuch der Phonetik TEUBNER, LEIPZIG

JOANETTE, Y., KELLER, E. & LECOURS, A.R. (IN PRESS) Sequences of phonemic approximations in aphasia BRAIN AND LANGUAGE

JOHANSON, D. & WHITE, T.D. 1979 A systematic assessment of early African hominids SCIENCE 203: 321-330

JOHNSON, D.H. 1974 The response of single auditory-nerve fibers in the cat to single tones: synchrony and average discharge rate PH.D. DISSERTATION, MASSACHUSETTS INSTITUTE OF TECHNOLOGY

JOHNSON-DAVIES, D. & PATTERSON, R.D. 1979 Psychophysical tuning curves: restricting the listening band to the signal region JOURNAL OF THE ACOUSTICAL SOCIETY OF AMERICA 65: 765-770

JOHNSTONE, B.M., TAYLOR, K.J. & BOYLE, A.J. 1970 Mechanics of the guinea pig cochlea JOURNAL OF THE ACOUSTICAL SOCIETY OF AMERICA 47: 504-509

JONES, D. 1957 The history and meaning of the term 'phoneme' IN PHONETICS IN LINGUISTICS, W.E. JONES & J. LAVER (EDS) 1973 187-204, LONGMAN, LONDON

JOOS, M. 1948 Acoustic Phonetics LANGUAGE MONOGRAPH 23

JORDAN, J. 1971 Studies of the origin of voice and vocalization in the chimpanzees FOLIA MORPHOLOGICA, PART III, WARSAW

JUSCZYK, P.W. & THOMPSON, E. 1978 Perception of a phonetic contrast in multi-syllabic utterances by 2-month old infants PERCEPTION AND PSYCHOPHYSICS 23: 105-109

KAGAYA, R. 1974 A fiberscopic and acoustic study of the Korean stops, affricates, and fricatives JOURNAL OF PHONETICS 2: 161-180

KAHN, D. 1976 Syllable-based generalizations in English phonology PH.D. DISSERTATION, MASSACHUSETTS INSTITUTE OF TECHNOLOGY

KAHN, D. 1978 On the identifiability of isolated vowels WORKING PAPERS IN PHONETICS 41: 26-31, UNIVERSITY OF CALIFORNIA AT LOS ANGELES

KALLIOINEN, V. 1965 Contribution à l'étude de l'intonation roumaine IN A. AVRAM, (ED) OMAGIU LUI ALEXANDRU ROSETTI LA 70 DE ANI, EDITURA ACADEMIEI, BUCHAREST

KAPLAN, R. 1972 Augmented transition networks as psychological models of sentence comprehension ARTIFICIAL INTELLIGENCE 3: 77-100

KAPLAN, R. 1975 Transient processing load in sentence comprehension PH.D. DISSERTATION, HARVARD UNIVERSITY

KARNICKAYA, E.G., MUSHIKOV, V.N., SLEPOKUROVA, N.A. & ZHUKOV, S.JA. 1975 Auditory processing of steady-state vowels IN G. FANT AND M.A.A. TATHAM (EDS) AUDITORY ANALYSIS AND PERCEPTION OF SPEECH, 37-53, ACADEMIC PRESS, LONDON

KAVANAGH, J.F. & MATTINGLY, I.G. 1972 Language by Eye and by Ear MASSACHUSETTS INSTITUTE OF TECHNOLOGY, CAMBRIDGE

KAY, R & MATTHEWS, D.R. 1972 On the existence in human auditory pathways of channels selectively tuned to the modulation present in frequency- modulated tones JOURNAL OF PHYSIOLOGY 225: 657-678

KAYE, K. 1977 Infants' effects upon their mothers' teaching strategies IN J.C. GLIDEWELL (ED) THE SOCIAL CONTEXT OF LEARNING AND DEVELOPMENT, 173-206, GARDNER PRESS/WILEY, NEW YORK

KEANE, A.H. 1895 Ethnology CAMBRIDGE UNIVERSITY PRESS

KELLER, E. 1975 Vowel errors in aphasia PH.D. DISSERTATION, UNIVERSITY OF TORONTO

KELLER, E. 1978 Parameters for vowel substitutions in Broca's aphasia BRAIN AND LANGUAGE 5: 265-285

KELLER, E., ROTHERNBERGER, A. & GOEPFERT, M. 1980 The perceptual and productive discrimination of vowels in aphasia BABBLE CONFERENCE, NIAGARA FALLS, ONTARIO

KELSO, J.S., HOLT, K.G., KUGLER, P.N. & TURVEY, M.Y. 1979 On the concept of coordinative structures as dissipative structures II. Empirical lines of convergence IN G.E. STELMACH & J. REQUIN (EDS), TUTORIALS IN MOTOR BEHAVIOUR NORTH-HOLLAND, AMSTERDAM

KENNEDY, J.G. 1977 Compensatory responses of the labial musculature to unanticipated disruption of articulation PH.D. DISSERTATION , UNIVERSITY OF WASHINGTON

KENT, R.D. 1976 Models of speech production IN N.J. LASS (ED) CONTEMPORARY ISSUES IN EXPERIMENTAL PHONETICS, 79-104, ACADEMIC PRESS, NEW YORK

KENT, R.D. & MINIFIE, F.D. 1977 Coarticulation in recent speech production models JOURNAL OF PHONETICS 5: 115-134

KENT, R.D. & MOLL, K.L. 1975 Articulatory timing in selected consonants BRAIN AND LANGUAGE 2: 304-323

KESSLER, C. 1971 The Acquisition of Syntax in Bilingual Children GEORGETOWN UNIVERSITY PRESS, WASHINGTON D.C.

KIANG, N.Y.S. 1975 Stimulus representation in the discharge patterns of auditory neurons IN D.B. TOWER (ED) THE NERVOUS SYSTEM, VOL 3, HUMAN COMMUNICATION AND ITS DISORDERS, 81-96, RAVEN PRESS, NEW YORK

KIANG, N.Y.S. 1979 Processing of speech by the auditory nervous system (an overview) JOURNAL OF THE ACOUSTICAL SOCIETY OF AMERICA (IN PRESS)

KIANG, N.Y.S., EDDINGTON, D.K. & DELGUTTE, B.1979 Fundamental considerations in designing auditory implants ACTA OTOLARYNGOLOGICA 87: 204-219

KIANG, N.Y.S., MOREST, D.K., GODFREY, D.A., GUINAN, J.J. KANE, E.C. 1973 Stimulus coding at caudal levels of the cat's auditory system. I. Response characteristics of single units IN A.R. MØLLER (ED) BASIC MECHANISMS IN HEARING, 455-475 ACADEMIC PRESS, NEW YORK

KIANG, N.Y.S. & MOXON, E.C. 1972 Physiological considerations in artificial stimulation of the inner ear ANNALS OF OTOLOGY 81: 714-730

KIANG, N.Y.S. & MOXON, E.C. 1974 Tails of tuning curves of auditory nerve fibers JOURNAL OF THE ACOUSTICAL SOCIETY OF AMERICA 55: 620-630

KIANG, N.Y.S., MOXON, E.C. & LEVINE, R.A. 1970 Auditory-nerve activity in cats with normal and abnormal cochleas IN G.E.W. WOLSTENHOLME AND J. KNIGHT (EDS) CIBA FOUNDATION SYMPOSIUM ON SENSORINEURAL HEARING LOSS, 241-273, J. & A. CHURCHILL, LONDON

KIANG, N.Y.S., WATANABE, T. THOMAS, E.C. & CLARK, L.F. 1965 Discharge Patterns of Single Fibers in the Cat's Auditory Nerve MASSACHUSETTS INSTITUTE OF TECHNOLOGY PRESS, CAMBRIDGE

KIM, D.O. & MOLNAR, C.E. 1975 Cochlear mechanics: measurements and models IN D.B. TOWER (ED) THE NERVOUS SYSTEM VOL 3: 57-68, HUMAN COMMUNICATION AND ITS DISORDERS, RAVEN PRESS, NEW YORK

KIM, D.O. & MOLNAR, C.E. 1979 A population study of cochlear nerve fibers: comparison of spatial distributions of average-rate and phase-locking measures of responses to single tones JOURNAL OF NEUROPHYSIOLOGY 42, 16-30

KIM, D.O., SIEGEL, J.H. & MOLNAR, C.E. 1979 Cochlear nonlinear effects in two-tone responses SCANDINAVIAN AUDIOLOGY (IN PRESS)

KIMBALL, J. 1973 Seven principles of surface structure parsing in natural language COGNITION 2: 15-47

KIMURA, D. 1979 Neuromotor mechanisms in the evolution of human communication IN H.D. STEKLIS AND M.J. RALEIGH (EDS) NEUROBIOLOGY OF SOCIAL COMMUNICATION IN PRIMATES: AN EVOLUTIONARY PERSPECTIVE, ACADEMIC PRESS, NEW YORK

KING, E.W. 1952 A roentgenographic study of pharyngeal growth ANGLE ORTHODONTIST 22: 23-27

KINGDON, R. 1958 The Groundwork of English Intonation LONGMANS, LONDON

KIPARSKY, P. 1968 Linguistic universals and linguistic change IN E. BACH AND T. HARMS (EDS) UNIVERSALS IN LINGUISTIC THEORY, HOLT, RINEHART & WINSTON, NEW YORK

KIPARSKY, P. 1973 Historical linguistics IN W. DINGWALL (ED) SURVEY OF LINGUISTICS, UNIVERSITY OF MARYLAND PRESS

KIPARSKY, P. 1979 Metrical structure assignment is cyclic LINGUISTIC INQUIRY 10: 421-442

KIPARSKY, P. & MENN, L. 1977 On the acquisition of phonology IN J. MACNAMARA (ED) LANGUAGE, LEARNING AND THOUGHT, ACADEMIC PRESS, NEW YORK

KIRAKOWSKI, J. 1977 Prosody and speech perception PH.D. DISSERTATION, UNIVERSITY OF EDINBURGH

KIRAKOWSKI, J. & MYERS, T. 1975 The effect of intonation on message intelligibility PAPER PRESENTED AT THE BAS SPRING CONFERENCE, NOTTINGHAM

KIRITANI, S. ITOH, K. & FUJIMURA, O. 1975 Tongue-pellet tracking by a computer-controlled x-ray microbeam system JOURNAL OF THE ACOUSTICAL SOCIETY OF AMERICA 57: 1516-1520

KLATT, D.H. 1974 The duration of 's' in English words JOURNAL OF SPEECH AND HEARING RESEARCH 17: 51-63

KLATT, D.H. 1975 Vowel lengthening is syntactically determined in a connected discourse JOURNAL OF PHONETICS 3: 129-140

KLATT, D. 1976 Structure of a phonological rule component for a synthesis-by-rule program IEEE TRANSACTIONS, ASSP-24: 391-398

KLATT, D.H. 1976 A digital filter bank for spectral matching PROCEEDINGS OF THE 1976 IEEE INTERNATIONAL CONFERENCE ON ACOUSTICS, SPEECH AND SIGNAL PROCESSING, PHILADELPHIA, APRIL 12-14, 1976, IEEE CATALOG NO. 76 CH1067-8 ASSP 537-540

KLATT, D.H. 1977 Review of the ARPA speech understanding project JOURNAL OF THE ACOUSTICAL SOCIETY OF AMERICA 62: 1345-1366

KLATT, D.H. 1979 Speech perception: a model of acoustic-phonetic analysis and lexical access JOURNAL OF PHONETICS 7 : 279-312

KLATT, D.H. & STEVENS, K.N. 1973 On the automatic recognition of continuous speech: implications from a spectogram-reading experiment IEEE TRANSACTIONS, AU-21: 210-217

KLIMA, E. & BELLUGI, U. 1979 The Signs of Language HARVARD UNIVERSITY PRESS, CAMBRIDGE MASSACHUSETTS

KLINGER, H. 1962 Imitated English cleft palate speech in a normal Spanish speaking child JOURNAL OF SPEECH AND HEARING DISORDERS 27: 379-381

KLOVSTAD, J.W. 1978 Computer automated speech perception system UNPUBLISHED PH.D. DISSERTATION, MASSACHUSETTS INSTITUTE OF TECHNOLOGY, CAMBRIDGE

KORDICK, E.A. 1975 Pointing in the acquisition of language PH.D. DISSERTATION, UNIVERSITY OF ILLINOIS: UNIVERSITY MICROFILMS, (MICROFICHE 76-6823)

KOSKI, A. & MIHALYFY, I. 1962 Hungarian: Basic Course FOREIGN SERVICE INSTITUTE, DEPARTMENT OF STATE, WASHINGTON

KOZHEVNIKOV, V. & CHISTOVICH, L. 1965 Rech', Artikulyatsiya, i Vospriyatiye, translated as: Speech: Articulation and Perception JOINT PUBLICATIONS RESEARCH SERVICE, JPRS NO. 30.543, WASHINGTON D.C.

KRISHNAMURTI, BH. 1978 Areal and lexical diffusion of sound change LANGUAGE 54: 1-20

KUEHN, D.P. & MOLL, K. 1972 Perceptual effects of forward coarticulation JOURNAL OF SPEECH AND HEARING RESEARCH 15: 654-664

KUEHN, D.P. & MOLL, K. 1976 A cinefluorographic investigation of CV and VC articulatory velocities JOURNAL OF PHONETICS 3: 303-320

KUGLER, P.N., KELSO, J.S. & TURVEY, M.T. 1979 On the concept of coordinative structures as dissipative structures I. Theoretical lines of convergence IN G.E. STELMACH & J. REQUIN (EDS), TUTORIALS IN MOTOR BEHAVIOR NORTH-HOLLAND, AMSTERDAM

KUHL, P.K. 1976 Speech perception in early infancy: the acquisition of speech-sound categories IN S.K. HIRSCH, D.H. ELDREDGE, I.J. HIRSCH AND S.R. SILVERMAN (EDS) HEARING AND DAVIS: ESSAYS HONORING HALLOWELL DAVIS, WASHINGTON UNIVERSITY PRESS

KUHL, P.K. 1978 Predispositions for the perception of speech-sound categories: a species-specific phenomenon? IN F.D. MINIFIE AND L.L. LLOYD (EDS) COMMUNICATIVE AND COGNITIVE ABILITIES - EARLY BEHAVIORAL ASSESSMENT, UNIVERSITY PARK PRESS, BALTIMORE

KUHL, P.K. & MILLER, J.D. 1975 Speech perception by the chinchilla: voiced-voiceless distinction in alveolar plosive consonants SCIENCE 190: 69-72

KUHL, P.K. & MILLER, J.D. 1978 Speech perception by the chinchilla: identification functions for synthetic stimuli JOURNAL OF THE ACOUSTICAL SOCIETY OF AMERICA 63: 905-917

KUHN, G.M. 1973 A two-pass procedure for synthesis by rule JOURNAL OF THE ACOUSTICAL SOCIETY OF AMERICA 54: 339A

KUNO, S. & OETTINGER, A.G. 1962 Multiple-path syntactic analyser INTERNATIONAL FEDERATION OF INFORMATION PROCESSING CONGRESS 62, MUNICH, GERMANY

KURODA, S. 1979 Grouping of the pygmy chimpanzee PRIMATES 20: 161-183

KUSCHEL, R. 1974 A lexicon of signs from a Polynesian outliner [sic] island KOBENHAVNS UNIVERSITET, PSYKOLOGISK SKRIFTSERIE 8

LABOV, W. 1972A The boundaries of words and their meanings IN C.-J. BAILEY AND R. SHUY (EDS) NEW WAYS OF ANALYZING VARIATION IN ENGLISH, GEORGETOWN UNIVERSITY PRESS, WASHINGTON D.C.

LABOV, W. 1972B The internal evolution of linguistic rules IN R.P. STOCKWELL AND R.K.S. MACAULAY (EDS) LINGUISTIC CHANGE AND GENERATIVE THEORY, 101-171, INDIANA UNIVERSITY PRESS, BLOOMINGTON

LABOV, W. 1973 The boundaries of words and their meanings IN C.-J. BAILEY AND R. SHUY (EDS) NEW WAYS OF ANALYZING VARIATIONS IN ENGLISH, GEORGETOWN UNIVERSITY PRESS, WASHINGTON D.C.

LACKNER, J.R. 1974 Proprioceptive facilitation of open-loop visual pointing PERCEPTUAL AND MOTOR SKILLS 39: 263-265

LACKNER, J.R. & GARRETT, M.F. 1972 Resolving ambiguity: effects of biasing context in unattended ear COGNITION 1: 359-372

LADD, D.R. 1978 The structure of intonational meaning PH.D. DISSERTATION, CORNELL UNIVERSITY

LADD, D.R. JR. 1980 The Structure of Intonational Meaning: Evidence from English INDIANA UNIVERSITY PRESS, BLOOMINGTON (IN PRESS)

LADEFOGED, P. 1971 Preliminaries to Linguistic Phonetics UNIVERSITY OF CHICAGO PRESS

LADEFOGED, P. 1975 A Course in Phonetics HARCOURT BRACE JOVANOVICH, NEW YORK

LADEFOGED, P. 1977 The abyss between phonetics and phonology CHICAGO LINGUISTIC SOCIETY 13: 225-235

LADEFOGED, P., DECLERK, J., LINDAU, M. & PAPCUN, G. 1972 An auditory-motor theory of speech production WORKING PAPERS IN PHONETICS 22: 48-75, UNIVERSITY OF CALIFORNIA AT LOS ANGELES

LADEFOGED, P., HARSHMAN, R, GOLDSTEIN L. & RICE, L. 1978 Generating vocal tract shapes from formant frequencies JOURNAL OF THE ACOUSTICAL SOCIETY OF AMERICA 64: 1027-1035

LAIDLER, K. 1978 Language in the orang-utan IN A. LOCK (ED) ACTION, GESTURE AND SYMBOL, CHAPTER 7, ACADEMIC PRESS, LONDON

LAITMAN, J.T. & CRELIN, E.S. 1976 Postnatal development of the basicranium and vocal tract region in man IN J.F. BOSMA (ED) SYMPOSIUM ON DEVELOPMENT OF THE BASICRANIUM, 206-219, US GOVERNMENT PRINTING OFFICE, WASHINGTON D.C.

LAITMAN, J.T., HEIMBUCH, R.C. & CRELIN, E.S. 1978 Developmental change in a basicranial line and its relationship to the upper respiratory system in living primates AMERICAN JOURNAL OF ANATOMY 152: 467-482

LAITMAN, J.T., HEIMBUCH, R.C. & CRELIN, E.S. 1979 The basicranium of fossil hominids as an indicator of their upper respiratory systems AMERICAN JOURNAL OF PHYSICAL ANTHROPOLOGY 51: 15-34

LAKOFF, G. 1973 Fuzzy grammar and the competence/performance terminology game IN C. CORUM ET AL (EDS) PAPERS FROM THE NINTH REGIONAL MEETING OF THE CHICAGO LINGUISTIC SOCIETY

LANGENDOEN, D.T. & BEVER, T.G. 1969 Can a not unhappy man be called a not sad one? IN S. ANDERSON AND P. KIPARSKY (EDS) A FESTSCHRIFT FOR MORRIS HALLE, 392-409, HOLT, NEW YORK

LASHLEY, K.S. 1951 The problem of serial order in behavior IN L.A. JEFFRESS (ED) CEREBRAL MECHANISMS IN BEHAVIOR, 112-136, WILEY, NEW YORK

LASS, N.J. & CAIN, C.J. 1972 A correlational study of listening rate preferences and listeners' oral reading rates JOURNAL OF AUDITORY RESEARCH 12: 308-312

LASSEN, N.A., INGVAR, D.H. & SKINHOJ, E. 1978 Brain function and blood flow SCIENTIFIC AMERICAN 239: 62-71

LEA, W.A. 1973 Segmental and suprasegmental influences on fundamental frequency contours IN L.H. HYMAN (ED) CONSONANT TYPES AND TONE, UNIVERSITY OF CALIFORNIA, LOS ANGELES

LEA, W.A. 1976A Use of intonational phrase boundaries to select syntactic hypotheses in a speech understanding system PAPER PRESENTED AT THE 92ND MEETING OF THE ACOUSTICAL SOCIETY OF AMERICA

LEA, W.A. 1976B A prosodically guided speech understanding system IEEE TRANSACTIONS, ASSP-23: 30-38

LEA, W.A. 1979 Trends in Speech Recognition PRENTICE-HALL, NEW YORK

LEAKEY, M.D. 1979 Footprints in the ashes of time NATIONAL GEOGRAPHIC 155: 446-457

LEANDERSON, R. & PERSSON, A. 1972 The effects of trigeminal nerve block on the articulatory EMG activity of facial muscles ACTA OTOLARYNGOLOGICA 74: 271-278

LEBEN, W.R. & ROBINSON, O.W. 1977 'Upside-down' phonology LANGUAGE 53: 1-20

LEED, R.L. 1968 The intonation of yes-no questions in Serbo-Croatian SLAVIC AND EAST EUROPEAN JOURNAL 12: 330-336

LEHISTE, I. 1960 A phonetic study of internal juncture SUPPLEMENT TO PHONETICA 5: 1-54

LEHISTE, I. 1970 Suprasegmentals MASSACHUSETTS INSTITUTE OF TECHNOLOGY PRESS, CAMBRIDGE

LEHISTE, I. 1977 Isochrony reconsidered JOURNAL OF PHONETICS 5: 253-263

LEHISTE, I. 1978 The syllable as a structural unit in Estonian IN A. BELL AND J.B. HOOPER (EDS) SYLLABLES AND SEGMENTS, 73-83, NORTH-HOLLAND, AMSTERDAM

LEHISTE, I. & IVIC, P. 1977 The intonation of yes-or-no questions - a new balkanism? PAPER PRESENTED AT SYMPOSIUM/CONFERENCE ON SOUTHEASTERN EUROPE, OHIO STATE UNIVERSITY

LEHISTE, I. & SHOCKEY, L. 1972 On the perception of coarticulation effects in VCV syllables JOURNAL OF SPEECH AND HEARING RESEARCH 15: 500-506

LE MAY, M. & GESCHWIND, N. 1975 Hemispheric differences in the brains of great apes BRAIN, BEHAVIOR AND EVOLUTION 11: 48-52

LENNEBERG, P. 1967 Biological Foundations of Language WILEY, NEW YORK

LEOPOLD, W. 1939-1947 Speech Development of a Bilingual Child: a Linguist's Record 4 VOLS, NORTHWESTERN UNIVERSITY PRESS

LEOPOLD, W.F. 1948 German LANGUAGE 24: 179-80

LESSER, V.R. FENNELL, R.D., ERMAN, L.D. & REDDY, D.R. 1975 Organization of the HEARSAY-II speech understanding system IEEE TRANSACTIONS, ASSP-23: 11-23

LIBERMAN, A.M. 1970 The grammar of speech and language COGNITIVE PSYCHOLOGY 1: 301-323

LIBERMAN, A.M., COOPER, F.S., SHANKWEILER, D.P. & STUDDERT-KENNEDY, M. 1967 Perception of the speech code PSYCHOLOGICAL REVIEW 74: 431-461

LIBERMAN, A.M., COOPER, F.S., HARRIS, K.S. & MACNEILAGE, P.F. 1962 A motor theory of speech perception IN G. FANT (ED) PROCEEDINGS OF THE SPEECH COMMUNICATION SEMINAR, ROYAL INSTITUTE OF TECHNOLOGY, STOCKHOLM

LIBERMAN, A.M., DELATTRE, P.C. & COOPER, F.S. 1958 Some cues for the distinction between voiced and voiceless stops in the initial position LANGUAGE AND SPEECH 1: 153-167

LIBERMAN, A.M., DELATTRE, P.C., GERSTMAN, L.J. & COOPER, F.S. 1956 Tempo of frequency change as a cue for distinguishing classes of speech sounds JOURNAL OF EXPERIMENTAL PSYCHOLOGY 52: 127-137

LIBERMAN, A.M., HARRIS, K.S., HOFFMAN, H.S. & GRIFFITH, B.C. 1957 The discrimination of speech sounds within and across phoneme boundaries JOURNAL OF EXPERIMENTAL PSYCHOLOGY 54: 358-368

LIBERMAN, A.M., INGEMANN, F., LISKER, L., DELATTRE, P.C. & COPPER, F.S. 1959 Minimal rules for synthesizing speech JOURNAL OF THE ACOUSTICAL SOCIETY OF AMERICA 31: 1490-1499

LIBERMAN, A.M., MATTINGLY, I.G. & TURVEY, M.T. 1972 Language codes and memory codes IN A.W. MELTON AND E. MARTIN (EDS) CODING PROCESSES IN HUMAN MEMORY, WINSTON, WASHINGTON D.C.

LIBERMAN, A.M. & STUDDERT-KENNEDY, M. 1978 Phonetic perception IN R. HELD, H. LEIBOWITZ AND H.L. TEUBER (EDS) HANDBOOK OF SENSORY PHYSIOLOGY, VOL VIII, PERCEPTION, SPRINGER-VERLAG, BERLIN

LIBERMAN, I.Y., SHANKWEILER, D. FISCHER, F.W. & CARTER, B. 1974 Reading and the awareness of linguistic segments JOURNAL OF EXPERIMENTAL CHILD PSYCHOLOGY 18: 201-212

LIBERMAN, M. 1975 The intonational system of English PH.D. DISSERTATION, MASSACHUSETTS INSTITUTE OF TECHNOLOGY, AVAILABLE FROM INDIANA UNIVERSITY LINGUISTICS CLUB

LIBERMAN, M. & PRINCE, A. 1977 On stress and linguistic rhythm LINGUISTIC INQUIRY 9(2): 249-336

LIBERMAN, M.C. 1978 Auditory-nerve response from cats raised in a low-noise chamber JOURNAL OF THE ACOUSTICAL SOCIETY OF AMERICA 63: 442-455

LIBERMAN, M. & STREETER, L.A. 1978 Use of non-sense syllable mimicry in the study of prosodic phenomena JOURNAL OF THE ACOUSTICAL SOCIETY OF AMERICA 63: 231-233

LIEBERMAN, P. 1967 Intonation, Perception and Language MASSACHUSETTS INSTITUTE OF TECHNOLOGY PRESS, CAMBRIDGE

LIEBERMAN, P. 1968 Primate vocalizations and human linguistic ability JOURNAL OF THE ACOUSTICAL SOCIETY OF AMERICA 44: 1574-1584

LIEBERMAN, P. 1970 Toward a unified phonetic theory LINGUISTIC INQUIRY I: 307-322

LIEBERMAN, P. 1973 On the evolution of language: a unified view COGNITION 2: 59-94

LIEBERMAN, P. 1975A On the Origins of Language: An Introduction to the Evolution of Human Speech MACMILLAN, NEW YORK

LIEBERMAN, P. 1975B More discussion of neanderthal speech LINGUISTIC INQUIRY 6: 325-329

LIEBERMAN, P. 1976A Structural harmony and neanderthal speech: a reply to Le May AMERICAN JOURNAL OF PHYSICAL ANTHROPOLOGY 45: 493-496

LIEBERMAN, P. 1976B Interactive models for evolution: neural mechanism, anatomy and behavior IN S.E. HARNAD, H.D. STEKLIS AND J. LANCASTER (EDS) ORIGINS AND EVOLUTION OF LANGUAGE AND SPEECH, ANNALS OF THE NEW YORK ACADEMY OF SCIENCE, 280: 660-672

LIEBERMAN, P. 1976C Phonetic features and physiology: a reappraisal JOURNAL OF PHONETICS 4: 91-112

LIEBERMAN, P. 1977 More on hominid evolution, speech and language CURRENT ANTHROPOLOGY 18: 550-551

LIEBERMAN, P. 1978 A reply to Carlisle and Siegel's assessment of neanderthal speech capabilities AMERICAN ANTHROPOLOGIST 80: 676-681

LIEBERMAN, P. 1979A Phonetics and physiology: some current issues IN G. PRIDEAUX (ED) PERSPECTIVES IN EXPERIMENTAL LINGUISTICS, JOHN BENJAMINS, AMSTERDAM

LIEBERMAN, P. 1979B Hominid evolution, supralaryngeal vocal tract physiology, and the fossil evidence for reconstructions BRAIN AND LANGUAGE 7: 101-126

LIEBERMAN, P. (IN PRESS) On the development of vowel production in young children IN G.H. YENI-KOMSHIAN, J.F. KAVANAGH AND C.A. FERGUSON (EDS), CHILD PHONOLOGY: PERCEPTION, PRODUCTION AND DEVIATION, ACADEMIC PRESS, NEW YORK

LIEBERMAN, P. & CRELIN, E.S. 1971 On the speech of neanderthal man LINGUISTIC INQUIRY 2: 203-222

LIEBERMAN, P., CRELIN, E.S. & KLATT, D.H. 1972 Phonetic ability and related anatomy of the newborn, adult human, neanderthal man, and the chimpanzee AMERICAN ANTHROPOLOGIST 74: 287-307

LIEBERMAN, P., HARRIS, K.S., WOLFF, P. & RUSSELL, L.H. 1972 Newborn infant cry and nonhuman primate vocalizations JOURNAL OF SPEECH AND HEARING RESEARCH 14: 718-727

LIEBERMAN, P., KLATT, D.L. & WILSON, W.A. 1969 Vocal tract limitations on the vowel repertoires of rhesus monkeys and other nonhuman primates SCIENCE 164: 1185-1187

LILJENCRANTS, J. & LINDBLOM, B. 1972 Numerical simulation of vowel quality systems: the role of perceptual contrast LANGUAGE 48: 839-862

LINDAU, M. 1978 Vowel features LANGUAGE 54: 541-562

LINDBLOM, B. 1963 Spectrographic study of vowel reduction JOURNAL OF THE ACOUSTICAL SOCIETY OF AMERICA 35: 1773-1781

LINDBLOM, B. 1967 Vowel duration and a model of lip-mandible coordination QUARTERLY PROGRESS AND STATUS REPORT 4: 1-29, SPEECH TRANSMISSION LABORATORY, ROYAL INSTITUTE OF TECHNOLOGY, STOCKHOLM

LINDBLOM, B. 1968 Temporal organisation of syllable production QUARTERLY PROGRESS AND STATUS REPORT 2(3), SPEECH TRANSMISSION LABORATORY, ROYAL INSTITUTE OF TECHNOLOGY, STOCKHOLM

LINDBLOM, B. 1975 Experiments in sound structure PLENARY ADDRESS, EIGHTH INTERNATIONAL CONGRESS OF PHONETIC SCIENCES, LEEDS, ENGLAND

LINDBLOM, B. & STUDDERT-KENNEDY, M. 1967 On the role of formant transitions in vowel recognition JOURNAL OF THE ACOUSTICAL SOCIETY OF AMERICA 42: 830-843

LINDBLOM, B. & SUNDBERG, J. 1971A Neurophysiological representation of speech sounds PAPER PRESENTED AT 15TH WORLD CONGRESS OF LOGOPEDICS AND PHONIATRICS, BUENOS AIRES

LINDBLOM, B. & SUNDBERG, J. 1971B Acoustical consequences of lip, tongue, jaw and larynx movements JOURNAL OF THE ACOUSTICAL SOCIETY OF AMERICA 50: 1160-1179

LINDBLOM, B., LUBKER, J. & GAY, T. 1979 Formant frequencies of some fixed-mandible vowels and a model of speech motor programming by predictive simulation JOURNAL OF PHONETICS 7: 147-162

LINDBLOM, B.,, MCALLISTER, R. & LUBKER, J. 1977 Compensatory articulation and the modelling of normal speech production behavior IN R. CARRE, R. DESCOUT AND M. WAJSKOP (EDS) PROCEEDINGS OF SYMPOSIUM ON ARTICULATION MODELLING, G.A.L.F., GRENOBLE

LISKER, L. & ABRAMSON, A.S. 1967 The voicing dimension: some experiments in comparative phonetics PROCEEDINGS OF THE SIXTH INTERNATIONAL CONGRESS OF PHONETIC SCIENCES, PRAGUE, 563-567, ACADEMIA, PRAGUE

LISKER, L. & ABRAMSON, A. 1964 A cross-language study of voicing in initial stops: acoustical measurements WORD 20: 384-422

LISKER, L. & ABRAMSON, A.S. 1967 Some effects of context on voice onset time in English stops LANGUAGE AND SPEECH 10: 1-28

LITTLEFIELD, W.M. 1973 Investigation of the linear range of the peripheral auditory system PH.D. DISSERTATION, WASHINGTON UNIVERSITY, ST. LOUIS, MISSOURI

LOCK, A. 1978 Action, Gesture and Symbol: The Emergence of Language ACADEMIC PRESS, LONDON

LOVINS, J.B. 1978 A study of 'nasal reduction' in English syllable codas A MIMEOGRAPH PAPER, A REVISED VERSION OF PAPER IN PAPERS FROM THE FOURTEENTH REGIONAL MEETING, CHICAGO LINGUISTIC SOCIETY

LOVINS, J.B., MACCHI, M.J. & FUJIMURA, O. 1979 A demisyllable inventory for speech synthesis TO BE PUBLISHED IN THE PROCEEDINGS OF THE 97TH MEETING OF THE ACOUSTICAL SOCIETY OF AMERICA, CAMBRIDGE,MASSACHUSETTS

LOWERRE, B.T. 1976 The HARPY speech recognition system PH.D. DISSERTATION, DEPARTMENT OF COMPUTER SCIENCE, CARNEGIE-MELLON UNIVERSITY, PITTSBURGH

LOWERRE, B. & REDDY, D.R. 1979 The Harpy speech understanding system IN W.A. LEA (ED) TRENDS IN SPEECH RECOGNITION

LUBKER, J. 1968 An electromyographic-cinefluorographic investigation of velar function during normal speech production CLEFT PALATE JOURNAL 5: 1-19

LUBKER, J., MCALLISTER, R. & CARLSON, J. 1975A Labial co-articulation in Swedish: a preliminary report IN G. FANT (ED) PROCEEDINGS OF THE SPEECH COMMUNICATION SEMINAR, 55-64, ALMQVIST AND WIKSELL, STOCKHOLM

LUBKER, J.F., MCALLISTER, R. & CARLSON, J. 1975B Electro-myographic studies of speech production EIGHTH INTERNATIONAL CONGRESS OF PHONETIC SCIENCES, LEEDS,ENGLAND

LUCE, R.D. 1959 Individual Choice Behavior WILEY, NEW YORK

LURIA, A.R. 1970 Traumatic Aphasia MOUTON, THE HAGUE

MACDONALD, J. & MCGURK, H. 1978 Visual influences on speech perception processes PERCEPTION AND PSYCHOPHYSICS 24: 253-257

MACKAY, D. 1966 To end ambiguous sentences PERCEPTION & PSYCHOPHYSICS 1: 426-436

MACKAY, D.G. 1970 Spoonerisms: the structure of errors in the serial order of behaviour NEUROPSYCHOLOGIA 8: 323-350

MACKAY, D.G. 1972 The structure of words and syllables: evidence from errors in speech COGNITIVE PSYCHOLOGY 3: 210-227

MACKAY, D.M. 1967 Ways of looking at perception IN W. WATHEN-DUNN (ED) MODELS FOR THE PERCEPTION OF SPEECH AND VISUAL FORM, 25-43, MASSACHUSETTS INSTITUTE OF TECHNOLOGY PRESS (REPRINTED IN P.C. DODWELL (ED) 1970 PERCEPTUAL PROCESSING, 487-503, APPLETON-CENTURY-CROFTS, NEW YORK)

MACKAY, D.M. 1968 The 'active/passive' controversy ZEITSCHRIFT FUR PHONETIK, SPRACHWISSENSCHAFT UND KOMMUNIKATIONSFORSCHUNG 21: 40-42

MACKEN, M.A. 1978 Permitted complexity in phonological development: one child's acquisition of Spanish consonants LINGUA 44: 219-253

MACKEN, M.A. 1980 The child's lexical representation: evidence from the 'puzzle-puddle-pickle' phenomenon JOURNAL OF LINGUISTICS 16: 1-17

MACKEN, M.A. & BARTON, D. 1978 The acquisition of the voicing contrast in English: a study of voice onset time in word-initial stop consonants JOURNAL OF CHILD LANGUAGE 1980 (IN PRESS)

MACMILLAN, N.A., KAPLAN, H.I. & CREELMAN, C.D. 1977 The psychophysics of categorical perception PSYCHOLOGICAL REVIEW 84: 452-471

MACNEILAGE, P.F. 1970 Motor control of serial ordering of speech PSYCHOLOGICAL REVIEW 77: 182-196

MACNEILAGE, P.F. 1979A Distinctive properties of speech motor control IN G.E. STELMACH AND J. REQUIN (EDS) TUTORIALS IN MOTOR BEHAVIOR, NORTH-HOLLAND, AMSTERDAM

MACNEILAGE, P.F. 1979B Speech production PROCEEDINGS OF THE NINTH INTERNATIONAL CONGRESS OF PHONETIC SCIENCES, VOL 1: 11-39, INSTITUTE OF PHONETICS, UNIVERSITY OF COPENHAGEN

MACNEILAGE, P.F. & DECLERK, J.L. 1969 On the motor control of coarticulation of CVC monosyllables JOURNAL OF THE ACOUSTICAL SOCIETY OF AMERICA 45: 1217-1233

MACNEILAGE, P.F. & SCHOLES, G.N. 1964 An electromyographic study of the tongue during vowel production JOURNAL OF SPEECH AND HEARING RESEARCH 7: 209-232

MACNEILAGE, P.F., KRONES, R. & HANSON, R. 1969 Closed-loop control of the initiation of jaw movement for speech PAPER PRESENTED AT THE 78TH MEETING OF THE ACOUSTICAL SOCIETY OF AMERICA, SAN DIEGO, NOVEMBER 4-7

MACNEILAGE, P.F., SUSSMAN, H.M., WESTBURY, J.R. & POWERS, R.K. 1979 Mechanical properties of single motor units in speech musculature JOURNAL OF THE ACOUSTICAL SOCIETY OF AMERICA 65: 1047-1052

MADDIESON, I. 1974A A note on tone and consonants IN I. MADDIESON (ED) STUDIES ON TONE FROM THE UCLA TONE PROJECT, 18-27, WORKING PAPERS IN PHONETICS NO. 27, UCLA PHONETICS LABORATORY, LOS ANGELES

MADDIESON, I. (ED) 1974B An annotated bibliography on tone WORKING PAPERS IN PHONETICS NO. 28, UCLA PHONETICS LABORATORY, LOS ANGELES

MAKARENKO, T. 1979 Notes on the intonation of special and yes-no questions in Romanian compared to English PAPER PRESENTED AT THE NINTH INTERNATIONAL CONGRESS OF PHONETIC SCIENCES, INSTITUTE OF PHONETICS, UNIVERSITY OF COPENHAGEN

MALECOT, A. 1960 Vowel nasality as a distinctive feature in American English LANGUAGE 36: 222-229

MALLERY, G. 1881 Sign language among North American Indians BUREAU OF AMERICAN ETHNOLOGY, ANNUAL REPORT 1: 263-552

MANDLER, R. 1976 Categorical perception along an oral-nasal continuum HASKINS LABORATORIES STATUS REPORT ON SPEECH RESEARCH SR-47: 147-154

MARCUS, S.M. 1978A A theory of syntactic recognition for natural language PH.D. DISSERTATION MASSACHUSETTS INSTITUTE OF TECHNOLOGY

MARCUS, S.M. 1978B Distinguishing "slit" and "split" - an invariant timing cue in speech perception PERCEPTION AND PSYCHOPHYSICS 23: 58-60

MARSHALL, J.C. 1980 On the biology of language acquisition IN D. CAPLAN (ED) BIOLOGICAL STUDIES OF MENTAL PROCESSES, MASSACHUSETTS INSTITUTE OF TECHNOLOGY PRESS

MARSLEN-WILSON, W. 1973 Linguistic structure and speech shadowing at very short latencies NATURE 244: 522-523

MARSLEN-WILSON, W. 1975 Sentence perception as an interactive parallel process SCIENCE 189: 226-228

MARSLEN-WILSON, W. 1976 Linguistic descriptions and psychological assumptions in the study of sentence perception IN R.J. WALES AND E. WALKER (EDS) NEW APPROACHES TO LANGUAGE MECHANISMS, NORTH-HOLLAND, AMSTERDAM

MARSLEN-WILSON, W. 1979A Sequential decision processes during spoken word recognition PAPER PRESENTED AT PSYCHONOMIC SOCIETY, SAN ANTONIO

MARSLEN-WILSON, W. 1979B Recognising spoken words IN PREPARATION

MARSLEN-WILSON, W. & WELSH A. 1978 Processing interactions and lexical access during word recognition in continuous speech COGNITIVE PSYCHOLOGY 10 : 29-63

MARTIN, J. 1972 Rhythmic (hierarchical) versus serial structure in speech and other behavior PSYCHOLOGICAL REVIEW 79: 487-509

MARX, J.L. 1980 Ape-language controversy flares up SCIENCE 207: 1330-1333

MASSARO, D.W. 1975 Experimental Psychology and Information Processing RAND MCNALLY, CHICAGO

MASSARO, D.W. 1978 A stage model of reading and listening VISIBLE LANGUAGE 12: 3-26

MASSARO, D.W. 1979 Reading and listening IN P.A. KOLERS, M.E. WROLSTAD, AND H. BOUMA (EDS) PROCESSING OF VISIBLE LANGUAGE, PLENUM, NEW YORK

MASSARO, D.W. & COHEN, M.M. 1976 The contribution of fundamental frequency and voice onset time to the /zi/-/si/ distinction JOURNAL OF THE ACOUSTICAL SOCIETY OF AMERICA 60: 704-717

MASSARO, D.W. & COHEN, M.M. 1977 The contribution of voice-onset time and fundamental frequency as cues to the /zi/-/si/ distinction PERCEPTION & PSYCHOPHYSICS 22: 373-382

MASSARO, D.W. & COHEN, M.M. Binary or continuous featural information? MANUSCRIPT IN PREPARATION

MASSARO, D.W. & ODEN, G.C. Evaluation and integration of acoustic features in speech perception JOURNAL OF THE ACOUSTICAL SOCIETY OF AMERICA (SUBMITTED)

MATTINGLY, I.G. 1968 Experimental methods for speech synthesis by rule IEEE TRANSACTIONS, AU16: 198-202

MATTINGLY, I.G. 1974 Speech synthesis for phonetic and phonological models IN T.A. SEBEOK (ED) CURRENT TRENDS IN LINGUISTICS, VOL 12, MOUTON, THE HAGUE

MCALLISTER, R. 1978 Temporal asymmetry in labial co-articulation PAPERS FROM THE INSTITUTE OF LINGUISTICS, UNIVERSITY OF STOCKHOLM, NO. 35

MCCAWLEY, J. 1979 Remarks on Cena's vowel shift experiment PAPER PRESENTED TO THE 15TH REGIONAL MEETING OF THE CHICAGO LINGUISTIC SOCIETY

MCCLEAN, M. 1978 Variation in perioral reflex amplitude prior to lip muscle contraction for speech JOURNAL OF SPEECH AND HEARING RESEARCH 21: 276-284

MCCLEAN, M., FOLKINS, J.W. & LARSON, C. The role of the perioral reflex in lip motor control for speech BRAIN AND LANGUAGE (IN PRESS)

MCGURK, H. & MACDONALD, J. 1976 Hearing lips and seeing voices NATURE 264: 746-748

MCNEILL, D. & LINDIG, K. 1973 The perceptual reality of phonemes, syllables, words and sentences JOURNAL OF VERBAL LEARNING AND VERBAL BEHAVIOR 12: 419-430

MEHLER, J. & BERTONCINI, J. 1979 Infants' perception of speech and other acoustic stimuli IN J. MORTON AND J. MARSHALL (EDS) PSYCHOLINGUISTICS SERIES II, ELEK SCIENTIFIC BOOKS, LONDON

MEHLER, J., BERTONCINI, J., BARRIERE, M. & JASSIK-GERSCHENFELD, D. 1978 Infant recognition of mother's voice PERCEPTION 7: 491-497

MEHLER, J., SEGUI, J. & CAREY, P. 1978 Tails of words: monitoring ambiguity JOURNAL OF VERBAL LEARNING AND VERBAL BEHAVIOR 17: 29-35

MELTZOFF, A. & MOORE, M.K. 1977 Imitation of facial and manual gestures by human neonates SCIENCE 198: 75-78

MENN, L. 1971 Phonotactic rules in beginning speech LINGUA 26: 225-251

MENN, L. 1978A Phonological units in beginning speech IN A. BELL AND J. HOOPER (EDS) SYLLABLES AND SEGMENTS, NORTH-HOLLAND, AMSTERDAM

MENN, L. 1978B Pattern, Control and Contrast in Beginning Speech INDIANA UNIVERSITY LINGUISTICS CLUB, BLOOMINGTON

MENN, L. 1979 Towards a psychology of phonology: child phonology as a first step PAPER SUBMITTED TO THE PROCEEDINGS OF THE THIRD ANNUAL MICHIGAN STATE UNIVERSITY CONFERENCE ON METATHEORY: APPLICATIONS OF LINGUISTIC THEORY IN THE HUMAN SCIENCES

MENYUK, P. & MENN, L. 1979 Perception and production of words and sounds IN P. FLETCHER AND M. GARMAN (EDS) LANGUAGE ACQUISITION: STUDIES IN FIRST LANGUAGE DEVELOPMENT, CAMBRIDGE UNIVERSITY PRESS

MENZEL, E., PREMACK, D. & WOODRUFF, G. 1978 Map reading by chimpanzees FOLIA PRIMATOLOGICA 29: 241-249

MENZERATH, P. & LACERDA, A. DE 1933 Koartikulation, Steurung und Lautabgrensung F. DUMMLER, BERLIN

MERCIER, G. 1979 Segmentation et reconnaissance phonétique de la parole continue PAPER PRESENTED AT THE NINTH INTERNATIONAL CONGRESS OF PHONETIC SCIENCES, I: 274, INSTITUTE OF PHONETICS, UNIVERSITY OF COPENHAGEN

MERMELSTEIN, P. 1967 Determination of the vocal-tract shape from measured formant frequencies JOURNAL OF THE ACOUSTICAL SOCIETY OF AMERICA 41: 1283-1294

MERMELSTEIN, P. 1975 Automatic segmentation of speech into syllable units JOURNAL OF THE ACOUSTICAL SOCIETY OF AMERICA 58: 880-883

MERZENICH, M.M., ROTH, G.L., ANDERSON, R.A., KNIGHT, P.L. & COLWELL, S.A. 1977 Some basic features of organization of the central auditory nervous system IN E.F. EVANS AND J.P. WILSON (EDS) PSYCHOPHYSICS AND PHYSIOLOGY OF HEARING, 485-496, ACADEMIC PRESS, LONDON

MIDDLEBROOKS, J.C. DYKES, R.W. & MERZENICH, M.M. 1980 Binaural response - specific bands in primary auditory cortex (A1) of the cat BRAIN RESEARCH 181: 31-48

MILES, F.A. & EVARTS, E.V. 1979 Concepts of motor organization ANNUAL REVIEW OF PSYCHOLOGY 30: 327-362

MILLER, G.A. 1956 The magical number seven plus or minus two, or, some limits on our capacity for processing information PSYCHOLOGICAL REVIEW 63: 81-96

MILLER, G.A. 1962 Decision units in the perception of speech IEEE TRANSACTIONS, IT-8: 81-83

MILLER, G.A. 1978 Semantic relations among words IN M. HALLE, J. BRESNAN AND G.A. MILLER (EDS) LINGUISTIC THEORY AND PSYCHOLOGICAL REALITY, MASSACHUSETTS INSTITUTE OF TECHNOLOGY, CAMBRIDGE

MILLER, G.A. & CHOMSKY, A.N. 1963 Finitary models of language users IN R. LUCE, R. BUSH, AND E. GALANTER (EDS) HANDBOOK OF MATHEMATICAL PSYCHOLOGY, VOL 2, WILEY, NEW YORK

MILLER, G.A., HEISE, G.A. & LICHTEN, W. 1951 The intelligibility of speech as a function of the context of the test materials JOURNAL OF EXPERIMENTAL PSYCHOLOGY 41: 329-335

MILLER, J.D. 1977 Perception of speech sounds in animals: evidence for speech processing by mammalian auditory mechanisms IN T.H. BULLOCK (ED) RECOGNITION OF COMPLEX ACOUSTIC SIGNALS, DAHLEM KONFERENZEN, BERLIN

MILLER, J.D. WIER, C.C., PASTORE, R.E., KELLY, W.J. & DOOLING, R.J. 1976 Discrimination and labeling of noise-buzz sequences with varying noise-lead times: an example of categorical perception JOURNAL OF THE ACOUSTICAL SOCIETY OF AMERICA 60: 410-417

MILLER, J.E. & FUJIMURA, O. 1979 A graphic display for combined presentation of acoustic and articulatory information TO BE PUBLISHED IN THE PROCEEDINGS OF THE 97TH MEETING OF THE ACOUSTICAL SOCIETY OF AMERICA, CAMBRIDGE

MILLER, J.L. 1977A Properties of feature detectors for VOT: the voiceless channel of analysis JOURNAL OF THE ACOUSTICAL SOCIETY OF AMERICA 62: 641-648

MILLER, J.L. 1977B Nonindependence of feature processing in initial consonants JOURNAL OF SPEECH AND HEARING RESEARCH 20: 519-528

MILLER, J.L. & LIBERMAN, A.M. 1979 Some effects of later-occurring information on the perception of stop consonant and semivowel PERCEPTION AND PSYCHOPHYSICS 25: 457-465

MILLS, C.A. 1980 Effects of context on reaction time to phonemes JOURNAL OF VERBAL LEARNING AND VERBAL BEHAVIOR 19: 75-83

MILLS, L. & ROLLMA, G.B. 1979 Left hemisphere selectivity for processing duration in normal subjects BRAIN AND LANGUAGE 7: 320-335

MILLS, M. & MELHUISH, E. 1974 Recognition of mother's voice in early infancy NATURE 252, NO. 5479: 123-124

MITCHELL, J. 1979 Tone and prosodic structure in Kikuyu UNPUBLISHED MANUSCRIPT, UNIVERSITY OF MASSACHUSETTS, AMHERST

MOHANAN, K.P. (IN PREPARATION) Lexicalist phonology

MOLL, K.L. 1962 Velopharyngeal closure on vowels JOURNAL OF SPEECH AND HEARING RESEARCH 5: 30-37

MOLL, K.L. & DANILOFF, R. 1971 The study of speech production as a human neuromotor system IN M. SAWASHIMA AND F.S. COOPER (EDS) DYNAMIC ASPECTS OF SPEECH PRODUCTION, UNIVERSITY OF TOKYO PRESS, TOKYO

MOLLER, A.R. 1977 Frequency selectivity of single auditory nerve fibres in response to broad band noise stimuli JOURNAL OF THE ACOUSTICAL SOCIETY OF AMERICA 62: 135-142

MOLLER, A.R. 1978 Coding of time-varying sounds in the cochlear nucleus AUDIOLOGY 17: 446-468

MOLNAR, C.E. 1974 Analysis of memoryless polynomial nonlinearities JOURNAL OF THE ACOUSTICAL SOCIETY OF AMERICA 56: S31 (A)

MOORE, B.C.J. 1978 Psychophysical tuning curves measured in simultaneous and forward masking JOURNAL OF THE ACOUSTICAL SOCIETY OF AMERICA 63: 524-532

MOORE, T.J. & CASHIN, J.L. 1974 Response patterns of cochlear nucleus neurons to excerpts from sustained vowels JOURNAL OF THE ACOUSTICAL SOCIETY OF AMERICA 56: 1565-1576

MORAIS, J., CARY, L., ALEGRIA, J. & BERTELSON, P. 1979 Does awareness of speech as a sequence of phones arise spontaneously? COGNITION 7: 323-331

MORSE, P.A. 1974 Infant speech perception: a preliminary model and review of the literature IN R.L. SCHIEFELBUSCH AND L.A. LLOYD (EDS) LANGUAGE PERSPECTIVES - ACQUISITION, RETARDATION, AND INTERVENTION, 19-54, UNIVERSITY PARK PRESS, BALTIMORE

MORSE, P.A. & SNOWDON, C.T. 1975 An investigation of categorical speech discrimination by rhesus monkeys PERCEPTION AND PSYCHOPHYSICS 17: 9-16

MORTON, J. 1969 Interaction of information in word recognition PSYCHOLOGICAL REVIEW 76: 165-178

MORTON, J. 1970 A functional model for memory IN D.A. NORMAN (ED) MODELS OF HUMAN MEMORY, ACADEMIC PRESS, NEW YORK

MORTON, J. & BROADBENT, D. 1967 Passive versus active recognition models, or is your homunculus really necessary? IN W. WATHEN-DUNN (ED) MODELS FOR THE PERCEPTION OF SPEECH AND VISUAL FORM, MASSACHUSETTS INSTITUTE OF TECHNOLOGY PRESS

MORTON, J. & LONG, J. 1976 Effect of word transitional probability on phoneme identification JOURNAL OF VERBAL LEARNING AND VERBAL BEHAVIOR 15: 43-51

MORTON, J. & SMITH, N.V. 1974 Some ideas concerning the acquisition of phonology COLLOQUES INTERNATIONAUX DU CNRS NO. 206, PROBLEMES ACTUELS DU PSYCHOLINGUISTIQUE, 161-176

MORTON, K. & TATHAM, M.A.A. 1980A Devoicing, aspiration and nasality - cases of universal misunderstanding? OCCASIONAL PAPERS 23: 90-103, DEPARTMENT OF LANGUAGE AND LINGUISTICS UNIVERSITY OF ESSEX

MORTON, K. & TATHAM, M.A.A. 1980B Production instructions OCCASIONAL PAPERS 23: 104-106, DEPARTMENT OF LANGUAGE AND LINGUISTICS UNIVERSITY OF ESSEX

MOSKOWITZ, B. 1973 On the status of vowel shift in English IN T.E. MOORE (ED) COGNITIVE DEVELOPMENT AND THE ACQUISITION OF LANGUAGE, ACADEMIC PRESS, NEW YORK

MOSLIN, E.J. & NIGRO, G. 1976 Apical stop production in mothers to children PAPER PRESENTED AT THE BOSTON UNIVERSITY CONFERENCE ON LANGUAGE DEVELOPMENT

MOULTON, W.G. 1947 Juncture in modern standard German LANGUAGE 23: 212-216

MRAYATI, M. & CARRE, R. 1975 Acoustic aspects of French nasal vowels JOURNAL OF THE ACOUSTICAL SOCIETY OF AMERICA 57: 549 (A)

MRAYATI, M. & CARRE, R. 1976 Forme du conduit vocal et caractéristiques acoustiques des voyelles françaises PHONETICA 33: 285-306

MRAYATI, M. & GUERIN, B. 1976 Etude des caractéristiques acoustiques des voyelles orales françaises par simulation du conduit vocal avec pertes LA REVUE D'ACOUSTIQUE 36: 18-32

MRAYATI, M. & GUERIN, B. 1977 Nasal vowel study sensitivity functions IN R. CARRE, R. DESCOUT AND M. WAJSKOP (EDS) SYMPOSIUM ON ARTICULATORY MODELING, G.A.L.F., GRENOBLE

MURPHY, C.M. 1978 Pointing in the context of a shared activity CHILD DEVELOPMENT 49: 371-380

MURRAY, L. 1980 Infants capacities for regulating interactions with their mothers, and the function of emotions PH.D. DISSERTATION, UNIVERSITY OF EDINBURGH

MYERS, T.F. 1970 Asymmetry and attention in phonic decoding IN A.F. SANDERS (ED) ATTENTION AND PERFORMANCE III, 158-177 NORTH-HOLLAND, AMSTERDAM

MYERS, T.F. 1979 Verbal and non-verbal interactivity IN T.F. MYERS (ED) THE DEVELOPMENT OF CONVERSATION AND DISCOURSE, 1-43 EDINBURGH UNIVERSITY PRESS

MYERS, T.F., ZHUKOVA,M., CHISTOVICH,L. & MUSHNIKOV, V. 1975 Auditory segmentation and the method of dichotic stimulation IN G.FANT AND M.A.A. TATHAM (EDS) AUDITORY ANALYSIS AND PERCEPTION OF SPEECH, 243-273 ACADEMIC PRESS, LONDON

MYERSON, R. 1976 A study of children's knowledge of certain word formation rules and the relationship of this knowledge to various forms of reading achievement PH.D. DISSERTATION, HARVARD UNIVERSITY

NAKATANI, L.H. & DUKES, K.D. 1977 Locus of segmental cues for word juncture JOURNAL OF THE ACOUSTICAL SOCIETY OF AMERICA 62: 714-719

NAKATANI, L.H. & SCHAFFER, J.A. 1978 Hearing 'words' without words: prosodic cues for word perception JOURNAL OF THE ACOUSTICAL SOCIETY OF AMERICA 63: 234-245

NAKIC, A. & BROWNE, W. 1975 The intonation of questions in Serbo-Croatian and English IN R. FILIPOVIC (ED) CONTRASTIVE ANALYSIS OF ENGLISH AND SERBO-CROATIAN, INSTITUTE OF LINGUISTICS, ZAGREB

NEARY, T. 1976 Phonetic features for vowels PH.D. DISSERTATION, UNIVERSITY OF CONNECTICUT

NEELEY, J. 1977 Semantic priming and retrieval from lexical memory: roles of inhibitionless spreading activation and limited capacity attention JOURNAL OF EXPERIMENTAL PSYCHOLOGY 106: 226-254

NEFF, N. 1977 Cortical and subcortical specialisation in auditory processing IN T.H. BULLOCK (ED) RECOGNITION OF COMPLEX ACOUSTIC SIGNALS, DAHLEM KONFERENZEN, BERLIN

NEGUS, V.E. 1949 The Comparative Anatomy and Physiology of the Larynx HAFNER, LONDON

NEISSER, U. 1967 Cognitive Psychology APPLETON-CENTURY-CROFTS, NEW YORK

NELSON, W.L. 1979 Automatic alignment of phonetic transcriptions of continuous speech utterances with corresponding speech-articulation data TO BE PUBLISHED IN THE PROCEEDINGS OF THE 97TH MEETING OF THE ACOUSTICAL SOCIETY OF AMERICA, CAMBRIDGE

NETSELL, R. & ABBS, J.H. 1977 Some possible uses of neuromotor speech disturbances in understanding the normal mechanism IN M. SAWASHIMA AND F.S. COOPER (EDS) DYNAMIC ASPECTS OF SPEECH PRODUCTION, 369-392, UNIVERSITY OF TOKYO PRESS, TOKYO

NETSELL, R., KENT, R. & ABBS, J. 1978 Adjustments of the tongue and lips to fixed jaw positions during speech: A preliminary report PAPER PRESENTED AT THE CONFERENCE ON SPEECH MOTOR CONTROL, UNIVERSITY OF WISCONSIN, MADISON, JUNE 2-3

NEWELL, A. 1978 HARPY, production systems and human cognition, REPORT NO. CMU-CS-78-140 DEPARTMENT OF COMPUTER SCIENCE, CARNEGIE-MELLON UNIVERSITY, PITTSBURGH

NEWELL, A., BARNETT, J., FORGIE, J.W., GREEN, C.C., KLATT, D.H., LICKLIDER, J.C.R., MUNSON, J., REDDY, D.R. & WOODS, W.A. 1973 Speech Understanding Systems: Final Report of a Study Group NORTH-HOLLAND PRESS, AMSTERDAM

NEWMAN, J.D. 1978 Perception of sounds used in species-specific communication: the auditory cortex and beyond JOURNAL OF MEDICAL PRIMATOLOGY 7: 98-105

NEWMAN, J.D. & SYMES, D. 1974 Arousal effects on unit responsiveness to vocalisations in the squirrel monkey auditory cortex BRAIN RESEARCH 78: 125-138

NEWMAN, J.E. & DELL, G.S. 1978 The phonological nature of phoneme monitoring: a critique of some ambiguity studies JOURNAL OF VERBAL LEARNING AND VERBAL BEHAVIOR 17: 359-374

NINIO, A. & BRUNER, J.S. 1977 The achievement and antecedents of labelling JOURNAL OF CHILD LANGUAGE 5: 1-15

NOOTEBOOM, S.G. 1969 The tongue slips into patterns IN NOMEN: LEYDEN STUDIES IN LINGUISTICS AND PHONETICS, A.G. SCIARONE ET AL (EDS) , 114-132, MOUTON, THE HAGUE

NOOTEBOOM, S.G. 1970 The target theory of speech production ANNUAL REPORT OF THE INSTITUUT VOOR PERCEPTIE ONDERZOEK 5: 51-55, EINDHOVEN

NOOTEBOOM, S.G. 1977 Forward and backward normalization of speech rate in the perception of vowel length SUBMITTED FOR PUBLICATION

NOOTEBOOM, S.G. 1979 Complex control of simple decisions in the perception of vowel length IN THE PROCEEDINGS OF THE NINTH INTERNATIONAL CONGRESS OF PHONETIC SCIENCES, VOL 2: 298-304, INSTITUTE OF PHONETICS, UNIVERSITY OF COPENHAGEN

NOOTEBOOM, S.G. & DOODEMAN, G.J.N. 1980 Perception of vowel length in spoken sentences JOURNAL OF THE ACOUSTICAL SOCIETY OF AMERICA (IN PRESS)

NOOTEBOOM, S.G. & SLIS, I. 1970 A note on the degree of opening and the duration of vowels in normal and "pipe" speech ANNUAL REPORT OF THE INSTITUUT VOOR PERCEPTIE ONDERZOEK 5: 55-58, EINDHOVEN

NOTTEBOHM, F. 1979 Origins and mechanisms in the establishment of cerebral dominance IN M.S. GAZZANIGA (ED) HANDBOOK OF BEHAVIORAL NEUROBIOLOGY, VOL 2, PLENUM, NEW YORK

NYE, P.W. & GAITENBY, J. 1973 Consonant intelligibility in synthetic speech and in a natural speech control (modified rhyme test results) STATUS REPORT ON SPEECH RESEARCH 33: 77-91, HASKINS LABORATORIES, NEW HAVEN

NYE, P.W. & GAITENBY, J. 1974 The intelligibility of synthetic monosyllable words in short, syntactically normal sentences STATUS REPORT ON SPEECH RESEARCH 37/38: 169-190, HASKINS LABORATORIES, NEW HAVEN

O'ROURKE, T.J. 1973 A Basic Course in Manual Communication COMMUNICATIVE SKILLS PROGRAM, NATIONAL ASSOCIATION OF THE DEAF, WASHINGTON D.C.

ODEN G.C. 1977 Integration of fuzzy logical information JOURNAL OF EXPERIMENTAL PSYCHOLOGY 3: 565-575

ODEN, G.C. & MASSARO, D.W. 1978 Integration of featural information in speech perception PSYCHOLOGICAL REVIEW 85: 172-191

OHALA, J. & OHALA, M. 1975 Testing hypotheses regarding the psychological manifestation of morpheme structure constraints PAPER PRESENTED TO THE ANNUAL MEETING OF THE LINGUISTICS SOCIETY OF AMERICA, SAN FRANCISCO

OHALA, J.J. 1970 Aspects of the control and production of speech WORKING PAPERS IN PHONETICS 15, UNIVERSITY OF CALIFORNIA AT LOS ANGELES

OHALA, J.J. 1971 Monitoring soft palate activity in speech PROJECT ON LINGUISTIC ANALYSIS REPORTS 13: J01-J015, UNIVERSITY OF CALIFORNIA AT BERKELEY

OHALA, J.J. 1972 How is pitch lowered? JOURNAL OF THE ACOUSTICAL SOCIETY OF AMERICA 52: 124

OHALA, J.J. 1974 Experimental historical phonology IN J.M. ANDERSON AND C. JONES (EDS) HISTORICAL LINGUISTICS II: THEORY AND DESCRIPTION IN PHONOLOGY, 353-389, NORTH-HOLLAND, AMSTERDAM

OHALA, J.J. 1975A Conditions for vowel devoicing and frication JOURNAL OF THE ACOUSTICAL SOCIETY OF AMERICA 58: S39

OHALA, J.J. 1975B The temporal regulation of speech IN G. FANT AND M.A.A. TATHAM (EDS) AUDITORY ANALYSIS AND PERCEPTION OF SPEECH, 431-453, ACADEMIC PRESS, LONDON

OHALA, J.J. 1975C Phonetic explanations for nasal sound patterns IN C.A. FERGUSON, L.M. HYMAN, AND J.J. OHALA (EDS) NASALFEST, 289-316, LANGUAGE UNIVERSALS PROJECT, UNIVERSITY OF STANFORD

OHALA, J.J. 1976 A model of speech aerodynamics REPORT OF THE PHONOLOGY LABORATORY 1: 93-107, UNIVERSITY OF CALIFORNIA AT BERKELEY

OHALA, J.J. 1977 The physiology of stress IN L.M. HYMAN (ED) STUDIES IN STRESS AND ACCENT, OCCASIONAL PAPERS IN LINGUISTICS 4: 145-168, UNIVERSITY OF SOUTHERN CALIFORNIA

OHALA, J.J. 1978A Southern Bantu vs. the world: the case of palatalization of labials PROCEEDINGS OF THE BERKELEY LINGUISTIC SOCIETY 4: 370-386

OHALA, J.J. 1978B Production of tone IN V.A. FROMKIN (ED) TONE: A LINGUISTIC SURVEY, 5-39, ACADEMIC PRESS, NEW YORK

OHALA, J.J. & EUKEL, B.W. 1978 Explaining the intrinsic pitch of vowels REPORT OF THE PHONOLOGY LABORATORY 2: 118-125, UNIVERSITY OF CALIFORNIA AT BERKELEY

OHALA, J.J. & LORENTZ, J. 1977 The story of [w]. An exercise in the phonetic explanation for sound patterns PROCEEDINGS OF THE BERKELEY LINGUISTIC SOCIETY 3: 577-599

OHALA, J.J. & LYBERG, B. 1976 Comments on 'Temporal interactions within a phrase and sentence context' [Journal of the Acoustical Society of America 56, 1258-1265 (1974)] JOURNAL OF THE ACOUSTICAL SOCIETY OF AMERICA 59: 990-992

OHALA, J.J. & RIORDAN, C.J. 1979 Passive vocal tract enlargement during voiced stops IN J.J. WOLF AND D.H. KLATT (EDS) SPEECH COMMUNICATION PAPERS, 97TH MEETING OF THE ACOUSTICAL SOCIETY OF AMERICA, 89-92

OHALA, J.J., HIKI, S., HUBLER, S. & HARSHMAN, R. 1968 Photoelectric methods of transducing lip and jaw movements in speech WORKING PAPERS IN PHONETICS 10: 135-144, UNIVERSITY OF CALIFORNIA AT LOS ANGELES

OHMAN, S.E.G. 1966 Coarticulation in CVC utterances: spectrographic measurements JOURNAL OF THE ACOUSTICAL SOCIETY OF AMERICA 39: 151-168

OHMAN, S.E.G. 1967 Numerical models of coarticulation JOURNAL OF THE ACOUSTICAL SOCIETY OF AMERICA 41: 310-320

OHMAN, S.E.G. 1975 What is it that we perceive when we perceive speech? IN A. COHEN & S.G. NOOTEBOOM (EDS) STRUCTURE AND PROCESS IN SPEECH PERCEPTION, SPRINGER-VERLAG, NEW YORK

OLLER, D.K. 1973 The effect of position in utterance on speech segment duration in English JOURNAL OF THE ACOUSTICAL SOCIETY OF AMERICA 54: 1235-1247

OLMSTED, D. 1971 Out of the Mouth of Babes MOUTON, THE HAGUE

OSHIKA, B.T. ZUE, V.W., WEEKS, R.V. & AURBACH, J. 1975 The role of phonological rules in speech understanding research IEEE TRANSACTIONS, ASSP-23: 104-112

OSTREICHER, H.J. & SHARF, D.J. 1976 Effects of coarticulation on the identification of deleted consonant and vowel sounds JOURNAL OF PHONETICS 4: 285-301

PAIVO, A. 1974 Imagery and Verbal Processes HOLT, RINEHART & WINSTON, NEW YORK

PALMER, A.R. & EVANS, E.F. 1979 On the peripheral coding of the level of individual frequency components of complex sounds at high sound levels EXPERIMENTAL BRAIN RESEARCH, SUPPLEMENTUM 2: 19-26

PALMER, F.R. (ED) 1970 Prosodic Analysis OXFORD UNIVERSITY PRESS, LONDON

PALMER, H. 1922 English Intonation, with Systematic Exercises HEFFER, CAMBRIDGE

PAPCUN, G., KRASHEN, S., TERBEEK, D., REMINGTON, R. & HARSHMAN, R. 1974 Is the left hemisphere specialized for speech, language and/or something else? JOURNAL OF THE ACOUSTICAL SOCIETY OF AMERICA 55: 319-327

PARKER, S.T. 1977 Piaget's sensorimotor period series in an infant macaque: a model for comparing unstereotyped behavior and intelligence in human and non-human primates IN S. CHEVALIER-SKOLNIKOFF AND F.N. POIRIER (EDS) PRIMATE BIO-SOCIAL DEVELOPMENT: BIOLOGICAL, SOCIAL AND ECOLOGICAL DETERMINANTS, 43-112, GARLAND, NEW YORK

PARKER, S.T. & GIBSON, K.R. 1979 A developmental model for the evolution of language and intelligence in early hominids BEHAVIORAL AND BRAIN SCIENCES (IN PRESS)

PARKINSON, S.R. & HUBBARD, L.L. 1974 Stimulus suffix effects in dichotic memory JOURNAL OF EXPERIMENTAL PSYCHOLOGY 102: 266-276

PASSY, P. 1890 Etudes sur les Changements Phonétiques LIBRAIRIE FIRMIN-DIDOT, PARIS

PASTORE, R.E., AHROON, W.A., BAFFUTO, K.J., FRIEDMAN, C., PUELEO, J.S. & FINK, E.A. 1977 Common-factor model of categorical perception JOURNAL OF EXPERIMENTAL PSYCHOLOGY: HUMAN PERCEPTION AND PERFORMANCE 3: 686-696

PATTERSON, R.D. 1976 Auditory filter shape derived from noise stimuli JOURNAL OF THE ACOUSTICAL SOCIETY OF AMERICA 59: 640-654

PERKELL, J.S. 1977 Articulatory modeling, phonetic features and speech production strategies IN R. CARRE, R. DESCOUT AND M. WAJSKOP (EDS) PROCEEDINGS OF THE SYMPOSIUM ON ARTICULATORY MODELLING, G.A.L.F., GRENOBLE

PERKELL, J.S. 1979A On the nature of distinctive features: implications of a preliminary vowel production study IN B. LINDBLOM AND S. OHMAN (EDS) FRONTIERS OF SPEECH COMMUNICATION RESEARCH, 365-380, ACADEMIC PRESS, LONDON

PERKELL, J.S. 1979B On the use of orosensory feedback: an interpretation of compensatory articulation results PROCEEDINGS OF THE NINTH INTERNATIONAL CONGRESS OF PHONETIC SCIENCES, VOL 2: 358-364, INSTITUTE OF PHONETICS, UNIVERSITY OF COPENHAGEN

PERKELL, J.S. 1980 Phonetic features and the physiology of speech production IN B. BUTTERWORTH (ED) LANGUAGE PRODUCTION, 337-372 ACADEMIC PRESS, LONDON

PERKELL, J.S., BOYCE, S.E. & STEVENS, K.N. 1979 Articulatory and acoustic correlates of the [s-š] distinction IN J.J. WOLF AND D.H. KLATT (EDS) SPEECH COMMUNICATION PAPERS PRESENTED AT THE 97TH MEETING OF THE ACOUSTICAL SOCIETY OF AMERICA, NEW YORK

PETERSON, G.E. & BARNEY, H.L. 1952 Control methods used in a study of the vowels JOURNAL OF THE ACOUSTICAL SOCIETY OF AMERICA 24: 175-184

PETERSON, M., BEECHER, M., ZOLOTH, S., MOODY, D. & STEBBINS, W. 1978 Neural lateralization of species-specific vocalizations by japanese macaques (macaca fuscata) SCIENCE 202: 324-327

PETERSON, M.R., BEECHER, M.D., ZOLOTH, S.R., MOODY, D.B. & STEBBINS, W.C. 1978 Species specific perceptual processing of vocal sounds by monkeys SCIENCE 202: 324-326

PETITTO, L.A. & SEIDENBERG, M.S. 1979 On the evidence for linguistic abilities in signing apes BRAIN AND LANGUAGE 8: 162-183

PFEIFFER, R.R. & KIM, D.O. 1975 Cochlear nerve fiber responses: distribution along the cochlear partition JOURNAL OF THE ACOUSTICAL SOCIETY OF AMERICA 58: 867-869

PICK, G.F. 1980 Level dependence of psychophysical frequency resolution and auditory filter shape JOURNAL OF THE ACOUSTICAL SOCIETY OF AMERICA (IN PRESS)

PICKETT, J.M. & DECKER, L.R. 1960 Time factors in perception of a double consonant LANGUAGE AND SPEECH 3: 11-17

PICKETT, J.M. & POLLACK, I. 1963 The intelligibility of excerpts from fluent speech: auditory versus structural context LANGUAGE AND SPEECH 6: 151-165

PICKLES, J.O. 1975 Normal critical bands in the cat ACTA OTOLARYNGOLOGICA 80: 245-254

PIERCE, J.R. 1969 Whither speech recognition JOURNAL OF THE ACOUSTICAL SOCIETY OF AMERICA 46: 1049-1051

PIKE, K.L. 1943 Phonetics UNIVERSITY OF MICHIGAN PRESS, ANN ARBOR

PIKE, K.L. 1967 Language in Relation to a Unified Theory of the Structure of Human Behavior 2ND EDITION, MOUTON, THE HAGUE

PISONI, D.B. 1971 On the nature of the categorical perception of speech sounds PH.D. DISSERTATION, UNIVERSITY OF MICHIGAN

PISONI, D.B. 1973 Auditory and phonetic memory codes in the discrimination of consonants and vowels PERCEPTION AND PSYCHOPHYSICS 13: 253-260

PISONI, D.B. 1975 Auditory short-term memory and vowel perception MEMORY AND COGNITION 1975 3: 7-18

PISONI, D.B. 1977 Identification and discrimination of the relative onset time of two-component tones: implications for voicing perception in stress JOURNAL OF THE ACOUSTICAL SOCIETY OF AMERICA 61: 1352-1361

PISONI, D.B. 1978 Speech perception IN W.K. ESTES (ED) HANDBOOK OF LEARNING AND COGNITIVE PROCESSES, VOL.6, 167-233, ERLBAUM, HILLSDALE, NEW JERSEY

PISONI, D.B. 1979 Some measures of intelligibility and comprehension CHAPTER PREPARED FOR MASSACHUSETTS INSTITUTE OF TECHNOLOGY SUMMER COURSE, CONVERSION OF UNRESTRICTED ENGLISH TEXT TO SPEECH, TO APPEAR IN J. ALLEN (ED) (UNTITLED)

PISONI, D.B. & SAWUSCH, J.R. 1975 Some stages of processing in speech perception IN A. COHEN AND S.G. NOOTEBOOM (EDS) STRUCTURE AND PROCESS IN SPEECH PERCEPTION, 16-35, SPRINGER-VERLAG, NEW YORK

PISONI, D.B. & TAHS, J. 1974 Reaction times to comparisons within and across phonetic categories PERCEPTION & PSYCHOPHYSICS 15: 285-290

PISONI, D.B., CARRELL, T.D. & SIMNICK, S.S. 1979 Does a listener need to recover the dynamic vocal tract gestures of a talker to recognize his vowels? SPEECH COMMUNICATION PAPERS PRESENTED AT 97TH MEETING OF THE ACOUSTICAL SOCIETY OF AMERICA, 19-23

PLOOIJ, F.X. 1978 Some basic traits of language in chimpanzees? IN A. LOCK (ED) ACTION, GESTURE AND SYMBOL, CHAPTER 6, ACADEMIC PRESS, LONDON

POIZNER, H. & BATTISON, R. 1979 L'asymétrie cérébrale et la langue des signes: études cliniques et expérimentales LANGAGES 56: 58-77

POLIT, A. & BIZZI, E. 1978 Processes controlling arm movements in monkeys SCIENCE 201: 1235

POLLACK, I. & PICKETT, J.M. 1958 Masking of speech by noise at high sound levels JOURNAL OF THE ACOUSTICAL SOCIETY OF AMERICA 30: 127-120

POLLACK, I. & PICKETT, J.M. 1964 The intelligibility of excerpts from fluent speech: auditory versus structural context LANGUAGE AND SPEECH 6: 151-165

PORT, R.F. 1977 The influence of tempo on stop closure duration as a cue for voicing and place STATUS REPORT ON SPEECH RESEARCH, SR-51/52, HASKINS LABORATORIES, NEW HAVEN

PORT, R.F. 1978 Effects of word-internal versus word-external tempo on the voicing boundary for medial stop closure JOURNAL OF THE ACOUSTICAL SOCIETY OF AMERICA, SUPPLEMENT NO. 1, S20

POSNER, M.I. & SNYDER, C.R. 1975 Attention and cognitive control IN R. SOLSO (ED) INFORMATION PROCESSING AND COGNITION, ERLBAUM, HILLSDALE, NEW JERSEY

PRATHER, P. & SWINNEY, D. 1977 Some effects of syntactic context upon lexical access PRESENTED AT A MEETING OF THE AMERICAN PSYCHOLOGICAL ASSOCIATION, SAN FRANCISCO, CALIFORNIA

PRIBRAM, K.H. 1971 Languages of the Brain PRENTICE-HALL, ENGLEWOOD CLIFFS (2ND EDITION, BROOKS/COLE, MONTEREY, 1977)

PRIBRAM, K.H. 1978 The place of pragmatics in the syntactic and semantic organization of language PAPER PRESENTED AT PAUSOLOGICAL IMPLICATIONS OF SPEECH PRODUCTION, KASSEL, GERMANY, JUNE 1978 TO BE PUBLISHED IN H. DECHERT AND M. RAUPACH (EDS) TEMPORAL VARIABLES IN SPEECH: STUDIES IN HONOUR OF FRIEDA GOLDMAN-EISLER, MOUTON, THE HAGUE

PRIBRAM, K.H. & TUBBS, W. 1967 Short-term memory, parsing and the primate frontal cortex SCIENCE 156: 1765-1767

PRIBRAM, K.H., KRUGER, L., ROBINSON, F. & BERMAN, A.J. 1955-56 The effects of precentral lesions on the behavior of monkeys JOURNAL OF BIOLOGY AND MEDICINE 28: 428-443

PRIBRAM, K.H., PLOTKIN, H.C., ANDERSON, R.M. & LEONG, D. 1977 Information sources in the delayed alternation task for normal and "frontal" monkeys NEUROPSYCHOLOGIA 15: 329-340

PRIESTLEY, T. 1977 An idiosyncratic strategy in the acquisition of phonology JOURNAL OF CHILD LANGUAGE 4: 45-65

PRINCE, A. 1980 Estonian quantity LINGUISTIC INQUIRY 11(3), MASSACHUSETTS INSTITUTE OF TECHNOLOGY

PUTNAM, A.H.B., DOHERTY, E.T. & SHIPP, T. 1976 Lip-larynx interaction models for intervocalic /p/ production JOURNAL OF THE ACOUSTICAL SOCIETY OF AMERICA 60: S63

READ, C. 1971 Pre-school children's knowledge of English phonology HARVARD EDUCATIONAL REVIEW 41: 1-34

READ, C. 1975 Children's categorization of speech sounds in English NATIONAL COUNCIL OF TEACHERS OF ENGLISH RESEARCH REPORT NO. 17, ERIC CLEARINGHOUSE ON LANGUAGE AND LINGUISTICS

REALE, R.A. & GEISLER, C.D. 1979 Auditory-nerve fiber encoding of two-tone approximations to steady-state vowels ABSTRACT OF THE SECOND MIDWINTER MEETING OF THE ASSOCIATION FOR RESEARCH IN OTOLARYNGOLOGY 74

REDDY, D.R. 1976 Speech recognition by machine: a review IEEE PROCEEDINGS, ASSP-64: 501-531

REDDY, D.R., LEE, D.E., FENNELL, R.D. & NEELY, R.B. 1976 The Hearsay-I speech understanding system: an example of the recognition process IEEE TRANSACTIONS, C-25: 422-431

REDDY, D.R. & ERMAN, L.D. 1975 Tutorial on system organisation for speech understanding IN D.R. REDDY (ED) SPEECH RECOGNITION, 457-459, ACADEMIC PRESS, NEW YORK

REGAN, D. & TANSLEY, B.W. 1979 Selective adaptation to frequency-modulated tones: evidence for an information processing channel selectively sensitive to frequency changes JOURNAL OF THE ACOUSTICAL SOCIETY OF AMERICA 65: 1249-1257

REMEZ, R.E., CUTTING, J. & STUDDERT-KENNEDY, M. 1980 Cross-series adaptation using song and string PERCEPTION AND PSYCHOPHYSICS 27: 524-530

RENSCH, C.R. 1978 Ballistic and controlled syllables in Otomanguean languages IN A. BELL AND J.B. HOOPER (EDS) SYLLABLES AND SEGMENTS, 85-92, NORTH-HOLLAND, AMSTERDAM

REPP, B.H. 1977 Interdependence of voicing and place decisions UNPUBLISHED MANUSCRIPT, HASKINS LABORATORIES, NEW HAVEN

REPP, B.H., HEALY, A.F. & CROWDER, R.G. 1979 Categories and context in the perception of isolated steady-state vowels JOURNAL OF EXPERIMENTAL PSYCHOLOGY 5: 129-145

REPP, B.H., LIBERMAN, A.M., ECCARDT, T. & PESETSKY, D. 1978 Perceptual integration of acoustic cues for stop, fricative and affricative manner JOURNAL OF EXPERIMENTAL PSYCHOLOGY 4: 621-637

RHODE, W.S. 1971 Observations of the vibration of the basilar membrane in squirrel monkeys using the Mossbauer technique JOURNAL OF THE ACOUSTICAL SOCIETY OF AMERICA 49: 1218-1231

RICHMAN, B. 1976 Some vocal distinctive features used by gelada monkeys JOURNAL OF THE ACOUSTICAL SOCIETY OF AMERICA 60: 718-724

RINGEL, R.L. & STEER, M.D. 1963 Some effects of tactile and auditory alterations on speech output JOURNAL OF SPEECH AND HEARING RESEARCH 6: 369-378

RIORDAN, C.J. 1977 Control of vocal tract length in speech JOURNAL OF THE ACOUSTICAL SOCIETY OF AMERICA 62: 998-1002

RIORDAN, C.J. 1978 Acoustic aspects of speech production PH.D. DISSERTATION, UNIVERSITY OF ESSEX

RISCHEL, J. 1961 Stress, juncture and syllabification in phonemic description IN M. HALLE (ED) PROCEEDINGS OF THE NINTH INTERNATIONAL CONGRESS OF LINGUISTS, 87-93, MOUTON, THE HAGUE

ROBINS, R.H. 1964 General Linguistics: An Introductory Survey LONGMANS, LONDON

ROMANES, G.J. 1888 Mental Evolution in Man: Origin of Human Faculty KEGAN PAUL, LONDON

ROSCH, E. 1973 On the internal structure of perceptual and semantic categories IN T.E. MOORE (ED) COGNITIVE DEVELOPMENT AND THE ACQUISITION OF LANGUAGE, ACADEMIC PRESS, NEW YORK

ROSE, J.E., BRUGGE, J.F., ANDERSON, D.J. & HIND, J.E. 1967 Phase-locked response to low frequency tones in single auditory nerve fibers of the squirrel monkey JOURNAL OF NEUROPHYSIOLOGY 30: 769-793

ROSE, J.E., KITZES, L.M., GIBSON, M.M. & HIND, J.E. 1974 Observations on phase-sensitive neurons of anteroventral cochlear nucleus of the cat: nonlinearity of cochlear output JOURNAL OF NEUROPHYSIOLOGY 37: 218-253

ROSEN, S.M. 1978 Range and frequency effects in consonant categorization SPEECH AND HEARING: WORK IN PROGRESS, 71-89, DEPARTMENT OF PHONETICS AND LINGUISTICS, UNIVERSITY COLLEGE LONDON

ROSS, J.R. 1972 Upstairs pruning NELS PRESENTATION

ROSS, J.R. 1974 Nouniness IN O. FUJIMURA (ED) THREE DIMENSIONS IN LINGUISTIC THEORY, TEC, TOKYO

ROSSI, M. 1975 Les contraintes phonologiques dans un système de reconnaissance de la parole 6IEME JOURNEES D'ETUDES SUR LA PAROLE, 150-188, G.A.L.F.

RUBIN, P., TURVEY, M.T. & VAN GELDER, P. 1976 Initial phonemes are detected faster in spoken words than in nonwords PERCEPTION AND PSYCHOPHYSICS 19: 394-398

RUDES, B. 1976 Lexical representations and variable rules in natural generative phonology GLOSSA 10.1: 111-150

RUMBAUGH, D., SAVAGE-RUMBAUGH, S. & GILL, T. 1978 Language skills, cognition, and the chimpanzee IN F. PENG (ED) SIGN LANGUAGE AND LANGUAGE ACQUISITION IN MAN AND APE, CHAPTER 6, AMERICAN ASSOCIATION FOR THE ADVANCEMENT OF SCIENCE, SYMPOSIUM 16, WASHINGTON D.C.

RUPERT, A.L., CASPARY, D.M. & MOUSHEGIAN, G. 1977 Response characteristics of cochlear nucleus neurons vowels sounds ANNALS OF OTOLOGY 86: 37-48

RUSKE, G. & SCHOTOLA, T. 1978 An approach to speech recognition using syllabic decision units IEEE PROCEEDINGS, ASSP CONFERENCE, 722-725, TULSA,

SACHS, J. 1967 Recognition memory for syntactic and semantic aspects of connected discourse PERCEPTION AND PSYCHOPHYSICS 2: 437-442

SACHS, J. 1977 The adaptive significance of linguistic input to prelinguistic infants IN C. SNOW AND C.A. FERGUSON (EDS) TALKING TO CHILDREN: LANGUAGE INPUT AND ACQUISITION, 51-61, CAMBRIDGE UNIVERSITY PRESS

SACHS, J. 1979 Topic selection in parent-child discourse DISCOURSE PROCESSES 2: 145-153

SACHS, M.B. & ABBAS, P.J. 1974 Rate versus level functions for auditory-nerve fibers in cats: tone-burst stimuli JOURNAL OF THE ACOUSTICAL SOCIETY OF AMERICA 56: 1835-1847

SACHS, M.B. & ABBAS, P.J. 1976 Phenomenological model for two-tone suppression JOURNAL OF THE ACOUSTICAL SOCIETY OF AMERICA 60: 1157-1163

SACHS, M.B. & KIANG, N.Y.S. 1968 Two-tone inhibition in auditory-nerve fibers JOURNAL OF THE ACOUSTICAL SOCIETY OF AMERICA 43: 1120-1128

SACHS, M.B. & YOUNG, E.D. 1979 Encoding of steady-state vowels in the auditory nerve: representation in terms of discharge rate JOURNAL OF THE ACOUSTICAL SOCIETY OF AMERICA (IN PRESS)

SANKOFF, D. (ED) 1978 Linguistic Variation ACADEMIC PRESS, NEW YORK

SAVIN, H.B. & BEVER, T.G. 1970 The nonperceptual reality of the phoneme JOURNAL OF VERBAL LEARNING AND VERBAL BEHAVIOR 9: 295-302

SAWUSCH, J.R. & NUSBAUM, H.C. 1979 Contextual effects in vowel perception I. Anchor induced contrast effects PERCEPTION AND PSYCHOPHYSICS 25: 292-302

SCAIFE, M. & BRUNER, J.S. 1975 The capacity for joint visual attention in the infant NATURE 253: 265-266

SCHANE, S.A. 1973 Generative Phonology PRENTICE HALL, ENGLEWOOD CLIFFS, NEW JERSEY

SCHLEICHER, A. 1863 Die Darwinsche Theorie und die Sprachwissenschaft BOHLAU, WEIMAR

SCHLESINGER, I. 1977 Production and Comprehension of Utterances ERLBAUM, HILLSDALE, NEW JERSEY

SCHOUTEN, M.E.H. 1980 The case against a speech mode of perception ACTA PSYCHOLOGICA 44: 71-98

SCHUELL, H., JENKINS, J.J. & JIMINEZ-PABON, E. 1964 Aphasia in Adults HARPER AND ROW , NEW YORK

SCHWARTZ, J. & TALLAT, P. 1980 Rate of acoustic change may underlie hemispheric specialization for speech perception SCIENCE 207: 1380-1381

SCOTT, D. (FORTHCOMING) Perception of phrase boundaries PH.D. DISSERTATION, UNIVERSITY OF SUSSEX

SCULLY, C. 1977 Interrelated acoustic factors in plosives PROCEEDINGS OF THE INSTITUTE OF ACOUSTICS 2-14: 1-4

SCULLY, C. 1979 Model prediction and real speech: fricative dynamics IN B. LINDBLOM AND S. OHMAN (EDS) FRONTIERS OF SPEECH COMMUNICATION RESEARCH, ACADEMIC PRESS, LONDON

SEARLE, C.L., JACOBSON, J.Z. & RAYMENT, S.G. 1979 Stop consonant discrimination based on human audition JOURNAL OF THE ACOUSTICAL SOCIETY OF AMERICA 65: 799-809

SEARS, T.A. & NEWSOM DAVIS, J. 1968 The control of respiratory muscles during voluntary breathing IN A. BOUHUYS (ED) SOUND PRODUCTION IN MAN, ANNALS OF THE NEW YORK ACADEMY OF SCIENCES 155: 183-190

SEGUI, J., FRAUENFELDER, U. & MEHLER, J. Phoneme monitoring, syllable monitoring and lexical access UNPUBLISHED MANUSCRIPT

SEIDENBERG, M.S. & PETITTO, L.A. 1979 Signing behavior in apes: a critical review COGNITION 7: 177-215

SELKIRK, E.O. 1972 The phrase phonology in English and French PH.D. DISSERTATION, MASSACHUSETTS INSTITUTE OF TECHNOLOGY

SELKIRK, E.O. 1978A On prosodic structure and its relation to syntactic structure PAPER PRESENTED AT THE CONFERENCE ON THE MENTAL REPRESENTATION OF PHONOLOGY, NOVEMBER 18-19, 1978

SELKIRK, E.O. 1978B The French foot: on the status of "mute" e STUDIES IN FRENCH LINGUISTICS, 1: 141-150

SELKIRK, E.O. 1979 The prosodic structure of French PAPER PRESENTED AT THE NINTH ANNUAL LINGUISTIC SYMPOSIUM ON ROMANCE LANGUAGES, GEORGETOWN UNIVERSITY

SELKIRK, E.O. 1980 The role of prosodic categories in English word stress LINGUISTIC INQUIRY 11(3), MASSACHUSETTS INSTITUTE OF TECHNOLOGY

SELKIRK, E.O. (FORTHCOMING) Phonology and Syntax: the Relation between Sound and Structure MASSACHUSETTS INSTITUTE OF TECHNOLOGY PRESS, CAMBRIDGE

SEMILOFF, H. 1976 An acoustic correlate of syllabicity in English JOURNAL OF THE ACOUSTICAL SOCIETY OF AMERICA 60: 592

SHAFTON, A. 1976 Conditions of Awareness RIVERSTONE PRESS, PORTLAND, OREGON

SHATTUCK, S.R. 1975 Speech errors and sentence production UNPUBLISHED DOCTORAL DISSERTATION, DEPARTMENT OF PSYCHOLOGY, MASSACHUSETTS INSTITUTE OF TECHNOLOGY, CAMBRIDGE

SHATTUCK-HUFNAGEL, S.R. 1979 Speech errors as evidence for a serial order mechanism in sentence production IN SENTENCE PROCESSING: PSYCHOLINGUISTIC STUDIES PRESENTED TO MERRILL GARRETT, W.E. COOPER & E.C.T. WALKER (EDS), ERLBAUM, HILLSDALE, NEW JERSEY

SHATTUCK-HUFNAGEL, S.R. & KLATT, D.H. 1979A The limited use of distinctive features and markedness in speech production: evidence from speech error data JOURNAL OF VERBAL LEARNING AND VERBAL BEHAVIOUR 18: 41-56

SHATTUCK-HUFNAGEL, S.R. & KLATT, D.H. 1979B Distinctive feature constraints on phoneme errors of different types PROCEEDINGS OF THE 9TH INTERNATIONAL CONGRESS OF PHONETIC SCIENCES, COPENHAGEN

SHERZER, J. 1973 Verbal and nonverbal deixis: the pointed lip gesture among the San Blas Cuna LANGUAGE IN SOCIETY 2: 117-131

SHOTTER, J. 1978 The cultural context of communication studies; theoretical and methodological issues IN A. LOCK (ED) ACTION, GESTURE AND SYMBOL, 43-78, ACADEMIC PRESS, LONDON

SIEGEL, J.H., KIM, D.O. & MOLNAR, C.E. 1977 Cochlear distortion products: effects of altering the Organ of Corti JOURNAL OF THE ACOUSTICAL SOCIETY OF AMERICA 61: S2 (A)

SIMON, H.J. & STUDDERT-KENNEDY, M. 1978 Selective anchoring and adaptation of phonetic and nonphonetic continua JOURNAL OF THE ACOUSTICAL SOCIETY OF AMERICA 64: 1338-1357

SINOTT, J.M., BEECHER, M.D., MOODY, D.B. & STEBBINS, W.C. 1976 Speech sound discrimination by monkeys and humans JOURNAL OF THE ACOUSTICAL SOCIETY OF AMERICA 60: 687-695

SLOBIN, D.I. 1975 The more it changes ... on understanding language by watching it move through time PAPERS AND REPORTS ON CHILD LANGUAGE DEVELOPMENT 10: 1-30 STANFORD UNIVERSITY

SMITH, B.L. 1978 Effects of place of articulation and vowel environment on "voiced" stop consonant production GLOSSA 12: 163-175

SMITH, N.V. 1973 The Acquisition of Phonology: A Case Study CAMBRIDGE UNIVERSITY PRESS

SMITH, N.V. 1975 Review of B.L. Derwing, Transformational grammar as a theory of language acquisition JOURNAL OF LINGUISTICS 11, 261-270

SMITH, N.V. 1979 Lexical representation and the acquisition of phonology STUDIES IN THE LINGUISTIC SCIENCES 8, UNIVERSITY OF ILLINOIS

SMITH, N.V. An audit of developmental phonology THIS VOLUME

SMITH, N.V. & WILSON, D. 1979 Modern Linguistics: the Results of Chomsky's Revolution PENGUIN, HARMONDSWORTH

SMITH, P.T. Linguistic information in spelling IN U. FRITH (ED) COGNITIVE PROCESSES IN SPELLING, ACADEMIC PRESS, LONDON, (IN PRESS)

SMITH, P.T. & BAKER, R.G. 1976 The influence of English spelling patterns on pronunciation JOURNAL OF VERBAL LEARNING AND VERBAL BEHAVIOR 15: 267-285

SNOW, C. 1972 Mothers' speech to children learning language CHILD DEVELOPMENT 549-565

SNOW, C. & FERGUSON, C.A. (EDS) 1977 Talking to children CAMBRIDGE UNIVERSITY PRESS

SONDHI, M.M. 1974 Model for wave propagation in a lossy vocal tract JOURNAL OF THE ACOUSTICAL SOCIETY OF AMERICA 55: 1070-1075

SONDHI, M.M. & GOPINATH, B. 1971 Determination of vocal tract shape from impulse response at the lips JOURNAL OF THE ACOUSTICAL SOCIETY OF AMERICA 49: 1067-1873

SPENCER, N.J. 1973 Differences between linguists and non-linguists in intuitions of grammaticality-acceptability JOURNAL OF PSYCHOLINGUISTIC RESEARCH 2: 83-98

SPINELLI, D.N. 1970 OCCAM, a content addressable memory model for the brain IN K.H. PRIBRAM AND D. BROADBENT (EDS) THE BIOLOGY OF MEMORY, 293-306, ACADEMIC PRESS, NEW YORK

SPINELLI, D.N., PRIBRAM, K.H. & WEINGARTEN, M. 1965 Centrifugal optic nerve responses evoked by auditory and somatic stimulation EXPERIMENTAL NEUROLOGY 12: 303-319

SPOENDLIN, H. 1973 The innervation of the cochlear receptor IN A.R. MOLLER (ED) BASIC MECHANISMS IN HEARING, 185-234, ACADEMIC PRESS, NEW YORK

SPOENDLIN, H. 1974 Neuroanatomy of the cochlea IN E. ZWICKER AND E. TERHARDT (EDS) FACTS AND MODELS IN HEARING, 18-32, SPRINGER-VERLAG, NEW YORK

SRULOVICZ, P. 1978 Neural timing as the physiological basis for aural frequency and amplitude measurement PH.D. DISSERTATION, TEL-AVIV UNIVERSITY

STAM, J.H. 1976 Inquiries into the Origin of Language HARPER AND ROW, NEW YORK

STAMPE, D. 1973 A dissertation on natural phonology PH.D. DISSERTATION, UNIVERSITY OF CHICAGO

STANLEY, R. 1967 Redundancy rules in phonology LANGUAGE 43: 393-436

STARI, R.E., HEINZ, P.M. & WRIGHT-WILSON, C. 1976 Vowel utterances of young infants JOURNAL OF THE ACOUSTICAL SOCIETY OF AMERICA 60, SUPPLEMENT 2, 43 (A)

STEINBERG, D. & KROHN, R. 1975 The psychological reality of Chomsky and Halle's vowel shift rule IN E. KOERNER (ED) THE TRANSFORMATIONAL PARADIGM AND MODERN LINGUISTIC THEORY, JOHN BENJAMINS, AMSTERDAM

STEVENS, K.N. 1960 Towards a model for speech recognition JOURNAL OF THE ACOUSTICAL SOCIETY OF AMERICA 32: 47-55

STEVENS, K.N. 1971A Perception of phonetic segments: Evidence from phonology, acoustics, and psychoacoustics IN D.L. HORTON AND J.J. JENKINS (EDS) THE PERCEPTION OF LANGUAGE, 216-235, MERRILL, COLUMBUS, OHIO

STEVENS, K.N. 1971B The role of rapid spectrum changes in the production and perception of speech IN FORM AND SUBSTANCE (FESTSCHRIFT FOR ELI FISCHER-JØRGENSEN),95-101, AKADEMISK, COPENHAGEN

STEVENS, K.N. 1972 The quantal nature of speech: evidence from articulatory-acoustic data IN E.E. DAVID, JR AND P.B. DENES (EDS) HUMAN COMMUNICATION: A UNIFIED VIEW, 51-66, MCGRAW-HILL, NEW YORK

STEVENS, K.N. 1975 Quantal configurations for vowels JOURNAL OF THE ACOUSTICAL SOCIETY OF AMERICA 57, SUPPLEMENT 1, S70 (A)

STEVENS, K.N. (IN PRESS) Acoustic correlates of some phonetic categories JOURNAL OF THE ACOUSTICAL SOCIETY OF AMERICA

STEVENS, K.N. & BLUMSTEIN, S.E. 1978 Invariant cues for place of articulation JOURNAL OF THE ACOUSTICAL SOCIETY OF AMERICA 64: 1358-1368

STEVENS, K.N. & BLUMSTEIN, S.E. (IN PRESS) The search for invariant acoustic correlates of phonetic features IN P.D. EIMAS AND J. MILLER (EDS) PERSPECTIVES ON THE STUDY OF SPEECH, CHAPTER 1, ERLBAUM, HILLSDALE, NEW JERSEY

STEVENS, K.N. & HALLE, M. 1967 Remarks on analysis by synthesis and distinctive features IN MODELS FOR THE PERCEPTION OF SPEECH AND VISUAL FORM, W. WATHEN-DUNN (ED), MASSACHUSETTS INSTITUTE OF TECHNOLOGY, CAMBRIDGE

STEVENS, K.N. & HOUSE, A.S. 1955 Development of a quantitative description of vowel articulation JOURNAL OF THE ACOUSTICAL SOCIETY OF AMERICA 27: 484-493

STEVENS, K.N. & KLATT, D.H. 1974 Role of formant transitions in the voiced-voiceless distinction for stops JOURNAL OF THE ACOUSTICAL SOCIETY OF AMERICA 55: 653-659

STEVENS, K.N., LIBERMAN, A.M., OHMAN, S.E.G. & STUDDERT-KENNEDY, M. 1969 Crosslanguage study of vowel perception LANGUAGE AND SPEECH 12: 1-23

STEVENS, K.N. & PERKELL, J.S. 1977 Speech physiology and phonetic features IN M. SAWASHIMA AND F.S. COOPER (EDS) DYNAMIC ASPECTS OF SPEECH PRODUCTION, 323-341, UNIVERSITY OF TOKYO PRESS, TOKYO

STOCKWELL, R.P. & MACAULAY, R.K.S. 1972 Linguistic Change and Generative Theory INDIANA UNIVERSITY PRESS, BLOOMINGTON

STOKOE, W.C. 1978 Sign languages and the verbal/non-verbal distinction IN T.A. SEBEOK (ED) SIGHT, SOUND AND SENSE, 157-172 INDIANA UNIVERSITY PRESS, BLOOMINGTON

STRANGE, W., VERBRUGGE, R.R., SHANKWEILER, D.P. & EDMAN, T.R. 1976 Consonantal environment specifies vowel identity JOURNAL OF THE ACOUSTICAL SOCIETY OF AMERICA 60: 213-224

STREETER, L.A. 1978 Acoustic determinants of phrase boundary perception JOURNAL OF THE ACOUSTICAL SOCIETY OF AMERICA 64: 1582-1592

STUDDERT-KENNEDY, M. & SHANKWEILER, D.P. 1970 Hemispheric specialization for speech JOURNAL OF THE ACOUSTICAL SOCIETY OF AMERICA 48: 479-596

SUGA, N. 1971 responses of inferior collicular neurones of bats to tone bursts with different rise times JOURNAL OF PHYSIOLOGY 217: 159-177

SUGA, N. 1973 Feature extraction in the auditory system of bats IN A.R. MØLLER (ED) BASIC MECHANISMS IN HEARING, 675-744, ACADEMIC PRESS, NEW YORK

SUGA, N., O'NEILL, W.E. & MANABE, T. 1979 Harmonic-sensitive neurones in the auditory cortex of the mustache bat SCIENCE 203: 270-274

SUMMERFIELD, Q. 1975A Aerodynamics versus mechanics in the control of voicing onset in consonant-vowel syllables SPEECH PERCEPTION, SERIES 2, NO. 4: 61-72, UNIVERSITY OF BELFAST

SUMMERFIELD, Q. 1975B How a full account of segmental perception depends on prosody and vice versa IN A. COHEN AND S.G. NOOTEBOOM (EDS) STRUCTURE AND PROCESS IN SPEECH PERCEPTION, SPRINGER-VERLAG, NEW YORK

SUMMERFIELD, Q. 1979A Timing in phonetic perception: extrinsic or intrinsic? IN W.J. BARRY AND K.J. KOHLER (EDS) "TIME" IN THE PRODUCTION AND PERCEPTION OF SPEECH, ARBEITSBERICHTE 12: 169-204, PHONETICS DEPARTMENT, UNIVERSITY OF KIEL

SUMMERFIELD, Q. 1979B Use of visual information for phonetic perception PHONETICA 36: 314-331

SUMMERFIELD, Q. & HAGGARD, M.P. 1972 Speech rate effects in perception of voicing SPEECH SYNTHESIS AND PERCEPTION, REPORT OF SPEECH RESEARCH IN PROGRESS, 6: 1-12, DEPARTMENT OF PSYCHOLOGY, THE QUEEN'S UNIVERSITY OF BELFAST

SUSSMAN, H. 1979 Motor equivalence and lip/jaw reciprocity: an artifact? TEXAS LINGUISTICS FORUM, 132-136, DEPARTMENT OF LINGUISTICS, UNIVERSITY OF TEXAS AT AUSTIN

SUSSMAN, H., MACNEILAGE, P.F. & HANSON, R.J. 1973 Labial and mandibular mechanics during the production of bilabial stop consonants JOURNAL OF SPEECH AND HEARING RESEARCH 16: 397-420

SUSSMAN, H.M. & WESTBURY, J.R. 1979 The effects of antagonistic gestures on temporal and amplitude parameters of anticipatory labial coarticulation JOURNAL OF THE ACOUSTICAL SOCIETY OF AMERICA 65, SUPPLEMENT NO. 1, S25

SUTTER, E. 1976 A revised conception of visual receptive fields based on pseudo-random spatio-temporal pattern stimuli IN P.Z. MARMARELIS AND G.D. MCCANN (EDS) PROCEEDINGS OF 1ST SYMPOSIUM ON TESTING AND IDENTIFICATION OF NONLINEAR SYSTEMS, 353-365, CALIFORNIA INSTITUTE OF TECHNOLOGY

SWINNEY, D. 1979 Lexical access during sentence comprehension: (re)consideration of context effects JOURNAL OF VERBAL LEARNING AND VERBAL BEHAVIOR, DECEMBER 1979 (IN PRESS)

SWINNEY, D. & CUTLER, A. 1979 The access and processing of idiomatic expressions JOURNAL OF VERBAL LEARNING AND VERBAL BEHAVIOR, OCTOBER 1979 (IN PRESS)

SWINNEY, D., ONIFER, W. & HIRSHKOWITZ, M. 1979 Accessing lexical ambiguities during sentence comprehension: effects of frequency-of-meaning and contextual bias MANUSCRIPT SUBMITTED FOR PUBLICATION

SWINNEY, D., ONIFER, W., PRATHER, P. & HIRSCHKOWITZ, M. 1979 Semantic facilitation across sensory modalities in the processing of individual words and sentences MEMORY & COGNITION 7: 159-165

SWINNEY, D.A. & PRATHER, P. 1980 Phonemic identification in a phoneme monitoring experiment: the variable role of uncertainty about vowel context PERCEPTION AND PSYCHOPHYSICS 27: 104-110

SWISHER, L.P. 1967 Auditory intensity discrimination in patients with temporal-lobe damage CORTEX 2: 1979-193

SYLVESTER-BRADLEY, B. & TREVARTHEN, C. 1978 "Baby-talk" as an adaptation to the infant's communication IN N. WATERSON AND C. SNOW (EDS) DEVELOPMENT OF COMMUNICATION: SOCIAL AND PRAGMATIC FACTORS IN LANGUAGE ACQUISITION, WILEY, LONDON

SYLVESTER-BRADLEY, B. (NEARING COMPLETION) The study of mother-infant relationship in the first six months of life PH.D. DISSERTATION, UNIVERSITY OF EDINBURGH

TAKAHASHI, H. & NIGAURI, Y. 1962 Relation of vowel articulation to the shape of vocal tract, with special reference to the mouth opening and the tongue STUDIA PHONOLOGICA 2: 71-82

TALLAL, P. & PIERCY 1975 Developmental aphasia: the perception of brief vowels and extended consonants NEUROPSYCHOLOGIA 13: 69-74

TANENHAUS, M.K. & CARROLL, J.M. 1975 The clausal processing hierarchy and .. nouniness IN R. GROSSMAN, J. SAN AND T. VANCE (EDS) PAPERS FROM THE PARASESSION ON FUNCTIONALISM, CHICAGO LINGUISTIC SOCIETY

TARTTER, V.C. & EIMAS, P.D. 1979 The role of auditory feature detectors in the perception of speech PERCEPTION AND PSYCHOPHYSICS 18: 293-298

TAUB, E., GOLDBERG, I. & TAUB, P. 1975 Deafferentation in monkeys: pointing at a target without visual feedback EXPERIMENTAL NEUROLOGY 46: 178-186

TEMPLIN, M. 1957 Certain language skills in children: their development and interrelationships INSTITUTE OF CHILD WELFARE MONOGRAPH 26, UNIVERSITY OF MINNESOTA PRESS, MINNEAPOLIS

TERRACE, H.S., PETITTO, L.A., SANDERS, R.J. & BEVER, T.G. 1979 Can an ape create a sentence? SCIENCE 206: 891-902

TERRELL, T. 1975 Functional constraints on deletion of word final 's' in Cuban Spanish BERKELEY LINGUISTIC SOCIETY 1

TERRELL, T. 1977 Constraints on the aspiration and deletion of final /s/ in Cuban and Puerto Rican Spanish THE BILINGUAL REVIEW 4: 35-51

THORNE, J.P., BRATLEY, P. & DEWAR, H. 1968 The syntactic analysis of English by machine IN D. MICHIE (ED) MACHINE INTELLIGENCE 3, ELSEVIER, NEW YORK

TIMBERLAKE, A. 1978 Uniform and Alternating Environments in Phonological Change MS, UCLA

TOMKINS, W. 1969 Indian Sign Language DOVER PUBLICATIONS, NEW YORK

TOPPER, S.T. 1975 Gesture language for a non-verbal severely retarded male MENTAL RETARDATION 13: 30-31

TOWNSEND, D. & BEVER, T.G. 1978 Inter-clause relations and clausal processing JOURNAL OF VERBAL LEARNING AND VERBAL BEHAVIOR 17: 509-521

TRAN DUC THAO 1973 Recherches sur l'Origine du Langage et de la Conscience EDITIONS SOCIALES, PARIS

TREISMAN, A. & GEFFEN, G. 1967 Selective attention: perception or response? QUARTERLY JOURNAL OF EXPERIMENTAL PSYCHOLOGY 19: 1-17

TREISMAN, A.M. 1964 Monitoring and storage of irrelevant messages in selective attention JOURNAL OF VERBAL LEARNING AND VERBAL BEHAVIOR 3: 449-459

TREISMAN, A.M. 1979 The psychological reality of levels of processing IN L. CERMAK AND F. CRAIK (EDS) LEVELS OF PROCESSING AND HUMAN MEMORY, ERLBAUM, HILLSDALE, NEW JERSEY

TREVARTHEN, C. 1974 The psychobiology of speech development IN E.H. LENNEBERG (ED) LANGUAGE AND BRAIN: DEVELOPMENTAL ASPECTS, NEUROSCIENCES RESEARCH PROGRAM BULLETIN 12: 570-585, BOSTON

TREVARTHEN, C. 1977 Descriptive analyses of infant communication behaviour IN H.R. SCHAFFER (ED) MOTHER-INFANT INTERACTION, 227-270, ACADEMIC PRESS, LONDON

TREVARTHEN, C. 1978 Modes of perceiving and modes of acting IN H.J. PICK (ED) PSYCHOLOGICAL MODES OF PERCEIVING AND PROCESSING INFORMATION, 99-136, ERLBAUM, HILLSDALE, NEW JERSEY

TREVARTHEN, C. 1979A Communication and cooperation in early infancy IN M. BULLOWA (ED) BEFORE SPEECH: THE BEGINNINGS OF HUMAN COMMUNICATION, 321-346, CAMBRIDGE UNIVERSITY PRESS, (IN PRESS)

TREVARTHEN, C. 1979B Instincts for human understanding and for cultural cooperation: their development in infancy IN M. VON CRANACH, K. FOPPA, W. LEPENIES AND D. PLOOG (EDS) HUMAN ETHOLOGY, 530-571, CAMBRIDGE UNIVERSITY PRESS, (IN PRESS)

TREVARTHEN, C. & HUBLEY, P. 1978 Secondary intersubjectivity: confidence, confiding and acts of meaning in the first year IN A.LOCK (ED) ACTION, GESTURE AND SYMBOL: THE EMERGENCE OF LANGUAGE, 183-229, ACADEMIC PRESS, LONDON

TRIM, J.L.M. 1964 Tonetic stress-marks for German IN D. ABERCROMBIE ET AL (EDS) IN HONOUR OF DANIEL JONES 374-383, LONGMANS, LONDON

TRUBETSKOY, N.S. 1939 Grundzuge der Phonologie TRAVAUX DU CERCLE LINGUISTIQUE DE PRAGUE, 7

TRUBY, H.M., BOSMA, J.F. & LIND, J. 1965 Newborn Infant Cry ALMQVIST AND WIKSELL, STOCKHOLM

TUAYCHAROEN, P. 1979 An account of speech development of a Thai child: from babbling to speech IN T.L. THONGKUM ET AL (EDS) STUDIES IN TAI AND MON-KHMER PHONETICS AND PHONOLOGY, IN HONOUR OF E.J.A. HENDERSON, CHULALONGKORN UNIVERSITY PRESS

TURVEY, M.T. 1977 Preliminaries to a theory of action with reference to vision IN R. SHAW AND J. BRANSFORD (EDS) PERCEIVING, ACTING AND KNOWING: TOWARD AN ECOLOGICAL PSYCHOLOGY, ERLBAUM HILLSDALE, NEW JERSEY

TYLOR, E.B. 1865 Early History of Mankind MURRAY, LONDON

UMEDA, N. 1976 Linguistic rules for text-to-speech synthesis IEEE PROCEEDINGS 64: 443-451

UMEDA, N. 1977 Consonant duration in English JOURNAL OF THE ACOUSTICAL SOCIETY OF AMERICA 61: 846-858

VAISSIERE, J. 1975A On French prosody QUARTERLY PROGRESS REPORT 114: 212-223, RESEARCH LABORATORY OF ELECTRONICS, MASSACHUSETTS INSTITUTE OF TECHNOLOGY

VAISSIERE, J. 1975B Further note on French prosody QUARTERLY PROGRESS REPORT 115: 251-261, RESEARCH LABORATORY OF ELECTRONICS, MASSACHUSETTS INSTITUTE OF TECHNOLOGY

VAISSIERE, J. 1976 Premiers essais de segmentation automatique de la parole continue à partir des variations du fondamental de la phrase RECHERCHES ACOUSTIQUES 2: 193-208, CNET, LANNION

VAISSIERE, J. 1977 Premiers essais d'utilisation de la durée pour la segmentation en mot dans un système de reconnaissance 8IEMES JOURNEES D'ETUDES SUR LA PAROLE, 345-352, G.A.L.F.

VENNEMANN, T. 1972 On the theory of syllabic phonology LINGUISTISCHE BERICHTE 18: 1-18

VENNEMANN, T. 1978 Rule inversion and lexical storage: the case of Sanskrit Visarga IN J. FISIAK (ED) RECENT DEVELOPMENTS IN HISTORICAL PHONOLOGY, 391-408, MOUTON, THE HAGUE

VERGNAUD, J.R. & HALLE, M. (IN PREPARATION) Metrical structure in phonology MANUSCRIPT, MASSACHUSETTS INSTITUTE OF TECHNOLOGY/ UNIVERSITY OF MASSACHUSETTS, AMHERST

VITZ, P. & WINKLER, B. 1973 Predicting judged 'similarity of sound' of English words JOURNAL OF VERBAL LEARNING AND VERBAL BEHAVIOR 12: 373-378

VIVES, R. 1979 Utilisation de l'information phonémique et syllabique pour la reconnaissance de mots prononcés isolément ou dans des phrases 10IEMES JOURNEES D'ETUDES SUR LA PAROLE, 375-384, G.A.L.F.

VIVES, R., LE CORRE, C., MERCIER, G. & VAISSIERE, J. 1977 Utilisation, pour la reconnaissance de la parole continue, de marqueurs prosodiques extraits de la fréquence du fondamental 7IEME JOURNEES D'ETUDES SUR LA PAROLE, 353-363, G.A.L.F.

VON RAFFLER-ENGEL, W. 1964 Il prelinguaggio infantile PAIDEIA (STUDIE GRAMMATICALI E LINGUISTICIE) 7, BRESCIA, ITALY

VON RAFFLER-ENGEL, W. 1970 The LAD, our underlying unconscious and more on 'felt sets' THE LANGUAGE SCIENCES, DECEMBER, 15-18

VON RAFFLER-ENGEL, W. 1974 Children's Acquisition of Kinesics CAMPUS FILM DISTRIBUTORS, SCARSDALE, NEW YORK

VON RAFFLER-ENGEL, W. 1975 The correlation of gestures and verbalization in first language acquisition IN A. KENDON, R.M. HARRIS AND M.R. KEY ORGANIZATION OF BEHAVIOR IN FACE-TO-FACE INTERACTION, 241-250, MOUTON, THE HAGUE

VON RAFFLER-ENGEL, W. 1976 A pluri-modal communicative approach to language acquisition IN W. VON RAFFLER-ENGEL AND Y. LEBRUN (EDS) BABY TALK AND INFANT SPEECH, SWETS AND ZEITLINGER, AMSTERDAM

VON RAFFLER-ENGEL, W. 1977 A pluri-modal approach to first language acquisition IN F.C.C. PENG (ED) DEVELOPMENT OF VERBAL AND NONVERBAL BEHAVIOR, 1-29, BUNKA HYORON, HIROSHIMA, JAPAN

VON RAFFLER-ENGEL, W. 1979 Developmental kinesics IN W. VON RAFFLER-ENGEL (ED) ASPECTS OF NONVERBAL COMMUNICATION , SWETS AND ZEITLINGER, AMSTERDAM

VON RAFFLER-ENGEL, W. & VON WEINSTEIN, S. 1977 Metakinesic behavior in the description of nonverbal behavior SERIES B, PAPER 32, LINGUISTIC AGENCY, UNIVERSITY OF TRIER, GERMANY

VYGOTSKY, L.S. 1962 Thought and Language TRANSLATED BY E. HANFMANN AND G. VAKAR, MASSACHUSETTS INSTITUTE OF TECHNOLOGY PRESS

WAKITA, H. 1973 Direct estimation of the vocal tract shape by inverse filtering of acoustic speech waveforms IEEE TRANSACTIONS, AU 21: 417-427

WAKITA, H. & DESCOUT, R. 1977 Determination of the area function IN R. CARRE, R. DESCOUT AND M. WAJSKOP (EDS) SYMPOSIUM ON ARTICULATORY MODELING, G.A.L.F., GRENOBLE

WAKITA, H. & FANT, G. 1978 Toward a better vocal tract modeling QUARTERLY PROGRESS AND STATUS REPORT 1: 9-29, SPEECH TRANSMISSION LABORATORY, ROYAL INSTITUTE OF TECHNOLOGY, STOCKHOLM

WALLACE, A.R. 1895 The expressiveness of speech, or mouth-gesture as a factor in the origin of language FORTNIGHTLY REVIEW 58: 528-543

WANNER, E., KAPLAN, R. & SHINER, S. 1975 Garden paths in relative clauses UNPUBLISHED PAPER, HARVARD UNIVERSITY

WANNER, E. & MARATSOS, M. 1978 An ATN approach to comprehension IN M. HALLE, J. BRESNAN, AND G. MILLER (EDS) LINGUISTIC THEORY AND PSYCHOLOGICAL REALITY, MASSACHUSETTS INSTITUTE OF TECHNOLOGY PRESS

WARREN, R.M. 1974A Auditory pattern recognition by untrained listeners PERCEPTION AND PSYCHOPHYSICS 15: 495-500

WARREN, R.M. 1974B Auditory temporal discrimination by trained listeners COGNITIVE PSYCHOLOGY 6: 237-256

WATERS, R.S. & WILSON, W.A. 1976 Speech perception by rhesus monkeys: the voicing distinction in synthesized labial and velar stop consonants PERCEPTION AND PSYCHOPHYSICS 19: 285-289

WATERSON, N. 1971A Child phonology: a prosodic view JOURNAL OF LINGUISTICS 7: 179-211

WATERSON, N. 1971B Some views on speech perception JOURNAL OF THE INTERNATIONAL PHONETIC ASSOCIATION 1: 81-96

WATERSON, N. 1976 Perception and production in the acquisition of phonology IN W. VON RAFFLER-ENGEL AND Y. LEBRUN (EDS) BABY TALK AND INFANT SPEECH, 294-322, SWETS AND ZEITLINGER, AMSTERDAM

WATERSON, N. 1978 Growth of complexity in phonological development IN N. WATERSON AND C. SNOW (EDS) THE DEVELOPMENT OF COMMUNICATION, 415-442, WILEY, NEW YORK

WATERSON, N. 1980A Prosodic phonology: an introduction to the theory PAPER DELIVERED AT ANNUAL CONFERENCE OF THE DANISH ASSOCIATION OF SPEECH AND HEARING THERAPISTS

WATERSON, N. 1980B Prosodic phonology: further illustration PAPER DELIVERED AT ANNUAL CONFERENCE OF THE DANISH ASSOCIATION OF SPEECH AND HEARING THERAPISTS

WATERSON, N. 1980C A tentative developmental model of phonological representation THIS VOLUME

WEIGL, E. & BIERWISCH, M. 1970 Neuropsychology and linguistics: topics of common research FOUNDATIONS OF LANGUAGE 6: 1-18 (REPRINTED IN H. GOODGLASS AND S. BLUMSTEIN (EDS) 1973 PSYCHOLINGUISTICS AND APHASIA, 11-28, THE JOHNS HOPKINS UNIVERSITY PRESS, BALTIMORE)

WERNICKE, C. 1874 Die Aphasische Symtomenkomplex COHN UND WEIGERT, BRESLAU

WEVER, E.G. 1949 Theory of Hearing WILEY, NEW YORK

WEVER, E.G. & VERNON, J.A. 1955 The effects of the tympanic muscle reflexes upon sound transmission ACTA OTOLARYNGOLOGICA 45: 433-439

WHITAKER, H.A. 1971 On the Representation of Language in the Human Brain LINGUISTIC RESEARCH, EDMONTON, ALBERTA

WHITE, G.M. 1976 Speech recognition, a tutorial overview IEEE TRANSACTIONS ON COMPUTERS, 40-53

WHITEHOUSE, P., CARAMAZZA, A. & ZURIF, E. 1978 Naming in aphasia: interacting effects of form and function BRAIN AND LANGUAGE 6: 63-74

WHITNEY, W.D. 1870 On the present state of the question as to the origin of language REPRINTED IN ORIENTAL AND LINGUISTIC STUDIES (1873), SCRIBNER, NEW YORK

WHORF, B.L. 1956 Language, Thought and Reality MASSACHUSETTS INSTITUTE OF TECHNOLOGY

WICKELGREN, W.A. 1969A Context-sensitive coding, associative memory, and serial order in (speech) behavior PSYCHOLOGICAL REVIEW 76: 1-15

WICKELGREN, W.A. 1969B Context-sensitive coding in speech recognition, articulation, and development IN K.N. LEIBOVIC (ED) INFORMATION PROCESSING IN THE NERVOUS SYSTEM, SPRINGER-VERLAG, NEW YORK

WICKELGREN, W.A. 1972 Context-sensitive coding and serial vs. parallel processing in speech IN J.H. GILBERT (ED) SPEECH AND CORTICAL FUNCTIONING, ACADEMIC PRESS, NEW YORK

WICKELGREN, W.A. 1976 Phonetic coding and serial order IN E.C. CARTERETTE AND M.P. FRIEDMAN (EDS) HANDBOOK OF PERCEPTION, LANGUAGE AND SPEECH, VOL 7, ACADEMIC PRESS, NEW YORK

WIENER, F.M. & ROSS, D.A. 1946 The pressure distribution in the auditory canal in a progressive sound field JOURNAL OF THE ACOUSTICAL SOCIETY OF AMERICA 18: 401-408

WIGHTMAN, F., MCGEE, T. & KRAMER, M. 1977 Factors influencing frequency selectivity in normal and hearing-impaired listeners IN E.F. EVANS AND J.P. WILSON (EDS) PSYCHOPHYSICS AND PHYSIOLOGY OF HEARING, 295-306, ACADEMIC PRESS, LONDON

WILBUR, R. 1979 Theoretical phonology and child phonology: argumentation and implications IN D. GOYVAERTS (ED) PHONOLOGY IN THE 1970S, E. STORY-SCIENTIA, GHENT

WILBUR, R. & MENN, L. 1974 The roles of rules in generative phonology PRESENTED AT THE SUMMER MEETING, LINGUISTIC SOCIETY OF AMERICA, AMHERST, MASSACHUSETTS

WILBUR, R. & MENN, L. 1975 Towards a redefinition of psychological reality: on the internal structure of the lexicon SAN JOSE STATE OCCASIONAL PAPERS, 215-221

WILSON, J.P. 1974 Psychoacoustical and neurophysiological aspects of auditory pattern recognition IN F.G. WORDEN AND F.O. SCHMITT (EDS) THE NEUROSCIENCES: THE THIRD STUDY PROGRAMM, 147-153, MASSACHUSETTS INSTITUTE OF TECHNOLOGY PRESS, CAMBRIDGE

WILSON, J.P. & JOHNSTONE, J.R. 1975 Basilar membrane vibration in guinea pig measured by capacitive probe JOURNAL OF THE ACOUSTICAL SOCIETY OF AMERICA 57: 705-723

WIND, J. 1970 On the Phylogeny and the Ontogeny of the Human Larynx WOLTERS-NOORDHOFF PUBLISHING, GRONINGEN

WINTER, P. & FUNKENSTEIN, H.H. 1973 The effect of species-specific vocalization on the discharge of auditory cortical cells in the awake squirrel monkey (saimire sciureus) EXPERIMENTAL BRAIN RESEARCH 18: 489-504

WITTGENSTEIN, L. 1974 Philosophical Grammar BLACKWELL, OXFORD

WOLF, J.J. & WOODS, W.A. 1979 The HWIM speech understanding system IN W.A. LEA (ED) TRENDS IN SPEECH RECOGNITION, 316-339, PRENTICE HALL, ENGLEWOOD CLIFFS, NEW JERSEY

WOOD, C.C. & DAY, R.S. 1975 Failure of selective attention to phonetic segments in consonant-vowel syllables PERCEPTION AND PSYCHOPHYSICS 17: 346-349

WOODRUFF, G. & PREMACK, D. 1979 Intentional communication in the chimpanzee: the development of deception COGNITION 7: 333-362

WOODS, S. 1978 Model experiments on lip, tongue, and larynx positions for palatal vowels ANNUAL REPORT OF THE INSTITUTE OF PHONETICS, UNIVERSITY OF COPENHAGEN 12: S-103-112

WOODS, W.A. 1970 Transition network grammars for national language analysis COMMUNICATIONS OF THE ACM 13: 591-606

WOODS, W.A. ET AL 1975 Speech understanding systems REPORT NO. 3188, BOLT BERANEK AND NEWMAN, CAMBRIDGE, MASSACHUSETTS

WOODS, W.A., ET AL 1976 Speech understanding systems: final technical progress report REPORT NO. 3438, (IN 5 VOLUMES), BOLT, BERANEK AND NEWMAN, CAMBRIDGE, MASSACHUSETTS

WOODS, W.A. & ZUE, V.W. 1976 Dictionary expansion via phonological rules for a speech understanding system IN CONFERENCE RECORD OF THE 1976 IEEE INTERNATIONAL CONFERENCE ON ACOUSTICS, SPEECH AND SIGNAL PROCESSING, C. TEACHER (ED), 161-164, IEEE CATALOG NO. 76CH1067-8 ASSP

WUNDT, W. 1900 Volkerpsychologie, Volume 1: Die Sprache ENGELMANN, LEIPZIG

WUNDT, W. 1973 The Language of Gesture TRANSLATED BY J.S. THAYER, ET AL, APPROACHES TO SEMIOTICS, PAPERBACK SERIES 6, MOUTON, THE HAGUE

YENI-KOMSHIAN, G. & BENSON, D. 1976 Anatomical study of cerebral asymmetry in the temporal lobe of humans, chimpanzees and rhesus monkeys SCIENCE 192: 387-389

YOUNG, E. & SACHS, M.B. 1973 Recovery from sound exposure in auditory-nerve fibers JOURNAL OF THE ACOUSTICAL SOCIETY OF AMERICA 54: 1535-1543

YOUNG, E.D. & SACHS, M.B. 1979 Representation of steady-state vowels in the temporal aspects of the discharge patterns of populations of auditory-nerve fibers JOURNAL OF THE ACOUSTICAL SOCIETY OF AMERICA (IN PRESS)

ZAZZO, R. 1957 Le problème de l'imitation chez le nouveau-né ENFANCE 2: 134-142

ZEN NIHON ROA REMMEI (ALL-JAPAN LEAGUE OF THE DEAF) 1977 Watashitachi no Shuwa TOKYO

ZIHLMAN, A. & CRAMER, D. 1978 Skeletal differences between pygmy (pan paniscus) and common chimpanzees (pan troglodytes) FOLIA PRIMATOLOGICA 29: 86-94

ZUE, V.W. 1976 Acoustic characteristics of stop consonants: a controlled study PH.D. DISSERTATION, MASSACHUSETTS INSTITUTE OF TECHNOLOGY

ZURIF, E.B., CARAMAZZA, A., MYERSON, R. & GALVIN, J. 1974 Semantic feature representations for normal and aphasic language BRAIN AND LANGUAGE 1: 167-187

ZWICKER, E. 1974 On a psychoacoustical equivalent of tuning curves IN E. ZWICKER AND E. TERHARDT (EDS) FACTS AND MODELS HEARING, 132-140, SPRINGER-VERLAG, HEIDELBERG

ZWICKER, E., & TERHARDT, E. 1979 Automatic speech recognition using psychoacoustics models JOURNAL OF THE ACOUSTICAL SOCIETY OF AMERICA 65: 487-498

ZWICKY, A. 1972 A note on a phonological hierarchy in English IN R.P. STOCKWELL AND R.K.S. MACAULAY (EDS) LINGUISTIC CHANGE AND GENERATIVE THEORY, INDIANA UNIVERSITY PRESS, BLOOMINGTON

ZWISLOCKI, J.J. & SOKOLICH, W.G. 1974 Neuro-mechanical frequency analysis in the cochlea IN E. ZWICKER AND E. TERHARDT (EDS) FACTS AND MODELS IN HEARING, 107-117, SPRINGER-VERLAG, NEW YORK